SIXTH EDITION

Learning Java
*An Introduction to Real-World
Programming with Java*

Marc Loy, Patrick Niemeyer, and Daniel Leuck

Beijing · Boston · Farnham · Sebastopol · Tokyo

Learning Java

by Marc Loy, Patrick Niemeyer, and Daniel Leuck

Published by O'Reilly Media, Inc., 1005 Gravenstein Highway North, Sebastopol, CA 95472.

O'Reilly books may be purchased for educational, business, or sales promotional use. Online editions are also available for most titles (*http://oreilly.com*). For more information, contact our corporate/institutional sales department: 800-998-9938 or *corporate@oreilly.com*.

Acquisitions Editor: Brian Guerin	**Indexer:** Potomac Indexing, LLC
Development Editor: Sarah Grey	**Interior Designer:** David Futato
Production Editor: Ashley Stussy	**Cover Designer:** Karen Montgomery
Copyeditor: Sonia Saruba	**Illustrator:** Kate Dullea
Proofreader: Piper Editorial Consulting, LLC	

May 2000:	First Edition
July 2002:	Second Edition
May 2005:	Third Edition
June 2013:	Fourth Edition
March 2020:	Fifth Edition
August 2023:	Sixth Edition

Revision History for the Sixth Edition

2023-08-16:   First Release

See *http://oreilly.com/catalog/errata.csp?isbn=9781098145538* for release details.

978-1-098-14553-8

[LSI]

Table of Contents

Preface

This book introduces the Java programming language and environment. Whether you are a software developer or just someone who uses the internet in your daily life, you've undoubtedly heard about Java. Its arrival was one of the most exciting developments in the history of the web, and Java applications continue to power business on the internet. Java is, arguably, the most popular programming language in the world, used by millions of developers on almost every kind of computer imaginable. Java has surpassed languages such as C++ and Visual Basic in terms of developer demand and has become the de facto language for certain kinds of development—especially for web-based services. Most universities are now using Java in their introductory courses alongside the other important modern languages. Perhaps you're using this text in one of your classes right now!

This book gives you a thorough grounding in Java fundamentals and grammar. *Learning Java*, Sixth Edition, attempts to live up to its name by mapping out the Java language and its class libraries, programming techniques, and idioms. We'll dig deep into interesting areas and at least scratch the surface of other popular topics. Other titles from O'Reilly pick up where we leave off and provide more comprehensive information on specific areas and applications of Java.

Whenever possible, we provide compelling, realistic, and fun examples and avoid merely cataloging features. The examples are simple but hint at what can be done. We won't be developing the next great "killer app" in these pages, but we hope to give you a starting point for many hours of experimentation and inspired tinkering that will lead you to develop one yourself.

Who Should Read This Book

This book is for computer professionals, students, technical people, and Finnish hackers. It's for everyone who has a need for hands-on experience using Java with an eye toward building real applications. This book could also be considered a crash course in object-oriented programming, threads, and user interfaces. As you learn about Java, you'll also learn a powerful and practical approach to software development, beginning with a deep understanding of the fundamentals of Java.

Superficially, Java looks like C or C++, so you'll have a tiny head start in using this book if you have some experience with one of these languages. If you do not, don't worry. In many respects, Java acts like more dynamic languages such as Smalltalk and Lisp. Knowledge of another object-oriented programming language will certainly help, although you may have to change some ideas and unlearn a few habits. Java is considerably simpler than languages such as C++ and Smalltalk. If you learn well from concise examples and personal experimentation, you'll like this book.

New Developments

We cover all of the important features of the latest "long-term support" release of Java, officially called Java Standard Edition (SE) 21, OpenJDK 21. Sun Microsystems (Java's keeper before Oracle) has changed the naming scheme many times over the years. Sun coined the term *Java 2* to cover the major new features introduced in Java version 1.2 and dropped the term *JDK* in favor of *SDK*. With the sixth release, Sun skipped from Java version 1.4 to Java 5.0 but revived the term JDK and kept its numbering convention. After that, we had Java 6, Java 7, and Java 8. Starting with Java 9, Oracle announced a regular (an expedited) release cadence. New versions are released twice a year, and we are at Java 21 as we write in 2023.

This release of Java reflects a mature language with occasional syntactic changes and updates to packages and libraries. We've tried to capture these new features and update every example in this book to reflect the current Java style and best practices.

New in This Edition (Java 15, 16, 17, 18, 19, 20, 21)

This edition of the book continues our tradition of rework to be as up-to-date as possible. It incorporates changes from recent releases of Java, from Java 15 through Java 21 (early access). New topics in this edition include:

- Virtual threads that allow for impressive performance gains in scenarios requiring many, many threads
- New coverage of functional streams for data processing
- Expanded coverage of lambda expressions
- Updated examples and analysis throughout the book
- Review questions and exercises to help reinforce topics discussed in each chapter

Using This Book

This book is organized as follows:

- Chapters 1 and 2 provide a basic introduction to Java concepts and a tutorial to give you a jump-start on Java programming.
- Chapter 3 discusses fundamental tools for developing with Java (the compiler, the interpreter, *jshell*, and the JAR file package).
- Chapters 4 and 5 introduce programming fundamentals, then describe the Java language itself, beginning with the basic syntax and covering classes and objects, exceptions, arrays, enumerations, annotations, and much more.
- Chapter 6 covers exceptions, errors, and the logging facilities native to Java.
- Chapter 7 covers collections alongside generics and parameterized types in Java.
- Chapter 8 covers text processing, formatting, scanning, string utilities, and many of the core API utilities.
- Chapter 9 covers the language's built-in thread facilities, including the new virtual threads.
- Chapter 10 covers Java file I/O and the NIO package.
- Chapter 11 covers function programming techniques in Java.
- Chapter 12 covers the basics of graphical user interface (GUI) development with Swing.
- Chapter 13 covers network communication for both clients and servers, as well as accessing web resources.

If you're like us, you don't read books from front to back. If you're really like us, you usually don't read the preface at all. However, on the off chance that you will see this in time, here are a few suggestions:

- If you are already a programmer and just need to learn Java in the next five minutes, you are probably looking for the examples. You might want to start by glancing at the tutorial in Chapter 2. If that doesn't float your boat, you should at least look at the information in Chapter 3, which explains how to use the compiler and interpreter. This should get you started.
- Chapter 12 discusses Java's graphics features and component architecture. You should read this if you are interested in writing desktop graphical Java applications.

- Chapter 13 is the place to head if you are interested in writing network applications or interacting with web-based services. Networking remains one of the more interesting and important parts of Java.

Online Resources

There are many online sources for information about Java.

Look at Oracle's official website (*https://oreil.ly/Lo8QZ*) for Java topics such as the software, updates, and Java releases. This is where you'll find the reference implementation of the JDK, which includes the compiler, the interpreter, and other tools.

Oracle also maintains the OpenJDK site (*https://oreil.ly/DrTm4*). This is the primary open source version of Java and the associated tools. We'll be using the OpenJDK for all the examples in this book.

You should also visit O'Reilly's site (*http://oreilly.com*). There you'll find information about other O'Reilly books for both Java and a growing array of other topics. You should also check out the online learning and conference options—O'Reilly is a real champion for education in all its forms.

And of course, you can check the home page for *Learning Java* (*https://oreil.ly/learning-java-6e*)!

Conventions Used in This Book

The font conventions used in this book are quite simple.

Italic is used for:

- Pathnames, filenames, and program names
- Internet addresses, such as domain names and URLs
- New terms where they are defined
- Program names, compilers, interpreters, utilities, and commands
- Emphasis on important points

`Constant width` is used for:

- Anything that might appear in a Java program, including method names, variable names, and class names
- Tags that might appear in an HTML or XML document
- Keywords, objects, and environment variables

Constant width bold is used for:

- Text that is typed by the user on the command line or in a dialog

Constant width italic is used for:

- Replaceable items in code

 This element signifies a tip or suggestion.

 This element signifies a general note.

 This element indicates a warning or caution.

In the main body of text, we always use a pair of empty parentheses after a method name to distinguish methods from variables, classes, and other creatures.

In the Java source listings, we follow the coding conventions most frequently used in the Java community. Class names begin with capital letters; variable and method names begin with lowercase. All the letters in the names of constants are capitalized. We don't use underscores to separate words in a long name; following common practice, we capitalize individual words (after the first) and run the words together. For example: `thisIsAVariable`, `thisIsAMethod()`, `ThisIsAClass`, and `THIS_IS_A_CONSTANT`. Also note that we differentiate between static and non-static methods when we refer to them. Unlike some books, we never write `Foo.bar()` to mean the `bar()` method of `Foo` unless `bar()` is a static method (paralleling the Java syntax in that case).

For source listings from example programs, the listing will begin with a comment indicating the related filename (and method name, if needed):

```
// filename: ch02/examples/HelloWorld.java

public static void main(String args[]) {
  System.out.println("Hello, world!");
}
```

You should feel free to look at the noted file in your editor or IDE. We encourage you to compile and run the examples. And we especially encourage tinkering!

For work in *jshell*, we will always retain the `jshell` prompt:

```
jshell> System.out.println("Hello, jshell!")
Hello, jshell!
```

Other snippets without a filename or *jshell* prompt are meant to illustrate valid syntax and structure, or to present a hypothetical approach to handling a programming task. These undecorated listings are not necessarily meant to be executed, although you are always encouraged to create your own classes for trying out any topic in the book.

Using Code Examples

This book is here to help you get your job done. In general, if example code is offered with this book, you may use it in your programs and documentation. You do not need to contact us for permission unless you're reproducing a significant portion of the code. For example, writing a program that uses several chunks of code from this book does not require permission. Selling or distributing examples from O'Reilly books does require permission. Answering a question by citing this book and quoting example code does not require permission. Incorporating a significant amount of example code from this book into your product's documentation does require permission.

We appreciate, but generally do not require, attribution. An attribution usually includes the title, author, publisher, and ISBN. For example: "*Learning Java* by Marc Loy, Patrick Niemeyer, and Daniel Leuck (O'Reilly). Copyright 2023 Marc Loy, 978-1-098-14553-8."

If you feel your use of code examples falls outside fair use or the permission given above, feel free to contact us at *permissions@oreilly.com*.

If you have a technical question or a problem using the code examples, please send email to *bookquestions@oreilly.com*.

O'Reilly Online Learning

O'REILLY® For more than 40 years, *O'Reilly Media* has provided technology and business training, knowledge, and insight to help companies succeed.

Our unique network of experts and innovators share their knowledge and expertise through books, articles, and our online learning platform. O'Reilly's online learning platform gives you on-demand access to live training courses, in-depth learning paths, interactive coding environments, and a vast collection of text and video from O'Reilly and 200+ other publishers. For more information, visit *https://oreilly.com*.

How to Contact Us

Please address comments and questions concerning this book to the publisher:

O'Reilly Media, Inc.
1005 Gravenstein Highway North
Sebastopol, CA 95472
800-889-8969 (in the United States or Canada)
707-829-7019 (international or local)
707-829-0104 (fax)
support@oreilly.com
https://www.oreilly.com/about/contact.html

We have a web page for this book where we list errata and any additional information. You can access this page at *https://oreil.ly/learning-java-6e*.

You can visit GitHub to grab the code examples (*https://github.com/l0y/learnjava6e*). More details on downloading and working with the examples are provided in Appendix A.

For news and information about our books and courses, visit *https://oreilly.com*.

Find us on LinkedIn: *https://linkedin.com/company/oreilly-media*

Follow us on Twitter: *https://twitter.com/oreillymedia*

Watch us on YouTube: *https://youtube.com/oreillymedia*

Acknowledgments

Many people have contributed to putting this book together, both in its *Exploring Java* incarnation and in its current form as *Learning Java*. Foremost, we would like to thank Brian Guerin, Senior Acquisitions Editor, and Zan McQuade, Content Director, for kicking off this edition. Indeed, we want to thank the entire team at O'Reilly, including Sarah Grey, Development Editor; Ashley Stussy, Production Editor; and Kristen Brown, Manager, Content Services. It's hard to imagine a company more dedicated to the success of their employees, authors, and readers. Sarah deserves a particularly loud shoutout for her work editing this sixth edition. Authors often thank their editors regardless of the genre of book, but this gratitude and praise is doubly important for technical topics. Sarah is a tireless collaborator who lifted our moods almost as regularly as she improved the quality of our writing.

Several reviewers provided valuable feedback as we prepared this edition. Duncan MacGregor directed several topics down more useful paths. Eric van Hoose tightened our prose. David Calabrese noted spots where new programmers might need more background. And Alex Faber helped validate the code for all of our examples and exercises. As with so many things, extra eyes are indispensable. We are lucky to have had such attentive pairs in our corner.

The original version of the glossary came from David Flanagan's book *Java in a Nutshell* (*http://oreil.ly/Java_Nutshell_5*) (O'Reilly). We also borrowed several class hierarchy diagrams from David's book. These diagrams were based on similar diagrams by Charles L. Perkins.

Finally, warm thanks to Ron Becker for sound advice and interesting ideas as seen from the perspective of a layman well removed from the programming world.

CHAPTER 1

A Modern Language

The greatest challenges and most exciting opportunities for software developers today lie in harnessing the power of networks. Applications created today, whatever their intended scope or audience, will almost certainly run on machines linked by a global network of computing resources. The increasing importance of networks is placing new demands on existing tools and fueling the demand for a rapidly growing list of completely new kinds of applications.

As users, we want software that works—consistently, anywhere, on any platform—and that plays well with other applications. We want dynamic applications that take advantage of a connected world, capable of accessing disparate and distributed information sources. We want truly distributed software that can be extended and upgraded seamlessly. We want intelligent applications that can roam the cloud for us, ferreting out information and serving as electronic emissaries. We have known for some time what kind of software we want, but it is really only in the past few years that we have begun to get it.

The problem, historically, has been that the tools for building these applications have fallen short. The requirements of speed and portability have been, for the most part, mutually exclusive, and security has been largely ignored or misunderstood. In the past, truly portable languages were bulky, interpreted, and slow. These languages were popular as much for their high-level functionality as for their portability. Fast languages usually provided speed by binding themselves to particular platforms, so they met the portability requirement only halfway. There were even a few languages that nudged programmers to write better, more secure code, but they were primarily offshoots of the portable languages and suffered from the same problems. Java is a modern language that addresses all three of these fronts: portability, speed, and security. This is why it remains a dominant language in the world of programming almost three decades after its introduction.

Enter Java

The Java programming language was designed to be a machine-independent programming language that is both safe enough to traverse networks and powerful enough to replace native executable code. Java addresses the issues raised here and played a starring role in the growth of the internet, leading to where we are today.

Java has become the premier platform for web-based applications and web services. These applications use technologies such as the Java Servlet API, Java Web Services, and many popular open source and commercial Java application servers and frameworks. Java's portability and speed make it the platform of choice for modern business applications. Java servers running on open source Linux platforms are at the heart of the business and financial world today.

Initially, most of the enthusiasm for Java centered on its capabilities for building embedded applications for the web, called *applets*. But in the early days, applets and other client-side graphical user interfaces (GUIs) written in Java were limited. Today, Java has Swing, a sophisticated toolkit for building GUIs. This development has allowed Java to become a viable platform for developing traditional client-side application software, although many other contenders have entered this crowded field.

This book will show you how to use Java to accomplish real-world programming tasks. In the coming chapters we'll introduce you to a wide selection of Java features, including text processing, networking, file handling, and building desktop applications with Swing.

Java's Origins

The seeds of Java were planted in 1990 by Sun Microsystems patriarch and chief researcher Bill Joy. At the time, Sun was competing in a relatively small workstation market, while Microsoft was beginning its domination of the more mainstream, Intel-based PC world. When Sun missed the boat on the PC revolution, Joy retreated to Aspen, Colorado, to work on advanced research. He was committed to the idea of accomplishing complex tasks with simple software and founded the aptly named Sun Aspen Smallworks.

Of the original members of the small team of programmers Joy assembled in Aspen, James Gosling will be remembered as the father of Java. Gosling first made a name for himself in the early 1980s as the author of Gosling Emacs, the first version of the popular Emacs editor that was written in C and ran under Unix. Gosling Emacs was soon eclipsed by a free version, GNU Emacs, written by Emacs's original designer. By that time, Gosling had moved on to design Sun's Network extensible Window System (NeWS), which briefly contended with the X Window System for control of the Unix GUI desktop in 1987. Although some people would argue that NeWS was superior to X, NeWS lost because Sun kept it proprietary and didn't publish source code, while the primary developers of X formed the X Consortium and took the opposite approach.

Designing NeWS taught Gosling the power of integrating an expressive language with a network-aware windowing GUI. It also taught Sun that the internet programming community will ultimately refuse to accept proprietary standards, no matter how good they may be. NeWS's failure sowed the seeds of Java's licensing scheme and open (if not quite "open source") code. Gosling brought what he had learned to Bill Joy's nascent Aspen project. In 1992, work on the project led to the founding of the Sun subsidiary FirstPerson, Inc. Its mission was to lead Sun into the world of consumer electronics.

The FirstPerson team worked on developing software for information appliances, such as cellular phones and personal digital assistants (PDAs). The goal was to enable the transfer of information and real-time applications over cheap infrared and traditional packet-based networks. Memory and bandwidth limitations dictated small, efficient code. The nature of the applications also demanded they be safe and robust. Gosling and his teammates began programming in C++, but they soon found themselves confounded by a language that was too complex, unwieldy, and insecure for the task. They decided to start from scratch, and Gosling began working on something he dubbed "C++ minus minus."

With the foundering of the Apple Newton (Apple's earliest handheld computer), it became apparent that the PDA's ship had not yet come in, so Sun shifted FirstPerson's efforts to interactive TV (ITV). The programming language of choice for ITV set-top boxes was to be the near ancestor of Java, a language called Oak. Even with its elegance and ability to provide safe interactivity, Oak could not salvage the lost cause of ITV. Customers didn't want it, and Sun soon abandoned the concept.

At that time, Joy and Gosling got together to decide on a new strategy for their innovative language. It was 1993, and the explosion of interest in the web presented a new opportunity. Oak was small, safe, architecture independent, and object-oriented. As it happens, these are also some of the requirements for a universal, internet-savvy programming language. Sun quickly changed focus, and, with a little retooling, Oak became Java.

Growing Up

It wouldn't be an overstatement to say that Java (and its developer-focused bundle, the Java Development Kit, or JDK) caught on like wildfire. Even before its first official release, when Java was still a nonproduct, nearly every major industry player jumped on the Java bandwagon. Java licensees included Microsoft, Intel, IBM, and virtually all major hardware and software vendors. However, even with all this support, Java took a lot of knocks and experienced some growing pains during its first few years.

A series of breach of contract and antitrust lawsuits between Sun and Microsoft over the distribution of Java and its use in Internet Explorer hampered its deployment on the world's most common desktop operating system—Windows. Microsoft's involvement with Java also became one focus of a larger federal lawsuit over serious anticompetitive practices at the company. Court testimony revealed the software giant had attempted to undermine Java by introducing incompatibilities in its version of the language. Meanwhile, Microsoft introduced its own Java-derived language called C# (C-sharp) as part of its .NET initiative and dropped Java from inclusion in Windows. C# has gone on to become a very good language in its own right, enjoying more innovation in recent years than has Java.

But Java continues to spread on a wide variety of platforms. As we begin looking at the Java architecture, you'll see that much of what is exciting about Java comes from the self-contained virtual machine environment in which Java applications run. Java was carefully designed so that this supporting architecture can be implemented either in software, for existing computer platforms, or in customized hardware. Hardware implementations of Java are used in some smart cards and other embedded systems. You can even buy "wearable" devices, such as rings and dog tags, that have Java interpreters embedded in them. Software implementations of Java are available for all modern computer platforms, right down to portable computing devices. Today, an offshoot of the Java platform is the basis for Google's Android operating system, which powers billions of phones and other mobile devices.

In 2010, Oracle Corporation bought Sun Microsystems and became the steward of the Java language. In a somewhat rocky start to its tenure, Oracle sued Google over its use of the Java language in Android and lost. In July 2011, Oracle released Java Standard Edition 7,[1] a significant Java release that included a new I/O package. In 2017, Java 9 introduced modules to address some long-standing issues with the way Java applications were compiled, distributed, and executed. Java 9 also kicked off a rapid update process leading to some Java versions being designated "long-term support" and the rest as standard, short-term versions. (More on these and other versions in "A Java Road Map" on page 20.) Oracle continues to lead Java development; however, it has also bifurcated the Java world by moving the main Java deployment environment to a costly commercial license, while offering a free subsidiary OpenJDK option that retains the accessibility many developers love and expect.

---

1 The Standard Edition (SE) moniker appeared early in Java's history when Sun released the J2EE platform, or Java 2 Enterprise Edition. The Enterprise Edition now goes by the name "Jakarta EE."

A Virtual Machine

Before we get much farther, it's useful to know a bit more about the environment Java needs to do its magic. It's OK if you don't understand everything we touch on in these next sections. Any unfamiliar term you might see will get its due in later chapters. We just want to provide you with an overview of Java's ecosystem. At the core of that ecosystem is the *Java Virtual Machine* (JVM).

Java is both a compiled and an interpreted language. Java source code is turned into simple binary instructions, much like ordinary microprocessor machine code. However, whereas C or C++ source is reduced to native instructions for a particular model of processor, Java source is compiled into a universal format—instructions for the virtual machine known as *bytecode*.

Java bytecode is executed by a Java runtime interpreter. The runtime system performs all the normal activities of a hardware processor, but it does so in a safe, virtual environment. It executes a stack-based instruction set and manages memory like an operating system. It creates and manipulates primitive data types and loads and invokes newly referenced blocks of code. Most importantly, it does all this in accordance with a strictly defined open specification that can be implemented by anyone who wants to produce a Java-compliant virtual machine. Together, the virtual machine and language definition provide a complete specification. There are no features of the base Java language left undefined or implementation dependent. For example, Java specifies the sizes and mathematical properties of all its primitive data types rather than leaving it up to the platform implementation.

The Java interpreter is relatively lightweight and small; it can be implemented in whatever form is desirable for a particular platform. The interpreter may be run as a separate application or it can be embedded in another piece of software, such as a web browser. Put together, this means that Java code is implicitly portable. The same Java application bytecode can run on any platform that provides a Java runtime environment, as shown in Figure 1-1. You don't have to produce alternative versions of your application for different platforms, and you don't have to distribute source code to end users.

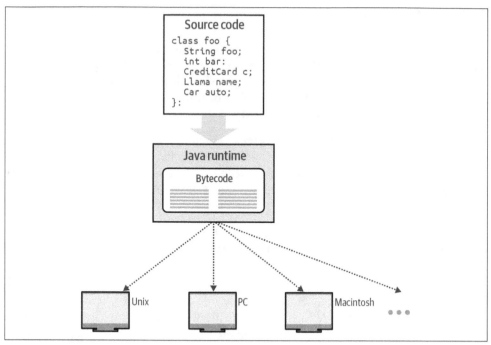

Figure 1-1. The Java runtime environment

The fundamental unit of Java code is the *class*. As in other object-oriented languages, classes are small, modular application components that hold executable code and data. Compiled Java classes are distributed in a universal binary format that contains Java bytecode and other class information. Classes can be maintained discretely and stored in files or archives locally or on a network server. Classes are located and loaded dynamically at runtime as they are needed by an application.

In addition to the platform-specific runtime system, Java has a number of fundamental classes that contain architecture-dependent methods. These *native methods* serve as the gateway between the Java virtual machine and the real world. They are implemented in a natively compiled language on the host platform and provide low-level access to resources such as the network, the windowing system, and the host filesystem. The vast majority of Java, however, is written in Java itself—bootstrapped from these basic parts—and is therefore portable. This includes important Java tools such as the Java compiler also written in Java and therefore available on all Java platforms in exactly the same way without porting.

Historically, interpreters have been considered slow, but Java is not a traditional interpreted language. In addition to compiling source code down to portable bytecode, Java has also been carefully designed so that software implementations of the runtime system can further optimize their performance by compiling bytecode to native machine code on the fly. This is called dynamic or *just-in-time* (JIT) compilation. With JIT compilation, Java code can execute as fast as native code and maintain its transportability and security.

This JIT feature is an often misunderstood point among those who want to compare language performance. There is only one intrinsic performance penalty that compiled Java code suffers at runtime for the sake of security and virtual machine design—array bounds checking. Everything else can be optimized to native code just as it can with a statically compiled language. Going beyond that, the Java language includes more structural information than many other languages, providing for more types of optimizations. Also remember that these optimizations can be made at runtime, taking into account the actual application behavior and characteristics. What can be done at compile time that can't be done better at runtime? Well, there is a trade-off: time.

The problem with a traditional JIT compilation is that optimizing code takes time. While a JIT compiler can produce decent results, it may suffer significant latency when the application starts up. This is generally not a problem for long-running server-side applications, but it is a serious problem for client-side software and applications that run on smaller devices with limited capabilities. To address this, Java's compiler technology, called HotSpot, uses a trick called *adaptive compilation*. If you look at what programs actually spend their time doing, it turns out that they spend almost all their time executing a relatively small part of the code again and again. The chunk of code that is executed repeatedly may be only a small fraction of the total program, but its behavior determines the program's overall performance. Adaptive compilation allows the Java runtime to take advantage of new kinds of optimizations that simply can't be done in a statically compiled language, hence the claim that Java code can run faster than C/C++ in some cases.

To take advantage of this adaptive ability, HotSpot starts out as a normal Java byte-code interpreter, but with a difference: it measures (profiles) the code as it is executing to see what parts are being executed repeatedly. Once it knows which parts of the code are crucial to performance, HotSpot compiles those sections into optimal native machine code. Since it compiles only a small portion of the program into machine code, it can afford to take the time necessary to optimize those portions. The rest of the program may not need to be compiled at all—just interpreted—saving memory and time. In fact, the Java VM can run in one of two modes: client and server, which determine whether it emphasizes quick startup time and memory conservation or flat-out performance. As of Java 9, you can also put *ahead-of-time* (AOT) compilation to use if minimizing your application startup time is really important.

A natural question to ask at this point is, why throw away all this good profiling information each time an application shuts down? Well, Sun partially broached this topic with the release of Java 5.0 through the use of shared, read-only classes that are stored persistently in an optimized form. This significantly reduced both the startup time and overhead of running many Java applications on a given machine. The technology for doing this is complex, but the idea is simple: optimize the parts of the program that need to go fast, and don't worry about the rest.

Of course, "the rest" does contain code that could be further optimized. In 2022, OpenJDK's Project Leyden (*https://oreil.ly/pZnd5*) kicked off with the intention of further reducing the startup time, minimizing the large size of Java applications, and reducing the time it takes for all of the previously mentioned optimizations to take full effect. The mechanisms proposed by Project Leyden are fairly complex, so we won't be discussing them in this book. But we wanted to highlight the constant work going into developing and improving Java and its ecosystem. Even some 30 years after its debut, Java remains a modern language.

Java Compared with Other Languages

Java's developers drew on many years of programming experience with other languages in their choice of features. It is worth taking a moment to compare Java at a high level with some of those languages, both for the benefit of those of you with other programming experience and for the newcomers who need to put things in context. While this book does expect you to have some comfort with computers and software applications in a generic sense, we do not expect you to have knowledge of any particular programming language. When we refer to other languages by way of comparison, we hope that the comments are self-explanatory.

At least three pillars are necessary to support a universal programming language today: portability, speed, and security. Figure 1-2 shows how Java compares to a few of the languages that were popular when it was created.

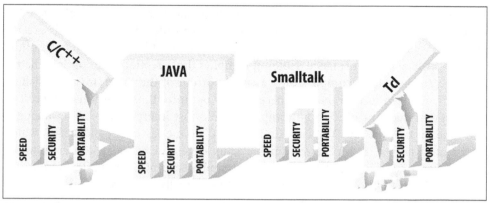

Figure 1-2. Programming languages compared

You may have heard that Java is a lot like C or C++, but that's really not true except at a superficial level. When you first look at Java code, you'll see that the basic syntax looks like C or C++. But that's where the similarities end. Java is by no means a direct descendant of C or a next-generation C++. If you compare language features, you'll see that Java actually has more in common with highly dynamic languages, such as Smalltalk and Lisp. In fact, Java's implementation is about as far from native C as you can imagine.

If you are familiar with the current language landscape, you will notice that C#, a popular language, is missing from this comparison. C# is largely Microsoft's answer to Java, admittedly with a number of niceties layered on top. Given their common design goals and approach (such as use of a virtual machine, bytecode, and a sandbox), the platforms don't differ substantially in terms of their speed or security characteristics. C# is more or less as portable as Java. Like Java, C# borrows heavily from C syntax but is really a closer relative of the dynamic languages. Most Java developers find it relatively easy to pick up C# and vice versa. The majority of the time you'll spend moving from one to the other will be in learning the standard library.

The surface-level similarities to these languages are worth noting, however. Java borrows heavily from C and C++ syntax, so you'll see terse language constructs, including an abundance of curly braces and semicolons. Java subscribes to the C philosophy that a good language should be compact; in other words, it should be sufficiently small and regular that a programmer can hold all of its capabilities in their head at once. Just as C is extensible with libraries, packages of Java classes can be added to the core language components to extend its vocabulary.

C has been successful because it provides a reasonably feature-packed programming environment, with high performance and an acceptable degree of portability. Java also tries to balance functionality, speed, and portability, but it does so in a very different way. C trades functionality for portability; Java initially traded speed for portability. Java also addresses security issues that C does not (although in modern systems, many of those concerns are now addressed in the operating system and hardware).

Scripting languages such as Perl, Python, and Ruby remain popular. There's no reason a scripting language can't be suitable for safe, networked applications. But most scripting languages are not well suited for serious, large-scale programming. The attraction to scripting languages is that they are dynamic; they are powerful tools for rapid development. Some scripting languages such as Tcl (more popular when Java was being developed) also help programmers accomplish specific tasks, such as quickly creating graphical interfaces, that more general-purpose languages find unwieldy. Scripting languages are also highly portable, albeit at the source code level.

Not to be confused with Java, JavaScript is an object-based scripting language originally developed by Netscape for the web browser. It serves as a web browser resident language for dynamic, interactive, web-based applications. JavaScript takes its name from its integration with and similarities to Java, but the comparison really ends there. There are, however, significant applications of JavaScript outside of the browser, such as Node.js,[2] and it continues to rise in popularity for developers in a variety of fields. For more information on JavaScript, check out *JavaScript: The Definitive Guide (https://oreil.ly/qj5Jt)* by David Flanagan (O'Reilly).

The problem with scripting languages is that they are rather casual about program structure and data typing. They have simplified type systems and generally don't provide for sophisticated scoping of variables and functions. These characteristics make them less suitable for building large, modular applications. Speed is another problem with scripting languages; the high-level, usually source-interpreted nature of these languages often makes them quite slow.

Advocates of individual scripting languages would take issue with some of these generalizations, and no doubt they'd be right in some cases. Scripting languages have improved in recent years—especially JavaScript, which has had an enormous amount of research poured into its performance. But the fundamental trade-off is undeniable: scripting languages were born as loose, less-structured alternatives to systems programming languages, and they are generally not ideal for large or complex projects for a variety of reasons.

Java offers some of the essential advantages of a scripting language: it is highly dynamic and has the added benefits of a lower-level language. Java has a powerful regular expression package that competes with Perl for working with text. It also has language features that streamline coding with collections, variable argument lists, static imports of methods, and other syntactic sugar that make it more concise.

Incremental development with object-oriented components, combined with Java's simplicity, make it possible to develop applications rapidly and change them easily. Studies have found that developing in Java is faster than in C or C++, strictly based on language features.[3] Java also comes with a large base of standard core classes for common tasks such as building GUIs and handling network communications. Maven Central is an external resource with an enormous range of libraries and packages that can be quickly bundled into your environment to help you tackle all manner of new programming problems. Along with these features, Java has the scalability and

---

2 If you are curious about Node.js, check out Andrew Mead's *Learning Node.js Development* (*https://oreil.ly/Dl_FL*) and Shelley Powers's *Learning Node* (*https://oreil.ly/ZRl15*) at the O'Reilly site.

3 See, for example, G. Phipps, "Comparing Observed Bug and Productivity Rates for Java and C++" (*https://oreil.ly/zgpMa*), *Software—Practice & Experience*, Volume 29, 1999.

software-engineering advantages of more static languages. It provides a safe structure on which to build higher-level frameworks (and even other languages).

As we've already said, Java is similar in design to languages such as Smalltalk and Lisp. However, these languages were used mostly as research vehicles rather than for developing large-scale systems. One reason is that these languages never developed a standard portable binding to operating system services, such as the C standard library or the Java core classes. Smalltalk is compiled to an interpreted bytecode format, and it can be dynamically compiled to native code on the fly, just like Java. But Java improves on the design by using a bytecode verifier to ensure the correctness of compiled Java code. This verifier gives Java a performance advantage over Smalltalk because Java code requires fewer runtime checks. Java's bytecode verifier also helps with security issues, something that Smalltalk doesn't address.

Throughout the rest of this chapter, we'll present a bird's-eye view of the Java language. We'll explain what's new and what's not-so-new about Java and why.

Safety of Design

You have no doubt heard a lot about the fact that Java is designed to be a safe language. But what do we mean by safe? Safe from what or whom? The Java security features that attract the most attention are those that make possible new types of dynamically portable software. Java provides several layers of protection from dangerously flawed code as well as more mischievous things such as viruses and Trojan horses. In the next section, we'll take a look at how the Java virtual machine architecture assesses the safety of code before it's run and how the Java *class loader* (the bytecode loading mechanism of the Java interpreter) builds a wall around untrusted classes. These features provide the foundation for high-level security policies that can allow or disallow various kinds of activities on an application-by-application basis.

In this section, though, we'll look at some general features of the Java programming language. Perhaps more important than the specific security features, although often overlooked in the security din, is the safety that Java provides by addressing common design and programming problems. Java is intended to be as safe as possible from the simple mistakes programmers make ourselves, as well as those we inherit from legacy software. The goal with Java has been to keep the language simple, provide tools that have demonstrated their usefulness, and let users build more complicated facilities on top of the language when needed.

Simplify, Simplify, Simplify…

With Java, simplicity rules. Since Java started with a clean slate, it avoided features that have proved messy or controversial in other languages. For example, Java doesn't allow programmer-defined operator overloading (which, in some languages, allows programmers to redefine the meanings of basic symbols like + and –). Java doesn't have a source code preprocessor, so it doesn't have things like macros, `#define` statements, or conditional source compilation. These constructs exist in other languages primarily to support platform dependencies, so in that sense, they should not be needed in Java. Conditional compilation is also commonly used for debugging, but Java's sophisticated runtime optimizations and features such as assertions solve the problem more elegantly.[4]

Java provides a well-defined *package* structure for organizing class files. The package system allows the compiler to handle some of the functionality of the traditional *make* utility (a tool for building executables from source code). The compiler can also work with compiled Java classes directly because all type information is preserved; there is no need for extraneous source "header" files, as in C/C++. All this means that Java code requires less context to read. Indeed, you may sometimes find it faster to look at the Java source code than to refer to class documentation.

Java also takes a different approach to some structural features that have been troublesome in other languages. For example, Java supports only a single inheritance class hierarchy (each class may have only one "parent" class) but allows multiple inheritance of interfaces. An *interface*, like an abstract class in C++, specifies the behavior of an object without defining its implementation. It is a very powerful mechanism that allows the developer to define a "contract" for object behavior that can be used and referred to independently of any particular object implementation. Interfaces in Java eliminate the need for multiple inheritance of classes and the associated problems.

As you'll see in Chapter 4, Java is a fairly simple and elegant programming language, and that is still a large part of its appeal.

Type Safety and Method Binding

One attribute of a language is the kind of *type checking* it uses. Generally, languages are categorized as *static* or *dynamic*, which refers to the amount of information about variables known at compile time versus what is known while the application is running.

In a strictly statically typed language such as C or C++, data types are etched in stone when the source code is compiled. The compiler benefits from this by having enough information to catch many kinds of errors before the code is executed. For example, the compiler would not allow you to store a floating-point value in an integer variable. The code then doesn't require runtime type checking, so it can be

---

4 Assertions are beyond the scope of this book, but they are a worthy topic for exploration after you've gained more of a foothold in Java. You'll find some basic details in the Oracle Java SE Documentation (*https://oreil.ly/-giQD*).

compiled to be small and fast. But statically typed languages are inflexible. They don't support collections as naturally as languages with dynamic type checking, and they make it impossible for an application to safely import new data types while it's running.

In contrast, a dynamic language such as Smalltalk or Lisp has a runtime system that manages the types of objects and performs necessary type checking while an application is executing. These kinds of languages allow for more complex behavior and are in many respects more powerful. However, they are also generally slower, less safe, and harder to debug.

The differences in languages have been likened to the differences among kinds of automobiles.[5] Statically typed languages such as C++ are analogous to a sports car: reasonably safe and fast, but useful only if you're driving on a nicely paved road. Highly dynamic languages such as Smalltalk are more like an off-road vehicle: they afford you more freedom but can be somewhat unwieldy. It can be fun (and sometimes faster) to go roaring through the backwoods, but you might also get stuck in a ditch or mauled by bears.

Another attribute of a language is the way it binds method calls to their definitions. In a static language such as C or C++, the definitions of methods are normally bound at compile time, unless the programmer specifies otherwise. Languages like Smalltalk, on the other hand, are called *late binding* because they locate the definitions of methods dynamically at runtime. Early binding is important for performance reasons; it lets an application run without the overhead incurred by searching for methods at runtime. But late binding is more flexible. It's also necessary in an object-oriented language where new types can be loaded dynamically and only the runtime system can determine which method to run.

Java provides some of the benefits of both C++ and Smalltalk; it's a statically typed, late-binding language. Every object in Java has a well-defined type that is known at compile time. This means the Java compiler can do the same kind of static type checking and usage analysis as C++. As a result, you can't assign an object to the wrong type of variable or call nonexistent methods on an object. The Java compiler goes even further and prevents you from using uninitialized variables and creating unreachable statements (see Chapter 4).

However, Java is fully runtime-typed as well. The Java runtime system keeps track of all objects and makes it possible to determine their types and relationships during execution. This means you can inspect an object at runtime to determine what it is. Unlike C or C++, the Java runtime system checks casts from one type of object to another, and it's possible to use new kinds of dynamically loaded objects with a

---

5 The credit for the car analogy goes to Marshall P. Cline, author of *C++ FAQ*.

degree of type safety. And because Java uses late binding, it's possible to write code that replaces some method definitions at runtime.

Incremental Development

Java carries all data type and method signature information with it from its source code to its compiled bytecode form. This means that Java classes can be developed incrementally. Your own Java source code can also be compiled safely with classes from other sources your compiler has never seen. In other words, you can write new code that references binary class files without losing the type safety you gain from having the source code.

Java does not suffer from the "fragile base class" problem. In languages such as C++, the implementation of a base class can be effectively frozen because it has many derived classes; changing the base class may require recompiling all of the derived classes. This is an especially difficult problem for developers of class libraries. Java avoids this problem by dynamically locating fields within classes. As long as a class maintains a valid form of its original structure, it can evolve without breaking other classes that are derived from it or use.

Dynamic Memory Management

Some of the most important differences between Java and lower-level languages (such as C or C++) involve how Java manages memory. Java eliminates ad hoc references to arbitrary areas of memory (*pointers*, in other languages) and adds some high-level data structures to the language. Java also cleans up unused objects (a process known as *garbage collection*) efficiently and automatically. These features eliminate many otherwise insurmountable problems with safety, portability, and optimization.

Garbage collection alone has saved countless programmers from the single largest source of programming errors in C or C++: explicit memory allocation and deallocation. In addition to maintaining objects in memory, the Java runtime system keeps track of all references to those objects. When an object is no longer in use, Java automatically removes it from memory. You can, for the most part, simply ignore objects you no longer use, with confidence that the interpreter will clean them up at an appropriate time.

Java uses a sophisticated garbage collector that runs in the background, which means that most garbage collecting takes place during idle times: between I/O pauses, mouse clicks, or keyboard hits. Some runtime systems, such as HotSpot, have more advanced garbage collection that can differentiate the usage patterns of objects (such as short-lived versus long-lived) and optimize their collection. The Java runtime can now tune itself automatically for the optimal distribution of memory for different kinds of applications based on their behavior. With this kind of runtime profiling, automatic memory management can be much faster than the most diligently programmer-managed resources, something that some old-school programmers still find hard to believe.

We've said that Java doesn't have pointers. Strictly speaking, this statement is true, but it's also misleading. What Java provides are *references*—a safer kind of pointer. A reference is a strongly typed handle for an object. All objects in Java, with the exception of primitive numeric types, are accessed through references. You can use references to build all the normal kinds of data structures a C programmer would be accustomed to building with pointers, such as linked lists, trees, and so forth. The only difference is that with references, you have to do so in a type-safe way.

References in Java cannot be changed in the same way as you alter pointers in languages like C. A reference is an atomic thing; you can't manipulate the value of a reference except by assigning it to an object. References are passed by value, and you can't reference an object through more than a single level of indirection. Protecting references is one of the most fundamental aspects of Java security. It means that Java code has to play by the rules; it can't peek into places it shouldn't to circumvent those rules.

Finally, we should mention that arrays (essentially indexed lists) in Java are true, first-class objects. They can be dynamically allocated and assigned like other objects. Arrays know their own size and type. Although you can't directly define or subclass array classes, they do have a well-defined inheritance relationship based on the relationship of their base types. Having true arrays in the language alleviates much of the need for pointer arithmetic, such as that used in C or C++.

Error Handling

Java's roots are in networked devices and embedded systems. For these applications, it's important to have robust and intelligent error management. Java has a powerful mechanism for handling *exceptions*, somewhat like that in newer implementations of C++. Exceptions provide a more natural and elegant way to deal with errors. Exceptions allow you to separate error-handling code from normal code, which makes for cleaner, more readable applications.

When an exception occurs, it causes the flow of program execution to be transferred to a predesignated "catch" block of code. The exception carries with it an object that contains information about the situation that caused the problem. The Java compiler requires that a method either declare the exceptions it can generate or catch and deal with them itself. This promotes error information to the same level of importance as arguments and return types for methods. As a Java programmer, you know precisely what exceptional conditions you must deal with, and you have help from the compiler in writing correct software that doesn't leave them unhandled.

Threads

Modern applications require a high degree of parallelism. Even a very single-minded application can have a complex user interface, which requires concurrent activities. As machines get faster, users become less patient with unrelated tasks that seize control of their time. Threads provide efficient multiprocessing and distribution of tasks for both client and server applications. Java makes threads easy to use because support for them is built into the language.

Concurrency is nice, but there's more to programming with threads than just performing multiple tasks simultaneously. In most cases, threads need to be *synchronized* (coordinated), which can be tricky without explicit language support. Java supports synchronization based on the *monitor* model—a sort of lock and key system for accessing resources. The keyword `synchronized` designates methods and blocks of code for safe, serialized access within an object. There are also simple, primitive methods for explicit waiting and signaling between threads interested in the same object.

Java has a high-level concurrency package that provides powerful utilities addressing common patterns in multithreaded programming, such as thread pools, coordination of tasks, and sophisticated locking. With the addition of the concurrency package and related utilities, Java provides some of the most advanced thread-related utilities of any language. And when you need many, many threads, you can tap into the world of Project Loom's virtual threads starting as a preview feature in Java 19.

Although some developers may never have to write multithreaded code, learning to program with threads is an important part of mastering programming in Java and something all developers should grasp. See Chapter 9 for a discussion of this topic. "Virtual Threads" on page 285 in particular introduces virtual threads and highlights some of their performance gains.

Scalability

As we noted earlier, Java programs primarily consist of classes. Over classes, Java provides *packages*, a layer of structure that groups classes into functional units. Packages provide a naming convention for organizing classes and a second tier of organizational control over the visibility of variables and methods in Java applications.

Within a package, a class is either publicly visible or protected from outside access. Packages form another type of scope that is closer to the application level. This lends itself to building reusable components that work together in a system. Packages also help in designing a scalable application that can grow without becoming a bird's nest of tightly coupled code. The reuse and scale issues are really only enforced with the module system added in Java 9.[6]

Safety of Implementation

It's one thing to create a language that prevents you from shooting yourself in the foot; it's quite another to create one that prevents others from shooting you in the foot.

Encapsulation is the concept of hiding data and behavior within a class; it's an important part of object-oriented design. It helps you write clean, modular software. In most languages, however, the visibility of data items is simply part of the relationship between the programmer and the compiler. It's a matter of semantics, not an assertion about the actual security of the data in the context of the running program's environment.

When Bjarne Stroustrup, the creator of C++, chose the keyword `private` to designate hidden members of classes in C++, he was probably thinking about shielding a developer from the messy details of another developer's code, not about shielding that developer's classes and objects from attack by someone else's viruses and Trojan horses. Arbitrary casting and pointer arithmetic in C or C++ make it trivial to violate access permissions on classes without breaking the rules of the language. Consider the following code:

```
// C++ code
class Finances {
    private:
        char creditCardNumber[16];
        // ...
};

main() {
    Finances finances;

    // Forge a pointer to peek inside the class
    char *cardno = (char *)&finances;
    printf("Card Number = %.16s\n", cardno);
}
```

In this little C++ drama, we have written some code that violates the encapsulation of the `Finances` class and pulls out some secret information. This sort of shenanigan—abusing an untyped pointer—is not possible in Java. If this example seems unrealistic, consider how important it is to protect the foundation (system) classes of the

---

6 Modules are beyond the scope of this book, but they are the sole focus of *Java 9 Modularity* (*https://oreil.ly/ TLbpl*) by Paul Bakker and Sander Mak (O'Reilly).

runtime environment from similar kinds of attacks. If untrusted code can corrupt the components that provide access to real resources such as the filesystem, network, or windowing system, it certainly has a chance at stealing your credit card numbers.

Java grew up with the internet—and all the untrusted sources that abound there. It used to require more security than it does now, but it retains a couple security features: a class loader handles loading classes from local storage or the network, and below that, all system security ultimately rests on the Java verifier, which guarantees the integrity of incoming classes.

The Java bytecode verifier is a special module and a fixed part of the Java runtime system. Class loaders, however, are components that may be implemented differently by different applications, such as servers or web browsers. All of these pieces need to be functioning properly to ensure security in the Java environment.

The Verifier

Java's first line of defense is the *bytecode verifier*. The verifier reads bytecode before it is run and makes sure it is well-behaved and obeys the basic rules of the Java bytecode specification. A trusted Java compiler won't produce code that does otherwise. However, it's possible for a mischievous person to deliberately assemble bad Java bytecode. It's the verifier's job to detect this.

Once code has been verified, it's considered safe from certain inadvertent or malicious errors. For example, verified code can't forge references or violate access permissions on objects (as in our credit card example). It can't perform illegal casts or use objects in unintended ways. It can't even cause certain types of internal errors, such as overflowing or underflowing the internal stack. These fundamental guarantees underlie all of Java's security.

You might be wondering, isn't this kind of safety implicit in lots of interpreted languages? Well, while it's true that you shouldn't be able to corrupt a BASIC interpreter with a bogus line of BASIC code, remember that the protection in most interpreted languages happens at a higher level. Those languages are likely to have heavyweight interpreters that do a great deal of runtime work, so they are necessarily slower and more cumbersome.

By comparison, Java bytecode is a relatively light, low-level instruction set. The ability to statically verify the Java bytecode before execution lets the Java interpreter run at full speed later with full safety, without expensive runtime checks. This was one of the fundamental innovations in Java.

The verifier is a type of mathematical "theorem prover." It steps through the Java bytecode and applies simple, inductive rules to determine certain aspects of how the bytecode will behave. This kind of analysis is possible because compiled Java bytecode contains a lot more type information than the object code of other languages of this kind. The bytecode also has to obey a few extra rules that simplify its behavior. First, most bytecode instructions operate only on individual data types. For example, with stack operations, there are separate instructions for object references and for each of the numeric types in Java. Similarly, there is a different instruction for moving each type of value into and out of a local variable.

Second, the type of object resulting from any operation is always known in advance. No bytecode operations consume values and produce more than one possible type of value as output. As a result, it's always possible to look at the next instruction and its operands and know the type of value that will result.

Because an operation always produces a known type, it's possible to determine the types of all items on the stack and in local variables at any point in the future by looking at the starting state. The collection of all this type information at any given time is called the *type state* of the stack. This is what Java tries to analyze before it runs an application. Java doesn't know anything about the actual values of stack and variable items at this time; it only knows what kind of items they are. However, this is enough information to enforce the security rules and to ensure that objects are not manipulated illegally.

To make it feasible to analyze the type state of the stack, Java places an additional restriction on how its bytecode instructions are executed: all paths to the same point in the code must arrive with exactly the same type state.

Class Loaders

Java adds a second layer of security with a *class loader*. A class loader is responsible for bringing the bytecode for Java classes into the interpreter. Every application that loads classes from the network must use a class loader to handle this task.

After a class has been loaded and passed through the verifier, it remains associated with its class loader. As a result, classes are effectively partitioned into separate name-spaces based on their origin. When a loaded class references another class name, the location of the new class is provided by the original class loader. This means that classes retrieved from a specific source can be restricted to interact only with other classes retrieved from that same location. For example, a Java-enabled web browser can use a class loader to build a separate space for all the classes loaded from a given URL. Sophisticated security based on cryptographically signed classes can also be implemented using class loaders.

The search for classes always begins with the built-in Java system classes. These classes are loaded from the locations specified by the Java interpreter's *classpath* (see Chapter 3). Classes in the classpath are loaded by the system only once and can't be replaced. This means that it's impossible for an application to replace fundamental system classes with its own versions that change their functionality.

Application and User-Level Security

There's a fine line between having enough power to do something useful and having all the power to do anything you want. Java provides the foundation for a secure environment in which untrusted code can be quarantined, managed, and safely executed. However, unless you are content with keeping that code in a little black box and running it just for its own benefit, you will have to grant it access to at least some system resources so that it can be useful. Every kind of access carries with it certain risks and benefits. For example, in the cloud service environment, the advantages of granting untrusted (unknown) code access to the cloud server's filesystem are that it can find and process large files faster than you could download them and process locally. The associated risks are that the code may instead sneak around the cloud server and possibly discover sensitive information it should not see.

At one extreme, the simple act of running an application gives it a resource—computation time—that it may put to good use or burn frivolously. It's difficult to prevent an untrusted application from wasting your time or even attempting a "denial of service" attack. At the other extreme, a powerful, trusted application may justifiably deserve access to all sorts of system resources (like the filesystem, process creation, or network interfaces); a malicious application could wreak havoc with these resources. The message here is that you must address important and sometimes complex security issues in your programs.

In some situations, it may be acceptable to simply ask the user to "okay" requests. The Java language provides the tools to implement any security policies you want. However, what policies you choose ultimately depends on whether or not you trust the identity and integrity of the code in question. This is where digital signatures come into play.

Digital signatures, together with certificates, are techniques for verifying that data truly comes from the source it claims to have come from and hasn't been modified en route. If the Bank of Boofa signs its checkbook application, you can verify that the app actually came from the bank rather than an imposter and hasn't been modified. Therefore, you can tell your system to trust code that has the Bank of Boofa's signature.

A Java Road Map

With the constant updates to Java, it's hard to keep track of what features are available now, what's promised, and what's been around for some time. The following sections constitute a road map that imposes some order on Java's past, present, and future. As for the versions of Java, Oracle's release notes contain good summaries with links to further details. If you're using older versions for work, consider reading over the Oracle technology resources documents (*https://oreil.ly/oi6eL*).

The Past: Java 1.0–Java 20

Java 1.0 provided the basic framework for Java development: the language itself, plus packages that let you write applets and simple applications. Although 1.0 is officially obsolete, a few applets still exist that conform to its API.

Java 1.1 superseded 1.0, incorporating major improvements in the Abstract Window Toolkit (AWT) package (Java's original GUI facility), a new event pattern, new language facilities such as reflection and inner classes, and many other critical features. Java 1.1 is the version that was supported natively by most versions of Netscape and Microsoft Internet Explorer for many years. For various political reasons, the browser world was frozen in this condition for a long time.

Java 1.2, dubbed "Java 2" by Sun, was a major release in December 1998. It provided many improvements and additions, mainly in terms of the set of APIs that were bundled into the standard distributions. The most notable additions were the inclusion of the Swing GUI package as a core API and a new, full-fledged 2D drawing API. Swing is Java's advanced UI toolkit with capabilities far exceeding the old AWT's. (Swing, AWT, and some other packages have been variously called the JFC, or Java Foundation Classes.) Java 1.2 also added a proper collections API to Java.

Java 1.3, released in early 2000, added minor features but was primarily focused on performance. With version 1.3, Java got significantly faster on many platforms, and Swing received many bug fixes. In this timeframe, Java enterprise APIs such as Servlets and Enterprise JavaBeans also matured.

Java 1.4, released in 2002, integrated a major new set of APIs and many long-awaited features. This included language assertions, regular expressions, preferences and logging APIs, a new I/O system for high-volume applications, standard support for XML, fundamental improvements in AWT and Swing, and a greatly matured Java Servlets API for web applications.

Java 5, released in 2004, was a major release that introduced many long-awaited language syntax enhancements, including generics, type-safe enumerations, the enhanced for-loop, variable argument lists, static imports, autoboxing and unboxing of primitives, as well as advanced metadata on classes. A new concurrency API provided powerful threading capabilities, and APIs for formatted printing and parsing similar to those in C were added. Remote Method Invocation (RMI) was also overhauled to eliminate the need for compiled stubs and skeletons. There were also major additions in the standard XML APIs.

Java 6, released in late 2006, was a relatively minor release that added no new syntactic features to the Java language but bundled new extension APIs such as those for XML and web services.

Java 7, released in 2011, represented a fairly major update. Several small tweaks to the language such as allowing strings in `switch` statements (more on both of those things later!) along with major additions such as the `java.nio` new I/O library were packed into the five years after the release of Java 6.

Java 8, released in 2014, completed a few of the features such as lambdas and default methods that had been dropped from Java 7 as the release date of that version was delayed again and again. This release also had some work done to the date and time support, including the ability to create immutable date objects, handy for use in the now-supported lambdas.

Java 9, released after a number of delays in 2017, introduced the Module System (Project Jigsaw) as well as a Read-Evaluate-Print Loop (REPL) for Java: *jshell*. We'll be using *jshell* for much of our quick explorations of many of Java's features throughout the rest of this book. Java 9 also removed JavaDB from the JDK.

Java 10, released shortly after Java 9 in early 2018, updated garbage collection and brought other features such as root certificates to the OpenJDK builds. Support for unmodifiable collections was added, and support for old look-and-feel packages (such as Apple's Aqua) was removed.

Java 11, released in late 2018, added a standard HTTP client and Transport Layer Security (TLS) 1.3. JavaFX and Java EE modules were removed. (JavaFX was redesigned to live on as a standalone library.) Java applets were also removed. Along with Java 8, Java 11 is part of Oracle's long-term support (LTS). Certain releases—Java 8, Java 11, Java 17, and Java 21—will be maintained for longer periods of time. Oracle is trying to change the way customers and developers engage with new releases, but good reasons still exist to stick with known versions. You can read more about Oracle's thoughts and plans for both LTS and non-LTS releases at the Oracle Technology Network's Oracle Java SE Support Roadmap (*https://oreil.ly/Ba97c*).

Java 12, released in early 2019, added minor language syntax enhancements such as a switch expressions preview.

Java 13, released in September 2019, includes more language feature previews, such as text blocks, as well as a big reimplementation of the Sockets API. Per the official design docs, this impressive effort provides "a simpler and more modern implementation that is easy to maintain and debug."

Java 14, released in March 2020, added more language syntax enhancement previews such as records, updated the garbage collection feature, and removed the Pack200 tools and API. It also moved the switch expression first previewed in Java 12 out of its preview state and into the standard language.

Java 15, released in September 2020, moved support for text blocks (multiline strings) out of preview, and added both hidden and sealed classes that allow new ways to restrict access to certain code. (Sealed classes were kept as a preview feature.) Text encoding support was also updated to Unicode 13.0.

Java 16, released in March 2021, kept sealed classes in preview but moved records out of preview. Networking APIs were expanded to include Unix domain sockets. It also added a list output option to the Streams API.

Java 17, released in September 2021 with LTS, upgraded sealed classes to a regular feature of the language. A preview of pattern matching for `switch` statements was added along with several improvements on macOS. Datagram sockets can now be used to join multicast groups.

Java 18, released in March 2022, finally made UTF-8 the default character set for Java SE APIs. It introduced a simple, static web server appropriate for prototyping or testing, and expanded the options for IP address resolution.

Java 19, released in September 2022, previewed virtual threads, structured concurrency, and record patterns. Unicode support moved to version 14.0, and some additional date-time formats were added.

Java 20, released in March 2023, finally removed several threading operations (stop/pause/resume) that were deprecated as unsafe over 20 years earlier in JDK 1.2. String parsing was improved to support graphemes, such as composed emoji symbols.

The Present: Java 21

This book includes all the latest and greatest improvements through the release of Java 21 in September 2023. With a six-month release cadence in place, newer versions of the JDK will almost certainly be available by the time you read this. As noted above, Oracle wants developers to treat these releases as feature updates. With the exception of the examples that cover virtual threads, Java 17 is sufficient for working with the code in this book. In the rare cases where we use a more recent feature, we will note the minimum version required. You will not need to "keep up" while reading, but if you are using Java for published projects, consider going over Oracle's official road map to see if staying current makes sense.

Feature overview

Here's a brief overview of the most important features of the current core Java API that live outside the standard library:

Java Database Connectivity (JDBC)
A general facility for interacting with databases (introduced in Java 1.1).

Remote Method Invocation (RMI)
Java's distributed objects system. RMI lets you call methods on objects hosted by a server running somewhere else on the network (introduced in Java 1.1).

Java Security
> A facility for controlling access to system resources, combined with a uniform interface to cryptography. Java Security is the basis for signed classes.

Java Desktop
> A catchall for a large number of features starting with Java 9, including the Swing UI components; "pluggable look and feel," which allows you to adapt and theme the entire UI itself; drag and drop; 2D graphics; printing; image and sound display, playback, and manipulation; and accessibility features that can integrate with special software and hardware for people with visual or other impairments.

Internationalization
> The ability to write programs that adapt themselves to the language and locale the user wants to use. The program automatically displays text in the appropriate language (introduced in Java 1.1).

Java Naming and Directory Interface (JNDI)
> A general service for looking up resources. JNDI unifies access to directory services, such as LDAP, Novell's NDS, and others.

The following are "standard extension" APIs. Some, such as those for working with XML and web services, are bundled with the standard edition of Java; some must be downloaded separately and deployed with your application or server:

JavaMail
> A uniform API for writing email software.

Java Media Framework
> Another catchall for coordinating the display of many different kinds of media that includes Java 2D, Java 3D, Java Speech (for both speech recognition and synthesis), Java Sound (high-quality audio), Java TV (for interactive television and similar applications), and others.

Java Servlets
> A facility that lets you write server-side web applications in Java.

Java Cryptography
> Actual implementations of cryptographic algorithms. (This package was separated from Java Security for legal reasons.)

eXtensible Markup Language/eXtensible Stylesheet Language (XML/XSL)
> Tools for creating and manipulating XML documents, validating them, mapping them to and from Java objects, and transforming them with stylesheets.

We'll try to touch on some of these features. Unfortunately for us (but fortunately for Java software developers), the Java environment has become so rich that it's impossible to cover everything in a single book. We'll note other books and resources that do cover any topics we can't tackle in depth.

The Future

Java is certainly not the new kid on the block these days, but it continues to be one of the most popular platforms for web and application development. This is especially true in the areas of web services, web application frameworks, and XML tools. While Java has not dominated mobile platforms in the way it seemed destined to, you can use the Java language and core APIs to program for Google's Android mobile OS, which is used on billions of devices around the world. In the Microsoft camp, the Java-derived C# language has taken over much .NET development and brought the core Java syntax and patterns to those platforms.

The JVM itself is also an interesting area of exploration and growth. New languages are cropping up to take advantage of the JVM's feature set and ubiquity. Clojure (*https://clojure.org*) is a robust functional language with a growing fan base cropping up in a range of work, from hobbyists to the biggest of the big-box stores. And Kotlin (*https://kotlinlang.org*) is a general-purpose language taking over Android development with gusto. It is gaining traction in new environments while retaining good interoperability with Java.

Probably the most exciting areas of change in Java today are found in the trends toward lighter-weight, simpler frameworks for business and toward integrating the Java platform with dynamic languages for scripting web pages and extensions. There is much more interesting work to come.

You have several choices for Java development environments and runtime systems. Oracle's Java Development Kit is available for macOS, Windows, and Linux. Visit Oracle's Java website (*https://oreil.ly/rDigu*) for more information about obtaining the latest official JDK.

Since 2017, Oracle has officially supported updates to the open source OpenJDK. Individuals and small (or even medium-sized) companies may find this free version sufficient. The releases lag behind the commercial JDK release and do not include Oracle's tech support, but Oracle has stated a firm commitment to maintaining free and open access to Java. All of the examples in this book were written and tested using the OpenJDK. You can get more details direct from the horse's (Oracle's?) mouth on the OpenJDK site (*https://openjdk.org*).

For quick installation of a free version of Java 19 (sufficient for almost all examples in this book, although we do note a few language features from later releases), Amazon offers its Corretto (*https://oreil.ly/DVjwL*) distribution online with friendly, familiar installers for all three major platforms. Chapter 2 will walk you through the basic Corretto installation on Windows, macOS, and Linux.

There is also an array of popular Java Integrated Development Environments (IDEs). We'll discuss one in this book: the free Community Edition of JetBrains's IntelliJ IDEA (*https://oreil.ly/gpGao*). This all-in-one development environment lets you write, test, and package software with advanced tools at your fingertips.

Exercises

At the end of each chapter, we'll provide a few questions and code exercises for you to review. The answers to the questions can be found in Appendix B. Solutions to code exercises are included with the other code examples on GitHub (*https://github.com/l0y/learnjava6e*). (Appendix A provides details on downloading and using the code for this book.) We encourage you to answer the questions and try the exercises. Don't worry if you have to go back into a chapter and read a little more to find an answer or look up some method name. That's the point! Learning how to use this book as a reference will come in handy down the road.

1. Which company currently maintains Java?
2. What is the name of the open source development kit for Java?
3. Name the two main components that play a role in Java's approach to securely running bytecode.

CHAPTER 2

A First Application

Before diving into our full discussion of the Java language, let's get our feet wet with some working code and splash around a bit. In this chapter, we'll build a friendly little application that illustrates many of the concepts used throughout the book. We'll take this opportunity to introduce general features of the Java language and applications.

This chapter also serves as a brief introduction to the object-oriented and multithreaded aspects of Java. If these concepts are new to you, we hope that encountering them here in Java for the first time will be a straightforward and pleasant experience. If you have worked with another object-oriented or multithreaded programming environment, you should especially appreciate Java's simplicity and elegance. This chapter is intended only to give you a bird's eye view of the Java language and a feel for how it is used. If you have trouble with any of the concepts introduced here, rest assured they will be covered in greater detail later in the book.

We can't stress enough the importance of experimentation as you learn new concepts here and throughout the book. Don't just read the examples—run them. Where we can, we'll show you how to use *jshell* (more on that in "Trying Java" on page 73) to try things in real time. The source code for the examples in this book can be found on GitHub (*https://github.com/l0y/learnjava6e*). Compile the programs and try them. Then, turn our examples into your examples: play with them, change their behavior, break them, fix them, and hopefully have some fun along the way.

Java Tools and Environment

Although it's possible to write, compile, and run Java applications with nothing more than Oracle's open source Java Development Kit (OpenJDK) and a simple text editor (such as vi or Notepad), today the vast majority of Java code is written with the benefit of an Integrated Development Environment (IDE). The benefits of using an IDE include an all-in-one view of Java source code with syntax highlighting, navigation help, source control, integrated documentation, building, refactoring, and deployment all at your fingertips. Therefore, we are going to skip an academic command-line treatment and start with a popular, free IDE—IntelliJ IDEA CE (Community Edition). If you are adverse to using an IDE, feel free to use the command-line commands `javac HelloJava.java` for compilation and `java HelloJava` to run the upcoming examples.

IntelliJ IDEA requires Java to be installed. This book covers Java 21 language features, so although the examples in this chapter will work with older versions, it's best to have JDK 21 installed to ensure that all examples in the book compile. (Java 19 does have all of the most important features available as well, although many are technically in "preview" mode.) The JDK includes several developer tools that we'll discuss in Chapter 3. You can check to see which version, if any, you have installed by typing `java -version` at the command line. If Java isn't present, or if it's a version older than JDK 19, you will want to install a newer version, as discussed in "Installing the JDK" on page 28. All you'll need for the examples in this book is the basic JDK.

Installing the JDK

It should be said at the outset that you are free to download and use the official, commercial JDK from Oracle (*https://oreil.ly/sYaZm*) for personal use. The versions available on Oracle's download page include the latest version and the most recent long-term support version (both are version 21 at the time of this writing), with links to older versions if legacy compatibility is something you must manage. Both Java 8 and Java 11, for example, remain workhorses on the backends of large organizations.

If you plan to use Java in any commercial or shared capacity, however, the Oracle JDK now comes with strict (and paid) licensing terms. For this and other more philosophical reasons, we primarily use the OpenJDK mentioned previously in "Growing Up" on page 3. Regrettably, this open source version does not include installers for all the different platforms. Being open source, however, means other groups are welcome to step in and provide any missing pieces, and several OpenJDK installer-based packages do exist. Amazon has consistently released timely installers under the Corretto (*https://oreil.ly/W7noE*) moniker. We'll go through Corretto's basic installation steps on Windows, Mac, and Linux in this chapter.

For those who want the latest release and don't mind a little configuration work, you should take a look at installing the OpenJDK. While not as simple as using typical native installers, installing the OpenJDK on your chosen operating system is usually just a matter of uncompressing the downloaded file into a folder and making sure a few environment variables (JAVA_HOME and PATH) are correctly set. Regardless of which operating system you use, if you are going to use the OpenJDK, you'll head to Oracle's OpenJDK download page (*http://jdk.java.net*). There they list the current releases as well as any early access versions that are available.

Installing Corretto on Linux

For the popular Debain and Red Hat distros, you can download the appropriate file (*.deb* or *.rpm*, respectively) and use your usual package manager to install the JDK. The file for generic Linux systems is a compressed tar file (*tar.gz*) that can be unpacked in any shared directory of your choice. We'll go through the steps to unpack and configure this compressed tar file since it works on most Linux distros. These steps use version 17 of Java, but they apply to all of the current and LTS Corretto downloads.

Decide where you want to install the JDK. We'll store ours in */usr/lib/jvm*, but other distros might use other locations, such as */opt*, */usr/share*, or */usr/local*. If you will be the only one using Java on your system, you can even unpack the file under your home directory. Using your favorite terminal app, change to the directory where you downloaded the file and run the following commands to install Java:

```
~$ cd Downloads

~/Downloads$ sudo tar xzf amazon-corretto-17.0.5.8.1-linux-x64.tar.gz \
  --directory /usr/lib/jvm

~/Downloads$ /usr/lib/jvm/amazon-corretto-17.0.5.8.1-linux-x64/bin/java -version
openjdk version "17.0.5" 2022-10-18 LTS
OpenJDK Runtime Environment Corretto-17.0.5.8.1 (build 17.0.5+8-LTS)
OpenJDK 64-Bit Server VM Corretto-17.0.5.8.1 (build 17.0.5+8-LTS, mixed mode,
  sharing)
```

You can see that the first line of the version information ends with the LTS initials. This is an easy way to determine if you are using a long-term support version. With Java successfully unpacked, you can configure your terminal to use this version by setting the JAVA_HOME and PATH environment variables:

```
$ export JAVA_HOME=/usr/lib/jvm/amazon-corretto-17.0.5.8.1-linux-x64
$ export PATH=$JAVA_HOME/bin:$PATH
```

You can test that this setup is working by checking the version of the Java using the -version flag, as shown in Figure 2-1.

You'll want to make those JAVA_HOME and PATH changes permanent by updating the startup or rc scripts for your shell. For example, if you use bash as your shell, you could add both of the export lines in Figure 2-1 to your *.bashrc* file.

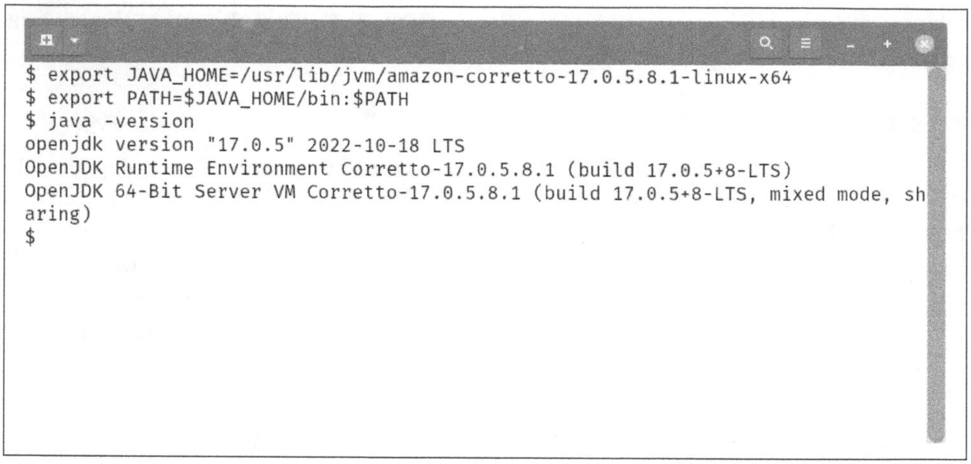

```
$ export JAVA_HOME=/usr/lib/jvm/amazon-corretto-17.0.5.8.1-linux-x64
$ export PATH=$JAVA_HOME/bin:$PATH
$ java -version
openjdk version "17.0.5" 2022-10-18 LTS
OpenJDK Runtime Environment Corretto-17.0.5.8.1 (build 17.0.5+8-LTS)
OpenJDK 64-Bit Server VM Corretto-17.0.5.8.1 (build 17.0.5+8-LTS, mixed mode, sh
aring)
$
```

Figure 2-1. Verifying your Java version in Linux

Installing Corretto on macOS

For users on macOS systems, the Corretto download (*https://oreil.ly/W7noE*) and installation process is straightforward. Select the version of the JDK you want to use, then select the *.pkg* link from the subsequent download page. Double-click the downloaded file to start the wizard.

The installation wizard shown in Figure 2-2 does not allow much real customization. The JDK will be installed on the disk running macOS in its own folder under the */Library/Java/JavaVirtualMachines* directory. It will be symbolically linked to */usr/bin/java*. While you can select an alternate installation location if you have separate hard disks with macOS, the defaults work well for the purposes of this book.

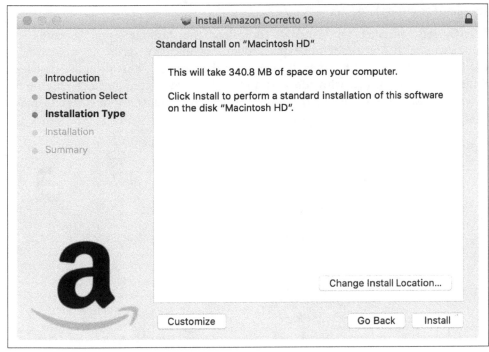

Figure 2-2. Corretto installation wizard in macOS

After you complete the installation, you can test Java by opening the *Terminal* app typically found in the *Utilities* folder under the global *Applications* folder. Type **java -version** and you should see output similar to Figure 2-3. We installed version 19 on this system, but you should see whatever version you downloaded reflected in the output.

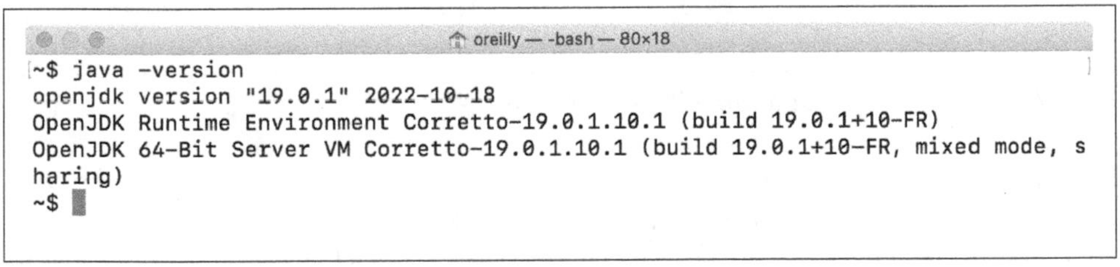

```
~$ java -version
openjdk version "19.0.1" 2022-10-18
OpenJDK Runtime Environment Corretto-19.0.1.10.1 (build 19.0.1+10-FR)
OpenJDK 64-Bit Server VM Corretto-19.0.1.10.1 (build 19.0.1+10-FR, mixed mode, s
haring)
~$ 
```

Figure 2-3. Verifying your Java version in macOS

Installing Corretto on Windows

The Corretto installer for Windows (download the *.msi* file from Amazon's site (*https://oreil.ly/W7noE*)) follows typical Windows install wizards, as seen in Figure 2-4. You can accept the defaults as you go through the short prompts, or tweak things if you are familiar with administrative tasks, such as configuring environment variables and registry entries. If you are prompted to allow the installer to make changes to your system, go ahead and say yes.

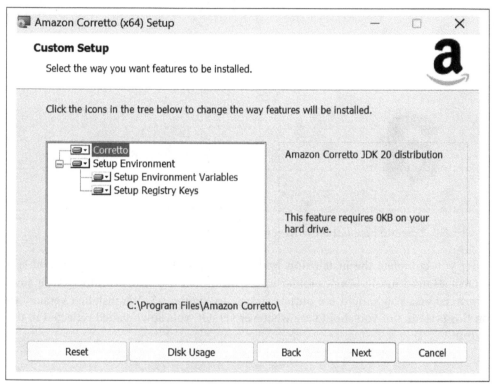

Figure 2-4. Corretto installation wizard in Windows

Perhaps you don't use a command line regularly in Windows, but the *Terminal* application in new versions of Windows (or *Command Prompt* application in older versions) serves the same purpose as similar apps in macOS or Linux. From your Windows menu, you can search for term or cmd, as shown in Figure 2-5.

Figure 2-5. Locating a terminal application in Windows

Click the appropriate result to start your terminal, and check for the version of Java by typing **java -version**. In our example, we were running version 19; you should see something similar to Figure 2-6 but with your version number.

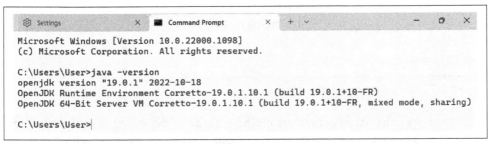

Figure 2-6. Checking the Java version in Windows

You can continue using the terminal, of course, but now you are also free to point other applications such as IntelliJ IDEA at your installed JDK and simply work with those tools. And speaking of IntelliJ IDEA, let's look at its installation steps in more detail.

Installing IntelliJ IDEA and Creating a Project

IntelliJ IDEA is an IDE available at the JetBrains website (*https://oreil.ly/Lo9Xk*). For the purposes of this book, and getting started with Java in general, the Community Edition is sufficient. The download is an executable installer or compressed archive: *.exe* for Windows, *.dmg* for macOS, and *.tar.gz* on Linux. The installers (and archives) all follow standard procedures and should feel familiar. If you want a little extra guidance, the installation guide (*https://oreil.ly/wjooh*) on the JetBrains site is a great resource.

Let's create a new project. Select File → New → Project from the application menu, and type **Learning Java** in the "Name" field at the top of the dialog, as shown in Figure 2-7. Select a JDK (version 19 or later will suffice) and make sure the "Add sample code" checkbox is selected.

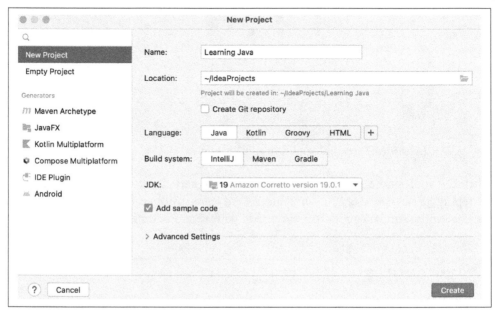

Figure 2-7. New Java project dialog

You may notice the list of generators on the left side of the dialog. The default "New Project" is perfect for our needs. But you can start other projects with templates for things like Kotlin or Android. The default includes a minimal Java class with a `main()` method that can be executed. The coming chapters will go into much more detail about the structure of Java programs and the commands and statements you can place in those programs. With the default option selected on the left, go ahead and click the Create button. (If you notice a prompt to download shared indexes, go ahead and say yes. The shared indexes are not critical, but they will make IDEA run a little faster.) You should end up with a simple project that includes a *Main.java* file, as shown in Figure 2-8.

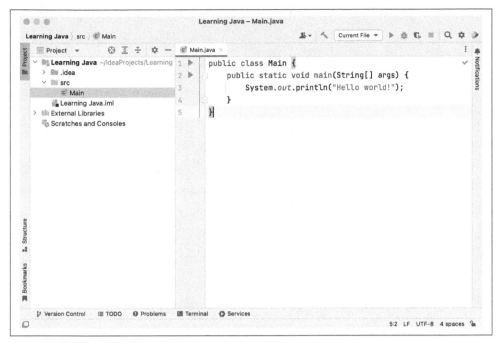

Figure 2-8. The `Main` *class in IDEA*

Congratulations! You now have a Java program. You'll run this example and then expand on it to give it a little more flair. The coming chapters will present more interesting examples piecing together more and more elements of Java. We'll always build these examples in a similar setup, though. These starting steps are good ones to get under your belt.

Running the Project

Starting from the simple template provided by IDEA should leave you in good shape to run your first program. Glance back at Figure 2-8. Notice the green triangles at lines 1 and 2 along the left side of the code editor, next to both the `Main` class as well as the `main()` method. IDEA understands that `Main` can be executed. You can click either of those buttons to run your code. (The `Main` class listed under the *src* folder in the project outline on the left has a tiny green "play" button as well.) You can right-click that class entry and select the `Run 'Main.main()'` option, as shown in Figure 2-9.

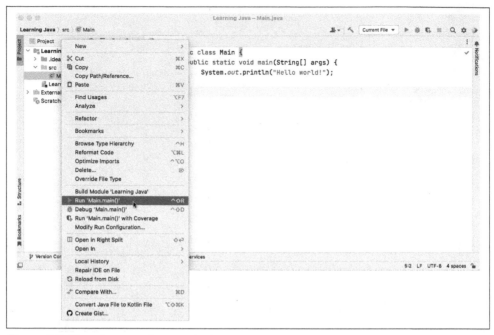

Figure 2-9. Running your Java project

Whether you use the editor margin buttons or the context menu, go ahead and run your code now. You should see your "Hello World!" message show up in the Run tab along the bottom of the editor, similar to Figure 2-10.

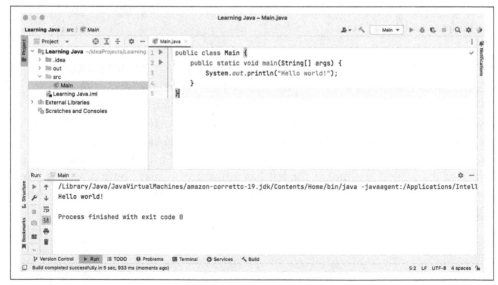

Figure 2-10. Our first output from a Java program

IDEs also include a handy terminal option. This allows you to open a tab or window that has a command prompt available. You may not need this option very often, but it can definitely come in handy. In IDEA, for example, you can open the terminal tab from the View → Tool Windows → Terminal menu option or by clicking the Terminal shortcut along the bottom of the main window, as shown in Figure 2-11.

Figure 2-11. The Terminal tab in IntelliJ IDEA

In VS Code, you can use the Terminal → New Terminal menu option to pull up a similar portion of the IDE, as shown in Figure 2-12.

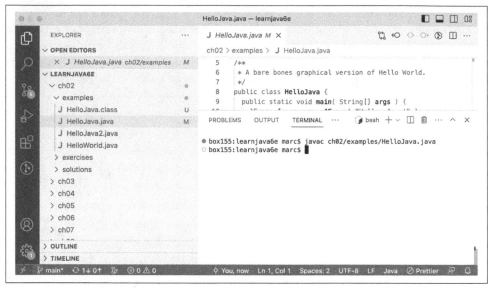

Figure 2-12. The Terminal tab in Microsoft's VS Code

Feel free to try out the terminal yourself. With a terminal window open in your IDE, navigate to the *Learning Java* folder. (Most IDEs will open the terminal at the base directory for your project automatically.) Use the *java* command to run our Main program, as shown in Figure 2-13.

Figure 2-13. Running a Java program in a terminal tab

Whichever route you chose, congratulations are due again—you have now run your first Java program!

Grabbing the Examples

The code examples and exercise solutions are available online at the book's GitHub repository (*https://github.com/l0y/learnjava6e*). GitHub has become the de facto cloud repository site for open source projects available to the public, as well as private, closed source projects. GitHub has many helpful tools beyond simple source-code storage and versioning. If you go on to develop an application or library that you want to share with others, it is worth setting up an account with GitHub and exploring it deeper. Happily, you can also just grab ZIP files of public projects without logging in, as shown in Figure 2-14.

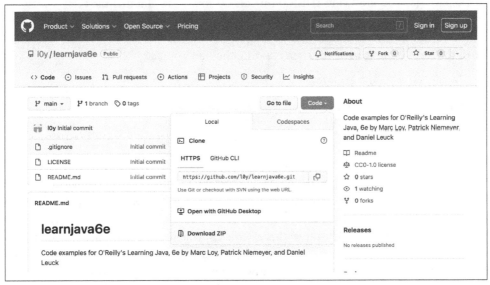

Figure 2-14. Downloading a ZIP file from GitHub

You should get a file called *learnjava6e-main.zip* (since you are grabbing an archive of the "main" branch of this repository). If you're familiar with GitHub from other projects, please feel free to clone the repository, but the static ZIP file contains everything you need to try the examples as you read through the rest of this book. When you unzip the download, you'll find folders for all of the chapters that have examples as well as a completed *game* folder that contains a fun, lighthearted apple tossing game to help illustrate many of the programming concepts presented throughout the book in one cohesive application. We'll go into more details on the examples and the game in coming chapters.

As mentioned previously, you can compile and run the examples from the ZIP file right from the command line. You can also import the code into your favorite IDE. Appendix A contains detailed information on how to best import these examples into IntelliJ IDEA, but other popular IDEs such as Microsoft's VS Code will also work.

HelloJava

In the tradition of introductory programming texts, we will begin with Java's equivalent of the archetypal "Hello World" application, HelloJava.

We'll end up taking a few passes at this example before we're done (HelloJava, HelloJava2, etc.), adding features and introducing new concepts along the way. But let's start with the minimalist version. Create a new file named *HelloJava.java* in your workspace. (If you are using IDEA, you can do this from the menus: File → New → Java Class. Then give it the name *HelloJava* with no suffix—the *.java* extension will be added to the filename automatically.) Go ahead and fill in the same main() method from the Main demo provided when creating the new project:

```
// ch02/examples/HelloJava.java

public class HelloJava {
  public static void main(String[] args) {
    System.out.println("Hello, Java!");
  }
}
```

This five-line program declares a class called HelloJava and that all-important main() method. It uses a predefined method called println() to write some text as output. This is a *command-line program*, which means that it runs in a terminal or DOS window and prints its output there. This approach is a bit old-school, so before we go any further, we're going to give HelloJava a graphical user interface (GUI). Don't worry about the code yet; just follow along with the progression here, and we'll come back for explanations in a moment.

In place of the line containing the println() method, we're going to use a JFrame object to put a window on the screen. We can start by replacing the println line with the following three lines:

```
// filename: ch02/examples/HelloJava.java
// method:   main()
    JFrame frame = new JFrame("Hello, Java!");
    frame.setSize(300, 150);
    frame.setVisible(true);
```

This snippet creates a JFrame object with the title "Hello, Java!" JFrame represents a graphical window. To display it, we simply configure its size on the screen using the setSize() method and make it visible by calling the setVisible() method.

If we stopped here, we would see an empty window on the screen with our "Hello, Java!" banner as its title. But we'd like our message inside the window, not just at the top. To put something in the window, we need a couple more lines. The following complete example adds a JLabel object to display the text centered in our window. The additional import line at the top is necessary to tell the Java compiler where to find the definitions of the JFrame and JLabel objects that we're using:

```
// ch02/examples/HelloJava.java
package ch02.examples;

import javax.swing.*;

public class HelloJava {
  public static void main(String[] args) {
    JFrame frame = new JFrame("Hello, Java!");
    frame.setSize(300, 150);
    JLabel label = new JLabel("Hello, Java!", JLabel.CENTER);
    frame.add(label);
    frame.setVisible(true);
  }
}
```

Now, to compile and run this source, either right-click your *HelloJava.java* class from the package explorer along the left and use the context menu, or click one of the green arrows in the left margin of the editor. See Figure 2-15.

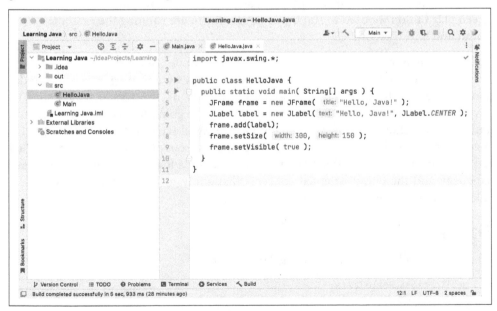

Figure 2-15. Running the HelloJava application

You should see the proclamation shown in Figure 2-16. Congratulations again, you have now run your second Java application! Take a moment to bask in the glow of your monitor.

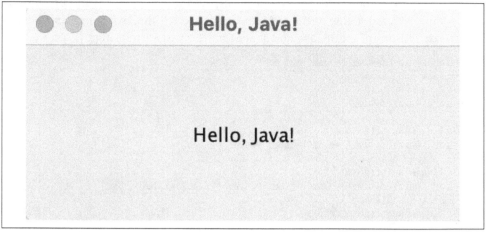

Figure 2-16. The output of the HelloJava application

Be aware that when you click on the window's close box, the window goes away, but your program is still running. (We'll fix this shutdown behavior soon.) To stop the Java application in IDEA, click the red square "stop" button to the right of the green play button we used to run the program. If you are running the example on the command line, type Ctrl-C.

HelloJava may be a small program, but there is quite a bit going on behind the scenes. Those few lines represent the tip of an impressive iceberg. What lies under the surface are the layers of functionality provided by the Java language and its Swing libraries. Remember that in this chapter, we're going to cover a lot of ground quickly in an effort to show you the big picture. We'll try to offer enough detail for a good understanding of what is happening in each example, but we'll defer detailed explanations until the appropriate chapters. This holds for both elements of the Java language and the object-oriented concepts that apply to them. With that said, let's take a look now at what's going on in our first example.

Classes

The first example defines a class named HelloJava:

```
public class HelloJava {
  // ...
}
```

Classes are the fundamental building blocks of most object-oriented languages. A *class* is a group of data items with associated functions that can perform operations on that data. The data items in a class are called *variables*, or sometimes *fields*; in Java, functions are called *methods*. The primary benefits of an object-oriented language are this association between data and functionality in class units and the ability of classes to *encapsulate* or hide details, freeing the developer from worrying about low-level details. We'll expand on these benefits in Chapter 5 where we fill out the structure of classes.

In an application, a class might represent something concrete, such as a button on a screen or the information in a spreadsheet, or something more abstract, such as a sorting algorithm or perhaps the sense of ennui in a video game character. A class representing a spreadsheet might, for example, have variables that represent the values of its individual cells and methods that perform operations on those cells, such as "clear a row" or "compute values."

Our HelloJava class is an entire Java application in a single class. It defines just one method, main(), which holds the body of our program:

```
public class HelloJava {
  public static void main(String[] args) {
    // ...
  }
}
```

It is this main() method that is called first when the application is started. The bit labeled String [] args allows us to pass *command-line arguments* to the application. We'll walk through the main() method in the next section.

Finally, although this version of HelloJava does not define any variables as part of its class, it does use two variables, frame and label, inside its main() method. We'll have more to say about variables soon as well.

The main() Method

As you saw when we ran our example, running a Java application means picking a particular class and passing its name as an argument to the Java virtual machine. When we did this, the java command looked in our HelloJava class to see if it contained the special method named main() with just the right form. It did, and the method was executed. If main() had not been there, we would have received an error message. The main() method is the entry point for applications. Every standalone Java application includes at least one class with a main() method that performs the necessary actions to start the rest of the program.

Our main() method sets up a window (a JFrame) to hold the visual output of the HelloJava class. Right now, main() is doing all the work in the application. But in an object-oriented application, we normally delegate responsibilities to many different classes. In the next incarnation of our example, we're going to perform just such a split—creating a second class—and we'll see that as the example subsequently evolves, the `main()` method remains more or less the same, simply holding the startup procedure.

Let's quickly walk through our `main()` method, just so you know what it does. First, `main()` creates a `JFrame`, the window that will hold our example:

```
JFrame frame = new JFrame("Hello, Java!");
```

The word `new` in this line of code is very important. `JFrame` is the name of a class that represents a window on the screen, but the class itself is just a template, like a building plan. The `new` keyword tells Java to allocate memory and actually create a particular `JFrame` object. In this case, the argument inside the parentheses tells the `JFrame` what to display in its title bar. We could have left out the "Hello, Java!" text and used empty parentheses to create a `JFrame` with no title, but only because the `JFrame` specifically allows us to do that.

When frame windows are first created, they are very small. Before we show the `JFrame`, let's set its size to something reasonable:

```
frame.setSize(300, 150);
```

This is an example of invoking a method on a particular object. In this case, the `setSize()` method is defined by the `JFrame` class, and it affects the particular `JFrame` object we've placed in the variable `frame`. Like the frame, we also create an instance of `JLabel` to hold our text inside the window:

```
JLabel label = new JLabel("Hello, Java!", JLabel.CENTER);
```

`JLabel` is much like a physical label. It holds some text at a particular position—in this case, on our frame. This is a very object-oriented concept: using an object to hold some text, instead of simply invoking a method to "draw" the text and moving on. The rationale for this will become clearer later.

Next, we have to place the label into the frame we created:

```
frame.add(label);
```

Here, we're calling a method named `add()` to place our label inside the `JFrame`. The `JFrame` is a kind of container that can hold things. We'll talk more about that later. `main()`'s final task is to show the frame window and its contents, which otherwise would be invisible. An invisible window makes for a pretty boring application:

```
frame.setVisible(true);
```

That's the whole `main()` method. As we progress through the examples in this chapter, it will remain mostly unchanged as the `HelloJava` class evolves around it.

Classes and Objects

A class is a blueprint for a part of an application; it holds methods and variables that make up that component. Many individual working copies of a given class can exist while an application is active. These individual incarnations are called *instances* of the class, or *objects*. Two instances of a given class may contain different data, but they always have the same methods.

As an example, consider a Button class. There is only one Button class, but an application can create many different Button objects, each one an instance of the same class. Furthermore, two Button instances might contain different data, perhaps giving each a different appearance and performing a different action. In this sense, a class can be considered a mold for making the object it represents, something like a cookie cutter stamping out working instances of itself in the memory of the computer. As you'll see later, there's a bit more to it than that—a class can in fact share information among its instances—but this explanation suffices for now. Chapter 5 has the whole story on classes and objects.

The term *object* in Java is very general and is sometimes used almost interchangeably with *class*. Objects are the abstract entities that all object-oriented languages refer to in one form or another. We will use *object* as a generic term for an instance of a class. We might, therefore, refer to an instance of the Button class as a button, a Button object, or, indiscriminately, as an object. You will see the term used frequently in the coming chapters, and Chapter 5 will go into much more detail on both classes and objects.

The main() method in the previous example creates a single instance of the JLabel class and shows it in an instance of the JFrame class. You could modify main() to create many instances of JLabel, perhaps each in a separate window.

Variables and Class Types

In Java, every class defines a new *type* (data type). You can declare a variable of this type and then it can hold instances of that class. A variable could, for example, be of type Button and hold an instance of the Button class, or of type SpreadSheetCell and hold a SpreadSheetCell object, just as it could be any of the simpler types, such as int or char. The fact that variables have types and cannot simply hold any kind of object is another important feature of Java that ensures the safety and correctness of code.

Setting aside the variables used inside the `main()` method for the moment, only one other variable is declared in our simple `HelloJava` example. It's found in the declaration of the `main()` method itself:

```
public static void main(String [] args) {
    // ...
}
```

Just like functions in other languages, a method in Java declares a list of *parameters* (variables) that it accepts as *arguments*, and it specifies the types of those parameters. In this case, the main `method` is requiring that when it is invoked, it be passed an array of `String` objects in the variable named `args`. The `String` is the fundamental object representing text in Java. As we hinted at earlier, Java uses the `args` parameter to pass any command-line arguments supplied to the Java virtual machine into your application. (We don't use them here, but we will later.)

Up to this point, we have loosely talked about variables as holding objects. In reality, variables that have class types don't hold objects—they refer to them. A *reference* is a pointer to or a handle for an object. If you declare a class-type variable without assigning it an object, it doesn't point to anything. It's assigned the default value of `null`, meaning "no value." If you try to use a variable with a null value as if it were pointing to a real object, a runtime error, `NullPointerException`, occurs.

Of course, object references have to come from somewhere. In our example, we created two objects using the `new` operator. We'll examine object creation in more detail a little later in the chapter.

HelloComponent

Thus far, our `HelloJava` example has contained itself in a single class. In fact, because of its simple nature, it has really just served as a single, large method. Although we have used a couple of objects to display our GUI message, our own code does not illustrate any object-oriented structure.

Well, we're going to correct that right now by adding a second class. To give us something to build on throughout this chapter, we're going to take over the job of the `JLabel` class (bye-bye, `JLabel`!) and replace it with our own graphical class: `HelloComponent`. Our `HelloComponent` class will start simple, just displaying our "Hello, Java!" message at a fixed position. We'll add capabilities later.

The code for our new class is simple; we only need a few more lines. First we need another `import` statement at the top of the *HelloJava.java* file:

```
import java.awt.*;
```

This line tells the compiler where to find the extra classes we need to fill out the logic of HelloComponent. And here's that logic:

```
class HelloComponent extends JComponent {
  public void paintComponent(Graphics g) {
    g.drawString("Hello, Java!", 125, 95);
  }
}
```

The HelloComponent class definition can go either above or below our HelloJava class. Then, to use our new class in place of the JLabel, simply replace the two lines referencing the label in the main() method with:

```
// Delete or comment out these two lines
//JLabel label = new JLabel("Hello, Java!", JLabel.CENTER);
//frame.add(label);

// And add this line
frame.add(new HelloComponent());
```

This time when you compile *HelloJava.java*, take a look at the generated *.class* files. (These files will be located in either your current directory if you are using a terminal or in the *Learn Java/out/production/Learn Java* folder where you chose to put IDEA projects. In IDEA itself, you can also expand the *out* folder in the project navigation pane on the left side.) Regardless of how you arranged the classes in your source, you should see two binary class files: *HelloJava.class* and *HelloComponent.class*. Running the code should look much like the JLabel version, but if you resize the window, you'll notice that our new component does not automatically adjust to center the text.

So what have we done, and why have we gone to such lengths to insult the perfectly good JLabel component? We've created our new HelloComponent class, extending a generic graphical class called JComponent. To *extend* a class simply means to add functionality to an existing class, creating a new one. We'll get into that process more in the next section.

In our current example, we have created a new kind of JComponent that contains a method called paintComponent(), which is responsible for drawing our message. The paintComponent() method takes one argument named (somewhat tersely) g, which is of type Graphics. When the paintComponent() method is invoked, a Graphics object is assigned to g, which we use in the body of the method. We'll say more about paintComponent() and the Graphics class in a moment. As for why, you'll understand when we add all sorts of new features to our new component later on.

Inheritance

Java classes are arranged in a parent-child hierarchy in which the parent and child are known as the *superclass* and *subclass*, respectively. We'll explore these concepts more in Chapter 5. In Java, every class has exactly one superclass (a single parent), but possibly many subclasses. The only exception to this rule is the `Object` class, which sits atop the entire class hierarchy; it has no superclass. (Feel free to peek ahead at the tiny slice of the Java class hierarchy shown in Figure 2-17.)

The declaration of our class in the previous example uses the keyword `extends` to specify that `HelloComponent` is a subclass of the `JComponent` class:

```
class HelloComponent extends JComponent { ... }
```

A subclass may *inherit* some or all of the variables and methods of its superclass. Inheritance provides the subclass access to the variables and methods of its superclass as if it has declared them itself. A subclass can add variables and methods of its own, and it can also *override* or change the meaning of inherited methods. When we use a subclass, overridden methods are hidden (replaced) by the subclass's own versions of them. In this way, inheritance provides a powerful mechanism whereby a subclass can refine or extend the functionality of its superclass.

For example, the hypothetical spreadsheet class might be subclassed to produce a new scientific spreadsheet class with special built-in constants. In this case, the source code for the scientific spreadsheet might declare variables for the special constants, but the new scientific class still has all of the variables (and methods) that constitute the normal functionality of a spreadsheet. Again, those standard elements are inherited from the parent spreadsheet class. This also means that the scientific spreadsheet maintains its identity as a spreadsheet; it can still do everything the simpler spreadsheet could do. That idea, that a more specific class can still perform all of the duties of a more general parent or ancestor, has profound implications. We call this idea *polymorphism*, and we'll continue to explore it throughout the book. Polymorphism is one of the foundations of object-oriented programming.

Our `HelloComponent` class is a subclass of the `JComponent` class and inherits many variables and methods not explicitly declared in our source code. This is what allows our tiny class to serve as a component in a `JFrame`, with just a few customizations.

The JComponent Class

The `JComponent` class provides the framework for building all kinds of UI components. Particular components—such as buttons, labels, and list boxes—are implemented as subclasses of `JComponent`.

We mentioned that subclasses can take an inherited method and override it to implement some particular behavior. But why would we want to change the behavior of something that presumably already works for the superclass? Many classes start with minimal functionality. The original programmers expect someone else to come along and add the interesting parts. JComponent is just such a class. It handles a great deal of the communication with the computer's windowing system for you, but it leaves room for you to add the specific details of presentation and behavior.

The paintComponent() method is an important method of the JComponent class; we override it to implement the way our particular component displays itself on the screen. The default behavior of paintComponent() doesn't do any drawing at all. If we hadn't overridden it in our subclass, our component would simply have been empty. Here, we're overriding paintComponent() to do something only slightly more interesting. We don't override any of the other inherited members of JComponent because they provide basic functionality and reasonable defaults for this (trivial) example. As HelloJava grows, we'll delve deeper into the inherited members and use additional methods. We will also add some application-specific methods and variables specifically for the needs of HelloComponent.

JComponent is really the tip of another iceberg called Swing. Swing is Java's UI toolkit, represented in our example by the import statement at the top; we'll discuss Swing in more detail in Chapter 12.

Relationships and Finger-Pointing

You can think of subclassing as creating an "is a" relationship, in which the subclass "is a" kind of its superclass. HelloComponent is therefore a kind of JComponent. When we refer to a kind of object, we mean *any instance of that object's class or any of its subclasses*. Later, we will look more closely at the Java class hierarchy and see that JComponent is itself a subclass of the Container class, which is further derived from a class called Component, and so on, as shown in Figure 2-17.

In this sense, a HelloComponent object is a kind of JComponent, which is a kind of Container, and all of these can ultimately be considered to be a kind of Component. It's from these classes that HelloComponent inherits its basic GUI functionality and (as we'll discuss later) the ability to have other graphical components embedded within it as well.

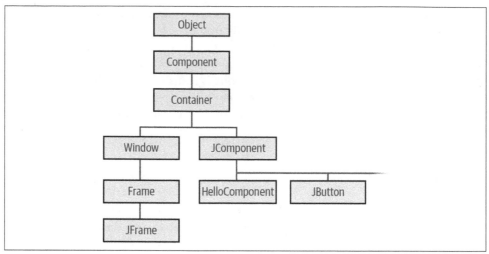

Figure 2-17. Part of the Java class hierarchy

Component is a subclass of the top-level Object class, so all these classes are types of Object. Every other class in the Java API inherits behavior from Object, which defines a few basic methods, as you'll see in Chapter 5. We'll continue to use the word *object* (lowercase *o*) in a generic way to refer to an instance of any class; we'll use Object to refer specifically to the type of that class.

Packages and Imports

We mentioned earlier that the first line of our example tells Java where to find some of the classes that we've been using:

```
import javax.swing.*;
```

Specifically, it tells the compiler that we are going to be using classes from the Swing GUI toolkit (in this case, JFrame, JLabel, and JComponent). These classes are organized into a Java *package* called javax.swing. In Java, a package is a group of classes that are related by purpose or by application. Classes in the same package have special access privileges with respect to one another and may be designed to work together closely.

Packages are named in a hierarchical fashion with dot-separated components, such as java.util and java.util.zip. Classes in a package typically live in nested folders matching their package name. They also take on the name of the package as part of their "full name" or, to use the proper terminology, their *fully qualified name*. For example, the fully qualified name of the JComponent class is javax.swing.JComponent. We could have referred to it by that name directly, in lieu of using the import statement:

```
class HelloComponent extends javax.swing.JComponent {...}
```

Using fully qualified names can get tiresome. The statement `import javax.swing.*` enables us to refer to all the classes in the `javax.swing` package by their simple names. We don't have to use fully qualified names to refer to the `JComponent`, `JLabel`, and `JFrame` classes.

As we saw when we added our second example class, there may be one or more `import` statements in a given Java source file. The `imports` effectively create a "search path" that tells Java where to look for classes that we refer to by their simple, unqualified names. (It's not really a path, but it avoids ambiguous names that can create errors.) The `imports` we've seen use the dot star (`.*`) notation to indicate that the entire package should be imported. But you can also specify just a single class. For example, our current example uses only the `Graphics` class from the `java.awt` package. We could have used `import java.awt.Graphics` instead of using the wildcard `*` to import all the Abstract Window Toolkit (AWT) package's classes. However, we are anticipating using several more classes from this package later.

The `java.` and `javax.` package hierarchies are special. Any package that begins with `java.` is part of the core Java API and is available on any platform that supports Java. The `javax.` package normally denotes a standard extension to the core platform, which may or may not be installed. However, in recent years, many standard extensions have been added to the core Java API without renaming them. The `javax.swing` package is an example; it is part of the core API in spite of its name. Figure 2-18 illustrates some of the core Java packages, showing a representative class or two from each.

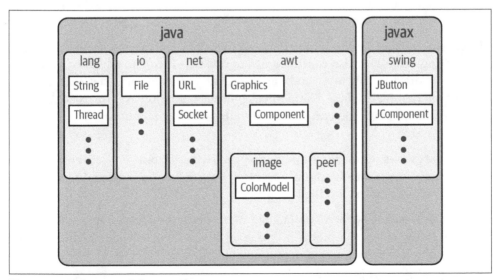

Figure 2-18. Some core Java packages

`java.lang` contains fundamental classes needed by the Java language itself; this package is imported automatically, and that is why we didn't need an `import` statement to use class names such as `String` or `System` in our examples. The `java.awt` package contains classes of the older, graphical windowing system; `java.net` contains the networking classes; and so on.

As you gain more experience with Java, you will realize that having a command of the packages available to you, what they do, and when and how to use them is a critical part of becoming a successful Java developer.

The paintComponent() Method

The source for our `HelloComponent` class defines a method, `paintComponent()`, that overrides the `paintComponent()` method of the `JComponent` class:

```
public void paintComponent(Graphics g) {
    g.drawString("Hello, Java!", 125, 95);
}
```

The `paintComponent()` method is called when it's time for our example to draw itself on the screen. It takes a single argument, a `Graphics` object, and doesn't return any type of value (`void`) to its caller.

Modifiers are keywords placed before classes, variables, and methods to alter their accessibility, behavior, or semantics. Here `paintComponent()` is declared as `public`, which means it can be invoked (called) by methods in classes other than `HelloComponent`. In this case, it's the Java windowing environment that is calling our `paintComponent()` method. A method or variable declared as `private`, by contrast, is accessible only from its own class.

The `Graphics` object, an instance of the `Graphics` class, represents a particular graphical drawing area. (It is also called a *graphics context*.) It contains methods that can be used to draw in this area, and variables that represent characteristics such as clipping or drawing modes. The particular `Graphics` object we are passed in the `paintComponent()` method corresponds to our `HelloComponent`'s area of the screen, inside our frame.

The `Graphics` class provides methods for rendering shapes, images, and text. In `HelloComponent`, we invoke the `drawString()` method of our `Graphics` object to scrawl our message at the specified coordinates.

As we've seen earlier, we access a method of an object by appending a dot (.) and its name to the object that holds it. We invoked the `drawString()` method of the `Graphics` object (referenced by our g variable) in this way:

```
g.drawString("Hello, Java!", 125, 95);
```

Here we can see how overriding an inherited method provides new functionality. On its own, an instance of JComponent has no idea what information to show the user or how to respond to things like mouse clicks. We extended JComponent and added a tiny bit of custom logic: we show a bit of text on the screen. But we can do much more!

HelloJava2: The Sequel

Now that we've got some basics down, let's make our application a little more interactive. The following minor upgrade allows us to drag the message text around with the mouse. If you're new to programming, though, the upgrade may not seem so minor. Fear not! We will look closely at all of the topics covered in this example in later chapters. For now, enjoy playing with the example and use it as an opportunity to get more comfortable creating and running Java programs, even if you don't feel as comfortable with the code inside.

We'll call this example HelloJava2 rather than cause confusion by continuing to expand the old one, but the primary changes here and further on lie in adding capabilities to the HelloComponent class and simply making the corresponding changes to the names to keep them straight (e.g., HelloComponent2, HelloComponent3, and so on). Having just seen inheritance at work, you might wonder why we aren't creating a subclass of HelloComponent and exploiting inheritance to build upon our previous example and extend its functionality. Well, in this case, that would not provide much advantage, so for clarity we simply start over.

Two slashes in a row indicate that the rest of the line is a comment. We've added a few comments to HelloJava2 to help you keep track of everything:

```
//file: HelloJava2.java
import java.awt.*;
import java.awt.event.*;
import javax.swing.*;

public class HelloJava2 {
  public static void main(String[] args) {
    JFrame frame = new JFrame("HelloJava2");
    frame.add(new HelloComponent2("Hello, Java!"));
    frame.setDefaultCloseOperation(JFrame.EXIT_ON_CLOSE);
    frame.setSize(300, 300);
    frame.setVisible(true);
  }
}

class HelloComponent2 extends JComponent
    implements MouseMotionListener {
  String theMessage;
  int messageX = 125, messageY = 95; // Coordinates of the message
```

```
  public HelloComponent2(String message) {
    theMessage = message;
    addMouseMotionListener(this);
  }

  public void paintComponent(Graphics g) {
    g.drawString(theMessage, messageX, messageY);
  }

  public void mouseDragged(MouseEvent e) {
    // Save the mouse coordinates and paint the message.
    messageX = e.getX();
    messageY = e.getY();
    repaint();
  }

  public void mouseMoved(MouseEvent e) { }
}
```

If you are using IDEA, create a new Java class named *HelloJava2* and copy the code above. If you are sticking with the terminal, place the text of this example in a new file called *HelloJava2.java*. Either way, you want to compile it as before. You should get new class files, *HelloJava2.class* and *HelloComponent2.class*, as a result.

If you are following in IDEA, click the Run button next to `HelloJava2`. If you are using a terminal, run the example using the following command:

```
C:\> java HelloJava2
```

Feel free to substitute your own victorious comment for the "Hello, Java!" message and enjoy many hours of fun, dragging the text around with your mouse. Notice that now when you click the window's close button, the application exits properly; we'll explain that later when we talk about events. Let's dive in and see what has changed.

Instance Variables

We have added some variables to the `HelloComponent2` class in our example:

```
int messageX = 125, messageY = 95;
String theMessage;
```

`messageX` and `messageY` are integers that hold the current coordinates of our movable message. We have set them to default values that should place the message roughly near the center of the window. Java integers are 32-bit signed numbers, so they can easily hold our coordinate values. The variable `theMessage` is of type `String` and can hold instances of the `String` class.

You should note that these three variables are declared inside the braces of the class definition but not inside any particular method in that class. These variables are called *instance* variables, and they belong to the object as a whole. Specifically, separate copies of them appear in each separate instance of the class. Instance variables are always visible to (and usable by) all the methods inside their class. Depending on their modifiers, they may also be accessible from outside the class.

Unless otherwise initialized (programmer jargon for setting the first value on something), instance variables are set to a default value of 0, false, or null, depending on their type. Numeric types are set to 0, Boolean variables are set to false, and class type variables always have their value set to null.

Instance variables differ from method arguments and other variables that are declared inside the scope of a particular method. The latter are called *local* variables. They are effectively private variables that can be seen only by code inside a method or other code block. Java doesn't initialize local variables, so you must assign values yourself. If you try to use a local variable that has not yet been assigned a value, your code generates a compile-time error. Local variables live only as long as the method is executing and then disappear, unless something else saves their value. Each time the method is invoked, its local variables are recreated and must be assigned values.

We have used the new variables to make our previously stodgy paintComponent() method more dynamic. Now all the arguments in the call to drawString() are determined by these variables.

Constructors

The HelloComponent2 class includes a special kind of a method called a *constructor*. A constructor is called to set up a new instance of a class. When a new object is created, Java allocates storage for it, sets instance variables to their default values, and calls the constructor method for the class to do whatever application-level setup is required.

A constructor always has the same name as its class. For example, the constructor for the HelloComponent2 class is called HelloComponent2(). Constructors don't have a return type, but you can think of them as creating an object of their class's type. Like other methods, constructors can have parameters. Their sole mission in life is to configure and initialize newly born class instances, possibly using information passed to them in these parameters.

An object is created with the new operator specifying the constructor for the class and any necessary arguments.[1] The resulting object instance is returned as a value. In our example, a new HelloComponent2 instance is created in the main() method by this line:

```
frame.add(new HelloComponent2("Hello, Java!"));
```

This line actually does two things. To make that clearer, we could write them as two separate lines that are a little easier to understand:

```
HelloComponent2 newObject = new HelloComponent2("Hello, Java!");
frame.add(newObject);
```

The first line is the important one, where a new HelloComponent2 object is created. The HelloComponent2 constructor takes a String as an argument and, as we have arranged things, uses that argument to set the message that is displayed in the window. With a little magic from the Java compiler, quoted text in Java source code is turned into a String object. (See Chapter 8 for a deeper discussion of the String class.) The second line simply adds our new component to the frame to make it visible, as we did in the previous examples.

While we're on the topic, if you'd like to make our message configurable, you can change the constructor call to the following:

```
HelloComponent2 newobj = new HelloComponent2(args[0]);
```

Now you can pass the text on the command line when you run the application using the following command:

```
C:\> java HelloJava2 "Hello, Java!"
```

args[0] refers to the first command-line parameter. Its meaning will become clearer when we discuss arrays in Chapter 4. If you are using an IDE, you will need to configure it to accept your parameters before running it. IntelliJ IDEA has something called a *run configuration* that you can edit from the same menus that pop up when you click the green play buttons. The run configuration has a number of options, but our interest is in the text field for "Program Arguments," as shown in Figure 2-19. Note that on both the command line and in the IDE, you must enclose your phrase in double quotes to make sure the text is considered one argument. If you leave off the quotes, Hello, and Java! would be two separate arguments.

---

1 The terms *parameter* and *argument* often get used interchangeably. That's mostly fine, but technically you provide parameters with a type and a name when defining methods or constructors. You supply arguments to fill those parameters when you call the method or constructor.

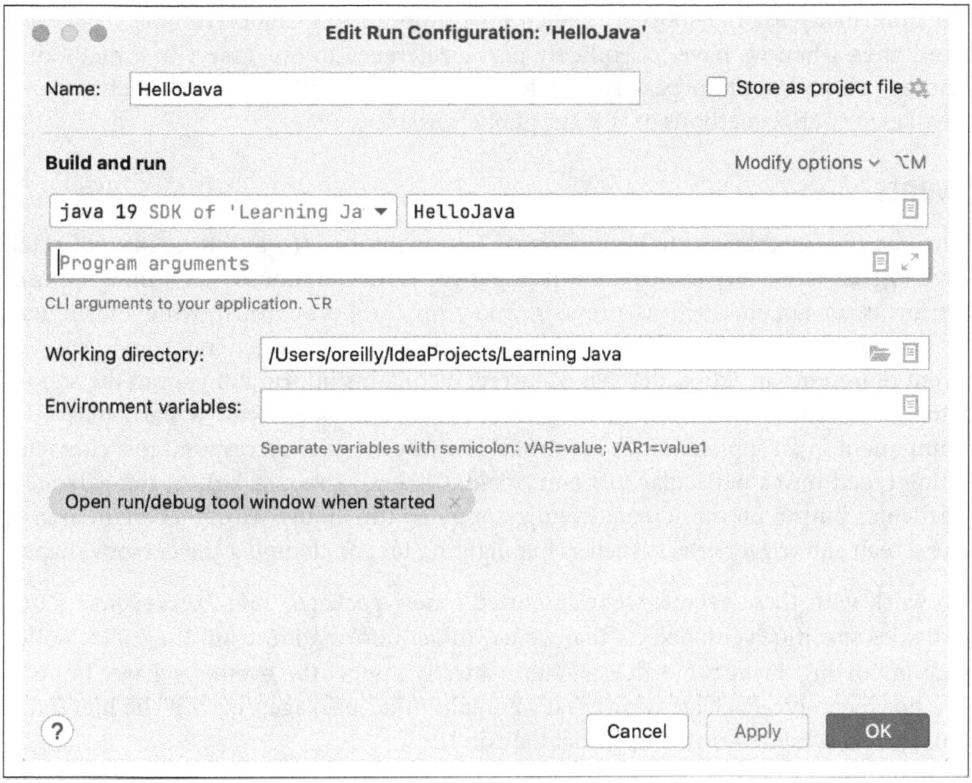

Figure 2-19. IDEA dialog for giving command-line parameters

HelloComponent2's constructor then does two things: it sets the text of theMessage instance variable and calls addMouseMotionListener(). This method is part of the event mechanism, which we'll discuss next. It tells the system, "Hey, I'm interested in anything that happens involving mouse motion":

```
public HelloComponent2(String message) {
    theMessage = message;
    addMouseMotionListener(this);
}
```

The special, read-only variable called this is used to explicitly refer to our object (the "current" object context) in the call to addMouseMotionListener(). A method can use this to refer to the instance of the object that holds it. The following two statements are therefore equivalent ways of assigning the value to theMessage instance variable:

```
theMessage = message;
```

or:

```
this.theMessage = message;
```

We'll normally use the shorter, implicit form to refer to instance variables, but we'll need this when we have to explicitly pass a reference to our object to a method in another class. We often pass such references so that methods in other classes can invoke our public methods or use our public variables.

Events

The last two methods of HelloComponent2, mouseDragged() and mouseMoved(), tell Java to pass along any information it might get from the mouse. Each time the user performs an action, such as pressing a key on the keyboard, moving the mouse, or perhaps banging their head against a touch screen, Java generates an *event*. An event represents an action that has occurred; it contains information about the action, such as its time and location. Most events are associated with a particular GUI component in an application. A keystroke, for instance, can correspond to a character being typed into a particular text entry field. Clicking a mouse button can activate a particular button on the screen. Even just moving the mouse within a certain area of the screen can trigger effects such as highlighting text or changing the cursor's shape.

To work with these events, we've imported a new package, java.awt.event, which provides specific Event objects that we use to get information from the user. (Notice that importing java.awt.* doesn't automatically import the event package. Imports are not recursive. Packages don't really contain other packages, even if the hierarchical naming scheme would imply that they do.)

There are dozens of event classes, including MouseEvent, KeyEvent, and Action Event. For the most part, the meaning of these events is fairly intuitive. A MouseEvent occurs when the user does something with the mouse, a KeyEvent occurs when the user presses or releases a key, and so on. ActionEvent is a little special; we'll see it at work in Chapter 12. For now, we'll focus on dealing with MouseEvents.

GUI components in Java generate events for specific kinds of user actions. For example, if you click the mouse inside a component, the component generates a mouse event. Objects can ask to receive the events from one or more components by registering a *listener* with the event source. For example, to declare that a listener wants to receive a component's mouse-motion events, you invoke that component's addMouseMotionListener() method, specifying the listener object as an argument. That's what our example is doing in its constructor. In this case, the component is calling its own addMouseMotionListener() method, with the argument this, meaning "I want to receive my own mouse-motion events."

That's how we register to receive events. But how do we actually get them? That's what the two mouse-related methods in our class are for. The mouseDragged() method is called automatically on a listener to receive the events generated when the user drags the mouse—that is, moves the mouse with any button clicked. The `mouseMoved()` method is called whenever the user moves the mouse over the area without clicking a button.

In this case, we've placed these methods in our `HelloComponent2` class and had it register itself as the listener. This is entirely appropriate for our new text-dragging component. More generally, good design usually dictates that event listeners be implemented as *adapter classes* that provide better separation of GUI and "business logic." An adapter class is a convenient intermediate class that implements all of the methods of an interface with some default behavior. We'll discuss events, listeners, and adapters in detail in Chapter 12.

Our `mouseMoved()` method is boring: it doesn't do anything. We ignore simple mouse motions and reserve our attention for dragging. But we have to supply some kind of implementation—even an empty one—since the `MouseMotionListener` interface includes it. Our `mouseDragged()` method, on the other hand, has some meat to it. This method is called repeatedly by the windowing system to give us updates on the position of the mouse as the user drags it around. Here it is:

```
public void mouseDragged(MouseEvent e) {
    messageX = e.getX();
    messageY = e.getY();
    repaint();
}
```

The lone parameter to `mouseDragged()` is a `MouseEvent` object, e, that contains all the information we need to know about this event. We ask the `MouseEvent` to tell us the x and y coordinates of the mouse's current position by calling its `getX()` and `getY()` methods. We save these in the `messageX` and `messageY` instance variables for use elsewhere.

The beauty of the event model is that you have to handle only the kinds of events you want. If you don't care about keyboard events, you just don't register a listener for them; the user can type all they want and you won't be bothered. If there are no listeners for a particular kind of event, Java won't even generate it. The result is that event handling is quite efficient.[2]

While we're discussing events, we should mention another small addition we slipped into `HelloJava2`:

```
frame.setDefaultCloseOperation(JFrame.EXIT_ON_CLOSE);
```

This line tells the frame to exit the application when its Close button is clicked. It's called the "default" close operation because this operation, like almost every other

---

2 Event handling in Java 1.0 was a very different story. Early on, Java did not have a notion of event listeners, and all event handling happened by overriding methods in base GUI classes. This was inefficient and led to poor design, with a proliferation of highly specialized components.

GUI interaction, is governed by events. We could register a window listener to be notified when the user clicks on the Close button and take whatever action we like, but this convenience method handles the common cases.

Finally, we've danced around a couple of other questions here. How does the system know that our class contains the necessary `mouseDragged()` and `mouseMoved()` methods? Where do these names come from? And why do we have to supply a `mouseMoved()` method that doesn't do anything? The answer to these questions has to do with interfaces. We'll touch on interfaces after clearing up some unfinished business with `repaint()`.

The repaint() Method

Because we change the coordinates for the message when we drag the mouse, we would like `HelloComponent2` to redraw itself. We do this by calling `repaint()`, which asks the system to redraw the screen at a later time. We can't call `paintComponent()` directly, even if we wanted to, because we don't have a graphics context to pass to it.

We can use the `repaint()` method of the `JComponent` class to request that our component be redrawn. `repaint()` causes the Java windowing system to schedule a call to our `paintComponent()` method at the next possible time; Java supplies the necessary `Graphics` object, as shown in Figure 2-20.

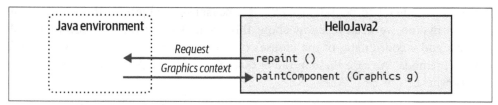

Figure 2-20. Invoking the repaint() method

This mode of operation isn't just an inconvenience brought about by not having the right graphics context handy. Its biggest advantage is that the repainting behavior is handled by something else, while we are free to go about our business. The Java system has a separate, dedicated thread of execution that handles all `repaint()` requests. It can schedule and consolidate `repaint()` requests as necessary, which helps to prevent the windowing system from being overwhelmed during painting-intensive situations like scrolling. Another advantage is that all the painting functionality must be encapsulated through our `paintComponent()` method; we aren't tempted to spread it throughout the application (which could make maintenance difficult).

Interfaces

Now it's time to tackle some of the questions we avoided earlier: how does the system know to call `mouseDragged()` when a mouse event occurs? Is it simply a matter of knowing that `mouseDragged()` is some magic name that our event-handling method must have? Not quite; the answer touches on the discussion of interfaces, which are one of the most important features of the Java language.

The first sign of an interface comes on the line of code that introduces the `HelloComponent2` class. We say that the class *implements* the `MouseMotionListener` interface:

```
class HelloComponent2 extends JComponent implements MouseMotionListener {
  // ...
  public void mouseMoved(MouseEvent e) {
    // Your own logic goes here
  }

  public void mouseDragged(MouseEvent e) {
    // Your own logic goes here
  }
}
```

Essentially, an *interface* is a list of methods that the class must have; this particular interface requires our class to have methods called `mouseDragged()` and `mouseMoved()`. The interface doesn't say what these methods have to do; indeed, our `mouseMoved()` doesn't do anything at all. It does say that the methods must take a `MouseEvent` as an argument and return no value (that's what `void` means).

An interface is a contract between you, the code developer, and the compiler. By saying that your class implements the `MouseMotionListener` interface, you're saying that these methods will be available for other parts of the system to call. If you don't provide them, a compilation error will occur. That's why we need a `mouseMoved()` method; even though the one we supplied doesn't do anything, the `MouseMotionListener` interface says we must have one.

The Java distribution comes with many interfaces that define what classes have to do. This idea of a contract between the compiler and a class is very important. There are many situations like the one we just saw where you don't care what class something is; you just care that it has some capability, such as listening for mouse events. Interfaces give us a way of acting on objects based on their capabilities without knowing or caring about their actual type. They are a tremendously important concept in how we use Java as an object-oriented language. We'll talk about them in detail in Chapter 5.

Chapter 5 also discusses how interfaces provide a sort of escape clause to the Java rule that any new class can extend only a single class ("single inheritance"). A class in Java can extend only one class but can implement as many interfaces as it wants. Interfaces can be used as data types, can extend other interfaces (but not classes), and can be inherited by classes (if class A implements interface B, subclasses of A also implement B). The crucial difference is that classes don't actually inherit methods from interfaces; the interfaces merely specify the methods the class must have.

Goodbye and Hello Again

Well, it's time to say goodbye to `HelloJava`. We hope that you have developed a feel for some of the features of the Java language and the basics of writing and running a Java program. This brief introduction should help you as you explore the details of programming with Java. If you are a bit bewildered by some of the material presented here, take heart. We'll be covering all the major topics presented here again in their own chapters throughout the book. This tutorial was meant to be something of a "trial by fire" to get the important concepts and terminology into your brain so that the next time you hear them you'll have a head start.

We will be getting to know the tools of the Java world better in the next chapter. We'll see details on the commands we have already introduced, such as *javac*, as well as go over other important utilities. Read on to say hello to several of your new best friends as a Java developer!

Review Questions

Here are a few review questions to make sure you caught the key topics in this chapter:

1. What command do you use to compile a Java source file?

2. How does the JVM know where to start when you run a Java class?

3. Can you extend more than one class when creating a new class?

4. Can you implement more than one interface when creating a new class?

5. Which class represents the main window in a graphical application?

Code Exercises

And for your first programming exercise,[3] create a `GoodbyeJava` class that works just like the first HelloJava program from "Running the Project" on page 35, but displays the message "Goodbye, Java!" instead. Try either the command-line version or the graphical version—or both! Feel free to copy as much of the original program as you like. Be sure to compile and run your `GoodbyeJava` class to help practice the process of executing a Java application. You will certainly get more practice along the way, but gathering a little more familiarity with either your IDE or the *javac* and *java* commands now will help as you read the next several chapters.

---

3 You can find the solutions to the programming challenges from each chapter in the *exercises* folder of the source code. Appendix A contains details on downloading and using the source code. Appendix B contains answers to the end-of-chapter questions as well as hints on code solutions for each chapter.

CHAPTER 3

Tools of the Trade

While you will almost certainly do the majority of your Java development in an IDE such as VS Code or IntelliJ IDEA, all of the core tools you need to build Java applications are included in the JDK that you downloaded in "Installing the JDK" on page 28. When we write Java source code, it is the Java compiler—*javac*—that turns our source into usable bytecode. When we want to test that bytecode, it is the Java command itself—*java*—that we use to execute our programs. When we have all of our classes compiled and working together, it is the Java archive tool—*jar*—that allows us to bundle up those classes for distribution. In this chapter, we'll discuss some of these command-line tools that you can use to compile, run, and package Java applications. There are many additional developer tools included in the JDK, such as *jshell* for interactive work or *javap* for decompiling class files. We won't have time to discuss all of them in this book, but anywhere another tool might be useful, we'll mention it. (And we will definitely be looking at *jshell*. It's great for quickly trying out a new class or method.)

We want you to be comfortable with these command-line tools even if you don't typically work in a terminal or command window. Some features of these tools aren't easily accessible through IDEs. You may also encounter times where an IDE is impractical or downright unavailable. System administrators and DevOps engineers, for example, often have only limited, text-based connections to their servers running in fancy data centers. If you need to fix a Java problem over such a connection, these command-line tools will be essential.

JDK Environment

After you install the JDK, the core *java* runtime command usually appears in your path (available to run) automatically, although not always. Additionally, many of the other commands provided with the JDK may not be available unless you add the Java *bin* directory to your execution path. To make sure you have access to all the tools, regardless of your setup, the following commands show how to correctly configure your development environment on Linux, macOS, and Windows. You define a new environment variable for Java's location and append that *bin* folder to the existing path variable. (Operating systems use *environment variables* to store bits of information that applications can use and potentially share as they run.) You will, of course, have to change the paths in our examples to match the version of Java you have installed:

```
# Linux
export JAVA_HOME=/usr/lib/jvm/jdk-21-ea14
export PATH=$PATH:$JAVA_HOME/bin

# Mac OS X
export JAVA_HOME=/Users/marc/jdks/jdk-21-ea14/Contents/Home
export PATH=$PATH:$JAVA_HOME/bin

# Windows
set JAVA_HOME=c:\Program Files\Java\jdk21
set PATH=%PATH%;%JAVA_HOME%\bin
```

On macOS, the situation may be more confusing because recent versions of the operating system ship with "stubs" for the Java commands installed. Apple no longer provides its own implementation of Java, so if you attempt to run one of these commands, the OS will prompt you to download Java at that time.

When in doubt, your go-to test for determining if Java is installed, and which version of the tools you are using, is to use the `-version` flag on the *java* and *javac* commands:

```
% java -version

openjdk version "21-ea" 2023-09-19
OpenJDK Runtime Environment (build 21-ea+14-1161)
OpenJDK 64-Bit Server VM (build 21-ea+14-1161, mixed mode, sharing)

% javac -version

javac 21-ea
```

The `ea` in our version output indicates this is an "early access" release. (Java 21 is still being tested as we write this edition.)

The Java VM

A Java virtual machine (VM) is software that implements the Java runtime system and executes Java applications. It can be a standalone application like the *java* command that comes with the JDK or built into a larger application like a web browser. Usually the interpreter itself is a native application, supplied for each platform, which then bootstraps other tools written in the Java language. Tools such as Java compilers and IDEs are often implemented directly in Java to maximize their portability and extensibility. Eclipse, for example, is a pure Java application.

The Java VM performs all the runtime activities of Java. It loads Java class files, verifies classes from untrusted sources, and executes the compiled bytecode. It manages memory and system resources. Good implementations also perform dynamic optimization, compiling Java bytecode into native machine instructions.

Running Java Applications

A standalone Java application must have at least one class containing a method called `main()`, which is the first code to be executed upon startup. To run the application, start the VM, specifying that class as an argument. You can also specify options to the interpreter as well as arguments to be passed to the application:

```
% java [interpreter options] class_name [program arguments]
```

The class should be specified as a fully qualified class name, including the package name, if any. Note, however, that you don't include the *.class* file extension. Here are a couple of examples that you can try from the terminal in the *ch03/examples* folder:

```
% cd ch03/examples
% java animals.birds.BigBird
% java MyTest
```

The interpreter searches for the class in the *classpath*, a list of directories and archive files where classes are stored. You can specify the classpath either by an environment variable similar to `JAVA_HOME` above, or with the command-line option `-classpath`. If both are present, Java uses the command-line option. We'll discuss the classpath in detail in the next section.

You can also use the *java* command to launch an "executable" Java ARchive (JAR) file:

```
% java -jar spaceblaster.jar
```

In this case, the JAR file includes metadata with the name of the startup class containing the `main()` method, and the classpath becomes the JAR file itself. We'll look more closely at JAR files in "JAR Files" on page 78.

If you're working primarily in an IDE, remember that you can still try those previous commands using the built-in terminal options we mentioned in "Running the Project" on page 35.

After loading the first class and executing its `main()` method, the application can reference other classes, start additional threads, and create its user interface or other structures, as shown in Figure 3-1.

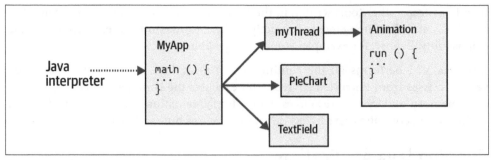

Figure 3-1. Starting a Java application

The `main()` method must have the right *method signature*. A method signature is the set of information that defines the method. It includes the method's name, arguments, and return type, as well as type and visibility modifiers. The `main()` method must be a `public`, `static` method that takes an array of `String` objects as its argument and does not return any value (`void`):

```
public static void main (String [] myArgs)
```

The fact that `main()` is a `public` and `static` method simply means that it is globally accessible and that it can be called directly by name. We'll discuss the implications of visibility modifiers such as `public` and the meaning of `static` in Chapter 4 and Chapter 5.

The `main()` method's single argument, the array of `String` objects, holds the command-line arguments passed to the application. The name of the parameter doesn't matter; only the type is important. In Java, the content of `myArgs` is an array. (More on arrays in Chapter 4.) In Java, arrays know how many elements they contain and can happily provide that information:

```
int numArgs = myArgs.length;
```

`myArgs[0]` is the first command-line argument, and so on.

The Java interpreter continues to run until the `main()` method of the initial class file returns and until any threads that it has started also exit. (More on threads in Chapter 9.) Special threads designated as *daemon* threads are automatically terminated when the rest of the application has completed.

System Properties

Although it is possible to read host environment variables from Java, Oracle discourages using them for application configuration. Instead, Java allows you to pass any number of *system property* values to the application when the VM is started. System properties are simply name-value string pairs that are available to the application through the static `System.getProperty()` method. You can use these properties as a more structured and portable alternative to command-line arguments and environment variables for providing general configuration information to your application at startup. You pass each system property to the interpreter on the command line using the *-D* option followed by *name=value*. For example:

```
% java -Dstreet=sesame -Dscene=alley animals.birds.BigBird
```

You can then access the value of the `street` property inside your program this way:

```
String street = System.getProperty("street");
```

An application can get its configuration in a myriad of other ways, of course, including via files or or over the network at runtime.

The Classpath

The concept of a *path* should be familiar to anyone who has worked on a DOS or Unix platform. It's an environment variable that provides an application with a list of places to look for some resource. The most common example is a path for executable programs. In a Unix shell, the `PATH` environment variable is a colon-separated list of directories that are searched, in order, when the user types the name of a command. The Java `CLASSPATH` environment variable, similarly, is a list of locations that both the interpreter and the compiler will search for packages and Java classes.

An element of the classpath can be a directory or a JAR file. JARs are simple archives that include extra files (metadata) that describe each archive's contents. JAR files are created with the JDK's *jar* utility. Many tools for creating ZIP archives are publicly available and can be used to inspect or create JAR files as well.[1] The archive format enables large groups of classes and their resources to be distributed in a single, compact file; the Java runtime automatically extracts individual class files from the archive, as needed. We'll look more closely at JARs and the *jar* command in "The jar Utility" on page 79.

The precise means and format for setting the classpath vary from system to system. Let's take a look at how to do it.

CLASSPATH on Unix and macOS

On a Unix system (including macOS), you set the `CLASSPATH` environment variable with a colon-separated list of directories and class archive files:

```
% export CLASSPATH=/home/vicky/Java/classes:/home/josh/lib/foo.jar:.
```

---

1 JAR files are mostly conventional ZIP files with that extra metadata. As such, Java also supports archives in the conventional ZIP format, but that is rarely used.

This example specifies a classpath with three locations: a directory in the user's home, a JAR file in another user's directory, and the current directory, which is always specified with a dot (.). The last component of the classpath, the current directory, is useful when you are tinkering with classes.

CLASSPATH on Windows

On a Windows system, the CLASSPATH environment variable is set with a semicolon-separated list of directories and class archive files:

```
C:\> set CLASSPATH=C:\home\vicky\Java\classes;C:\home\josh\lib\foo.jar;.
```

The Java launcher and the other command-line tools know how to find the *core classes*, which are the classes included in every Java installation. The classes in the `java.lang`, `java.io`, `java.net`, and `javax.swing` packages, for example, are all core classes, so you do not need to include a library or directory for these classes in your classpath.

CLASSPATH Wildcards

The CLASSPATH environment variable may also include "*" wildcards that match all JAR files within a directory. For example:

```
% export CLASSPATH=/home/sarah/libs/*
```

To find other classes, the Java interpreter searches the elements of the classpath in the order they are listed. The search combines the path location and the components of the fully qualified class name. For example, consider a search for the class `animals.birds.BigBird`, as shown in Figure 3-2. Searching the classpath directory */usr/lib/java* means that the interpreter looks for an individual class file at */usr/lib/java/animals/birds/BigBird.class*. Searching a ZIP or JAR archive on the classpath, say */home/sarah/zoo.jar*, means that the interpreter looks for the file *animals/birds/BigBird.class* within that archive.

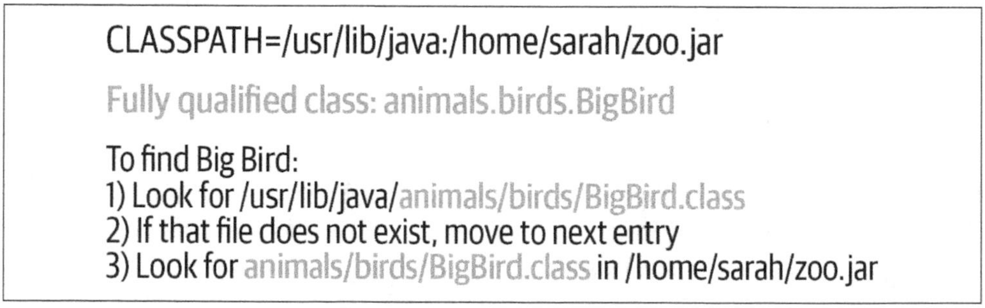

> CLASSPATH=/usr/lib/java:/home/sarah/zoo.jar
>
> Fully qualified class: animals.birds.BigBird
>
> To find Big Bird:
> 1) Look for /usr/lib/java/animals/birds/BigBird.class
> 2) If that file does not exist, move to next entry
> 3) Look for animals/birds/BigBird.class in /home/sarah/zoo.jar

Figure 3-2. Finding a fully qualified name in the classpath

For the Java runtime, *java*, and the Java compiler, *javac*, the classpath can also be specified with the *-classpath* option. On a Linux or macOS machine, for example:

```
% javac -classpath /home/pat/classes:/utils/utils.jar:. Foo.java
```

It's essentially the same on Windows, but you have to follow the system path separator (a semicolon) and use drive letters to start absolute paths.

If you don't specify the CLASSPATH environment variable or command-line option, the classpath defaults to the current directory (.); this means that the files in your current directory are normally available. If you change the classpath and don't include the current directory, these files will no longer be accessible.

We suspect that many of the problems that newcomers have when first learning Java are classpath related. Pay particular attention to setting and checking the classpath when getting started. If you're working inside an IDE, it may remove some or all of the burden of managing the classpath. Ultimately, however, understanding the classpath and knowing exactly what is in it when your application runs is very important to your long-term sanity.

Modules

Java 9 introduced the *modules* approach to Java applications. Modules allow for more fine-grained, performant application deployments—even when the application in question is (very) large. (Modules are not required, even for large applications. You can continue using the classic classpath approach if it fits your needs.) Using modules requires extra setup so we won't be tackling them in this book, but larger, commercially distributed apps may be module based. You can check out *Java 9 Modularity* (*https://oreil.ly/Wjs1q*) by Paul Bakker and Sander Mak (O'Reilly) for more details and help modularizing your own large projects if you start looking to share your work beyond just posting source code to public repositories.

The Java Compiler

The *javac* command-line utility is the compiler in the JDK. The compiler is written entirely in Java, so it's available for any platform that supports the Java runtime system. *javac* turns Java source code into a compiled class that contains Java bytecode. By convention, source files are named with a *.java* extension; the resulting class files have a *.class* extension. Each source code file is considered a single compilation unit. (As you'll see in Chapter 5, classes in a given compilation unit share certain features, such as package and import statements.)

javac allows one public class per file and insists that the file must have the same name as the class. If the filename and class name don't match, *javac* issues a compilation error. A single file can contain multiple classes, as long as only one of the classes is public and is named for the file. Avoid packing too many classes into a single source file. Packing classes together in a *.java* file only superficially associates them.

Go ahead and create a new file named *Bluebird.java* in the *ch03/examples/animals/birds* folder. You can use your IDE for this step, or you can just open any old text editor and make a new file. Once you have created the file, place the following source code in the file:

```
package animals.birds;

public class Bluebird {
}
```

Next, compile it with:

```
% cd ch03/examples
% javac animals/birds/Bluebird.java
```

Our tiny file doesn't do anything yet, but compiling it should work fine. You should not see any errors.

Unlike the Java interpreter, which takes just a class name as its argument, *javac* needs a filename (including the *.java* extension) to process. The previous command produces the class file *Bluebird.class* in the same directory as the source file. While it's nice to see the class file in the same directory as the source for this example, for most real applications, you need to store the class file in an appropriate place in the classpath.

You can use the *-d* option with *javac* to specify an alternative directory for storing the class files *javac* generates. The specified directory is used as the root of the class hierarchy, so *.class* files are placed in this directory or in a subdirectory, depending on whether the class is contained in a package. (The compiler creates intermediate subdirectories automatically, if necessary.) For example, we could use the following command to create the *Bluebird.class* file at */home/vicky/Java/classes/animals/birds/Bluebird.class*:

```
% javac -d /home/vicky/Java/classes Bluebird.java
```

You can specify multiple *.java* files in a single *javac* command; the compiler creates a class file for each source file given. But you don't need to list the other classes your class references as long as they are in the classpath in either source or compiled form. During compilation, Java resolves all other class references using the classpath.

The Java compiler is more intelligent than your average compiler. For example, *javac* compares the modification times of the source and class files for all classes and recompiles them as necessary. A compiled Java class remembers the source file from which it was compiled, and as long as the source file is available, *javac* can recompile it, if necessary. If, in the previous example, class `BigBird` references another class, say, `animals.furry.Grover`, *javac* looks for the source file *Grover.java* in an `animals.furry` package and recompiles the file, if necessary, to bring the *Grover.class* class file up-to-date.

By default, however, *javac* checks only source files that are referenced directly from other source files. This means that if you have an out-of-date class file that is referenced only by an up-to-date class file, it may not be noticed and recompiled. For that and many other reasons, most projects use a real build utility such as Gradle (*https://gradle.org*) to manage builds, packaging, and more.

Finally, it's important to note that *javac* can compile an application even if only the compiled (binary) versions of some of the classes are available. You don't need source code for all your objects. Java class files contain all the data type and method signature information that source files contain, so compiling against binary class files is as good as compiling with Java source code. (If you need to make changes, of course, you still need source files.)

Trying Java

Java 9 introduced a utility called *jshell*, which allows you to try out bits of Java code and see the results immediately. *jshell* is a REPL—a Read-Evaluate-Print Loop. Many languages have them, and prior to Java 9 there were many third-party variations available, but nothing was built into the JDK itself. Let's look a little more carefully at its capabilities.

You can use a terminal or command window from your operating system, or you can open a terminal tab in IntelliJ IDEA, as shown in Figure 3-3. Just type **jshell** at your command prompt and you'll see a bit of version information along with a quick reminder about how to view help from within the REPL.

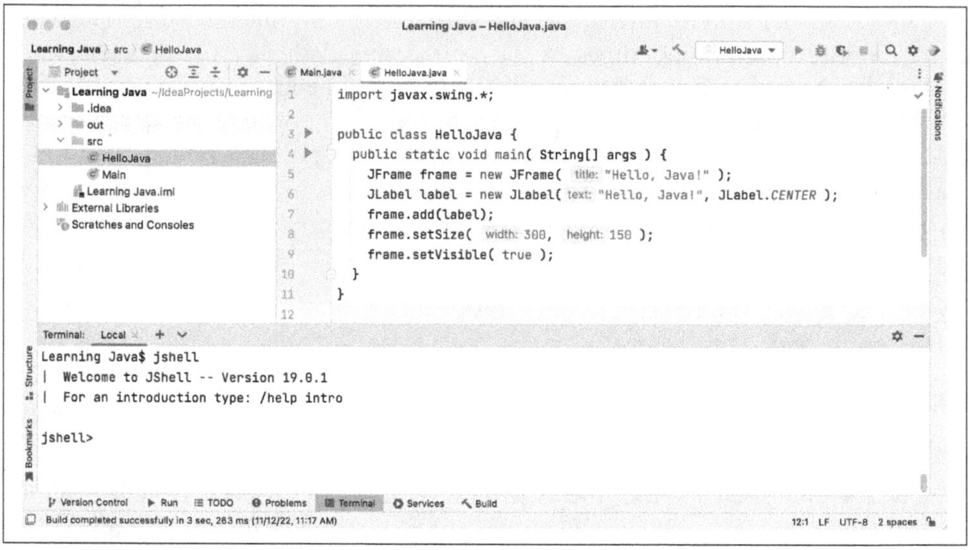

Figure 3-3. Starting jshell inside IDEA

Let's go ahead and try that help command now:

```
|  Welcome to JShell -- Version 19.0.1
|  For an introduction type: /help intro

jshell> /help intro
|
|                                intro
|                                =====
|
|  The jshell tool allows you to execute Java code, getting immediate results.
|  You can enter a Java definition (variable, method, class, etc),
|  like:  int x = 8
|  or a Java expression, like:  x + x
|  or a Java statement or import.
|  These little chunks of Java code are called 'snippets'.
|
|  There are also the jshell tool commands that allow you to understand and
|  control what you are doing, like:  /list
|
|  For a list of commands: /help
```

jshell is quite powerful, and we won't be using all of its features in this book. However, we will certainly be using it to try Java code here and throughout most of the remaining chapters. Think back to our `HelloJava2` example, "HelloJava2: The Sequel" on page 53. You can create UI elements like that `JFrame` right in the REPL and then manipulate them—all while getting immediate feedback! No need to save, compile, run, edit, save, compile, run, etc. Let's try:

```
jshell> JFrame frame = new JFrame("HelloJava2")
|  Error:
|  cannot find symbol
|    symbol:   class JFrame
|  JFrame frame = new JFrame("HelloJava2");
|  ^----^
|  Error:
|  cannot find symbol
|    symbol:   class JFrame
|  JFrame frame = new JFrame("HelloJava2");
|                     ^----^
```

Oops! *jshell* is smart and feature rich, but it is also quite literal. Remember that if you want to use a class not included in the default package, you have to import it. That's true in Java source files, and it's true when using *jshell*. Let's try again:

```
jshell> import javax.swing.*

jshell> JFrame frame = new JFrame("HelloJava2")
frame ==> javax.swing.JFrame[frame0,0,23,0x0,invalid,hidden ... led=true]
```

That's better. A little strange, probably, but better. Our `frame` object has been created. That extra information after the `==>` arrow is just the details about our `JFrame`, such as its size (`0x0`) and position on-screen (`0,23`). Other types of objects will show other details. Let's give our frame some width and height like we did before and get our frame on the screen where we can see it:

```
jshell> frame.setSize(300,200)

jshell> frame.setLocation(400,400)

jshell> frame.setVisible(true)
```

You should see a window pop up right before your very eyes! It will be resplendent in modern finery, as shown in Figure 3-4.

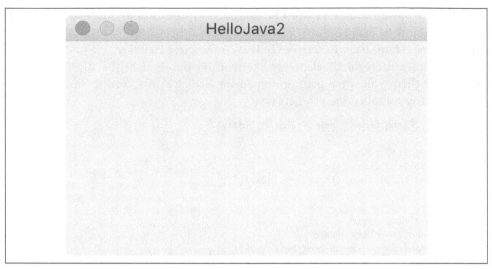

Figure 3-4. Showing a JFrame from jshell

By the way, don't worry about making mistakes in the REPL. You'll see an error message, but you can just correct whatever was wrong and keep going. As a quick example, imagine making a typo when trying to change the size of the frame:

```
jshell> frame.setsize(300,100)
|  Error:
|  cannot find symbol
|    symbol:   method setsize(int,int)
|  frame.setsize(300,100)
|  ^----------^
```

Java is case-sensitive so `setSize()` is not the same as `setsize()`. *jshell* gives you the same kind of error information that the Java compiler would but presents it inline. Correct that mistake and watch the frame get a little smaller (Figure 3-5)!

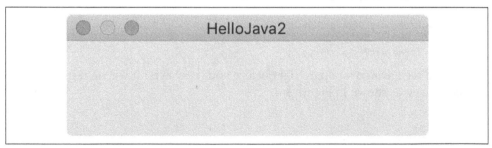

Figure 3-5. Changing the size of our frame

Amazing! Well, all right, perhaps it is less than useful, but we're just starting. Let's add some text using the `JLabel` class:

```
jshell> JLabel label = new JLabel("Hi jshell!")
label ==> javax.swing.JLabel[,0,0,0x0, ...rticalTextPosition=CENTER]

jshell> frame.add(label)
$8 ==> javax.swing.JLabel[,0,0,0x0, ...text=Hi, ...]
```

Neat, but why didn't our label show up in the frame? We'll go into much more detail on this in Chapter 11, but Java allows some graphical changes to build up before realizing them on your screen. This can be an immensely efficient trick, but it can sometimes catch you off guard. Let's force the frame to redraw itself (Figure 3-6):

```
jshell> frame.revalidate()

jshell> frame.repaint()
```

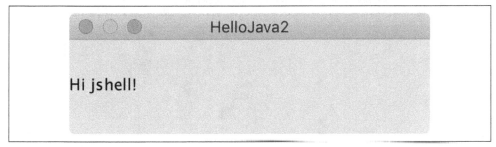

Figure 3-6. Adding a JLabel to our frame

Now we can see our label. Some actions will automatically trigger a call to `revalidate()` or `repaint()`. Any component already added to our frame before we make it visible, for example, would appear right away when we do show the frame. Or we can remove the label similarly to how we added it. Watch again to see what happens when we change the size of the frame immediately after removing our label (Figure 3-7):

```
jshell> frame.remove(label) // as with add(), things don't change immediately

jshell> frame.setSize(400,150)
```

Figure 3-7. Removing a label and resizing our frame

See? We have a new, slimmer window and no label—all without forced repainting. We'll do more work with UI elements in later chapters, but let's try one more tweak to our label just to show you how easy it is to try out new ideas or methods you looked up in the documentation. We can center the label's text, for example, resulting in something like Figure 3-8:

```
jshell> frame.add(label)
$45 ==> javax.swing.JLabel[,0,0,300x278,...,text=Hi jshell!,...]

jshell> frame.revalidate()

jshell> frame.repaint()

jshell> label.setHorizontalAlignment(JLabel.CENTER)
```

Figure 3-8. Centering the text on our label

We know this was another whirlwind tour with several bits of code that might not make sense yet. Why is CENTER in all caps? Why is the class name JLabel used before our center alignment? We can't answer every question right now, but we hope that typing along, probably making a few small mistakes, correcting them, and seeing the results make you want to know more. We want to make sure you have the tools to continue playing along as you go through the rest of this book. Like so many other skills, programming benefits from doing, in addition to reading!

JAR Files

Java ARchive (JAR) files are Java's suitcases. They are the standard and portable way to pack up all the parts of your Java application into a compact bundle for distribution or installation. You can put whatever you want into a JAR file: Java class files, serialized objects, data files, images, audio, etc. A JAR file can also carry one or more digital signatures that attest to its integrity and authenticity, attached to the file as a whole or to individual items in the file.

The Java runtime system can load class files directly from an archive in your CLASSPATH environment variable, as described earlier. Nonclass files (data, images, etc.) contained in your JAR file can also be retrieved from the classpath by your application using the `getResource()` method. Using this feature, your code doesn't have to know whether any resource is in a plain file or a member of a JAR archive. Whether a given class or data file is an item in a JAR file or an individual file on the classpath, you can always refer to it in a standard way and let Java's class loader resolve the location.

Items stored in JAR files are compressed with the standard ZIP file compression.[2] Compression makes downloading classes over a network much faster. A quick survey of the standard Java distribution shows that a typical class file shrinks by about 40% when it is compressed. Text files containing English words, such as HTML or ASCII, often compress to one-tenth their original size or less. (On the other hand, image files don't normally get smaller when compressed, as most common image formats are themselves compression formats.)

The jar Utility

The *jar* utility provided with the JDK is a simple tool for creating and reading JAR files. Its user interface isn't particularly friendly. It mimics the Unix tape archive command, *tar*. If you're familiar with *tar*, you'll recognize the following incantations which all share the form laid out in Figure 3-9:

```
jar -cvf jarFile path [ path ] [ … ]
```
Create *jarFile* containing *path*(s).

```
jar -tvf jarFile [ path ] [ … ]
```
List the contents of *jarFile*, optionally showing just *path*(s).

```
jar -xvf jarFile [ path ] [ … ]
```
Extract the contents of *jarFile*, optionally extracting just *path*(s).

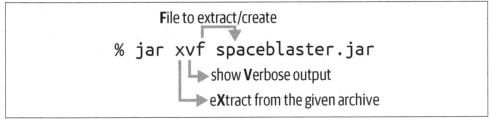

Figure 3-9. Important elements of the jar command-line utility

In these commands, the flag letters c, t, and x tell *jar* whether it is creating an archive, listing an archive's contents, or extracting files from an archive. The f flag means that the next argument is the name of the JAR file on which to operate.

---

2 You can even use standard ZIP utilities to inspect or unpack JAR files.

The optional v flag tells the *jar* command to be verbose when displaying information about files. In verbose mode, you get information about file sizes, modification times, and compression ratios.

Subsequent items on the command line (pretty much anything aside from the letters telling *jar* what to do and the file on which *jar* should operate) are taken as names of archive items. If you're creating an archive, the files and directories you list are placed in it. If you're extracting, only the filenames you list are extracted from the archive. (If you don't list any files, *jar* extracts everything in the archive.)

For example, let's say we have just completed our new game, Space Blaster. All the files associated with the game are in three directories. The Java classes themselves are in the *spaceblaster/game* directory, *spaceblaster/images* contains the game's images, and *spaceblaster/docs* contains associated game data. We can pack all this in an archive with this command:

```
% jar -cvf spaceblaster.jar spaceblaster/
```

Because we requested verbose output, *jar* tells us what it is doing:

```
added manifest
adding: spaceblaster/(in = 0) (out= 0)(stored 0%)
adding: spaceblaster/docs/(in = 0) (out= 0)(stored 0%)
adding: spaceblaster/docs/help1.html(in = 502) (out= 327)(deflated 34%)
adding: spaceblaster/docs/help2.html(in = 562) (out= 360)(deflated 35%)
adding: spaceblaster/game/(in = 0) (out= 0)(stored 0%)
adding: spaceblaster/game/Game.class(in = 362) (out= 270)(deflated 25%)
adding: spaceblaster/game/Planetoid.class(in = 606) (out= 418)(deflated 31%)
adding: spaceblaster/game/SpaceShip.class(in = 1084) (out= 629)(deflated 41%)
adding: spaceblaster/images/(in = 0) (out= 0)(stored 0%)
adding: spaceblaster/images/planetoid.png(in = 3434) (out= 3439)(deflated 0%)
adding: spaceblaster/images/spaceship.png(in = 2760) (out= 2765)(deflated 0%)
```

jar creates the file *spaceblaster.jar* and adds the directory *spaceblaster*, adding the directories and files within *spaceblaster* to the archive. In verbose mode, *jar* reports the savings gained by compressing the files in the archive.

We can unpack the archive with this command:

```
% jar -xvf spaceblaster.jar
```

Unpacking a JAR file is just like unzipping a ZIP file. The folders get created where you issued the command, and the files are placed in the correct hierarchy. We can also extract an individual file or directory by supplying one more command-line argument:

```
% jar -xvf spaceblaster.jar spaceblaster/docs/help2.html
```

This will extract the *help2.html* file, but it will be placed in the *spaceblaster/docs* folder—both of which may be created if need be. Of course, you normally don't have to unpack a JAR file to use its contents; Java tools know how to extract files from archives automatically. If you just want to see what is inside a JAR file, you can list the contents of our JAR with the command:

```
% jar -tvf spaceblaster.jar
```

Here's the output. It lists all the files, their sizes, and their creation times:

```
   0 Tue Feb 07 18:33:20 EST 2023 META-INF/
  63 Tue Feb 07 18:33:20 EST 2023 META-INF/MANIFEST.MF
   0 Mon Feb 06 19:21:24 EST 2023 spaceblaster/
   0 Mon Feb 06 19:31:30 EST 2023 spaceblaster/docs/
 502 Mon Feb 06 19:31:30 EST 2023 spaceblaster/docs/help1.html
 562 Mon Feb 06 19:30:52 EST 2023 spaceblaster/docs/help2.html
   0 Mon Feb 06 19:41:14 EST 2023 spaceblaster/game/
 362 Mon Feb 06 19:40:22 EST 2023 spaceblaster/game/Game.class
 606 Mon Feb 06 19:40:22 EST 2023 spaceblaster/game/Planetoid.class
1084 Mon Feb 06 19:40:22 EST 2023 spaceblaster/game/SpaceShip.class
   0 Mon Feb 06 16:30:06 EST 2023 spaceblaster/images/
3434 Mon Feb 06 16:30:06 EST 2023 spaceblaster/images/planetoid.png
2760 Mon Feb 06 16:27:26 EST 2023 spaceblaster/images/spaceship.png
```

If you leave out the verbose flag for the extraction or creation actions, you won't see any output at all (unless something goes wrong). Leaving out the verbose flag for the table-of-contents action simply prints the path and name of each file or directory without any extra information.

JAR manifests

Note that the *jar* command automatically adds a directory called *META-INF* to our archive. The *META-INF* directory holds files describing the contents of the JAR file. It always contains at least one file: *MANIFEST.MF*. The *MANIFEST.MF* file usually contains a "packing list" naming important files in the archive, along with a user-definable set of attributes for each entry.

The manifest is a text file containing a set of lines in the form keyword: value. The manifest is, by default, mostly empty and contains only JAR file version information:

```
Manifest-Version: 1.0
Created-By: 1.7.0_07 (Oracle Corporation)
```

It is also possible to sign JAR files with a digital signature. When you do this, digest (checksum) information is added to the manifest for each archived item (as shown next), and the *META-INF* directory holds digital signature files for items in the archive:

```
Name: com/oreilly/Test.class
SHA1-Digest: dF2GZt8G11dXY2p4olzzIc5RjP3=
...
```

You can add your own information to the manifest descriptions by specifying your own supplemental, manifest file when you create the archive. This is one possible place to store other simple kinds of attribute information about the files in the archive, perhaps version or authorship information.

For example, we can create a file with the following *keyword: value* lines:

```
Name: spaceblaster/images/planetoid.gif
RevisionNumber: 42.7
Artist-Temperament: moody
```

To add this information to the manifest in our archive, place it in a file called *myManifest.mf*[3] in your current directory and give the following *jar* command:

```
% jar -cvmf myManifest.mf spaceblaster.jar spaceblaster
```

Notice we included an additional option in the compact list of flags, m, which specifies that *jar* should read additional manifest information from the file given on the command line. How does *jar* know which file is which? Because m is before f, it expects to find the manifest file name information before the name of the JAR file it will create. If you think that's awkward, you're right; get the names in the wrong order, and *jar* does the wrong thing. Happily, it is easy to correct: simply delete the incorrect file and create a new one with the names in the right order.

If you're curious, an application can read its own manifest information from a JAR file using the `java.util.jar.Manifest` class. Its details are beyond the scope of what we need for this book, but feel free to check out the `java.util.jar` package in the documentation. Java applications can do quite a bit with the contents of JAR files.

Making a JAR file runnable

Now back to our new manifest file. Aside from attributes, you can put a few special values in the manifest file. One of these, `Main-Class`, allows you to specify one class containing the primary `main()` method for an application contained in the JAR:

```
Main-Class: spaceblaster.game.Game
```

Chapter 5 has more information on package names. If you add this to your JAR file manifest (using the m option described earlier), you can run the application directly from the JAR:

```
% java -jar spaceblaster.jar
```

Sadly, most operating systems have dropped the ability to double-click a JAR application from their file browsers. Professional desktop applications written in Java these

---

3 The actual name is entirely up to you, but the *.mf* file extension is common.

days typically have an executable wrapper (such as a *.bat* file in Windows or a *.sh* file in Linux or macOS) for better compatibility.

Tool Wrap-Up

There are obviously quite a few tools in the Java ecosystem—they got the name right with the initial bundling of everything into the Java Development "Kit." You won't use every tool mentioned above right away, so don't worry if the list of utilities seems a little overwhelming. We will focus on using the *javac* compiler and the *jshell* interactive utility as you wade farther into the Java waters. Our goal for this chapter is to make sure you know what tools are out there so that you can come back for details when you need them.

Review Questions

1. What statement gives you access to the Swing components in you application?

2. What environment variable determines where Java will look for class files when compiling or executing?

3. What options do you use to look at the contents of a JAR file without unpacking it?

4. What entry is required in the *MANIFEST.MF* file to make a JAR file executable?

5. What tool allows you to try out Java code in an interactive fashion?

Code Exercises

Your programming challenges for this chapter don't require any programming. Instead, we want to look at creating and executing JAR files. This exercise allows you to practice launching a Java application from a JAR file. First, locate the interactive review application, *lj6review.jar*, in the *quiz* folder wherever you installed the examples. Use the `-jar` flag with the *java* command (Java 17 or higher) to start the review app:

```
% cd quiz
% java -jar lj6review.jar
```

Once it starts, you can test your memory and your new skills by answering the review questions from all of the chapters in this book. Not all at once, of course! But you can keep coming back to the review app as you read further. The app presents the same questions found at the end of each chapter in a multiple-choice format. If you get an answer wrong, we've included some brief explanations that will help point you in the right direction.

The source code for this small review application is included in the *quiz/src* folder if you want to take a look behind the scenes.

Advanced Code Exercises

For an extra challenge, create an executable JAR file. Compile *HelloJar.java* and include the resulting class files (there should be two) along with the *manifest.mf* file in your archive. Name the JAR file *hello.jar*. You do need to make one modification: you'll have to update the *manifest.mf* file to indicate the main class. In this application, the HelloJar class contains the main() method required to launch. When this is completed, you should be able to execute the following command from a terminal window or the terminal tab in your IDE:[4]

```
% java -jar hello.jar
```

A friendly graphical greeting similar to our HelloComponent example from "Hello-Component" on page 46 should pop up on your screen. Don't cheat! We use some of the methods mentioned in "JAR manifests" on page 81 to read the contents of the manifest file. If you simply compile and run the application without making a JAR file, your greeting will not be quite as congratulatory.

Finally, look at the source code of the program if you like. It includes a few new elements of Java that we'll be tackling in the next chapter.

---

4 If you have any trouble building this JAR file, the exercise solutions in Appendix B contain more detailed steps to help.

CHAPTER 4

The Java Language

As humans, we learn the subtleties of spoken language through trial and error. We learn where to put the subject in relation to the verb and how to handle things like tenses and plurals. We certainly learn advanced language rules in school, but even the youngest students can ask their teachers intelligible questions. Computer languages have similar features: there are "parts of speech" that work as composable building blocks. There are ways of declaring facts and asking questions. In this chapter, we look at those fundamental programming units in Java. Trial and error remains a great teacher, so we'll also look at how to play with these new units and practice your skills.

Since Java's syntax is derived from C, we make some comparisons to features of that language, but no prior knowledge of C is necessary. Chapter 5 builds on this chapter by talking about Java's object-oriented side and completing the discussion of the core language. Chapter 7 discusses generics and records, features that enhance the way types work in the Java language, allowing you to write certain kinds of classes more flexibly and safely.

After that, we dive into the Java APIs and see what we can do with the language. The rest of this book is filled with brief examples that do useful things in a variety of areas. If you are left with any questions after these introductory chapters, we hope they'll be answered as you look at the code. There is always more to learn, of course! We'll try to point out other resources along the way that might benefit folks looking to continue their Java journey beyond the topics we cover.

For readers just beginning their programming journey, the web will likely be a constant companion. Many, many sites, Wikipedia articles, blog posts, and, well, the entirety of Stack Overflow (*https://oreil.ly/XHO1v*) can help you dig into particular topics or answer small questions that might arise. For example, while this book covers the Java language and how to start writing useful programs with Java and its tools, we don't cover lower, core programming topics such as algorithms (*https://oreil.ly/hXXGL*) in much detail. These programming fundamentals will naturally appear in our discussions and code examples, but you might enjoy a few hyperlink tangents to help cement certain ideas or fill in the gaps we must necessarily leave.

As we have mentioned before, many terms in this chapter will be unfamiliar. Don't worry if you are occasionally a little confused. The sheer breadth of Java means we have to leave out explanations or background details from time to time. As you progress, we hope you'll have the chance to revisit some of these early chapters. New information can work a bit like a jigsaw puzzle. It's easier to fit a new piece if you already have some other, related pieces connected. When you've spent some time writing code and this book becomes more of a reference for you and less of a guide, you'll find the topics in these first chapters make more sense.

Text Encoding

Java is a language for the internet. Since individual users speak and write in many different human languages, Java must be able to handle a large number of languages as well. It handles internationalization through the Unicode character set, a worldwide standard that supports the scripts of most languages.[1] The latest version of Java bases its character and string data on the Unicode 14.0 standard, which uses at least two bytes to represent each symbol internally. As you may recall from "The Past: Java 1.0–Java 20" on page 21, Oracle endeavors to keep up with new releases of the Unicode standard. Your version of Java may include a newer version of Unicode.

Java source code can be written using Unicode and stored in any number of character encodings. This makes Java a fairly friendly language for including non-English content. Programmers can use Unicode's rich set of characters not only for displaying information to the user but also in their own class, method, and variable names.

The Java char type and String class natively support Unicode values. Internally, the text is stored using either character or byte arrays; however, the Java language and APIs make this transparent to you, and you generally will not have to think about it. Unicode is also very ASCII friendly (ASCII is the most common character encoding for English). The first 256 characters are defined to be identical to the first 256 characters in the ISO 8859-1 (Latin-1) character set, so Unicode is effectively backward compatible with the most common English character sets. Furthermore, one of the most common file encodings for Unicode, called UTF-8, preserves ASCII

---

1 Check out the official Unicode site (*http://www.unicode.org*) for more information. Curiously, one of the scripts listed as "obsolete and archaic" and not currently supported by the Unicode standard is Javanese—a historical language of the people of the Indonesian island of Java.

values in their single byte form. This encoding is used by default in compiled Java class files, so storage remains compact for English text.

Most platforms can't display all currently defined Unicode characters. As a work-around, Java programs can be written with special Unicode escape sequences. A Unicode character can be represented with this escape sequence:

```
\uxxxx
```

xxxx is a sequence of one to four hexadecimal digits. The escape sequence indicates an ASCII-encoded Unicode character. This is also the form Java uses to output (print) Unicode characters in an environment that doesn't otherwise support them. Java comes with classes to read and write Unicode character streams in specific encodings, including UTF-8.

As with many long-lived standards in the tech world, Unicode was originally designed with so much extra space that no conceivable character encoding could ever possibly require more than 64K characters. Sigh. Naturally we have sailed past that limit and some UTF-32 encodings are in popular circulation. Most notably, emoji characters scattered throughout messaging apps are encoded beyond the standard range of Unicode characters. (For example, the canonical smiley emoji has the Unicode value 1F600.) Java supports multibyte UTF-16 escape sequences for such characters. Not every platform that supports Java will support emoji output, but you can fire up *jshell* to find out if your environment can show emoji characters (see Figure 4-1).

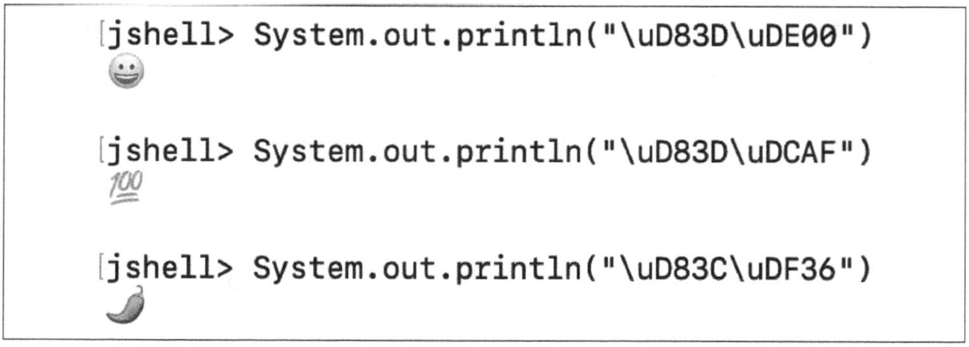

Figure 4-1. Printing emojis in the macOS Terminal app

Be careful about using such characters, though. We had to use a screenshot to make sure you could see the little cuties in *jshell* running on a Mac. You can use *jshell* to test your own system. You can put up a minimal graphical application similar to our HelloJava class from "HelloJava" on page 40. Create a JFrame, add a JLabel, and make the frame visible:

```
jshell> import javax.swing.*
```

```
jshell> JFrame f = new JFrame("Emoji Test")
f ==> javax.swing.JFrame[frame0 ...=true]

jshell> f.add(new JLabel("Hi \uD83D\uDE00"))
$12 ==> javax.swing.JLabel[ ...=CENTER]

jshell> f.setSize(300,200)

jshell> f.setVisible(true)
```

Hopefully you see the smiley, but it will depend on your system. Figure 4-2 shows the results we got when doing this exact test on macOS and Linux.

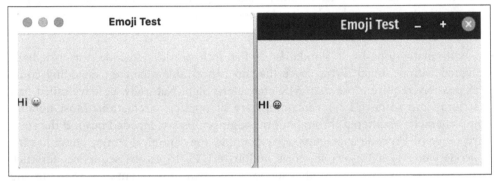

Figure 4-2. Testing emoji presentation on various systems

It's not that you can't use or support emoji in your applications, you just have to be aware of differences in output features. Make sure your users have a good experience wherever they are running your code.

 When importing the graphical components from the Swing package, be careful to use the correct `javax` prefix rather than the standard `java` prefix. More on all things Swing in Chapter 12.

Comments

Now that we know how the text of our programs is stored, we can concentrate on what to store! Programmers often include *comments* in their code to help explain complex bits of logic or to provide a guide to reading the code for other programmers. (Quite often the "other programmer" is yourself several months or years later.) The text in a comment is completely ignored by the compiler. Comments have no impact on the performance or functionality of your application. As such, we are big fans of writing good comments. Java supports both C-style *block comments* that can span multiple lines delimited by /* and */ and C++-style *line comments* indicated by //:

```
/*  This is a
       multiline
           comment.    */

// This is a single-line comment
// and so // is this
```

Block comments have both a beginning and end sequence and can cover large ranges of text. However, they cannot be "nested," meaning that you can't put a block comment inside of another block comment without running afoul of the compiler. Single-line comments have only a start sequence and are delimited by the end of a line; extra // indicators inside a single line have no effect. Line comments are useful for short comments within methods; they don't conflict with block comments. You can still wrap larger chunks of code in which the single-line comments appear with a block comment. This is often called *commenting out* a section of code—a common trick for debugging large applications. Since the compiler ignores all comments, you can put comments on lines or around blocks of code to see how a program behaves when that code is removed.[2]

Javadoc Comments

A special block comment beginning with /** indicates a *doc comment*. A doc comment is designed to be extracted by automated documentation generators, such as the JDK's own *javadoc* program or the context-aware tooltips in many IDEs. A doc comment is terminated by the next */, just as with a regular block comment. Within the doc comment, lines beginning with @ are interpreted as special instructions for the documentation generator, giving it information about the source code. By convention, each line of a doc comment begins with a *, as shown in the following example, but this is optional. Any leading spacing and the * on each line are ignored:

```
/**
 * I think this class is possibly the most amazing thing you will
 * ever see. Let me tell you about my own personal vision and
 * motivation in creating it.
 * <p>
 * It all began when I was a small child, growing up on the
 * streets of Idaho. Potatoes were the rage, and life was good...
 *
 * @see PotatoPeeler
 * @see PotatoMasher
 * @author John 'Spuds' Smith
```

---

2 Using a comment to "hide" code can be safer than simply deleting the code. If you want the code back, you just take out the comment delimiter(s).

```
 * @version 1.00, 19 Nov 2022
 */
class Potato { ... }
```

The *javadoc* command-line tool creates HTML documentation for classes by reading the source code and pulling out the embedded comments and @ tags. In this example, the tags create author and version information in the class documentation. The @see tags produce hypertext links to the related class documentation.

The compiler also looks at the doc comments; in particular, it is interested in the @deprecated tag, which means that the method has been declared obsolete and should be avoided in new programs. The compiled class includes information on any deprecated methods so the compiler can warn you whenever you use a deprecated feature in your code (even if the source isn't available).

Doc comments can appear above class, method, and variable definitions, but some tags may not apply to all of these. For example, the @exception tag can only be applied to methods. Table 4-1 summarizes the tags used in doc comments.

Table 4-1. Doc comment tags

Tag	Description	Applies to
@see	Associated class name	Class, method, or variable
@code	Source code content	Class, method, or variable
@link	Associated URL	Class, method, or variable
@author	Author name	Class
@version	Version string	Class
@param	Parameter name and description	Method
@return	Description of return value	Method
@exception	Exception name and description	Method
@deprecated	Declares an item to be obsolete	Class, method, or variable
@since	Notes API version when item was added	Variable

Javadoc tags in doc comments represent *metadata* about the source code; that is, they add descriptive information about the structure or contents of the code that is not, strictly speaking, part of the application. Some additional tools extend the concept of Javadoc-style tags to include other kinds of metadata about Java programs that are carried with the compiled code and can more readily be used by the application to affect its compilation or runtime behavior. The Java *annotations* facility provides a more formal and extensible way to add metadata to Java classes, methods, and variables. This metadata is also available at runtime.

Annotations

The @ prefix serves another role in Java that can look similar to tags. Java supports the notion of *annotations* as a means of marking certain content for special treatment. You apply annotations to code *outside* of comments. The annotation can provide information useful to the compiler or to your IDE. For example, the @SuppressWarn ings annotation causes the compiler (and often your IDE as well) to hide warnings about potential problems such as unreachable code. As you get into creating more interesting classes in "Advanced Class Design" on page 167, you may see your IDE add @Overrides annotations to your code. This annotation tells the compiler to perform some extra checks; these checks are meant to help you write valid code and catch errors before you (or your users) run your program.

You can even create custom annotations to work with other tools or frameworks. While a deeper discussion of annotations is beyond the scope of this book, we wanted you to know about them, as tags like @Overrides will show up both in our code and in examples or blog posts you might find online.

Variables and Constants

While adding comments to your code is critical to producing readable, maintainable files, at some point you have to start writing some compilable content. Programming is the art of manipulating that content. In just about every language, such information is stored in variables and constants for easier use by the programmer. Java has both. *Variables* store information that you plan to change and reuse over time (or information that you don't know ahead of time, such as a user's email address). *Constants* store information that is, well, constant. We've seen examples of both elements even in our tiny starter programs. Recall our simple graphical label from "HelloJava" on page 40:

```
import javax.swing.*;

public class HelloJava {
  public static void main(String[] args) {
    JFrame frame = new JFrame("Hello, Java!");
    JLabel label = new JLabel("Hello, Java!", JLabel.CENTER);
    frame.add(label);
    frame.setSize(300, 300);
    frame.setVisible(true);
  }
}
```

In this snippet, frame is a variable. We load it up in line 5 with a new instance of the JFrame class. Then we get to reuse that same instance in line 7 to add our label. We reuse the variable again to set the size of our frame in line 8 and to make it visible in line 9. All that reuse is exactly where variables shine.

Line 6 contains a constant: `JLabel.CENTER`. Constants contain a specific value that never changes throughout your program. Information that doesn't change may seem like a strange thing to store—why not just use the information itself each time? Constants can be simpler to use than their data; `Math.PI` is probably easier to remember than the value `3.141592653589793` it represents. And since you get to select the name of the constants in your own code, another benefit is that you can describe the information in a useful way. `JLabel.CENTER` may seem a little opaque still, but the word `CENTER` at least gives you a hint about what's happening.

Using named constants also allows for simpler changes down the road. If you code something like the maximum number of some resource you use, altering that limit is much easier if all you have to do is change the initial value given to the constant. If you use a literal number like 5, every time your code needs to check that maximum, you would have to hunt through all of your Java files to track down every occurrence of a 5 and change it as well—if that particular 5 was in fact referring to the resource limit. That type of manual search and replace is prone to error, quite above and beyond being tedious.

We'll see more details on the types and initial values of variables and constants in the next section. As always, feel free to use *jshell* to explore and discover some of those details on your own! Due to interpreter limitations, you cannot declare your own top-level constants in *jshell*. You can still use constants defined for classes like `JLabel.CENTER` or define them in your own classes.

Try typing the following statements into *jshell* to calculate and store the area of a circle in a variable using `Math.PI`. This exercise also proves that reassigning constants won't work. (And again, we have to introduce a few new concepts like *assignment*—putting a value into a variable—and the multiplication operator *. If these commands still feel strange, read on. We'll go over all of the new elements in more detail throughout the rest of this chapter.)

```
jshell> double radius = 42.0;
radius ==> 42.0

jshell> Math.PI
$2 ==> 3.141592653589793

jshell> Math.PI = 3;
|  Error:
|  cannot assign a value to final variable PI
|  Math.PI = 3;
|  ^-----^

jshell> double area = Math.PI * radius * radius;
area ==> 5541.769440932396

jshell> radius = 6;
```

```
radius ==> 6.0

jshell> area = Math.PI * radius * radius;
area ==> 113.09733552923255

jshell> area
area ==> 113.09733552923255
```

Notice the compiler error when we try to set `Math.PI` to 3. You could change `radius` and even `area` after you declare and initialize them. But variables hold only one value at a time, so the latest calculation is the only thing that remains in the variable `area`.

Types

The *type system* of a programming language describes how its *data elements* (the variables and constants we just touched on) are associated with storage in memory and how they are related to one another. In a *statically typed* language, such as C or C++, the type of a data element is a simple, unchanging attribute that often corresponds directly to some underlying hardware phenomenon, such as a register or a pointer value. In a *dynamically typed* language, such as Smalltalk or Lisp, variables can be assigned arbitrary elements and can effectively change their type throughout their lifetime. A considerable amount of overhead goes into validating what happens in these languages at runtime. Scripting languages, such as Perl, achieve ease of use by providing drastically simplified type systems in which only certain data elements can be stored in variables, and values are unified into a common representation, such as strings.

Java combines many of the best features of both statically and dynamically typed languages. As in a statically typed language, every variable and programming element in Java has a type that is known at compile time, so the runtime system doesn't normally have to check the validity of assignments between types while the code is executing. Unlike traditional C or C++, Java also maintains runtime information about objects and uses this to allow truly dynamic behavior. Java code may load new types at runtime and use them in fully object-oriented ways, allowing *casting* (converting between types) and full *polymorphism* (combining features from multiple types). Java code may also "reflect" upon or examine its own types at runtime, allowing advanced kinds of application behavior, such as interpreters that can interact with compiled programs dynamically.

Java data types fall into two categories. *Primitive types* represent simple values that have built-in functionality in the language; they represent numbers, boolean (true or false) values, and characters. *Reference types* (or class types) include objects and arrays; they are called reference types because they "refer to" a large data type that is passed "by reference," as we'll explain shortly. *Generics* are reference types that refine an existing type while still providing compile-time type safety. For example,

Java has a `List` class that can store a series of items. Using generics, you can create a `List<String>` which is a `List` that can only contain `Strings`. Or we could create a list of `JLabel` objects with `List<JLabel>`. We'll see much more of generics in Chapter 7.

Primitive Types

Numbers, characters, and boolean values are fundamental elements in Java. Unlike some other (perhaps more pure) object-oriented languages, they are not objects. For those situations where it's desirable to treat a primitive value as an object, Java provides "wrapper" classes. (More on this later.) The major advantage of treating primitive values as special is that the Java compiler and runtime can more readily optimize their implementation. Primitive values and computations can still be mapped down to hardware, as they always have been in lower-level languages.

An important portability feature of Java is that primitive types are precisely defined. For example, you never have to worry about the size of an `int` on a particular platform; it's always a 32-bit, signed number. The "size" of a numeric type determines how big (or how precise) a value you can store. For example, the `byte` type is an 8-bit, signed value for storing small numbers, from -128 to 127.[3] The aforementioned `int` type can handle most numeric needs, storing values between (roughly) +/- two billion. Table 4-2 summarizes Java's primitive types and their capacities.

Table 4-2. Java primitive data types

Type	Definition	Approximate range or precision
`boolean`	Logical value	`true` or `false`
`char`	16-bit, Unicode character	64K characters
`byte`	8-bit, signed integer	-128 to 127
`short`	16-bit, signed integer	-32,768 to 32,767
`int`	32-bit, signed integer	-2.1e9 to 2.1e9
`long`	64-bit, signed integer	-9.2e18 to 9.2e18
`float`	32-bit, IEEE 754, floating-point value	6-7 significant decimal places
`double`	64-bit, IEEE 754	15 significant decimal places

---

3 Java uses a technique called "two's complement" to store integers. This technique uses one bit at the beginning of the number to determine whether it is a positive or negative value. A quirk of this technique is that the negative range is always larger by one.

Those of you with a C background may notice that the primitive types look like an idealization of C scalar types on a 32-bit machine, and you're absolutely right. That's how they're supposed to look. Java's designers made a few changes, such as supporting 16-bit characters for Unicode and dropping ad hoc pointers. But overall, the syntax and semantics of Java primitive types derive from C.

But why have sizes at all? Again, that goes back to efficiency and optimization. The number of goals in a soccer match rarely crest the single digits—they would fit in a byte variable. The number of fans watching that match, however, would need something bigger. The total amount of money spent by all of the fans at all of the soccer matches in all of the World Cup countries would need something bigger still. By picking the right size, you give the compiler the best chance at optimizing your code, thus making your application run faster, consume fewer system resources, or both.

Some scientific or cryptographic applications require you to store and manipulate very large (or very small) numbers, and value accuracy over performance. If you need bigger numbers than the primitive types offer, you can check out the BigInteger and BigDecimal classes in the java.math package. These classes offer near-infinite size or precision. (If you want to see these big numbers in action, we use BigInteger to calculate factorial values in "Creating a custom reducer" on page 375.)

Floating-point precision

Floating-point operations in Java follow the IEEE 754 (*https://oreil.ly/ssh7S*) international specification, which means that the result of floating-point calculations is normally the same on different Java platforms. However, Java allows for extended precision on platforms that support it. This can introduce extremely small-valued and arcane differences in the results of high-precision operations. Most applications would never notice this, but if you want to ensure that your application produces *exactly* the same results on different platforms, you can use the special keyword strictfp as a class modifier on the class containing the floating-point manipulation (we cover classes in Chapter 5). The compiler then prohibits these platform-specific optimizations.

Variable declaration and initialization

You declare variables inside of methods and classes with a type name, followed by one or more comma-separated variable names. For example:

```
int foo;
double d1, d2;
boolean isFun;
```

You can optionally initialize a variable with an expression of the appropriate type when you declare it:

```
int foo = 42;
double d1 = 3.14, d2 = 2 * 3.14;
boolean isFun = true;
```

Variables that are declared as members of a class are set to default values if they aren't initialized (see Chapter 5). In this case, numeric types default to the appropriate flavor of zero, characters are set to the null character (\0), and boolean variables have the value `false`. (Reference types also get a default value, `null`, but more on that soon in "Reference Types" on page 98.)

Local variables, which are declared inside a method and live only for the duration of a method call, on the other hand, must be explicitly initialized before they can be used. As we'll see, the compiler enforces this rule, so there is no danger of forgetting.

Integer literals

Integer literals can be specified in binary (base 2), octal (base 8), decimal (base 10), or hexadecimal (base 16). Binary, octal, and hexadecimal bases are mostly used when dealing with low-level file or network data. They represent useful groupings of individual bits: 1, 3, and 4 bits, respectively. Decimal values have no such mapping, but they are much more human friendly for most numeric information. A decimal integer is specified by a sequence of digits beginning with one of the characters 1–9:

```
int i = 1230;
```

A binary number is denoted by the leading characters 0b or 0B (zero "b"), followed by a combination of zeros and ones:

```
int i = 0b01001011;        // i = 75 decimal
```

Octal numbers are distinguished from decimal numbers by a simple leading zero:

```
int i = 01230;             // i = 664 decimal
```

A hexadecimal number is denoted by the leading characters 0x or 0X (zero "x"), followed by a combination of digits and the characters a–f or A–F, which represent the decimal values 10–15:

```
int i = 0xFFFF;            // i = 65535 decimal
```

Integer literals are of type `int` unless they are suffixed with an L, denoting that they are to be produced as a `long` value:

```
long l = 13L;
long l = 13;          // equivalent: 13 is converted from type int
long l = 40123456789L;
long l = 40123456789;  // error: too big for an int without conversion
```

(The lowercase letter l will also work, but it should be avoided because it often looks like the number 1.)

When a numeric type is used in an assignment or an expression involving a "larger" type with a greater range, it can be *promoted* to the bigger type. In the second line of the previous example, the number 13 has the default type of int, but it's promoted to type long for assignment to the long variable.

Certain other numeric and comparison operations also cause this kind of arithmetic promotion, as do mathematical expressions involving more than one type. For example, when multiplying a byte value by an int value, the compiler promotes the byte to an int first:

```
byte b = 42;
int i = 43;
int result = b * i;   // b is promoted to int before multiplication
```

You can never go the other way and assign a numeric value to a type with a smaller range without an explicit *cast*, a special syntax you can use to tell the compiler exactly what type you need:

```
int i = 13;
byte b = i;        // Compile-time error, explicit cast needed
byte b = (byte) i; // OK
```

The cast in the third line is the (byte) phrase before our variable i. Conversions from floating-point to integer types always require an explicit cast because of the potential loss of precision.

Last and maybe least, you can add a bit of formatting to your numeric literals by utilizing the "_" (underscore) character between digits. If you have particularly large strings of digits, you can break them up as in the following examples:

```
int RICHARD_NIXONS_SSN = 567_68_0515;
int for_no_reason = 1___2___3;
int JAVA_ID = 0xCAFE_BABE;
long grandTotal = 40_123_456_789L;
```

Underscores may only appear between digits, not at the beginning or end of a number or next to the L long integer signifier. Try out some big numbers in *jshell*. Notice that if you try to store a long value without the L signifier, you'll get an error. You can see how the formatting really is just for your convenience. It is not stored; only the actual value is kept in your variable or constant:

```
jshell> long m = 41234567890;
|  Error:
|  integer number too large
|  long m = 41234567890;
|          ^
```

```
jshell> long m = 40123456789L;
m ==> 40123456789

jshell> long grandTotal = 40_123_456_789L;
grandTotal ==> 40123456789
```

Try some other examples. It can be useful to get a sense of what you find readable. It can also help you learn the kinds of promotions and castings that are available or required. Nothing like immediate feedback to drive home these subtleties!

Floating-point literals

Floating-point values can be specified in decimal or scientific notation. Floating-point literals are of type `double` unless they are suffixed with an `f` or `F`, denoting that they are a smaller-precision `float` value. And just as with integer literals, you may use the underscore character to format floating-point numbers—but again, only between digits. You can't place them at the beginning, at the end, next to the decimal point, or next to the F signifier of the number:

```
double d = 8.31;
double e = 3.00e+8;
float f = 8.31F;
float g = 3.00e+8F;
float pi = 3.1415_9265F;
```

Character literals

A literal character value can be specified either as a single-quoted character or an escaped ASCII or Unicode sequence, also inside single quotes:

```
char a = 'a';
char newline = '\n';
char smiley = '\u263a';
```

You'll most often deal with characters collected into a `String`, but there are still places where individual characters are useful. For example, if you handle keyboard input in your application, you might need to process individual key presses one `char` at a time.

Reference Types

In an object-oriented language like Java, you create new, complex data types from simple primitives by creating a *class*. Each class then serves as a new type in the language. For example, if we create a new class called `Car` in Java, we are also implicitly creating a new type called `Car`. The type of an item governs how it's used and where it can be assigned. As with primitives, an item of type `Car` can, in general, be assigned to a variable of type `Car` or passed as an argument to a method that accepts a `Car` value.

A type is not just a simple attribute. Classes can have relationships with other classes and so do the types that they represent. All classes in Java exist in a parent-child hierarchy, where a child class or *subclass* is a specialized kind of its parent class. The corresponding types have the same relationship, where the type of the child class is considered a subtype of the parent class. Because child classes inherit all of the functionality of their parent classes, an object of the child's type is in some sense equivalent to or an extension of the parent type. An object of the child type can be used in place of an object of the parent's type.

For example, if you create a new class, Dog, that extends Animal, the new type, Dog, is considered a subtype of Animal. Objects of type Dog can then be used anywhere an object of type Animal can be used; an object of type Dog is said to be assignable to a variable of type Animal. This is called *subtype polymorphism* and is one of the primary features of an object-oriented language. We'll look more closely at classes and objects in Chapter 5.

Primitive types in Java are used and passed "by value." This means that when a primitive value like an int is assigned to a variable or passed as an argument to a method, its *value* is copied. Reference types (class types), on the other hand, are always accessed "by reference." A *reference* is a handle or a name for an object. What a variable of a reference type holds is a "pointer" to an object of its type (or of a subtype, as described earlier). When you assign the reference to a variable or pass it to a method, only the reference is copied, not the object to which it's pointing. A reference is like a pointer in C or C++, except that its type is strictly enforced. The reference value itself can't be explicitly created or changed. You must assign an appropriate object to give a reference type variable a reference value.

Let's run through an example. We declare a variable of type Car, called myCar, and assign it an appropriate object:[4]

```
Car myCar = new Car();
Car anotherCar = myCar;
```

myCar is a reference-type variable that holds a reference to the newly constructed Car object. (For now, don't worry about the details of creating an object; again, we'll cover that in Chapter 5.) We declare a second Car type variable, anotherCar, and assign it to the same object. There are now two identical references : myCar and anotherCar, but only one actual Car object instance. If we change things in the state of the Car object itself, we see the same effect by looking at it with either reference. We can see behind the scenes a little bit by trying this with *jshell*:

---

4 The comparable code in C++ would be:
```
Car& myCar = *(new Car());
Car& anotherCar = myCar;
```

```
jshell> class Car {}
|  created class Car

jshell> Car myCar = new Car()
myCar ==> Car@21213b92

jshell> Car anotherCar = myCar
anotherCar ==> Car@21213b92

jshell> Car notMyCar = new Car()
notMyCar ==> Car@66480dd7
```

Notice the result of the creation and assignments. Here you can see that Java reference types come with a pointer value (21213b92, the right side of the @) and their type (Car, the left side of the @). When we create a new Car object, notMyCar, we get a different pointer value. myCar and anotherCar point to the same object; notMyCar points to a second, separate object.

Inferring types

Modern versions of Java have continually improved the ability to infer variable types in many situations. Starting with Java 10, you can use the var keyword in conjunction with the declaration and initiation of a variable, and allow the compiler to infer the correct type:

```
jshell> class Car2 {}
|  created class Car2

jshell> Car2 myCar2 = new Car2()
myCar2 ==> Car2@728938a9

jshell> var myCar3 = new Car2()
myCar3 ==> Car2@6433a2
```

Notice the (admittedly ugly) output when you create myCar3 in *jshell*. Although we did not explicitly give the type as we did for myCar2, the compiler can easily understand the correct type to use, and we do, in fact, get a Car2 object.

Passing references

Object references are passed to methods in the same way. In this case, either myCar or anotherCar would serve as equivalent arguments to some hypothetical method, called myMethod(), in our hypothetical class:

```
myMethod(myCar);
```

An important, but sometimes confusing, distinction is that the reference itself is a value (a memory address). That value is copied when you assign it to a variable or pass it in a method call. Given our previous example, the argument passed to a method (a local variable from the method's point of view) is actually a third reference to the Car object, in addition to myCar and anotherCar.

The method can alter the state of the Car object through that reference by calling the Car object's methods or altering its variables. However, myMethod() can't change the caller's notion of the reference to myCar: that is, the method can't change the caller's myCar to point to a different Car object; it can change only its own reference. This will be more obvious when we talk about methods later.

Reference types always point to objects (or null), and objects are always defined by classes. Similar to native types, if you don't initialize an instance or class variable when you declare it, the compiler will assign it the default value of null. Also, like native types, local variables that have a reference type are *not* initialized by default so you must set your own value before using them. However, two special kinds of reference types—arrays and interfaces—specify the type of object they point to in a slightly different way.

Arrays in Java are an interesting kind of object automatically created to hold a collection of some other type of object, known as the *base type*. An individual element in the array will have that base type. (So one element of an array of type int[] will be an int, and an element of an array of type String[] will be a String.) Declaring an array implicitly creates the new class type designed as a container for its base type, as you'll see later in this chapter.

Interfaces are a bit sneakier. An interface defines a set of methods and gives that set a corresponding type. An object that implements the methods of the interface can be referred to by that interface type, as well as its own type. Variables and method arguments can be declared to be of interface types, just like other class types, and any object that implements the interface can be assigned to them. This adds flexibility in the type system and allows Java to cross the lines of the class hierarchy and make objects that effectively have many types. We'll cover interfaces in Chapter 5 as well.

Generic types or *parameterized types*, as we mentioned earlier, are an extension of the Java class syntax that allows for additional abstraction in the way classes work with other Java types. Generics allow the programmer to specialize a class without changing any of that class's code. We cover generics in detail in Chapter 7.

A Word About Strings

Strings in Java are objects; they are therefore a reference type. String objects do, however, have some special help from the Java compiler that makes them look more like primitive types. Literal string values in Java source code, a series of characters or escape sequences between double quotes, are turned into String objects by the compiler. You can use a String literal directly, pass it as an argument to methods, or assign it to a String type variable:

```
System.out.println("Hello, World...");
String s = "I am the walrus...";
String t = "John said: \"I am the walrus...\"";
```

The + symbol in Java is *overloaded* to work with strings as well as regular numbers. Overloading is a term used in languages that allow you to use the same method name or operator symbol when working with distinct data types. With numbers, + performs addition. With strings, + performs *concatenation*, which is what programmers call sticking two strings together. While Java allows arbitrary overloading of methods (more in "Method Overloading" on page 154), + is one of the few overloaded operators in Java:

```
String quote = "Fourscore and " + "seven years ago,";
String more = quote + " our" + " fathers" +  " brought...";

// quote is now "Fourscore and seven years ago,"
// more is now " our fathers brought..."
```

Java builds a single String object from the concatenated string literals and provides it as the result of the expression. (More on all things String in Chapter 8.)

Statements and Expressions

Java *statements* appear inside methods and classes. They describe all activities of a Java program. Variable declarations and assignments, such as those in the previous section, are statements, as are basic language structures such as if/then conditionals and loops. (More on these structures later in this chapter.) Here are a few statements in Java:

```
int size = 5;
if (size > 10)
  doSomething();
for (int x = 0; x < size; x++) {
  doSomethingElse();
  doMoreThings();
}
```

Expressions produce values; Java evaluates an expression to produce a result. That result can then be used as part of another expression or in a statement. Method calls, object allocations, and, of course, mathematical expressions are examples of expressions:

```
// These are all valid Java expressions
new Object()
Math.sin(3.1415)
42 * 64
```

One of the tenets of Java is to keep things simple and consistent. To that end, when there are no other constraints, evaluations and initializations in Java always occur in the order in which they appear in the code—from left to right, top to bottom. You'll see this rule used in the evaluation of assignment expressions, method calls, and array indexes, to name a few cases. In some other languages, the order of evaluation is more complicated or even implementation dependent. Java removes this element of danger by precisely and simply defining how the code is evaluated.

This doesn't mean you should start writing obscure and convoluted statements, however. Relying on the order of evaluation of expressions in complex ways is a bad programming habit, even when it works. It produces code that is hard to read and harder to modify.

Statements

In any program, statements perform the real magic. Statements help us implement those algorithms we mentioned at the beginning of this chapter. In fact, they don't just help, they are precisely the programming ingredient we use; each step in an algorithm will correspond to one or more statements. Statements generally do one of four things:

- Gather input to assign to a variable
- Write output (to your terminal, to a JLabel, etc.)
- Make a decision about which statements to execute
- Repeat one or more other statements

Statements and expressions in Java appear within a *code block*. A code block contains a series of statements surrounded by an open curly brace ({) and a close curly brace (}). The statements in a code block can include variable declarations and most of the other sorts of statements and expressions we mentioned earlier:

```
{
  int size = 5;
  setName("Max");
  // more statements could follow...
}
```

In a sense, methods are just code blocks that take parameters and can be called by their names—for example, a hypothetical method setUpDog() might start out like this:

```
setUpDog(String name) {
  int size = 5;
  setName(name);
  // do any other setup work ...
}
```

Variable declarations are *scoped* in Java. They are limited to their enclosing code block—that is, you cannot see or use a variable outside of the nearest set of braces:

```
{
  // Scopes are like Vegas...
  // What's declared in a scope, stays in that scope
  int i = 5;
}

i = 6;  // Compile-time error, no such variable i
```

In this way, you can use code blocks to arbitrarily group statements and variables. The most common use of code blocks, however, is to define a group of statements for use in a conditional or iterative statement.

if/else conditionals

One of the key concepts in programming is the notion of making a decision. "If this file exists" or "If the user has a WiFi connection" are examples of the decisions computer programs and apps make all the time. Java uses the popular `if/else` statement for many of these types of decisions.[5] Java defines an `if/else` clause as follows:

```
if (condition)
   statement1;
else
   statement2;
```

In English, you could read that `if/else` statement as "if the condition is true, perform `statement1`. Otherwise, perform `statement2`."

The `condition` is a Boolean expression and must be enclosed in parentheses. A *Boolean expression*, in turn, is either a *Boolean value* (`true` or `false`) or an expression that evaluates to one of those values.[6] For example, `i == 0` is a Boolean expression that tests whether the integer `i` holds the value `0`:

```
// filename: ch04/examples/IfDemo.java
    int i = 0;
    // you can use i now to do other work and then
    // we can test it to see if anything has changed
    if (i == 0)
      System.out.println("i is still zero");
    else
      System.out.println("i is most definitely not zero");
```

---

5 We say popular because many programming languages have this same conditional statement.

6 The word "Boolean" comes from the English mathematician, George Boole, who laid the groundwork for logic analysis. The word is rightly capitalized, but many computer languages have a "boolean" type that uses lowercase—including Java. You will invariably see both variations online.

The whole of the preceding example is itself a statement and could be nested within another `if`/`else` clause. The `if` clause has the common functionality of taking two different forms: a "one-liner" or a block. We'll see this same pattern with other statements like the loops discussed in the next section. If you only have one statement to execute (like the simple `println()` calls in the previous snippet), you can place that lone statement after the `if` test or after the `else` keyword. If you need to execute more than one statement, you use a block. The block form looks like this:

```
if (condition) {
  // condition was true, execute this block
  statement;
  statement;
  // and so on...
} else {
  // condition was false, execute this block
  statement;
  statement;
  // and so on...
}
```

Here, all the enclosed statements in the block are executed for whichever branch is taken. We can use this form when we need to do more than just print a message. For example, we could guarantee that another variable, perhaps j, is not negative:

```
// filename: ch04/examples/IfDemo.java
  int j = 0;
  // you can use j now to do work like i before,
  // then make sure that work didn't drop
  // j's value below zero
  if (j < 0) {
    System.out.println("j is less than 0! Resetting.");
    j = 0;
  } else {
    System.out.println("j is positive or 0. Continuing.");
  }
```

Notice that we used curly braces for the `if` clause, with two statements, and for the `else` clause, which still has a single `println()` call. You can always use a block if you want. But if you only have one statement, the block with its braces is optional.

switch statements

Many languages support a "one of many" conditional commonly known as a *switch* or *case* statement. Given one variable or expression, a `switch` statement provides multiple options that might match. And we do mean *might*. A value does not have to match any of the `switch` options; in that case nothing happens. If the expression does match a `case`, that branch is executed. If more than one `case` would match, the first match wins.

The most common form of the Java `switch` statement takes an integer (or a numeric type argument that can be automatically promoted to an integer type) or a string, and selects among a number of alternative, constant `case` branches:[7]

```
switch (expression) {
  case constantExpression :
    statement;
  [ case constantExpression :
    statement;  ]
  // ...
  [ default :
    statement;  ]
}
```

The case expression for each branch must evaluate to a different constant integer or string value at compile time. Strings are compared using the `String equals()` method, which we'll discuss in more detail in Chapter 8.

You can specify an optional `default` case to catch unmatched conditions. When executed, the switch simply finds the branch matching its conditional expression (or the default branch) and executes the corresponding statement. But that's not the end of the story. Perhaps counterintuitively, the `switch` statement then continues executing branches after the matched branch until it hits the end of the switch or a special statement called `break`. Here are a couple of examples:

```
// filename: ch04/examples/SwitchDemo.java
int value = 2;

switch(value) {
  case 1:
    System.out.println(1);
  case 2:
    System.out.println(2);
  case 3:
    System.out.println(3);
}
// prints both 2 and 3
```

Using `break` to terminate each branch is more common:

```
// filename: ch04/examples/SwitchDemo.java
int value = GOOD;

switch (value) {
  case GOOD:
    // something good
    System.out.println("Good");
```

---

7 We won't be covering other forms here, but Java also supports using enumeration types and class matching in switch statements.

```
        break;
      case BAD:
        // something bad
        System.out.println("Bad");
        break;
      default:
        // neither one
        System.out.println("Not sure");
        break;
    }
    // prints only "Good"
```

In this example, only one branch—GOOD, BAD, or the default—is executed. The "keep going" behavior of switch is justified when you want to cover several possible case values with the same statement(s) without resorting to duplicating a bunch of code:

```
// filename: ch04/examples/SwitchDemo.java
    int value = MINISCULE;
    String size = "Unknown";

    switch(value) {
      case MINISCULE:
      case TEENYWEENY:
      case SMALL:
        size = "Small";
        break;
      case MEDIUM:
        size = "Medium";
        break;
      case LARGE:
      case EXTRALARGE:
        size = "Large";
        break;
    }

    System.out.println("Your size is: " + size);
```

This example effectively groups the six possible values into three cases. And this grouping feature can now appear directly in expressions. Java 12 offered *switch expressions* as a preview feature that was honed and made permanent with Java 14.

For example, rather than printing out the size names in the example above, we could assign our size label directly to a variable:

```
// filename: ch04/examples/SwitchDemo.java

    int value = EXTRALARGE;

    String size = switch(value) {
      case MINISCULE, TEENYWEENY, SMALL -> "Small";
      case MEDIUM -> "Medium";
      case LARGE, EXTRALARGE -> "Large";
```

```
    default -> "Unknown";
}; // note the semicolon! It completes the switch statement

System.out.println("Your size is: " + size);
// prints "Your size is Large"
```

Note the new "arrow" (a hyphen followed by the greater-than symbol) syntax. You still use separate `case` entries, but with this expression syntax, the case values are given in one comma-separated list rather than as separate, cascading entries. You then use `->` between the list and the value to return. This form can make the `switch` expression a little more compact and (hopefully) more readable.

do/while loops

The other major concept in controlling which statement gets executed next (*control flow* or *flow of control* in programmerese) is repetition. Computers are really good at doing things over and over. Repeating a block of code is done with a loop. There are a number of different loop statements in Java. Each type of loop has advantages and disadvantages. Let's look at these different types now.

The `do` and `while` iterative statements run as long as a Boolean expression (often referred to as the loop's condition) returns a `true` value. The basic structure of these loops is straightforward:

```
while (condition)
  statement; // or block

do
  statement; // or block
while (condition);
```

A `while` loop is perfect for waiting on some external condition, such as getting new email:

```
while(mailQueue.isEmpty())
  wait();
```

Of course, this hypothetical `wait()` method needs to have a limit (typically a time limit such as waiting for one second) so that it finishes and gives the loop another chance to run. But once you do have some email, you also want to process all of the messages that arrived, not just one. Again, a `while` loop is perfect. You can use a block of statements inside curly braces if you need to execute more than one statement in your loop. Consider a simple countdown printer:

```
// filename: ch04/examples/WhileDemo.java

        int count = 10;
        while(count > 0) {
          System.out.println("Counting down: " + count);
          // maybe do other useful things
          // and decrement our count
          count = count - 1;
        }
        System.out.println("Done");
```

In this example, we use the > comparison operator to monitor our count variable. We want to keep working while the countdown is positive. Inside the body of the loop, we print out the current value of count and then reduce it by one before repeating. When we eventually reduce count to 0, the loop will halt because the comparison returns false.

Unlike while loops which test their conditions first, a do-while loop (or more often just a do loop) always executes its statement body at least once. A classic example is validating input from a user. You know you need to get some information, so you request that information in the body of the loop. The loop's condition can test for errors. If there's a problem, the loop will start over and request the information again. That process can repeat until your request comes back without errors and you know you have good information.

```
        do {
          System.out.println("Please enter a valid email: ");
          String email = askUserForEmail();
        } while (email.hasErrors());
```

Again, the body of a do loop executes at least once. If the user gives us a valid email address the first time, we just don't repeat the loop.

The for loop

Another popular loop statement is the for loop. It excels at counting. The most general form of the for loop is also a holdover from the C language. It can look a little messy, but it compactly represents quite a bit of logic:

```
        for (initialization; condition; incrementor)
          statement; // or block
```

The variable initialization section can declare or initialize variables that are limited to the scope of the for body. The for loop then begins a possible series of rounds in which the condition is first checked and, if true, the body statement (or block) is executed. Following each execution of the body, the incrementor expressions are evaluated to give them a chance to update variables before the next round begins. Consider a classic counting loop:

```
// filename: ch04/examples/ForDemo.java

    for (int i = 0; i < 100; i++) {
      System.out.println(i);
      int j = i;
      // do any other work needed
    }
```

This loop will execute 100 times, printing values from 0 to 99. We declare and initialize a variable, i, to zero. We use the condition clause to see if i is less than 100. If it is, then Java executes the body of the loop. In the increment clause, we bump i up by one. (We'll see more on the comparison operators like < and >, as well as the increment shortcut ++ in the next section, "Expressions" on page 114.) After i is incremented, the loop goes back to check the condition. Java keeps repeating these steps (condition, body, increment) until i reaches 100.

Remember that the variable j is local to the block (visible only to statements within it) and will not be accessible to the code after the for loop. If the condition of a for loop returns false on the first check (for example, if we set i to 1,000 in the initialization clause), the body and incrementor section will never be executed.

You can use multiple comma-separated expressions in the initialization and incrementation sections of the for loop. For example:

```
// filename: ch04/examples/ForDemo.java

    // generate some coordinates
    for (int x = 0, y = 10; x < y; x++, y--) {
      System.out.println(x + ", " + y);
      // do other stuff with our new (x, y)...
    }
```

You can also initialize existing variables from outside the scope of the for loop within the initializer block. You might do this if you wanted to use the end value of the loop variable elsewhere. This practice is generally frowned upon: it's prone to mistakes and can make your code difficult to reason about. Nonetheless, it is legal and you may hit a situation where this behavior makes the most sense to you:

```
    int x;
    for(x = 0; x < someHaltingValue; x++) {
      System.out.print(x + ": ");
      // do whatever work you need ...
    }
    // x is still valid and available
    System.out.println("After the loop, x is: " + x);
```

In fact, you can leave out the initialization step completely if you want to work with a variable that already has a good starting value:

```
int x = 1;
for(; x < someHaltingValue; x++) {
  System.out.print(x + ": ");
  // do whatever work you need ...
}
```

Note that you do still need the semicolon that normally separates the initialization step from the condition.

The enhanced for loop

Java's auspiciously dubbed "enhanced `for` loop" acts like the `foreach` statement in some other languages, iterating over a series of values in an array or other type of collection:

```
for (varDeclaration : iterable)
  statement_or_block;
```

The enhanced `for` loop can be used to loop over arrays of any type as well as any kind of Java object that implements the `java.lang.Iterable` interface. (We'll have more to say on arrays, classes, and interfaces in Chapter 5.) This includes most of the classes of the Java Collections API (see Chapter 7). Here are a couple of examples:

```
// filename: ch04/examples/EnhancedForDemo.java

int [] arrayOfInts = new int [] { 1, 2, 3, 4 };
int total = 0;

for(int i  : arrayOfInts) {
  System.out.println(i);
  total = total + i;
}
System.out.println("Total: " + total);

// ArrayList is a popular collection class
ArrayList<String> list = new ArrayList<String>();
list.add("foo");
list.add("bar");

for(String s : list)
  System.out.println(s);
```

Again, we haven't discussed arrays or the `ArrayList` class and its special syntax in this example. What we're showing here is the syntax of the enhanced `for` loop iterating over both an array and a list of string values. The brevity of this form makes it popular whenever you need to work with a collection of items.

break/continue

The Java `break` statement and its friend `continue` can also be used to cut a loop or conditional statement short by jumping out of it. A `break` causes Java to stop the current loop (or `switch`) statement and skip the rest of the body. Java picks up executing the code that comes after the loop. In the following example, the `while` loop goes on endlessly until the `watchForErrors()` method returns `true`, triggering a `break` statement that stops the loop and proceeds at the point marked "after the `while` loop":

```
while(true) {
  if (watchForErrors())
    break;
  // No errors yet so do some work...
}
// The "break" will cause execution to
// resume here, after the while loop
```

A `continue` statement causes `for` and `while` loops to move on to their next iteration by returning to the point where they check their condition. The following example prints the numbers 0 through 9, skipping the number 5:

```
// filename: ch04/examples/ForDemo.java

for (int i = 0; i < 10; i++) {
  if (i == 5)
    continue;
  System.out.println(i);
}
```

The `break` and `continue` statements look like those in the C language, but Java's forms have the additional ability to take a label as an argument and jump out multiple levels to the scope of the labeled point in the code. This usage is not very common in day-to-day Java coding but may be important in special cases. Here is what that looks like:

```
labelOne:
  while (condition1) {
    // ...
    labelTwo:
      while (condition2) {
        // ...
        if (smallProblem)
          break; // Will break out of just this loop

        if (bigProblem)
          break labelOne; // Will break out of both loops
      }
    // after labelTwo
  }
// after labelOne
```

Enclosing statements, such as code blocks, conditionals, and loops, can be labeled with identifiers like `labelOne` and `labelTwo`. In this example, a `break` or `continue` without an argument has the same effect as the earlier examples. A `break` causes processing to resume at the point labeled "after labelTwo"; a continue immediately causes the labelTwo loop to return to its condition test.

We could use the statement break labelTwo in the smallProblem statement. It would have the same effect as an ordinary break, but break labelOne, as seen with the bigProblem statement, breaks out of both levels and resumes at the point labeled "after labelOne." Similarly, continue labelTwo would serve as a normal continue, but continue labelOne would return to the test of the labelOne loop. Multilevel break and continue statements remove the main justification for the much maligned goto statement in C/C++.[8]

There are a few Java statements we aren't going to discuss right now. The try, catch, and finally statements are used in exception handling, as we'll discuss in Chapter 6. The synchronized statement in Java is used to coordinate access to statements among multiple threads of execution; see Chapter 9 for a discussion of thread synchronization.

Unreachable statements

On a final note, we should mention that the Java compiler flags *unreachable statements* as compile-time errors. An unreachable statement is one that the compiler determines will never be called. Of course, many methods or bits of code may never actually be called in your program, but the compiler detects only those that it can "prove" are never called with some clever checking at compile time. For example, a method with an unconditional return statement in the middle of it causes a compile-time error, as does a method with a conditional that the compiler can tell will never be fulfilled:

```
if (1 < 2) {
    // This branch always runs and the compiler knows it
    System.out.println("1 is, in fact, less than 2");
    return;
} else {
    // unreachable statements, this branch never runs
    System.out.println("Look at that, seems we got \"math\" wrong.");
}
```

You have to correct the unreachable errors before you can complete the compilation. Fortunately, most instances of this error are just typos that are easily fixed. On the rare occasion that this compiler check uncovers a fault in your logic and not your syntax, you can always rearrange or delete the code that cannot be executed.

---

8 Jumping to named labels is still considered bad form (*https://oreil.ly/4M1Rm*).

Expressions

An expression produces a result, or value, when it is evaluated. The value of an expression can be a numeric type, as in an arithmetic expression; a reference type, as in an object allocation; or the special type, void, which is the declared type of a method that doesn't return a value. In the last case, the expression is evaluated only for its *side effects*; that is, the work it does aside from producing a value. The compiler knows the type of an expression. The value produced at runtime will either have this type or, in the case of a reference type, a compatible (assignable) subtype. (More on that compatibility in Chapter 5.)

We've seen several expressions already in our example programs and code snippets. We'll also see many more examples of expressions in the section "Assignment" on page 116.

Operators

Operators help you combine or alter expressions in various ways. They "operate" expressions. Java supports almost all standard operators from the C language. These operators also have the same precedence in Java as they do in C, as shown in Table 4-3.[9]

Table 4-3. Java operators

Precedence	Operator	Operand type	Description
1	++, ——	Arithmetic	Increment and decrement
1	+, -	Arithmetic	Unary plus and minus
1	~	Integral	Bitwise complement
1	!	Boolean	Logical complement
1	(*type*)	Any	Cast
2	*, /, %	Arithmetic	Multiplication, division, remainder
3	+, -	Arithmetic	Addition and subtraction
3	+	String	String concatenation
4	<<	Integral	Left shift
4	>>	Integral	Right shift with sign extension
4	>>>	Integral	Right shift with no extension
5	<, <=, >, >=	Arithmetic	Numeric comparison
5	instanceof	Object	Type comparison
6	==, !=	Primitive	Equality and inequality of value

---

9 You might remember the term *precedence*—and its cute mnemonic, "Please Excuse My Dear Aunt Sally"—from high school algebra. Java evaluates (p)arentheses first, then any (e)xponents, then (m)ultiplication and (d)ivision, and finally (a)ddition and (s)ubtraction.

Precedence	Operator	Operand type	Description
6	==, !=	Object	Equality and inequality of reference
7	&	Integral	Bitwise AND
7	&	Boolean	Boolean AND
8	^	Integral	Bitwise XOR
8	^	Boolean	Boolean XOR
9	|	Integral	Bitwise OR
9	|	Boolean	Boolean OR
10	&&	Boolean	Conditional AND
11	||	Boolean	Conditional OR
12	?:	N/A	Conditional ternary operator
13	=	Any	Assignment

We should also note that the percent (%) operator is not strictly a modulo but a remainder, and it can have a negative value. Try playing with some of these operators in *jshell* to get a better sense of their effects. If you're somewhat new to programming, it is particularly useful to get comfortable with operators and their order of precedence. You'll regularly encounter expressions and operators even when performing mundane tasks in your code:

```
jshell> int x = 5
x ==> 5

jshell> int y = 12
y ==> 12

jshell> int sumOfSquares = x * x + y * y
sumOfSquares ==> 169

jshell> int explicitOrder = (((x * x) + y) * y)
explicitOrder ==> 444

jshell> sumOfSquares % 5
$7 ==> 4
```

Java also adds some new operators. As we've seen, you can use the + operator with String values to perform string concatenation. Because all integer types in Java are signed values, you can use the >> operator to perform a right-arithmetic-shift operation with sign extension. The >>> operator treats the operand as an unsigned number[10] and performs a right-arithmetic-shift with no sign extension. As programmers,

---

10 Computers represent integers in one of two ways: signed integers, which allow negative numbers, and unsigned, which do not. A signed byte, for example, has the range -128...127. An unsigned byte has the range 0...255.

we don't need to manipulate the individual bits in our variables nearly as much as we used to, so you likely won't see these shift operators very often. If they do crop up in encoding or binary data parsing examples you read online, feel free to pop into *jshell* to see how they work. This type of play is one of our favorite uses for *jshell*!

Assignment

While declaring and initializing a variable is considered a statement with no resulting value, variable assignment alone is, in fact, an expression:

```
int i, j;    // statement with no resulting value
int k = 6;   // also a statement with no result
i = 5;       // both a statement and an expression
```

Normally, we rely on assignment for its side effects alone, as in the first two lines above, but an assignment can be used as a value in another part of an expression. Some programmers will use this fact to assign a given value to multiple variables at once:

```
j = (i = 5);
// both j and i are now 5
```

Relying on order of evaluation extensively (in this case, using compound assignments) can make code obscure and hard to read. We don't recommend it, but this type of initialization does show up in online examples.

The null value

The expression null can be assigned to any reference type. It means "no reference." A null reference can't be used to reference anything, and attempting to do so generates a NullPointerException at runtime. Recall from "Reference Types" on page 98 that null is the default value assigned to uninitialized class and instance variables; be sure to perform your initializations before using reference type variables to avoid that exception.

Variable access

The dot (.) operator is used to select members of a class or object instance. (We'll talk about members in detail in the following chapters.) It can retrieve the value of an instance variable (of an object) or a static variable (of a class). It can also specify a method to be invoked on an object or class:

```
int i = myObject.length;
String s = myObject.name;
myObject.someMethod();
```

A reference-type expression can be used in compound evaluations (multiple uses of the dot operation in one expression) by selecting further variables or methods on the result:

```
int len = myObject.name.length();
int initialLen = myObject.name.substring(5, 10).length();
```

The first line finds the length of our `name` variable by invoking the `length()` method of the `String` object. In the second case, we take an intermediate step and ask for a substring of the `name` string. The `substring` method of the `String` class also returns a `String` reference, for which we ask the length. Compounding operations like this is also called *chaining* method calls. One chained selection operation that we've used a lot already is calling the `println()` method on the variable `out` of the `System` class:

```
System.out.println("calling println on out");
```

Method invocation

Methods are functions that live within a class and may be accessible through the class or its instances, depending on the kind of method. Invoking a method means to execute its body statements, passing in any required parameter variables and possibly getting a value in return. A method invocation is an expression that results in a value. The value's type is the *return type* of the method:

```
System.out.println("Hello, World...");
int myLength = myString.length();
```

Here, we invoked the methods `println()` and `length()` on different objects. The `length()` method returned an integer value; the return type of `println()` is void (no value). It's worth emphasizing that `println()` produces *output*, but no *value*. We can't assign that method to a variable like we did above with `length()`:

```
jshell> String myString = "Hi there!"
myString ==> "Hi there!"

jshell> int myLength = myString.length()
myLength ==> 9

jshell> int mistake = System.out.println("This is a mistake.")
|  Error:
|  incompatible types: void cannot be converted to int
|  int mistake = System.out.println("This is a mistake.");
|                ^------------------------------------^
```

Methods make up the bulk of a Java program. While you could write some trivial applications that exist entirely inside a lone `main()` method of a class, you will quickly find you need to break things up. Methods not only make your application more readable, they also open the doors to complex, interesting, and *useful* applications that simply are not possible without them. Indeed, look back at our graphical Hello World applications in "HelloJava" on page 40. We used several methods defined for the `JFrame` class.

These are simple examples, but in Chapter 5 you'll see that it gets a little more complex when there are methods with the same name but different parameter types in the same class, or when a method is redefined in a subclass.

Statements, expressions, and algorithms

Let's assemble a collection of statements and expressions of these different types to accomplish an actual goal. In other words, let's write some Java code to implement an algorithm. A classic example of an algorithm is Euclid's process for finding the greatest common denominator (GCD) of two numbers. It uses a simple (if tedious) process of repeated subtraction. We can use Java's `while` loop, an `if/else` conditional, and some assignments to get the job done:

```
// filename: ch04/examples/EuclidGCD.java

int a = 2701;
int b = 222;
while (b != 0) {
  if (a > b) {
    a = a - b;
  } else {
    b = b - a;
  }
}
System.out.println("GCD is " + a);
```

It's not fancy, but it works—and it is exactly the type of task computer programs are great at performing. This is what you're here for! Well, you're probably not here for the greatest common denominator of 2701 and 222 (37, by the way), but you are here to start formulating the solutions to problems as algorithms and translating those algorithms into executable Java code.

Hopefully a few more pieces of the programming puzzle are starting to fall into place. But don't worry if these ideas are still fuzzy. This whole coding process takes a lot of practice. For one of the coding exercises in this chapter, we want you to try getting that block of code above into a real Java class inside the `main()` method. Try changing the values of `a` and `b`. In Chapter 8 we'll look at converting strings to numbers, so that you can find the GCD simply by running the program again, passing two numbers as parameters to the `main()` method, as shown in Figure 2-10, without recompiling.

Object creation

Objects in Java are allocated with the `new` operator:

```
Object o = new Object();
```

The argument to `new` is the *constructor* for the class. The constructor is a method that always has the same name as the class. The constructor specifies any required parameters to create an instance of the object. The value of the new expression is a reference of the type of the created object. Objects always have one or more constructors, though they may not always be accessible to you.

We look at object creation in detail in Chapter 5. For now, just note that object creation is also a type of expression and that the result is an object reference. A minor oddity is that the binding of new is "tighter" than that of the dot (.) selector. A popular side effect of this detail is that you can create a new object and invoke a method on it without assigning the object to a reference type variable. For example, you might need the current hour of the day—but not the rest of the information found in a Date object. You don't need to retain a reference to the newly created date, you can simply grab the attribute you need through chaining:

```
jshell> int hours = new Date().getHours()
hours ==> 13
```

The Date class is a utility class that represents the current date and time. Here we create a new instance of Date with the new operator and call its getHours() method to retrieve the current hour as an integer value. The Date object reference lives long enough to service the getHours() method call and is then cut loose and eventually garbage-collected (see "Garbage Collection" on page 159).

Calling methods from a fresh object reference in this way is a matter of style. It would certainly be clearer to allocate an intermediate variable of type Date to hold the new object and then call its getHours() method. However, combining operations like we did to get the hours above is common. As you learn Java and get comfortable with its classes and types, you'll probably take up some of these patterns. Until then, however, don't worry about being "verbose" in your code. Clarity and readability are more important than stylistic flourishes as you work through this book.

The instanceof operator

You use the instanceof operator to determine the type of an object at runtime. It tests to see if an object is of the same type or a subtype of the target type. (Again, more on this class hierarchy to come!) This is the same as asking if the object can be assigned to a variable of the target type. The target type may be a class, interface, or array type. instanceof returns a boolean value that indicates whether the object matches the type. Let's try it in *jshell*:

```
jshell> boolean b
b ==> false

jshell> String str = "something"
str ==> "something"

jshell> b = (str instanceof String)
b ==> true
```

```
jshell> b = (str instanceof Object)
b ==> true

jshell> b = (str instanceof Date)
|  Error:
|  incompatible types: java.lang.String cannot be converted to java.util.Date
|  b = (str instanceof Date)
|         ^-^
```

Notice the final `instanceof` test returns an error. With its strong sense of types, Java can often catch impossible combinations at compile time. Similar to unreachable code, the compiler won't let you proceed until you fix the issue.

The `instanceof` operator also correctly reports whether the object is of the type of an array:

```
if (myVariable instanceof byte[]) {
    // now we're sure myVariable is an array of bytes
    // go ahead with your array work here...
}
```

It is also important to note that the value `null` is not considered an instance of any class. The following test returns `false`, no matter what type you give to the variable:

```
jshell> String s = null
s ==> null

jshell> Date d = null
d ==> null

jshell> s instanceof String
$7 ==> false

jshell> d instanceof Date
$8 ==> false

jshell> d instanceof String
|  Error:
|  incompatible types: java.util.Date cannot be converted to java.lang.String
|  d instanceof String
|  ^
```

So `null` is never an "instance of" any class, but Java still tracks the types of your variables and will not let you test (or cast) between incompatible types.

Arrays

An array is a special type of object that can hold an ordered collection of elements. The type of the elements of the array is called the *base type* of the array; the number of elements it holds is a fixed attribute called its *length*. Java supports arrays of all primitive types as well as reference types. To create an array with a base type of byte, for example, you could use the type byte[]. Similarly, you can create an array with the base type of String with String[].

If you have done any programming in C or C++, the basic syntax of Java arrays should look familiar. You create an array of a specified length and access the elements with the *index* operator, []. Unlike those languages, however, arrays in Java are true, first-class objects. An array is an instance of a special Java array class and has a corresponding type in the type system. This means that to use an array, as with any other object, you first declare a variable of the appropriate type and then use the new operator to create an instance of it.

Array objects differ from other objects in Java in three respects:

- Java implicitly creates a special Array class type for us whenever we declare a new type of array. It's not strictly necessary to know about this process in order to use arrays, but it will help in understanding their structure and their relationship to other objects in Java later.

- Java lets us use the [] operator to access and assign array elements so that arrays look like many experienced programmers expect. We could implement our own classes that act like arrays, but we would have to settle for having methods such as get() and set() instead of using the special [] notation.

- Java provides a corresponding special form of the new operator that lets us construct an instance of an array with a specified length with the [] notation or initialize it directly from a structured list of values.

Arrays make it easy to work with chunks of related information, such as the lines of text in a file, or the words in one of those lines. We use them often in examples throughout the book; you'll see many examples of creating and manipulating arrays with the [] notation in this and coming chapters.

Array Types

An array variable is denoted by a base type followed by the empty brackets, []. Alternatively, Java accepts a C-style declaration with the brackets placed after the array name.

The following declarations are equivalent:

```
int[] arrayOfInts;    // preferred
int [] arrayOfInts;   // spacing is optional
int arrayOfInts[];    // C-style, allowed
```

In each case, we declare arrayOfInts as an array of integers. The size of the array is not yet an issue because we are only declaring a variable of an array type. We have not yet created an actual instance of the `array` class, nor its associated storage. It's not even possible to specify the length of an array when declaring an array type variable. The size is strictly a function of the array object itself, not the reference to it.

Arrays of reference types can be created in the same way:

```
String[] someStrings;
JLabel someLabels[];
```

Array Creation and Initialization

You use the `new` operator to create an instance of an array. After the `new` operator, we specify the base type of the array and its length with a bracketed integer expression. We can use this syntax to create array instances with actual storage for our recently declared variables. Since expressions are allowed, we can even do a little calculating inside the brackets:

```
int number = 10;
arrayOfInts = new int[42];
someStrings = new String[ number + 2 ];
```

We can also combine the steps of declaring and allocating the array:

```
double[] someNumbers = new double[20];
Component[] widgets = new Component[12];
```

Array indices start with zero. Thus, the first element of `someNumbers[]` has index 0, and the last element has index 19. After creation, the array elements themselves are initialized to the default values for their type. For numeric types, this means the elements are initially zero:

```
int[] grades = new int[30];
// first element grades[0] == 0
// ...
// last element grades[19] == 0
```

The elements of an array of objects are references to the objects—just like individual variables they point to—but they do not actually contain instances of the objects. The default value of each element is therefore `null` until we assign instances of appropriate objects:

```
String names[] = new String[42];
// names[0] == null
// names[1] == null
// ...
```

This is an important distinction that can cause confusion. In many other languages, the act of creating an array is the same as allocating storage for its elements. In Java, a newly allocated array of objects actually contains only reference variables, each with the value null.[11] That's not to say that there is no memory associated with an empty array; memory is needed to hold those references (the empty "slots" in the array). Figure 4-3 illustrates the names array of the previous example.

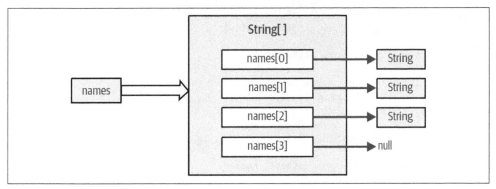

Figure 4-3. A Java array

We build our names variable as an array of strings (String[]). This particular String[] object contains four String type variables. We have assigned String objects to the first three array elements. The fourth has the default value null.

Java supports the C-style curly braces {} construct for creating an array and initializing its elements:

```
jshell> int[] primes = { 2, 3, 5, 7, 7+4 };
primes ==> int[5] { 2, 3, 5, 7, 11 }

jshell> primes[2]
$12 ==> 5

jshell> primes[4]
$13 ==> 11
```

An array object of the proper type and length is implicitly created, and the values of the comma-separated list of expressions are assigned to its elements. Note that we did not use the new keyword or the array type here. Java infers the use of new from the assignment.

---

11 The analog in C or C++ is an array of pointers. However, pointers in C or C++ are themselves two-, four-, or eight-byte values. Allocating an array of pointers is, in actuality, allocating the storage for some number of those pointer values. An array of references is conceptually similar, although references are not themselves objects. We can't manipulate references or parts of references other than by assignment, and their storage requirements (or lack thereof) are not part of the high-level Java language specification.

We can also use the {} syntax with an array of objects. In this case, each expression must evaluate to an object that can be assigned to a variable of the base type of the array or the value null. Here are some examples:

```
jshell> String[] verbs = { "run", "jump", "hide" }
verbs ==> String[3] { "run", "jump", "hide" }

jshell> import javax.swing.JLabel

jshell> JLabel yesLabel = new JLabel("Yes")
yesLabel ==> javax.swing.JLabel...

jshell> JLabel noLabel = new JLabel("No")
noLabel ==> javax.swing.JLabel...

jshell> JLabel[] choices={ yesLabel, noLabel,
   ...> new JLabel("Maybe") }
choices ==> JLabel[3] { javax.swing.JLabel ... ition=CENTER] }

jshell> Object[] anything = { "run", yesLabel, new Date() }
anything ==> Object[3] { "run", javax.swing.JLabe ... 2023 }
```

The following declaration and initialization statements are equivalent:

```
JLabel[] threeLabels = new JLabel[3];
JLabel[] threeLabels = { null, null, null };
```

Obviously, the first example is better when you have a large number of things to store. Most programmers use the curly brace initialization only when they have real objects ready to store in the array.

Using Arrays

The size of an array object is available in the public variable length:

```
jshell> char[] alphabet = new char[26]
alphabet ==> char[26] { '\000', '\000' ... , '\000' }

jshell> String[] musketeers = { "one", "two", "three" }
musketeers ==> String[3] { "one", "two", "three" }

jshell> alphabet.length
$24 ==> 26

jshell> musketeers.length
$25 ==> 3
```

length is the only accessible field of an array; it is a variable, not a method as in many other languages. Happily, the compiler tells you when you accidentally use parentheses like alphabet.length(), as everyone does now and then.

Array access in Java is just like array access in many other languages; you access an element by putting an integer-valued expression between brackets after the name of the array. This syntax works both for accessing individual, existing elements and for assigning new elements. We can get our second musketeer like this:

```
// remember the first index is 0!
jshell> System.out.println(musketeers[1])
two
```

The following example creates an array of JButton objects called keyPad. It then fills the array with buttons, using our square brackets and the loop variable as the index:

```
JButton[] keyPad = new JButton[10];
for (int i=0; i < keyPad.length; i++)
  keyPad[i] = new JButton("Button " + i);
```

Remember that we can also use the enhanced for loop to iterate over array values. Here we'll use it to print all the values we just assigned:

```
for (JButton b : keyPad)
  System.out.println(b);
```

Attempting to access an element that is outside the range of the array generates an ArrayIndexOutOfBoundsException. This is a type of RuntimeException, so you can either catch and handle it yourself if you really expect it, or ignore it, as we will discuss in Chapter 6. Here's a taste of the try/catch syntax Java uses to wrap such potentially problematic code:

```
String [] states = new String [50];

try {
  states[0] = "Alabama";
  states[1] = "Alaska";
  // 48 more...
  states[50] = "McDonald's Land";  // Error: array out of bounds
} catch (ArrayIndexOutOfBoundsException err) {
  System.out.println("Handled error: " + err.getMessage());
}
```

It's a common task to copy a range of elements from one array into another. One way to copy arrays is to use the low-level arraycopy() method of the System class:

```
System.arraycopy(source, sourceStart, destination, destStart, length);
```

The following example doubles the size of the names array from an earlier example:

```
String[] tmpVar = new String [ 2 * names.length ];
System.arraycopy(names, 0, tmpVar, 0, names.length);
names = tmpVar;
```

Here we allocate and assign a temporary variable, tmpVar, as a new array, twice the size of names. We use arraycopy() to copy the elements of names to the new array.

Finally, we assign a temporary array to `names`. If there are no remaining references to the old array of names after assigning the new array to `names`, the old array will be garbage-collected on the next pass.

Perhaps an easier way to accomplish the same task is to use the `copyOf()` or `copyOfRange()` methods from the `java.util.Arrays` class:

```
jshell> byte[] bar = new byte[] { 1, 2, 3, 4, 5 }
bar ==> byte[5] { 1, 2, 3, 4, 5 }

jshell> byte[] barCopy = Arrays.copyOf(bar, bar.length)
barCopy ==> byte[5] { 1, 2, 3, 4, 5 }

jshell> byte[] expanded = Arrays.copyOf(bar, bar.length+2)
expanded ==> byte[7] { 1, 2, 3, 4, 5, 0, 0 }

jshell> byte[] firstThree = Arrays.copyOfRange(bar, 0, 3)
firstThree ==> byte[3] { 1, 2, 3 }

jshell> byte[] lastThree = Arrays.copyOfRange(bar, 2, bar.length)
lastThree ==> byte[3] { 3, 4, 5 }

jshell> byte[] plusTwo = Arrays.copyOfRange(bar, 2, bar.length+2)
plusTwo ==> byte[5] { 3, 4, 5, 0, 0 }
```

The `copyOf()` method takes the original array and a target length. If the target length is larger than the original array length, then the new array is padded (with zeros or nulls) to the desired length. The `copyOfRange()` takes a starting index (inclusive) and an ending index (exclusive) and a desired length, which will also be padded, if necessary.

Anonymous Arrays

Often it is convenient to create *throwaway* arrays: arrays that are used in one place and never referenced anywhere else. Such arrays don't need names because you never refer to them again in that context. For example, you may want to create a collection of objects to pass as an argument to some method. It's easy enough to create a normal, named array, but if you don't actually work with the array (if you use the array only as a holder for some collection), you shouldn't need to name that temporary holder. Java makes it easy to create "anonymous" (unnamed) arrays.

Let's say you need to call a method named `setPets()`, which takes an array of `Animal` objects as arguments. Provided `Cat` and `Dog` are subclasses of `Animal`, here's how to call `setPets()` using an anonymous array:

```
Dog pete = new Dog ("golden");
Dog mj = new Dog ("black-and-white");
Cat stash = new Cat ("orange");
setPets (new Animal[] { pete, mj, stash });
```

The syntax looks similar to the initialization of an array in a variable declaration. We implicitly define the size of the array and fill in its elements using the curly brace notation. However, because this is not a variable declaration, we have to explicitly use the new operator and the array type to create the array object.

Multidimensional Arrays

Java supports multidimensional arrays in the form of arrays of other arrays. You create a multidimensional array with C-like syntax, using multiple bracket pairs, one for each dimension. You also use this syntax to access elements at various positions within the array. Here's an example of a multidimensional array that represents a hypothetical chessboard:

```
ChessPiece[][] chessBoard;
chessBoard = new ChessPiece[8][8];
chessBoard[0][0] = new ChessPiece.Rook;
chessBoard[1][0] = new ChessPiece.Pawn;
chessBoard[0][1] = new ChessPiece.Knight;
// setup the remaining pieces
```

Figure 4-4 illustrates the array of arrays we create.

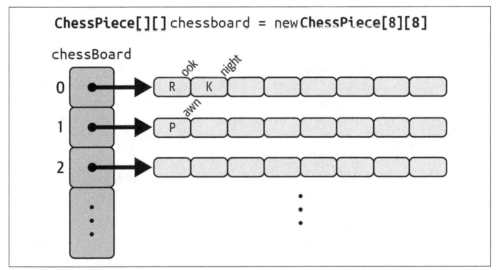

Figure 4-4. An array of arrays of chess pieces

Here, chessBoard is declared as a variable of type ChessPiece[][] (an array of ChessPiece arrays). This declaration implicitly creates the type ChessPiece[] as well. The example illustrates the special form of the new operator used to create a multidimensional array. It creates an array of ChessPiece[] objects and then, in turn, makes each element into an array of `ChessPiece` objects. We then index `chessBoard` to specify values for particular `ChessPiece` elements.

Of course, you can create arrays with more than two dimensions. Here's a slightly impractical example:

```
Color [][][] rgb = new Color [256][256][256];
rgb[0][0][0] = Color.BLACK;
rgb[255][255][0] = Color.YELLOW;
rgb[128][128][128] = Color.GRAY;
// Only 16 million to go!
```

We can specify a partial index of a multidimensional array to get a subarray of array type objects with fewer dimensions. In our example, the variable `chessBoard` is of type `ChessPiece[][]`. The expression `chessBoard[0]` is valid and refers to the first element of `chessBoard`, which, in Java, is of type `ChessPiece[]`. For example, we can populate our chessboard one row at a time:

```
ChessPiece[] homeRow = {
  new ChessPiece("Rook"), new ChessPiece("Knight"),
  new ChessPiece("Bishop"), new ChessPiece("King"),
  new ChessPiece("Queen"), new ChessPiece("Bishop"),
  new ChessPiece("Knight"), new ChessPiece("Rook")
};

chessBoard[0] = homeRow;
```

We don't necessarily have to specify the dimension sizes of a multidimensional array with a single `new` operation. The syntax of the `new` operator lets us leave the sizes of some dimensions unspecified. The size of at least the first dimension (the most significant dimension of the array) has to be specified, but the sizes of any number of trailing, less significant array dimensions may be left undefined. We can assign appropriate array-type values later.

We can create a simplified board of Boolean values which could hypothetically track the occupied status of a given square using this technique:

```
boolean [][] checkerBoard = new boolean [8][];
```

Here, `checkerBoard` is declared and created, but its elements, the eight `boolean[]` objects of the next level, are left empty. With this type of initialization, `checkerBoard[0]` is `null` until we explicitly create an array and assign it, as follows:

```
checkerBoard[0] = new boolean [8];
checkerBoard[1] = new boolean [8];
// ...
checkerBoard[7] = new boolean [8];
```

The code of the previous two snippets is equivalent to:

```
boolean [][] checkerBoard = new boolean [8][8];
```

One reason you might want to leave dimensions of an array unspecified is so that you can store arrays given to us later.

Note that because the length of the array is not part of its type, the arrays in the checkerboard do not necessarily have to be of the same length; that is, multidimensional arrays don't have to be rectangular. Consider the "triangular" array of integers shown in Figure 4-5 where row one has one column, row two has two columns, and so on.

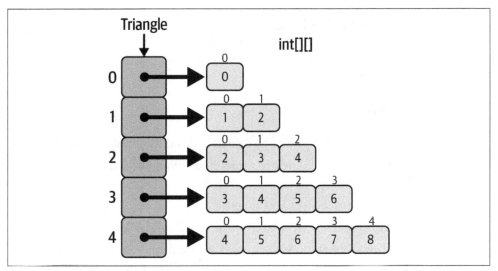

Figure 4-5. A triangular array of arrays

The exercises at the end of the chapter give you a chance to set up this array and initialize it yourself!

Types and Classes and Arrays, Oh My!

Java has a wide variety of types for storing information, each with its own way of representing literal bits of that information. Over time, you'll gain familiarity and comfort with ints and doubles and chars and Strings. But don't rush—these fundamental building blocks are exactly the kind of thing *jshell* was designed to help you explore. It's always worth a moment to check your understanding of what a variable can store. Arrays in particular might benefit from a little experimentation. You can try out the different declaration techniques and confirm that you have a grasp of how to access the individual elements inside single-dimensional and multidimensional structures.

You can also play with simple flow-of-control statements in *jshell* like our if branching and while looping statements. It requires a little patience to type in the occasional multiline snippet, but we can't overstate how useful play and practice are as you load more and more details of Java into your brain. Programming languages are certainly not as complex as human languages, but they still have many similarities. You can gain literacy in Java just as you have in English (or the language you're using to read this book, if you have a translation). You will start to get a feel for what the code is meant to do even if you don't immediately understand the particulars.

Some parts of Java, like arrays, are definitely full of particulars. We noted earlier that arrays are instances of special array classes in the Java language. If arrays have classes, where do they fit into the class hierarchy and how are they related? These are good questions, but we need to talk more about the object-oriented aspects of Java before answering them. That's the subject of Chapter 5. For now, take it on faith that arrays fit into the class hierarchy.

Review Questions

1. What text encoding format is used by default by Java in compiled classes?

2. What characters are used to enclose a multiline comment? Can those comments be nested?

3. Which looping constructs does Java support?

4. In a chain of `if/else if` tests, what happens if multiple conditions are true?

5. If you wanted to store the US stock market's total capitalization (roughly $31 trillion at the close of fiscal year 2022) as whole dollars, what primitive data type could you use?

6. What does the expression `18 - 7 * 2` evaluate to?

7. How would you create an array to hold the names of the days of the week?

Code Exercises

For your coding practice, we'll build on two of the examples from this chapter:

1. Implement Euclid's GCD algorithm as a full class named `Euclid`. Recall the basics of the algorithm:

```
int a = 2701;
int b = 222;
while (b != 0) {
  if (a > b) {
    a = a - b;
  } else {
    b = b - a;
  }
}
System.out.println("GCD is " + a);
```

For your output, can you think of a way to show the user the original values of a and b in addition to the common denominator? The ideal output would look something like this:

```
% java Euclid
The GCD of 2701 and 222 is 37
```

2. Try creating the triangular array from the previous section into a simple class or in *jshell*. Here's one way:

```
int[][] triangle = new int[5][];
for (int i = 0; i < triangle.length; i++) {
  triangle[i] = new int [i + 1];
  for (int j = 0; j < i + 1; j++)
    triangle[i][j] = i + j;
}
```

Now expand that code to print the contents of triangle to the screen. To help, recall that you can print the value of an array element with the System.out.println() method:

```
System.out.println(triangle[3][1]);
```

Your output will probably be a long, vertical line of numbers like this:

```
0
1
2
2
3
4
3
4
5
6
4
5
6
7
8
```

Advanced Exercises

1. If you're up for a bit more of a challenge, try arranging the output in a visual triangle. The statement above prints one element on a line by itself. The built-in `System.out` object has another output method: `print()`. This method does not print a newline after it prints whatever argument was passed in. You can chain together several `System.out.print()` calls to produce one line of output:

   ```
   System.out.print("Hello");
   System.out.print(" ");
   System.out.print("triangle!");
   System.out.println(); // We do want to complete the line
   // Output:
   // Hello triangle!
   ```

   Your final output should look similar to this:

   ```
   % java Triangle
   0
   1 2
   2 3 4
   3 4 5 6
   4 5 6 7 8
   ```

Objects in Java

In this chapter, we get to the heart of Java and explore its object-oriented aspects. The term *object-oriented design* refers to the art of decomposing an application into some number of *objects*, which are self-contained application components that work together. The goal is to break your problem down into smaller problems that are simpler and easier to handle and maintain. Object-based designs have proven themselves over the years, and object-oriented languages such as Java provide a strong foundation for writing applications—from the very small to the very large. Java was designed from the ground up to be an object-oriented language, and all of the Java APIs and libraries are built around solid object-based design patterns.

An object design *methodology* is a system or a set of rules created to help you break down your application into objects. Often this means mapping real-world entities and concepts (sometimes called the *problem domain*) into application components. Various methodologies attempt to help you factor your application into a good set of reusable objects. This is good in principle, but the problem is that good object-oriented design is still more art than science. While you can learn from off-the-shelf design methodologies, none of them will help you in all situations. The truth is that there is no substitute for experience.

We won't try to push you into a particular methodology here; there are shelves full of books to do that.[1] Instead, we'll provide some common-sense hints along the way as you get started.

---

[1] Once you have some experience with basic object-oriented concepts, you might want to look at *Design Patterns: Elements of Reusable Object-Oriented Software* by Erich Gamma et al. (Addison-Wesley). This book catalogs useful object-oriented designs that have been refined over the years. Many of these patterns appear in the design of the Java APIs.

Classes

Classes are the building blocks of a Java application. A *class* can contain methods (functions), variables, initialization code, and, as we'll discuss later, other classes. Separate classes that describe individual parts of a more complex idea are often bundled in *packages*, which help you organize larger projects. (Every class belongs to some package, even the simple examples we've seen so far.) An *interface* can describe some specific commonalities between otherwise disparate classes. Classes can be related to each other by extension or to interfaces by implementation. Figure 5-1 illustrates the ideas in this very dense paragraph.

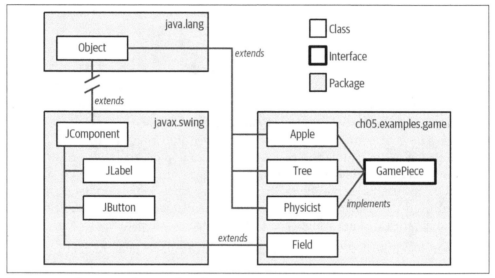

Figure 5-1. Class, interface, and package overview

`Object` (in the upper-left corner) is the foundational class at the heart of every other class in Java. It is part of the core Java package, `java.lang`. Java also has a package for its graphical UI elements called `javax.swing`. Inside that package, the `JComponent` class defines all of the low-level, common properties of graphical things, like frames and buttons and canvases. The `JLabel` class, for example, *extends* the `JComponent` class. That means `JLabel` inherits details from `JComponent` but adds things specific to labels. You might have noticed that `JComponent` itself extends from `Object`, or at least, it eventually extends back to `Object`. For brevity's sake, we have left out the intermediate classes and packages in between.

You can define your own classes and packages as well. For instance, the `ch05.examples.game` package in the lower-right corner is a custom package we built for a simple game that allows physicists to throw apples. (Newton will have his revenge!) In this package, we have some classes, like `Apple` and `Field`, that are part of our application. You can also see the GamePiece interface, which will contain some common, required elements for all game pieces and is implemented by the Apple, Tree, and Physicist classes. (In our game, the Field class is where all of the game pieces will be shown, but it is not a game piece itself. Notice that it does *not* implement the GamePiece interface.)

This chapter will go into much more detail, with more examples of each concept. We heartily recommend that you try the examples as you go and use the *jshell* tool (discussed in "Trying Java" on page 73) to help cement your understanding of new topics.

Declaring and Instantiating Classes

A class serves as a blueprint for making *instances*, which are runtime objects (individual copies) that implement the class structure. You declare a class with the class keyword and a name of your choosing. In our game, for example, the physicists, apples, and trees are all good targets for becoming classes. Inside a class, we add variables that store details or other useful information, and methods that describe what we can do to and with instances of this class.

Let's get started with a class for our apples. By (strong!) convention, class names start with capital letters. That makes Apple a good name to use. We won't try to get every detail about our game apples into the class right away, just a few elements to help illustrate how a class, variables, and methods fit together:

```
package ch05.examples;

class Apple {
  float mass;
  float diameter = 1.0f;
  int x, y;

  boolean isTouching(Apple other) {
    // Code will eventually go here that performs
    // distance calculations and returns true if
    // this apple is touching another apple
  }

  // More methods will go here as we fill out more
  // details of our apple
}
```

The Apple class contains four variables: mass, diameter, x, and y. It also defines a method called isTouching(), which takes a reference to another Apple as an argument and returns a boolean value as a result. Variables and method declarations can appear in any order, but variable initializers can't make "forward references" to other variables that appear later. (In our little snippet, the diameter variable could use the mass variable to help calculate its initial value, but mass could not use the diameter variable to do the same.) Once we've defined the Apple class, we can create an Apple object (an instance of that class) for our game, like so:

```
// Two steps, the declaration then the instantiation
Apple a1;
a1 = new Apple();

// Or all in one line...
Apple a2 = new Apple();
```

Recall that our declaration of the variable a1 doesn't create an Apple object; it simply creates a variable that refers to an object of type Apple. We still have to create the object, using the new keyword, as shown in the second line of the preceding code snippet. But you can combine those steps into a single line just as we did for the a2 variable. The same separate actions occur under the hood, of course. Sometimes the combined declaration and initialization will feel more readable than the multiline version.

Now that we've created an Apple object, we can access its variables and methods, as we've seen in several of our examples from Chapter 4 or even our graphical "Hello" app from "HelloJava" on page 40. Although this is not very exciting, we could now build another class, PrintAppleDetails, that is a complete application to create an Apple instance and print its details:

```
package ch05.examples;

public class PrintAppleDetails {
  public static void main(String args[]) {
    Apple a1 = new Apple();
    System.out.println("Apple a1:");
    System.out.println("  mass: " + a1.mass);
    System.out.println("  diameter: " + a1.diameter);
    System.out.println("  position: (" + a1.x + ", " + a1.y +")");
  }
}
```

If you compile and run this example, you should see the following output in your terminal or in the terminal window of your IDE:

```
Apple a1:
  mass: 0.0
  diameter: 1.0
  position: (0, 0)
```

But hmm, why doesn't a1 have a mass? If you look back at how we declared the variables for our Apple class, we only initialized diameter. All the other variables get the Java-assigned default value of 0 since they are numeric types.[2] We would ideally like to have a more interesting apple. Let's see how to provide those interesting bits.

Accessing Fields and Methods

Once you have a reference to an object, you can use and manipulate its variables and methods using the dot notation you saw in Chapter 4. Let's create a new class, PrintAppleDetails2, provide some values for the mass and position of our a1 instance, and then print the new details:

```
package ch05.examples;

public class PrintAppleDetails2 {
  public static void main(String args[]) {
    Apple a1 = new Apple();
    System.out.println("Apple a1:");
    System.out.println("  mass: " + a1.mass);
    System.out.println("  diameter: " + a1.diameter);
    System.out.println("  position: (" + a1.x + ", " + a1.y +")");
    // fill in some information on a1
    a1.mass = 10.0f;
    a1.x = 20;
    a1.y = 42;
    System.out.println("Updated a1:");
    System.out.println("  mass: " + a1.mass);
    System.out.println("  diameter: " + a1.diameter);
    System.out.println("  position: (" + a1.x + ", " + a1.y +")");
  }
}
```

Here's the new output:

```
Apple a1:
  mass: 0.0
  diameter: 1.0
  position: (0, 0)
Updated a1:
  mass: 10.0
  diameter: 1.0
  position: (20, 42)
```

Great! a1 is looking a little better. But look at the code again. We had to repeat the three lines that print the object's details. That type of exact replication calls out for a *method*.

Methods allow us to "do stuff" inside a class. As a simple example, we could improve the Apple class by providing these print statements in a method:

---

2 The char also gets a 0 but usually expressed as the null character, \0. A boolean variable gets the default of false, and reference types get the default of null.

```
public class Apple {
  float mass;
  float diameter = 1.0f;
  int x, y;

  // other apple-related variables and methods

  public void printDetails() {
    System.out.println("  mass: " + mass);
    System.out.println("  diameter: " + diameter);
    System.out.println("  position: (" + x + ", " + y +")");
  }
}
```

With those detail statements relocated, we can create `PrintAppleDetails3` that does its job more succinctly than its predecessor:

```
package ch05.examples;

public class PrintAppleDetails3 {
  public static void main(String args[]) {
    Apple a1 = new Apple();
    System.out.println("Apple a1:");

    // We can use our new method!
    a1.printDetails();

    // fill in some information on a1
    a1.mass = 10.0f;
    a1.x = 20;
    a1.y = 42;
    System.out.println("Updated a1:");
    // And look! We can easily reuse the same method
    a1.printDetails();
  }
}
```

Take another look at the `printDetails()` method we added to the `Apple` class. Inside a class, we can access variables and call methods of the class directly by name. The print statements just use the simple names like `mass` and `diameter`.

Or consider filling out the `isTouching()` method. We can use our own x and y coordinates without any special prefix. But to access the coordinates of some other apple, we need to go back to the dot notation. Here's one way to write that method using some math (more of this in "The java.lang.Math Class" on page 258) and the `if/then` statement we saw in "if/else conditionals" on page 104:

```
// File: ch05/examples/Apple.java

  public boolean isTouching(Apple other) {
    double xdiff = x - other.x;
    double ydiff = y - other.y;
    double distance = Math.sqrt(xdiff * xdiff + ydiff * ydiff);
    if (distance < diameter / 2 + other.diameter / 2) {
      return true;
    } else {
      return false;
    }
  }
}
```

Let's fill out a bit more of our game and create a `Field` class that uses a few `Apple` objects. It creates instances as member variables and works with those objects in the `setupApples()` and `detectCollision()` methods, invoking `Apple` methods and accessing variables of those objects through the references `a1` and `a2`, visualized in Figure 5-2:

```
package ch05.examples;

public class Field {
  Apple a1 = new Apple();
  Apple a2 = new Apple();

  public void setupApples() {
    a1.diameter = 3.0f;
    a1.mass = 5.0f;
    a1.x = 20;
    a1.y = 40;
    a2.diameter = 8.0f;
    a2.mass = 10.0f;
    a2.x = 70;
    a2.y = 200;
  }

  public void detectCollisions() {
    if (a1.isTouching(a2)) {
      System.out.println("Collision detected!");
    } else {
      System.out.println("Apples are not touching.");
    }
  }
}
```

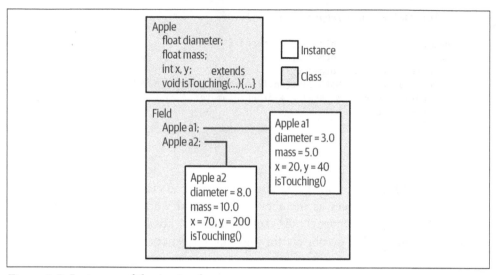

Figure 5-2. Instances of the Apple class

We can prove that `Field` has access to the apples' variables and methods with another iteration of our application, `PrintAppleDetails4`:

```
package ch05.examples;

public class PrintAppleDetails4 {
  public static void main(String args[]) {
    Field f = new Field();
    f.setupApples();
    System.out.println("Apple a1:");
    f.a1.printDetails();
    System.out.println("Apple a2:");
    f.a2.printDetails();
    f.detectCollisions();
  }
}
```

We should see the familiar apple details followed by an answer to whether or not the two apples are touching:

```
% java PrintAppleDetails4
Apple a1:
  mass: 5.0
  diameter: 3.0
  position: (20, 40)
Apple a2:
  mass: 10.0
  diameter: 8.0
  position: (70, 200)
Apples are not touching.
```

Great, just what we expected.

Before reading further, try changing the positions of the apples to make them touch. Do you get the expected output?

Access modifiers preview

Several factors affect whether class members can be accessed from another class. You can use the visibility modifiers public, private, and protected to control access; classes can also be placed into a *package*, which affects their scope. The private modifier, for example, designates a variable or method for use only by other members of the class itself. In the previous example, we could change the declaration of our variable diameter to private:

```
class Apple {
  // ...
  private float diameter;
  // ...
}
```

Now we can't access diameter from Field:

```
class Field {
  Apple a1 = new Apple();
  Apple a2 = new Apple();
  // ...
  void setupApples() {
    a1.diameter = 3.0f; // Compile-time error
    // ...
    a2.diameter = 8.0f; // Compile-time error
    // ...
  }
  // ...
}
```

If we still need to access diameter in some capacity, we would usually add public getDiameter() and setDiameter() methods to the Apple class:

```
public class Apple {
  private float diameter = 1.0f;
  // ...

  public void setDiameter(float newDiameter) {
    diameter = newDiameter;
  }

  public float getDiameter() {
    return diameter;
  }
  // ...
}
```

Creating methods like this is a good design rule because it allows future flexibility in changing the type or behavior of the value. We'll look more at packages, access modifiers, and how they affect the visibility of variables and methods later in this chapter.

Static Members

As we've said, instance variables and methods are associated with and accessed through an instance of the class (that is, through a particular object, like a1 or f in the previous examples). In contrast, members that are declared with the `static` modifier live in the class and are shared by all instances of the class. Variables declared with the `static` modifier are called *static variables* or *class variables*; similarly, these kinds of methods are called *static methods* or *class methods*. Static members are useful as flags and identifiers, that can be accessed from anywhere. We can add a static variable to our `Apple` example to store the value of acceleration due to gravity. This lets us calculate the trajectory of a tossed apple when we start animating our game:

```
class Apple {
  // ...
  static float gravAccel = 9.8f;
  // ...
}
```

We have declared the new `float` variable `gravAccel` as `static`. That means it is associated with the class, not with an individual instance, and if we change its value (either directly or through any instance of `Apple`), the value changes for all `Apple` objects, as shown in Figure 5-3.

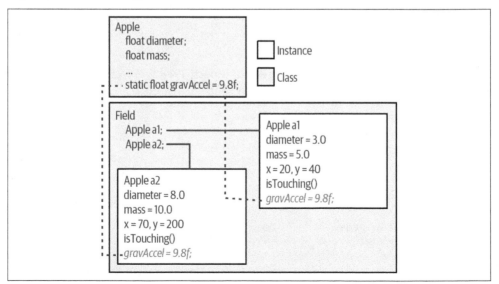

Figure 5-3. Static variables shared by all instances of a class

You can access static members similarly to the way you access instance members. Inside our `Apple` class, we can refer to `gravAccel` like any other variable:

```
class Apple {
  // ...
  float getWeight () {
    return mass * gravAccel;
  }
  // ...
}
```

However, since static members exist in the class itself, independent of any instance, we can also access them directly through the class. If we want to toss apples on Mars, for example, we don't need an `Apple` object like `a1` or `a2` to get or set the variable `gravAccel`. Instead, we can use the class to change the variable to reflect conditions on Mars:

```
Apple.gravAccel = 3.7f;
```

This changes the value of `gravAccel` for the class and all its instances. We don't have to manually set each instance of `Apple` to fall on Mars. Static variables are useful for any kind of data that is shared among classes at runtime. For instance, you can create methods to register your object instances so that they can communicate, or so that you can keep track of all of them. It's also common to use static variables to define constant values. In this case, we use the `static` modifier along with the `final` modifier. So, if we cared only about apples under the influence of the Earth's gravitational pull, we might change `Apple` as follows:

```
class Apple {
  // ...
  static final float EARTH_ACCEL = 9.8f;
  // ...
}
```

We have followed a common convention here and named our constant with capital letters and underscores (if the name has more than one word). The value of EARTH_ACCEL is a constant; you can access it through the class `Apple` or its instances, but you can't change its value.

It's important to use the combination of `static` and `final` only for things that are really constant. The compiler is allowed to "inline" such values within classes that reference them. This means that if you change a `static final` variable, you may have to recompile all code that uses that class (this is really the only case where you have to do that in Java). Static members are also useful for values needed in the construction of an instance itself. In our example, we might declare a number of static values to represent various sizes of `Apple` objects:

```
class Apple {
  // ...
  static int SMALL = 0, MEDIUM = 1, LARGE = 2;
  // ...
}
```

We might then use these options in a method that sets the size of an `Apple`, or in a special constructor, as we'll discuss shortly:

```
Apple typicalApple = new Apple();
typicalApple.setSize(Apple.MEDIUM);
```

Again, inside the `Apple` class, we can use static members directly by name, as well. There's no need for the `Apple.` prefix:

```
class Apple {
  // ...
  void resetEverything() {
    setSize (MEDIUM);
    // ...
  }
  // ...
}
```

Methods

So far, our example classes have been fairly simple. We keep a few bits of information around—apples have mass, fields have a couple of apples, etc. But we have also touched on the idea of making those classes do stuff. All of our various `PrintAppleDe tails` classes have a list of steps that get executed when we run the program, for example. As we noted briefly before, in Java, those steps are bundled into a method. In the case of `PrintAppleDetails`, that is the `main()` method.

Everywhere you have steps to take or decisions to make, you need a method. In addition to storing variables like the `mass` and `diameter` in our `Apple` class, we also added a few pieces of code that contained actions and logic. Methods are so fundamental to classes that we had to create a few even before getting here to the formal discussion of them! Think back to the `printDetails()` method in `Apple` or the `setupApples()` method in `Field`. Even our very first, simple program required a `main()` method.

Hopefully, the methods we have discussed so far have been straightforward enough to follow just from context. But methods can do much more than print out a few variables or calculate a distance. They can contain local variable declarations and other Java statements that are executed when the method is invoked. Methods may also return a value to the caller. They always specify a return type, which can be a primitive type, a reference type, or the special `void`, which indicates no returned value. Methods may take arguments, which are values supplied by the caller of the method.

Here's a simple example of a method that takes arguments:

```
class Bird {
  int xPos, yPos;

  double fly (int x, int y) {
    double distance = Math.sqrt(x*x + y*y);
    flap(distance);
    xPos = x;
    yPos = y;
    return distance;
  }
  // other bird things ...
}
```

In this example, the class Bird defines a method, fly(), that takes as arguments two integers: x and y. It returns a double type value as a result, using the return keyword.

Our method has a fixed number of arguments (two); however, methods can have *variable-length argument lists*, which allow the method to specify that it can take any number of arguments and sort them out itself at runtime.[3]

Local Variables

Our fly() method declares a local variable called distance, which it uses to compute the distance flown. A local variable is temporary; it exists only within the scope (the block) of its method. Local variables are allocated when a method is invoked; they are normally destroyed when the method returns. They can't be referenced from outside the method itself. If the method is executing concurrently in different threads, each thread has its own version of the method's local variables. A method's arguments also serve as local variables within the scope of the method; the only difference is that they are initialized by being passed in from the caller of the method.

An object created within a method and assigned to a local variable may or may not persist after the method has returned. As we'll see in detail in "Object Destruction" on page 158, it depends on whether any references to the object remain. If an object is created, assigned to a local variable, and never used anywhere else, that object is no longer referenced when the local variable disappears from scope, so garbage collection removes the object. If, however, we assign the object to an instance variable of an object, pass it as an argument to another method, or pass it back as a return value, it may be saved by another variable holding its reference.

---

3 We don't go into the details of such argument lists, but if you're curious and would like to do a little reading on your own, search online for the programmer-speak keyword "varargs."

Shadowing

If a local variable or method argument and an instance variable have the same name, the local variable *shadows*, or hides, the name of the instance variable within the scope of the method. This might sound like an odd situation, but it happens fairly often when the instance variable has a common or obvious name. For example, we could add a move method to our Apple class. Our method will need a new coordinate telling it where to place the apple. An easy choice for the coordinate arguments would be x and y. But we already have instance variables of the same name that hold the current position of the apple:

```java
class Apple {
  int x, y;

  public void moveTo(int x, int y) {
    System.out.println("Moving apple to " + x + ", " + y);
    // actual move logic would go here ...
  }
}
```

If the apple is currently at position (20, 40) and you call moveTo(40, 50), what do you think that println() statement will show? Inside moveTo(), the x and y names refer only to the method arguments with those names. The output would be:

```
Moving apple to 40, 50
```

If we can't get to the x and y instance variables, how can we move the apple? Turns out Java understands shadowing and provides a mechanism for working around these situations.

The "this" reference

You can use the special reference this any time you need to refer explicitly to the current object or a member of the current object. Often you don't need to use this, because the reference to the current object is implicit; such is the case when using unambiguously named instance variables inside a class. But you can use this to refer explicitly to instance variables in an object, even if they are shadowed. The following example shows how to use this to allow argument names that shadow instance variable names. This is a fairly common technique because it saves having to make up alternative names. Here's how we could implement our moveTo() method with shadowed variables:

```java
class Apple {
  int x, y;
  float diameter = 1.0f;

  public void moveTo(int x, int y) {
    System.out.println("Moving apple to " + x + ", " + y);
```

```
      // store the new x value
      this.x = x;
      // store the new y value if it is high enough
      if (y > diameter) {
        this.y = y;
      } else {
        // otherwise set y to the height of the apple
        this.y = (int)diameter;
      }
    }
  }
```

In this example, the expression `this.x` refers to the instance variable x and assigns it the value of the local variable x, which would otherwise hide its name. We do the same for `this.y` but add a little protection to make sure we don't move the apple below our ground. Notice that `diameter` is not shadowed in this method. Since we don't have a `diameter` argument in `moveTo()`, we don't have to say `this.diameter` when we use it.

The only reason we need to use `this` in the previous example is because we've used argument names that hide our instance variables, and we want to refer to the instance variables. You can also use the `this` reference any time you want to pass a reference to "the current" enclosing object to some other method, like we did for the graphical version of our "Hello Java" application in "HelloJava2: The Sequel" on page 53.

Static Methods

Static methods (sometimes called class methods), like static variables, belong to the class and not to individual instances of the class. What does this mean? Well, foremost, a *static method* lives outside of any particular instance. It can be invoked through the class name and dot operator, without any objects around. Because it is not bound to a particular object, a static method can only access other static members (static variables and other static methods) of the class. It can't directly see any instance variables or call any instance methods, because to do so it would have to ask, "on which instance?" Static methods can be called from instances using the same syntax as instance methods, but the important thing is that they can also be used independently.

Our `isTouching()` method uses a static method, `Math.sqrt()`, which is defined by the `java.lang.Math` class; we'll explore this class in detail in Chapter 8. For now, the important thing to note is that `Math` is the name of a class and not an instance of a `Math` object.[4] Because static methods can be invoked wherever the class name

---

4 It turns out the `Math` class cannot be instantiated at all. It contains only static methods. Trying to call `new Math()` would result in a compiler error.

is available, class methods are closer to C-style functions. Static methods are particularly useful for utility methods that perform work that is useful either independently of instances or in working on instances. For example, in our `Apple` class, we could enumerate all of the available sizes as human-readable strings from the constants we created in "Accessing Fields and Methods" on page 137:

```java
class Apple {
    public static final int SMALL = 0;
    public static final int MEDIUM = 1;
    public static final int LARGE = 2;
    // other apple things...

    public static String[] getAppleSizes() {
        // Return names for our constants
        return new String[] { "SMALL", "MEDIUM", "LARGE" };
    }
}
```

Here, we've defined a static method, `getAppleSizes()`, that returns an array of strings containing apple size names. We make the method static because the list of sizes is the same regardless of what size any given instance of `Apple` might be. We can still use `getAppleSizes()` from within an instance of `Apple` if we want, just like an instance method. We could change the (nonstatic) `printDetails` method to print a size name rather than an exact diameter, for example:

```java
public void printDetails() {
    System.out.println("  mass: " + mass);
    // Print the exact diameter:
    //System.out.println("  diameter: " + diameter);
    // Or a nice, human-friendly approximate
    String niceNames[] = getAppleSizes();
    if (diameter < 5.0f) {
        System.out.println(niceNames[SMALL]);
    } else if (diameter < 10.0f) {
        System.out.println(niceNames[MEDIUM]);
    } else {
        System.out.println(niceNames[LARGE]);
    }
    System.out.println("  position: (" + x + ", " + y +")");
}
```

However, we can also call it from other classes, using the `Apple` class name with the dot notation. For example, the very first `PrintAppleDetails` class could use similar logic to print a summary statement using our static method and static variables, like so:

```java
public class PrintAppleDetails {
    public static void main(String args[]) {
        String niceNames[] = Apple.getAppleSizes();
        Apple a1 = new Apple();
```

```
      System.out.println("Apple a1:");
      System.out.println("  mass: " + a1.mass);
      System.out.println("  diameter: " + a1.diameter);
      System.out.println("  position: (" + a1.x + ", " + a1.y +")");
      if (a1.diameter < 5.0f) {
        System.out.println("This is a " + niceNames[Apple.SMALL] + " apple.");
      } else if (a1.diameter < 10.0f) {
        System.out.println("This is a " + niceNames[Apple.MEDIUM] + " apple.");
      } else {
        System.out.println("This is a " + niceNames[Apple.LARGE] + " apple.");
      }
    }
  }
```

Here we have our trusty instance of the Apple class, a1, but we don't need a1 to get the list of sizes. Notice that we load the list of nice names *before* a1 even exists. But everything still works, as seen in the output:

```
Apple a1:
  mass: 0.0
  diameter: 1.0
  position: (0, 0)
This is a SMALL apple.
```

Static methods also play an important role in various design patterns, where you limit the use of the new operator for a class to one method—a static method called a *factory method*. We'll talk more about object construction in "Constructors" on page 155. There's no naming convention for factory methods, but it is common to see usage like this:

```
    Apple bigApple = Apple.createApple(Apple.LARGE);
```

We won't be writing any factory methods, but you're likely to find them in the wild, especially when looking up questions on sites like Stack Overflow.

Initializing Local Variables

Unlike instance variables, which receive default values if we don't provide an explicit one, local variables must be initialized before they can be used. You'll get a compile-time error if you try to access a local variable without first assigning it a value:

```
// instance variables always get default values if
// you don't initialize them
int foo;

void myMethod() {
  // local variables do not get default values
  int bar;

  foo += 1;  // This is ok, foo has the value 0
  bar += 1;  // compile-time error, bar is uninitialized
```

```
    bar = 99;  // This is ok, we're setting bar's initial value
    bar += 1;  // Now this calculation is ok
  }
```

Notice that this doesn't imply you always have to initialize local variables when you declare them, just that you must assign some value to them before the first time you reference them. More subtle possibilities arise when making assignments inside conditionals:

```
void myMethod {
  int bar;
  if (someCondition) {
    bar = 42;
  }
  bar += 1;   // Still a compile-time error, bar may not be initialized
}
```

In this example, bar is initialized only if someCondition is true. The compiler doesn't let you make this wager, so it flags the use of bar after our if statement as an error.

We could correct this situation in several ways. We could initialize the variable to a default value in advance or move the usage inside the conditional. We could also make sure the flow of control doesn't reach the uninitialized variable through some other means, depending on what makes sense for our particular application. For example, we could simply make sure that we assign bar a value in both an else branch if someCondition is false. Or we could return from the method abruptly:

```
void myMethod {
  int bar;
  if (someCondition) {
    bar = 42;
  } else {
    return;
  }
  bar += 1;  // This is ok!
}
```

In this case, either someCondition is true and bar is set to 42, or it is false and control returns from myMethod(). There's no chance of reaching bar in an uninitialized state, so the compiler allows this use of bar after the conditional.

Why is Java so picky about local variables? One of the most common (and insidious) sources of errors in other languages, like C or C++, is forgetting to initialize local variables. Local variables in those languages start with seemingly random values and cause all kinds of frustration for the programmer. Java tries to help out and forces you to assign good, known values.

Argument Passing and References

In the beginning of Chapter 4, we described the distinction between primitive types, which are passed by value (by copying), and objects, which are passed by reference. Now that you've got a better handle on methods in Java, let's walk through an example:

```
// declare a method with some arguments
void myMethod(int num, SomeKindOfObject o) {
  // do some useful stuff with num and o
}

// use the method
int i = 0;
SomeKindOfObject obj = new SomeKindOfObject();
myMethod(i, obj);
```

This chunk of code calls myMethod(), passing it two arguments. The first argument, i, is passed by value; when the method is called, the value of i is copied into the method's first parameter (a local variable) named num. If myMethod() changes the value of num, it changes only its local variable. Our i will not be affected.

In the same way, Java places a copy of the reference to obj into the argument o of myMethod(). But since it is a reference, both obj and o refer to the same object. Any changes made through either o or obj affect the actual object instance. If we change the value of, say, o.size, the change is visible both as o.size (inside myMethod()) and as obj.size (in the caller after myMethod() completes). However, if myMethod() reassigns the reference o to point to a different object, that assignment only affects its local variable reference. Assigning o to something else doesn't affect the caller's variable obj, which still refers to the original object.

Passing references to methods gives us a taste of the other use for the this keyword we mentioned earlier. You can use this to pass a reference for the current object to some other object. Let's look at a bit of code to see how this (no pun intended) works:

```
class Element {
  int num;
  double weight;

  void printMyDetails() {
    System.out.println(this);
  }
}
```

Our example is contrived, of course, but the syntax is correct. Inside the printMyDe tails() method, we call our old friend, System.out.println(). The argument we pass to println() is this, meaning we want the current element object printed. We'll be working with more complex object relationships in later chapters, and we will often need access to the current instance. The `this` keyword gives us that access.

Wrappers for Primitive Types

As we touched on briefly in "Primitive Types" on page 94, there is a schism in the Java world between class types (objects) and primitive types (numbers, characters, and Boolean values). Java accepts this trade-off for efficiency reasons. When you're crunching numbers, you want your computations to be lightweight; having to use objects for primitive types complicates performance optimizations. It's not common, but sometimes you need to store a primitive value as an object. For those occasions, Java supplies a standard wrapper class for each of the primitive types, as shown in Table 5-1.

Table 5-1. Primitive type wrappers

Primitive	Wrapper
void	java.lang.Void
boolean	java.lang.Boolean
char	java.lang.Character
byte	java.lang.Byte
short	java.lang.Short
int	java.lang.Integer
long	java.lang.Long
float	java.lang.Float
double	java.lang.Double

An instance of a wrapper class encapsulates a single value of its corresponding type. It's an immutable object that serves as a container to hold the value and lets you retrieve it later. You can construct a wrapper object from a primitive value or from a `String` representation of the value. The following statements are equivalent:

```
Float pi = new Float(3.14);
Float pi = new Float("3.14");
```

The numeric wrapper constructors throw a `NumberFormatException` when they encounter an error parsing a string.

Each of the numeric wrappers implements the `java.lang.Number` interface, which provides "value" methods to access its value in all the primitive forms. You can retrieve scalar values with the methods `doubleValue()`, `floatValue()`, `longValue()`, `intValue()`, `shortValue()`, and `byteValue()`:

```
Double size = new Double (32.76);

double d = size.doubleValue();    // 32.76
float f = size.floatValue();      // 32.76f
long l = size.longValue();        // 32L
int i = size.intValue();          // 32
```

This code is equivalent to casting the primitive double value to the various types.

The most common need for these wrappers is when you want to pass a primitive value to a method that requires an object. For example, in Chapter 7, we'll look at Java collections, a sophisticated set of classes for dealing with object groups, such as lists, sets, and maps. Collections work only with object types, so primitives must be wrapped when stored in them. As we'll see in the next section, Java makes this wrapping process transparent and automatic. For now, however, let's do it ourselves. As we'll see, a List is an extensible collection of Objects. We can use wrappers to hold simple numbers in a List (along with other objects):

```
// Manually wrapping an integer
List myNumbers = new ArrayList();
Integer thirtyThree = new Integer(33);
myNumbers.add(thirtyThree);
```

Here, we have created an Integer wrapper object so that we can insert the number into the List, using the add() method, which accepts an object. Later, when we are extracting elements from the List, we can recover the int value as follows:

```
// Manually unwrapping an integer
Integer theNumber = (Integer)myNumbers.get(0);
int n = theNumber.intValue();         // 33
```

Happily, Java can do much of this work automatically. Java calls the automatic wrapping and unwrapping of primitive types *autoboxing*. As we alluded to earlier, allowing Java to do this for us makes the code more concise and secure. The usage of the wrapper class is mostly hidden from us by the compiler, but it is still being used internally. Here's one more example that includes extra type information (*generics* in computer language parlance) and uses autoboxing:

```
// Using autoboxing and generics
List<Integer> myNumbers = new ArrayList<Integer>();
myNumbers.add(33);
int n = myNumbers.get(0);
```

Notice we don't create any explicit instances of the Integer wrapper, although we do include that extra type information in angle brackets (<Integer>) when we declare our variable. We'll see more of generics in Chapter 7.

Method Overloading

Method overloading is the ability to define multiple methods with the same name in a class; when the method is invoked, the compiler picks the correct one based on the arguments passed to the method. This implies that overloaded methods must have different numbers or types of arguments. (In "Overriding methods" on page 171, we'll look at *method overriding*, which occurs when we declare methods with identical signatures in subclasses.)

Method overloading (also called *ad hoc polymorphism*) is a powerful and useful feature. The idea is to create methods that act in the same way on different types of arguments. This creates the illusion that a single method can operate on many types of arguments. The `print()` method in the standard `PrintStream` class is a good example of method overloading in action. As you've probably deduced by now, you can print a string representation of just about anything using this expression:

```
System.out.print(argument);
```

The variable `out` is a reference to an object (a `PrintStream`) that defines nine different, "overloaded" versions of the `print()` method. The versions take arguments of the following types: `Object`, `String`, `char[]`, `char`, `int`, `long`, `float`, `double`, and `boolean`:

```
class PrintStream {
  void print(Object arg) { ... }
  void print(String arg) { ... }
  void print(char[] arg) { ... }
  // ...
}
```

You can invoke the `print()` method with any of these types as an argument, and the value will be printed in an appropriate way. In a language without method overloading, this requires something more cumbersome, such as a uniquely named method for printing each type of object. In that case, it's your responsibility to figure out what method to use for each data type.

In Java, `print()` has been overloaded to support two reference types: `Object` and `String`. What if we try to call `print()` with some other reference type? Say, a `Date` object? When there's not an exact type match, the compiler searches for an acceptable, *assignable* match. Since `Date`, like all classes, is a subclass of `Object`, a `Date` object can be assigned to a variable of type `Object`. It's therefore an acceptable match, and the compiler selects the `Object` version of the method.

What if there's more than one possible match? For example, what if we want to print the literal `"Hi there"`? That literal is assignable to either `String` (since it is a `String`) or to `Object`, the parent class of `String`. Here, the compiler decides which match is "better" and selects that method. In this case, it selects the `String` version.

The intuitive explanation for selecting the String version is that the String class is "closer" to the type of our literal "Hi there" in the inheritance hierarchy. It is a *more specific* match. A slightly more rigorous way of specifying it would be to say that a given method is more specific than another method if the argument types of the first method are all assignable to the argument types of the second method. In this case, the String method is more specific because type String is assignable to type Object. The reverse is not true.

If you're paying close attention, you may have noticed we said that the compiler resolves overloaded methods. Method overloading is not something that happens at runtime; this is an important distinction. Making this decision during compilation means that once the overloaded method is selected, the choice is fixed until the code is recompiled, even if the class containing the called method is later revised and an even more specific overloaded method is added.

This compile-time selection is in contrast to *overridden* methods, which are located at runtime and can be found even if they didn't exist when the calling class was compiled. In practice, this distinction will not usually be relevant to you, as you will likely recompile all of the necessary classes at the same time. We'll talk about method overriding later in the chapter.

Object Creation

Objects in Java are allocated on a system "heap" memory space. Unlike some other languages, however, we needn't manage that memory ourselves. Java takes care of memory allocation and deallocation for you. Java explicitly allocates storage for an object when you create it with the new operator. More importantly, objects are removed by garbage collection when they're no longer referenced.

Constructors

Objects are allocated with the new operator using a *constructor*. A constructor is a special method with the same name as its class and no return type. It's called when a new class instance is created, which gives the class an opportunity to set up the object for use. Constructors, like other methods, can accept arguments and can be overloaded. They are not, however, inherited like other methods:

```
class Date {
  int day;
  // other date variables ...

  // Simple "default" constructor
  Date() {
    day = currentDay();
  }
```

```
Date(String date) {
    day = parseDay(date);
}

// other Date methods ...
}
```

In this snippet, the class Date has two constructors. The first takes no arguments; it's known as the *default constructor*. Default constructors play a special role: if you don't define any constructors for a class, the compiler will supply an empty default constructor for you. The default constructor is what gets called whenever you create an object by calling its constructor with no arguments.

Here we have implemented the default constructor so that it sets the instance variable day by calling a hypothetical method, currentDay(), which presumably knows how to look up the current day. The second constructor takes a String argument. In this case, the String contains a date string that can be parsed to set the day variable. Given these constructors, we can create a Date object in the following ways:

```
Date now = new Date();
Date christmas = new Date("Dec 25, 2022");
```

In each case, Java chooses the appropriate constructor at compile time based on the rules for overloaded method selection.

If we later remove all references to an allocated object, it'll be garbage-collected, as we'll discuss shortly:

```
christmas = null;  // christmas is now fair game for the garbage collector
```

Setting this reference to null means it's no longer pointing to the "Dec 25, 2022" date object. Setting the variable christmas to any other value would have the same effect. Unless another variable also refers to the original date object, the date is now inaccessible and can be garbage-collected. We're not suggesting that you have to set references to null to get the values garbage-collected. Often this just happens naturally when local variables fall out of scope, but instance variables of objects live as long as the object itself lives (through references to it), and static variables live effectively forever.

A few more notes: you can declare constructors with the same visibility modifiers (public, private, or protected) as other methods, to control their accessibility. You can't, however, make constructors abstract, final, or synchronized. We'll talk in detail about abstract, final, and visibility modifiers later in this chapter, and we'll cover synchronized in Chapter 9.

Working with Overloaded Constructors

A constructor can refer to another constructor in the same class or the immediate superclass using special forms of the this and super references. We'll discuss the first case here and return to that of the superclass constructor after we have talked more about creating subclasses (often referred to simply as subclassing) and inheritance. A constructor can invoke another overloaded constructor in its class using the self-referential method call this() with appropriate arguments to select the desired constructor. If a constructor calls another constructor, *it must do so as its first statement*:

```java
class Car {
  String model;
  int doors;

  Car(String model, int doors) {
    this.model = model;
    this.doors = doors;
    // other, complicated stuff
  }

  Car(String model) {
    this(model, 4 /* doors */);
  }
}
```

In this example, the class Car has two constructors. The first, more explicit one accepts arguments specifying the car's model and its number of doors. The second constructor takes just the model as an argument and, in turn, calls the first constructor with a default value of four doors. The advantage of this approach is that you can have a single constructor do all the complicated setup work; other, more convenient constructors simply feed the appropriate arguments to that primary constructor.

The special call to this() must appear as the first statement in our delegating constructor. The syntax is restricted in this way because there's a need to identify a clear chain of command when calling constructors. At the end of the chain, Java invokes the constructor of the superclass (if we don't do it explicitly in our code) to ensure that inherited members are initialized properly before we proceed.

There's also a point in the chain, just after invoking the constructor of the superclass, where the initializers of the current class's instance variables are evaluated. Before that point, we can't even reference the instance variables of our class. We'll explain this situation again in complete detail after we have talked about inheritance.

For now, all you need to know is that you can invoke a second constructor (delegate to it) only as the first statement of your constructor. For example, the following code is illegal and causes a compile-time error:

```
Car(String m) {
  int doors = determineDoors();
  this(m, doors);    // Error: constructor call
                            // must be first statement
}
```

The simple model name constructor can't do any additional setup before calling the more explicit constructor. It can't even refer to an instance member for a constant value:

```
class Car {
  final int default_doors = 4;

  Car(String m) {
    this(m, default_doors); // Error: referencing
                            // uninitialized variable
  }
}
```

The instance variable `defaultDoors` is not initialized until a later point in the chain of constructor calls setting up the object, so the compiler doesn't let us access it yet. Fortunately, we can solve this particular problem by using a static variable instead of an instance variable:

```
class Car {
  static final int DEFAULT_DOORS = 4;

  Car(String m) {
    this(m, DEFAULT_DOORS);  // Okay!
  }
}
```

The static members of a class are initialized when the class is first loaded into the virtual machine. The compiler can determine the value of these static members so it's safe to access them in a constructor.

Object Destruction

Now that we've seen how to create objects, it's time to talk about how to destroy them. If you're accustomed to programming in C or C++, you've probably spent time hunting down *memory leaks* in your code. Programmers accidentally allow memory to leak by creating objects (which consume memory) and forgetting to destroy them (which returns the allocated memory) once the objects are no longer needed. Java takes care of object destruction for you; you don't have to worry about traditional memory leaks, and you can concentrate on more important programming tasks.[5]

Garbage Collection

Java uses a technique known as *garbage collection* to remove objects that are no longer needed. The garbage collector is Java's Grim Reaper. It lingers in the background, stalking objects and awaiting their demise. It finds and watches them, periodically counting references to them to see when their time has come. When all references to an object are gone and it's no longer accessible, the garbage-collection mechanism declares the object *unreachable* and reclaims its space back to the available pool of resources. An unreachable object is one that can no longer be found through any combination of "live" references in the running application.

Garbage collection uses a variety of algorithms; the Java virtual machine architecture doesn't require a particular scheme. It's worth noting, however, how some implementations of Java have accomplished this task. In the beginning, Java used a technique called "mark and sweep." In this scheme, Java first walks through the tree of all accessible object references and marks them as alive. It then scans the heap, looking for identifiable objects that are *not* marked. Using this technique, Java can find objects on the heap because they are stored in a characteristic way and have a particular signature of bits in their handles that's unlikely to be reproduced naturally. This kind of algorithm doesn't become confused by the problem of cyclic references, in which objects can mutually reference each other and appear alive even when they are dead (Java handles this problem automatically). This scheme wasn't the fastest method, however, and caused pauses in programs. Since then, implementations have become much more sophisticated.

Modern Java garbage collectors effectively run continuously without forcing any lengthy delay in execution of the Java application. Because they are part of a runtime system, they can also accomplish some things that could not be done statically. For instance, Java divides the memory heap into several areas for objects with different estimated life spans. Short-lived objects are placed on a special part of the heap, which drastically reduces the time required to recycle them. Objects that live longer can be moved to other, less volatile parts of the heap. In recent implementations, the garbage collector can even "tune" itself by adjusting the heap partition sizes based on the actual application performance. The improvement in Java's garbage collection since the early releases has been remarkable and is one of the reasons that Java is now

---

5 It's still possible to write code in Java that holds on to objects forever (by accident, we're sure), consuming more and more memory. This isn't really a leak as much as it is hoarding. Such hoarding in Java is usually easier to track down than a leak in C.

roughly equivalent in speed to many traditional languages that place the burden of memory management on the shoulders of the programmer.

In general, you do not have to concern yourself with the garbage-collection process. But one garbage-collection method can be useful for debugging. You can prompt the garbage collector to make a clean sweep explicitly by invoking the System.gc() method. This method is completely implementation dependent and may do nothing, but you can use it if you want some guarantee that Java has at least tried to clean up memory before you do an activity.

Packages

Even when we stick to simple examples, you may have noticed that solving problems in Java requires creating classes. For our game classes above, we have our apples and our trees and our playing field, to name just a few. For more complex applications or libraries, you can have hundreds or even thousands of classes. You need a way to organize things, and Java uses the notion of a *package* to accomplish this task. Let's look at some examples.

Recall our second Hello World example in Chapter 2. The first few lines in the file show us a lot of information about where the code lives:

```java
package ch02.examples;

import javax.swing.*;

public class HelloJava {
  public static void main(String[] args) {
    JFrame frame = new JFrame("Hello, Java!");
    JLabel label = new JLabel("Hello, Java!", JLabel.CENTER);
    // ...
  }
}
```

We named the Java file *HelloJava.java* according to the main class (HelloJava) in that file. When we talk about organizing things that go in files, you might naturally think of using folders to organize those files in turn. That is essentially what Java does. In this example, we use the package keyword and assign a package name of ch02.examples. Packages map onto folder names much the way classes map onto filenames. From the directory where you installed the examples for this book, then, this class should be found in the file *ch02/examples/HelloJava.java*. Take a look back at Figure 5-1 where we have some classes grouped into their packages. If you were looking at the Java source code for the Swing components we used in HelloJava, for example, you would find a folder named *javax*, and under that, one named *swing*, and under that you would find files like *JFrame.java* and *JLabel.java*.

Each class belongs to exactly one package. Package names follow the same general rules as other Java identifiers and are all lowercase by convention. If you don't specify a package, Java assigns your class to the "default" package. Using the default package is fine for one-off demos, but you should otherwise use `package` for your classes. The default package has several limitations—for example, a class in the default package cannot be used with *jshell*—and is not meant to be used beyond testing.

Importing Classes

One of Java's biggest strengths lies in the vast collection of supporting libraries available under both commercial and open source licensing. Need to export a PDF? There's a library for that. Need to import a spreadsheet? There's a library for that. Need to turn on that smart lightbulb in the basement from a web server in the cloud? There's a library for that, too. If computers are doing some task or other, you will almost always find a Java library to help you write code to perform that task as well.

To use any of these wonderful libraries, you *import* them with the cleverly named `import` keyword. We used `import` with our `HelloJava` example so we could add the frame and label components from the Swing graphical library. You can import individual classes or entire packages. Let's look at some examples.

Importing Individual classes

In programming, you'll often hear the maxim that "less is more." Less code is more maintainable. Less overhead means more throughput, and so on. (Although in pursuing this way of coding, we do want to remind you to follow another famous quote from no less a thinker than Einstein: "Everything should be made as simple as possible, but no simpler.") If you need only one or two classes from an external package, you can import exactly those classes. This makes your code a little more readable—others know exactly what classes you'll be using.

Let's reexamine that earlier snippet of `HelloJava`. We used a blanket import (more on that in the next section), but we could tighten things up a bit by importing just the classes we need, like so:

```
package ch02.examples;

import javax.swing.JFrame;
import javax.swing.JLabel;

public class HelloJava {
  public static void main(String[] args) {
    JFrame frame = new JFrame("Hello, Java!");
    JLabel label = new JLabel("Hello, Java!", JLabel.CENTER);
    // ...
  }
}
```

This type of import setup is certainly more verbose, but again, it means anyone reading or compiling your code knows its exact dependencies. Many IDEs even have an "Optimize Imports" function that will automatically find those dependencies and list them individually. Once you get in the habit of listing and seeing these explicit imports, it is surprising how useful they become when orienting yourself in a new (or perhaps long-forgotten) class.

Importing entire packages

Of course, not every package lends itself to individual imports. That same Swing package, `javax.swing`, is a great example. If you are writing a graphical desktop application, you'll almost certainly use Swing—and lots and lots of its components. You can import every class in the package using the syntax we glossed over earlier:

```java
import javax.swing.*;

public class HelloJava {
  public static void main(String[] args) {
    JFrame frame = new JFrame("Hello, Java!");
    JLabel label = new JLabel("Hello, Java!", JLabel.CENTER);
    // ...
  }
}
```

The * is a sort of wildcard for class imports. This version of the `import` statement tells the compiler to have every class in the package ready to use. You'll see this type of import quite often for many of the common Java packages, such as AWT, Swing, utilities, and I/O. Again, it works for any package, but where it makes sense to be more specific, you'll gain some compile-time performance boosts and improve the readability of your code.

 While it might seem natural for a wildcard `import` to include both the classes of the named package as well as the classes from any subpackages, Java does not allow recursive imports. If you need some classes from `java.awt` and some more classes from `java.awt.event`, you must supply separate `import` lines for each package.

Skipping imports

You have another option for using external classes from other packages—you can use their fully qualified names right in your code. For example, our `HelloJava` class used the `JFrame` and `JLabel` classes from the `javax.swing` package. We could import only the `JLabel` class if we wanted:

```
import javax.swing.JLabel;

public class HelloJava {
  public static void main(String[] args) {
    javax.swing.JFrame frame = new javax.swing.JFrame("Hello, Java!");
    JLabel label = new JLabel("Hello, Java!", JLabel.CENTER);
    // ...
  }
}
```

This might seem overly verbose for one line where we create our frame, but in larger classes with already lengthy lists of imports, one-off usages can actually make your code more readable. Such a fully qualified entry often points to the sole use of this class within a file. If you were using that class many times, you would import it or its package. This type of full-name usage is never a requirement, but you will see it in the wild from time to time.

Custom Packages

As you continue learning Java and write more code and solve larger problems, you will undoubtedly start to collect a larger and larger number of classes. You can use packages to help organize that collection. You use the package keyword to declare a custom package. You then place the file with your class inside a folder structure corresponding to the package name. As a quick reminder, packages use all lowercase names (by convention) separated by periods, such as in our graphical interface package, javax.swing.

Another convention applied widely to package names is something called "reverse domain name" naming. Apart from the packages associated directly with Java, third-party libraries and other contributed code are usually organized using the domain name of the company or individual's email address. For example, the Mozilla Foundation has contributed a variety of Java libraries to the open source community. Most of those libraries and utilities will be in packages starting with Mozilla's domain, *mozilla.org*, in reverse order: org.mozilla. This reverse naming has the handy (and intended) side effect of keeping the folder structure at the top fairly small. It is not uncommon for good-sized projects to use libraries from only the com and org top-level domains.

If you are building your own packages separate from any company or contract work, you can use your email address and reverse it, similar to company domain names. Another popular option for code distributed online is to use the domain of your hosting provider. GitHub, for example, hosts many, *many* Java projects for hobbyists and enthusiasts. You might create a package named com.github.myawesomeproject (where myawesomeproject would obviously be replaced by your actual project name). Be aware that repositories at sites like GitHub often allow names that are not valid in package names. You might have a repo named my-awesome-project, but dashes are not allowed in any portion of a package name. Often such illegal characters are simply omitted to create a valid name.

You may have already noticed we placed the various examples from this book in packages. While organizing classes *within* packages is a woolly topic with no great best practices available, we've taken an approach designed to make the examples easy to locate as you're reading the book. For any complete examples in a chapter, you'll see a package like ch05.examples. For the ongoing game example, we use a game subpackage. We put the end-of-chapter exercises in ch05.exercises.

 When you compile a packaged class, you need to tell the compiler where the actual file resides within the filesystem, so you use its path, with the package elements separated by your filesystem separator (typically / or \). When you run a packaged class, on the other hand, you specify its fully qualified, dot-separated name.

If you are using an IDE, it will happily manage these package issues for you. Simply create and organize your classes and continue to identify the main class that kicks off your program.

Member Visibility and Access

We've talked a bit about the access modifiers you can use when declaring variables and methods. Making something public means anyone, anywhere, can see your variable or call your method. Making something protected means any subclass can access the variable, call the method, or override the method to provide some alternate functionality more appropriate to your subclass. The private modifier means the variable or method is available only within the class itself.

Packages affect protected members. In addition to being accessible by any subclass, such members are visible and can be overridden by other classes in the same package. Packages also come into play if you leave off the modifier altogether. Consider some example text components in the custom package mytools.text, as shown in Figure 5-4.

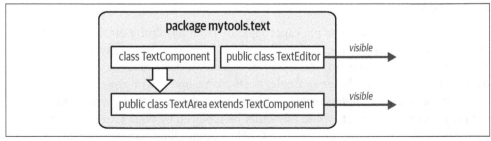

Figure 5-4. Packages and class visibility

The class `TextComponent` has no modifier. It has *default* visibility or "package private" visibility. This means that other classes *in the same package* can access the class, but any classes outside the package cannot. This can be very useful for implementation-specific classes or internal helpers. You can use the package private elements freely in building your code, but other programmers can use only your `public` and `protected` elements. Figure 5-5 shows more details, with both subclasses and external classes using variables and methods for a sample class.

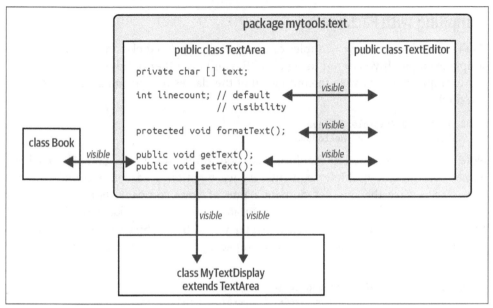

Figure 5-5. Packages and member visibility

Notice that extending the `TextArea` class gives you access to the public `getText()` and `setText()` methods as well as the `protected` method `formatText()`. But `MyText Display` (more on subclasses and `extends` shortly in "Subclassing and Inheritance" on page 167) does not have access to the package-private variable `linecount`. Within the `mytools.text` package where we create the `TextEditor` class, however, we can get to `linecount` as well as those methods that are `public` or `protected`. Our internal storage for the content, `text`, remains private and unavailable to anyone other than the `TextArea` class itself.

Table 5-2 summarizes the levels of visibility available in Java; it runs generally from most to least restrictive. Methods and variables are always visible within a declaring class itself, so the table doesn't address that scope.

Table 5-2. Visibility modifiers

Modifier	Visibility outside the class
private	None
No modifier (default)	Classes in the package
protected	Classes in package and subclasses inside or outside the package
public	All classes

Compiling with Packages

You've already seen a few examples of using a fully qualified class name to compile a simple example. If you're not using an IDE, you have other options available to you. For example, you may wish to compile all of the classes in a given package. If so, you can do this:

```
% javac ch02/examples/*.java
% java ch02.examples.HelloJava
```

Note that for commercial applications, you often see more complex package names that include multiple segments. As we mentioned earlier, a common practice is to reverse the internet domain name of your company. For example, this book from O'Reilly might more appropriately use a full package prefix such as com.oreilly.learningjava6e. Each chapter would be a subpackage under that prefix. Compiling and running classes in such packages is fairly straightforward, if a bit wordy:

```
% javac com/oreilly/learningjava6e/ch02/examples/*.java
% java com.oreilly.learningjava6e.ch02.examples.HelloJava
```

The *javac* command also understands basic class dependency. If your main class uses a few other classes in the same source hierarchy—even if they are not all in the same package—compiling that main class will "pick up" the other, dependent classes and compile them as well.

Beyond simple programs with a few classes in a single package, though, you really are more likely to rely on your IDE or a build management tool such as Gradle or Maven. Those tools are outside the scope of this book, but there are many references for them online. Maven in particular is popular for managing large projects with many dependencies. See *Maven: The Definitive Guide* (*https://oreil.ly/ya4DY*) (O'Reilly) by Maven creator Jason Van Zyl and his team at Sonatype for a true exploration of the features and capabilities of this powerful tool.[6]

---

6 Maven sufficiently changed the landscape for dependency management in Java and even other JVM-based languages so you can now find tools such as Gradle (*https://gradle.org*), which were based on Maven's success.

Advanced Class Design

You may recall from "HelloJava2: The Sequel" on page 53 that we had two classes in the same file. That simplified the writing and compiling process but didn't grant either class any special access to the other. As you start thinking about more complex problems, you will encounter cases where more advanced class design that does grant special access is not just handy but critical to writing maintainable code.

Subclassing and Inheritance

Classes in Java exist in a hierarchy. You can declare a class in Java as a *subclass* of another class using the `extends` keyword. A subclass *inherits* variables and methods from its *superclass* and can use them as if they were declared within the subclass itself:

```java
class Animal {
  float weight;

  void eat() {
    // do eating stuff
  }
  // other animal stuff
}

class Mammal extends Animal {
  // inherits weight
  int heartRate;

  // inherits eat()
  void breathe() {
    // respire
  }
}
```

In this example, an object of type `Mammal` has both the instance variable `weight` and the method `eat()`. They are inherited from `Animal`.

A class can *extend* only one other class. To use the proper terminology, Java allows *single inheritance* of a class implementation. Later in this chapter, we'll talk about interfaces, which take the place of *multiple inheritance* found in other languages.

A subclass can be further subclassed. Normally, subclassing specializes or refines a class by adding variables and methods (you cannot remove or hide variables or methods by subclassing). For example:

```
class Cat extends Mammal {
  // inherits weight and heartRate
  boolean longHair;

  // inherits eat() and breathe()
  void purr() {
    // make nice sounds
  }
}
```

The Cat class is a type of Mammal that is ultimately a type of Animal. Cat objects inherit all the characteristics of Mammal objects and, in turn, Animal objects. Cat also provides additional behavior in the form of the purr() method and the longHair variable. We can denote the class relationship in a diagram, as shown in Figure 5-6.

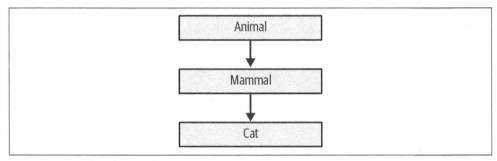

Figure 5-6. A class hierarchy

A subclass inherits all members of its superclass not designated as private. As we'll discuss shortly, other levels of visibility affect which inherited members of the class can be seen from outside of the class and its subclasses, but at a minimum, a subclass always has the same set of visible members as its parent. For this reason, the type of a subclass can be considered a *subtype* of its parent, and instances of the subtype can be used anywhere instances of the supertype are allowed. Consider the following example:

```
Cat simon = new Cat();
Animal creature = simon;
```

The Cat instance simon in this example can be assigned to the Animal type variable creature because Cat is a subtype of Animal. Similarly, any method accepting an Animal object would accept an instance of a Cat or any Mammal type as well. This is an important aspect of polymorphism in an object-oriented language such as Java. We'll see how it can be used to refine a class's behavior, as well as add new capabilities to it.

Shadowed variables

We have seen that a local variable of the same name as an instance variable *shadows* (hides) the instance variable. Similarly, an instance variable in a subclass can shadow an instance variable of the same name in its parent class, as shown in Figure 5-7.

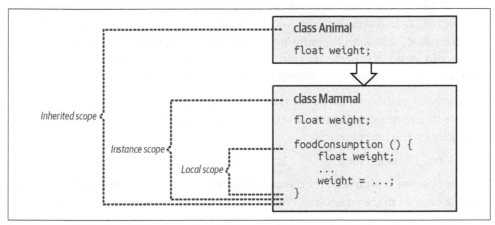

Figure 5-7. The scope of shadowed variables

The variable `weight` is declared in three places: as a local variable in the method `foodConsumption()` of the class `Mammal`, as an instance variable of the class `Mammal` itself, and as an instance variable of the class `Animal`. The actual variable you would reference in the code would depend on the scope in which you are working and how you qualify the reference to it.

In the previous example, all variables were of the same type. A slightly more plausible use of shadowed variables would involve changing their types. We could, for example, shadow an `int` variable with a `double` variable in a subclass that needs decimal values instead of integer values. We can do this without changing the existing code because, as its name suggests, when we shadow variables, we don't replace them but rather mask them instead. Both variables still exist; methods of the superclass see the original variable, and methods of the subclass see the new version. What variables the various methods see is determined at compile time.

Here's a simple example:

```
class IntegerCalculator {
  int sum;
  // other integer stuff ...
}

class DecimalCalculator extends IntegerCalculator {
  double sum;
  // other floating point stuff ...
}
```

In this example, we shadow the instance variable `sum` to change its type from `int` to `double`.[7] Methods defined in the class `IntegerCalculator` see the integer variable `sum`, while methods defined in `DecimalCalculator` see the floating-point variable `sum`. However, both variables actually exist for a given instance of `DecimalCalculator`, and they can have independent values. In fact, any methods that `DecimalCalculator` inherits from `IntegerCalculator` actually see the integer variable `sum`. If that sounds confusing—it certainly can be. Shadowing is something you should avoid when possible. But it isn't always possible to avoid, so we want to make sure you have seen some examples, albeit contrived ones.

Because both variables exist in `DecimalCalculator`, we need a way to reference the variable inherited from `IntegerCalculator`. We do that using the `super` keyword as a qualifier on the reference:

```
int s = super.sum;
```

Inside of `DecimalCalculator`, the `super` keyword used in this manner selects the `sum` variable defined in the superclass. We'll explain the use of `super` more fully in a bit.

Another important point about shadowed variables has to do with how they work when we refer to an object by way of a less derived type (a parent type). For example, we can refer to a `DecimalCalculator` object as an `IntegerCalculator` by using it via a variable of type `IntegerCalculator`. If we do so and then access the variable `sum`, we get the integer variable, not the decimal one:

```
DecimalCalculator dc = new DecimalCalculator();
IntegerCalculator ic = dc;

int s = ic.sum;        // accesses IntegerCalculator sum
```

The same would be true if we accessed the object using an explicit cast to the `IntegerCalculator` type or when passing an instance into a method that accepts that parent type.

To reiterate, the usefulness of shadowed variables is limited. It's much better to abstract the use of variables like this in other ways than to use tricky scoping rules. However, it's important to understand the concepts here before we talk about doing the same thing with methods. We'll see a different and more dynamic type of behavior when methods shadow other methods, or to use the correct terminology, *override* other methods. Overriding methods in a subclass is quite common and can be very powerful.

---

7 Note that a better way to design our calculators would be to have an abstract `Calculator` class with two separate subclasses: `IntegerCalculator` and `DecimalCalculator`.

Overriding methods

We have seen that we can declare overloaded methods (methods with the same name but a different number or type of arguments) within a class. Overloaded method selection works in the way we described on all methods available to a class, including inherited ones. This means that a subclass can define additional overloaded methods that add to the overloaded methods provided by a superclass.

A subclass can do more than that; it can define a method that has exactly the *same* method signature (name and argument types) as a method in its superclass. In that case, the method in the subclass *overrides* the method in the superclass and effectively replaces its implementation, as shown in Figure 5-8. Overriding methods to change the behavior of objects is called *subtype polymorphism*. It's the usage most people think of when they talk about the power of object-oriented languages.

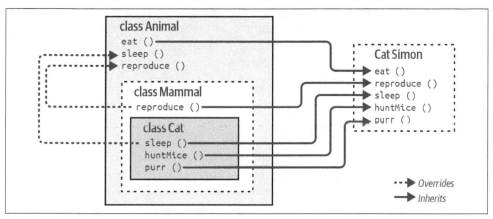

Figure 5-8. Method overriding

In Figure 5-8, `Mammal` overrides the `reproduce()` method of `Animal`, perhaps to specialize the method for the behavior of mammals giving birth to live young.[8] The `Cat` object's sleeping behavior is also overridden to be different from that of a general `Animal`, perhaps to accommodate catnaps. The `Cat` class also adds the more unique behaviors of purring and hunting mice.

From what you've seen so far, overridden methods probably look like they shadow methods in superclasses, just as variables do. But overridden methods are actually more powerful than that. When there are multiple implementations of a method in the inheritance hierarchy of an object, the one in the "most derived" class (the

---

8 The platypus is a highly unusual egg-laying mammal. We could override the `reproduce()` behavior again for `Platypus` in its own subclass of `Mammal`.

furthest down the hierarchy) always overrides the others, even if we refer to the object through a reference of one of the superclass types.[9]

For example, if we have a `Cat` instance assigned to a variable of the more general type `Animal`, and we call its `sleep()` method, we still get the `sleep()` method implemented in the `Cat` class, not the one in `Animal`:

```
Cat simon = new Cat();
Animal creature = simon;
// ...
creature.sleep();        // accesses Cat sleep();
```

In other words, for purposes of behavior (invoking methods), a `Cat` acts like a `Cat`, regardless of whether you refer to it as such. You might remember that accessing a shadowed variable through our `Animal` variable `creature` would find that variable in the `Animal` class, not the `Cat` class. However, because methods are located *dynamically*, searching subclasses first, the runtime will invoke the appropriate method in the `Cat` class, even though we are treating it more generally as an `Animal` object. This means that the *behavior* of objects is dynamic. We can deal with specialized objects as if they were more general types and still take advantage of their specialized implementations of behavior.

Abstract Classes and Methods

Sometimes you don't have a good default behavior for a method. Think about how animals communicate. Dogs bark. Cats meow. Cows moo. There really is no standard sound. In Java, you can create an *abstract* method that defines exactly what a method should look like, without specifying any particular behavior. You use the `abstract` modifier when declaring the method. And rather than providing a body, you simply end the definition with a semicolon. Consider a `makeSound()` method for our animals:

```
public class Animal {
  float weight;
  // other animal traits ...

  public abstract void makeSound(int duration);
  // other animal behaviors ...
}
```

---

9 An overridden method in Java acts like a `virtual` method in C++.

Notice that our method to make a sound has a complete signature (recall "Running Java Applications" on page 67). It is void (it has no return value), and it takes one argument of type int. But it has no body. This type of method is explicitly designed to be overridden. You cannot call an abstract method; you'll get a compile-time error. You must create a new subclass that provides the logic for the abstract method before you can use it:

```
public class Cat extends Animal {
  // ...
  public void makeSound(int duration) {
    for (int count = 0; count < duration; count++) {
      // assume our sound takes one second to make and we can
      // repeat the sound to match the requested duration
      System.out.println("meow!");
    }
  }
  // ...
}
```

With an instance of Cat, we can now call the makeSound() method and the compiler knows what to do. But because Animal now contains an abstract method, we can't create an instance of that class. To use Animal we have to create a subclass and fill out makeSound() like we did with our Cat.

In fact, if we do include an abstract method in our class, we also have to declare the class itself as abstract. Our snippet of Animal above would not compile. We use the same abstract keyword for the class:

```
public abstract class Animal {
  // Notice the class definition needs the "abstract" modifier

  public abstract void makeSound(int duration);
  // ...
}
```

This declaration tells the compiler (and other developers) that you designed this class to be part of a larger program. You expect (actually, require) subclasses to extend your abstract class and fill in any missing details. Those subclasses, in turn, can be instantiated and can do real work.

Abstract classes can still contain typical, complete-with-body methods, too. In the case of Animal, for example, we could add some helper methods for the animal's weight:

```java
public abstract class Animal {
  private double weight;
  // ...
  public abstract void makeSound(int duration);
  // ...

  public void setWeight(double w) {
    this.weight = w;
  }

  public double getWeight() {
    return weight;
  }
}
```

This is common and a good design practice. Your `Animal` class contains as much of the basic, shared information and behavior as possible. But for things that are not shared, you create a subclass with the desired traits and actions.

Interfaces

Java expands on the concept of abstract methods with interfaces. It's often desirable to specify a group of abstract methods defining some behavior for an object without tying it to any implementation at all. In Java, this is called an *interface*. An interface defines a set of methods that a class must implement. A class in Java can declare that it *implements* an interface if it implements the required methods. Unlike extending an abstract class, a class implementing an interface doesn't have to inherit from any particular part of the inheritance hierarchy or use a particular implementation.

Interfaces are kind of like Scouting merit badges. A scout who has learned to build a birdhouse can walk around wearing a cloth patch or sash with a picture of one. This says to the world, "I know how to build a birdhouse." Similarly, an interface is a list of methods that define some set of behavior for an object. Any class that implements each method listed in the interface can declare at compile time that it implements the interface and wear, as its merit badge, an extra type—the interface's type.

Interface types act like class types. You can declare variables to be of an interface type, you can declare arguments of methods to accept interface types, and you can specify that the return type of a method is an interface type. In each case, you're saying that any object that implements the interface (i.e., wears the right merit badge) can fill that role. In this sense, interfaces are orthogonal to the class hierarchy. They cut across the boundaries of what kind of object an item *is* and deal with it only in terms of what it can *do*. You can implement as many interfaces as you need for any given class. Interfaces in Java replace much of the need for multiple inheritance in other languages (and all the messy complications that come from true multiple inheritance).

An interface looks, essentially, like a purely abstract class (a class with *only* abstract methods). You define an interface with the interface keyword and list its methods with no bodies, just prototypes (signatures):

```
interface Driveable {
  boolean startEngine();
  void stopEngine();
  float accelerate(float acc);
  boolean turn(Direction dir);
}
```

The previous example defines an interface called Driveable with four methods. It's acceptable, but not necessary, to declare the methods in an interface with the abstract modifier; we haven't done that here. More importantly, the methods of an interface are always considered public, and you can optionally declare them as so. Why public? Well, the user of the interface wouldn't necessarily be able to see them otherwise, and interfaces are generally intended to describe the behavior of an object, not its implementation.

Interfaces define capabilities, so it's common to name interfaces after their capabilities. Driveable, Runnable, and Updateable are good interface names. Any class that implements all the methods can then declare that it implements the interface by using a special implements clause in its class definition. For example:

```
class Automobile implements Driveable {
  // Automobile traits could go here ...

  // build all the Driveable methods
  public boolean startEngine() {
    if (notTooCold)
      engineRunning = true;
    // ...
  }

  public void stopEngine() {
    engineRunning = false;
  }

  public float accelerate(float acc) {
    // ...
  }

  public boolean turn(Direction dir) {
    // ...
  }

  // Do other car things ...
}
```

Here, the class `Automobile` implements the methods of the `Driveable` interface and declares itself a type of `Driveable` using the `implements` keyword.

As shown in Figure 5-9, another class, such as `Lawnmower`, can also implement the `Driveable` interface. The figure illustrates the `Driveable` interface being implemented by two different classes. While it's possible that both `Automobile` and `Lawnmower` could derive from some primitive kind of vehicle, they don't have to in this scenario.

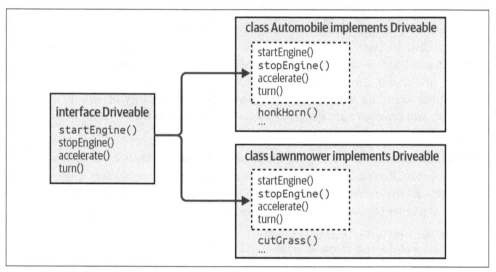

Figure 5-9. Implementing the `Driveable` interface

After declaring the interface, we have a new type, `Driveable`. We can declare variables of type `Driveable` and assign them any instance of a `Driveable` object:

```
Automobile auto = new Automobile();
Lawnmower mower = new Lawnmower();
Driveable vehicle;

vehicle = auto;
vehicle.startEngine();
vehicle.stopEngine();

vehicle = mower;
vehicle.startEngine();
vehicle.stopEngine();
```

Both `Automobile` and `Lawnmower` implement `Driveable`, so they can be considered interchangeable objects of that type.

As we mentioned earlier, interfaces play a critical role in Java's power and popularity. We will be using them throughout the remaining chapters. If they don't quite make sense, keep reading and working on the code exercises. You'll get much more practice with them. Practice doesn't always make perfect, but it definitely does make something less weird and opaque.

Inner Classes

All of the classes we've seen so far in this book have been *top-level*, "freestanding" classes declared at the file and package level. But classes in Java can actually be declared at any level of scope, within any set of curly braces—in other words, almost anywhere that you could put any other Java statement. These *inner classes* belong to another class or method as a variable would and may have their visibility limited to its scope in the same way.

Inner classes are a useful and aesthetically pleasing facility for structuring code. Their cousins, *anonymous inner classes*, are an even more powerful shorthand that make it seem as if you can create new kinds of objects dynamically within Java's statically typed environment. In Java, anonymous inner classes play part of the role of *closures* in other languages, giving the effect of handling state and behavior independently of classes. (You can also use *lambdas* in many places where inner or anonymous inner classes work. Lambdas encapsulate bits of logic and are common in many functional languages and LISPs. We'll look at them in much more detail in Chapter 11.)

However, as we delve into their inner workings, we'll see that inner classes are not quite as aesthetically pleasing or dynamic as they seem. Inner classes are pure syntactic sugar; the Java runtime does not support them. Instead, the compiler maps the code of an inner class to a cleverly named regular class. As a programmer, you may never need to know this; you can simply rely on inner classes like any other language construct. However, you should know a little about how they work to better understand the compiled code and to watch for a few potential side effects.

Inner classes are essentially nested classes. For example:

```
class Animal {
  double weight;

  class Brain {
    double volume;
    // more brain stuff ...
  }
}
```

Here, the class `Brain` is an inner class: it is a class declared inside the scope of the `Animal` class. Although the details of what that means require a bit of explanation, we'll start by saying that Java tries to make the meaning, as much as possible, the same as for the other members (methods and variables) living at that level of scope. For example, let's add a method to the `Animal` class:

```
class Animal {
  double weight;

  class Brain {
    double volume;
    // more brain stuff ...
  }

  void performBehavior() { ... }
}
```

The inner class `Brain`, the method `performBehavior()`, and the `weight` variable are within the scope of `Animal`. Therefore, anywhere within `Animal`, we can refer to `Brain`, `performBehavior()`, and `weight` directly, by name. Within `Animal`, we can call the constructor for `Brain` (`new Brain()`) to get a `Brain` object or invoke `perform Behavior()` to carry out that method's function. But none of these elements are generally accessible outside of the class `Animal` without some additional qualification.

Within the body of the inner `Brain` class and the body of the `performBehavior()` method, we have direct access to the `weight` variable as well as all the other methods and variables of the `Animal` class. So, just as the `performBehavior()` method could work with the `Brain` class and create instances of `Brain`, methods within the `Brain` class can invoke the `performBehavior()` method of `Animal` or work with the `weight` variable. The `Brain` class "sees" all of the methods and variables of the `Animal` class directly in its scope.

A brain's access to the variables and methods of `Animal` has important consequences. From within `Brain`, we can invoke the method `performBehavior()`; that is, from within an instance of `Brain`, we can invoke the `performBehavior()` method of an instance of `Animal`. Well, which instance of `Animal`? If we have several `Animal` objects around (say, a few `Cats` and `Dogs`), we need to know whose `performBehavior()` method we are calling. What does it mean for a class definition to be "inside" another class definition? The answer is that a `Brain` object always lives within a single instance of `Animal`: the one that it was told about when it was created. We'll call the object that contains any instance of `Brain` its *enclosing instance*.

A `Brain` object cannot live outside of an enclosing instance of an `Animal` object. Anywhere you see an instance of `Brain`, it will be tethered to an instance of `Animal`. Although it is possible to construct a `Brain` object from elsewhere (perhaps another class), `Brain` always requires an enclosing instance of `Animal` to "hold" it. If you ever do find a `Brain` of the `Animal` class, it will still be explicitly associated with `Animal` as the `Animal.Brain` class. Just as with the `performBehavior()` method, modifiers can be applied to restrict its visibility. All of the usual visibility modifiers apply, and inner classes can also be declared `static`, as we'll discuss in later chapters.

Anonymous Inner Classes

Now we get to the best part. As a general rule, the more deeply encapsulated and limited in scope our classes are, the more freedom we have in naming them. We saw this in our earlier iterator example. This is not just a purely aesthetic issue. Naming is an important part of writing readable, maintainable code. Generally, use the most concise, meaningful names possible. As a corollary, avoid doling out names for temporary objects that are going to be used only once.

Anonymous inner classes are an extension of the syntax of the new operation. When you create an anonymous inner class, you combine a class declaration with the allocation of an instance of that class, effectively creating a "one-time only" class and an instance in one operation. After the new keyword, you specify either the name of a class or an interface, followed by a class body. The class body becomes an inner class. It either extends the specified class or, in the case of an interface, is expected to implement the interface. A single instance of the class is created and returned as the value.

For example, we could revisit the graphical application from "HelloJava2: The Sequel" on page 53. As you might recall, that app creates a HelloComponent2 that extends JComponent and implements the MouseMotionListener interface. (Does that example make a little more sense now?) We never expect HelloComponent2 to respond to mouse motion events coming from other components. It might make more sense to create an anonymous inner class specifically to move our "Hello" label around.

Indeed, since HelloComponent2 is really meant only for use by our demo, we could *refactor* (a common developer process to optimize or improve code that is already working) that separate class into an inner class. Now that we know a little more about constructors and inheritance, we could also make our class an extension of JFrame rather than building a frame inside our main() method. And to put a little icing on this newly refactored cake, we can move our mouse listener code into an anonymous inner class devoted to our custom component.

Here's our HelloJava3 with these nifty refactorings in place:

```
package ch05.examples;

import java.awt.*;
import java.awt.event.*;
import javax.swing.*;

public class HelloJava3 extends JFrame {
  public static void main(String[] args) {
    HelloJava3 demo = new HelloJava3();
    demo.setVisible(true);
  }
```

```
public HelloJava3() {
  super("HelloJava3");
  add(new HelloComponent3("Hello, Inner Java!"));
  setDefaultCloseOperation(JFrame.EXIT_ON_CLOSE);
  setSize(300, 300);
}

class HelloComponent3 extends JComponent {
  String theMessage;
  int messageX = 125, messageY = 95; // message coordinates

  public HelloComponent3(String message) {
    theMessage = message;
    addMouseMotionListener(new MouseMotionListener() {
      public void mouseDragged(MouseEvent e) {
        messageX = e.getX();
        messageY = e.getY();
        repaint();
      }

      public void mouseMoved(MouseEvent e) { }
    });
  }

  public void paintComponent(Graphics g) {
    g.drawString(theMessage, messageX, messageY);
  }
}
}
```

Try compiling and running this example. It should behave exactly like the original
HelloJava2 application. The real difference is how we have organized the classes
and who can access them (and the variables and methods inside them). HelloJava3
probably looks a little cumbersome compared to HelloJava2, and it is verbose for
such a small demo.

The power of inner classes and interfaces will start to shine as you develop more
complex applications. Practicing with the structure and rules of these features will
help you write more maintainable code in the long run.

Organizing Content and Planning for Failure

Classes are the single most important idea in Java. They form the core of every
executable program, portable library, or helper. We looked at the contents of classes
and how classes relate to each other in a larger project. We know more about how to
create and destroy objects based on the classes we write. And we've seen how inner
classes (and anonymous inner classes) can help us write more maintainable code.
We'll be seeing more of these inner classes as we get into deeper topics such as threads
in Chapter 9 and Swing in Chapter 12.

As you build your classes, here are a few guidelines to keep in mind:

Hide as much of your implementation as possible

Never expose more of the internals of an object than you need to. This is key to building maintainable, reusable code. Avoid using public variables in your objects, with the notable exception of constants. Instead, define *accessor* methods to set and return values. This is useful even if they are simple types—think of methods like `getWeight()` and `setWeight()`. You'll be able to modify and extend your objects' behavior down the road without breaking other classes that rely on them.

Use composition instead of inheritance

Specialize objects only when you must. When you use an object in its existing form, as a piece of a new object, you are *composing* objects. When you change or refine the behavior of an object (by subclassing), you are using *inheritance*. Try to reuse objects by composition rather than inheritance whenever possible. When you compose objects, you are taking full advantage of existing tools. Inheritance involves breaking down the encapsulation of an object, so do it only when there's a real advantage. Ask yourself if you really need to inherit the whole class (do you want it to be a "kind" of that object?) or if you can just include an instance of that class in your own class and delegate some work to that included instance.

Minimize relationships between objects and try to organize related objects in packages

Java packages (recall Figure 5-1) can also hide classes that are not of general interest. Expose only classes that you intend other people to use. The more loosely coupled your objects, the easier it will be to reuse them later.

We can apply these principles even on small projects. The *ch05/examples* folder contains simple versions of the classes and interfaces we'll use to create our apple tossing game. Take a moment to see how the `Apple`, `Tree`, and `Physicist` classes implement the `GamePiece` interface—like the `draw()` method every class includes. Notice how `Field` extends `JComponent` and how the main game class, `AppleToss`, extends `JFrame`. You can see these simple pieces playing together in Figure 5-10.

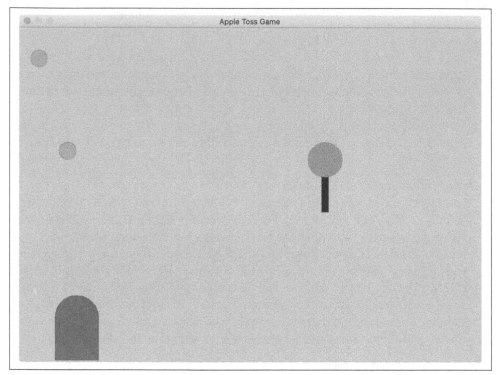

Figure 5-10. Our very first game classes in action

The final code exercise for this chapter will help you get started. Look over the comments in the classes. Try tweaking a few things. Add another tree. More play is always good. We'll be building on these classes throughout the remaining chapters, so getting comfortable with how they fit together will make it easier.

Regardless of how you organize the members in your classes, the classes in your packages, or the packages in your project, you'll have to contend with errors. Some will be simple syntax errors you'll fix in your editor. Other errors are more interesting and may crop up only while your program is actually running. The next chapter will cover Java's notion of these problems and help you handle them.

Review Questions

1. What is the primary organizing unit in Java?

2. What operator do you use to create an object (or instance) from a class?

3. Java does not support classic multiple inheritance. What mechanisms does Java provide as alternatives?

4. How can you organize multiple, related classes?

5. How do you include classes from other packages for use in your own code?

6. What do you call a class defined inside the scope of another class? What are some features that make such a class useful in some circumstances?

7. What do you call a method designed to be overridden that has a name, return type, and argument list, but no body?

8. What is an overloaded method?

9. If you want to make sure no other class can use a variable you have defined, what access modifier should you use?

Code Exercises

1. For your first coding practice, create a small zoo of communicative creatures. The *ch05/exercises/Zoo.java* file contains a complete outline for creating a few animals and having them "speak" using inner classes. Start by filling in the `speak()` method of the included `Gibbon` class using the completed `Lion` inner class as an example. When you compile and run your `Zoo`, you should see output like this (with your own animal noises, of course):

```
% cd ch05/exercises
% javac Zoo.java
% java Zoo
Let&rsquo;s listen to some animals!
The lion goes "roar"
The gibbon goes "hoot"
```

2. Now add your own animal to the zoo. Create a new inner class similar to `Lion`. Fill in the appropriate sound for your animal, and add them to the output section of the `listen()` method. Your new output will look something like:

```
% java Zoo
Let&rsquo;s listen to some animals!
The lion goes "roar"
The gibbon goes "hoot"
The seal goes "bark"
```

3. Let's clean up that `listen()` method. We currently use separate `print()` and `println()` methods for each animal. If we add another animal (or several), that

will require copying and pasting and tweaking the output lines—tasks that can introduce errors. Add another abstract method to `Animal` called `getSpecies()`. In the subclasses, this method should return the name of the animal as a `String`, such as "lion" or "seal" from the examples above.

With that method in place, refactor the output section to put your animals in a small array, and then use a loop to produce the output. (Feel free to edit your existing `Zoo` class. Our solution is in a new class, `Zoo2`, so that you can look over the solution to this problem as well as the solution to the previous exercise.)

4. Run the apple tossing game. Compile and run the `ch05.exercises.game.Apple Toss` class in the *ch05/exercises/game* folder using the steps discussed earlier in "Custom Packages" on page 163.

Advanced Exercises

1. For a more advanced challenge, let's expand our apple tossing game by creating a new type of obstacle. Use the `Tree` class as a template and create a `Hedge` class. You can draw your hedge as a green rectangle. To draw a rectangle:

```
public void paintComponent(Graphics g) {
  // x and y set the upper left corner
  g.fillRect(x,y,width,height);
}
```

Add a hedge to your field. The final game should look something like Figure 5-11.

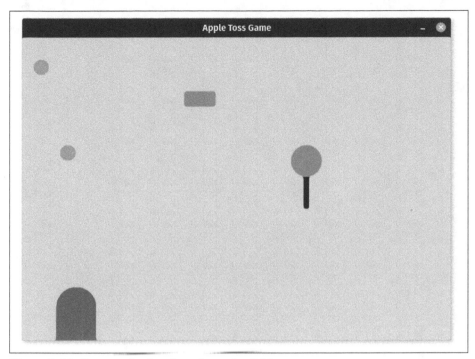

Figure 5-11. Our new hedge obstacle on the field

We will continue to expand this game throughout the book, but feel free to do some of your own expanding now. Play around with drawing other shapes or change the colors of the current elements. The online documentation (*https://oreil.ly/_dhQy*) for the Graphics class will be helpful.

CHAPTER 6

Error Handling

You will always encounter errors in the real world. How you handle them helps show the quality of your code.

Java has its roots in embedded systems—software that runs inside specialized devices, such as the handheld computers, cellular phones, and fancy toasters that we might consider part of the internet of things (IoT) these days. In those applications, it's especially important that software errors be handled robustly. Most users would agree that it's unacceptable for their phone to crash on a regular basis or for their toast (and perhaps their house) to burn because some software failed. Given that we can't eliminate the possibility of software errors, recognizing and dealing with application-level errors methodically is a good step in the right direction.

Some languages leave the responsibility for handling errors entirely with the programmer. The language itself provides no help in identifying error types and no tools for dealing with them easily. In the C language, for example, functions generally indicate a failure by returning an "unreasonable" value (like the idiomatic -1 or a null). As the programmer, you must know what constitutes a bad result and what it means. It's often awkward to work around the limitations of passing error values in the normal path of data flow.[1] An even worse problem is that certain types of errors can legitimately occur almost anywhere, and it's slow and costly to test for them explicitly at every point in the software.

In this chapter we'll consider how Java tackles the problem of problems. We'll go over the notion of exceptions to look at how and why they occur, as well as how and where

---

[1] The somewhat obscure setjmp() and longjmp() statements in C can save a point in the execution of code and later return to it unconditionally from a deeply buried location. In a limited sense, this is the functionality of exceptions in Java that we explore in this chapter.

to handle them. We'll also be looking at errors and assertions. *Errors* are more serious problems that often cannot be fixed at runtime but can still be logged for debugging. *Assertions* are a popular way of inoculating your code against exceptions or errors by verifying ahead of time that safe conditions exist.

Exceptions

Java offers an elegant solution to aid the programmer in addressing common coding and runtime problems through exceptions. (Java exception handling is similar to, but not quite the same as, exception handling in C++.) An *exception* indicates an unusual condition or an error condition. When a problem occurs, the runtime transfers control (or "throws") to a specially designated section of your code that can handle (or "catch") the condition. In this way, error handling is independent of the normal flow of the program. We don't need special return values for all of our methods; errors are handled by a separate mechanism. Java can pass control a long distance from a deeply nested routine and handle errors in a single location when that is desirable, or an error can be handled immediately at its source. A few standard Java methods still return a special value such as -1, but these are generally limited to situations where expecting and handling a special value is relatively straightforward.[2]

You must specify any known exceptions your methods can throw, and the compiler makes sure that callers of the method handle them. In this way, Java treats information about what errors a method can produce with the same level of importance as its argument and return types. You may still decide to punt and ignore some errors, but in Java you must do so explicitly. (We'll discuss runtime exceptions and errors, which don't require this explicit declaration, in a moment.)

Exceptions and Error Classes

Exceptions are represented by instances of the class `java.lang.Exception` and its subclasses. Subclasses of `Exception` can hold specialized information (and possibly behavior) for different kinds of exceptional conditions. However, more often they are simply "logical" subclasses that serve only to identify a new exception type. Figure 6-1 shows the subclasses of `Exception` in the `java.lang` package. It should give you a feel for how exceptions are organized. Most packages define their own exception types, which usually are subclasses of `Exception` itself or of its important subclass `RuntimeException`, which we'll get to in a moment.

---

2 For example, the `getHeight()` method of the AWT `Image` class returns -1 if the height isn't known yet. No error has occurred; the height will be available once the image is loaded. In this situation, throwing an exception would be excessive and could impact performance.

For example, let's look at another important exception class: `java.io.IOException`. The `IOException` class extends `Exception` and has many subclasses of its own for typical I/O problems, such as a `FileNotFoundException`. Notice how explicit (and useful) the class name is. Many network exceptions further extend `IOException` —they do involve input and output—but following conventions, exceptions like `MalformedURLException` belong to the `java.net` package alongside other networking classes.

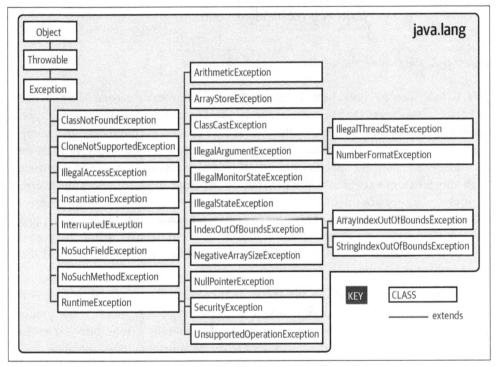

Figure 6-1. The `java.lang.Exception` subclasses

The runtime creates an `Exception` object at the point where the error condition arises. It can be designed to hold any information necessary to describe the exceptional condition. It also includes a full stack trace for debugging. A *stack trace* is the (occasionally unwieldy) list of all the methods called and the order in which they were called from your `main()` method up to the point where the exception was thrown. (We'll look at these useful lists in more detail in "Stack Traces" on page 195.) The `Exception` object is passed as an argument to the handling block of code, along with the flow of control. This is where the terms *throw* and *catch* come from: the `Exception` object is thrown from one point in the code and caught by another, where execution resumes, as shown in Figure 6-2.

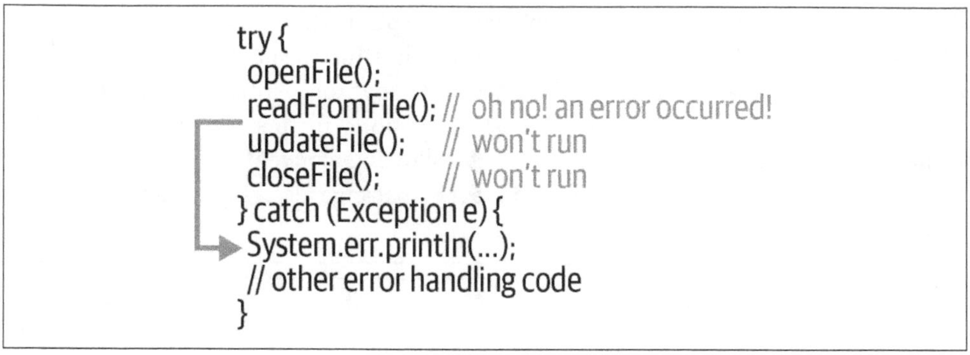

```
try {
  openFile();
  readFromFile(); // oh no! an error occurred!
  updateFile();   // won't run
  closeFile();    // won't run
} catch (Exception e) {
  System.err.println(...);
  // other error handling code
}
```

Figure 6-2. The flow of control when an exception occurs

Java also defines the `java.lang.Error` class for unrecoverable errors. The subclasses of `Error` in the `java.lang` package are shown in Figure 6-3. A notable `Error` type is `AssertionError`, which is used by the Java `assert` statement (more on this statement later in this chapter) to indicate a failure. A few other packages define their own subclasses of `Error`, but subclasses of `Error` are much less common (and less useful) than subclasses of `Exception`. You generally won't need to worry about these errors in your code; they are intended to indicate fatal problems or virtual machine errors, which usually cause the Java interpreter to display a message and exit. Java's designers actively discourage developers from trying to catch or recover from these errors because they are supposed to indicate a fatal program bug, possibly in the JVM itself, not a routine condition.

Both `Exception` and `Error` are subclasses of `Throwable`. The `Throwable` class is the base class for objects that can be "thrown" with the `throw` statement. While you can technically extend `Throwable` yourself, you should generally extend only `Exception`, `Error`, or one of their subclasses if you want to create your own throwable type.

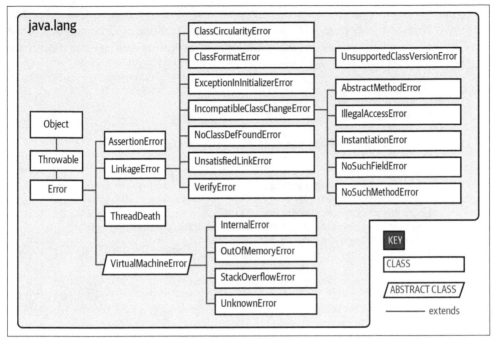

Figure 6-3. The java.lang.Error subclasses

Exception Handling

To catch and handle an _Italicized Textixexception, you wrap blocks of your code in
try/catch guarding statements:

```
try {
  readFromFile("foo");
  // do other file things ...
} catch (Exception e) {
  // Handle error
  System.out.println("Exception while reading file: " + e);
}
```

In this example, any exceptions that occur within the body of the try portion of the
statement are directed to the catch clause for possible handling. The catch clause
acts like a method; it specifies the type of exception it wants to handle. If it's invoked,
the clause receives the Exception object as an argument. Here, we receive the object
in the variable e and print it along with a message.

We can try this ourselves. Recall the simple program to calculate the greatest common denominator (GCD) using the Euclid algorithm back in Chapter 4. We could
augment that program to allow the user to pass in the two numbers a and b as
command-line arguments via that args[] array in the main() method. However, that

array is of type String. If we cheat a little bit and steal some code from "Parsing Primitive Numbers" on page 244, we can use a text parsing method to turn those strings into int values. However, that parsing method can throw an exception if we don't pass a valid number. Here's a look at our new Euclid2 class:

```java
public class Euclid2 {
  public static void main(String args[]) {
    int a = 2701;
    int b = 222;
    // Only try to parse arguments if we have exactly 2
    if (args.length == 2) {
      try {
        a = Integer.parseInt(args[0]);
        b = Integer.parseInt(args[1]);
      } catch (NumberFormatException nfe) {
        System.err.println("Arguments were not both numbers.");
        System.err.println("Using defaults.");
      }
    } else {
      System.err.print("Wrong number of arguments");
      System.err.println(" expected 2).");
      System.err.println("Using defaults.");
    }
    System.out.print("The GCD of " + a + " and " + b + " is ");
    while (b != 0) {
      if (a > b) {
        a = a - b;
      } else {
        b = b - a;
      }
    }
    System.out.println(a);
  }
}
```

Notice that we limit our try/catch to just the potentially problematic code. It's common to see several different try/catch blocks in a method. This small scope allows us to better tailor the code in the catch block to whatever problems we're anticipating. In this case, we know we might get some bad input from the user, so we can check for the (very) specific NumberFormatException and print a friendly message for the user.

If we run this program from a terminal window or use the command-line arguments option in our IDE like we did in Figure 2-10, we can now find the GCD of several number pairs without recompiling:

```
$ javac ch06/examples/Euclid2.java
$ java ch06.examples.Euclid2
The GCD of 18 and 6 is 6

$ java ch06.examples.Euclid2 547832 2798
The GCD of 547832 and 2798 is 2
```

But if we pass in arguments that are not numeric, we'll get that `NumberFormatExcep tion` and see our error message. Note, however, that our code recovers gracefully and still provides some output. This recovery is the essence of error handling:

```
$ java ch06.examples.Euclid2 apples oranges
Arguments were not both numbers.
Using defaults.
The GCD of 2701 and 222 is 37
```

A `try` statement can have multiple `catch` clauses that specify different types (subclasses) of `Exception`:

```
try {
  readFromFile("foo");
  // do any other file things
} catch (FileNotFoundException e) {
  // Handle file not found
} catch (IOException e) {
  // Handle read error
} catch (Exception e) {
  // Handle all other errors
}
```

The `catch` clauses are evaluated in order, and Java picks the first assignable match. At most, one `catch` clause is executed, which means that the exceptions should be listed from most specific to most generic. In the previous example, we anticipate that the hypothetical `readFromFile()` method can throw two different kinds of exceptions: one for a file not found and another for a more general read error. Maybe the file exists but we don't have permission to open it. `FileNotFoundException` is a subclass of `IOException`, so if we had swapped the first two `catch` clauses, the more general `IOException` clause would catch the missing file exception.

What if we completely reverse the order of the `catch` clauses? You can assign any subclass of `Exception` to the parent type `Exception`, so that clause catches *every* exception. If you use a `catch` with type `Exception`, always put it as the last possible clause. It acts like the `default` case in a `switch` statement and handles any remaining possibilities.

One advantage of the `try/catch` scheme is that any statement in the `try` block can assume that all previous statements in the block succeeded. A problem won't arise suddenly because you forgot to check the return value from a method. If an earlier statement fails, execution jumps immediately to a `catch` clause; later statements inside the `try` are never executed.

There is an alternative to using multiple `catch` clauses. You can handle multiple discrete exception types in a single `catch` clause, using the *or syntax* (written using the pipe character, "|"):

```
try {
  // read from network...
  // write to file..
} catch (ZipException | SSLException e) {
  logException(e);
}
```

Using this "|" syntax, we receive both types of exception in the same `catch` clause.

What is the actual type of the e variable that we are passing to our log method? What can we do with it? In this case, e's type will be neither `ZipException` nor `SSLException` but `IOException`, which is the nearest common ancestor (the closest parent class type to which they are both assignable) for the two exceptions. In many cases, the nearest common type among the two or more argument exception types may simply be `Exception`, the parent of all exception types.

The difference between catching these discrete exception types with a multiple-type `catch` clause and simply catching the common parent exception type is that we are limiting our `catch` to only these specifically enumerated exception types. We will not catch any of the other `IOException` types. Combining multiple-type `catch` clauses with ordering the clauses from specific to broad types gives you great flexibility in handling exceptions. You can consolidate error-handling logic where appropriate and avoid repeating code. There are more nuances to this feature, and we will return to it after we have discussed "throwing" and "re-throwing" exceptions.

Bubbling Up

What if we hadn't caught the exception? Where would it have gone? Well, if there is no enclosing `try/catch` statement, the exception pops up from the method in which it originated (halting further execution of that method) and is thrown from that method up to its caller. If that calling method has a `try` clause, control passes to the corresponding `catch` clause. Otherwise, the exception continues propagating up the call stack, from one method to its caller. The exception bubbles up until it's caught or until it pops out of the top of the program and terminates it with a runtime error message. Sometimes there's a bit more to it; the compiler might force you to deal with the exception along the way. "Checked and Unchecked Exceptions" on page 196 talks about this distinction in more detail.

Let's look at another example. In Figure 6-4, the method getContent() invokes the method openConnection() from within a try/catch statement (step 1 in the figure). In turn, openConnection() invokes the method sendRequest() (step 2), which calls the method write() to send some data.

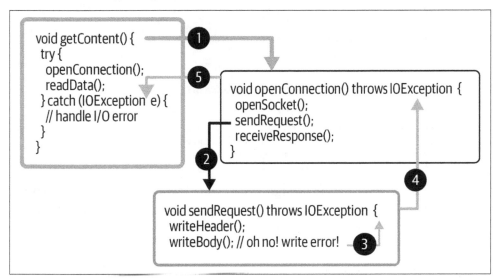

Figure 6-4. Exception propagation

In this figure, the second call to write() throws an IOException (step 3). Since sendRequest() doesn't contain a try/catch statement to handle the exception, it's thrown again from the point where it was called in the method openConnection() (step 4). But openConnection() doesn't catch the exception either, so it's thrown once more (step 5). Finally, it's caught by the try statement in getContent() and handled by its catch clause. Notice that each throwing method must declare that it can throw a particular type of exception with a throws clause. We'll discuss this in "Checked and Unchecked Exceptions" on page 196.

Adding a high-level try statement early in your code can also help handle errors that might bubble up from background threads. We'll discuss threads in much more detail in Chapter 9, but uncaught exceptions can lead to debugging headaches in larger, more complex programs.

Stack Traces

Because an exception can bubble up quite a distance before it is caught and handled, we need a way to determine exactly where it was thrown. It's also important to know how that problematic code was reached. Which methods called which other methods to get to that point? For debugging, all exceptions can dump a *stack trace* that lists their method of origin and all the nested method calls they took to arrive there. Most commonly, the user sees a stack trace when it is printed using the `printStackTrace()` method:

```
try {
  // complex, deeply nested task
} catch (Exception e) {
  // dump information about where the exception occurred
  e.printStackTrace(System.err);
}
```

Such a stack trace for an exception might look like this:

```
java.io.FileNotFoundException: myfile.xml
        at java.io.FileInputStream.<init>(FileInputStream.java)
        at java.io.FileInputStream.<init>(FileInputStream.java)
        at MyApplication.loadFile(MyApplication.java:137)
        at MyApplication.main(MyApplication.java:5)
```

This stack trace indicates that line 5 (in your source code) of the `main()` method of the class `MyApplication` called the method `loadFile()`. The `loadFile()` method then tried to construct a `FileInputStream` at line 137, which threw the `FileNotFoundException`.

Once the stack trace reaches Java system classes (like `FileInputStream`), the line numbers may be lost. This can also happen if the code has been optimized. Usually, there is a way to disable the optimization temporarily to find the exact line numbers, but sometimes other debugging techniques may be required. We'll look at many of those techniques later in this chapter.

Methods in the `Throwable` class allow you to retrieve the stack trace information programmatically, by using the `getStackTrace()` method. (Recall that `Throwable` is the parent class of `Exception` and `Error`.) This method returns an array of `StackTraceElement` objects, each of which represents a method call on the stack. You can ask a `StackTraceElement` for details about that method's location using the methods `getFileName()`, `getClassName()`, `getMethodName()`, and `getLineNumber()`. Element zero of the array is the top of the stack, the final line of code that caused the exception; subsequent elements step back one method call each until the original `main()` method is reached in the last element.

Checked and Unchecked Exceptions

We mentioned earlier that Java forces us to be explicit about our error handling, but it's not necessary to require that every conceivable type of error be handled explicitly in every situation. Java exceptions are therefore divided into two categories: *checked* and *unchecked*. Most application-level exceptions are checked, which means that any method that throws one must declare it with a special `throws` clause in its definition, like this:

```
void readFile(String s) throws IOException, InterruptedException {
  // do some I/O work, maybe using threads for background processing
}
```

Our `readFile()` method anticipates throwing two types of exceptions: by generating them itself (as we'll discuss in "Throwing Exceptions" on page 197) and by ignoring ones that occur within it. For now, all you need to know is that methods have to declare the checked exceptions they can throw or allow to be thrown.

The `throws` clause tells the compiler that a method is a possible source of that type of checked exception and that anyone calling that method must be prepared to deal with it. The caller must then either use a `try/catch` block to handle it or, in turn, declare that it can throw the exception from itself.

In contrast, exceptions that are subclasses of either the class `java.lang.RuntimeException` or the class `java.lang.Error` are unchecked. See Figure 6-1 for the subclasses of `RuntimeException`. It's not a compile-time error to ignore the possibility of these exceptions; methods also don't have to declare they can throw them. In all other respects, unchecked exceptions behave the same as other exceptions. You are free to catch them if you wish, but in this case you aren't required to.

Checked exceptions are intended to cover application-level problems, such as missing files and unavailable network hosts. As good programmers (and upstanding citizens), we should design software to recover gracefully from these kinds of conditions. Unchecked exceptions are intended for system-level problems, such as "array index out of bounds." While these may indicate application-level programming errors, they can occur almost anywhere. Fortunately, because they are unchecked exceptions, you don't have to wrap every one of your array operations in a `try/catch` statement or declare all of the calling methods as a potential source of them.

To sum up, checked exceptions are problems that a reasonable application should try to handle gracefully. Unchecked exceptions (runtime exceptions or errors) are problems from which we would not normally expect our software to recover, but you can provide a polite and hopefully informative message to the user about what happened. Error types, such as "out of memory" errors, are conditions we typically cannot recover from.

Throwing Exceptions

We can throw our own exceptions—either instances of `Exception`, one of its existing subclasses, or our own specialized exception classes. All we have to do is create an instance of the appropriate exception class and throw it with the `throw` statement:

```
throw new IOException();
```

Execution stops and is transferred to the nearest enclosing `try`/`catch` statement that can handle the exception type. Notice we didn't put the new exception into a variable. There is little point in keeping a reference to the `IOException` object we've created here, as the `throw` statement immediately halts the current flow through our code.

An alternative constructor for exceptions lets us specify a string with an error message:

```
throw new IOException("Sunspots!");
```

You can retrieve this string by using the `Exception` object's `getMessage()` method. Often, though, you can just print the exception object itself to get the message and stack trace.

By convention, all types of `Exception` have a `String` constructor like this. The "Sunspots!" message is whimsical but not very helpful. Normally, you will throw a more specific subclass of `Exception`, which captures extra details about the fault or at least provides a more useful string explanation. Here's another example:

```
public void checkRead(String s) throws SecurityException {
  // ...
  if (new File(s).isAbsolute() || (s.indexOf("..") != -1))
    throw new SecurityException(
        "Access to file : "+ s +" denied.");
  // ...
}
```

In this code, we partially implement a method to check for an illegal path. If we find one, we throw a `SecurityException` with some information about the transgression.

Of course, we could include any other information that is useful in our own specialized subclasses of `Exception`. Often, though, just having a new type of exception is good enough because it's sufficient to help direct the flow of control. For example, if we are building a program to read and parse the contents of a web page, we might want to make our own kind of exception to indicate a particular failure:

```
class ParseException extends Exception {
  private int lineNumber;

  ParseException() {
    super();
    this.lineNumber = -1;
  }

  ParseException(String desc, int lineNumber) {
    super(desc);
    this.lineNumber = lineNumber;
  }

  public int getLineNumber() {
```

```
    return lineNumber;
  }
}
```

See "Constructors" on page 155 for a full description of classes and class constructors. The body of our `Exception` class here simply allows a `ParseException` to be created in the conventional ways (either generically or with a little extra information). Now that we have our new exception type, we can guard against any poorly formatted content like this:

```
// Get some input from a file and parse it
try {
  parseStream(input);
} catch (ParseException pe) {
  // Bad input... We can even tell them which line was bad!
  System.err.println("Bad input on line " + pe.getLineNumber());
} catch (IOException ioe) {
  // Other, low-level communications problem
}
```

Even without special information like the line number where our input caused a problem, our custom exception lets us distinguish a parse error from some other I/O error in the same chunk of code.

Chaining and re-throwing exceptions

Sometimes you'll want to take some action based on an exception and then turn around and throw a new exception in its place. This is common when building frameworks where low-level detailed exceptions are handled and represented by higher-level exceptions that can be managed more easily. For example, you might want to catch an `IOException` in a communications package, possibly perform some cleanup, and then throw a higher-level exception of your own, maybe something like `LostServerConnection`.

You can do this in the obvious way by simply catching the exception and then throwing a new one, but then you lose important information, including the stack trace of the original "causal" exception. To deal with this, you can use the technique of *exception chaining*. This means that you include the causal exception in the new exception that you throw. Java has explicit support for exception chaining. The base `Exception` class can be constructed with an exception as an argument or the standard `String` message and an exception:

```
throw new Exception("Here's the story...", causalException);
```

You can get access to the wrapped exception later with the `getCause()` method. More importantly, Java automatically prints both exceptions and their respective stack traces if you print the exception or if it is shown to the user.

You can add this kind of constructor to your own exception subclasses (delegating to the parent constructor). You can also take advantage of this pattern by using the `Throwable` method `initCause()` to set the causal exception explicitly after constructing your own exception and before throwing it:

```
try {
  // ...
} catch (IOException cause) {
  Exception e =
    new IOException("What we have here is a failure to communicate...");
  e.initCause(cause);
  throw e;
}
```

Sometimes it's enough to simply do some logging or take some intermediate action and then re-throw the original exception:

```
try {
  // ...
} catch (IOException cause) {
  log(cause); // Log it
  throw cause;  // re-throw it
}
```

You see this pattern crop up when you have exceptions that don't contain enough information to handle locally. You can do something with what information is available (like printing an error message to help during debugging), but you don't have enough information to recover from the problem. You have to pass on the exception and hope that some calling method with more resources will know what to do.

try Creep

The `try` statement imposes a condition on the statements that it guards. It says that if an exception occurs within it, the remaining statements will be abandoned. This has consequences for local variable initialization. If the compiler can't determine whether a local variable assignment placed inside a `try`/`catch` block will happen, it won't let us use the variable. For example:

```
void myMethod() {
  int foo;

  try {
    foo = getResults();
  }
  catch (Exception e) {
    // handle our exception ...
  }

  int bar = foo; // Compile-time error: foo may not have been initialized
}
```

In this example, we can't use foo in the indicated place because there's a chance it was never assigned a value. One option is to move the assignment for bar inside the try statement:

```
try {
  foo = getResults();
  int bar = foo;  // Okay because we get here only
                  // if previous assignment succeeds
}
catch (Exception e) {
  // handle our exception ...
}
```

Sometimes this works just fine. However, now we have the same problem if we want to use bar later in myMethod(). If we're not careful, we might end up pulling everything into the try statement. The situation changes, however, if we transfer control out of the method in the catch clause:

```
try {
  foo = getResults();
}
catch (Exception e) {
  // log our exception or show the user a warning message
  return;
}
int bar = foo;  // Okay because we get here only
                // if previous try block succeeds
```

The compiler is smart enough to know that if an error had occurred in the try clause, we wouldn't have reached the bar assignment, so it allows us to refer to foo. Your code may have different requirements; we just want you to be aware of the options.

The finally Clause

What if we have something important to do before we exit our method from one of the catch clauses? To avoid duplicating the code in each catch branch and to make the cleanup more explicit, you can use the finally clause. A finally clause can be added after a try block and its associated catch clauses. Any statements in the body of the finally clause are guaranteed to be executed no matter how control leaves the try body, whether an exception is thrown or not:

```
try {
  // Do something here
}
catch (FileNotFoundException e) {
  // handle a missing file ...
}
catch (IOException e) {
  // handle other file problems ...
}
```

```
catch (Exception e) {
  // eek, handle even bigger problems ...
}
finally {
  // Any cleanup here is always executed
}
```

In this example, the statements at the cleanup point are executed eventually, no matter how control leaves the `try`. If control transfers to one of the `catch` clauses, the statements in `finally` are executed after the `catch` completes. If none of the `catch` clauses handles the exception, the `finally` statements are executed before the exception propagates to the next level.

Even if the statements in the `try` execute cleanly, or if we perform a `return`, `break`, or `continue`, the statements in the `finally` clause are still executed. To guarantee that some operations will run, we can even use `try` and `finally` without any `catch` clauses:

```
try {
  // Do something here that might cause an exception
  return;
} finally {
  System.out.println("Whoo-hoo!");
}
```

Exceptions that occur in a `catch` or `finally` clause are handled normally; the search for an enclosing `try`/`catch` begins outside the offending `try` statement, after the `finally` has been executed.

try with Resources

A common use of the `finally` clause is to ensure that resources used in a `try` clause are cleaned up, no matter how the code exits the block. Consider opening a network socket (more on these in Chapter 13):

```
try {
  Socket sock = new Socket(...);
  // work with the socket
} catch(IOException e) {
  // handle our network problem ...
} finally {
  if (sock != null) { sock.close(); }
}
```

What we mean by "cleaning up" here is deallocating expensive resources or closing connections to things such as files, network sockets, or databases. In some cases, these resources might get cleaned up on their own eventually as Java reclaims the garbage, but at best, that would happen at an unknown time in the future. At worst, the cleanup may never happen or may not happen before you run out of resources. You should always guard against these situations.

In the real world, however, there are two problems with staying on top of such resource allocation. First, it requires extra work to carry out a proper cleanup pattern in all of your code, including important things like null checks, as shown in our hypothetical example. Second, if you are juggling multiple resources in a single `finally` block, you have the possibility of your cleanup code itself throwing an exception (e.g., on `close()`) and leaving the job unfinished.

The "try with resources" form of the `try` clause can help. In this extended form, you place one or more resource initialization statements within parentheses after the `try` keyword. Those resources will automatically be "closed" for you when control leaves the `try` block:

```
try (
  Socket sock = new Socket("192.168.100.1", 80);
  FileWriter file = new FileWriter("foo");
)
{
  // work with sock and file
} catch (IOException e) {
  // ...
}
// Both sock and file have been cleaned up by this point
```

In this example, we initialize both a `Socket` object and a `FileWriter` object within the try-with-resources clause, and we can use them within the body of the `try` statement. When control leaves the `try` statement, either after successful completion or because of an exception, Java automatically closes both resources by calling their respective `close()` methods. Java closes these resources in the *reverse of the order* in which you constructed them, so you can accommodate any dependencies among them.

Java supports this behavior for any class that implements the `AutoCloseable` interface (which, at current count, over one hundred different built-in classes do). The `close()` method of this interface is prescribed to release all resources associated with the object, and you can implement this easily in your own classes as well. Now when using try-with-resources, we don't have to add any code specifically to close the file or socket; it is done for us automatically.

Another problem that try-with-resources solves is the pesky situation where an exception is thrown during a close operation. Looking back to the prior example in which we used a `finally` clause to do our cleanup, if an exception had been raised by the `close()` method, the new exception would have been thrown at that point, completely abandoning the original exception from the body of the `try` clause. But try-with-resources preserves the original exception. If an exception occurs within the body of the `try` and one or more exceptions are raised during the subsequent auto-closing operations, it is the original exception from the body of the `try` that will bubble up to the caller. Let's look at an example:

```
try (
  // potential exception #3
  Socket sock = new Socket("192.168.100.1", 80);
  // potential exception #2
  FileWriter file = new FileWriter("foo");
)
{
  // work with sock and file // potential exception #1
}
```

Once the `try` has begun, if an exception occurs at exception point #1, Java will attempt to close both resources in reverse order, leading to potential exceptions at locations #2 and #3. In this case, the calling code will still receive exception #1. Exceptions #2 and #3 are not lost, however; they are merely "suppressed." You can retrieve them via the `getSuppressed()` method of the exception thrown to the caller. This method returns an array of all of the suppressed exceptions.

Performance Issues

Because of the way the Java VM is implemented, using a `try` block to guard against an exception being thrown is free, meaning it doesn't add any overhead to the execution of your code. However, throwing an exception is not free. When an exception is thrown, Java has to locate the appropriate `try/catch` block and perform other time-consuming activities at runtime.

That's why you should throw exceptions only in truly "exceptional" circumstances and avoid using them for expected conditions, especially when performance is an issue. For example, if you have a loop, it may be better to perform a small test on each pass and avoid a `try` block rather than potentially throwing an exception several times over the run of the loop. On the other hand, if the exception is thrown only once in a gazillion times, you may want to eliminate the overhead of your small checks and not worry about the cost of throwing that very rare exception. The general rule should be that exceptions are used for abnormal situations, not routine or expected conditions (such as the end of a file or a missing web resource).

Assertions

Java supports assertions as another mechanism for validating the state of your program. An *assertion* is a simple pass/fail test of some condition, performed while your application is running. You can use assertions to "sanity check" your code. Assertions are distinct from other kinds of tests because they check conditions that should never be violated at a logical level: if the assertion fails, it means some code you wrote is not doing its job and the application generally halts with an appropriate error message. Assertions are supported directly by the Java language, and they can be turned on or off at runtime to remove any performance penalty associated with including them in your code.

Using assertions to test for the correct behavior of your application is a simple but powerful technique for ensuring software quality. It fills a gap between those aspects of software that the compiler can check automatically and those more generally checked by "unit tests" or human testing. Assertions test your own assumptions about program behavior and turn those assumptions into guarantees (at least while assertions are activated).

If you have programmed before, you may have seen something like the following:[3]

```
if (!condition)
    throw new AssertionError("fatal error: 42");
```

An assertion in Java is equivalent to this example, but you use the `assert` keyword. It takes a Boolean condition and an optional expression value. If the assertion fails, an `AssertionError` is thrown, which usually causes Java to bail out of the application. The idea behind bailing out is that an assertion failure reveals a logical flaw in your code—and it is your responsibility as the programmer to find and fix that flaw.

The optional expression may evaluate to either a primitive value or object type. Either way, its sole purpose is to be turned into a string and shown to the user if the assertion fails. Most often you'll use a string message explicitly. Here are some examples:

```
assert false;
assert (array.length > min);
assert a > 0 : a  // shows value of a to the user
assert foo != null :  "foo is null!" // shows message "foo is null!" to user
```

In the event of failure, the first two assertions print only a generic message. The third prints the value of a, and the last prints the `foo is null!` message.

The important thing about assertions is not just that they are more terse than the equivalent `if` condition, but that you can enable or disable them when you run the application. Disabling assertions means that their test conditions are not even evaluated, so there is no performance penalty for including them in your code (other than, perhaps, still consuming a small bit of space in the class files when they are loaded).

---

3 If you have done some programming, we hope your error messages are not this opaque! The more helpful and explanatory your messages, the better.

Enabling and Disabling Assertions

You turn assertions on or off at runtime. When disabled, assertions still exist in the class files but are not executed and do not consume CPU time. You can enable and disable assertions for an entire application, package by package, or even class by class. Remember, assertions are meant to be sanity checks for *you* during development. They are not usually meant to be seen by your end users. Using them as you work on your project but disabling them for "production" is a common tactic.

By default, assertions are turned off in Java. To enable them for your code, use the java command flag -ea or -enableassertions:

```
% java -ea MyApplication
```

To turn on assertions for a particular class, append the class name:

```
% java -ea:com.oreilly.examples.Myclass MyApplication
```

To turn on assertions just for particular packages, append the package name with trailing ellipses (...):

```
% java -ea:com.oreilly.examples... MyApplication
```

When you enable assertions for a package, Java also enables all subordinate package names (e.g., com.oreilly.examples.text). However, you can be more selective by using the corresponding -da or -disableassertions flag to negate individual packages or classes. You can combine all this to achieve arbitrary groupings, like this:

```
% java -ea:com.oreilly.examples... \
    -da:com.oreilly.examples.text \
    -ea:com.oreilly.examples.text.MonkeyTypewriters \
    MyApplication
```

This example enables assertions for the com.oreilly.examples package as a whole, excludes the package com.oreilly.examples.text, but then turns exceptions on for the MonkeyTypewriters class in that package.

Using Assertions

An assertion enforces a rule about something that should be stable in your code and would otherwise go unchecked. You can use an assertion for added safety anywhere you want to verify your assumptions about program behavior that the compiler may not be able to check.

A common situation that cries out for an assertion is testing for multiple conditions or values where one should always be found. In this case, a failing assertion as the default or "fall through" behavior indicates the code is broken. For example, suppose we have a value called direction that should always contain one of two constants, LEFT or RIGHT:

```
if (direction == LEFT)
  goLeft();
else if (direction == RIGHT)
  goRight()
else
  assert false : "bad direction";
```

The same applies to the default case of a switch:

```
switch (direction) {
  case LEFT:
    goLeft();
    break;
  case RIGHT:
    goRight();
    break;
  default:
    assert false;
}
```

In general, you should not use assertions for checking the validity of arguments to methods. You want that validating behavior to be part of your application, not just a quality control test that can be turned off. Methods require valid input as part of their *preconditions*, and you should usually throw an exception if any preconditions are not met. Using exceptions elevates the preconditions to part of the method's "contract" with the user. However, checking the correctness of the results of your methods with assertions before returning them can be useful. These wrap-up checks are called *postconditions*.

Sometimes determining what is or is not a precondition depends on your point of view. For example, when a method is used internally within a class, its preconditions may already be guaranteed by the methods that call it. Public methods of the class should probably throw exceptions when their preconditions are violated, but a private method might use assertions because its callers are always closely related code that should obey the correct behavior.

Real-World Exceptions

Java's adoption of exceptions as an error-handling technique makes it much simpler for developers to write robust code. The compiler forces you to think about checked exceptions ahead of time. Unchecked exceptions will definitely pop up, but assertions can help you watch out for those runtime problems and hopefully prevent a crash.

The try-with-resources feature makes it even simpler for developers to keep their code clean and "do the right thing" when interacting with limited system resources, such as files and network connections. As we noted at the beginning of the chapter, other languages certainly have facilities or customs for dealing with these problems. Java, as a language, works hard to help you thoughtfully consider issues that can arise in your code. The more you work through resolving those issues, the more stable your application (and the happier your users) will be.

Many of our examples so far have been straightforward and have not really required any fancy error checking. Rest assured we'll be exploring more interesting code with, many things that merit exception handling. Later chapters will cover topics like multithreaded programming and networking. Those topics are rife with situations that can go wrong at runtime, such as a big calculation running amok or a WiFi connection dropping. Pardon the pun, but you'll be trying all of these new exception tricks soon enough!

Review Questions

1. What statement should you use to manage potential exceptions in your code?

2. Which exceptions does the compiler require you to handle or throw?

3. Where do you place any cleanup code that you want to always run after using some resources in a try block?

4. Do assertions have much of a performance penalty when they are disabled?

Code Exercises

1. The *Pause.java* program in the *ch06/exercises* folder will not compile. It uses a method, Thread.sleep(), to pause the program for five seconds. That sleep() method can throw a checked exception. Fix the program so it compiles and runs. (We'll be seeing more of threads and Thread.sleep() in Chapter 9.)

2. The exercises include another variation of our "Hello, World" program from Chapter 2 called HelloZero. Use an assertion to make sure that the initial x and y coordinates for the graphical message are greater than zero.

   Try running the program and enabling assertions. What happens if you assign a negative number to one of the coordinates? Run the program again but leave assertions disabled. (Recall that "disabled" is the default behavior, so just don't enable them.) What happens in this case?

Advanced Exercises

1. Let's pretend that a greatest common denominator (GCD) of 1 is an error condition that we need to flag. Create a new class, Euclid3, that will do the usual work of finding the GCD but will throw an exception if that common denominator is 1. (Feel free to start by copying any of your other Euclidean classes.) Create a custom exception class called GCDException that stores the offending pair of numbers as details of the exception.

   Modify Euclid3 to test for a GCD of 1 and throw your new GCDException if that is the result. (Supplying two prime numbers is a quick way to guarantee a result of 1.)

   Before you add any exception handling code, try compiling. Did *javac* warn you about the exception? It should! Go ahead and add a try/catch guard or edit the definition of main() to throw your exception. If you do handle the new exception, be sure to print a nice error message to the user that includes the "bad" numbers from the caught exception.

CHAPTER 7

Collections and Generics

As we start to use our growing knowledge of objects to handle more and more interesting problems, one recurring question will emerge. How do we store the data we're manipulating in the course of solving those problems? We'll definitely use variables of all the different types, but we'll also need bigger, fancier storage options. The arrays we discussed back in "Arrays" on page 120 are a start, but arrays have some limitations. In this chapter we will see how to get efficient, flexible access to large amounts of data using Java's idea of collections. We'll also see how to deal with the various types of data we want to store in these big containers like we do with individual values in variables. That's where generics come in. We'll get to those in "Type Limitations" on page 217.

Collections

Collections are data structures that are fundamental to all types of programming. Whenever we need to refer to a group of objects, we have some kind of collection. At the core language level, Java supports collections in the form of arrays. But arrays are static, and because they have a fixed length, they are awkward for groups of things that grow and shrink over the lifetime of an application. Arrays are also bad at representing abstract relationships between objects. In the early days, the Java platform had only two basic classes to address these needs: the `java.util.Vector` class, which represents a dynamic list of objects, and the `java.util.Hashtable` class, which holds a map of key/value pairs. Today, Java has a more comprehensive approach called the *collections framework*. The framework standardizes how you work with a variety of collections. The older classes still exist, but they have been retrofitted into the framework (with some eccentricities) and are generally no longer used.

Though conceptually simple, collections are one of the most powerful parts of any programming language. They implement data structures that lie at the heart of managing complex problems. A great deal of basic computer science is devoted to describing the most efficient ways to implement certain types of algorithms over collections. (How do you quickly find something in a large collection? How do you sort items in a collection? How do you add or remove items efficiently?) Having these tools at your disposal and understanding how to use them can make your code both much smaller and faster. It can also save you from reinventing the wheel.

The original collections framework had two major drawbacks. The first was that collections were by necessity untyped and worked only with undifferentiated Objects instead of specific types like Dates and Strings. This meant that you had to perform a type cast every time you took an object out of a collection. This flew in the face of Java's compile-time type safety. But in practice, this was less a problem than it was just plain cumbersome and tedious. The second issue was that, for practical reasons, collections could work only with objects and not with primitive types. This meant that any time you wanted to put a number or other primitive type into a collection, you had to store it in a wrapper class first and unpack it later upon retrieving it. This combination of factors made code working with collections less readable and more dangerous.

Generic types (again, more on this in "Type Limitations" on page 217) make it possible for truly type-safe collections to be under the control of the programmer. Alongside generics, autoboxing and unboxing of primitive types means that you can generally treat objects and primitives as equals where collections are concerned. The combination of these new features adds a bit of safety and can significantly reduce the amount of code you write. As we'll see, all of the collections classes now take advantage of these features.

The collections framework is based around a handful of interfaces in the java.util package. These interfaces are divided into two hierarchies. The first hierarchy descends from the Collection interface. This interface (and its descendants) represents a container that holds other objects. The second, separate hierarchy is based on the Map interface, another container that represents a group of key/value pairs where the key can be used to retrieve the value in an efficient way.

The Collection Interface

The mother of all collections is an interface appropriately named Collection. It serves as a container that holds other objects, its *elements*. It doesn't specify exactly how the objects are organized; it doesn't say, for example, whether duplicate objects are allowed or whether the objects are ordered in any way. These kinds of details are left to child interfaces or implementing classes. Nevertheless, the Collection interface defines some basic operations common to all collections:

```
public boolean add( element )
```
Adds the supplied object to this collection. If the operation succeeds, this method returns `true`. If the object already exists in this collection and the collection does not permit duplicates, `false` is returned. Furthermore, some collections are read-only. Those collections throw an `UnsupportedOperationException` if this method is called.

```
public boolean remove( element )
```
Removes the specified object from this collection. Like the `add()` method, this method returns `true` if the object is removed from the collection. If the object doesn't exist in this collection, `false` is returned. Read-only collections throw an `UnsupportedOperationException` if this method is called.

```
public boolean contains( element )
```
Returns `true` if the collection contains the specified object.

```
public int size()
```
Returns the number of elements in this collection.

```
public boolean isEmpty()
```
Returns `true` if this collection has no elements.

```
public Iterator iterator()
```
Examines all the elements in this collection. This method returns an `Iterator`, which is an object you can use to step through the collection's elements. We'll talk more about iterators in the next section.

Additionally, the methods `addAll()`, `removeAll()`, and `containsAll()` accept another `Collection` and add, remove, or test for all of the elements of the supplied collection.

Collection Types

The `Collection` interface has three child interfaces. `Set` represents a collection in which duplicate elements are not allowed. `List` is a collection whose elements have a specific order. The `Queue` interface is a buffer for objects with a notion of a "head" element that's next in line for processing.

Set

`Set` has no methods besides the ones it inherits from `Collection`. It simply enforces its no-duplicates rule. If you try to add an element that already exists in a `Set`, the `add()` method simply returns `false`. `SortedSet` maintains elements in a prescribed order; like a sorted list that cannot contain duplicates. You can retrieve subsets (which are also sorted) using the `subSet()`, `headSet()`, and `tailSet()` methods.

These methods accept one or two elements that mark the boundaries. The `first()` and `last()` calls provide access to the first and last elements, respectively. And the `comparator()` method returns the object used to compare elements (more on this in "A Closer Look: The sort() Method" on page 232).

`NavigableSet` extends `SortedSet` and adds methods for finding the closest match greater or lesser than a target value within the sort order of the `Set`. You can implement this interface efficiently using techniques such as skip lists, which make finding ordered elements fast.

List

The next child interface of `Collection` is `List`. A `List` is an ordered collection, similar to an array but with methods for manipulating the position of elements in the list:

`public boolean add(E element )`
    Adds the specified element to the end of the list.

`public void add(int index , E element )`
    Inserts the given object at the supplied position in the list. If the position is less than zero or greater than the list length, an `IndexOutOfBoundsException` will be thrown. The element that was previously at the supplied position, and all elements after it, are moved up one index position.

`public void remove(int index )`
    Removes the element at the specified position. All subsequent elements move down one index position.

`public E get(int index )`
    Returns the element at the given position but does not change the list.

`public Object set(int index , E element )`
    Changes the element at the given position to the specified object. There must already be an object at the index or else an `IndexOutOfBoundsException` is thrown. No other elements of the list are affected.

The type `E` in these methods refers to the parameterized element type of the `List` class. `Collection`, `Set`, and `List` are all interface types. This is an example of the Generics feature we hinted at in the introduction to this chapter, and we'll look at concrete implementations of these shortly.

Queue

A `Queue` is a collection that acts like a buffer for elements. The queue maintains the insertion order of items placed into it and has the notion of a "head" item. Queues may be first in, first out (FIFO or "in order") or last in, first out (LIFO, sometimes "most recent" or "reverse" order), depending on the implementation:

public boolean offer(E element), public boolean add(E element)
>   The offer() method attempts to place the element into the queue, returning true if successful. Different Queue types may have different limits or restrictions on element types (including capacity). This method differs from the add() method inherited from Collection in that it returns a Boolean value instead of throwing an exception to indicate that the collection cannot accept the element.

public E poll(), public E remove()
>   The poll() method removes the element at the head of the queue and returns it. This method differs from the Collection method remove() in that if the queue is empty, null is returned instead of throwing an exception.

public E peek()
>   Returns the head element *without* removing it from the queue. If the queue is empty, null is returned.

The Map Interface

The collections framework also includes the java.util.Map, which is a collection of key/value pairs. Other names for a map are "dictionary" or "associative array." Maps store and retrieve elements with key values; they are very useful for things like caches and minimalist databases. When you store a value in a map, you associate a key object with that value. When you need to look up the value, the map retrieves it using the key.

With generics (that E type again), a Map type is parameterized with two types: one for the keys and one for the values. The following snippet uses a HashMap, which is an efficient but unordered type of map implementation that we'll discuss later:

```
Map<String, Date> dateMap = new HashMap<String, Date>();
dateMap.put("today", new Date());
Date today = dateMap.get("today");
```

In legacy code, maps simply map Object types to Object types and require an appropriate cast to retrieve values.

The basic operations on Map are straightforward. In the following methods, the type K refers to the key parameter type, and the type V refers to the value parameter type:

public V put(K *key* , V *value*)
>   Adds the specified key/value pair to the map. If the map already contains a value for the specified key, the old value is replaced and returned as the result.

```
public V get(K key)
```
Retrieves the value corresponding to key from the map.

```
public V remove(K key)
```
Removes the value corresponding to key from the map. The value removed is returned.

```
public int size()
```
Returns the number of key/value pairs in this map.

You can retrieve all the keys or values in the map using the following methods:

```
public Set keySet()
```
This method returns a Set that contains all the keys in this map.

```
public Collection values()
```
Use this method to retrieve all the values in this map. The returned Collection can contain duplicate elements.

```
public Set entrySet()
```
This method returns a Set that contains all the key/value pairs (as Map.Entry objects) in this map.

Map has one child interface, SortedMap. A SortedMap maintains its key/value pairs sorted in a particular order according to the keys. It provides the subMap(), head Map(), and tailMap() methods for retrieving sorted map subsets. Like SortedSet, it also provides a comparator() method, which returns an object that determines how the map keys are sorted. We'll talk more about that in "A Closer Look: The sort() Method" on page 232. Java 7 added a NavigableMap with functionality parallel to that of NavigableSet; namely, it adds methods to search the sorted elements for an element greater or lesser than a target value.

Finally, we should make it clear that although they're related, Map is not literally a type of Collection (Map does not extend the Collection interface). You might wonder why. All of the methods of the Collection interface would appear to make sense for Map, except for iterator(). A Map, again, has two sets of objects: keys and values, and separate iterators for each. This is why a Map does not implement a Collection. If you do want a Collection-like view of a Map with both keys and values, you can use the entrySet() method.

One more note about maps: some map implementations (including Java's standard HashMap) allow null to be used as a key or value, but others do not.

Type Limitations

Generics are about abstraction. Generics let you create classes and methods that work in the same way on different types of objects. The term *generic* comes from the idea that we'd like to be able to write general algorithms that can be broadly reused for many types of objects rather than having to adapt our code to fit each circumstance. This concept is not new; it is the impetus behind object-oriented programming itself. Java generics do not so much add new capabilities to the language as they make reusable Java code easier to write and easier to read.

Generics take reuse to the next level by making the *type* of the objects we work with an explicit parameter of the generic code. For this reason, generics are also referred to as *parameterized types*. In the case of a generic class, the developer specifies a type as a parameter (an argument) whenever they use the generic type. The class is parameterized by the supplied type to which the code adapts itself.

In other languages, generics are sometimes referred to as *templates*, which is more of an implementation term. Templates are like intermediate classes, waiting for their type parameters so that they can be used. Java takes a different path, which has both benefits and drawbacks that we'll describe in detail in this chapter.

There is much to say about Java generics. Some of the fine points may seem a bit obscure at first, but don't get discouraged. The vast majority of what you'll do with generics—using existing classes such as `List` and `Set`, for example—is easy and intuitive. Designing and creating your own generics requires a more careful understanding and will come with a little patience and tinkering.

We begin our discussion in that intuitive space with the most compelling case for generics: the container classes and collections we just covered. Next, we take a step back and look at the good, bad, and ugly of how Java generics work. We conclude by looking at a couple of real-world generic classes in Java.

Containers: Building a Better Mousetrap

Recall that in an object-oriented programming language like Java, *polymorphism* means that objects are always interchangeable to some degree. Any child of a type of object can serve in place of its parent type and, ultimately, every object is a child of `java.lang.Object`: the object-oriented "Eve," so to speak.

It is natural for the most general types of containers in Java to work with the type `Object` so that they can hold just about anything. By *containers*, we mean classes that hold instances of other classes in some way. The Java collections framework we looked at in the previous section is the best example of containers. `List`, to recap, holds an ordered collection of elements of type `Object`. And `Map` holds an association of key/value pairs, with the keys and values also being of the most general type,

Object. With a little help from wrappers for primitive types, this arrangement has served us well. But (not to get too Zen on you), a "collection of any type" is also a "collection of no type," and working with Objects pushes a great deal of responsibility onto the developer.

It's kind of like a costume party for objects where everybody is wearing the same mask and disappears into the crowd of the collection. Once objects are dressed as the Object type, the compiler can no longer see the real types and loses track of them. It's up to the user to pierce the anonymity of the objects later by using a type cast. And like attempting to yank off a partygoer's fake beard, you'd better have the cast correct or you'll get an unwelcome surprise:

```
Date date = new Date();
List list = new ArrayList();
list.add(date);
// other code that might add or remove elements ...
Date firstElement = (Date)list.get(0); // Is the cast correct? Maybe.
```

The List interface has an add() method that accepts any type of Object. Here, we assigned an instance of ArrayList, which is simply an implementation of the List interface, and added a Date object. Is the cast in this example correct? It depends on what happens in the elided "other code" period of time.

The Java compiler knows this type of activity is fraught and currently issues warnings when you add elements to a simple ArrayList, as above. We can see this with a little *jshell* detour. After importing from the java.util and javax.swing packages, try creating an ArrayList and add a few disparate elements:

```
jshell> import java.util.ArrayList;

jshell> import javax.swing.JLabel;

jshell> ArrayList things = new ArrayList();
things ==> []

jshell> things.add("Hi there");
|  Warning:
|  unchecked call to add(E) as a member of the raw type java.util.ArrayList
|  things.add("Hi there");
|  ^-------------------^
$3 ==> true

jshell> things.add(new JLabel("Hi there"));
|  Warning:
|  unchecked call to add(E) as a member of the raw type java.util.ArrayList
|  things.add(new JLabel("Hi there"));
|  ^---------------------------------^
$5 ==> true
```

```
jshell> things
things ==> [Hi there, javax.swing.JLabel[...,text=Hi there,...]]
```

You can see that the warning is the same no matter what type of object you add(). In the last step, where we display the contents of things, both the plain String object and the JLabel object are happily in the list. The compiler is not worried about using disparate types; it is helpfully warning you that it will not know whether casts such as the (Date) cast above will work at runtime.

Can Containers Be Fixed?

It's natural to ask if there is a way to make this situation better. What if we know that we are only going to put Dates into our list? Can't we just make our own list that only accepts Date objects, get rid of the cast, and let the compiler help us again? The answer, perhaps surprisingly, is no. At least, not in a very satisfying way.

Our first instinct may be to try to "override" the methods of ArrayList in a subclass. But of course, rewriting the add() method in a subclass would not actually override anything; it would add a new *overloaded* method:

```
public void add(Object o) { ... } // still here
public void add(Date d) { ... }   // overloaded method
```

The resulting object still accepts any kind of object—it just invokes different methods to get there.

Moving along, we might take on a bigger task. For example, we might write our own DateList class that does not extend ArrayList but rather delegates the guts of its methods to the ArrayList implementation. With a fair amount of tedious work, that would get us an object that does everything a List does but works with Dates in a way that both the compiler and the runtime environment can understand and enforce. However, we've now shot ourselves in the foot because our container is no longer an implementation of List. That means we can't use it interoperably with all of the utilities that deal with collections, such as Collections.sort(), or add it to another collection with the Collection addAll() method.

To generalize, the problem is that instead of refining the behavior of our objects, what we really want to do is to change their contract with the user. We want to adapt their method signatures to a more specific type, and polymorphism doesn't allow that. So are we stuck with Objects for our collections? That's where generics come in.

Enter Generics

As we noted when introducing the type limitations in the previous section, generics enhance the syntax of classes that allow us to specialize the class for a given type or set of types. A generic class requires one or more *type parameters* wherever we refer to the class type. It uses them to customize itself.

If you look at the source or Javadoc for the List class, for example, you'll see it defines something like this:

```
public class List< E > {
  // ...
  public void add(E element) { ... }
  public E get(int i) { ... }
}
```

The identifier E between the angle brackets (<>) is a *type parameter*.[1] It indicates that the class List is generic and requires a Java type as an argument to make it complete. The name E is arbitrary, but there are conventions that we'll see as we go on. In this case, the type parameter E represents the type of elements we want to store in the list. The List class refers to the type parameter within its body and methods as if it were a real type, to be substituted later. The type parameter may be used to declare instance variables, arguments to methods, and the return type of methods. In this case, E is used as the type for the elements we'll be adding via the add( ) method and for the return type of the get( ) method. Let's see how to use it.

The same angle bracket syntax supplies the type parameter when we want to use the List type:

```
List<String> listOfStrings;
```

In this snippet, we declared a variable called listOfStrings using the generic type List with a type parameter of String. String refers to the String class, but we could have a specialized List with any Java class type. For example:

```
List<Date> dates;
List<java.math.BigDecimal> decimals;
List<HelloJava> greetings;
```

Completing the type by supplying its type parameter is called *instantiating the type*. It is also sometimes called *invoking the type*, by analogy with invoking a method and supplying its arguments. Whereas with a regular Java type we simply refer to the type by name, a generic type like List<> must be instantiated with parameters wherever it is used.[2] Specifically, this means that we must instantiate the type everywhere types can appear: as the declared type of a variable (as shown in this code snippet), as the

---

1 You may also see the term *type variable* used. The Java Language Specification mostly uses *parameter* so that's what we try to stick with, but you may see both names used in the wild.

2 That is, unless you want to use a generic type in a nongeneric way. We'll talk about "raw" types later in this chapter.

---

type of a method parameter, as the return type of a method, or in an object allocation expression using the new keyword.

Returning to our listOfStrings, what we have now is effectively a List in which the type String has been substituted for the type variable E in the class body:

```
public class List< String > {
  // ...
  public void add(String element) { ... }
  public String get(int i) { ... }
}
```

We have specialized the List class to work with elements of type String and *only* elements of type String. This method signature is no longer capable of accepting an arbitrary Object type.

List is just an interface. To use the variable, we'll need to create an instance of some actual implementation of List. As we did in our introduction, we'll use ArrayList. As before, ArrayList is a class that implements the List interface, but in this case, both List and ArrayList are generic classes. As such, they require type parameters to instantiate them where they are used. Of course, we'll create our ArrayList to hold String elements to match our List of Strings:

```
List<String> listOfStrings = new ArrayList<String>();
// Or shorthand in Java 7.0 and later
List<String> listOfStrings = new ArrayList<>();
```

As always, the new keyword takes a Java type and parentheses with possible arguments for the class's constructor. In this case, the type is ArrayList<String>—the generic ArrayList type instantiated with the String type.

Declaring variables (as shown in the first line of the preceding example) is a bit cumbersome because it requires us to provide the generic parameter type twice: once on the left side in the variable type and once on the right in the initialing expression. And in complicated cases, the generic types can get very lengthy and nested within one another.

The compiler is smart enough to infer the type of the initializing expression from the type of the variable to which you are assigning it. This is called *generic type inference* and boils down to the fact that you can use shorthand on the right side of your variable declarations by leaving out the contents of the <> notation, as shown in the example's second version.

We can now use our specialized List with strings. The compiler prevents us from even trying to put anything other than a String object (or a subtype of String if there were any) into the list. It also allows us to fetch String objects with the get() method without requiring any cast:

```
jshell> ArrayList<String> listOfStrings = new ArrayList<>();
listOfStrings ==> []

jshell> listOfStrings.add("Hey!");
$8 ==> true

jshell> listOfStrings.add(new JLabel("Hey there"));
|  Error:
|  incompatible types: javax.swing.JLabel cannot be converted to java.lang.String
|  listOfStrings.add(new JLabel("Hey there"));
|                    ^--------------------^

jshell> String s = strings.get(0);
s ==> "Hey!"
```

Let's take another example from the Collections API. The `Map` interface provides a dictionary-like mapping that associates key objects with value objects. Keys and values do not have to be of the same type. The generic `Map` interface requires two type parameters: one for the key type and one for the value type. The Javadoc looks like this:

```
public class Map< K, V > {
  // ...
  public V put(K key, V value) { ... } // returns any old value
  public V get(K key) { ... }
}
```

We can make a `Map` that stores `Employee` objects by `Integer` "employee ID" numbers, like this:

```
Map< Integer, Employee > employees = new HashMap<Integer, Employee>();
Integer bobsId = 314; // hooray for autoboxing!
Employee bob = new Employee("Bob", ...);

employees.put(bobsId, bob);
Employee employee = employees.get(bobsId);
```

Here, we used `HashMap`, which is a generic class that implements the `Map` interface. We instantiated both types with the type parameters `Integer` and `Employee`. The `Map` now works only with keys of type `Integer` and holds values of type `Employee`.

The reason we used `Integer` here to hold our number is that the type parameters to a generic class must be class types. We can't parameterize a generic class with a primitive type, such as `int` or `boolean`. Fortunately, autoboxing of primitives in Java (see "Wrappers for Primitive Types" on page 152) almost makes it appear as if we can by allowing us to use primitive types as though they were wrapper types.

Dozens of other APIs beyond Collections use generics to let you adapt them to specific types. We'll talk about them as they occur throughout the book.

Talking About Types

Before we move on to more important things, we should say a few words about the way we describe a particular parameterization of a generic class. Because the most common and compelling case for generics is for container-like objects, it's common to think in terms of a generic type "holding" a parameter type. In our example, we called our `List<String>` a "list of strings" because, sure enough, that's what it was. Similarly, we might have called our employee map a "Map of Employee IDs to Employee Objects." However, these descriptions focus a little more on what the classes *do* than on the type itself.

Take instead a single object container called `Trap< E >` that could be instantiated on an object of type `Mouse` or of type `Bear`; that is, `Trap<Mouse>` or `Trap<Bear>`. Our instinct is to call the new type a "mouse trap" or "bear trap." We can think of our list of strings as a new type, as well. We could talk about a "string list" or describe our employee map as a new "integer employee object map" type. You may use whatever verbiage you prefer, but these latter descriptions focus more on the notion of the generic as a *type* and may help you keep the terms straight when we discuss how generic types are related in the type system. There we'll see that the container terminology turns out to be a little counterintuitive.

In the following section, we'll discuss generic types in Java from a different perspective. We've seen a little of what they can do; now we need to talk about how they do it.

"There Is No Spoon"

In the movie *The Matrix*,[3] the hero Neo is offered a choice: take the blue pill and remain in the world of fantasy, or take the red pill and see things as they really are. In dealing with generics in Java, we are faced with a similar ontological dilemma. We can go only so far in any discussion of generics before we are forced to confront the reality of how they are implemented. Our fantasy world is one created by the compiler to make our lives writing code easier to accept. Our reality (though not quite the dystopian nightmare in the movie) is a harsher place, filled with unseen dangers and questions. Why don't casts and tests work properly with generics? Why can't I implement what appear to be two different generic interfaces in one class? Why

---

3 For those of you who might like some context for the title of this section, here is where it comes from. Our hero, Neo, is learning about his powers.
Boy: Do not try and bend the spoon. That's impossible. Instead, only try to realize the truth.
Neo: What truth?
Boy: There is no spoon.
Neo: There is no spoon?
Boy: Then you'll see that it is not the spoon that bends, it is only yourself.
—The Wachowskis. *The Matrix*. 136 minutes. Warner Brothers, 1999.

can I declare an array of generic types, even though there is no way in Java to create such an array?!?

We'll answer these questions and more in the rest of this chapter, and you won't even have to wait for the sequel. You'll be bending spoons (well, types) in no time. Let's get started.

Erasure

The design goals for Java generics were formidable: add a radical new syntax to the language that safely introduces parameterized types with no impact on performance and, oh, by the way, make it backward compatible with all existing Java code and don't change the compiled classes in any serious way. It's amazing that they actually satisfied these conditions and no surprise that it took a while. But as always, some necessary compromises led to some headaches.

To accomplish this feat, Java employs a technique called *erasure*. Erasure relates to the idea that since most everything we do with generics applies statically at compile time, generic information does not need to be carried over into the compiled classes. The generic nature of the classes, enforced by the compiler, can be "erased" in the binary classes, maintaining compatibility with nongeneric code.

While Java does retain information about the generic features of classes in the compiled form, this information is used mainly by the compiler. The Java runtime does not know anything about generics at all (and does not waste any resources on them).

We can use *jshell* to confirm the runtime notion of a parameterized List<E> still being a List:

```
jshell> import java.util.*;

jshell> List<Date> dateList = new ArrayList<Date>();
dateList ==> []

jshell> dateList instanceof List
$3 ==> true
```

But our generic dateList clearly does not implement the List methods just discussed:

```
jshell> dateList.add(new Object())
|  Error:
|  incompatible types: java.lang.Object cannot be converted to java.util.Date
|  dateList.add(new Object())
|                    ^----------^
```

This illustrates the somewhat eclectic nature of Java generics. The compiler believes in them, but the runtime says they are an illusion. What if we try something a little simpler and check that our dateList is a List<Date>:

```
jshell> dateList instanceof List<Date>;
|  Error:
|  illegal generic type for instanceof
|  dateList instanceof List<Date>;
|                      ^--------^
```

This time the compiler simply puts its foot down and says, "No." You can't test for a generic type in an `instanceof` operation. Since there are no discernible classes for different parameterizations of `List` at runtime (every `List` is still a `List`), there is no way for the `instanceof` operator to tell the difference between one incarnation of `List` and another. All of the generic safety checking was done at compile time, so at runtime we're just dealing with a single actual `List` type.

Here's what really happened: the compiler erased all of the angle bracket syntax and replaced the type parameters in our `List` class with a type that can work at runtime with any allowed type: in this case, `Object`. We would seem to be back where we started, except that the compiler still has the knowledge to enforce our usage of the generics in the code at compile time and can, therefore, handle the cast for us. If you decompile a class using a `List<Date>` (the *javap* command with the *-c* option shows you the bytecode, if you dare), you will see that the compiled code actually contains the cast to `Date`, even though we didn't write it ourselves.

We can now answer one of the questions posed at the beginning of the section: "Why can't I implement what appear to be two different generic interfaces in one class?" We can't have a class that implements two different generic `List` instantiations because they are really the same type at runtime, and there is no way to tell them apart:

```
public abstract class DualList implements List<String>, List<Date> { }
// Error: java.util.List cannot be inherited with different arguments:
//    <java.lang.String> and <java.util.Date>
```

Fortunately, there are always workarounds. In this case, for example, you can use a common superclass or create multiple classes. The alternatives may not be as elegant, but you can almost always land on a clean answer—even if it is a little verbose.

Raw Types

Although the compiler treats different parameterizations of a generic type as different types (with different APIs) at compile time, we have seen that only one real type exists at runtime. For example, both `List<Date>` and `List<String>` share the plain old Java class `List`. `List` is called the *raw type* of the generic class. Every generic has a raw type. It is the base, "plain" Java form from which all of the generic type information has been removed and the type variables replaced by a general Java type like `Object`.

It is possible to use raw types in Java. However, the Java compiler generates a warning wherever they are used in an "unsafe" way. Outside *jshell*, the compiler still notices these problems:

```
// nongeneric Java code using the raw type
List list = new ArrayList(); // assignment ok
list.add("foo"); // Compiler warning on usage of raw type
```

This snippet uses the raw List type just as old-fashioned Java code prior to Java 5 would have. The difference is that now the Java compiler issues an *unchecked warning* about the code if we attempt to insert an object into the list:

```
% javac RawType.java
Note: RawType.java uses unchecked or unsafe operations.
Note: Recompile with -Xlint:unchecked for details.
```

The compiler instructs us to use the -Xlint:unchecked option to get more specific information about the locations of unsafe operations:

```
% javac -Xlint:unchecked MyClass.java
RawType.java:6: warning: [unchecked] unchecked call to add(E)
as a member of the raw type List
    list.add("foo");
           ^
  where E is a type-variable:
    E extends Object declared in interface List
```

Note that creating and assigning the raw ArrayList does not generate a warning. It is only when we try to use an "unsafe" method (one that refers to a type variable) that we get the warning. This means that it's still OK to use older-style, nongeneric Java APIs that work with raw types. We get warnings only when we do something unsafe in our own code.

One more thing about erasure before we move on. In the previous examples, the type variables were replaced by the Object type, which could represent any type applicable to the type variable E. Later, we'll see that this is not always the case. We can place limitations or *bounds* on the parameter types, and, when we do, the compiler can be more restrictive about the erasure of the type, for example:

```
class Bounded< E extends Date > {
    public void addElement(E element) { ... }
}
```

This parameter type declaration says that the element type E must be a subtype of the Date type. In this case, the erasure of the addElement() method is therefore more restrictive than Object, and the compiler uses Date:

```
    public void addElement(Date element) { ... }
```

Date is called the *upper bound* of this type, meaning that it is the top of the object hierarchy here. You can only instantiate the parameterized type on a Date or on a "lower" (more derived, or subclassed) type.

Now that we have a handle on what generic types really are, we can go into a little more detail about how they behave.

Parameterized Type Relationships

We know now that parameterized types share a common, raw type. This is why our parameterized List<Date> is just a List at runtime. In fact, we can assign any instantiation of List to the raw type if we want:

```
List list = new ArrayList<Date>();
```

We can even go the other way and assign a raw type to a specific instantiation of the generic type:

```
List<Date> dates = new ArrayList(); // unchecked warning
```

This statement generates an unchecked warning on the assignment, but after that, the compiler trusts that the list contained only Dates prior to the assignment. You can try casting new ArrayList() to List<Date>, but that won't address the warning. We'll talk about casting to generic types in "Casts" on page 229.

Whatever the runtime types, the compiler is running the show. It does not let us assign things that are clearly incompatible:

```
List<Date> dates = new ArrayList<String>(); // Compile-time Error!
```

Of course, the ArrayList<String> does not implement the methods of List<Date> required by the compiler, so these types are incompatible.

But what about more interesting type relationships? The List interface, for example, is a subtype of the more general Collection interface. Can you take a particular instantiation of the generic List and assign it to some instantiation of the generic Collection? Does it depend on the type parameters and their relationships? Clearly, a List<Date> is not a Collection<String>. But is a List<Date> a Collection<Date>? Can a List<Date> be a Collection<Object>?

We'll just blurt out the answer here first, then walk through it and explain. The rule for the simple types of generic instantiations we've discussed so far is that *inheritance applies only to the "base" generic type and not to the parameter types*. Furthermore, assignability applies only when the two generic types are instantiated on *exactly the same parameter type*. In other words, there is still one-dimensional inheritance, following the base generic class type, but with the additional restriction that the parameter types must be identical.

For example, since a List is a type of Collection, we can assign instantiations of List to instantiations of Collection when the type parameter is exactly the same:

```
Collection<Date> cd;
List<Date> ld = new ArrayList<Date>();
cd = ld; // Ok!
```

This code snippet says that a List<Date> is a Collection<Date>—pretty intuitive. But trying the same logic on a variation in the parameter types fails:

```
List<Object> lo;
List<Date> ld = new ArrayList<Date>();
lo = ld; // Compile-time Error!  Incompatible types.
```

Although our intuition tells us that the Dates in that List could all live happily as Objects in a List, the assignment is an error. We'll explain precisely why in the next section, but for now just note that the type parameters are not exactly the same and that there is no inheritance relationship among parameter types in generics.

This is a case where it helps to think of the instantiation in terms of types and not in terms of what the instantiated objects do. These are not really a "list of dates" and a "list of objects"—more like a DateList and an ObjectList, the relationship of which is not immediately obvious.

Try to pick out what's OK and what's not OK in the following example:

```
Collection<Number> cn;
List<Integer> li = new ArrayList<Integer>();
cn = li;
```

It is possible for an instantiation of List to be an instantiation of Collection, but only if the parameter types are exactly the same. Inheritance doesn't follow the parameter types, so the final assignment in this example fails.

Earlier we mentioned that this rule applies to the simple types of instantiations we've discussed so far in this chapter. What other types are there? Well, the kinds of instantiations we've seen so far where we plug in an actual Java type as a parameter are called *concrete type instantiations*. Later, we'll talk about *wildcard instantiations*, which are like mathematical set operations on types (think unions and intersections). It's possible to make more exotic instantiations of generics where the type relationships are actually two-dimensional, depending both on the base type and the parameterization. But don't worry: this doesn't come up very often and is not as scary as it sounds.

Why Isn't a List<Date> a List<Object>?

It's a reasonable question. Why shouldn't we be able to assign our List<Date> to a List<Object> and work with the Date elements as Object types?

The reason gets back to the heart of the rationale for generics: changing programming contracts. In the simplest case, supposing a DateList type extends an Object List type, the DateList would have all of the methods of ObjectList and we could insert Objects into it. Now, you might object that generics let us change the method signatures, so that doesn't apply anymore. That's true, but there is a bigger problem.

If we could assign our DateList to an ObjectList variable, we could use Object methods to insert elements of types other than Date into it.

We could *alias* (provide an alternate, broader type) the DateList as an ObjectList. Using the aliased object, we could try to trick it into accepting some other type:

```
DateList dateList = new DateList();
ObjectList objectList = dateList; // Can't really do this
objectList.add(new Foo()); // should be runtime error!
```

We'd expect to get a runtime error when the actual DateList implementation was presented with the wrong type of object.

And therein lies the problem. Java generics have no runtime representation. Even if this functionality were useful, there is no way for Java to know what to do at runtime. This feature is simply dangerous—it allows for an error at runtime that can't be caught at compile time. In general, we'd like to catch type errors at compile time.

You might think Java could guarantee the type safety of your code if it compiles with no unchecked warnings by disallowing these assignments. Unfortunately it can't, but that limitation has nothing to do with generics; it has to do with arrays. (If this all sounds familiar to you, it's because we mentioned this issue in Chapter 4 in relation to Java arrays.) Array types have an inheritance relationship that allows this kind of aliasing to occur:

```
Date [] dates = new Date[10];
Object [] objects = dates;
objects[0] = "not a date"; // Runtime ArrayStoreException!
```

Arrays have runtime representations as different classes. They check themselves at runtime, throwing an ArrayStoreException in situations like this. The Java compiler cannot guarantee the type safety of your code if you use arrays in this way.

Casts

We've now talked about relationships between generic types and even between generic types and raw types. But we haven't really explored the concept of casts in the world of generics.

No cast was necessary when we interchanged generics with their raw types. But we triggered unchecked warnings from the compiler:

```
List list = new ArrayList<Date>();
List<Date> dl = list;  // unchecked warning
```

Normally, we use a cast in Java to work with two types that could be assignable. For example, we could attempt to cast an Object to a Date because it is plausible that the Object could be a Date value. The cast then performs the check at runtime to see if we are correct.

Casting between unrelated types is a compile-time error. For example, we can't even try to cast an `Integer` to a `String`. Those types have no inheritance relationship. What about casts between compatible generic types?

```
Collection<Date> cd = new ArrayList<Date>();
List<Date> ld = (List<Date>)cd; // Ok!
```

This code snippet shows a valid cast from a more general `Collection<Date>` to a `List<Date>`. The cast is plausible here because a `Collection<Date>` is assignable from and could actually be a `List<Date>`.

Similarly, the following cast catches our mistake: we have aliased a `TreeSet<Date>` as a `Collection<Date>` and tried to cast it to a `List<Date>`:

```
Collection<Date> cd = new TreeSet<Date>();
List<Date> ld = (List<Date>)cd; // Runtime ClassCastException!
ld.add(new Date());
```

There is one case where casts are not effective with generics, however, and that is when trying to differentiate the types based on their parameter types:

```
Object o = new ArrayList<String>();
List<Date> ld = (List<Date>)o; // unchecked warning, ineffective
Date d = ld.get(0); // unsafe at runtime, implicit cast may fail
```

Here, we aliased an `ArrayList<String>` as a plain `Object`. Next, we cast o to a `List<Date>`. Unfortunately, Java does not know the difference between a `List<String>` and a `List<Date>` at runtime, so the cast is fruitless. The compiler warns us by generating an unchecked warning at the location of the cast. When we try to use the cast object, `ld`, we might find out that it is incorrect. Casts on generic types are ineffective at runtime because of erasure and the lack of type information.

Converting Between Collections and Arrays

While not related by direct inheritance or shared interfaces, converting between collections and arrays is still straightforward. For convenience, you can retrieve the elements of a collection as an array using the following methods:

```
public Object[] toArray()
public <E> E[] toArray(E[] a)
```

The first method returns a plain `Object` array. With the second form, we can be more specific and get back an array of the correct element type. If we supply an array of sufficient size, it will be filled in with the values. But if the array is too short (for instance, zero length), Java will create a new array of the *same type but the required length* and return it instead. So you can just pass in an empty array of the correct type like this:

```
Collection<String> myCollection = ...;
String [] myStrings = myCollection.toArray(new String[0]);
```

This trick is a little awkward. It would be nice if Java let us specify the type explicitly using a `Class` reference, but for some reason, it doesn't.

Going the other way, you can convert an array of objects to a `List` collection with the static `asList()` method of the `java.util.Arrays` helper class:

```
String [] myStrings = { "a", "b", "c" };
List list = Arrays.asList(myStrings);
```

The compiler is also smart enough to recognize a valid assignment to a `List<String>` variable.

Iterator

An *iterator* is an object that lets you step through a sequence of values. This kind of operation comes up so often that it has a standard interface: `java.util.Iterator`. The `Iterator` interface has three interesting methods:

`public E next()`
This method returns the next element (an element of generic type E) of the associated collection.

`public boolean hasNext()`
This method returns `true` if you have not yet stepped through all the `Collection`'s elements. In other words, it returns `true` if you can call `next()` to get the next element.

`public void remove()`
This method removes the most recent object returned from `next()` from the associated `Collection`.

The following example shows how to use an `Iterator` to print out every element of a collection:

```
public void printElements(Collection c, PrintStream out) {
  Iterator iterator = c.iterator();
  while (iterator.hasNext()) {
    out.println(iterator.next());
  }
}
```

After using `next()` to get the next element, you can sometimes `remove()` it. Working your way through a to-do list, for example, might follow a pattern: "get an item, process the item, remove the item." But the removal feature of iterators is not always appropriate and not all iterators implement `remove()`. It doesn't make sense to be able to remove an element from a read-only collection, for example.

If element removal is not allowed, an `UnsupportedOperationException` is thrown from this method. If you call `remove()` before first calling `next()`, or if you call `remove()` twice in a row, you'll get an `IllegalStateException`.

Looping over collections

A form of the `for` loop, described in "The for loop" on page 109, can operate over all `Iterable` types, which means it can iterate over all types of `Collection` objects as that interface extends `Iterable`. For example, it can now step over all of the elements of a typed collection of `Date` objects, like so:

```
Collection<Date> col = ...
for (Date date : col) {
  System.out.println(date);
}
```

This feature of the Java built-in `for` loop is called the "enhanced" `for` loop (as opposed to the pregenerics, numeric-only `for` loop). The enhanced `for` loop applies only to `Collection` type collections, not `Map`s. But looping over a map can be useful in some situations. You can use the `Map` methods `keySet()` or `values()` (or even `entrySet()` if you want each key/value pair as a single entity) to get a collection from your map that *does* work with this enhanced `for` loop:

```
Map<Integer, Employee> employees = new HashMap<>();
// ...
for (Integer id : employees.keySet()) {
  System.out.print("Employee " + id);
  System.out.println(" => " + employees.get(id));
}
```

The collection of keys is a simple, unordered set. The enhanced `for` loop above will show all of your employees, but their printed order might appear somewhat random. If you wanted them listed in order of their IDs or perhaps their names, you would need to sort the keys or values first. Fortunately, sorting is a very common task—and the collections framework can help.

A Closer Look: The sort() Method

Poking around in the `java.util.Collections` class, we find all kinds of static utility methods for working with collections. Among them is this goody—the static generic method `sort()`:

```
<T extends Comparable<? super T>> void sort(List<T> list) { ... }
```

Another nut for us to crack. Let's focus on the last part of the bound:

```
Comparable<? super T>
```

This is a wildcard instantiation that we mentioned in "Parameterized Type Relationships" on page 227. In this case, it is an interface, so we can read the extends in the sort() return type as implements if it helps.

Comparable holds a compareTo() method for some parameter type. A Comparable<String> means that the compareTo() method takes type String. Therefore, Comparable<? super T> is the set of instantiations of Comparable on T and all of its superclasses. A Comparable<T> suffices and, at the other end, so does a Comparable<Object>.

What this means in English is that the elements must be comparable to their own type, or some supertype of their own type for the sort() method to use them. This ensures that the elements can all be compared to one another, but it's not as restrictive as saying that they must all implement the compareTo() method themselves. Some of the elements may inherit the Comparable interface from a parent class that knows how to compare only to a supertype of T, and that is exactly what is allowed.

Application: Trees on the Field

There is a lot of theory in this chapter. Don't be afraid of theory—it can help you predict behavior in novel scenarios and inspire solutions to new problems. But practice is just as important, so let's revisit the game that we started in "Classes" on page 134. In particular, it's time to store more than one object of each type.

In Chapter 13 we'll cover networking and look at creating a two-player setup that would require storing multiple physicists. For now, we still have one physicist who can throw one apple at a time. But we can populate our field with several trees for target practice.

Let's add six trees. We'll use a pair of loops so you can easily increase the tree count if you wish. Our Field currently stores a lone tree instance. We can upgrade that storage to a typed list (we'll call it trees). From there we can approach adding and removing trees in a number of ways:

- We could create some methods for Field that work with the list and maybe enforce some other game rules (like managing a maximum number of trees).

- We could just use the list directly since the List class already has nice methods for most of the things we want to do.

- We could use some combination of those approaches: special methods where it makes sense for our game, and direct manipulation everywhere else.

Since we do have some game rules that are peculiar to our Field, we'll take the first approach here. (But look at the examples and think about how you might alter them to use the list of trees directly.) We'll start with an `addTree()` method. One benefit of this approach is that we can also relocate the creation of the tree instance to our method rather than creating and manipulating the tree separately. Here's one way to add a tree at a desired point on the field:

```
List<Tree> trees = new ArrayList<>();
// other field state

public void addTree(int x, int y) {
  Tree tree = new Tree();
  tree.setPosition(x,y);
  trees.add(tree);
}
```

With that method in place, we could add a couple of trees quite quickly:

```
Field field = new Field();
// other setup code
field.addTree(100,100);
field.addTree(200,100);
```

Those two lines add a pair of trees side by side. Let's go ahead and write the loops we need to create our six trees:

```
Field field = new Field();
// other setup code
for (int row = 1; row <= 2; row++) {
  for (int col = 1; col <=3; col++) {
    field.addTree(col * 100, row * 100);
  }
}
```

Can you see now how easy it would be to add eight or nine or a hundred trees? Computers are really good at repetition.

Hooray for creating our forest of apple targets! We left off a few critical details, though. Most importantly, we need to show our new forest on the screen. We also need to update our drawing method for the `Field` class so that it understands and uses our list of trees correctly. Eventually we'll do the same for our physicists and apples as we add more functionality to our game. We'll also need a way to remove elements that are no longer active. But first, let's see our forest!

```
// File: Field.java
  protected void paintComponent(Graphics g) {
    g.setColor(fieldColor);
    g.fillRect(0,0, getWidth(), getHeight());
    for (Tree t : trees) {
      t.draw(g);
    }
    physicist.draw(g);
    apple.draw(g);
  }
```

Since we are already in the Field class where our trees are stored, there is no need to write a separate function to pull out an individual tree and paint it. We can use the nifty enhanced for loop structure and quickly get all of our trees on the field, as shown in Figure 7-1.

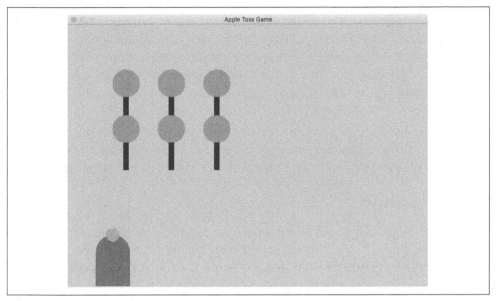

Figure 7-1. Rendering all the trees in our List

Useful Features

Java collections and generics are very powerful and useful additions to the language. Although some of the details we delved into in the latter half of this chapter may seem daunting, the common usage is very simple and compelling: generics make collections better. As you begin to use generics more, you will find that your code becomes more readable and more maintainable. Collections allow for elegant, efficient storage. Generics make explicit what you previously had to infer from usage.

Review Questions

1. If you want to store a contact list with names and phone numbers, which kind of collection would work best?

2. What method do you use to get an iterator for the items in a Set?

3. How can you turn a List into an array?

4. How can you turn an array into a List?

5. What interface should you implement to sort a list using the `Collections.sort()` method?

Code Exercises

1. The class `EmployeeList` in the *ch07exercises* folder contains a few employees loaded into a map of employee IDs and `Employee` objects, similar to the one used in several examples above. We mentioned printing these employees in a sorted fashion, but didn't show any code. Try to sort the employees by their ID numbers. You'll likely need to use the `keySet()` method and then create a temporary—but sortable—list from that set.

2. In Advanced Exercise 5.1, you created a new obstacle class, `Hedge`. Update the game so that you can have multiple hedges similar to the multiple trees. Make sure all of your trees and hedges paint correctly when you run the program.

Advanced Exercises

1. In Code Exercise 1 above, you probably sorted the keys of the map and then used the correctly sorted keys to get the corresponding employee. For a bit more of a challenge, implement the `Comparable` interface in your `Employee` class. You can decide how you want to organize the employees: by ID, by last name, by full name, or maybe some combination of those attributes. Rather than sorting the `keySet()` collection, try sorting your newly comparable employees directly by building a temporary list from the `values()` of your map.

CHAPTER 8

Text and Core Utilities

If you've been reading this book sequentially, you've read all about the core Java language constructs, including the object-oriented aspects of the language and the use of threads. Now it's time to shift gears and start talking about the collection of classes that compose the standard Java packages and come with every Java implementation. Java's core packages are one of its most distinguishing features. Many other object-oriented languages have similar features, but none has as extensive a set of standardized classes and tools as Java does. This is both a reflection of—and a reason for—Java's success.

Strings

We'll start by taking a closer look at the Java String class (or, more specifically, java.lang.String). Because working with Strings is so fundamental, it's important to understand how they are implemented and what you can do with them. A String object encapsulates a sequence of Unicode characters. Internally, these characters are stored in a regular Java array, but the String object guards this array jealously and gives you access to it only through its own API. This is to support the idea that Strings are *immutable*; once you create a String object, you can't change its value. Lots of operations on a String object appear to change the characters or length of a string, but what they really do is return a new String object that copies or internally references the needed characters of the original. Java implementations make an effort to consolidate identical strings used in the same class into a shared-string pool and to share parts of Strings where possible.

The original motivation for all of this was performance. Immutable Strings can save memory and the Java VM can optimize their use for speed. But they aren't magic. You should have a basic understanding of the `String` class to avoid creating an excessive number of `String` objects in places where performance is an issue.[1]

Constructing Strings

Literal strings, defined in your source code, are declared with double quotes and can be assigned to a `String` variable:

```
String quote = "To be or not to be";
```

Java automatically converts the literal string into a `String` object and assigns it to the variable.

Strings keep track of their own length, so `String` objects in Java don't require special terminators. You can get the length of a `String` with the `length()` method. You can also test for a zero-length string by using `isEmpty()`:

```
int length = quote.length();
boolean empty = quote.isEmpty();
```

Strings can take advantage of the only overloaded operator in Java, the + operator, for string concatenation. The following two lines produce equivalent strings:

```
String name = "John " + "Smith";
// or, equivalently:
String name = "John ".concat("Smith");
```

For chunks of text larger than a name, Java 13 introduced text blocks. We can store a poem with fairly little effort by using three double-quotes to mark the beginning and end of the multiline block. This feature even preserves leading space in a clever way: the leftmost nonspace character becomes the left "edge." Spaces to the left of that edge on subsequent lines are ignored, but spaces after that edge are retained. Consider redoing our poem in *jshell*:

```
jshell> String poem = """
   ...> Twas brillig, and the slithy toves
   ...>     Did gyre and gimble in the wabe:
   ...> All mimsy were the borogoves,
   ...>     And the mome raths outgrabe.
   ...> """;
poem ==> "Twas brillig, and ... the mome raths outgrabe.\n"

jshell> System.out.print(poem);
Twas brillig, and the slithy toves
    Did gyre and gimble in the wabe:
```

---

1 When in doubt, measure it! If your `String`-manipulating code is clean and easy to understand, don't rewrite it until someone proves to you that it is too slow. Chances are that they will be wrong. And don't be fooled by relative comparisons. A millisecond is a thousand times slower than a microsecond, but it still may be negligible to your application's overall performance.

```
All mimsy were the borogoves,
   And the mome raths outgrabe.

jshell>
```

Embedding lengthy text in source code is not normally something you want to do. For text longer than a few dozen lines, Chapter 10 looks at ways to load `String`s from files.

In addition to making strings from literal expressions, you can construct a `String` directly from an array of characters:

```
char [] data = new char [] { 'L', 'e', 'm', 'm', 'i', 'n', 'g' };
String lemming = new String(data);
```

You can also construct a `String` from an array of bytes:

```
byte [] data = new byte [] { (byte)97, (byte)98, (byte)99 };
String abc = new String(data, "ISO8859_1");
```

In this case, the second argument to the `String` constructor is the name of a character-encoding scheme. The `String` constructor uses it to convert the raw bytes in the specified encoding to the internal encoding chosen by the runtime. If you don't specify a character encoding, the default encoding scheme on your system is used.[2]

Conversely, the `charAt()` method of the `String` class lets you access the characters of a `String` in an array-like fashion:

```
String s = "Newton";
for (int i = 0; i < s.length(); i++)
    System.out.println(s.charAt(i) );
```

This code prints the characters of the string one at a time.

The notion that a `String` is a sequence of characters is also codified by the `String` class implementing the interface `java.lang.CharSequence`, which prescribes the methods `length()` and `charAt()` as a way to get a subset of the characters.

Strings from Things

Objects and primitive types in Java can be turned into a default textual representation as a `String`. For primitive types like numbers, the string should be fairly obvious; for object types, it is under the control of the object itself. We can get the string representation of an item with the static `String.valueOf()` method. Various overloaded versions of this method accept each of the primitive types:

---

2 On most platforms the default encoding is UTF-8. You can get more details on character sets, default sets, and standard sets supported by Java in the official Javadoc documentation (*https://oreil.ly/UarRO*) for the `java.nio.charset.Charset` class.

```
String one = String.valueOf(1); // integer, "1"
String two = String.valueOf(2.384f);  // float, "2.384"
String notTrue = String.valueOf(false); // boolean, "false"
```

All objects in Java have a `toString()` method that is inherited from the `Object` class. For many objects, this method returns a useful result that displays the contents of the object. For example, a `java.util.Date` object's `toString()` method returns the date it represents formatted as a string. For objects that do not provide a representation, the string result is just a unique identifier that you can use for debugging. The `String.valueOf()` method, when called for an object, invokes the object's `toString()` method and returns the result. The only real difference in using this method is that if you pass it a null object reference, it returns the `String` "null" for you, instead of producing a `NullPointerException`:

```
Date date = new Date();
// Equivalent, e.g., "Fri Dec 19 05:45:34 CST 1969"
String d1 = String.valueOf(date);
String d2 = date.toString();

date = null;
d1 = String.valueOf(date);  // "null"
d2 = date.toString();   // NullPointerException!
```

String concatenation uses the `valueOf()` method internally, so if you "add" an object or primitive using the plus operator (+), you get a `String`:

```
String today = "Today's date is :" + date;
```

You'll sometimes see people use the empty string and the plus operator (+) as shorthand to get the string value of an object. For example:

```
String two = "" + 2.384f;
String today = "" + new Date();
```

It's a bit of a cheat, but it does work and it is visually succinct.

Comparing Strings

The standard `equals()` method can compare strings for *equality*; they must contain exactly the same characters in the same order. You can use a different method, `equalsIgnoreCase()`, to check the equivalence of strings in a case-insensitive way:

```
String one = "FOO";
String two = "foo";

one.equals(two);                // false
one.equalsIgnoreCase(two);   // true
```

A common mistake for novice programmers in Java is to compare strings with the == operator when they actually need the `equals()` method. Remember that strings are objects in Java, and == tests for object *identity*: that is, whether the two arguments being tested are the same object. In Java, it's easy to make two strings that have the same characters but are not the same string object. For example:

```
String foo1 = "foo";
String foo2 = String.valueOf(new char [] { 'f', 'o', 'o' });

foo1 == foo2          // false!
foo1.equals(foo2)  // true
```

This mistake is particularly dangerous because it often works for the common case in which you are comparing *literal strings* (strings declared with double quotes right in the code). The reason for this is that Java tries to manage strings efficiently by combining them. At compile time, Java finds all the identical strings within a given class and makes only one object for them. This is safe because strings are immutable and cannot change, but it does leave room for this comparison problem.

The `compareTo()` method compares the lexical value of the `String` to another `String`, using the Unicode specification to compare the relative positions of two strings within the "alphabet." (We use quotes as Unicode has many more characters than just the letters of the English alphabet.) It returns an integer that is less than, equal to, or greater than zero:

```
String abc = "abc";
String def = "def";
String num = "123";

if (abc.compareTo(def) < 0) { ... }  // true
if (abc.compareTo(abc) == 0) { ... } // true
if (abc.compareTo(num) > 0) { ... }  // true
```

You can't really use the actual value returned by `compareTo()` beyond these three possibilities. Any negative number, be it -1, -5, or -1,000, simply means the first string is "less than" the second string. The `compareTo()` method compares strings strictly by their characters' positions in the Unicode specification. This works for simple text but does not handle all language variations well. If you need more sophisticated comparisons with broader internationalization support, check out the documentation for the `java.text.Collator` class (*https://oreil.ly/KrVCG*).

Searching

The `String` class provides several simple methods for finding fixed substrings within a string. The `startsWith()` and `endsWith()` methods compare an argument string with the beginning and end of the `String`, respectively:

```
String url = "http://foo.bar.com/";
if (url.startsWith("http:"))  // true
```

The indexOf() method searches for the first occurrence of a character or substring and returns the starting character position, or -1 if the substring is not found:

```
String abcs = "abcdefghijklmnopqrstuvwxyz";
int i = abcs.indexOf('p');     // 15
int i = abcs.indexOf("def");   // 3
int I = abcs.indexOf("Fang");  // -1
```

Similarly, lastIndexOf() searches backward through the string for the last occurrence of a character or substring.

The contains() method handles the very common task of checking to see whether a given substring is contained in the target string:

```
String log = "There is an emergency in sector 7!";
if (log.contains("emergency")) pageSomeone();

// equivalent to
if (log.indexOf("emergency") != -1) ...
```

For more complex searching, you can use the Regular Expression API, which allows you to look for and parse complex patterns. We'll talk about regular expressions later in this chapter.

String Method Summary

Table 8-1 summarizes the methods provided by the String class. We've included several methods not discussed in this chapter. Feel free to try these methods out in *jshell* or look up the documentation online (*https://oreil.ly/lbM1R*).

Table 8-1. String methods

Method	Functionality
charAt()	Gets a particular character in the string
compareTo()	Compares the string with another string
concat()	Concatenates the string with another string
contains()	Checks whether the string contains another string
copyValueOf()	Returns a string equivalent to the specified character array
endsWith()	Checks whether the string ends with a specified suffix
equals()	Compares the string with another string
equalsIgnore Case()	Compares the string with another string, ignoring case
getBytes()	Copies characters from the string into a byte array
getChars()	Copies characters from the string into a character array
hashCode()	Returns a hashcode for the string
indexOf()	Searches for the first occurrence of a character or substring in the string

Method	Functionality
intern()	Fetches a unique instance of the string from a global shared-string pool
isBlank()	Returns true if the string is zero length or contains only whitespace
isEmpty()	Returns true if the string is zero length
lastIndexOf()	Searches for the last occurrence of a character or substring in a string
length()	Returns the length of the string
lines()	Returns a stream of lines separated by line terminators
matches()	Determines if the whole string matches a regular expression pattern
regionMatches()	Checks whether a region of the string matches the specified region of another string
repeat()	Returns a concatenation of this string, repeated a given number of times
replace()	Replaces all occurrences of a character in the string with another character
replaceAll()	Replaces all occurrences of a regular expression pattern with a pattern
replaceFirst()	Replaces the first occurrence of a regular expression pattern with a pattern
split()	Splits the string into an array of strings using a regular expression pattern as a delimiter
startsWith()	Checks whether the string starts with a specified prefix
strip()	Removes leading and trailing whitespace as defined by `Character.isWhitespace()` (*https://oreil.ly/NK1Nl*)
stripLeading()	Removes leading whitespace, similar to `strip()`
stripTrailing()	Removes trailing whitespace, similar to `strip()`
substring()	Returns a substring from the string
toCharArray()	Returns the array of characters from the string
toLowerCase()	Converts the string to lowercase
toString()	Returns the string value of an object
toUpperCase()	Converts the string to uppercase
trim()	Removes leading and trailing whitespace, defined here as any character with a Unicode position (called its *codepoint*) less than or equal to 32 (the "space" character)
valueOf()	Returns a string representation of a value

Things from Strings

Parsing and formatting text is a large, open-ended topic. So far in this chapter, we've looked at only primitive operations on strings—creation, searching, and turning simple values into strings. Now we'd like to move on to more structured forms of text. Java has a rich set of APIs for parsing and printing formatted strings, including numbers, dates, times, and currency values. We'll cover most of these topics in this chapter, but we'll wait to discuss date and time formatting in "Local Dates and Times" on page 263.

We'll start with *parsing*—reading primitive numbers and values from strings, and chopping long strings into tokens. Then we'll take a look at regular expressions, the most powerful text-parsing tool Java offers. Regular expressions let you define your own patterns of arbitrary complexity, search for them, and parse them from text.

Parsing Primitive Numbers

In Java, numbers, characters, and booleans are primitive types—not objects. But for each primitive type, Java also defines a *primitive wrapper* class. Specifically, the java.lang package includes the following classes: Byte, Short, Integer, Long, Float, Double, Character, and Boolean. We talked about these in "Wrappers for Primitive Types" on page 152, but we bring them up now because these classes hold static utility methods that parse their respective types from strings. Each of these primitive wrapper classes has a static "parse" method that reads a String and returns the corresponding primitive type. For example:

```
byte b = Byte.parseByte("16");
int n = Integer.parseInt("42");
long l = Long.parseLong("99999999999");
float f = Float.parseFloat("4.2");
double d = Double.parseDouble("99.99999999");
boolean b = Boolean.parseBoolean("true");
```

You can find other ways to convert from strings to base types and back again, but these wrapper class methods are straightforward and easy to read. And in the case of Integer and Long, you can also supply an optional *radix* argument (the base of a number system; decimal numbers have a radix of 10, for example) to convert strings with octal or hexadecimal numbers. (Nondecimal data sometimes pops up when dealing with things such as cryptographic signatures or email attachments.)

Tokenizing Text

You'll rarely encounter strings with just one number to parse or with only the word you need. It's a more common programming task to parse a longer string of text into individual words, or *tokens*, that are separated by some set of *delimiter characters*, such as spaces or commas.

Programmers talk about tokens as a generic way to discuss different values or types present in a piece of text. A token might be a simple word, a username, an email address, or a number. Let's take a look at some examples.

Consider the sample text below. The first line contains words separated by single spaces. The remaining pair of lines involves comma-delimited fields:

```
Now is the time for all good people

Check Number, Description,      Amount
4231,         Java Programming, 1000.00
```

Java has several (unfortunately overlapping) methods and classes for handling situations like this. We'll use the powerful `split()` method from the `String` class. It utilizes regular expressions to allow you to break up a string based on arbitrary patterns. We'll talk about regular expressions shortly, but to show you how this works, we'll just give you the necessary magic now.

The `split()` method accepts a regular expression that describes a delimiter. It uses that expression to chop the string into an array of smaller `String`s:

```
String text1 = "Now is the time for all good people";
String [] words = text1.split("\\s");
// words = "Now", "is", "the", "time", ...

String text2 = "4231,          Java Programming, 1000.00";
String [] fields = text2.split("\\s*,\\s*");
// fields = "4231", "Java Programming", "1000.00"
```

In the first example, we used the regular expression \\s, which matches a single whitespace character (space, tab, or carriage return). Calling `split()` on our `text1` variable returns an array of eight strings. In the second example, we used a more complicated regular expression, \\s*,\\s*, which matches a comma surrounded by any amount of optional whitespace. This reduced our text to three nice, tidy fields.

Regular Expressions

Now it's time to take a brief detour on our trip through Java and enter the land of *regular expressions*. A regular expression, or *regex* for short, describes a text pattern. Regular expressions are used with many tools—including the `java.util.regex` package, text editors, and many scripting languages—to provide sophisticated text-searching and string-manipulation capabilities.

Regular expressions can help you find all of the phone numbers in a large file. They can help you find all of the phone numbers with a particular area code. They can help you find all of the phone numbers that do *not* have a particular area code. You can use a regular expression to find links in the source of a web page. You can even use regular expressions to do some editing in a text file. You could look for phone numbers with the area code in parentheses, say (123) 456-7890, and replace it with the simpler 123-456-7890 format, for example. And key to the power of regular expressions, you can find *every* phone number in your block of text with parentheses and convert it—not just one specific phone number.

If you are already familiar with the concept of regular expressions and how they are used with other languages, you may wish to skim through this section, but don't skip it entirely. At the very least, you'll need to look at "The java.util.regex API" on page 252 later in this chapter, which covers the Java classes necessary to use them. If you're wondering exactly what regular expressions are, then grab a can or a cup of your favorite beverage and get ready. You are about to learn about the most powerful tool in the arsenal of text manipulation, as well as a tiny language within a language, all in the span of a few pages.

Regex Notation

A regular expression (regex) describes a pattern in text. By *pattern*, we mean just about any feature you can imagine identifying in text from the literal characters alone, without actually understanding their meaning. This includes features such as words, word groupings, lines and paragraphs, punctuation, upper- or lowercase, and more generally, strings and numbers with a specific structure to them. (Think of things like phone numbers, email addresses, or zip codes.) With regular expressions, you can search the dictionary for all the words that have the letter "q" without its pal "u" next to it, or words that start and end with the same letter. Once you have constructed a pattern, you can use simple tools to hunt for it in text or to determine if a given string matches it.

Write once, run away

Regular expressions constitute a simple form of programming language. Think for a moment about the examples we cited earlier. We would need something like a language to describe even simple patterns—such as email addresses—that have common elements but also some variation in form.

A computer science textbook would classify regular expressions at the bottom of the hierarchy of computer languages, in terms of both what they can describe and what you can do with them. They are still capable of being quite sophisticated, however. As with most programming languages, the elements of regular expressions are simple, but you can combine them to create something quite complex. And that potential complexity is where things start to get sticky.

Since regexes work on strings, which can be found everywhere in Java code, it is convenient to have a very compact notation. But compact notation can be cryptic, and experience shows that it is much easier to write a complex statement than to read it again later. Such is the curse of the regular expression. You may find yourself in a moment of late-night, caffeine-fueled inspiration, writing a single glorious pattern to simplify the rest of your program down to one line. When you return to read that line the next day, however, it may look like Egyptian hieroglyphics to you. Simpler is generally better, but if you can break your problem more clearly into several steps, maybe you should.

Escaped characters

Now that you've been properly warned, we have to throw one more thing at you before we build you back up. Not only can the regex notation get a little hairy, but it is also somewhat ambiguous when used with ordinary Java strings. An important part of the notation is the escaped character—a character with a backslash in front of it. For example, in regex notation, the escaped d character, \d, (backslash "d") is a shorthand for any single digit character (0–9). However, you cannot simply write \d as part of a Java string, because Java uses the backslash for its own special characters and to specify Unicode character sequences (\uxxxx). Fortunately, Java gives us a replacement: an *escaped backslash*: two backslashes (\\). It represents a literal backslash. The rule is, when you want a backslash to appear in your regex, you must escape it with an extra one:

```
"\\d" // Java string that yields \d in a regex
```

It gets weirder! Because regex notation itself uses a backslash to denote special characters, it must provide the same "escape hatch" for itself. You need to double up backslashes if you want your regex to match a literal backslash. It looks like this:

```
"\\\\"  // Java string yields two backslashes; regex yields one
```

Most of the "magic" operator characters in this section operate on the character that precedes them, so you must escape them if you want their literal meaning. This includes such characters as ., *, +, {}, and (). An expression that can match formal US phone numbers (with the area code inside a pair of parentheses) looks like this:

```
"\\(\\d\\d\dd\\) \\d\\d\\d-\\d\\d\\d\\d"
```

If you need to create part of an expression that has lots of literal characters in it, you can use the special delimiters \Q and \E to help you. Any text appearing between \Q and \E is automatically escaped. (You still need the Java `String` escapes—double backslashes for backslash, but not quadruple.) There is also a static method called `Pattern.quote()` that does the same thing, returning a properly escaped version of whatever string you give it.

We have one more suggestion to help maintain your cool when working with these examples. Write out the plain regex using a comment line above the real Java string (where you must double up all backslashes). We also tend to include a comment with an example of the text we hope to match. Here's that US phone number example again with this commenting approach:

```
// US phone number: (123) 456-7890
// regex: \(\d\d\d\) \d\d\d-\d\d\d\d
"\\(\\d\\d\dd\\) \\d\\d\\d-\\d\\d\\d\\d"
```

And don't forget about *jshell*! It can be a very powerful playground for testing and tweaking your patterns. We'll see several examples of testing patterns with *jshell* in "The java.util.regex API" on page 252. But first, let's look at more of the elements you can use to construct patterns.

Characters and character classes

Now, let's dive into the actual regex syntax. The simplest form of a regular expression is plain, literal text, which has no special meaning and is matched directly (character for character) in the input. This can be a single character or more. For example, in the following string, the pattern s can match the character "s" in the words "rose" and "is":

```
"A rose is $1.99."
```

The pattern "rose" can match only the literal word rose. But this isn't very interesting. Let's crank things up a notch by introducing some special characters and the notion of character "classes":

Any character: dot (.)
> The special character dot (.) matches any single character. The pattern .ose matches "rose," "nose," "_ose" (space followed by "ose"), or any other character followed by the sequence "ose." Two dots match any two characters ("prose," "close"), and so on. The dot operator is very broad; it normally stops only for a *line terminator* (a newline, carriage return, or combination of both). Think of . as representing the class of all characters.

Whitespace or nonwhitespace character: \s, \S
> The special character \s matches whitespace. *Whitespace* includes any character that relates to visual space in text or that marks the end of a line. Common whitespace characters include the literal space character (what you get when you press the space bar on your keyboard), \t (tab), \r (carriage return), \n (newline), and \f (formfeed). The corresponding special character \S does the inverse, matching any character that is *not* whitespace.

Digit or nondigit character: \d, \D
> \d matches any of the digits from 0 to 9. \D does the inverse, matching all characters except digits.

Word or nonword character: \w, \W
> \w matches characters typically found in "words," such as upper- and lowercase letters A–Z, a–z, the digits 0–9, and the underscore character (_). \W matches everything except those characters.

Custom character classes

You can define your own character classes using square brackets ([ ]) around the characters you want. Here are some examples:

```
[abcxyz]      // matches any of a, b, c, x, y, or z
[02468]       // matches any even digit
```

```
[aeiouAEIOU] // matches any vowel, upper- or lowercase
[AaEeIiOoUu] // also matches any vowel
```

The special x-y *range notation* can be used as shorthand for consecutive runs of alphanumeric characters:

```
[LMNOPQ]      // Explicit class of L, M, N, O, P, or Q
[L-Q]         // Equivalent shorthand version
[12345]       // Explicit class of 1, 2, 3, 4, or 5
[1-5]         // Equivalent shorthand version
```

Placing a caret (^) as the first character inside the brackets inverts the character class, matching any character *except* those included in the brackets:

```
[^A-F]    // G, H, I, ..., a, b, c, 1, 2, $, #... etc.
[^aeiou]  // Any character that isn't a lowercase vowel
```

Nesting character classes simply concatenates them into a single class:

```
[A-F[G-Z]\s] // A-Z plus whitespace
```

You can use the && logical AND notation (similar to the Boolean operator we saw in "Operators" on page 114) to take the *intersection* (characters in common):

```
[a-p&&[l-z]] // l, m, n, o, p
[A-Z&&[^P]]  // A through Z except P
```

Position markers

The pattern [Aa] rose (including an upper- or lowercase A) matches three times in the following phrase:

```
"A rose is a rose is a rose"
```

Position characters allow you to designate the relative location of a match within a line. The most important are ^ and $, which match the beginning and end of a line, respectively:

```
^[Aa] rose  // matches "A rose" at the beginning of line
[Aa] rose$  // matches "a rose" at end of line
```

To be a little more precise, ^ and $ match the beginning and end of "input," which is usually a single line. If you are working with multiple lines of text and wish to match the beginnings and endings of lines within a single large string, you can turn on "multiline" mode with a flag, as described later in "Special options" on page 251.

The position markers \b and \B match a word boundary (whitespace, punctuation, or the beginning or end of a line), or a nonword boundary (the middle of a word), respectively. For example, the first pattern matches "rose" and "rosemary," but not "primrose." The second pattern matches "primrose" and "prose," but not "rose" at the beginning of a word or by itself:

```
\brose      // rose, rosemary, roses; NOT prose
\Brose      // prose, primrose; NOT rose or rosemary
```

You often use these position markers when you need to look for or exclude prefixes or suffixes.

Iteration (multiplicity)

Simply matching fixed-character patterns will not get us very far. Next, we look at operators that count the number of occurrences of a character (or more generally, of a pattern, as we'll see in "Pattern" on page 252):

Any (zero or more iterations): asterisk (*)
Placing an asterisk (*) after a character or character class means "allow any number of that type of character"—in other words, zero or more. For example, the following pattern matches a digit with any number of leading zeros (possibly none):

```
0*\d   // match a digit with any number of leading zeros
```

Some (one or more iterations): plus sign (+)
The plus sign (+) means "one or more" iterations and is equivalent to XX* (pattern followed by pattern asterisk). For example, the following pattern matches a number with one or more digits, plus optional leading zeros:

```
0*\d+   // match a number (one or more digits) with optional
        // leading zeros
```

It may seem redundant to match the zeros at the beginning of an expression because zero is a digit and is thus matched by the \d+ portion of the expression anyway. However, we'll show later how you can pick apart the string using a regex and get at just the pieces you want. In this case, you might want to strip off the leading zeros and keep only the digits.

Optional (zero or one iteration): question mark (?)
The question mark operator (?) allows exactly zero or one iteration. For example, the following pattern matches a credit card expiration date, which may or may not have a slash in the middle:

```
\d\d/?\d\d   // match four digits with optional slash in the middle
```

Range (between x and y iterations, inclusive): {x,y}
The {x,y} curly brace range operator is the most general iteration operator. It specifies a precise range to match. A range takes two arguments: a lower bound and an upper bound, separated by a comma. This regex matches any word with five to seven characters, inclusive:

```
\b\w{5,7}\b   // match words with 5, 6, or 7 characters
```

At least x or more iterations (y is infinite): {x,}

If you omit the upper bound, simply leaving a dangling comma in the range, the upper bound becomes infinite. This is a way to specify a minimum of occurrences with no maximum.

Alternation

The vertical bar (|) operator denotes the logical OR operation, also called *alternation* or *choice*. The | operator does not operate on individual characters but instead applies to everything on either side of it. It splits the expression in two unless constrained by parentheses grouping. For example, a slightly naive approach to parsing dates might be the following:

```
\w+, \w+ \d+, \d+|\d\d/\d\d/\d\d  // pattern 1 OR pattern 2
```

In this expression, the left matches patterns such as "Fri, Oct 12, 2001," and the right matches "10/12/01."

The following regex might be used to match email addresses with one of three domains (*net, edu,* and *gov*):

```
\w+@[\w.]+\.(net|edu|gov)
// email address ending in .net, .edu, or .gov
```

This pattern is by no means complete in terms of true, valid email addresses. But it does highlight how you can use alternation to help build regular expressions with some useful characteristics.

Special options

Several special options affect the way the regex engine performs its matching. These options can be applied in two ways:

- You can supply one or more special arguments (flags) to the `Pattern.compile()` step (discussed in "The java.util.regex API" on page 252).
- You can include a special block of code in your regex.

We'll show the latter approach here. To do this, include one or more flags in a special block (?x), where x is the flag for the option we want to turn on. Generally, you do this at the beginning of the regex. You can also turn off flags by adding a minus sign (?-x), which allows you to apply flags to select parts of your pattern.

The following flags are available:

Case-insensitive: (?i)

The (?i) flag tells the regex engine to ignore character case while matching. For example:

```
(?i)yahoo    // matches Yahoo, yahoo, yahOO, etc.
```

Dot all: (?s)

The (?s) flag turns on "dot all" mode, allowing the dot character to match anything, including end-of-line characters. It is useful if you are matching patterns that span multiple lines. The s stands for "single-line mode," a somewhat confusing name derived from Perl.

Multiline: (?m)

By default, ^ and $ don't really match the beginnings and ends of lines (as defined by carriage return or newline combinations). Instead, they match the beginning or end of the entire input text. In many cases, "one line" is synonymous with the entire input.

If you have a big block of text to process, you'll often break that block into separate lines for other reasons. If you do that, checking any given line for a regular expression will be straightforward, and ^ and $ will behave as expected. However, if you want to use a regex with the entire input string containing multiple lines (separated by those carriage return or newline combinations), you can turn on multiline mode with (?m). This flag causes ^ and $ to match the beginning and end of the individual lines *within* the block of text, *as well as* the beginning and end of the entire block. Specifically, this means the spot before the first character, the spot after the last character, and the spots just before and after line terminators inside the string.

Unix lines: (?d)

The (?d) flag limits the definition of the line terminator for the ^, $, and . special characters to Unix-style newline only (\n). By default, carriage return newline (\r\n) is also allowed.

The java.util.regex API

Now that we've covered the theory of how to construct regular expressions, the hard part is over. All that's left is to investigate the Java API to see how to apply these expressions.

Pattern

As we've said, the regex patterns that we write as strings are, in actuality, little programs describing how to match text. At runtime, the Java regex package compiles these little programs into a form that it can execute against some target text. Several simple convenience methods accept strings directly to use as patterns.

The static method `Pattern.matches()` takes two strings—a regex and a target string —and determines if the target matches the regex. This is very convenient if you want to do a quick test once in your application. For example:

```
Boolean match = Pattern.matches("\\d+\\.\\d+f?", myText);
```

This line of code can test whether the string `myText` contains a Java-style floating-point number such as "42.0f." Note that the string must match completely to be considered a match. If you want to see if a small pattern is contained within a larger string but don't care about the rest of the string, you have to use a `Matcher`, as described in "The Matcher" on page 255.

Let's try another (simplified) pattern that we could use in our game once we start letting multiple players compete against each other. Many login systems use email addresses as the user identifier. Such systems aren't perfect, of course, but an email address will work for our needs. We would like to invite users to input their email address, but we want to make sure it looks valid before using it. A regular expression can be a quick way to perform such a validation.[3]

Much like writing algorithms to solve programming problems, designing a regular expression requires you to break your pattern matching problem into bite-sized pieces. If we think about email addresses, a few patterns stand out right away. The most obvious is the @ in the middle of every address. A naive (but better than nothing!) pattern relying on that fact could be built like this:

```
String sample = "my.name@some.domain";
Boolean validEmail = Pattern.matches(".*@.*", sample);
```

But that pattern is too permissive. It will certainly recognize valid email addresses, but it will also recognize many invalid ones like `"bad.address@"` or `"@also.bad"` or even `"@@"`. Let's test these out in *jshell*:

```
jshell> String sample = "my.name@some.domain";
sample ==> "my.name@some.domain"

jshell> Pattern.matches(".*@.*", sample)
Pattern.matches(".*@.*", sample)$2 ==> true

jshell> Pattern.matches(".*@.*", "bad.address@")
Pattern.matches(".*@.*", "bad.address@")$3 ==> true

jshell> Pattern.matches(".*@.*", "@@")
Pattern.matches(".*@.*", "@@")$4 ==> true
```

---

3 Validating email addresses turns out to be much trickier than we can address here. Regular expressions can cover most valid addresses, but if you are doing validation for a commercial or other professional application, you may want to investigate third-party libraries, such as those available from Apache Commons (*https:// oreil.ly/JEjEk*).

Try to cook up a few more bad examples of your own. You'll quickly see that our simple email pattern is definitely too simple.

How can we make better matches? One quick adjustment would be to use the + modifier instead of the *. The upgraded pattern now requires at least one character on each side of the @. But we know a few other things about email addresses. For example, the left "half" of the address (the name portion) cannot contain the @ character. For that matter, neither can the domain portion. We can use a custom character class for this next upgrade:

```
String sample = "my.name@some.domain";
Boolean validEmail = Pattern.matches("[^@]+@[^@]+", sample);
```

This pattern is better but still allows several invalid addresses such as "still@bad" since domain names have at least a name followed by a period (.) followed by a top-level domain (TLD) such as "oreilly.com." So maybe a pattern like this:

```
String sample = "my.name@some.domain";
Boolean validEmail = Pattern.matches("[^@]+@[^@]+\\.(com|org)", sample);
```

That pattern fixes our issue with an address like "still@bad", but we've gone a bit too far the other way. There are many, many TLDs—too many to reasonably list even if we ignore the problem of maintaining that list as new TLDs are added.[4] So let's step back a little. We'll keep the "dot" in the domain portion, but remove the specific TLD and just accept a simple run of letters:

```
String sample = "my.name@some.domain";
Boolean validEmail = Pattern.matches("[^@]+@[^@]+\\.[a-z]+", sample);
```

Much better. We can add one last tweak to make sure we don't worry about the case of the address since all email addresses are case-insensitive. Just tack on the (?i) flag at the beginning of our pattern string:

```
String sample = "my.name@some.domain";
Boolean validEmail = Pattern.matches("(?i)[^@]+@[^@]+\\.[a-z]+", sample);
```

Again, this is by no means a perfect email validator, but it is definitely a good start and suffices for our hypothetical login system:

```
jshell> Pattern.matches("(?i)[^@]+@[^@]+\\.[a-z]+", "good@some.domain")
$1 ==> true

jshell> Pattern.matches("(?i)[^@]+@[^@]+\\.[a-z]+", "good@oreilly.com")
$2 ==> true

jshell> Pattern.matches("(?i)[^@]+@[^@]+\\.[a-z]+", "oreilly.com")
$3 ==> false
```

---

4 You are welcome to apply for your own, custom global TLD (*https://oreil.ly/lMRnm*) if you have a few hundred thousand dollars lying around.

```
jshell> Pattern.matches("(?i)[^@]+@[^@]+\\.[a-z]+", "bad@oreilly@com")
$4 ==> false

jshell> Pattern.matches("(?i)[^@]+@[^@]+\\.[a-z]+", "me@oreilly.COM")
$5 ==> true

jshell> Pattern.matches("[^@]+@[^@]+\\.[a-z]+", "me@oreilly.COM")
$6 ==> false
```

In these examples, we typed in the full `Pattern.matches(…)` line only once. After that it was a simple up arrow, edit, and then hit Return for the subsequent five lines. Can you spot the flaw in our final pattern that causes the match to fail?

 If you want to tinker around with the validation pattern and expand or improve it, remember you can "reuse" lines in *jshell* with the keyboard arrow keys. Use the up arrow to retrieve the previous line. Indeed, you can use the up arrow and down arrow to navigate all of your recent lines. Within a line, use the left arrow and right arrow to move around and delete/add/edit your command. Then just press the Return key to run the newly altered command—you do not need to move the cursor to the end of the line before pressing Return.

The Matcher

A `Matcher` associates a pattern with a string and provides tools for testing, finding, and iterating over matches of the pattern against it. The `Matcher` is "stateful." For example, the `find()` method tries to find the next match each time it is called. But you can clear the `Matcher` and start over by calling its `reset()` method.

To create a `Matcher` object, you first need to compile your pattern string into a `Pattern` object using the static `Pattern.compile()` method. With that pattern object in hand, you can use the `matcher()` method to get your `Matcher`, like so:

```
String myText = "Lots of text with hyperlinks and stuff ...";
Pattern urlPattern = Pattern.compile("https?://[\\w./]*");
Matcher matcher = urlPattern.matcher(myText);
```

If you're just interested in "one big match"—that is, you're expecting your string to either match the pattern or not—you can use `matches()` or `lookingAt()`. These correspond roughly to the methods `equals()` and `startsWith()` of the `String` class. The `matches()` method asks if the string matches the pattern in its entirety (with no string characters left over) and returns `true` or `false`. The `lookingAt()` method does the same, except that it asks only whether the string starts with the pattern and doesn't care if the pattern uses up all the string's characters.

More generally, you'll want to be able to search through the string and find one or more matches. To do this, you can use the `find()` method. Each call to `find()` returns `true` or `false` for the next match of the pattern and internally notes the position of the matching text. You can get the starting and ending character positions with the `Matcher` `start()` and `end()` methods, or you can simply retrieve the matched text with the `group()` method. For example:

```
import java.util.regex.*;

// ...

    String text="A horse is a horse, of course of course...";
    String pattern="horse|course";

    Matcher matcher = Pattern.compile(pattern).matcher(text);
    while (matcher.find())
      System.out.println(
        "Matched: '"+matcher.group()+"' at position "+matcher.start());
```

The previous snippet prints the starting location of the words "horse" and "course" (four in all):

```
Matched: 'horse' at position 2
Matched: 'horse' at position 13
Matched: 'course' at position 23
Matched: 'course' at position 33
```

Splitting strings

A very common need is to parse a string into a bunch of fields based on some delimiter, such as a comma. It's such a common problem that the `String` class contains a method for doing just this. The `split()` method accepts a regular expression and returns an array of substrings broken around that pattern. Consider the following string and `split()` calls:

```
    String text = "Foo, bar ,   blah";
    String[] badFields = text.split(",");
    // { "Foo", " bar ", "   blah" }
    String[] goodFields = text.split("\\s*,\\s*");
    // { "Foo", "bar", "blah" }
```

The first `split()` returns a `String` array, but the naive use of `,` to separate the string means the space characters in our `text` variable remain stuck to the more interesting characters. We get "Foo" as a single word, as expected, but then we get "bar<space>" and finally "<space><space><space>blah". Yikes! The second `split()` also yields a `String` array, but this time containing the expected "Foo", "bar" (with no trailing space), and "blah" (with no leading spaces).

If you are going to use an operation like this more than a few times in your code, you should probably compile the pattern and use its `split()` method, which is identical to the version in `String`. The `String` `split()` method is equivalent to:

```
Pattern.compile(pattern).split(string);
```

As we noted before, there is a lot to learn about regular expressions above and beyond the few regex capabilities we covered here. Check out the documentation on patterns (*https://oreil.ly/L8BUD*). Play around on your own using *jshell*. Modify the *ch08/examples/ValidEmail.java* file and see if you can create a better email validator! This is definitely a topic that benefits from practice.

Math Utilities

Of course, string manipulation and pattern matching are not the only types of operations Java can do. Java supports integer and floating-point arithmetic directly in the language. Higher-level math operations are supported through the `java.lang.Math` class. As you have seen, wrapper classes for primitive data types allow you to treat them as objects. Wrapper classes also hold some methods for basic conversions.

Let's start with a quick look at the built-in arithmetic in Java. Java handles errors in integer arithmetic by throwing an `ArithmeticException`:

```
int zero = 0;

try {
    int i = 72 / zero;
} catch (ArithmeticException e) {
    // division by zero
}
```

To generate the error in this example, we created the intermediate variable `zero`. The compiler is somewhat crafty. It would have caught us if we had tried to divide by `0` directly.

Floating-point arithmetic expressions, on the other hand, don't throw exceptions. Instead, they take on the special out-of-range values shown in Table 8-2.

Table 8-2. Special floating-point values

Value	Mathematical representation
POSITIVE_INFINITY	1.0/0.0
NEGATIVE_INFINITY	-1.0/0.0
NaN	0.0/0.0

The following example generates an infinite result:

```
double zero = 0.0;
double d = 1.0/zero;

if (d == Double.POSITIVE_INFINITY)
    System.out.println("Division by zero");
```

The special value NaN (not a number) indicates the result of dividing zero by zero. This value has the special mathematical distinction of not being equal to itself (NaN ! = NaN evaluates to true). Use Float.isNaN() or Double.isNaN() to test for NaN.

The java.lang.Math Class

The java.lang.Math class is Java's math library. It holds a suite of static methods covering all of the usual mathematical operations like sin(), cos(), and sqrt(). The Math class isn't very object-oriented (you can't create an instance of Math). Instead, it's really just a convenient holder for static methods that are more like global functions. As we saw in Chapter 5, it's possible to use the static import functionality to import the names of static methods and constants like this directly into the scope of our class and use them by their simple, unqualified names.

Table 8-3 summarizes the methods in java.lang.Math.

Table 8-3. Methods in java.lang.Math

Method	Argument type(s)	Functionality
Math.abs(a)	int, long, float, double	Absolute value
Math.acos(a)	double	Arc cosine
Math.asin(a)	double	Arc sine
Math.atan(a)	double	Arc tangent
Math.atan2(a,b)	double	Angle part of rectangular-to-polar coordinate transform
Math.ceil(a)	double	Smallest whole number greater than or equal to a
Math.cbrt(a)	double	Cube root of a
Math.cos(a)	double	Cosine
Math.cosh(a)	double	Hyperbolic cosine
Math.exp(a)	double	Math.E to the power a
Math.floor(a)	double	Largest whole number less than or equal to a
Math.hypot(a,b)	double	Precision calculation of the sqrt() of a2 + b2
Math.log(a)	double	Natural logarithm of a
Math.log10(a)	double	Log base 10 of a
Math.max(a, b)	int, long, float, double	The value a or b closer to Long.MAX_VALUE
Math.min(a, b)	int, long, float, double	The value a or b closer to Long.MIN_VALUE

Method	Argument type(s)	Functionality
`Math.pow(a, b)`	`double`	a to the power b
`Math.random()`	None	Random-number generator
`Math.rint(a)`	`double`	Converts double value to integral value in double format
`Math.round(a)`	`float, double`	Rounds to whole number
`Math.signum(a)`	`float, double`	Get the sign of the number at 1.0, −1.0, or 0
`Math.sin(a)`	`double`	Sine
`Math.sinh(a)`	`double`	Hyperbolic sine
`Math.sqrt(a)`	`double`	Square root
`Math.tan(a)`	`double`	Tangent
`Math.tanh(a)`	`double`	Hyperbolic tangent
`Math.toDegrees(a)`	`double`	Convert radians to degrees
`Math.toRadians(a)`	`double`	Convert degrees to radians

The methods `log()`, `pow()`, and `sqrt()` can throw a runtime `ArithmeticException`. The methods `abs()`, `max()`, and `min()` are overloaded for all the scalar values (`int`, `long`, `float`, and `double`) and return the corresponding type. Versions of `Math.round()` accept either `float` or `double` and return `int` or `long`, respectively. The rest of the methods operate on and return double values:

```
double irrational = Math.sqrt(2.0); // 1.414...
int bigger = Math.max(3, 4);  // 4
long one = Math.round(1.125798); // 1
```

Just to highlight the convenience of that static import option, try these simple functions in *jshell*:

```
jshell> import static java.lang.Math.*

jshell> double irrational = sqrt(2.0)
irrational ==> 1.4142135623730951

jshell> int bigger = max(3,4)
bigger ==> 4

jshell> long one = round(1.125798)
one ==> 1
```

`Math` also contains the static final double constants `E` and `PI`. To find the perimeter of a circle, for example:

```
double circumference = diameter  * Math.PI;
```

Math in action

We've already touched on using the Math class and its static methods in "Accessing Fields and Methods" on page 137. We can use it again to make our game a little more fun by randomizing where the trees appear. The Math.random() method returns a random double greater than or equal to 0 and less than 1. Add in a little arithmetic and rounding or truncating, and you can use that value to create random numbers in any range you need. In particular, converting this value into a desired range follows this formula:

```
int randomValue = min + (int)(Math.random() * (max - min));
```

Try it! Try to generate a random four-digit number in *jshell*. You could set the min to 1,000 and the max to 10,000, like so:

```
jshell> int min = 1000
min ==> 1000

jshell> int max = 10000
max ==> 10000

jshell> int fourDigit = min + (int)(Math.random() * (max - min))
fourDigit ==> 9603

jshell> fourDigit = min + (int)(Math.random() * (max - min))
fourDigit ==> 9178

jshell> fourDigit = min + (int)(Math.random() * (max - min))
fourDigit ==> 3789
```

To place our trees, we'll need two random numbers for the x and y coordinates. We can set a range that will keep the trees on the screen by thinking about a margin around the edges. For the x coordinate, one way to do that might look like this:

```
private int goodX() {
    // at least half the width of the tree plus a few pixels
    int leftMargin = Field.TREE_WIDTH_IN_PIXELS / 2 + 5;
    // now find a random number between a left and right margin
    int rightMargin = FIELD_WIDTH - leftMargin;

    // And return a random number starting at the left margin
    return leftMargin + (int)(Math.random() * (rightMargin - leftMargin));
}
```

Set up a similar method for finding a y value, and you should start to see something like the image shown in Figure 8-1. You could even get fancy and use the isTouching() method we discussed back in Chapter 5 to avoid placing any trees in direct contact with our physicist. Here's our upgraded tree setup loop:

```
for (int i = field.trees.size(); i < Field.MAX_TREES; i++) {
    Tree t = new Tree();
```

```
    t.setPosition(goodX(), goodY());

    // Trees can be close to each other and overlap,
    // but they shouldn't intersect our physicist
    while(player1.isTouching(t)) {
        // We do intersect this tree, so let's try again
        System.err.println("Repositioning an intersecting tree...");
        t.setPosition(goodX(), goodY());
    }
    field.addTree(t);
}
```

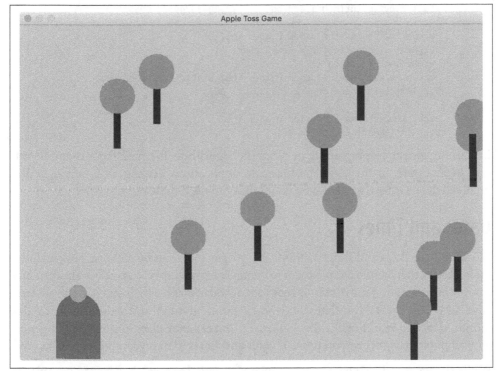

Figure 8-1. Randomly distributed trees

Try quitting the game and launching it again. You should see the trees in different places each time you run the application.

Big/Precise Numbers

If the long and double types are not large or precise enough for you, the java.math package provides two classes, BigInteger and BigDecimal, that support arbitrary-precision numbers. These full-featured classes have a bevy of methods for performing arbitrary-precision[5] math and precisely controlling rounding of remainders. In the following example, we use `BigDecimal` to add two very large numbers and then create a fraction with a 100-digit result:

```
long l1 = 9223372036854775807L; // Long.MAX_VALUE
long l2 = 9223372036854775807L;
System.out.println(l1 + l2); // -2 ! Not good.

try {
  BigDecimal bd1 = new BigDecimal("9223372036854775807");
  BigDecimal bd2 = new BigDecimal(9223372036854775807L);
  System.out.println(bd1.add(bd2) ); // 18446744073709551614

  BigDecimal numerator = new BigDecimal(1);
  BigDecimal denominator = new BigDecimal(3);
  BigDecimal fraction =
      numerator.divide(denominator, 100, BigDecimal.ROUND_UP);
  // 100-digit fraction = 0.333333 ... 3334
}
catch (NumberFormatException nfe) { }
catch (ArithmeticException ae) { }
```

If you implement cryptographic or scientific algorithms for fun, `BigInteger` is crucial. `BigDecimal`, in turn, can be found in applications dealing with currency and financial data. Other than that, you're not likely to need these classes.

Dates and Times

Working with dates and times without the proper tools can be a chore. Java includes three classes that handle simple cases for you. The `java.util.Date` class encapsulates a point in time. The `java.util.GregorianCalendar` class, which extends the abstract `java.util.Calendar`, translates between a point in time and calendar fields like month, day, and year. Finally, the `java.text.DateFormat` class knows how to generate and parse string representations of dates and times in many languages and locales.

While the `Date` and `Calendar` classes covered many use cases, they lacked granularity and were missing other features. Several third-party libraries cropped up, all aimed at making it easier for developers to work with dates and times and time durations. Java 8 provided much needed improvements in this area with the addition of the `java.time` package. The rest of this chapter explores this package, but you will still encounter many, many `Date` and `Calendar` examples in the wild, so it's useful to know

---

5 The `float` type is "single-precision," and `double` is, well, double-precision. (Hence its name!) A `double` can retain numbers with roughly twice the precision as a `float`. Arbitrary-precision simply means that you can have as many digits as you need before and after the decimal point. To be fair, NASA uses a value for π with only 15 digits of precision, which `double` can handle fine.

they exist. As always, the online docs (*https://oreil.ly/Behlk*) are an invaluable source for reviewing parts of the Java API we don't tackle here.

Local Dates and Times

The `java.time.LocalDate` class represents a date without time information for your local region. Think of an annual event such as the winter solstice on December 21. Similarly, `java.time.LocalTime` represents a time without any date information. Perhaps your alarm clock goes off at 7:15 every morning. The `java.time.LocalDateTime` stores both date and time values for things like appointments with your eye doctor (so you can keep reading books on Java). All of these classes offer static methods for creating new instances, either using appropriate numeric values with the method `of()` or by parsing strings with `parse()`. Let's pop into *jshell* and try creating a few examples:

```
jshell> import java.time.*

jshell> LocalDate.of(2019,5,4)
$2 ==> 2019-05-04

jshell> LocalDate.parse("2019-05-04")
$3 ==> 2019-05-04

jshell> LocalTime.of(7,15)
$4 ==> 07:15

jshell> LocalTime.parse("07:15")
$5 ==> 07:15

jshell> LocalDateTime.of(2019,5,4,7,0)
$6 ==> 2019-05-04T07:00

jshell> LocalDateTime.parse("2019-05-04T07:15")
$7 ==> 2019-05-04T07:15
```

Another great static method for creating these objects is `now()`, which provides the current date, time, or date-and-time as you might expect:

```
jshell> LocalTime.now()
$8 ==> 15:57:24.052935

jshell> LocalDate.now()
$9 ==> 2023-03-31

jshell> LocalDateTime.now()
$10 ==> 2023-03-31T15:57:37.909038
```

Great! After importing the `java.time` package, you can create instances of each of the `Local...` classes for specific moments or for "right now." You may have noticed the objects created with `now()` include seconds and nanoseconds in the time. You can supply those values to the `of()` and `parse()` methods if you want or need them. Not much exciting there, but once you have these objects, you can do a lot with them. Read on!

Comparing and Manipulating Dates and Times

One of the big advantages of using `java.time` classes is the consistent set of methods available for comparing and changing dates and times. For example, many chat applications will show you "how long ago" a message was sent. The `java.time.temporal` subpackage has just what we need: the `ChronoUnit` interface. It contains several date and time units such as `MONTHS`, `DAYS`, `HOURS`, `MINUTES`, etc. These units can be used to calculate differences. For example, we could calculate how long it takes us to create two example date-times in *jshell* using the `between()` method:

```
jshell> LocalDateTime first = LocalDateTime.now()
first ==> 2023-03-31T16:03:21.875196

jshell> LocalDateTime second = LocalDateTime.now()
second ==> 2023-03-31T16:03:33.175675

jshell> import java.time.temporal.*

jshell> ChronoUnit.SECONDS.between(first, second)
$12 ==> 11
```

A visual spot check shows that it did indeed take about 11 seconds to type in the line that created our `second` variable. Check out the docs for `ChronoUnit` (*https://oreil.ly/BhCr2*) for a complete list, but you get the full range, from nanoseconds up to millennia.

Those units can also help you manipulate dates and times with the `plus()` and `minus()` methods. To set a reminder for one week from today, for example:

```
jshell> LocalDate today = LocalDate.now()
today ==> 2023-03-31

jshell> LocalDate reminder = today.plus(1, ChronoUnit.WEEKS)
reminder ==> 2023-04-07
```

Neat! But this `reminder` example brings up another bit of manipulation you may need to perform from time to time. You might want a reminder at a particular time on the 7th. You can convert between dates, times, and date-times easily enough with the `atDate()` or `atTime()` methods:

```
jshell> LocalDateTime betterReminder = reminder.atTime(LocalTime.of(9,0))
betterReminder ==> 2023-04-07T09:00
```

Now you'll get a reminder at 9 A.M. Except, what if you set that reminder in Atlanta and then flew to San Francisco? When would the alarm go off? `LocalDateTime` is, well, local! So the `T09:00` portion is still 9 A.M. wherever you are when you run the program. But if you are handling something like scheduling a meeting, you can't ignore the different time zones involved. Fortunately the `java.time` package has thought of that, too.

Time Zones

The authors of the new `java.time` package encourage you to use the local variations of the time and date classes where possible. Adding support for time zones means adding complexity to your app—they want you to avoid that complexity if possible. But there are many scenarios where support for time zones is unavoidable. You can work with "zoned" dates and times using the `ZonedDateTime` and `OffsetDateTime` classes. The zoned variant understands named time zones and things like daylight saving adjustments. The offset variant is a constant, simple numeric offset from UTC/Greenwich.

Most user-facing uses of dates and times will use the named zone approach, so let's look at creating a zoned date-time. To attach a zone, we use the `ZoneId` class, which has the common `of()` static method for creating new instances. You can supply a region zone as a `String` to get your zoned value:

```
jshell> LocalDateTime piLocal = LocalDateTime.parse("2023-03-14T01:59")
piLocal ==> 2023-03-14T01:59

jshell> ZonedDateTime piCentral = piLocal.atZone(ZoneId.of("America/Chicago"))
piCentral ==> 2023-03-14T01:59-05:00[America/Chicago]
```

And now you can do things like make sure your friends in Paris can join you at the correct moment using the verbosely but aptly named `withZoneSameInstant()` method:

```
jshell> ZonedDateTime piAlaMode =
piCentral.withZoneSameInstant(ZoneId.of("Europe/Paris"))
piAlaMode ==> 2023-03-14T07:59+01:00[Europe/Paris]
```

If you have other friends who aren't conveniently located in a major metropolitan region but you want them to join as well, you can use the `systemDefault()` method of `ZoneId` to pick up their time zone programmatically:

```
jshell> ZonedDateTime piOther =
piCentral.withZoneSameInstant(ZoneId.systemDefault())
piOther ==> 2023-03-14T02:59-04:00[America/New_York]
```

We were running *jshell* on a laptop in the Eastern time zone of the United States. `piOther` comes out exactly as hoped. The `systemDefault()` zone ID is a very handy way to quickly tailor date-times from other zones to match what your user's clock and calendar are most likely to say. In commercial applications you may want to let the user tell you their preferred zone, but `systemDefault()` is usually a good guess.

Parsing and Formatting Dates and Times

For creating and showing our local and zoned date-times using strings, we've been relying on the default formats that follow ISO values. These generally work wherever we need to accept or display dates and times. But as every programmer knows, "generally" is not "always." Fortunately, you can use the utility class `java.time.for mat.DateTimeFormatter` to help with parsing input and formatting output.

The core of `DateTimeFormatter` centers on building a format string that governs both parsing and formatting. You build up your format with the pieces listed in Table 8-4. We are listing only a portion of the options available here, but these should get you through the bulk of the dates and times you will encounter. Note that case matters when using the characters mentioned!

Table 8-4. Popular and useful `DateTimeFormatter` elements

Character	Description	Example
a	am-pm-of-day	PM
d	day-of-month	10
E	day-of-week	Tue; Tuesday; T
G	era	BCE, CE
k	clock-hour-of-day (1-24)	24
K	hour-of-am-pm (0-11)	0
L	month-of-year	Jul; July; J
h	clock-hour-of-am-pm (1-12)	12
H	hour-of-day (0-23)	0
m	minute-of-hour	30
M	month-of-year	7; 07
s	second-of-minute	55
S	fraction-of-second	033954
u	year (without era)	2004; 04
y	year-of-era	2004; 04
z	time-zone name	Pacific Standard Time; PST
Z	zone-offset	+0000; -0800; -08:00

To put together a common US short format, for example, you could use the M, d, and y characters. You build the formatter using the static `ofPattern()` method. Now you can use (and reuse) the formatter with the `parse()` method of any of the date or time classes:

```
jshell> import java.time.format.DateTimeFormatter

jshell> DateTimeFormatter shortUS =
   ...> DateTimeFormatter.ofPattern("MM/dd/yy")
shortUS ==> Value(MonthOfYe ...) ... (YearOfEra,2,2,2000-01-01)

jshell> LocalDate valentines = LocalDate.parse("02/14/23", shortUS)
valentines ==> 2023-02-14

jshell> LocalDate piDay = LocalDate.parse("03/14/23", shortUS)
piDay ==> 2023-03-14
```

And as we mentioned earlier, the formatter works in both directions. Just use the format() method of your formatter to produce a string representation of your date or time:

```
jshell> LocalDate today = LocalDate.now()
today ==> 2023-12-14

jshell> shortUS.format(today)
$30 ==> "12/14/23"

jshell> shortUS.format(piDay)
$31 ==> "03/14/23"
```

Of course, formatters work for times and date-times as well!

```
jshell> DateTimeFormatter military =
   ...> DateTimeFormatter.ofPattern("HHmm")
military ==> Value(HourOfDay,2)Value(MinuteOfHour,2)

jshell> LocalTime sunset = LocalTime.parse("2020", military)
sunset ==> 20:20

jshell> DateTimeFormatter basic =
   ...> DateTimeFormatter.ofPattern("h:mm a")
basic ==> Value(ClockHourOfAmPm)': ... ,SHORT)

jshell> basic.format(sunset)
$42 ==> "8:20 PM"

jshell> DateTimeFormatter appointment =
DateTimeFormatter.ofPattern("h:mm a MM/dd/yy z")
appointment ==>
Value(ClockHourOfAmPm)':' ...
0-01-01)' 'ZoneText(SHORT)
```

Notice in the ZonedDateTime portion that follows that we put the time zone identifier (the z character) at the end—probably not where you were expecting it!

```
jshell> ZonedDateTime dentist =
ZonedDateTime.parse("10:30 AM 11/01/23 EST", appointment)
dentist ==> 2023-11-01T10:30-04:00[America/New_York]
```

```
jshell> ZonedDateTime nowEST = ZonedDateTime.now()
nowEST ==> 2023-12-14T09:55:58.493006-05:00[America/New_York]

jshell> appointment.format(nowEST)
$47 ==> "9:55 AM 12/14/23 EST"
```

We wanted to illustrate the power of these formats. You can design a format to accommodate a very wide range of input or output styles. Legacy data and poorly designed web forms come to mind as direct examples where `DateTimeFormatter` can help.

Parsing Errors

Even with all this parsing power at your fingertips, things will sometimes go wrong. Regrettably, the exceptions you see are often too vague to be immediately useful. Consider the following attempt to parse a time with hours, minutes, and seconds:

```
jshell> DateTimeFormatter withSeconds =
    ...> DateTimeFormatter.ofPattern("hh:mm:ss")
withSeconds ==>
Value(ClockHourOfAmPm,2)':' ...
Value(SecondOfMinute,2)

jshell> LocalTime.parse("03:14:15", withSeconds)
|  Exception java.time.format.DateTimeParseException:
|  Text '03:14:15' could not be parsed: Unable to obtain
|  LocalTime from TemporalAccessor: {MinuteOfHour=14, MilliOfSecond=0,
|  SecondOfMinute=15, NanoOfSecond=0, HourOfAmPm=3,
|  MicroOfSecond=0},ISO of type java.time.format.Parsed
|        at DateTimeFormatter.createError (DateTimeFormatter.java:2020)
|        at DateTimeFormatter.parse (DateTimeFormatter.java:1955)
|        at LocalTime.parse (LocalTime.java:463)
|        at (#33:1)
|  Caused by: java.time.DateTimeException:
|   Unable to obtain LocalTime from ...
|        at LocalTime.from (LocalTime.java:431)
|        at Parsed.query (Parsed.java:235)
|        at DateTimeFormatter.parse (DateTimeFormatter.java:1951)
|        ...
```

Yikes! Java will throw a `DateTimeParseException` any time it cannot parse the string input. Java will also throw the exception in cases like our example above; the fields were correctly parsed from the string, but they did not supply enough information to create a `LocalTime` object. It may not be obvious, but our time, "3:14:15," could be either mid-afternoon or very early in the morning. Our choice of the hh pattern for the hours turns out to be the culprit. We can either pick an hour pattern that uses an unambiguous 24-hour scale or we can add an explicit A.M./P.M. element:

```
jshell> DateTimeFormatter valid1 =
    ...> DateTimeFormatter.ofPattern("hh:mm:ss a")
```

```
valid1 ==> Value(ClockHourOfAmPm,...y,SHORT)

jshell> DateTimeFormatter valid2 =
   ...> DateTimeFormatter.ofPattern("HH:mm:ss")
valid2 ==> Value(HourOfDay,2)': ... Minute,2)

jshell> LocalTime piDay1 =
   ...> LocalTime.parse("03:14:15 PM", valid1)
piDay1 ==> 15:14:15

jshell> LocalTime piDay2 =
   ...> LocalTime.parse("03:14:15", valid2)
piDay2 ==> 03:14:15
```

If you ever get a `DateTimeParseException` but your input looks like a correct match for the format, double-check that your format itself includes everything necessary to create your date or time. One parting thought on these exceptions: you may need to use the nonmnemonic u character for parsing years if your dates don't naturally include an era designator such as CE.

There are many, *many* more details on `DateTimeFormatter`. For this, more than for most utility classes, it's worth a trip to read the docs online (*https://oreil.ly/rhosl*).

Formatting Dates and Times

Now that you know how to create, parse, and store dates and times, you need to display that handy data. Happily, you can build nice, human-readable strings using the same formatter you built to parse dates and times from strings. Remember our `withSeconds` and `military` formatters? You can pick up the current time and quickly turn it into either format, like this:

```
jshell> DateTimeFormatter withSeconds =
   ...> DateTimeFormatter.ofPattern("hh:mm:ss")
withSeconds ==> Value(ClockHou ... OfMinute,2)

jshell> DateTimeFormatter military =
   ...> DateTimeFormatter.ofPattern("HHmm")
military ==> Value(HourOfDay,2)Value(MinuteOfHour,2)

jshell> LocalTime t = LocalTime.now()
t ==> 09:17:34.356758

jshell> withSeconds.format(t)
$7 ==> "09:17:34"

jshell> military.format(t)
$8 ==> "0917"
```

You can use any date or time pattern you build from the parts shown in Table 8-4 to produce this formatted output. Hop into *jshell* and try creating a few formats. You can use the LocalTime.now() and LocalDate.now() methods to create some easy targets for your formatting tests.

Timestamps

One other popular date-time concept that java.time understands is timestamps. In any situation where you need to track the flow of information, you'll need a record of exactly when the information is produced or modified. You will still see the java.util.Date class used to store these moments in time, but the java.time.Instant class carries everything you need for a timestamp and comes with all the other benefits of the other classes in the java.time package:

```
jshell> Instant time1 = Instant.now()
time1 ==> 2019-12-14T15:38:29.033954Z

jshell> Instant time2 = Instant.now()
time2 ==> 2019-12-14T15:38:46.095633Z

jshell> time1.isAfter(time2)
$54 ==> false

jshell> time1.plus(3, ChronoUnit.DAYS)
$55 ==> 2019-12-17T15:38:29.033954Z
```

If dates or times appear in your work, the java.time package makes for a welcome helper. You have a mature, well-designed set of tools for dealing with this data—no third-party libraries needed!

Other Useful Utilities

We've looked at some of Java's building blocks, including strings and numbers, as well as one of the most popular combinations of those strings and numbers—dates—in the LocalDate and LocalTime classes. We hope this range of utilities has given you a sense of how Java works with many of the elements you are likely to encounter.

Be sure to read the documentation on the java.util, java.text, and java.time packages for more utilities that may come in handy. For example, you could look into using java.util.Random for generating the random coordinates of the trees in Figure 8-1. Sometimes "utility" work is actually complex and requires careful attention to detail. Searching online for code examples or even complete libraries written by other developers may speed up your own efforts.

Next up, we'll start building on these fundamental concepts. Java remains as popular as it is because it includes support for more advanced techniques in addition to the basics. One of those techniques is the "thread" features, which are baked right in. Threads provide better access to modern, powerful systems, keeping your applications performant even while handling many complex tasks. We'll show you how to take advantage of this signature feature in Chapter 9.

Review Questions

1. Which class contains the constant π? Do you need to import that class to use π?

2. Which package contains better replacements for the original `java.util.Date` class?

3. Which class should you use to format a date for user-friendly output?

4. What symbol would you use in a regular expression to help match the words "yes" and "yup"?

5. How would you convert the string "42" into the integer 42?

6. How would you compare two strings (such as "yes" and "YES") to see if they match, ignoring any capitalization?

7. Which operator concatenates strings?

Code Exercises

Let's revisit our graphical Hello Java application and upgrade it using some new utilities and string features discussed in this chapter. You can start with the `Hello Chapter8` class in the *exercises/ch08* folder. We want the program to support some command-line arguments for the message and initial position.

Your program should accept 0, 1, or 2 arguments:

- Zero arguments should place the text "Hello, utilities!" at the center to start.
- One argument should be treated as the message to display; it should be centered to start:
  — Remember that multiword messages must be enclosed in quotes.
  — If the message is the word `today`, your code should generate a formatted date to use as the message.
- Two arguments represent the message and initial coordinates for where to display it:
  — The coordinates should be a quoted string containing a pair of numbers separated by a comma and optional whitespace. These are all valid coordinate strings:

— 150,150

— 50, 50

— 100, 220

— The coordinates argument may also be the word `random`, meaning your code should generate a random initial position.

Here are some examples:

```
$ java HelloChapter8
// "Hello, utilities!" centered in the window
$ java HelloChapter8 "It works!"
// "It works!" centered in the window
$ java HelloChapter8 "I feel cornered" "20,20"
// "I feel cornered" in the upper left corner
```

If the user tries to pass three or more arguments, your code should generate an error message and exit.

Start by testing the number of arguments. If your program gets at least one argument, use the first argument for the message. If it gets two, you'll need to split the coordinates and convert them to numbers. If you get the `random` argument, be sure to generate random numbers that will keep the message visible. (You can assume some reasonable default length for the message; it's OK if some of a longer message gets truncated on the right side.)

Test out your solution with a few runs. Try different coordinates. Try the randomized option. Try the randomized option a few times successively to make sure the starting position really does change. What happens if you misspell `random` in the second argument?

For a further upgrade: try to write a regular expression to accept some variations on `random` while still ignoring the case:

- `random`
- `rand`
- `rndm`
- `r`

As always, you can find a few hints for this problem in Appendix B. Our solutions are in the *ch08/exercises* folder of the source code.

CHAPTER 9

Threads

We take for granted that modern computer systems can manage many applications and operating system (OS) tasks running concurrently and make it appear that all the software is running simultaneously. Most systems today have multiple processors or multiple cores or both, and they can achieve an impressive degree of concurrency. The OS still juggles applications at a higher level but turns its attention from one to the next so quickly that they also appear to run at once.

 In programming, *concurrent* operation denotes multiple, typically unrelated tasks running at the same time. Think of a fast-food cook preparing multiple orders on a grill. *Parallel* operation usually involves breaking up a large task into related subtasks that can be run alongside each other to produce the final result more quickly. Our cook could prepare a bacon double cheeseburger "in parallel" by tossing two patties and some bacon on the grill at the same time. In either case, programmers talk more generally about these tasks and subtasks occurring *simultaneously*. That's not to say everything starts and stops at the same exact instant, but it does mean that the execution times for those tasks overlap.

In the old days, the unit of concurrency for an operating system was the application or *process*. To the OS, a process was more or less a black box that decided what to do on its own. If an application required greater concurrency, it could get it only by running multiple processes and communicating between them, but this was a heavyweight approach and not very elegant.

Later, operating systems added the concept of threads. Conceptually, a *thread* is a flow of control within a program. (You may have heard of a "thread of execution," for example.) Threads provide fine-grained concurrency within a process under the application's own control. Threads have existed for a long time but have historically been tricky to use. The Java concurrency utilities address common patterns and practices in multithreaded applications and raise them to the level of tangible methods and classes. Collectively, this means that Java supports threading at both higher and lower levels.

This broad support makes it easier for programmers to write multithreaded code, and for compilers and runtimes to optimize that code. It also means that Java's APIs take full advantage of threading, so it's important that you gain some degree of familiarity with these concepts early in your exploration of Java. Not all developers will need to write applications that explicitly use threads or concurrency, but most will use some feature that involves them.

Threads are integral to the design of many Java APIs, especially those involved in client-side applications, graphics, and sound. For example, when we look at GUI programming in Chapter 12, you'll see that a component's paint() method isn't called directly by the application but rather by a separate drawing thread within the Java runtime system. At any given time, many such background threads may be performing activities alongside your application—yet you still get timely updates to your screen. On the server side, Java threads are there as well, servicing every request and running your application. It's important to understand how your code fits into that environment.

In this chapter, we'll talk about writing applications that create and use their own threads explicitly. We'll talk about the low-level thread support built into the Java language first and then discuss the java.util.concurrent thread utilities package. We'll also tackle the new virtual threads previewed in Java 19 under the moniker of Project Loom.

Introducing Threads

A thread is similar to the notion of a *process*, or running program, except that different threads within the same application are much more closely related and share much of the same state than different programs running on the same machine. It's kind of like a golf course that many golfers use at the same time. The threads cooperate to share a working area. They take turns and wait for other threads. They have access to the same objects, including static and instance variables, within their application. However, threads have their own copies of local variables, just as players share the golf course or a golf cart but do not share clubs or balls.

Multiple threads in an application have the same problems as golfers on a course—in a word, *synchronization*. Just as you can't have two sets of players playing the same green at the same time, you can't have several threads trying to access the same variables without some kind of coordination. Otherwise, someone is bound to get hurt. A thread can reserve the right to use an object until it's finished with its task, just as a golf party gets exclusive rights to the green until each of that party's players finishes. And a thread that is more important can raise its priority, asserting its right to "play through."

The devil is in the details, of course, and those details have long made threads difficult to use. Fortunately, Java makes creating, controlling, and coordinating threads simpler by integrating some of these concepts directly into the language.

It's common to stumble over threads when you first work with them. Creating a thread will exercise many of your new Java skills all at once. Just remember that two players are always involved in running a thread: a Java `Thread` object that represents the thread itself, and an arbitrary target object that contains the method the thread will execute. Later, we will see ways to combine these two roles, but those approaches just change the packaging, not the relationship.

The Thread Class and the Runnable Interface

All execution in Java is associated with a `Thread` object, beginning with a "main" thread that the JVM starts to launch your application. A new thread is born when you create an instance of the `java.lang.Thread` class. The `Thread` object represents a real thread in the Java interpreter and serves as a handle for controlling and coordinating its execution. With it, you can start the thread, wait for it to complete, cause it to sleep for a time, or interrupt its activity.

The constructor for the `Thread` class accepts information about where the thread should begin its execution. We would like to tell it what method to run. There are a number of ways to do this. The classic approach uses the `java.lang.Runnable` interface to mark an object that contains a "runnable" method.

`Runnable` defines a single, general-purpose `run()` method:

```
public interface Runnable {
    abstract public void run();
}
```

Every thread begins its life by executing the `run()` method in a `Runnable` object, which is the "target object" passed to the thread's constructor. The `run()` method can contain any code, but it must be public, take no arguments, have no return value, and throw no checked exceptions.

Any class that contains an appropriate `run()` method can declare that it implements the `Runnable` interface. An instance of this class becomes a runnable object that can serve as the target of a new thread. If you don't want to put the `run()` method directly in your object (and very often you don't), you can always make an adapter class that serves as the Runnable for you. The adapter's run() method can then call any method it wants after the thread is started. We'll show examples of these options later.

Creating and starting threads

A newly born thread remains idle until we give it a figurative slap on the bottom by calling its start() method. The thread then wakes up and proceeds to execute the run() method of its target object. start() can be called only once in the lifetime of a thread. Once a thread starts, it continues running until the target object's run() method either returns or throws an unchecked exception.

The following class, Animator, implements a run() method to drive a drawing loop. We could use something similar in our game to update the playing Field:

```
class Animator implements Runnable {
  boolean animating = true;

  public void run() {
    while (animating) {
      // move active apples one "frame"
      // repaint the field
      // pause
      // ...
    }
  }
}
```

To use it, create a Thread object, pass it an instance of Animator as its target object, and invoke its start() method:

```
Animator myAnimator = new Animator();
Thread myThread = new Thread(myAnimator);
myThread.start();
```

We created an instance of our Animator class and passed it as the argument to the constructor for myThread. As shown in Figure 9-1, when we call the start() method, myThread begins to execute Animator's run() method.

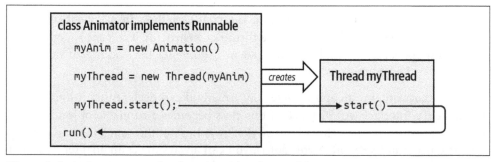

Figure 9-1. Animator as an implementation of Runnable

Let the show begin!

A natural-born thread

The `Runnable` interface lets you make an arbitrary object the target of a thread, as in the previous example. This is the most important general usage of the `Thread` class. In most situations where you need to use threads, you'll create a class (possibly a simple adapter class) that implements the `Runnable` interface.

Another design option for creating a thread makes our target class a subclass of a type that is already runnable. As it turns out, the `Thread` class itself conveniently implements the `Runnable` interface; it has its own `run()` method, which we can override directly to do our bidding:

```
class Animator extends Thread {
  boolean animating = true;

  public void run() {
    while (animating) {
      // draw Frames
      // do other stuff ...
    }
  }
}
```

The skeleton of our `Animator` class looks much the same as before, except that our class is now a subclass of `Thread`. To go along with this scheme, the default constructor of the `Thread` class makes itself the default target—that is, by default, the `Thread` executes its own `run()` method when we call the `start()` method, as shown in Figure 9-2. Now our subclass can just override the `run()` method in the `Thread` class. (`Thread` itself defines an empty `run()` method.)

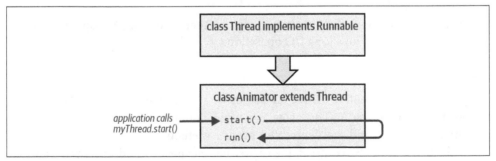

Figure 9-2. Animator as a subclass of Thread

Next, we create an instance of `Animator` and call its `start()` method (which it also inherited from `Thread`):

```
Animator bouncy = new Animator();
bouncy.start();
```

Extending `Thread` may seem like a convenient way to bundle a thread and its target `run()` method. However, this approach often isn't the best design. If you extend `Thread` to implement a thread, you are saying you need a new type of object that is a kind of `Thread`, which exposes all of the public methods of the `Thread` class. While there is something satisfying about taking an object that's primarily concerned with performing a task and making it a `Thread`, the actual situations where you'll want to create a subclass of `Thread` should not be very common. In most cases, it is more natural to let the requirements of your program dictate the class structure and use `Runnable`s to connect the execution and logic of your program.

Controlling Threads

Now that you have seen the `start()` method used to begin executing a new thread, let's look at instance methods that let you explicitly control a thread's behavior at runtime:

`Thread.sleep()` *method*
> Causes the currently executing thread to wait for a designated period of time (give or take), without consuming much (or possibly any) CPU time.

`wait()` *and* `join()` *methods*
> Coordinate the execution of two or more threads. We'll discuss them in detail when we talk about thread synchronization later in this chapter.

`interrupt()` *method*
> Wakes up a thread that is sleeping in a `sleep()` or `wait()` operation or is otherwise blocked on a long I/O operation.[1]

Deprecated methods

We should also mention three deprecated thread-control methods: `stop()`, `suspend()`, and `resume()`. The `stop()` method complements `start()`; it destroys the thread. `start()` and the deprecated `stop()` method can be called only once in the thread's life cycle. By contrast, the deprecated `suspend()` and `resume()` methods arbitrarily pause and then restart the execution of a thread.

---

1 Historically, `interrupt()` has not worked consistently in all Java implementations.

Although these deprecated methods still exist in the latest version of Java (and will probably be there forever), they shouldn't be used in new code development. The problem with both stop() and suspend() is that they seize control of a thread's execution in an uncoordinated, harsh way.

You can create and monitor a few variables as a better way to affect the execution of a thread (if these variables are boolean, you might see them referred to as "flags"). The early thread examples in this book use this technique in one way or another. Later examples will introduce some of the other control features available through the concurrency classes.

The sleep() method

Programmers often need to tell a thread to sit idle, or "sleep," for some period of time. You may need to wait for some external resource to become available, for example. Even our simple animation threads takes small pauses between frames. While a thread is asleep, or otherwise blocked from input of some kind, it doesn't consume CPU time or compete with other threads for processing. For such pauses, we can call the static method Thread.sleep(), which affects the currently executing thread. The call causes the thread to go idle for a specified number of milliseconds:

```
try {
    // The current thread
    Thread.sleep(1000);
} catch (InterruptedException e) {
    // someone woke us up prematurely
}
```

The sleep() method may throw an InterruptedException if it is interrupted by another thread via the interrupt() method (more below). As you saw in the previous code, the thread can catch this exception and take the opportunity to perform some action—such as checking a variable to determine whether or not the thread should exit—and then go back to sleep.

The join(), wait(), and notify() methods

If you need to coordinate a thread's activities by waiting for another thread to complete its task, you can use the join() method. Calling a thread's join() method causes that thread to block until the target thread completes. Alternatively, you can call join() with a number of milliseconds to wait as an argument. In this form, the calling thread waits until either the target thread completes or the specified period elapses. This is a very coarse form of thread synchronization.

If you need to coordinate a thread's activities with some other resource, such as checking the state of a file or network connection, you can use the wait() and notify() methods. Calling wait() on a thread will pause it, similar to using join(), but it will remain paused either until it gets `interrupt()`-ed by some other thread, or until you call `notify()` on the thread yourself.

Java supports more general and powerful mechanisms for coordinating thread activity in the `java.util.concurrent` package. We'll show you more of this package later in the chapter.

The interrupt() method

The `interrupt()` method does more or less what it says on the tin. It interrupts the normal flow of execution for a thread. If that thread was idle in a `sleep()`, `wait()`, or lengthy I/O operation, it will wake up. When you interrupt a thread, its *interrupt status* flag is set. You can test this flag with the `isInterrupted()` method. You can also use an alternate form, `isInterrupted(boolean)`, to indicate whether or not you want the thread to clear its interrupt status after retrieving the current value.

While you probably won't use `interrupt()` that often, it can definitely come in handy. If you have ever grown impatient while a desktop application tries—and fails —to connect to a server or database, you have experienced one of those moments where an interruption might be the right thing.

Let's simulate this scenario with a small graphical application. We'll show a label on the screen and move it to a new, random location every five seconds. During that five-second pause, a click anywhere on the screen will interrupt the pause. We'll change the message and then start the random move cycle again. You can run the full example from *ch09/examples/Interruption.java*, but Figure 9-3 highlights the flow and effect of calling `interrupt()`.

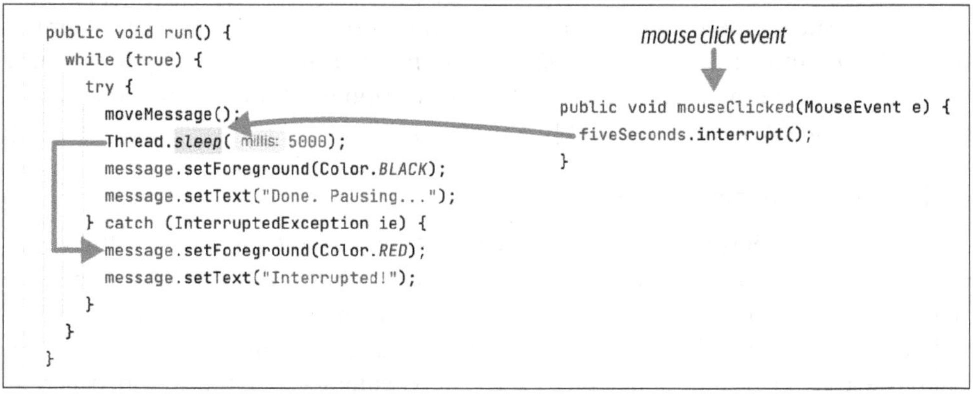

```
public void run() {                          mouse click event
  while (true) {
    try {
      moveMessage();                         public void mouseClicked(MouseEvent e) {
      Thread.sleep( millis: 5000);             fiveSeconds.interrupt();
      message.setForeground(Color.BLACK);    }
      message.setText("Done. Pausing...");
    } catch (InterruptedException ie) {
      message.setForeground(Color.RED);
      message.setText("Interrupted!");
    }
  }
}
```

Figure 9-3. Interrupting a thread

Revisiting Animation with Threads

Managing animations is a common task in graphical interfaces. Sometimes the animations are subtle transitions; other times they are the focus of the application, as with our apple tossing game. We'll look at two ways to handle the animation: using simple threads alongside the sleep() functions, and using a timer. Pairing one of those options with some type of stepping or "next frame" function is a popular approach that is also easy to understand.

You can use a thread similar to "Creating and starting threads" on page 276 to produce real animation. The basic idea is to paint or position all of your animated objects, pause, move them to their next spots, and then repeat. Let's take a look at how we draw some pieces of our game field without animation first. We'll include a new List for any active apples in addition to the existing lists for trees and hedges. You can pull up this code in your editor from the *ch09/examples/game* folder:

```
// From the Field class...
  protected void paintComponent(Graphics g) {
    g.setColor(fieldColor);
    g.fillRect(0,0, getWidth(), getHeight());
    physicist.draw(g);
    for (Tree t : trees) { t.draw(g); }
    for (Hedge h : hedges) { h.draw(g); }
    physicist.draw(g);
    for (Apple a : apples) { a.draw(g); }
  }

// And from the Apple class...
  public void draw(Graphics g) {
    // Make sure our apple will be red, then paint it!
    g.setColor(Color.RED);
    g.fillOval(x, y, scaledLength, scaledLength);
  }
```

We start by painting the background field, then the trees and hedges, then our physicist, and finally any apples. Painting the apples last guarantees that they will show "on top" of the other elements.

What changes on the screen as you play? There are really only two "moveable" items: the apple our physicist is aiming, and any apples actively flying after being tossed. The physicist aims in response to user input (by moving the mouse or clicking a button). That doesn't require separate animation, so we'll add this functionality in Chapter 12. For now, we can concentrate on handling flying apples.

Our game's animation step should move every apple that is active, according to the rules of gravity. First, we add a `toss()` method to our `Apple` class where we can set up the initial conditions for our apple using information from our physicist. (Since the physicist is not yet interactive, we'll fake some data.) Then we make one move for a given apple in the `step()` method:

```
// File: ch09/examples/game/Apple.java

    // Parameters provided by the physicist
    public void toss(float angle, float velocity) {
      lastStep = System.currentTimeMillis();
      double radians = angle / 180 * Math.PI;
      velocityX = (float)(velocity * Math.cos(radians) / mass);
      // Start negative since "up" means smaller values of y
      velocityY = (float)(-velocity * Math.sin(radians) / mass);
    }

    public void step() {
      // Make sure the apple is still moving
      // using our lastStep tracker as a sentinel
      if (lastStep > 0) {
        // Apply the law of gravity to the apple's vertical position
        long now = System.currentTimeMillis();
        float slice = (now - lastStep) / 1000.0f;
        velocityY = velocityY + (slice * Field.GRAVITY);
        int newX = (int)(centerX + velocityX);
        int newY = (int)(centerY + velocityY);
        setPosition(newX, newY);
      }
    }
```

We start by calculating how fast the apple will move (the `velocityX` and `velocityY` variables) in the `toss()` method. In our `step()` method, we update the apple's position based on those two velocities, then adjust the vertical velocity based on how strong our gravity is. It's not very fancy, but it will produce a nice arc for the apples. We then put that code in a loop that will do the update calculations, repaint the field and apples, pause, and repeat:

```
// File: ch09/examples/game/Field.java

// duration of an animation frame in milliseconds
public static final int STEP = 40;

// ...
// A simple inner class with our run() method
class Animator implements Runnable {
  public void run() {
    // "animating" is a global variable that allows us
    // to stop animating and conserve resources
    // if there are no active apples to move
    while (animating) {
```

```
        System.out.println("Stepping " + apples.size() +
            " apples");
        for (Apple a : apples) {
          a.step();
        }
        // Reach back to our outer class instance to repaint
        Field.this.repaint();
        // And get rid of any apples on the ground
        cullFallenApples();
        try {
          Thread.sleep(STEP);
        } catch (InterruptedException ie) {
          System.err.println("Animation interrupted");
          animating = false;
        }
      }
    }
  }
}
```

We'll use this implementation of Runnable in a simple thread. Our Field class will keep an instance of the thread around and contains the following simple start method:

```
// File: ch09/examples/game/Field.java
  Thread animationThread;

  // other state and methods ...

  void startAnimation() {
    animationThread = new Thread(new Animator());
    animationThread.start();
  }
```

We'll discuss events in "Events" on page 413; you'll use those events to launch an apple on command. For now, we'll just launch one apple automatically, as shown in Figure 9-4.

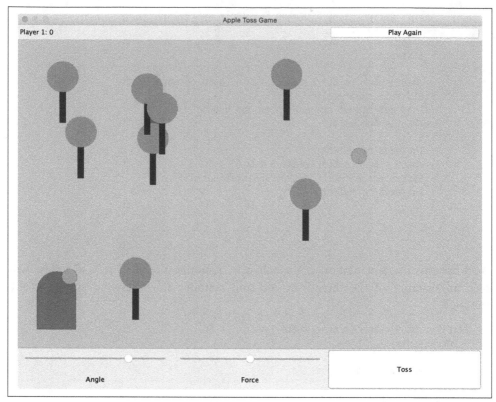

Figure 9-4. Tossable apples in action

It doesn't look like much as a still screenshot, but it is amazing in person. ;^)

Death of a Thread

All good things come to an end. A thread continues to execute until one of the following three things happens:

- It explicitly returns from its target `run( )` method.
- It encounters an uncaught runtime exception.
- The nasty, deprecated `stop( )` method is called.

What happens if none of these things occurs, and the `run( )` method for a thread never terminates? The thread can live on, even after the code that created it has finished. You have to be aware of how threads eventually terminate, or your application can end up leaving orphaned threads running that consume resources unnecessarily, or even keep the application alive when it would otherwise quit.

In many cases, you want background threads that do simple, periodic tasks in an application. You can create one of these background workers using the `setDaemon()` method to mark a thread as a *daemon* thread. Daemon threads can terminate like other threads, but if the application that started them is quitting, they should be killed and discarded when no other nondaemon application threads remain.[2] Normally, the Java interpreter continues to run until all threads have completed. But when daemon threads are the only threads still alive, the interpreter will exit.

Here's a "devilish" outline using daemon threads:

```
class Devil extends Thread {
  Devil() {
    setDaemon(true);
    start();
  }
  public void run() {
    // perform some tasks
  }
}
```

In this example, the `Devil` thread sets its daemon status when it is created. If any `Devil` threads remain when our application is otherwise complete, the runtime system terminates them for us. We don't have to worry about cleaning them up.

One final note about killing threads gracefully. New developers often encounter a common problem the first time they create an application using a graphical Swing component: their application never exits. The Java VM seems to hang indefinitely after everything is finished and the application window is closed. Java creates a UI thread to process input and painting events. This UI thread is not a daemon thread, so it doesn't exit automatically when other application threads have completed. The developer must call `System.exit()` explicitly. If you think about it, this makes sense. Because most GUI applications are event-driven and wait for user input, they would otherwise exit after their startup code completes.

Virtual Threads

Previewed in Java 19 and finalized in Java 21, Project Loom[3] brings lightweight, virtual threads to Java. One of the main goals of Project Loom is to improve the thread ecosystem in Java so that developers can put less energy into keeping multithreaded applications stable and more energy into solving higher-level problems.

---

2 The term daemon (often pronounced day-mun in Unix circles) was inspired by Maxwell's demon (*https://oreil.ly/YGQMt*) and refers to the Greek term for a lesser deity, not a malevolent spirit.

3 Many Java enhancements start out as works-in-progress with spiffy names like "Loom."

Preview Feature Tangent

What do we mean by "previewed in Java 19"? Starting with Java 12, Oracle began introducing some language features as *previews*. These preview features are well-specified and fully implemented but not wholly baked. Oracle may still make substantial modifications in future releases. Eventually, these features will either become permanent parts of the JDK or they will be removed. Oracle produces a language update page for each new release of Java that contains a nice history of recent changes to the language as well as an overview of preview features (*https://oreil.ly/5MuMw*) in general.

Because any given preview feature may end up being dropped from Java, Oracle requires you to include special flags when you compile or run an application that uses it. This requirement is a small guardrail to make sure you don't accidentally use code that may not work with a future release of Java.

Configuring IDEs for preview features

If you use an IDE for the demos and exercises, you may need to configure it to support preview features. IntelliJ IDEA, for example, does not support preview features by default. You need to change a setting in the File → Project Structure dialog, as shown in Figure 9-5.

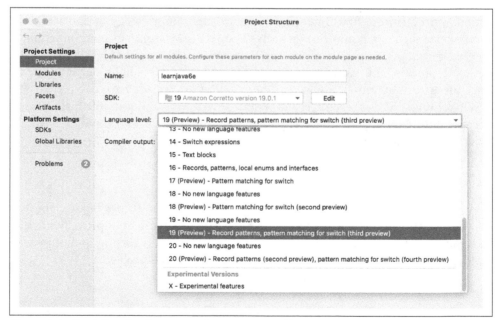

Figure 9-5. Enabling Java's preview features in IntelliJ IDEA

After choosing the version of Java you want in the SDK drop-down, you can enable preview feature support by choosing the appropriate option under the Language level drop-down. (The features that IDEA lists next to the version numbers is not an exhaustive list.) Click OK after setting the language level, and IDEA should be ready to compile and run any code with preview features.

Renaming preview source files

The VirtualDemo class (*ch09/examples/VirtualDemo.java.preview*) uses a virtual thread to pause briefly before issuing our favorite "Hello Java" greeting. Before you can compile or run it, you'll need to rename it. We added the *.preview* suffix to any file that includes a preview feature in the code. The suffix stops IDEs like IntelliJ IDEA from proactively compiling them until you've had a chance to configure preview support, as we mentioned in the previous section.

You can use the context (right-click) menu in IntelliJ IDEA to rename the file under the Refactor menu item. You can also rename a file quickly from a terminal in Linux or macOS using the *mv* command:

```
% cd ch09/examples
% mv VirtualDemo.java.preview VirtualDemo.java
% cd ../..
```

In a Windows terminal or command prompt, you can use the *rename* command:

```
C:\> cd ch09\examples
C:\> rename VirtualDemo.java.preview VirtualDemo.java
C:\> cd ..\..
```

Compiling classes with preview features

Oracle added a pair of command-line options for compiling code with preview features. If you try to compile our VirtualDemo source file with Java 19, for example, you'll likely see an error similar to this:

```
% javac --version
javac 19.0.1

% javac VirtualDemo.java
VirtualDemo.java:4: error: startVirtualThread(Runnable)
 is a preview API and is disabled by default.
    Thread thread = Thread.startVirtualThread(runnable);
                          ^
  (use --enable-preview to enable preview APIs)
```

The error gives us a hint as to how we should proceed. Let's try adding the suggested flag and compiling again:

```
% javac --enable-preview VirtualDemo.java
error: --enable-preview must be used with either -source or --release
```

Rats! Another, different error. At least it also includes some hints. To compile, you need to provide *two* flags: `--enable-preview` and then either `-source` or `--release`.[4] The compiler uses `-source` to specify which language rules apply to the source code being compiled. (The compiled bytecode is still targeted at the same version of Java as your JDK.) You can use the `--release` option to specify both the source version and the bytecode version.

While there are many scenarios where you might need to compile for older systems, preview features are meant for use with the current version of the JDK. As such, when we use any preview features in the book, we'll be pairing `--enable-preview` with `--release` and simply give the same release version as our version of Java. Returning to our virtual thread preview feature, for example, we can use Java 19 to try it out. Our final, correct *javac* call looks like this:

```
% javac --version
javac 19.0.1

% javac --enable-preview --release 19 VirtualDemo.java
Note: VirtualDemo.java uses preview features of Java SE 19.
Note: Recompile with -Xlint:preview for details.
```

The "notes" that appear after your compilation completes are purely informational. They remind you that your code relies on an unstable feature that may not be available in the future. The note is not meant to dissuade you from using these features, but if you are planning to share your code with other users or developers, you will have some extra compatibility contraints to remember.

If you're curious, you can use the `-Xlint:preview` option mentioned in the notes to see exactly what preview code caused the warning:

```
src$ javac --enable-preview --release 19 -Xlint:preview VirtualDemo.java
VirtualDemo.java:4: warning: [preview] startVirtualThread(Runnable)
 is a preview API and may be removed in a future release.
    Thread thread = Thread.startVirtualThread(runnable);
                         ^
1 warning
```

No surprises there, but then again, this is just a tiny demo program. With larger programs or code developed in teams, that extra `-Xlint:preview` flag can be very handy.

---

4 Sadly, the single- versus double-dash prefixes on these options are not typos. Command-line arguments have quite a storied history in their own right, and Java and its tools are old enough to have inherited some of the legacy patterns while still needing to accommodate modern approaches. Most options work with either prefix, but occasionally you have to obey what seems like an unwritten rule. When in doubt, tools like *javac* support another option: `-help` (or `--help`). Supplying that argument will print out a concise list of options and relevant details.

Running preview class files

Running Java classes that include preview features also requires the `--enable-preview` flag. If you try to run `VirtualDemo` with Java 19 as you would any other class, you'll get an error like this:

```
% java VirtualDemo
Error: LinkageError occurred while loading main class VirtualDemo
        java.lang.UnsupportedClassVersionError: Preview features are not
        enabled for VirtualDemo (class file version 63.65535).
        Try running with '--enable-preview'
```

Again, you can use the flag mentioned in the error, `--enable-preview`, and you're good to go:

```
% java --enable-preview VirtualDemo
Hello virtual thread! ID: 20
```

If you want to play with a preview feature in *jshell*, you can also provide the same `--enable-preview` flag:

```
% jshell --enable-preview
```

Including that flag would allow a Java 19 *jshell* session to use virtual threads, just as it allowed us to run our demo program above.

A Quick Comparison

The Loom team designed its virtual threads to be easy to use if you already have some skill with Java threads. Let's rework the trivial thread example that we used to test the `--enable-preview` flag to show both types of thread:

```
public class VirtualDemo2 {
  public static void main(String args[]) throws Exception {
    Runnable runnable = new Runnable() {
      public void run() {
        Thread t = Thread.currentThread();
        System.out.println("Hello thread! " +
          (t.isVirtual() ? "virtual " : "platform ") +
          "ID: " + t.threadId());
      }
    };
    Thread thread1 = new Thread(runnable);
    thread1.start();
    Thread thread2 = Thread.startVirtualThread(runnable);
    thread1.join();
    thread2.join();
  }
}
```

In this reworking, we expanded our anonymous `Runnable` inner class to do a little sleuthing on the current thread. We print out the thread's identification number and whether or not it's a virtual thread. But look how similar (and simple) the lines are that launch the two threads: they both accept our `runnable` object and "fit" in the `Thread` class. For developers with established code, switching to use these virtual threads should be straightforward. Here's the output after compiling and running (with the appropriate preview flags, of course):

```
$ javac --enable-preview --source 19 VirtualDemo2.java
Note: VirtualDemo.java uses preview features of Java SE 19.
Note: Recompile with -Xlint:preview for details.

$ java --enable-preview VirtualDemo2
Hello thread! virtual ID: 21
Hello thread! platform ID: 20
```

Both threads run as expected. One thread does indeed report itself as a virtual thread. We use the word *platform* to describe the other thread, since that's what the Oracle documentation calls them. Platform threads represent a direct, one-to-one relationship with the *native* threads your operating system (the platform) provides. Virtual threads, on the other hand, have an indirect, many-to-one relationship with native threads from the operating system, as shown in Figure 9-6.

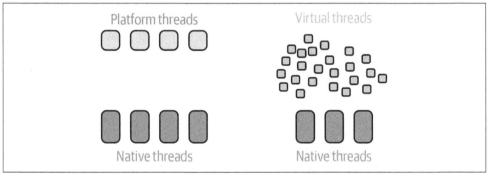

Figure 9-6. Platform and virtual threads map differently to native threads

This separation is one of the key design features of virtual threads. It allows Java to have many (many!) threads going at once without the performance costs of creating and managing corresponding native threads. Virtual threads are designed to be inexpensive to create and highly performant once they are up and running.

Synchronization

Every thread has a mind of its own. Normally, a thread goes about its business without any regard for what other threads in the application are doing. Threads may be *time-sliced*, which means they can run in arbitrary spurts and bursts as directed by the OS. On a multiprocessor or multicore system, it is even possible for many different threads to be running simultaneously on different CPUs. This section is about coordinating the activities of two or more threads so that they can work together and use the same variables and methods (without colliding, like players on the golf course).

Java provides a few simple structures for synchronizing the activities of threads. They are all based on the concept of monitors, a widely used synchronization scheme. You don't have to know the details about how monitors work to be able to use them, but it may help you to have Figure 9-7 in mind.

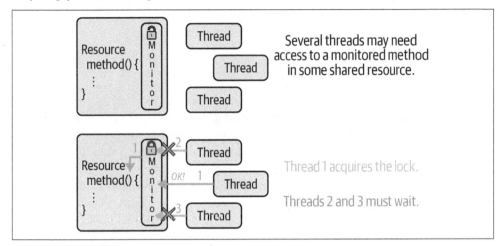

Figure 9-7. Synchronizing access with a monitor

A *monitor* is essentially a lock. The lock is attached to a resource that many threads may need to access but that should be accessed by only one thread at a time. It's very much like a restroom with a lock on the door; if it's unlocked, you can enter, and you lock the door while you are using it. If the resource is not being used, a thread can acquire the lock and access the resource. When the thread is done, it relinquishes the lock, just as you unlock the restroom door and leave it open for the next person (or thread).

If another thread already has the lock for the resource, however, all other threads must wait until the current thread is done and releases the lock. This is just like when the restroom is occupied when you arrive: you have to wait until the current user is done and unlocks the door.

Java makes it fairly easy to synchronize access to resources. The language handles setting up and acquiring locks; all you need to do is specify the resources to synchronize.

Serializing Access to Methods

The most common reason to synchronize threads in Java is to serialize their access to a resource (like an object or variable)—in other words, to make sure that only one thread at a time can manipulate that object.[5] In Java, every class and every instance of a class has its own lock. The synchronized keyword marks places where a thread must acquire the lock before proceeding.

For example, suppose we implement a SpeechSynthesizer class that contains a say() method. We don't want multiple threads calling say() at the same time because we wouldn't be able to understand anything the synthesizer says. So we mark the say() method as synchronized, which means that a thread must acquire the lock on the SpeechSynthesizer object before it can speak:

```java
class SpeechSynthesizer {
  synchronized void say(String words) {
    // speak the supplied words
  }
}
```

When say() has completed, the calling thread gives up the lock, which allows the next waiting thread to acquire the lock and run the method. It doesn't matter whether the thread is owned by the SpeechSynthesizer itself or some other object; every thread must acquire the same lock from the SpeechSynthesizer instance. If say() were a class (static) method instead of an instance method, we could still mark it as synchronized. In this case, because no instance object is involved, the lock is on the SpeechSynthesizer class object itself.

Often, you want to synchronize multiple methods of the same class so that only one method modifies or examines the data in the class at a time. All static synchronized methods in a class use the same class-object lock. By the same token, all instance methods in a class use the same instance-object lock. This guarantees that only one of a set of synchronized methods is running at a time. For example, a SpreadSheet class might contain several instance variables that represent cell values, as well as some methods that manipulate all of the cells in a row:

```java
class SpreadSheet {
  int cellA1, cellA2, cellA3;

  synchronized int sumRow() {
    return cellA1 + cellA2 + cellA3;
  }

  synchronized void setRow(int a1, int a2, int a3) {
    cellA1 = a1;
    cellA2 = a2;
```

---

5 Don't confuse the term *serialize* in this context with Java *object serialization*, which is a mechanism for making objects persistent. The underlying meaning (to place one thing after another) is the same, however. In the case of object serialization, the object's data is laid out, byte for byte, in a certain order. With threads, each thread gets access to the synchronized resource in turn.

```
    cellA3 = a3;
  }
  // other spreadsheet stuff ...
}
```

The methods setRow() and sumRow() both access the cell values. You can see that problems might arise if one thread was changing the values of the variables in setRow() at the same moment another thread was reading the values in sumRow(). To prevent this, we mark both methods as synchronized. When threads encounter synchronized resources, only one thread runs at a time. If a thread is in the middle of executing setRow() when another thread attempts to call sumRow(), the second thread must wait until the first one finishes executing setRow() before it runs sumRow(). This synchronization allows us to preserve the consistency of the Spread Sheet. The best part is that all this locking and waiting is handled by Java; it's invisible to the programmer.

In addition to synchronizing entire methods, the synchronized keyword can be used in a special construct to guard smaller blocks of code inside a method. In this form, it also takes an explicit argument that specifies which object's lock to acquire:

```
synchronized (myObject) {
  // Functionality that needs exclusive access to resources
}
```

This synchronized block can appear in any method. When a thread reaches it, the thread must acquire the lock on myObject before proceeding. In this way, we can synchronize methods (or parts of methods) in different classes in the same way as methods in the same class.

This means that a synchronized instance method is equivalent to a method with its statements synchronized on the current object:

```
synchronized void myMethod () {
  // method body
}
```

is equivalent to:

```
void myMethod () {
  synchronized (this) {
    // method body
  }
}
```

We can demonstrate the basics of synchronization with a classic "producer/consumer" scenario. Say we have some producers creating new resources and consumers grabbing and using those same resources: for instance a series of web crawlers picking up images online. The "producer" in this could be a thread (or multiple threads) doing the actual work of loading and parsing web pages to look for images and their URLs. We can tell it to place those URLs in a common queue. The "consumer" thread(s) would pick up the next URL in the queue and download the image to the filesystem or a database. We won't try to do all of the real I/O here (more on URLs and networking in Chapter 13), but let's set up some producing and consuming threads to show you how the synchronization works.

Synchronizing a queue of URLs

Let's look first at the queue where the URLs will be stored. It's just a list where we can append URLs (as Strings) to the end and pull them off from the front. We'll use a LinkedList similar to the ArrayList we saw in Chapter 7. We want a structure designed for efficient access and manipulation:

```
package ch09.examples;

import java.util.LinkedList;

public class URLQueue {
  LinkedList<String> urlQueue = new LinkedList<>();

  public synchronized void addURL(String url) {
    urlQueue.add(url);
  }

  public synchronized String getURL() {
    if (!urlQueue.isEmpty()) {
      return urlQueue.removeFirst();
    }
    return null;
  }

  public boolean isEmpty() {
    return urlQueue.isEmpty();
  }
}
```

Note that not every method is synchronized! Any thread can ask if the queue is empty without holding up other threads that might be adding or removing items. This *does* mean that isEmpty() might report a wrong answer—if the timing of different threads is exactly wrong. Fortunately, our system is somewhat fault-tolerant, so the efficiency of not locking the queue just to check its size wins out over more perfect knowledge.[6]

---

6 Even with the ability to tolerate minor discrepancies in the state of objects, modern, multicore systems can wreak havoc without perfect knowledge of the application. And perfection is difficult! If you expect to work with threads in the real world, *Java Concurrency in Practice* (*https://jcip.net*) by Brian Goetz et al. (Addison-Wesley) is *required* reading.

Now that we know how we'll be storing and retrieving the URLs, we can create the producer and consumer classes. The producer will run a loop to simulate a web crawler by making up fake URLs. It will prefix those URLs with a producer ID, and then store them in our queue. Here's the run() method for URLProducer:

```
public void run() {
  for (int i = 1; i <= urlCount; i++) {
    String url = "https://some.url/at/path/" + i;
    queue.addURL(producerID + " " + url);
    System.out.println(producerID + " produced " + url);
    try {
      Thread.sleep(delay.nextInt(500));
    } catch (InterruptedException ie) {
      System.err.println("Producer " + producerID + " interrupted. Quitting.");
      break;
    }
  }
}
```

The consumer class is similar, with the obvious exception of taking URLs out of the queue. It will pull a URL out, prefix it with a consumer ID, and start over until the producers are done producing and the queue is empty:

```
public void run() {
  while (keepWorking || !queue.isEmpty()) {
    String url = queue.getURL();
    if (url != null) {
      System.out.println(consumerID + " consumed " + url);
    } else {
      System.out.println(consumerID + " skipped empty queue");
    }
    try {
      Thread.sleep(delay.nextInt(1000));
    } catch (InterruptedException ie) {
      System.err.println("Consumer " + consumerID +
          " interrupted. Quitting.");
      break;
    }
  }
}
```

We can start by running our simulation with very small numbers: two producers and two consumers. Each producer will create only three URLs:

```
public class URLDemo {
  public static void main(String args[]) {
    URLQueue queue = new URLQueue();
    URLProducer p1 = new URLProducer("P1", 3, queue);
    URLProducer p2 = new URLProducer("P2", 3, queue);
    URLConsumer c1 = new URLConsumer("C1", queue);
    URLConsumer c2 = new URLConsumer("C2", queue);
    System.out.println("Starting...");
```

```
    Thread tp1 = new Thread(p1);
    tp1.start();
    Thread tp2 = new Thread(p2);
    tp2.start();
    Thread tc1 = new Thread(c1);
    tc1.start();
    Thread tc2 = new Thread(c2);
    tc2.start();
    try {
      // Wait for the producers to finish creating urls
      tp1.join();
      tp2.join();
    } catch (InterruptedException ie) {
      System.err.println("Interrupted waiting for producers to finish");
    }
    c1.setKeepWorking(false);
    c2.setKeepWorking(false);
    try {
      // Now wait for the workers to clean out the queue
      tc1.join();
      tc2.join();
    } catch (InterruptedException ie) {
      System.err.println("Interrupted waiting for consumers to finish");
    }
    System.out.println("Done");
  }
}
```

Even with these tiny numbers involved, you can still see the effects of using multiple threads to do the work:

```
Starting...
C1 skipped empty queue
C2 skipped empty queue
P2 produced https://some.url/at/path/1
P1 produced https://some.url/at/path/1
P1 produced https://some.url/at/path/2
P2 produced https://some.url/at/path/2
C2 consumed P2 https://some.url/at/path/1
P2 produced https://some.url/at/path/3
P1 produced https://some.url/at/path/3
C1 consumed P1 https://some.url/at/path/1
C1 consumed P1 https://some.url/at/path/2
C2 consumed P2 https://some.url/at/path/2
C1 consumed P2 https://some.url/at/path/3
C1 consumed P1 https://some.url/at/path/3
Done
```

The threads don't take perfect, round-robin turns, but every thread does get at least some work time. And the consumers are not locked to specific producers. The idea is to make efficient use of limited resources. Producers can keep adding tasks without worrying about how long each task will take or whom to assign it to. Consumers, in turn, can grab a task without worry about other consumers. If one consumer gets handed a simple task and finishes before other consumers, it can go back and get a new task right away.

Try running this example yourself and bump up some of those numbers. What happens with hundreds of URLs? What happens with hundreds of producers or consumers? At scale, this type of multitasking is almost required. You won't find large programs out there that don't use threads to manage at least some of their background work. Java's own graphical package, Swing, needs a separate thread to keep the UI responsive and correct, no matter how small your application is.

Synchronizing virtual threads

What about virtual threads? Do they have the same concurrency concerns? Mostly yes. Though lightweight, virtual threads still represent the standard "thread of execution" concept. They can still interrupt each other in messy ways and must still coordinate access to shared resources. But happily, the design goals of Project Loom come to the rescue. We can reuse all of our synchronizing tricks with virtual threads. In fact, to virtual thread-ify our URL producing-and-consuming demo, all we need to do is replace the chunk of code in the `main()` method that starts the threads:

```
// file: URLDemo2.java
    System.out.println("Starting virtual threads...");
    // Convert these two-step lines:
    //Thread tp1 = new Thread(p1);
    //tp1.start();

    // To these simpler, create-and-start lines:
    Thread vp1 = Thread.startVirtualThread(p1);
    Thread vp2 = Thread.startVirtualThread(p2);
    Thread vc1 = Thread.startVirtualThread(c1);
    Thread vc2 = Thread.startVirtualThread(c2);
```

The virtual threads honor the `synchronized` keyword in our `URLQueue` methods and understand the `join()` calls just like platform threads. If you compile `URLDemo2.java` and run it (don't forget you may need to enable preview features), you will see the same output as before, with small variations from the random pauses, of course.

We said virtual threads *mostly* have the same concurrency concerns as platform threads. We added that because creating and running virtual threads is a lot cheaper than managing a pool of platform threads so you don't overwhelm the operating system. (Recall that each platform thread is mapped to one native thread.) You don't pool virtual threads—you just make more.

Accessing Class and Instance Variables from Multiple Threads

In the `SpreadSheet` example, we guarded access to a set of instance variables with a synchronized method in order to avoid a thread changing one of the variables while another thread was reading the others, to keep them coordinated.

But what about individual variable types? Do they need to be synchronized? Normally, no. Almost all operations on primitives and object reference types in Java happen *atomically*: that is, the JVM handles them in one step, with no opportunity for two threads to collide. This prevents threads from looking at references while other threads are accessing them.

 Watch out—the JVM specification does not guarantee it will handle `double` and `long` primitive types atomically. Both of these types represent 64-bit values. The problem has to do with how the JVM's stack works. You should synchronize access to your `double` and `long` instance variables through accessor methods or use an atomic wrapper class, which we'll describe in "Concurrency Utilities" on page 305.

Scheduling and Priority

Java makes few guarantees about how it schedules threads. Almost all thread scheduling is left up to the Java implementation and, to some degree, the application. Java's designers could have specified a scheduling algorithm, but a single algorithm isn't suitable for all the roles that Java can play. Instead, Java's designers put the burden on you to write robust code that works no matter the scheduling algorithm, and let the implementation tune the algorithm for the best fit.

The priority rules in the Java language specification are carefully worded to be a general guideline for thread scheduling. You should be able to rely on this behavior overall (statistically), but it is not a good idea to write code that relies on very specific features of the scheduler to work properly. Instead, use the control and synchronization tools described in this chapter to coordinate your threads.[7]

Every thread has a priority. In general, any time a thread of a higher priority than the current thread becomes runnable (is started, stops sleeping, or is notified), it preempts the lower-priority thread and begins executing. On some systems, threads with the same priority are scheduled *round-robin*, which means once a thread starts to run, it continues until it does one of the following:

---

7 *Java Threads* by Scott Oaks and Henry Wong (O'Reilly) includes a detailed discussion of synchronization, scheduling, and other thread-related issues.

- Sleeps, by calling `Thread.sleep()` or `wait()`
- Waits for a lock, in order to run a `synchronized` method
- Blocks an I/O, for example, in a `read()` or `accept()` call
- Explicitly yields control, by calling `yield()`
- Terminates by completing its target method[8]

This situation looks something like Figure 9-8.

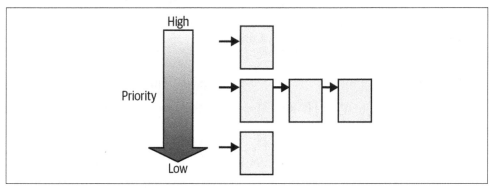

Figure 9-8. Priority-preemptive round-robin scheduling

You can set a priority on a platform thread with the `setPriority()` method and you can see a thread's current priority using the complementary `getPriority()` call. The priorities must fall within a range, bounded by the `Thread` class constants `MIN_PRIOR ITY` and `MAX_PRIORITY`. The default priority is held in the constant `NORM_PRIORITY`.

 Virtual threads all run with `NORM_PRIORITY`. If you call `setPrior ity()` on a virtual thread, the new priority you pass will simply be ignored.

Thread State

At any given time in its life cycle, a thread is in one of five general states. You can query them using the `getState()` method of the `Thread` class:

NEW
The thread has been created but has not yet started.

---

8 Technically, a thread can also terminate with the deprecated `stop()` call (*https://oreil.ly/AbbQk*), but as we noted at the start of the chapter, this is bad for myriad reasons.

RUNNABLE

The thread is in its normal active state, even if it is blocked in an I/O operation, like a read or write to a file or a network connection.

BLOCKED

The thread is blocked, waiting to enter a synchronized method or code block. This includes times when a thread has been awakened by a notify() and is attempting to reacquire its lock after a wait().

WAITING, TIMED_WAITING

The thread is waiting for another thread via a call to wait() or join(). In the case of TIMED_WAITING, the call has a timeout.

TERMINATED

The thread has completed due to a return, an exception, or being stopped.

You can show the state of all platform threads in the current thread group with the following snippet of code:

```
Thread [] threads = new Thread [ 64 ]; // max threads to show
int num = Thread.enumerate(threads);
for(int i = 0; i < num; i++)
    System.out.println(threads[i] +":"+ threads[i].getState());
```

The Thread.enumerate() call will populate our threads array up to its length. You probably won't use this method in general programming, but it is interesting and useful for experimenting and learning about Java threads.

Time-Slicing

In addition to prioritization, all modern systems (with the exception of some embedded and "micro" Java environments) implement thread *time-slicing*. In a time-sliced system, thread processing is chopped up so that each thread runs for a short period of time before the context is switched to the next thread, as shown in Figure 9-9.

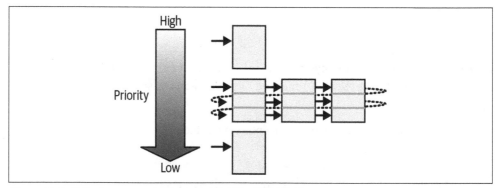

Figure 9-9. Priority-preemptive time-sliced scheduling

Higher-priority threads still preempt lower-priority threads in this scheme. Adding time-slicing mixes up the processing among threads of the same priority; on a multiprocessor machine, threads may even be run simultaneously. This can change the behavior of applications that don't use threads and synchronization properly.

Strictly speaking, because Java doesn't guarantee time-slicing, you shouldn't write code that relies on this type of scheduling; any software you write should function under round-robin scheduling. If you're wondering what your particular flavor of Java does, try the following experiment:

```java
public class Thready {
  public static void main(String args []) {
    new Thread(new ShowThread("Foo")).start();
    new Thread(new ShowThread("Bar")).start();
  }

  static class ShowThread implements Runnable {
    String message;

    ShowThread(String message) {
      this.message = message;
    }
    public void run() {
      while (true)
        System.out.println(message);
    }
  }
}
```

When you run this example, you will see how your Java implementation does its scheduling. The `Thready` class starts up two `ShowThread` objects. `ShowThread` is a thread that goes into an unending loop[9] (generally bad form, but useful for this demonstration) and prints its message. Because we don't specify a priority for either thread, they both inherit the priority of their creator, so they have the same priority. Under a round-robin scheme, only `Foo` should be printed; `Bar` should never appear. In a time-slicing implementation, you should occasionally see the `Foo` and `Bar` messages alternate.

The *ch09/examples* folder also contains a `VirtualThready` example if you want to see how virtual threads behave. They run with a "work-stealing" scheduler. (Feel free to dive into the official Oracle docs (*https://oreil.ly/qzfe0*) on the fork/join framework where this algorithm is laid out.) We had to add some `join()` calls to the virtual thread version. Unlike the platform threads, virtual threads will not keep the JVM "awake" without these explicit requests to wait for the threads to complete.

---

9 You can type Control-C to exit the demo when you get tired of seeing Foos fly by.

Priorities

Thread priorities are a general guideline for how the JVM should allocate time among competing threads. Unfortunately, Java platform threads are mapped to native threads in such complex ways that you can't rely upon the exact meaning of priorities. Instead, consider them a hint to the JVM.

Let's play with the priority of our threads:

```
class Thready2 {
  public static void main(String args []) {
    Thread foo = new ShowThread("Foo");
    foo.setPriority(Thread.MIN_PRIORITY);
    Thread bar = new ShowThread("Bar");
    bar.setPriority(Thread.MAX_PRIORITY);

    foo.start();
    bar.start();
  }
}
```

You might expect that with this change to our Thready2 class, the Bar thread will take over completely. If you run this code on an old Solaris implementation of Java 5.0, that's exactly what happens. The same is not true on most modern versions of Java. Similarly, if you change the priorities to values other than min and max, you may not see any difference at all. The subtleties of priority and performance relate to how Java threads and priorities are mapped to real threads in the OS. For this reason, you should generally reserve adjusting thread priorities for system and framework development.

Thread Performance

The use of threads has dictated the form and functionality of several Java packages.

The Cost of Synchronization

Acquiring locks to synchronize threads takes time, even when there is no contention. In older implementations of Java, this time could be significant. With newer JVMs, it is almost negligible. However, unnecessary low-level synchronization can still slow applications by blocking threads where concurrent access could be allowed. To avoid this penalty, two important APIs, the Java collections framework and the Swing API, were specifically crafted to put synchronization under the developer's control.

The java.util collections framework replaces earlier, simple Java aggregate types—namely, Vector and Hashtable—with more fully featured and, notably, unsynchronized types (List and Map). The collections framework instead defers to application code to synchronize access to collections when necessary, and provides special "fail fast" functionality to help detect concurrent access and throw an exception. It also provides synchronization "wrappers" that can provide safe access in the old style. Special concurrent-access-friendly implementations of the Map and Queue collections are included as part of the java.util.concurrent package. These implementations go even further and allow a high degree of concurrent access without any user synchronization.

The Java Swing API takes a different approach to providing speed and safety. Swing uses a single thread to modify its components, with an exception: the *event dispatch thread*, also called the event queue. Swing solves performance problems and any event ordering issues by forcing a single super-thread to control the GUI. The application accesses the event dispatch thread indirectly by pushing commands onto a queue through a simple interface. We'll see how to do just that in Chapter 12.

Thread Resource Consumption

A fundamental pattern in Java is to start many threads to handle asynchronous external resources, such as socket connections. For maximum efficiency, a web developer might be tempted to create a thread for each client connection on a server. When each client has its own thread, I/O operations can block and resume as needed. But as efficient as this may be in terms of throughput for a given client, it is a very inefficient use of server resources.

Threads consume memory; each thread has its own "stack" for local variables, and switching between running threads (known as *context switching*) adds overhead to the CPU. Threads are relatively lightweight. It is possible to have hundreds or thousands running on a large server. But after a certain point, the cost of managing the existing threads starts to outweigh the benefits of starting more threads. Creating a thread per client is not always a scalable option.

An alternative approach is to create "thread pools" where a fixed number of threads pull tasks from a queue and return for more work when they are finished. This recycling of threads makes for solid scalability, but it has often been difficult to implement efficiently for servers in Java. Basic I/O (for things like sockets) in Java does not fully support nonblocking operations. The java.nio package, New I/O (or simply NIO), has asynchronous I/O channels. Channels can perform nonblocking reads and writes. They also have the ability to test the readiness of streams for moving data. Threads can close channels asynchronously, making for graceful interactions. We'll discuss NIO in the coming chapters on working with files and network connections.

Java provides thread pools and job "executor" services as part of the java.util.concurrent package. This means you don't have to write these yourself. We'll summarize them when we discuss the concurrency utilities in Java.

Virtual Thread Performance

Project Loom set out to improve thread performance—especially when thousands or millions of threads are involved. The code of a run() method isn't any faster or slower when you run it on a platform thread versus a virtual thread. What is faster, though, is creating and managing those threads.

Let's take another look at our URLDemo class. Rather than four threads total, let's crank that number up to several thousand. We'll drop our producers and prepopulate the queue with URLs so we can focus on our new consumers. We'll make consumers whose only job is to consume one URL—no random, artificial delay before going back for another URL. This behavior mimics a real use case for virtual threads: a single server that handles millions of small requests in a short period. We'll also modify our print statements to show up at milestones rather than after every single URL is consumed. Our new URLDemo3 will take two optional command-line arguments: the number of URLs to create (default is 100,000) and whether to use platform or virtual threads (default is platform), so we can compare the difference in performance.

Check out the source code for URLConsumer3 in the *ch09/examples* folder to see the tweaks we made for this new variation. Then let's look more carefully at the processing loop in the main() method to see how it handles the new consumers. Here's the relevant section:

```
// Create and populate our shared queue object
URLQueue queue = new URLQueue();
for (int u = 1; u <= count; u++) {
  queue.addURL("http://some.url/path/" + u);
}

// Now the fun begins! Make one consumer for every URL
for (int c = 0; c < count; c++) {
  URLConsumer3 consumer = new URLConsumer3("C" + c, queue);
  if (useVirtual) {
    Thread.startVirtualThread(consumer);
  } else {
    new Thread(consumer).start();
  }
}
```

This code doesn't try to reuse consumers. There are valid reasons not to reuse threads in the real world, by the way. You have to manually clean up some shared data between uses, for example. Forget that bit of "administrivia" and you might leak sensitive information. (If you were processing bank transactions, you wouldn't want to accidentally use the previous account number.) You can often simplify your code by assuming a single thread will do all of the work and then terminate. This is true whether or not you're using virtual threads.

We tried this version with 1,000,000 URLs on a middling Linux desktop system. The platform threads cleared the queue in just under one minute (58.661 s according to the coarse `time` utility). Not bad! The virtual threads, on the other hand, cleared the queue in just under *2 seconds* (1.867 s). The testing for a milestone URL to print is trivial. It's not the task each consumer does that slows things down. The real bottleneck with platform threads is asking the operating system for a new, expensive resource thousands of times. Project Loom removes a lot of that expense. Using virtual threads is not a guarantee of better performance, but in cases like this, it certainly can be a benefit!

Concurrency Utilities

So far in this chapter, we've demonstrated how to create and synchronize threads at a low level, using Java language primitives. The `java.util.concurrent` package and subpackages build on this functionality, adding important threading utilities and codifying some common design patterns by supplying standard implementations. Roughly in order of generality, these areas include:

Thread-aware Collections implementations
> The `java.util.concurrent` package augments the Java Collections API in Chapter 7 with several implementations for specific threading models. These include timed wait and blocking implementations of the `Queue` interface, as well as nonblocking, concurrent-access optimized implementations of the `Queue` and `Map` interfaces. The package also adds "copy on write" `List` and `Set` implementations for extremely efficient "almost always read" cases. These may sound complex, but they cover some common cases very well.

Executors
> `Executors` run tasks, including `Runnables`, and abstract the concept of thread creation and pooling from the user (meaning you don't have to write your own). `Executors` are intended to be a high-level replacement for creating new threads to service a series of jobs. Along with `Executor`, the `Callable` and `Future` interfaces allow management, value return, and exception handling.

Low-level synchronization constructs
> The `java.util.concurrent.locks` package holds a set of classes, including `Lock` and `Condition`, that parallels the Java language-level synchronization primitives and promotes them to the level of a concrete API. For example, the `LockSupport` helper class includes two methods, `park()` and `unpark()`, that replace the deprecated `suspend()` and `resume()` methods from the `Thread` class. The locks package also adds the concept of nonexclusive reader/writer locks, allowing for greater concurrency in synchronized data access.

High-level synchronization constructs
>   This includes the classes `CyclicBarrier`, `CountDownLatch`, `Semaphore`, and `Exchanger`. These classes implement common synchronization patterns drawn from other languages and systems, and they can serve as the basis for new high-level tools.

Atomic operations (sounds very James Bond, doesn't it?)
>   The `java.util.concurrent.atomic` package provides wrappers and utilities for atomic, "all-or-nothing" operations on primitive types and references. This includes simple combination atomic operations like testing a value before setting it, and getting and incrementing a number in one operation.

With the possible exception of optimizations done by the Java VM for the `atomic` operations package, all of these utilities are implemented in pure Java, on top of the standard Java language synchronization constructs. This means that they are in a sense only convenience utilities and don't truly add new capabilities to the language. Their main role is to offer standard patterns and idioms in Java threading, making them safer and more efficient to use. A good example of this is the `Executor` utility, which allows a user to manage a set of tasks in a predefined threading model without having to delve into creating threads at all. Higher-level APIs like this both simplify coding and allow for greater optimization of the common cases.

Upgrading Our Queue Demo

Many of the concurrency features built into Java will be more useful to you on larger, more complex projects. But we can still upgrade our meager URL processing demo by using the thread-safe `ConcurrentLinkedQueue` class from the `java.util.concur rent` package. We can parameterize its type and do away with our custom `URLQueue` class entirely:

```
// Directory: ch09/examples
// in URLDemo4.java
   ConcurrentLinkedQueue<String> queue =
       new ConcurrentLinkedQueue<>();

// in URLProducer4.java, just "add" instead of "addURL"
   queue.add(producerID + " " + url);

// in URLConsumer4.java, "poll" rather than "getURL"
   String url = queue.poll();
   // ...
```

We do have to tweak the consumer and producer code a little, but only a little, and mostly just to use the normal queue operation names of `add` and `poll` instead of our custom, URL-centric method names. But we don't have to worry about the `URLQueue` class at all. Sometimes you will need custom data structures because the real world is messy. But if you can use one of the synchronized storage options built in, you know you're getting robust storage and access that you can safely use in your multithreaded application.

Another upgrade to consider is the atomic convenience classes. You might recall that our consumer class has a Boolean flag that can be set to false to end the consumer's processing loop. Since it's reasonable to assume that multiple threads might have access to our consumer, we can remake that flag as an instance of the `AtomicBoolean` class to make sure that warring threads can't clobber our poor flag. (We could make our accessor method `synchronized`, of course, but we want to highlight some of the existing options already in the JDK.) Here's a look at the interesting parts of `URLConsumer4`:

```
AtomicBoolean keepWorking;
//...

public void run() {
  while (keepWorking.get() || !queue.isEmpty()) {
    String url = queue.poll();
    //...
  }
}

public void setKeepWorking(boolean newState) {
  keepWorking.set(newState);
}
```

Using `AtomicBoolean` requires a smidge more typing—calling set/get methods rather than simple assignments or comparisons—but you get all the safe handling you could wish for. When you have complex, multithreaded logic everywhere, you might do your own state management. In situations where you don't have much other code that requires synchronization, though, these convenience classes can be very convenient indeed.

Structured Concurrency

Beyond the impressive improvements that virtual threads bring to highly concurrent applications, Project Loom also brings structured concurrency to Java. You may have heard about "parallel programming" in the threaded world. You have the option of pursuing a parallel programming solution when you can break a larger problem into smaller problems that can be solved separately and at the same time (in parallel, get it?).

This notion of a large task that can be turned into subtasks shares many similarities with our demo that uses producers and consumers, but the two types of problems are not entirely the same. One big difference lies in how to handle errors. If we failed to create a consumer in our `URLDemo` classes, for example, we could just create another one and continue on. But if a subtask fails in a parallel computation, it isn't as obvious how to recover. Should all of the other subtasks be canceled? What if some of them have already completed? What if we want to cancel the larger "parent" task?

Java 19 introduced an incubator feature, the `StructuredTaskScope` class, to better encapsulate the work done with subtasks. (If you were to call a preview feature like virtual threads a "beta" enhancement, incubator features would be an "alpha" enhancement.) You can read about the design goals and implementation details in JEP 428 (*https://oreil.ly/HBbfE*). We won't work with structured concurrency or executors in this book, but it is important to know that Java has many tools available to developers who are working with parallel and concurrent applications. Indeed, the support it provides to developers in this arena is precisely why Java remains such a popular workhorse in production backends.

So Many Threads to Pull

While we won't be looking any deeper at the concurrency packages in this chapter, we want you to know where you might dig next if concurrency is interesting to you or proves useful in the type of problems you encounter at work. As we (foot)noted in "Synchronizing a queue of URLs" on page 294, *Java Concurrency In Practice (https:// jcip.net)* by Brian Goetz, is required reading for real-world, multithreaded projects. We also want to give a shout-out to Doug Lea, the author of *Concurrent Programming in Java* (Addison-Wesley), who led the group that added these packages to Java and is largely responsible for creating them.

Alongside threads, Java's native support for basic file input and output (I/O) figures prominently in production applications. We'll look at the main classes for typical I/O in the next chapter.

Review Questions

1. What is a thread?
2. What keyword can you add to a method if you want threads to "take turns" when calling it? (Meaning no two threads should be executing the method at the same time to avoid corrupting shared data.)
3. What flags allow you to compile a Java program that includes preview feature code?
4. What flags allow you to run a Java program that includes preview feature code?
5. How many platform threads can one native thread support?
6. How many virtual threads can one native thread support?
7. Is the statement x = x + 1; an atomic action for the variable x?

8. What package includes thread-safe versions of popular collection classes like Queue and Map?

Code Exercises

1. Let's build a clock! Using a needle and thread—er, a JLabel and a Thread—make a small graphical clock application. The *Clock.java* file in the *ch09/exercises* folder contains a skeleton app that puts up a small window with a simple JLabel object. We bumped up the size of the label's font to make things more readable. Your clock should show hours, minutes, and seconds, at a minimum. Create a thread that will sleep for one second and then increment the clock's display. Feel free to revisit the date and time formatting examples from "Formatting Dates and Times" on page 269.

2. The apple tossing game in the *ch09/exercises/game* folder currently uses a platform thread for its first foray into the world of animation following the discussion in "Revisiting Animation with Threads" on page 281. Compile and run it to see an apple launch itself when the game starts. The apple won't hit anything, but it will move in an arc as though tossed. We'll make this animation more interesting and more interactive in Chapter 12.

   Once you have a feel for the intended animation, convert the platform thread to a virtual thread. Compile your new version and verify it still works as expected. (Remember that, depending on your version of Java, you may need to compile and run with the extra preview flags.)

CHAPTER 10

File Input and Output

The ability to store data in files and retrieve it later is crucial to desktop and enterprise applications. In this chapter, we'll look at some of the most popular classes in the `java.io` and `java.nio` packages. These packages offer a rich set of tools for basic input and output (I/O) and also provide the framework on which all file and network communication in Java is built. Figure 10-1 shows the breadth of the `java.io` package.

We'll start by looking at the stream classes in `java.io`, which are subclasses of the basic `InputStream`, `OutputStream`, `Reader`, and `Writer` classes. Then we'll examine the `File` class and discuss how you can read and write files using classes in `java.io`. We also take a quick look at data compression and serialization. Along the way, we introduce the `java.nio` package. The "new" I/O package (or NIO) adds significant functionality tailored for building high-performance services. NIO centers on working with *buffers* (where you store stuff to make more efficient use of other resources) and *channels* (where you can efficiently put stuff that can be just as efficiently picked up by others). In some cases, NIO also provides better APIs that can be used in place of some `java.io` features.[1]

---

[1] While NIO was introduced with Java 1.4—so not very new anymore—it was newer than the original, basic package and the name has stuck.

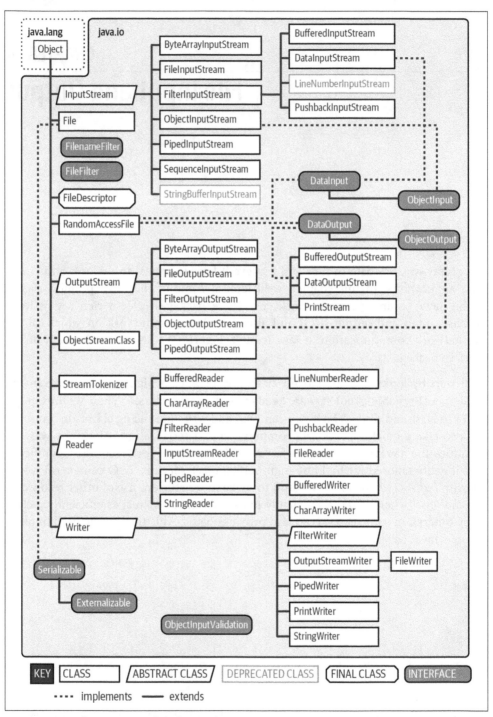

Figure 10-1. The `java.io` *class hierarchy*

Streams

Most I/O in Java is based on streams. Conceptually, a *stream* represents a flow of data with a *writer* at one end and a *reader* at the other. When you are working with the `java.io` package to perform terminal input and output, reading or writing files, or communicating through network sockets in Java (more on networking in Chapter 13), you are using various types of streams. When we look at the NIO package, we'll find a similar concept called a *channel*. The main difference between the two is that streams are oriented around bytes or characters, while channels are oriented around "buffers" containing those data types. A *buffer* is typically a fast, temporary storage for data that makes it easier to optimize throughput. They both perform roughly the same job. Let's start with streams. Here's a quick overview of the most popular stream classes:

`InputStream`, `OutputStream`
> Abstract classes that define the basic functionality for reading or writing an unstructured sequence of bytes. All other byte streams in Java are built on top of the basic `InputStream` and `OutputStream`.

`Reader`, `Writer`
> Abstract classes that define the basic functionality for reading or writing a sequence of character data, with support for Unicode. All other character streams in Java are built on top of `Reader` and `Writer`.

`InputStreamReader`, `OutputStreamWriter`
> Classes that bridge byte and character streams by converting according to a specific character-encoding scheme such as ASCII or Unicode. (Remember: in Unicode, a character is not necessarily one byte!)

`DataInputStream`, `DataOutputStream`
> Specialized stream filters that add the ability to read and write multibyte data types, such as numeric primitives and `String` objects in a standardized format.

`ObjectInputStream`, `ObjectOutputStream`
> Specialized stream filters that are capable of writing whole groups of serialized Java objects and reconstructing them.

`BufferedInputStream`, `BufferedOutputStream`, `BufferedReader`, `BufferedWriter`
> Specialized stream filters that add buffering for additional efficiency. For real-world I/O, a buffer is almost always used.

`PrintStream`, `PrintWriter`
> Specialized streams that simplify printing text.

`PipedInputStream`, `PipedOutputStream`, `PipedReader`, `PipedWriter`
>   Paired classes that move data within an application. Data written into a `PipedOut` `putStream` or `PipedWriter` is read from its corresponding `PipedInputStream` or `PipedReader`.

`FileInputStream`, `FileOutputStream`, `FileReader`, `FileWriter`
>   Implementations of `InputStream`, `OutputStream`, `Reader`, and `Writer` that read from and write to files on the local filesystem.

Streams in Java are one-way streets. The `java.io` input and output classes represent only the ends of a simple stream. For bidirectional conversations, you'll use one of each type of stream.

`InputStream` and `OutputStream`, as shown in Figure 10-2, are abstract classes that define the lowest-level interface for all byte streams. They contain methods for reading or writing an unstructured flow of byte-level data. Because these classes are abstract, you can't create a generic input or output stream.

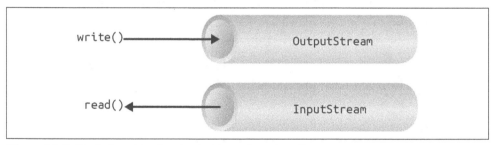

Figure 10-2. Basic input and output stream functionality

Java implements subclasses of these for activities such as reading from and writing to files or communicating with network connections. Because all byte streams inherit the structure of `InputStream` or `OutputStream`, the various kinds of byte streams can be used interchangeably. A method specifying an `InputStream` as an argument can accept any subclass of `InputStream`. Specialized types of streams can also be layered or wrapped around basic streams to add features such as buffering, filtering, compression, or handling higher-level data types.

`Reader` and `Writer` are very much like `InputStream` and `OutputStream`, except that they deal with characters instead of bytes. As true character streams, these classes correctly handle Unicode characters, which is not always the case with byte streams. Often, a bridge is needed between these character streams and the byte streams of physical devices, such as disks and networks. `InputStreamReader` and `OutputStream` `Writer` are special classes that use a character-encoding scheme like ASCII or UTF-8 to translate between character and byte streams.

This section describes several stream types, with the exception of `FileInputStream`, `FileOutputStream`, `FileReader`, and `FileWriter`. We postpone the discussion of file streams until the next section, where we cover accessing the filesystem in Java.

Basic I/O

The prototypical example of an `InputStream` object is the *standard input* of a Java application. Like `stdin` in C or `cin` in C++, this is the source of input to a command-line (non-GUI) program. It is an input stream from the environment—usually a terminal window or possibly the output of another command. The `java.lang.System` class, a general repository for system-related resources, provides a reference to the standard input stream in the static variable `System.in`. It also provides a *standard output stream* and a *standard error stream* in the `out` and `err` variables, respectively.[2] The following example shows the correspondence:

```
InputStream stdin = System.in;
OutputStream stdout = System.out;
OutputStream stderr = System.err;
```

This snippet hides the fact that `System.out` and `System.err` aren't just `OutputStream` objects but more specialized and useful `PrintStream` objects. We'll explain these later in "PrintWriter and PrintStream" on page 321, but for now we can reference `out` and `err` as `OutputStream` objects because they are derived from `OutputStream`.

You can read a single byte at a time from standard input with the `InputStream`'s `read()` method. If you look closely at the online documentation (*https://oreil.ly/GSEj0*), you'll see that the `read()` method of the base `InputStream` class is an abstract method. What lies behind `System.in` is a particular implementation of `InputStream` that provides the real implementation of the `read()` method:

```
try {
  int val = System.in.read();
} catch (IOException e) {
  // ...
}
```

Although we said that the `read()` method reads a byte value, the return type in the example is `int`, not `byte`. That's because the `read()` method of basic input streams in Java uses a convention carried over from the C language to indicate the end of a stream with a special value. Byte values are returned in the range 0 to 255, and the special value of `-1` is used to indicate that the end of the stream has been reached.

---

2 Standard error (`stderr`) is a stream usually reserved for error-related text messages that should be shown to the user of a command-line application. It is different from standard output (`stdout`), which is often redirected to a log file or another application and not seen by the user.

You test for this condition when using the simple `read()` method. You can then cast the value to a byte, if needed. The following example reads each byte from an input stream and prints its value:

```
try {
  int val;
  while((val=System.in.read()) != -1) {
    System.out.println((byte)val);
  }
} catch (IOException e) {
  // Oops. Handle the error or print an error message
}
```

As we've shown in the examples, the `read()` method can also throw an `IOException` if there is an error reading from the underlying stream source. Various subclasses of `IOException` may indicate that a source (such as a file or network connection) has had an error. Additionally, higher-level streams that read data types more complex than a single byte may throw `EOFException` ("end of file"), which indicates an unexpected or premature end of a stream.

An overloaded form of `read()` fills a byte array with as much data as possible up to the capacity of the array and returns the number of bytes read:

```
byte [] buff = new byte [1024];
int got = System.in.read(buff);
```

In theory, we can also check the number of bytes available for reading at a given time on an `InputStream` using the `available()` method. With that information, we could create an array of exactly the right size:

```
int waiting = System.in.available();
if (waiting > 0) {
  byte [] data = new byte [ waiting ];
  System.in.read(data);
  // ...
}
```

However, the reliability of this technique depends on whether the underlying stream implementation can detect how much data it can retrieve. It generally works for files but should not be relied upon for all types of streams.

These `read()` methods block until at least some data is read (at least one byte). You must, in general, check the returned value to determine how much data you got and if you need to read more. (We look at nonblocking I/O later in this chapter.) The `skip()` method of `InputStream` provides a way of jumping over a number of bytes. Depending on the implementation of the stream, skipping bytes may be more efficient than reading them.

The close() method shuts down the stream and frees up any associated system resources. It's important for performance to remember to close most types of streams when you are finished using them. In some cases, streams may close automatically when objects are garbage-collected, but it is not a good idea to rely on this behavior. The try-*with-resources* feature discussed in "try with Resources" on page 202 makes automatically closing streams and other closeable entities easier. We'll see some examples of that in "File Streams" on page 328. The interface java.io.Closeable identifies all types of stream, channel, and related utility classes that can be closed.

Character Streams

In early versions of Java, some InputStream and OutputStream types included methods for reading and writing strings, but most of them operated by naively assuming that a 16-bit Unicode character was equivalent to an 8-bit byte in the stream. This works for Latin-1 (ISO 8859-1) characters, but not for the world of other encodings used with different languages.

The java.io Reader and Writer character stream classes were introduced as streams that handle character data only. When you use these classes, you think only in terms of characters and string data. You allow the underlying implementation to handle the conversion of bytes to a specific character encoding. As you'll see, there are some direct implementations of Reader and Writer, such as those for reading and writing files.

More generally, two special classes, InputStreamReader and OutputStreamWriter, bridge the gap between character streams and byte streams. These are, respectively, a Reader and a Writer that can be wrapped around any underlying byte stream to make it a character stream. An encoding scheme converts between the bytes (which may come in groups representing multibyte characters) and Java's two-byte characters. An encoding scheme can be specified by name in the constructor of Input StreamReader or OutputStreamWriter. For convenience, the default constructor uses the system's default encoding scheme.

Let's see how to use readers and the java.text.NumberFormat class to retrieve numeric input from the user at the command line. We'll assume that the bytes coming from System.in use the system's default encoding scheme:

```
// file: ch10/examples/ParseKeyboard.java

try {
  InputStream in = System.in;
  InputStreamReader charsIn = new InputStreamReader(in);
  BufferedReader bufferedCharsIn = new BufferedReader(charsIn);

  String line = bufferedCharsIn.readLine();
  int i = NumberFormat.getInstance().parse(line).intValue();
```

```
    // ...
} catch (IOException e) {
    // ...
} catch (ParseException pe) {
    // ...
}
```

First, we wrap an `InputStreamReader` around `System.in`. This reader converts the incoming bytes of `System.in` to characters using the default encoding scheme. Then, we wrap a `BufferedReader` around the `InputStreamReader`. `BufferedReader` adds the `readLine()` method, which we can use to grab a full line of text (up to a platform-specific, line-terminator character combination) into a `String`. The string is then parsed into an integer using the techniques described in Chapter 8. Try it yourself. When prompted, try providing different input. What happens if you enter a "0"? What if you only enter your first name?

We have just taken a byte-oriented input stream, `System.in`, and safely converted it to a `Reader` for reading characters. If we wished to use an encoding other than the system default, we could have specified it in the `InputStreamReader`'s constructor, like so:

```
InputStreamReader reader = new InputStreamReader(System.in, "UTF-8");
```

For each character that is read from the reader, the `InputStreamReader` reads one or more bytes and performs the necessary conversion to Unicode.

We'll return to the topic of character encodings in "The New I/O File API" on page 331 when we discuss the `java.nio.charset` package, which allows you to find and use encoders and decoders. Both `InputStreamReader` and `OutputStreamWriter` can accept a `Charset` codec object as well as a character-encoding name.

Stream Wrappers

What if you want to do more than read and write a sequence of bytes or characters? We can use a *filter stream*, which is a type of `InputStream`, `OutputStream`, `Reader`, or `Writer` that wraps another stream and adds new features. A filter stream takes the target stream as an argument in its constructor, does some additional processing of its own, and then delegates calls to the target. For example, we can construct a `BufferedInputStream` to wrap the system standard input:

```
InputStream bufferedIn = new BufferedInputStream(System.in);
```

The `BufferedInputStream` reads ahead and buffers a certain amount of data. It wraps an additional layer of functionality around the underlying stream. Figure 10-3 shows this arrangement for a `DataInputStream`, which can read higher-level data types, such as Java primitives and strings.

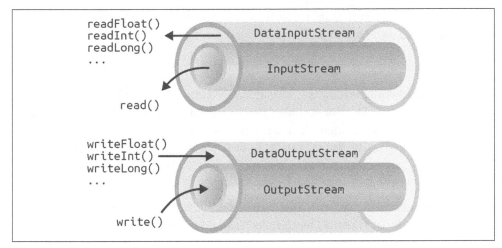

Figure 10-3. Layered streams

As you can see from the previous code snippet, the `BufferedInputStream` filter is a type of `InputStream`. Because filter streams are themselves subclasses of the basic stream types, they can be used as arguments to the construction of other filter streams. This allows filter streams to be layered on top of one another to provide different combinations of features. For example, we could first wrap our `System.in` with a `BufferedInputStream` to benefit from buffering our input, and then wrap the `BufferedInputStream` with a `DataInputStream` for reading special data types with buffering.

Java provides base classes for creating new types of filter streams: `FilterInput Stream`, `FilterOutputStream`, `FilterReader`, and `FilterWriter`. These superclasses provide the basic machinery for a filter by delegating all their method calls to their underlying stream. To create your own filter stream, you can extend these classes and override various methods to add the additional processing you need.

Data streams

`DataInputStream` and `DataOutputStream` are filter streams that let you read or write strings (as opposed to individual characters) and primitive data types composed of more than a single byte. `DataInputStream` and `DataOutputStream` implement the `DataInput` and `DataOutput` interfaces, respectively. These interfaces define methods for reading or writing strings and all of the Java primitive types, including numbers and Boolean values. `DataOutputStream` encodes these values in a way that can be read back correctly on any machine and then writes them to its underlying byte stream. `DataInputStream` picks up the encoded data from its underlying byte stream and decodes it into its original types and values.

You can construct a `DataInputStream` from an `InputStream` and then use a method such as `readDouble()` to read a primitive data type:

```
DataInputStream dis = new DataInputStream(System.in);
double d = dis.readDouble();
```

This snippet wraps the standard input stream in a `DataInputStream` and uses it to read a `double` value. The `readDouble()` method reads bytes from the stream and constructs a `double` from them. The `DataInputStream` methods expect the bytes of numeric data types to be in *network byte order*, a standard that specifies that the high-order bytes of any multibyte values are sent first (also known as *big-endian*; see "Byte order" on page 342).

The `DataOutputStream` class provides write methods that correspond to the read methods in `DataInputStream`. The complement to our input snippet looks like this:

```
double d = 3.1415926;
DataOutputStream dos = new DataOutputStream(System.out);
dos.writeDouble(d);
```

 DataOutputStream and DataInputStream work with binary data, not human-readable text. Typically, you would use a DataInput Stream to read content that was produced by a DataOutputStream. These filter streams are perfect for working directly with things like image files.

The `readUTF()` and `writeUTF()` methods of `DataInputStream` and `DataOutput Stream` read and write a Java `String` of Unicode characters using the UTF-8 character encoding. As discussed in Chapter 8, UTF-8 is an ASCII-compatible encoding of Unicode characters that is very widely used. Not all encodings are guaranteed to preserve all Unicode characters, but UTF-8 does. You can also use UTF-8 with `Reader` and `Writer` streams by specifying it as the encoding name.

Buffered streams

The `BufferedInputStream`, `BufferedOutputStream`, `BufferedReader`, and `Buffered Writer` classes add a data buffer of a specified size to the stream path. A buffer can increase efficiency by reducing the number of physical read or write operations that correspond to `read()` or `write()` method calls, as seen in Figure 10-4.

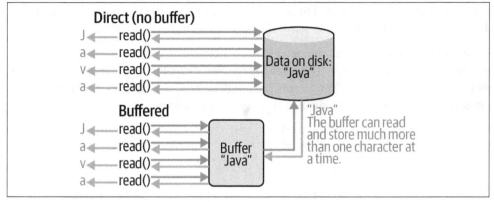

Figure 10-4. Reading data with and without a buffer

You create a buffered stream with an appropriate input or output stream and a buffer size. (You can also wrap another stream around a buffered stream so that it benefits from the buffering.) Here's a simple buffered input stream:

```
BufferedInputStream bis = new BufferedInputStream(myInputStream, 32768);
// bis will store up to 32K of data from myInputStream at a time
// we can then read from bis at any time
byte b = bis.read();
```

In this example, we specify a buffer size of 32 KB. If we leave off the size of the buffer in the constructor, Java creates a reasonably sized buffer for us. (Currently the default is 8 KB.) On our first call to `read()`, `bis` tries to fill our entire 32 KB buffer with data, if it's available. Thereafter, calls to `read()` retrieve data from the buffer, which is refilled as necessary.

A `BufferedOutputStream` works in a similar way. Calls to `write()` store the data in a buffer; data is actually written to the underlying stream only when the buffer fills up. You can also use the `flush()` method to write out the contents of a `BufferedOutput Stream` at any time. The `flush()` method is actually a method of the `OutputStream` class itself. It allows you to be sure that all data in any underlying streams has been saved or sent.

The `BufferedReader` and `BufferedWriter` classes work just like their byte-based counterparts, except that they operate on characters instead of bytes.

PrintWriter and PrintStream

Another useful wrapper is `java.io.PrintWriter`. This class provides a suite of over-loaded `print()` methods that turn their arguments into strings and push them out the stream. A complementary set of `println()` convenience methods appends a new line to the end of the strings. For formatted text output, `printf()` and the identical `format()` methods allow you to write C `printf`-style formatted text to the stream.

`PrintWriter` is an unusual character stream because it can wrap either an `Output Stream` or another `Writer`. `PrintWriter` is the more capable big brother of the legacy `PrintStream` byte stream. The `System.out` and `System.err` streams are `PrintStream` objects, which you have already seen throughout this book:

```
System.out.print("Hello, world...\n");
System.out.println("Hello, world...");
System.out.printf("The answer is %d\n", 17);
System.out.println(3.14);
```

When you create a `PrintWriter` object, you can pass an additional Boolean value to the constructor, specifying whether it should "auto-flush." If this value is `true`, the `PrintWriter` automatically performs a `flush()` on the underlying `OutputStream` or `Writer` each time it sends a newline:

```
// Stream automatically flushes after a newline.
PrintWriter pw = new PrintWriter(myOutputStream, true);
pw.println("Hello!");
```

When you use this technique with a buffered output stream, it acts like a terminal that outputs data line by line.

The other big advantage that `PrintStream` and `PrintWriter` have over regular character streams is that they shield you from exceptions thrown by the underlying streams. Unlike methods in other stream classes, the methods of `PrintWriter` and `PrintStream` do not throw IOExceptions. Instead, they provide a method to explicitly check for errors, if required. This makes the common operation of printing text a lot easier. You can check for errors with the `checkError()` method:

```
System.out.println(reallyLongString);
if (System.out.checkError()) {
  // uh oh
}
```

This feature of `PrintStream` and `PrintWriter` means you can generally output text to a variety of destinations without wrapping every print statement in a `try` block. But it still gives you access to any errors that occur if you are writing important information and want to guarantee that nothing went wrong.

The java.io.File Class

A popular destination for printed output is a file. The `java.io.File` class encapsulates access to information about a file or directory. You can use `File` to get attribute information about a file, list the entries in a directory, and perform basic filesystem operations, such as deleting a file or making a new directory. While the `File` object handles these "meta" operations, it doesn't provide the API for reading and writing file data; you'll need file streams for that.

File constructors

You can create an instance of File from a String pathname:

```
File fooFile = new File("/tmp/foo.txt");
File barDir = new File("/tmp/bar");
```

You can also create a file with a relative path that starts in the current working directory of the JVM:

```
File f = new File("foo");
```

You can determine the current working directory by reading the user.dir property in the System properties list:

```
System.getProperty("user.dir"); // e.g.,"/Users/pat"
```

An overloaded version of the File constructor lets you specify the directory path and filename as separate String objects:

```
File fooFile = new File("/tmp", "foo.txt");
```

With yet another variation, you can specify the directory with a File object and the filename with a String:

```
File tmpDir = new File("/tmp"); // File for directory /tmp
File fooFile = new File (tmpDir, "foo.txt");
```

None of these File constructors actually creates a file or directory, and it is not an error to create a File object for a nonexistent file. The File object is just a handle for a file or directory whose properties you may wish to read, write, or test. For example, you can use the exists() instance method to learn whether the file or directory exists. Many applications perform this test prior to saving to a file, for example. If the chosen file doesn't exist, hooray! The application can safely save its data. If the file does already exist, you often get an overwrite warning to make sure you want to replace the old file.

Path localization

In Java, pathnames are expected to follow the conventions of the local filesystem. The Windows filesystem uses distinct *roots* (top-level directories) with drive letters (for example, "C:") and a backslash (\) instead of the single root and forward slash (/) path separator that is used in Linux and macOS systems.

Java tries to compensate for this difference. For example, on Windows platforms, it accepts paths with either forward slashes or backslashes. On macOS and Linux, however, it only accepts forward slashes.

Your best bet is to make sure you follow the filename conventions of the host filesystem. If your application has a GUI that is opening and saving files at the user's request, you should be able to handle that functionality with the Swing JFileChooser class. This class encapsulates a graphical file-selection dialog box. The methods of the JFileChooser take care of system-dependent filename features for you.

If your application needs to deal with files on its own behalf, however, things get a little more complicated. The File class contains a few **static** variables to make this task easier. File.separator defines a String that specifies the file separator on the local host (e.g., / on Unix and macOS systems, and \ on Windows systems); File.separatorChar provides the same information as a char.

You can use this system-dependent information in several ways. Probably the simplest way to localize pathnames is to pick a convention that you use internally, such as the forward slash (/), and do a String replace to substitute for the localized separator character:

```
// we'll use forward slash as our standard
String path = "mail/2023/june";
path = path.replace('/', File.separatorChar);
File mailbox = new File(path);
```

Alternatively, you could work with the components of a pathname and build the local pathname when you need it:

```
String [] path = { "mail", "2004", "june", "merle" };

StringBuffer sb = new StringBuffer(path[0]);
for (int i=1; i< path.length; i++) {
  sb.append(File.separator + path[i]);
}
File mailbox = new File(sb.toString());
```

Remember that Java interprets backslash characters (\) in source code as escape characters when they're used in a String. To get a literal backslash, you have to double up: \\.

To grapple with the issue of filesystems with multiple "roots" (for example, C:\ on Windows), the File class provides the static method listRoots(), which returns an array of File objects corresponding to the filesystem root directories. You can try this out in *jshell*:

```
jshell> import java.io.File;

// On a Linux box:
jshell> File.listRoots()
$2 ==> File[1] { / }
```

```
// On Windows:
jshell> File.listRoots()
$3 ==> File[2] { C:\, D:\ }
```

Again, in a GUI application, a graphical file chooser dialog generally shields you from this problem.

File operations

Once we have a File object, we can use it to perform a number of standard operations on the file or directory it represents. Several methods let us ask questions about the File. For example, isFile() returns true if the File represents a regular file, while isDirectory() returns true if it's a directory. isAbsolute() indicates whether the File encapsulates an absolute or relative path specification. A *relative path* is relative to the application's working directory. An *absolute path* is a system-dependent notion that means that the path isn't tied to the working directory or current drive. In Unix and macOS, an absolute path starts with a forward slash: */Users/pat/foo.txt*. In Windows, it is a full path including the drive letter: *C:\Users\pat\foo.txt* (and, again, it can be on a different drive letter than the working directory if there are multiple drives in the system).

Components of the pathname are available through the methods getName(), get Path(), getAbsolutePath(), and getParent(). The getName() method returns a String for the filename without any directory information. If the File has an absolute path specification, getAbsolutePath() returns that path. Otherwise, it returns the relative path appended to the current working directory (attempting to make it an absolute path). The getParent() method returns the parent directory of the file or directory.

The string returned by getPath() or getAbsolutePath() may not follow the same case conventions as the underlying filesystem. You can retrieve the filesystem's own (or "canonical") version of the file's path by using the method getCanonicalPath(). In Windows, for example, you can create a File object whose getAbsolutePath() is *C:\Autoexec.bat* but whose getCanonicalPath() is *C:\AUTOEXEC.BAT*; both actually point to the same file. This is useful for comparing filenames or for showing them to the user.

You can get or set the modification time of a file or directory with the lastModified() and setLastModified() methods. The value is a long that is the number of milliseconds since the *epoch* (the name for the "first" date in Unix: January 1, 1970, 00:00:00 GMT). We can also get the size of the file, in bytes, with length().

Here's a fragment of code that prints some information about a file:

```
File fooFile = new File("/tmp/foo.txt");

String type = fooFile.isFile() ? "File " : "Directory ";
String name = fooFile.getName();
long len = fooFile.length();
System.out.println(type + name + ", " + len + " bytes ");
```

If the File object corresponds to a directory, we can list the files in the directory with the list() method or the listFiles() method:

```
File tmpDir = new File("/tmp");
String [] fileNames = tmpDir.list();
File [] files = tmpDir.listFiles();
```

list() returns an array of String objects that contains filenames. listFiles() returns an array of File objects. Note that in neither case are the files guaranteed to be in any kind of order (alphabetical, for example). You can use the Collections API to sort strings alphabetically, like so:

```
List list = Arrays.asList(fileNames);
Collections.sort(list);
```

If the File refers to a nonexistent directory, we can create the directory with mkdir() or mkdirs(). The mkdir() method creates at most a single directory level, so any intervening directories in the path must already exist. mkdirs() creates all directory levels necessary to create the full path of the File specification. In either case, if the directory cannot be created, the method returns false. Use renameTo() to rename a file or directory, and delete() to delete a file or directory.

Although you can create a directory using the File object, you don't typically use File to create a file; that's normally done implicitly when you write data to it with a FileOutputStream or FileWriter, as we'll discuss in a moment. The exception is the createNewFile() method, which you can use to create a new zero-length file at the File's location.

The createNewFile() operation is guaranteed to be atomic[3] with respect to all other file creation in the filesystem. Java returns a Boolean value from createNewFile() that tells you whether the file was created or not. Creating a new file this way is useful when you also use deleteOnExit(), which flags the file to be automatically removed when the Java VM exits. This combination allows you to guard resources or make an application that can only be run in a single instance at a time.

Another file creation method that is related to the File class itself is the static method createTempFile(), which creates a file in a specified location using an automatically

---

3 The term is borrowed from the world of threads and means the same thing: an atomic file creation cannot be interrupted by another thread.

generated, unique name. You typically use `createTempFile()` in conjunction with `deleteOnExit()`. Network applications use this combination frequently to create short-lived files for storing requests or building responses.

The `toURL()` method converts a file path to a `file:` URL object. URLs are a kind of abstraction that allow you to point to any kind of object anywhere on a network. Converting a `File` reference to a URL may be useful for consistency with more general utilities that deal with URLs. Java's NIO, for example, uses URLs to reference new types of filesystems that are implemented directly in Java code.

Table 10-1 summarizes the methods provided by the `File` class.

Table 10-1. File methods

Method	Return type	Description
canExecute()	boolean	Is the file executable?
canRead()	boolean	Is the file (or directory) readable?
canWrite()	boolean	Is the file (or directory) writable?
createNewFile()	boolean	Creates a new file.
createTempFile (String *pfx*, String*sfx*)	File	Static method to create a new file, with the specified prefix and suffix, in the default temp file directory
delete()	boolean	Deletes the file (or directory).
deleteOnExit()	Void	When it exits, the Java runtime system deletes the file.
exists()	boolean	Does the file (or directory) exist?
getAbsolute Path()	String	Returns the absolute path of the file (or directory).
getCanonical Path()	String	Returns the absolute, case-correct, and relative-element-resolved path of the file (or directory).
getFreeSpace()	long	Gets the number of bytes of unallocated space on the partition holding this path or 0 if the path is invalid.
getName()	String	Returns the name of the file (or directory).
getParent()	String	Returns the name of the parent directory of the file (or directory).
getPath()	String	Returns the path of the file (or directory). (Not to be confused with toPath().)
getTotalSpace()	long	Gets the size of the partition that contains the file path, in bytes, or 0 if the path is invalid.
getUseable Space()	long	Gets the number of bytes of user-accessible unallocated space on the partition holding this path or 0 if the path is invalid. This method attempts to take into account user write permissions.
isAbsolute()	boolean	Is the filename (or directory name) absolute?
isDirectory()	boolean	Is the item a directory?
isFile()	boolean	Is the item a file?

Method	Return type	Description
isHidden()	boolean	Is the item hidden? (System dependent.)
lastModified()	long	Returns the last modification time of the file (or directory).
length()	long	Returns the length of the file.
list()	String []	Returns a list of files in the directory.
listFiles()	File[]	Returns the contents of the directory as an array of File objects.
listRoots()	File[]	Returns an array of root filesystems, if any (e.g., C:/, D:/).
mkdir()	boolean	Creates the directory.
mkdirs()	boolean	Creates all directories in the path.
renameTo(File dest)	boolean	Renames the file (or directory).
setExecutable()	boolean	Sets execute permissions for the file.
setLastModified()	boolean	Sets the last-modified time of the file (or directory).
setReadable()	boolean	Sets read permissions for the file.
setReadOnly()	boolean	Sets the file to read-only status.
setWriteable()	boolean	Sets the write permissions for the file.
toPath()	java.nio.file.Path	Convert the file to an NIO file path. (Not to be confused with getPath().)
toURL()	java.net.URL	Generates a URL object for the file (or directory).

File Streams

You're probably sick of hearing about files already—and we haven't even written a byte yet! Well, now the fun begins. Java provides two fundamental streams for reading from and writing to files: FileInputStream and FileOutputStream. These streams provide the basic byte-oriented InputStream and OutputStream functionality that is applied to reading and writing files. They can be combined with the filter streams described earlier to work with files in the same way as other stream communications.

You can create a FileInputStream from a String pathname or a File object:

```
FileInputStream in = new FileInputStream("/etc/motd");
```

When you create a FileInputStream, the Java runtime system attempts to open the specified file. Thus, the FileInputStream constructors can throw a FileNotFoundException if the specified file doesn't exist, or an IOException if some other I/O error occurs. You must catch these exceptions in your code. Wherever possible, it's a good idea to get in the habit of using the try-with-resources construct to automatically close files for you when you are finished with them:

```
    try (FileInputStream fin = new FileInputStream("/etc/motd") ) {
        // ....
        // fin will be closed automatically if needed
        // upon exiting the try clause.
    }
```

When you first create the stream, its `available()` method and the `File` object's `length()` method should return the same value.

To read characters from a file as a `Reader`, you can wrap an `InputStreamReader` around a `FileInputStream`. You can also use the `FileReader` class, which is provided as a convenience. `FileReader` is just a `FileInputStream` wrapped in an `InputStream Reader` with some defaults.

The following class, `ListIt`, is a small utility that prints the contents of a file or directory to standard output:

```
//file: ch10/examples/ListIt.java
import java.io.*;

class ListIt {
    public static void main (String args[]) throws Exception {
        File file =  new File(args[0]);

        if (!file.exists() || !file.canRead()) {
            System.out.println("Can't read " + file);
            return;
        }

        if (file.isDirectory()) {
            String [] files = file.list();
            for (String file : files)
                System.out.println(file);
        } else {
            try {
                Reader ir = new InputStreamReader(
                    new FileInputStream(file) );

                BufferedReader in = new BufferedReader(ir);
                String line;
                while ((line = in.readLine()) != null)
                    System.out.println(line);
            }
            catch (FileNotFoundException e) {
                System.out.println("File Disappeared");
            }
        }
    }
}
```

`ListIt` constructs a `File` object from its first command-line argument and tests the `File` to see whether it exists and is readable. If the `File` is a directory, `ListIt` outputs the names of the files in the directory. Otherwise, `ListIt` reads and outputs the file, line by line. Give it a try! Can you use `ListIt` on *ListIt.java*?

For writing files, you can create a `FileOutputStream` from a `String` pathname or a `File` object. Unlike `FileInputStream`, however, the `FileOutputStream` constructors don't throw a `FileNotFoundException`. If the specified file doesn't exist, the `FileOutputStream` creates the file. The `FileOutputStream` constructors can throw an `IOException` if some other I/O error occurs, so you still need to handle this exception.

If the specified file does exist, the `FileOutputStream` opens it for writing. When you subsequently call the `write()` method, the new data overwrites the current contents of the file. If you need to append data to an existing file, you can use a form of the constructor that accepts a Boolean append flag:

```
FileOutputStream fooOut =
    new FileOutputStream(fooFile); // overwrite fooFile
FileOutputStream pwdOut =
    new FileOutputStream("/etc/passwd", true); // append
```

Another way to append data to files is with `RandomAccessFile`, which we'll discuss shortly.

Just as with reading, to write characters (instead of bytes) to a file, you can wrap an `OutputStreamWriter` around a `FileOutputStream`. If you want to use the default character-encoding scheme, you can use the `FileWriter` class instead, which is provided as a convenience.

The following snippet reads a line of data from standard input and writes it to the file */tmp/foo.txt*:

```
String s = new BufferedReader(
    new InputStreamReader(System.in) ).readLine();
File out = new File("/tmp/foo.txt");
FileWriter fw = new FileWriter (out);
PrintWriter pw = new PrintWriter(fw);
pw.println(s);
pw.close();
```

Notice how we wrapped the `FileWriter` in a `PrintWriter` to facilitate writing the data. Also, to be a good filesystem citizen, call the `close()` method when you're done. Here, closing the `PrintWriter` closes the underlying `Writer` for us.

RandomAccessFile

The `java.io.RandomAccessFile` class provides the ability to read *and* write data at any location in a file. `RandomAccessFile` implements both the `DataInput` and `DataOutput` interfaces, so you can use it to read and write strings and primitive types anywhere in the file just as if it were a `DataInputStream` and `DataOutputStream`. However, because the class provides random, rather than sequential, access to file data, it's not a subclass of either `InputStream` or `OutputStream`.

You can create a `RandomAccessFile` from a `String` pathname or a `File` object. The constructor also takes a second `String` argument that specifies the mode of the file. Use the string `"r"` for a read-only file or `"rw"` for a read/write file:

```
try {
  RandomAccessFile users = new RandomAccessFile("Users", "rw")
} catch (IOException e) { ... }
```

When you create a `RandomAccessFile` in read-only mode, Java tries to open the specified file. If the file doesn't exist, `RandomAccessFile` throws an `IOException`. If, however, you're creating a `RandomAccessFile` in read/write mode, the object creates the file if it doesn't exist. The constructor can still throw an `IOException` if some other I/O error occurs, so you still need to handle this exception.

After you have created a `RandomAccessFile`, you can call any of the normal reading and writing methods, just as you would with a `DataInputStream` or `DataOutputStream`. If you try to write to a read-only file, the write method throws an `IOException`.

What makes a `RandomAccessFile` special is the `seek()` method. This method takes a `long` value and uses it to set the location for reading and writing in the file. You can use the `getFilePointer()` method to get the current location. If you need to append data to the end of the file, use `length()` to determine that location, then `seek()` to it. You can write or seek beyond the end of a file, but you can't read beyond the end of a file. The `read()` method throws an `EOFException` if you try to do this.

Here's an example of writing data for a simple database:

```
users.seek(userNum * RECORDSIZE);
users.writeUTF(userName);
users.writeInt(userID);
```

In this snippet, we assume that the `String` length for `userName`, along with any data that comes after it, fits within the specified record size.

The New I/O File API

We are now going to turn our attention from the original, "classic" Java File API to the NIO File API. As we mentioned earlier, the NIO File API can be thought of as either a replacement for or a complement to the classic API. The new API moves Java toward a higher performance and more flexible style of I/O supporting *selectable* and asynchronously interruptible *channels*. (More on selecting and using channels soon.)

When working with files, the new API's strength is providing a fuller abstraction of the filesystem in Java.

In addition to better support for existing, real-world filesystem types—including the new and welcomed ability to copy and move files, manage links, and get detailed file attributes like owners and permissions—NIO allows you to implement entirely new types of filesystems directly in Java. The best example of this is the ZIP filesystem provider. You can "mount" a ZIP archive file as a filesystem. You can work with the files within the archive directly using the standard APIs, just like any other filesystem.

The NIO File package also provides some utilities that would have saved Java developers a lot of repeated code over the years, including directory tree change monitoring, filesystem traversal, filename "globbing" (the jargon for using wildcards in filenames), and convenience methods to read entire files directly into memory.

We'll cover the basic NIO File API in this section and return to the topic of buffers and channels at the end of the chapter. In particular, we'll talk about `ByteChannels` and `FileChannel`, which you can think of as alternate, buffer-oriented streams for reading and writing files and other types of data.

FileSystem and Path

There are three main players in the `java.nio.file` package:

FileSystem
> An underlying storage mechanism and serves as a factory[4] for `Path` objects.

FileSystems
> A factory for `FileSystem` objects.

Path
> The location of a file or directory within the filesystem.

Files
> A utility class that contains a rich set of static methods for manipulating `Path` objects to perform all of the basic file operations analogous to the classic API.

The `FileSystems` (plural) class is our starting point. Let's create a couple of filesystems:

```
// The default host computer filesystem
FileSystem fs = FileSystems.getDefault();
```

---

4 In OO programming, the term *factory* typically refers to a static helper that can construct and tailor some object. A factory (or factory method) is similar to a constructor, but that additional tailoring can add details to the new object that might be difficult (or impossible) to specify in a constructor.

```
// A custom filesystem for ZIP files, no special properties
Map<String,String> props = new HashMap<>();
URI zipURI = URI.create("jar:file:/Users/pat/tmp/MyArchive.zip");
FileSystem zipfs = FileSystems.newFileSystem(zipURI, props);
```

As shown in this snippet, we ask for the default filesystem to manipulate files in the host computer's environment. We also use the FileSystems class to construct another FileSystem by taking a *uniform resource identifier* (or URI, a special identifier similar to a URL) that references a custom filesystem type. We use jar:file as our URI protocol to indicate we are working with a JAR or ZIP file.

FileSystem implements Closeable, and when a FileSystem is closed, all open file channels and other streaming objects associated with it are closed as well. Attempting to read or write to those channels will throw an exception at that point. Note that the default filesystem (associated with the host computer) cannot be closed.

Once you have a FileSystem, you can use it as a factory for Path objects that represent files or directories. You can obtain a Path using a string representation just like the classic File class. Subsequently, you can use that Path object with methods of the Files utility to create, read, write, or delete the item:

```
Path fooPath = fs.getPath("/tmp/foo.txt");
OutputStream out = Files.newOutputStream(fooPath);
```

This example opens an OutputStream to write to the file *foo.txt*. By default, if the file does not exist, it will be created, and if it does exist, it will be truncated (set to zero length) before new data is written—but you can change these results using options. We'll talk more about Files methods in the next section.

The Path class implements the java.lang.Iterable interface, which can be used to iterate through its literal path components, such as the slash-separated tmp and foo.txt in the preceding snippet. (If you want to traverse the path to find other files or directories, you might be more interested in the DirectoryStream and FileVisitor that we'll discuss later.) Path also implements the java.nio.file.Watchable interface, which allows it to be monitored for changes.

Path has convenience methods for resolving paths relative to a file or directory:

```
Path patPath =  fs.getPath("/User/pat/");

Path patTmp = patPath.resolve("tmp"); // "/User/pat/tmp"

// Same as above, using a Path
Path tmpPath = fs.getPath("tmp");
Path patTmp = patPath.resolve(tmpPath); // "/User/pat/tmp"

// Resolving a given absolute path against any path just yields given path
Path absPath = patPath.resolve("/tmp"); // "/tmp"
```

```
// Resolve sibling to Pat (same parent)
Path danPath = patPath.resolveSibling("dan"); // "/Users/dan"
```

In this snippet, we've shown the Path methods resolve() and resolveSibling() used to find files or directories relative to a given Path object. The resolve() method is generally used to append a relative path to an existing Path representing a directory. If the argument provided to the resolve() method is an absolute path, it will just yield the absolute path (it acts kind of like the Unix or DOS cd command). The resolveSibling() method works the same way, but it is relative to the parent of the target Path; this method is useful for describing the target of a move() operation.

Path to classic files and back

To bridge the classic and new APIs, corresponding toPath() and toFile() methods have been provided in java.io.File and java.nio.file.Path, respectively, to convert to the other form. Of course, the only types of Paths that can be produced from File are paths representing files and directories in the default host filesystem:

```
Path tmpPath = fs.getPath("/tmp");
File file = tmpPath.toFile();
File tmpFile = new File("/tmp");
Path path = tmpFile.toPath();
```

NIO File Operations

Once we have a Path, we can operate on it with static methods of the Files utility to create the path as a file or directory, read and write to it, and interrogate and set its properties. We'll list the bulk of them and then discuss some of the more important ones as we proceed.

Table 10-2 summarizes these methods of the java.nio.file.Files class. As you might expect, because the Files class handles all types of file operations, it contains a large number of methods. To make the table more readable, we have elided overloaded forms of the same method (those taking different kinds of arguments), and we grouped corresponding and related types of methods together.

Table 10-2. NIO Files methods

Method	Return type	Description
copy()	long or Path	Copy a stream to a file path, file path to stream, or path to path. Returns the number of bytes copied or the target Path. A target file may optionally be replaced if it exists (the default is to fail if the target exists). Copying a directory results in an empty directory at the target (the contents are not copied). Copying a symbolic link copies the linked file's data (producing a regular file copy).

Method	Return type	Description
createDirectory(), createDirectories()	Path	Create a single directory or all directories in a specified path. createDirectory() throws an exception if the directory already exists. createDirectories() will ignore existing directories and only create as needed.
createFile()	Path	Create an empty file. The operation is atomic and will only succeed if the file does not exist. (This property can be used to create flag files to guard resources, etc.)
createLink(), createSymbolicLink(), isSymbolicLink(), readSymbolicLink(), createLink()	boolean or Path	Create a hard or symbolic link, test to see if a file is a symbolic link, or read the target file pointed to by the symbolic link. Symbolic links are files that reference other files. Regular ("hard") links are low-level mirrors of a file where two filenames point to the same underlying data. If you don't know which to use, use a symbolic link.
createTempDirectory(), createTempFile()	Path	Create a temporary, guaranteed, uniquely named directory or file with the specified prefix. Optionally, place it in the system default temp directory.
delete(), deleteIfExists()	void	Delete a file or an empty directory. deleteIfExists() will not throw an exception if the file does not exist.
exists(), notExists()	boolean	Determine whether the file exists (notExists() simply returns the opposite). Optionally, specify whether links should be followed (by default they are).
getAttribute(), setAttribute(), getFile AttributeView(), readAttributes()	Object, Map, or FileAttribute View	Get or set filesystem-specific file attributes such as access and update times, detailed permissions, and owner information using implementation-specific names.
getFileStore()	FileStore	Get a FileStore object that represents the device, volume, or other type of partition of the filesystem on which the path resides.
getLastModifiedTime(), set LastModifiedTime()	FileTime or Path	Get or set the last modified time of a file or directory.
getOwner(), setOwner()	UserPrincipal	Get or set a UserPrincipal object representing the owner of the file. Use toString() or getName() to get a string representation of the username.
getPosixFilePermissions(), setPosixFilePermissions()	Set or Path	Get or set the full POSIX user-group-other style read and write permissions for the path as a Set of PosixFile Permission enum values.
isDirectory(), isExecutable(), isHidden(), isReadable(), isRegular File(), isWriteable()	boolean	Test file features such as whether the path is a directory and other basic attributes.
isSameFile()	boolean	Test to see whether the two paths reference the same file (which may potentially be true even if the paths are not identical).

Method	Return type	Description
move()	Path	Move a file or directory by renaming or copying it, optionally specifying whether to replace any existing target. Rename will be used unless a copy is required to move a file across file stores or filesystems. Directories can be moved using this method only if the simple rename is possible or if the directory is empty. If a directory move requires copying files across file stores or filesystems, the method throws an IOException. (In this case, you must copy the files yourself. See walkFileTree().)
newBufferedReader(), new BufferedWriter()	BufferedReader or BufferedWriter	Open a file for reading via a BufferedReader, or create and open a file for writing via a BufferedWriter. In both cases, a character encoding is specified.
newByteChannel()	SeekableByteChannel	Create a new file or open an existing file as a seekable byte channel. (See the full discussion of NIO later in this chapter.) Consider using FileChannel.open() as an alternative.
newDirectoryStream()	DirectoryStream	Return a DirectoryStream for iterating over a directory hierarchy. Optionally, supply a glob pattern or filter object to match files.
newInputStream(), newOutputStream()	InputStream or OutputStream	Open a file for reading via an InputStream, or create and open a file for writing via an OutputStream. Optionally, specify file truncation for the output stream; if overwriting, the default is to truncate the existing file.
probeContentType()	String	Return the MIME type of the file if it can be determined by installed FileTypeDetector services or null if unknown.
readAllBytes(), readAllLines()	byte[] or List<String>	Read all data from the file as a byte [] or all characters as a list of strings using a specified character encoding.
size()	long	Get the size, in bytes, of the file at the specified path.
walkFileTree()	Path	Apply a FileVisitor to the specified directory tree, optionally specifying whether to follow links and a maximum depth of traversal.
write()	Path	Write an array of bytes or a collection of strings (with a specified character encoding) to the file at the specified path and close the file, optionally specifying append and truncation behavior. The default is to truncate and write the data.

With these methods, we can fetch input or output streams, or buffered readers and writers, to a given file. We can also create paths as files and directories, and iterate through file hierarchies. We'll discuss directory operations in the next section.

As a reminder, the resolve() and resolveSibling() methods of Path are useful for constructing targets for the copy() and move() operations:

```
// Move the file /tmp/foo.txt to /tmp/bar.txt
Path foo = fs.getPath("/tmp/foo.txt");
Files.move(foo, foo.resolveSibling("bar.txt"));
```

For quickly reading and writing the contents of files without streaming, we can use the various `readAll…` and `write` methods that move byte arrays or strings in and out of files in a single operation:

```
// Read and write collection of String (e.g., lines of text)
Charset asciiCharset = Charset.forName("US-ASCII");
List<String> csvData = Files.readAllLines(csvPath, asciiCharset);
Files.write(newCSVPath, csvData, asciiCharset);

// Read and write bytes
byte [] data = Files.readAllBytes(dataPath);
Files.write(newDataPath, data);
```

These are convenient for files that easily fit into memory.

The NIO Package

Let's return to the `java.nio` package and round out our discussion of core Java I/O. One aspect of NIO is simply to update and enhance features of the classic `java.io` package. Much of the general NIO functionality does indeed overlap with existing APIs. However, NIO was first introduced to address specific issues of scalability for large systems, especially in networked applications. The following sections outline the basic elements of NIO.

Asynchronous I/O

Most of the need for the NIO package was driven by the desire to add *nonblocking* and *selectable* I/O to Java. Prior to NIO, most read and write operations in Java were bound to threads and were forced to block for unpredictable amounts of time. Although certain APIs, such as Sockets (which we'll see in "Sockets" on page 446), provided specific means to limit how long an I/O call could take, this was a workaround to compensate for the lack of a more general mechanism. In many languages, even those without threading, I/O could still be done efficiently by setting I/O streams to a nonblocking mode and testing them for their readiness to send or receive data. In a nonblocking mode, a read or write does only as much work as can be done immediately—filling or emptying a buffer and then returning. Combined with the ability to test for readiness, this allows a single-threaded application to continuously service many channels efficiently. The main thread "selects" a channel that is ready, works with it until it blocks, and then moves on to another. On a single-processor system, this is fundamentally equivalent to using multiple threads.

In addition to nonblocking and selectable I/O, the NIO package enables closing and interrupting I/O operations asynchronously. As discussed in Chapter 9, prior to NIO there was no reliable way to stop or wake up a thread blocked in an I/O operation. With NIO, threads blocked in I/O operations always wake up when interrupted or when another thread closes the channel. Additionally, if you interrupt a thread while it is blocked in an NIO operation, its channel is automatically closed. (Closing the channel because the thread is interrupted might seem too strong, but usually it's the right thing to do. Leaving it open could result in unexpected behavior or subject the channel to unwanted manipulation.)

Performance

Channel I/O is designed around the concept of buffers, which are a sophisticated form of array, tailored to communication tasks. The NIO package supports the concept of *direct buffers*—buffers that maintain their memory outside the Java VM in the host operating system. Because all real I/O operations ultimately have to work with the host OS by maintaining the buffer space there, using direct buffers can make many operations more efficient. Data moving between two external endpoints can be transferred without first copying it into Java and back out.

Mapped and Locked Files

NIO provides two general-purpose file-related features not found in `java.io`: memory-mapped files and file locking. A *memory-mapped* file behaves as if all of its content is in an array in memory rather than on a disk. Memory-mapped files are beyond the scope of this chapter, but if you work with lots of data and occasionally need really fast read/write access, look up the `MappedByteBuffer` documentation (*https://oreil.ly/yNLMn*) online.

File locking supports both shared and exclusive locks on regions of files—useful for concurrent access by multiple applications. We'll look at file locking in "File locking" on page 347.

Channels

While `java.io` deals with streams, `java.nio` works with channels. A *channel* is an endpoint for communication. Although in practice channels are similar to streams, the underlying notion of a channel is simultaneously more abstract and more primitive. Whereas streams in `java.io` are defined in terms of input or output with methods to read and write bytes, the basic channel interface says nothing about how communications happen. It simply has the notion of being open or closed, supported via the methods `isOpen()` and `close()`. Implementations of channels for files, network sockets, or arbitrary devices then add their own methods for operations, such as reading, writing, or transferring data. NIO provides the following channels:

- `FileChannel`

- `Pipe.SinkChannel`, `Pipe.SourceChannel`
- `SocketChannel`, `ServerSocketChannel`, `DatagramChannel`

We'll cover `FileChannel` and its asynchronous cousin, `AsynchronousFileChannel`, in "FileChannel" on page 345. (The asynchronous version essentially buffers all of its operations through a thread pool and reports results back through an asynchronous API.) The `Pipe` channels are simply the channel equivalents of the `java.io` `Pipe` facilities. The socket and datagram channels play in Java's networking world, which we'll look at in Chapter 13. The network-related channels have asynchronous versions as well: `AsynchronousSocketChannel`, `AsynchronousServerSocketChannel`, and `AsynchronousDatagramChannel`.

All these basic channels implement the `ByteChannel` interface, designed for channels that have read and write methods like I/O streams. `ByteChannels`, however, read and write `ByteBuffers`, as opposed to plain byte arrays.

In addition to these channel implementations, you can bridge channels with `java.io` I/O streams and readers and writers for interoperability. However, if you mix these features, you may not get the full benefits and performance NIO offers.

Buffers

Most of the utilities of the `java.io` and `java.net` packages operate on byte arrays. The corresponding tools of the NIO package are built around `ByteBuffers` (with a character-based buffer, `CharBuffer`, for text). Byte arrays are simple, so why are buffers necessary? They serve several purposes:

- They formalize the usage patterns for buffered data, provide for things like read-only buffers, and keep track of read/write positions and limits within a large buffer space. They also provide a mark/reset facility like that of `java.io` `.BufferedInputStream`.
- They provide additional APIs for working with raw data representing primitive types. You can create buffers that "view" your byte data as a series of larger primitives, such as `shorts`, `ints`, or `floats`. The most general type of data buffer, `ByteBuffer`, includes methods that let you read and write all primitive types just like `DataInputStream` and `DataOutputStream` do for streams.
- They abstract the underlying storage of the data, allowing Java to optimize throughput. Specifically, buffers may be allocated as direct buffers that use native buffers of the host operating system instead of arrays in Java's memory. The NIO `Channel` facilities that work with buffers can recognize direct buffers automatically and try to optimize their interactions with them. For example, a read from a file channel into a Java byte array normally requires Java to copy the data for

the read from the host operating system into Java's memory. With a direct buffer, the data can remain in the host operating system, outside Java's normal memory space, until and unless it is needed.

Buffer operations

The base `java.nio.Buffer` class is something like an array with state. It does not specify what type of elements it holds (that is for subtypes to decide), but it does define functionality that is common to all data buffers. A `Buffer` has a fixed size, called its *capacity*. Although all the standard `Buffer`s provide "random access" to their contents, a `Buffer` generally expects to be read and written sequentially, so `Buffer`s maintain the notion of a *position* where the next element is read or written. In addition to position, a `Buffer` can maintain two other pieces of state information: a *limit*, which typically denotes the available data in read mode and the capacity of the file in write mode, and a *mark*, which can be used to remember an earlier position for future recall.

Implementations of `Buffer` add specific, typed get and put methods that read and write the buffer contents. For example, `ByteBuffer` is a buffer of bytes and it has `get()` and `put()` methods that read and write bytes and arrays of bytes (along with many other useful methods we'll discuss later). Getting from and putting to the `Buffer` changes the position marker, so the `Buffer` keeps track of its contents somewhat like a stream. Attempting to read or write past the limit marker generates a `BufferUnderflowException` or `BufferOverflowException`, respectively.

The mark, position, limit, and capacity values always obey the following formula:

```
mark <= position <= limit <= capacity
```

The position for reading and writing the `Buffer` is always between the mark, which serves as a lower bound, and the limit, which serves as an upper bound. The capacity represents the physical extent of the buffer space.

You can set the position and limit markers explicitly with the `position()` and `limit()` methods. Several convenience methods are provided for common usage patterns. The `reset()` method sets the position back to the mark. If no mark has been set, an `InvalidMarkException` is thrown. The `clear()` method resets the position to 0 and makes the limit the capacity, readying the buffer for new data (the mark is discarded). Note that the `clear()` method does not actually do anything to the data in the buffer; it simply changes the position markers.

The `flip()` method is used for the common pattern of writing data into the buffer and then reading it back out. `flip` makes the current position the limit and then resets the current position to 0 (any mark is thrown away), which saves having to keep track of how much data was read. Another method, rewind(), simply resets the position to 0, leaving the limit alone. You might use it to write the same size of data again. Here is a snippet of code that uses these methods to read data from a channel and write it to two channels:

```
ByteBuffer buff = ...
while (inChannel.read(buff) > 0) { // position = ?
  buff.flip();    // limit = position; position = 0;
  outChannel.write(buff);
  buff.rewind();  // position = 0
  outChannel2.write(buff);
  buff.clear();   // position = 0; limit = capacity
}
```

This might be confusing the first time you look at it because here, the read from the Channel is actually a write to the Buffer and vice versa. Because this example writes all the available data up to the limit, either flip() or rewind() have the same effect in this case.

Buffer types

The various buffer implementations add get and put methods for reading and writing specific data types. Each of the Java primitive types has an associated buffer type: ByteBuffer, CharBuffer, ShortBuffer, IntBuffer, LongBuffer, FloatBuffer, and DoubleBuffer. Each provides get and put methods for reading and writing its type and arrays of its type. Of these, ByteBuffer is the most flexible. Because it has the "finest grain" of all the buffers, it has been given a full complement of get and put methods for reading and writing all the other data types as well as byte. Here are some ByteBuffer methods:

```
byte get()
char getChar()
short getShort()
int getInt()
long getLong()
float getFloat()
double getDouble()

void put(byte b)
void put(ByteBuffer src)
void put(byte[] src, int offset, int length)
void put(byte[] src)
void putChar(char value)
void putShort(short value)
void putInt(int value)
void putLong(long value)
void putFloat(float value)
void putDouble(double value)
```

All the standard buffers also support random access. For each of the aforementioned methods of `ByteBuffer`, an additional form takes an index, for example:

```
getLong(int index)
putLong(int index, long value)
```

But that's not all! `ByteBuffer` can also provide "views" of itself as any of the coarse-grained types. For example, you can fetch a `ShortBuffer` view of a `ByteBuffer` with the `asShortBuffer()` method. The `ShortBuffer` view is *backed* by the `ByteBuffer`, which means that they work on the same data, and changes to either one affect the other. The view buffer's extent starts at the `ByteBuffer`'s current position, and its capacity is a function of the remaining number of bytes, divided by the new type's size. (For example, `shorts` consume two bytes each, `floats` four, and `longs` and `doubles` take eight.) View buffers are convenient for reading and writing large blocks of a contiguous type within a `ByteBuffer`.

`CharBuffers` are interesting as well, primarily because of their integration with `Strings`. Both `CharBuffers` and `Strings` implement the `java.lang.CharSequence` interface. This is the interface that provides the standard `charAt()` and `length()` methods. Many other parts of Java (such as the `java.util.regex` package) allow you to use a `CharBuffer` or a `String` interchangeably. In this case, the `CharBuffer` acts like a modifiable `String` with user-configurable, logical start and end positions.

Byte order

Because we're talking about reading and writing types larger than a byte, the question arises: in what order do the bytes of multibyte values (like `shorts` and `ints`) get written? There are two camps in this world: *big-endian* and *little-endian*.[5] Big-endian means that the most significant bytes come first; little-endian is the reverse. If you're writing binary data for consumption by some native application, this is important. Intel-compatible computers use little-endian, and many workstations that run Unix use big-endian. The `ByteOrder` class encapsulates the choice. You can specify the byte order to use with the `ByteBuffer order()` method, using the identifiers `ByteOrder.BIG_ENDIAN` and `ByteOrder.LITTLE_ENDIAN`, like so:

```
byteArray.order(ByteOrder.BIG_ENDIAN);
```

You can retrieve the native ordering for your platform using the static `ByteOrder.nativeOrder()` method. We know you're curious:

```
jshell> import java.nio.ByteOrder;
```

---

5 The terms *big-endian* and *little-endian* come from Jonathan Swift's novel *Gulliver's Travels*, where they denoted two camps of Lilliputians: those who eat eggs from the big end and those who eat them from the little end.

```
jshell> ByteOrder.nativeOrder()
$4 ==> LITTLE_ENDIAN
```

We ran this on a Linux desktop with an Intel chip. Give it a try on your own system!

Allocating buffers

You can create a buffer either by allocating it explicitly using `allocate()` or by wrapping an existing plain Java array type. Each buffer type has a static `allocate()` method that takes a capacity (size), and a `wrap()` method that takes an existing array:

```
CharBuffer cbuf = CharBuffer.allocate(64*1024);
ByteBuffer bbuf = ByteBuffer.wrap(someExistingArray);
```

A direct buffer is allocated in the same way, with the `allocateDirect()` method:

```
ByteBuffer bbuf2 = ByteBuffer.allocateDirect(64*1024);
```

As we described earlier, direct buffers can use operating system memory structures that are optimized for use with some kinds of I/O operations. The trade-off is that allocating a direct buffer is a little slower and heavier-weight operation than a plain buffer, so you should try to use them for longer-term buffers.

Character Encoders and Decoders

Character encoders and decoders turn characters into raw bytes and vice versa, mapping from the Unicode standard to particular encoding schemes. Encoders and decoders have long existed in Java for use by `Reader` and `Writer` streams and in the methods of the `String` class that work with byte arrays. However, early on there was no API for working with encoding explicitly; you simply referred to encoders and decoders wherever necessary by name as a `String`. The `java.nio.charset` package formalized the idea of a Unicode character set encoding with the `Charset` class.

The `Charset` class is a factory for `Charset` instances, which know how to encode character buffers to byte buffers and decode byte buffers to character buffers. You can look up a character set by name with the static `Charset.forName()` method and use it in conversions:

```
Charset charset = Charset.forName("US-ASCII");
CharBuffer charBuff = charset.decode(byteBuff);   // to ascii
ByteBuffer byteBuff = charset.encode(charBuff);   // and back
```

You can also test to see if an encoding is available with the static `Charset.isSuppor ted()` method.

The following character sets are guaranteed to be supplied:

- US-ASCII
- ISO-8859-1

- UTF-8

- UTF-16BE (big-endian)

- UTF-16LE (little-endian)

- UTF-16

You can list all the encoders available on your platform using the static `available Charsets()` method:

```
Map map = Charset.availableCharsets();
Iterator it = map.keySet().iterator();
while (it.hasNext())
  System.out.println(it.next());
```

The result of `availableCharsets()` is a map, because character sets may have "aliases" and appear under more than one name.

In addition to the buffer-oriented classes of the `java.nio` package, the `InputStream Reader` and `OutputStreamWriter` bridge classes of the `java.io` package work with `Charset` as well. You can specify the encoding as a `Charset` object or by name.

CharsetEncoder and CharsetDecoder

You can get more control over the encoding and decoding process by creating an instance of `CharsetEncoder` or `CharsetDecoder` (a codec) with the `Charset newEn coder()` and `newDecoder()` methods. In the previous snippet, we assumed that all the data was available in a single buffer. More often, however, we might have to process data as it arrives in chunks. The encoder/decoder API allows for this by providing more general `encode()` and `decode()` methods that take a flag specifying whether more data is expected. The codec needs to know this because it might have been left hanging in the middle of a multibyte character conversion when the data ran out. If it knows that more data is coming, it does not throw an error on this incomplete conversion.

In the following snippet, we use a decoder to read from a `ByteBuffer bbuff` and accumulate character data into a `CharBuffer cbuff`:

```
CharsetDecoder decoder = Charset.forName("US-ASCII").newDecoder();

boolean done = false;
while (!done) {
  bbuff.clear();
  done = (in.read(bbuff) == -1);
  bbuff.flip();
  decoder.decode(bbuff, cbuff, done);
}
cbuff.flip();
// use cbuff. . .
```

Here, we look for the end of input condition on the in channel to set the flag done. Note that we take advantage of the flip() method on ByteBuffer to set the limit to the amount of data read and reset the position, setting us up for the decode operation in one step. In case of problems, both encode() and decode() return a result object, CoderResult, that can determine the progress of encoding. The methods isError(), isUnderflow(), and isOverflow() on the CoderResult specify why encoding stopped: for an error, a lack of bytes on the input buffer, or a full output buffer, respectively.

FileChannel

Now that we've covered the basics of channels and buffers, it's time to look at a real channel type. The FileChannel is the NIO equivalent of the java.io.RandomAccess File, but it provides several enhanced features in addition to some performance optimizations. In particular, you can use a FileChannel in place of a plain java.io file stream if you wish to use file locking, memory-mapped file access, or highly optimized data transfer between files or between file and network channels. These are all fairly advanced use cases, but if you do backend work or handle large quantities of data, they will definitely come in handy.

You can create a FileChannel for a Path using the static FileChannel.open() method:

```
FileSystem fs = FileSystems.getDefault();
Path p = fs.getPath("/tmp/foo.txt");

// Open default for reading
try (FileChannel channel = FileChannel.open(p)) {
  // read from the channel ...
}

// Open with options for writing
import static java.nio.file.StandardOpenOption.*;

try (FileChannel channel =
    FileChannel.open(p, WRITE, APPEND, ...) ) {
  // append to foo.txt if it already exists,
  // otherwise, create it and start writing ...
}
```

By default, open() creates a read-only channel for the file. We can open a channel for writing or appending and control other, more advanced features such as atomic create and data syncing by passing additional options, as shown in the second part of the previous example. Table 10-3 summarizes these options.

Table 10-3. java.nio.file.StandardOpenOption

Option	Description
APPEND	Open the file for writing; all writes are positioned at the end of the file.
CREATE	Use with WRITE to open the file and create it if needed.
CREATE_NEW	Use with WRITE to create a file atomically; failing if the file already exists.
DELETE_ON_CLOSE	Attempt to delete the file when it is closed or, if open, when the VM exits.
READ, WRITE	Open the file for read-only or write-only (default is read-only). Use both for read-write.
SPARSE	Use when creating a new file; requests the file be sparse. On filesystems where this is supported, a sparse file handles very large, mostly empty files without allocating as much real storage for empty portions.
SYNC, DSYNC	Wherever possible, guarantee that write operations block until all data is written to storage. SYNC does this for all file changes including data and metadata (attributes), whereas DSYNC adds this requirement only for the data content of the file.
TRUNCATE_EXISTING	Use WRITE on an existing file; set the file length to zero upon opening it.

A FileChannel can also be constructed from a classic FileInputStream, FileOutput Stream, or RandomAccessFile:

```
FileChannel readOnlyFc = new FileInputStream("file.txt")
    .getChannel();
FileChannel readWriteFc = new RandomAccessFile("file.txt", "rw")
    .getChannel();
```

FileChannels created from these file input and output streams are read-only or write-only, respectively. To get a read/write FileChannel, you must construct a Ran domAccessFile with read/write options, as in the previous example.

Using a FileChannel is just like a RandomAccessFile, but it works with a ByteBuffer instead of byte arrays:

```
ByteBuffer bbuf = ByteBuffer.allocate(...);
bbuf.clear();
readOnlyFc.position(index);
readOnlyFc.read(bbuf);
bbuf.flip();
readWriteFc.write(bbuf);
```

You can control how much data is read and written either by setting buffer position and limit markers or using another form of read/write that takes a buffer starting position and length. You can also read and write to a random position by supplying indexes with the read and write methods:

```
readWriteFc.read(bbuf, index)
readWriteFc.write(bbuf, index2);
```

In each case, the actual number of bytes read or written depends on several factors. The operation tries to read or write to the limit of the buffer, and the vast majority of the time, that is what happens with local file access. The operation is guaranteed to block only until at least one byte has been processed. Whatever happens, the number of bytes processed is returned and the buffer position is updated accordingly, preparing you to repeat the operation until it is complete, if needed. This is one of the conveniences of working with buffers; they can manage the count for you. Like standard streams, the channel `read()` method returns -1 upon reaching the end of input.

The size of the file is always available with the `size()` method. It can change if you write past the end of the file. Conversely, you can truncate the file to a specified length with the `truncate()` method.

Concurrent access

`FileChannels` are safe for use by multiple threads and guarantee a consistent view of that data across channels in the same VM. Unless you specify the SYNC or DSYNC options, however, channels do not guarantee how quickly writes are propagated to the storage mechanism. If you only intermittently need to be sure that data is safe before moving on, you can use the `force()` method to flush changes to disk. This method takes a Boolean argument indicating whether file metadata, including timestamp and permissions, must be included. Some systems keep track of reads on files as well as writes, so you can save a lot of updates if you set the flag to `false`, which indicates that you don't care about syncing that metadata immediately.

As with all `Channels`, any thread may close a `FileChannel`. Once closed, all the channel's read/write and position-related methods throw a `ClosedChannelException`.

File locking

`FileChannels` support exclusive and shared locks on regions of files through the `lock()` method:

```
FileLock bigLock = fileChannel.lock();

int start = 0, len = fileChannel2.size();
FileLock readLock = fileChannel2.lock(start, len, true);
```

Locks may be either shared or exclusive. An *exclusive* lock prevents others from acquiring a lock of any kind on the specified file or file region. A *shared* lock allows others to acquire overlapping shared locks but not exclusive locks. These are useful as write and read locks, respectively. When you are writing, you don't want others to be able to write until you're done, but when reading, you need only to block others from writing, not from reading.

The `lock()` method with no arguments in the previous example attempts to acquire an exclusive lock for the whole file. The second form accepts starting and length parameters, as well as a flag indicating whether the lock should be shared (`true`) or exclusive (`false`). The `FileLock` object returned by the `lock()` method can be used to release the lock:

```
bigLock.release();
```

File locks are only guaranteed to be *cooperative*. They work when all threads honor them; they do not necessarily prevent a non-cooperating thread from reading or writing a locked file. In general, the only way to guarantee that locks are obeyed is for both parties to attempt to acquire the lock and proceed only if that attempt is successful.

Also, shared locks are not implemented on some systems, in which case all requested locks are exclusive. You can test whether a lock is shared with the `isShared()` method.

`FileChannel` locks are held until the channel is closed or interrupted, so performing locks within a `try`-with-resources statement will help ensure that locks are released more robustly:

```
try (FileChannel channel = FileChannel.open(p, WRITE) ) {
  channel.lock();
  // ...
}
```

FileChannel Example

Let's see some concrete usage of our channels and buffers. We'll create a small text file that includes a count of how many times it has been accessed by our program. Our program, then, will open the file, read the current count, increment that count, and then write (well, overwrite) the count back to the file. You can try out a complete version of the snippets below in the *AccessNIO.java* file in the *ch10/examples* folder.

You could absolutely tackle this project using the standard I/O classes in `java.io`. The NIO suite is not meant to replace the old classes wholesale, but to add functionality that is missing in the standard classes without breaking any code that relies on those classes. If you find NIO a little complex or dense, feel free to ignore it until you need some of those missing features, like file locking or manipulating metadata.

Our first task is to see if our access-counting file exists (*access.txt* in this example, but the name is arbitrary). If not, we need to create it (and set the internal access counter to 1). We can use a `Path` object with the `Files` static helper methods to get going:

```
public class AccessNIO {
  String accessFileName = "access.txt";
  Path   accessFilePath = Path.of(accessFileName);
  int    accessCount = 0;
  FileChannel accessChannel;

  public AccessNIO() {
    // ...
    boolean initial = !Files.exists(accessFilePath);
    accessChannel = FileChannel.open(accessFilePath, CREATE, READ, WRITE);
    // ...
  }
}
```

If the file doesn't exist yet, we can write out an initial message ("This file has been accessed 0 times.") and then rewind to the beginning of the new file. This gives us the same baseline to work from as though the file had existed all along:

```
if (initial) {
  String msg = buildMessage(); // helper for consistency
  accessChannel.write(ByteBuffer.wrap(msg.getBytes()));
  accessChannel.position(0);
}
```

If the file does exist, we need to make sure we can read from and write to it. We can gather this information with the `accessChannel` object we created in the constructor. We could certainly add other tests and more verbose error messages, but these minimal checks are useful:

```
public boolean isReady() {
  return (accessChannel != null && accessChannel.isOpen());
}
```

Now we come to our primary use case. The file exists and has some content. We have the appropriate permissions for everything we want to do. We'll start by opening the file in a read/write mode and reading its contents into a string:

```
int fsize = (int)accessChannel.size();
// Give ourselves extra room in case the count
// goes over a digit boundary (9 -> 10, 99 -> 100, etc.)
ByteBuffer in = ByteBuffer.allocate(fsize + 2);
accessChannel.read(in);
String current = new String(in.array());
```

We want the file to be human-readable on its own, so we won't take advantage of FileChannel's ability to read and write binary data. We can use our knowledge of how the single line of text is structured to parse our access count:

```
int countStart = 28;
// We know where the count number starts, so get
// everything from that position to the next space
String rawCount = current.substring(countStart,
    current.indexOf(" ", countStart));
accessCount = Integer.parseInt(rawCount) + 1;
```

Finally, we can reset our position and overwrite the previous line with our new, updated line. Notice that we also truncate our file to the end of the saved message. We gave ourselves extra room to accommodate a bigger number, but we don't want excess space in the actual file:

```
String msg = buildMessage();
accessChannel.position(0);
accessChannel.write(ByteBuffer.wrap(msg.getBytes()));
accessChannel.truncate(accessChannel.position());
accessChannel.close();
```

Try compiling and running this example a few times. Does the count go up as expected? What happens if you open the file in another program like a text editor? Unfortunately, Java NIO only *feels* like magic. Accessing the file using any other program will not necessarily change its contents according to the rules of our little example.

wrap() Up

Almost any application bound for distribution will need to handle file I/O. Java has robust support for working efficiently with local files, including access to metadata for both files and directories. Java's commitment to a broad compatibility shows up in the range of character encodings available when working with text files. Java is certainly known for working with nonlocal files, as well. We'll tackle network I/O and web resources in Chapter 13.

Review Questions

1. How could you check to see if a given file already exists?

2. If you have to work with a legacy text file using an old encoding scheme, such as ISO 8859, how might you set up a reader to properly convert that content to something like UTF-8?

3. Which package has the best classes for nonblocking file I/O?

4. Which type of input stream might you use to parse a binary file, such as a JPEG-compressed image?

5. What are the three standard text streams built into the System class?

6. Absolute paths begin at a root (/ or C:\, for example). Where do relative paths begin? More specifically, where are relative paths relative to?

7. How do you retrieve a NIO channel from an existing FileInputStream?

Code Exercises

For these exercises, a skeleton Count.java file is in the *ch10/exercises* folder, but feel free to start with your own class. We iterate on a single project, so you can use your solution from the first exercise as the starting point for the second, and so on. Because testing the program requires supplying different files on the command line, you may find it easier to run this program from a terminal or command window. You can certainly use the terminal tab in your IDE, too:

1. Using the classes of the java.io package, create a small program that will print the size of a file specified on the command line. For example:
   ```
   C:\> java Count ../examples/ListIt.java
   Analyzing ListIt.java
     Size: 1011 bytes
   ```

   If no file argument is given, print an error message to System.err.

2. Expand on the previous exercise to open the given file and count the number of lines. (For these simple exercises, it's OK to assume the file being analyzed is a text file.) If you want a little practice with some of the tools from Chapter 8, split each line based on whitespace and include a word count in the output. (You can use regular expressions to split words on fancier patterns such as punctuation, but that's not required.)
   ```
   C:\> java Count ../examples/ListIt.java
   Analyzing ListIt.java
     Size: 1011 bytes
     Lines: 36
     Words: 178
   ```

   As before, if no file argument is given, print an error message to System.err.

3. Convert your previous solution to use NIO classes like Path and Files instead of readers. You can use any part of the java.nio and java.nio.file packages that you like. You will almost certainly still need the java.io.IOException class from the "old" I/O, of course.

Advanced Exercises

1. Accept a second command-line containing the name of a statistics log file. Rather than printing the various counts back to the terminal, append a line containing the current timestamp, the name of the file, and its three counts. The exact format of the line isn't really important, but it should look something like this:

   ```
   2023-02-02 08:14:25 Count1.java  36  147  1002
   ```

   You can use either your NIO or your old I/O (OIO?) solution as your starting point. If you go with the NIO version, try to use a `ByteBuffer` and a `FileChannel` to do the writing.

   If only one command-line argument is provided, revert to printing the stats out to the screen as before. If no arguments are provided, or if the second argument is not writable, print an error to `System.err`.

   Run this version a few times on a few files. Check your log to make sure each new result is correctly appended to the end of the log file and is not overwriting it.

CHAPTER 11

Functional Approaches in Java

Java is—and remains—an object-oriented language. All of the design patterns and class types we saw in Chapter 5 are still core to how most developers write Java code. Java is also flexible, with individual and corporate contributors proposing and making improvements. As *functional programming* (FP) moves back into the limelight, Java is keeping up. FP represents an alternate way to approach programming: functions, rather than objects, are the focus.

Starting as far back as Java 8, Java has supported a reasonable set of functional features with the `java.util.function` package. This package includes several classes and interfaces that allow developers to use popular functional approaches to problem-solving. We'll explore some of these approaches in this chapter, but we want to emphasize that verb, *allow*. If you don't enjoy functional programming, you can safely ignore this chapter. We hope you'll try some of the examples, though. There are some nice features that can make your code more compact while retaining its readability.

Functions 101

The roots of functional programming extend all the way back to the 1930s, with American mathematician Alonzo Church and his lambda calculus. Church wasn't running his calculus on any hardware, but lambda calculus formalized a way of problem-solving that would lead to early programming languages written for real, operating machines.[1] The Lisp language was developed in the 1950s at MIT and ran on early iterations of modern computers like the IBM 700 series. If you can picture

---

1 Indeed, Church's student and computing pioneer Alan Turing proved that the lambda calculus was equivalent to Turing's own system (the foundational Turing machine) for performing computation.

an old black-and-white photo with bookshelf-sized walls of blinking lights, you've got the right idea for how far back FP ideas and patterns go in the history of computing.

But FP is not the only way to program a computer. Other paradigms, such as procedural programming and object-oriented programming (OOP), regularly vie for popularity. Happily, you can accomplish the same goals in any of those paradigms. The paradigm you choose usually comes down to the problem domain and more than a bit of personal preference.

Consider the simple tasks of adding two numbers and assigning that result to a variable. We can do this in object-oriented languages like Java, in functional languages like Clojure,[2] or procedural languages like C:

```
// Java objects
BigInteger five = new BigInteger(5);
BigInteger twelve = new BigInteger(12);
BigInteger sum = five.add(twelve);

// Clojure
(def five 5)
(def twelve 12)
(def sum (+ five twelve))

// C
int five = 5;
int twelve = 12;
int sum = five + twelve;
```

Java hit the digital scene as OOP was (again) on the rise, and it reflects those roots. Still, FP has always had its evangelists. Java 8 offered some substantial additions to the language and opened the door for fans of functional programming to work with Java. Let's take a look at some of those additions and see how they integrate with the larger world of Java.

Lambdas

Inspired by the lambda calculus, *lambda expressions* (or more simply, lambdas) form the core unit of functional programming in Java. Lambdas are a means of encapsulating a bit of logic. In a functional language, functions are "first-class citizens" and can be created, stored, referenced, used, and passed around just like objects in Java. To mimic that, uh, functionality, Java 8 introduced some new syntax alongside several special interfaces. These additions allow you to quickly define a function that can replace an entire inner class. The result of that definition is still an object under the hood, of course, but one whose "objectness" is mostly hidden.

---

2 We mention Clojure rather than the myriad other modern functional languages because it runs on the JVM and can integrate with Java classes and methods. Neat!

We'll cover lambda expressions and those special interfaces in more detail throughout the rest of this section. Then we'll look at a popular, concrete example of using these expressions to do real work.

Lambda Expressions

Lambda expressions are small bits of code that can accept parameters and return values, just like methods. Unlike methods, though, you can easily pass a lambda as an argument to some other method or store it in a variable like you might with an object reference. FP proponents prize this ability to move code around like data. It allows you to write interesting and dynamic code without the clutter of creating inner or anonymous inner classes.

Lambdas are not meant to provide a performance boost. Although judicious use of lambdas often makes for more compact, more concise source code, that compression does not remove any complexity. Lambdas may require less typing, but they don't do less work.

Recall the `run()` method used by threads, which we saw so often in Chapter 9. We created more than a few small classes that implemented the `Runnable` interface to supply a "body" to our threads. Small classes that do not include any state as instance variables are prime candidates for using lambdas: you have a well-defined task that you use in a well-defined situation.

Let's revisit one of our thread demonstrations and then take a peek at how we could use a lambda expression as an alternative to the explicit use of `Runnable`. We'll simplify the `VirtualDemo` class from "Death of a Thread" on page 284 and concentrate on the anonymous inner class:

```
public class VirtualDemo2 {
  public static void main(String args[]) throws Exception {
    Runnable runnable = new Runnable() {
      public void run() {
        System.out.println("Hello thread! ID: " +
            Thread.currentThread().threadId());
      }
    };
    Thread t = Thread.startVirtualThread(runnable);
    t.join();
  }
}
```

We create a new instance of `Runnable` with a simple `run()` method that prints a greeting and the thread's ID number:

```
% java --enable-preview VirtualDemo2
Hello thread! ID: 20
```

Great. Everything works as expected. Now let's replace that `runnable` variable with a lambda expression:

```
public class VirtualDemo3 {
  public static void main(String args[]) throws Exception {
    Thread t = Thread.startVirtualThread(() ->
      System.out.println("Hello thread! ID: " +
          Thread.currentThread().threadId())
    );
    t.join();
  }
}
```

We still start a new virtual thread, and we still store that thread in a variable (t, in both examples), but there is no evidence of the `Runnable` interface. We passed a somewhat strange argument to the `startVirtualThread()` method instead of a reference to some object. That "strange argument" is our lambda expression, annotated in Figure 11-1.

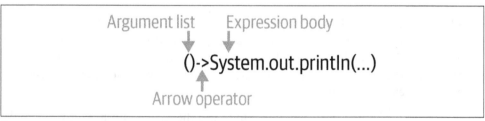

Figure 11-1. Basic structure of a lambda expression

This particular lambda is very simple. We don't pass it any arguments, and it does not return a value. Often that's all you need. But lambdas are capable of much more. Lambda expressions also support arguments, can return values, and can have more interesting bodies.

Passing arguments

If we think about lambdas as bits of code, it's reasonable to compare them to regular methods. Regular methods do encapsulate logic, just like lambdas. But many of the methods we've seen in previous chapters also accept arguments. Can we supply arguments to a lambda?

Consider an iterator that walks through the elements of a Java collection. We saw several examples in Chapter 7. In those examples, we used an iterator inside a loop, with the body of the loop doing something with the given element of the collection on each pass. Recall our tree-painting loop from "Application: Trees on the Field" on page 233:

```
// File: Field.java
  protected void paintComponent(Graphics g) {
    g.setColor(fieldColor);
    g.fillRect(0,0, getWidth(), getHeight());
    for (Tree t : trees) {
      t.draw(g);
    }
    // ...
  }
```

The alternate `for` loop uses the iterator from `trees` to get every individual tree, and then tells that tree to draw itself on our field. We could replace that loop with a lambda and the `forEach()` method of the `Iterable` interface:

```
// File: Field.java
  protected void paintComponent(Graphics g) {
    g.setColor(fieldColor);
    g.fillRect(0,0, getWidth(), getHeight());
    trees.forEach(t -> t.draw(g));
    // ...
  }
```

You can see the same arrow operator, but instead of an empty pair of parentheses, we have a variable, `t` on the lefthand side. That variable receives one tree at a time from the `trees` collection, just like the alternate `for` loop from the first snippet. And just like the body of that `for` loop, you can use the current tree on the righthand side of the expression. With this arrangement, we get a slightly more concise version of our loop, but it retains its readability. You can use this handy trick with any collection that implements the `Iterable` interface.

 Terms like *concise* and *readable* are subjective judgments. Proponents of FP definitely find the more compact syntax of lambdas easier to read, but those folks are already comfortable with the notation. We hope you'll try the examples and exercises in this chapter to gain a little of that familiarity. We do like lambdas and use them in a number of situations, but they are never required. If you don't find lambdas useful or readable after trying them out, you don't need to use them in your own code.

You may have noticed that our first lambda expression for a simple thread body took no arguments, so we used an empty set of parentheses on the lefthand side. But in this most recent example, we had one argument and no parentheses. The single argument form is so common that the compiler allows this shorthand with no parentheses. If you have no arguments, or more than one argument, the parentheses are required.

Expression bodies

Lambda expressions shine in situations where you would otherwise use an anonymous inner class. You can't substitute lambdas for all situations that call for anonymous inner classes, but there are a surprising number of spots throughout Java that do work with lambdas. With this variety of applications comes the need for more complex computing beyond print statements. If you need to perform a few statements or work with a temporary variable, for example, you can enclose the body of the expression in curly braces, just like a method.

Imagine the trees in our game are seasonal. You could specify the color of their leaves before drawing them. You can still use a lambda:

```
trees.forEach(t -> {
  t.setLeafColor(getSeasonalColor());
  t.draw(g);
});
```

Presumably our fictitious `getSeasonalColor()` method does some nice date-based calculating and returns an appropriate color. Notice that you can use methods (and most variables) from the rest of the class inside our lambda expression. Lambdas are quite powerful. But part of their power comes from judicious use—a 20-line expression body would probably hurt the readability of your code. But if you have a few lambdas with a few lines, you're in good shape.

Beyond keeping your lambdas readable, we want to point out a few quirks that might crop up for you. If you do want to use a local variable from the enclosing scope, it must be "effectively final" per the documentation. Recall that `final` variables can't be modified. *Effectively final* variables are ones that *are not* modified even though they might not have the official `final` keyword in their declaration. If you try to use a nonfinal, local variable, the compiler will complain. Happily, this restriction only applies to local variables. You are free to use (and even modify) variables declared as members of the enclosing class.

The other quirk revolves around the keyword `this`. If you recall from "The "this" reference" on page 146, `this` gives you a reference to the current object. It's handy when methods or constructors have argument names that overlap with member variables:

```
public class Position {
  int x, y;

  public Position(int x, int y) {
    this.x = x;
    this.y = y;
  }
  // ...
}
```

While you might reasonably think that `this` inside a lambda body would refer to the lambda itself, it actually still refers to the enclosing class. This quirk means you can use `this` inside a lambda just as you would with the constructor in the previous example. It makes sure your lambdas have access to the stuff in your class, even if a local variable would otherwise shadow something.

Returning values

Whether your lambda is a pithy one-liner or includes a readability-busting dozen lines, you can also return a value. A (deceptively) simple example is an incrementing function that takes an integer argument and returns an integer that is one more than the input. The expression itself would look something like this:

```
x -> x + 1
```

In this form, Java will compute the answer to `x + 1` and return it. If we have a multiline body that should return a value, we can use the `return` keyword:

```
x -> {
  System.out.println("Input: " + x);
  return x + 1;
}
```

Explicit returns can be handy when you have `if` statements in the body. But the simpler form is preferable if your expression fits.

Functional Interfaces

You may be wondering how Java categorizes our simple lambda expression. Is it an `int` like the input, or the result? Is it an object like so much of Java? Is it something we haven't seen yet? Let's see if *jshell* can shed any light:

```
jshell> x -> x + 1
|  Error:
|  incompatible types: java.lang.Object is not a functional interface
|  x -> x + 1
|  ^--------^
```

Hmm, not really what we were hoping for, but that phrase *functional interface* is a clue. Let's try that `var` keyword we saw in "Inferring types" on page 100 and see if our lambda expression can be inferred:

```
jshell> var inc = x -> x + 1
|  Error:
|  cannot infer type for local variable inc
|    (lambda expression needs an explicit target-type)
|  var inc = x -> x + 1;
|  ^------------------^
```

Shoot. *jshell* did recognize our lambda expression, but that recognition isn't enough to establish a type.

So what is a lambda expression's type? In the case of our simple incrementing lambda, it turns out to be an `IntFunction`, a function that accepts one `int` as an argument and returns an `int`. The `IntFunction` interface lives in the `java.util.function` package alongside several other functional interfaces. Each interface in this package represents a different "shape" that a lambda expression can take. Let's try it:

```
jshell> import java.util.function.*

jshell> IntFunction inc = x -> x + 1
inc ==> $Lambda$24/0x0000000840087840@23ab930d
```

Hooray! We didn't get an error! (Although that resulting value looks rather daunting.) Happily, we don't need to worry about the internal details of our lambda, as long as we can apply it to some data. But just how would we apply it?

Take a look at the online documentation (*https://oreil.ly/pgX7J*) for the interface and you'll see it has one method, `apply()`, appropriately enough:

```
jshell> inc.apply(7)
$16 ==> 8
```

Another hooray! Our incrementor increments! The other interfaces have a similar method defined.

The shapes that we mentioned cover the different arrangements of the arguments and results of lambda expressions. If we wanted to work with `double` values instead of `int`s, for example, we could use the `DoubleFunction` interface. If we want to supply an object as an argument but don't need to return a value, we could use the `Consumer<T>` interface. (Since `Consumer` works on reference types, it is parameterized. If we really did want to store a lambda that accepted a string, we would use the type `Consumer<String>`.) Or maybe we have a lambda that takes no arguments but generates a `long` value: the `LongSupplier` interface will do the trick. We won't reproduce the full list of functional interfaces here, but it's worth looking at the package summary (*https://oreil.ly/ksK1Z*) online.

As you find more situations where you can use lambdas, you'll see how all these different shapes get used. But it's important to point out that the term *functional interface* can apply to any interface that has a single abstract method (often abbreviated as SAM in the documentation). In Chapter 12, for example, we'll use lambdas to handle user interface events like clicking a button. Button events are reported to `ActionListeners`. The `ActionListener` interface has one abstract method, `action Performed()`, so it qualifies as a functional interface, even though it was part of Java long before these functional features were added.

Method References

One other feature is associated with Java's functional approach: a *method reference*. Sometimes your lambda expressions are really just wrappers for other methods. Consider the very popular task of printing out the contents of a collection. We could use the `forEach()` method we just learned about and print the elements of a list using a lambda:

```
jshell> List<String> names = new ArrayList<>()
names ==> []
jshell> names.add("Kermit");
$3 ==> true
jshell> names.add("Fozzie");
$4 ==> true
jshell> names.add("Gonzo");
$5 ==> true
jshell> names.add("Piggy");
$6 ==> true

jshell> names.forEach(n -> System.out.println(n))
Kermit
Fozzie
Gonzo
Piggy
```

You can see that our lambda expression simply shuttles each string to the `System.out.println()` method. This is just the right candidate for a method reference.

We specify such a reference with a double-colon operator separating the method from its object (or its class, in the case of a `static` method):

```
jshell> names.forEach(System.out::println)
Kermit
Fozzie
Gonzo
Piggy
```

Very compact and still readable. Method references only work in a narrow set of circumstances, but they are popular options wherever they're allowed. As with lambda expressions in general, there is no real performance benefit versus using a lambda. Indeed, the Java compiler creates a lambda expression out of our method reference behind the scenes:

```
jshell> Consumer<String> printer = System.out::println
printer ==> $Lambda$27/0x0000000840087440@63c12fb0
```

Feel free to use method references where they fit, but it's also fine to stick with an explicit lambda expression if you find it easier to read.

Practical Lambdas: Sorting

Gosh, that was a lot of theory! It's time to put these lambda expressions to use in some code you often find in real applications: sorting data. Sorting is a common task; we talked about it in "A Closer Look: The sort() Method" on page 232 while discussing collections. Where do lambdas fit in?

To put any list in order, you need a way of comparing two elements in the list so you know which one should come before the other. Some lists—say a list of employee salaries or a list of file and subfolder names in a given directory—have a fairly natural ordering that suffices in most cases. But sometimes you need a more complex ordering, like sorting the subfolders to the top before the files. You could implement the Comparable interface like you did before, or create a custom class that implements the closely related Comparator interface, but you could also supply a lambda.

For a lambda expression to help with sorting, it needs to behave like the compare() method of Comparator. We need an expression that takes two arguments, say a and b, and returns one of three int values:

- Something less than zero if a < b
- Something greater than zero if a > b
- Zero if a == b

The magic of lambdas allows us to decide *how* we organize a list in a dynamic way. The java.util.Collections helper class contains a sort() method that accepts a collection to sort, along with a comparator to provide the ordering. We can use a lambda to do that comparing. For example, we could create a simple lambda to sort our names list in alphabetical order:

```
jshell> Collections.sort(names, (a, b) -> a.compareTo(b))

jshell> names
names ==> [Fozzie, Gonzo, Kermit, Piggy]
```

Arranged as expected, although we could have used any of Java's sorting tricks to get this default ordering. Let's reverse the ordering:

```
jshell> Collections.sort(names, (a, b) -> b.compareTo(a))

jshell> names
names ==> [Piggy, Kermit, Gonzo, Fozzie]
```

Neat! All we had to do was swap the order of the arguments using the compareTo() method.

Lambdas can do more, of course, especially when you need to order something a little more complex than a list of names. Imagine taking the trees in our apple tossing game and sorting them by their distance from the origin, (0,0), using a slightly more interesting lambda:

```
Collections.sort(trees, (t1, t2) -> {
  var t1x = t1.getPositionX();
  var t1y = t1.getPositionY();
  var t2x = t2.getPositionX();
  var t2y = t2.getPositionY();
  var dist1 = Math.sqrt(t1x * t1x + t1y * t1Y);
  var dist2 = Math.sqrt(t2x * t2x + t2y * t2y);
  return dist1 - dist2;
});
```

We made this expression body more verbose than necessary to emphasize that lamb-das can have many lines of code. This lambda probably strains readability, but it also highlights a handy side effect of such expressions: you get to see the code being used to sort right where the sorting is done. This self-documenting feature is another reason FP has so many proponents.

Streams

As we've noted before, lambda expressions don't do anything that you couldn't accomplish using other features of Java, but they provide a different way to think about problems. In that same vein, the Java Streams API (not to be confused with all of the various "Stream" classes, like `PrintStream` in the `java.io` package) provides a different way to think about data.

You can get a stream from one of the classes in the `java.util.stream` package or by using the `stream()` method of a collection. A stream provides a steady flow of objects, and you perform *operations* on each object as you encounter it. Operations can filter out unwanted objects, count them, or even alter them before passing them along. In situations where you have very large amounts of data, streams offer a concise way to process all of that data. As a programmer, you can concentrate on how you handle a single object and let the stream do the work of getting those single objects ready for you.

Sources and Operations

To try out streams, we'll need a source of data. An easy start is using the `stream()` method on any class implementing the `Collection` interface or one of its descend-ants. (Arrays don't have a built-in stream option, but you can create one easily enough with the `Stream.of()` static method.)

Once we have a stream going, we can operate on it. We'll look at many more operations next, but a popular and simple starting point is the `count()` operation. Not surprisingly, this operation counts each element of the stream as it goes by and produces a single result. For example, we can use our `names` list in *jshell* and find out how many friends are in our list:

```
jshell> names
names ==> [Fozzie, Gonzo, Kermit, Piggy]

jshell> names.stream().count()
$24 ==> 4
```

Admittedly, this example doesn't do anything amazing, but we'll build up to more complex operations. The important thing to note is the way we attach an operation to our stream. The `stream()` returns a stream object, and we use the dot operator (`.`) immediately to get our count.

We could use another operation to print out our names:

```
jshell> names.stream().forEach(System.out::println)
Fozzie
Gonzo
Kermit
Piggy
```

We supplied a method reference to the `forEach()` operation, but you can also provide a lambda that takes one argument (the current name from the stream) and does not return a value.

Stream reuse

You may have noticed that we did not store our stream in a variable for reuse between our `count()` example and the similar `forEach()` example. Streams are one-way and single use. You can actually store a stream in a variable, but if you try to reuse the stream after you have processed it, you'll get an error:

```
jshell> Stream<String> nameStream = names.stream()
nameStream ==> java.util.stream.ReferencePipeline$Head@621be5d1

jshell> nameStream.count()
$27 ==> 4

jshell> nameStream.forEach(System.out::println)
|   Exception java.lang.IllegalStateException: stream has
|      already been operated upon or closed
|         at AbstractPipeline.sourceStageSpliterator
|            (AbstractPipeline.java:279)
|         at ReferencePipeline$Head.forEach
|            (ReferencePipeline.java:658)
|         at (#28:1)
```

We created a parameterized `Stream` object for our stream of `String` objects. We successfully started the stream and used the `count()` operation, but we failed to use that same stream for our `forEach()` operation. Processing a stream does not alter the original source, so you can safely start a new stream as often as needed. But once a stream has ended, it cannot be restarted.

Stream generators

Another source of stream data is a *generator*. Generators create data according to some rule. Some generators produce a fixed value over and over, while others produce random content. You can generate simple things like numbers or complex things like objects. If getting real data is an expensive operation, you can use generators to more easily test your stream logic. Similarly, you can use a generator to create good (or quirky, or error-filled) data to test other parts of your application.

The `Stream.generate()` method takes an instance of the `Supplier` interface. A supplier has one job: to supply an infinite stream of elements. It has one method: `get()`, which returns an element of the appropriate type. And the element's type is really the only restriction that Java places on your generator. Let's try generating something simple: a steady stream of the number 42:

```
jshell> Stream.generate(() -> 42).limit(3).forEach(System.out::println)
42
42
42
```

Our `Supplier` in this case is the very simple lambda, `() → 42`. There are no arguments, and every time the lambda expression is used or evaluated, the result is 42. Notice that we follow our `generate()` method with a new method, `limit()`, that sits between the generator and our `println()` step. On their own, generators generate forever. We'll discuss `limit()` and other related methods in the next section, but we need something in the short term to rein in our generators. If you don't believe us, try removing that piece. Just be ready to hit Ctrl-C quickly (and repeatedly) to stop the onslaught of infinite 42s!

We can implement the `Supplier` interface (or any of its base-type cousins such as `IntSupplier`) in a class when we need a more interesting set of generated data. Consider a stream of random day names. We need a random number generator and a list of valid days. Those requirements would probably make for a messy inline lambda, but they're trivial in a small class:

```
import java.util.Random;
import java.util.stream.Stream;
import java.util.function.Supplier;

public class WeekDayGenerator implements Supplier<String> {
  private static String[] days =
    { "Sun", "Mon", "Tue", "Wed", "Thu", "Fri", "Sat" };
  private Random randSrc = new Random();

  public String get() {
```

```
    return days[randSrc.nextInt(days.length)];
  }

  public static void main(String args[]) {
    Stream.generate(new WeekDayGenerator())
        .limit(5)
        .forEach(System.out::println);
  }
}
```

The `main()` method here isn't necessary, but it makes it easy to test. Just compile and run the class from the *ch11/examples* folder. You should see five random days of the week:

```
% cd ch11/examples
% javac WeekDayGenerator.java
% java WeekDayGenerator
Sun
Thu
Fri
Sun
Mon
```

Try running it a few times just to confirm that the random feature is working. Your generating class can be as rich as necessary. You just need to make sure `get()` returns an appropriate object or value: notice we implemented a parameterized version of our interface: `Suppler<String>`, and our `get()` method returns `String`. Now you're good to go!

Stream iterators

In addition to generators, streams can be built from iterators. These iterators aren't quite the same as the iterators you use to walk through a collection, but the idea is similar. *Stream iterators* have the same notion of a "next" value as collection iterators, but for streams, that next value comes from performing a calculation on the previous value. If you need a range of sequential numbers, for example, an iterator is ideal:

```
jshell> IntStream.iterate(1, i -> i + 1).limit(5).forEach(System.out::println)
1
2
3
4
5
```

The `iterate()` source method takes two arguments: a starting value and a lambda expression. The lambda takes one argument and uses it to create the next element. That second element will be put back through the same lambda expression to create the third, and so on. We certainly could have done that with a custom `Supplier`, but for many sequences, iterators offer a simpler entry point. And you aren't restricted to iterating on numbers—you can iterate on any object type that suits your needs. As long as you have a way to calculate the next object for the stream, you can use an iterator as a source. Let's try creating a sequence of LocalDate objects as an example:

```
jshell> import java.time.LocalDate

jshell> import java.time.temporal.ChronoUnit

jshell> Stream.iterate(LocalDate.now(),
   ...>    d -> d.plus(1, ChronoUnit.DAYS)).limit(5).forEach(System.out::println)
2023-02-10
2023-02-11
2023-02-12
2023-02-13
2023-02-14
```

We use the LocalDate.now() static method to get the current date for our starting value. The iterating expression takes a LocalDate object as input, uses the plus() method to add one day, and returns the new LocalDate. (And we end on such a lovely date.)

Filtering Streams

Both the count() and the forEach() operations in the previous snippets are examples of *terminal* operations. Terminal operations "terminate" a stream. You can have only one, final terminating operation when processing a stream. The limit() operation, in contrast, is an example of an *intermediate* operation. An intermediate operation may alter or remove some of the data in the stream, but the stream continues. Filtering is a popular type of intermediate operation, and limiting the number of elements that continue on down the stream is a form of filtering. But you can filter for all kinds of reasons. You can filter to select desirable data or to toss out undesirable data. You can filter out duplicates. You can input a stream of objects to your filter and have it output an essentially new stream for use by the next operation.

As luck would have it, generic filters are just lambdas that return boolean values. This is the Predicate shape from the big list of functional interfaces in the java.util.function package. You send one argument in, and either true or false comes out. For example, we could use a filter to count the names that contain the letter "o" like so:

```
jshell> names.stream().filter(n -> n.indexOf("o") > -1).count()
$30 ==> 2
```

Our filtering lambda takes one name and uses the indexOf() operation to see if the name contains an "o". Since indexOf() returns an int value, we compare it to an impossible index, -1, to create the required boolean result. If the predicate returns true, that name will be passed along. If the predicate returns false, the name is simply dropped from the stream.

The important detail again is the "in the middle" nature of a filter. We can keep doing things with our stream. It's common to stack multiple filters, for example. Each filter selects different desired elements (or removes unwanted elements, depending on how you look at it). Another popular built-in filter is the distinct() operation that weeds out duplicates. Let's add some repeated names to our list and try using two intermediate operations:

```
jshell> names.add("Gonzo")
$32 ==> true

jshell> names
names ==> [Fozzie, Gonzo, Kermit, Piggy, Gonzo]

jshell> names.stream().
   ...> filter(n -> n.indexOf("o") > -1).count()
$34 ==> 3

jshell> names.stream().
   ...> filter(n -> n.indexOf("o") > -1).
   ...> distinct().count()
$35 ==> 2
```

You can stack as many filters as you need, although it's still important to keep your code readable. (If you have a gauntlet of 20 filters, you may want to reconsider how you process the source for the stream.) But you can do more than simply filter the elements in your stream: you can turn them into something else!

Mapping Streams

In streams, *mapping* is the process of altering an element in a stream before passing it along. Like filtering, you use a lambda expression to perform the alteration. You can map simple changes, like adding sales tax to a stream of prices, or you can create complex maps that convert one type of object into a wholly different type. Or you can do both! Mapping is also an intermediate operation, so you can stack map operations just as you did with filters. Indeed, you will see many examples online of programmers mixing maps and filters to achieve their final result.

Let's start by trying the task of adding sales tax. We'll start with a short list of double values and a 5% tax. We can map() the tax onto the prices like so:

```
jshell> double[] prices = { 5.99, 9.99, 20.0, 8.5};
prices ==> double[4] { 5.99, 9.99, 20.0, 8.5 }

jshell> DoubleStream.of(prices).forEach(System.out::println)
5.99
9.99
20.0
8.5
```

```
jshell> DoubleStream.of(prices).map(p -> p*1.05).
   ...>    forEach(System.out::println)
6.2895
10.489500000000001
21.0
8.925
```

The formatting of our prices isn't very polished, but the tax has been correctly applied. While we have them handy, we can try out another useful terminal operation, sum(), to add up all the prices:

```
jshell> DoubleStream.of(prices).map(p -> p*1.05).sum()
$7 ==> 46.70400000000001
```

Again, the output isn't nicely formatted, but we summed up an entire array of numbers in one line!

Mapping object attributes

You can also use maps to peer inside objects. Let's create a simplified variation of our Employee class from Chapter 7 with an additional salary attribute. We'll call this version a PaidEmployee:

```java
public class PaidEmployee {
    private int id;
    private String name;
    private int salary; // annual, in whole dollars

    public PaidEmployee(String fullname, int id, int salary) {
        this.name = fullname;
        this.id = id;
        this.salary = salary;
    }

    public String getName() { return name; }
    public int getID() { return id; }
    public int getSalary() { return salary; }
}
```

In a stream of employees, we can now use map() to extract specific attributes, like their names. Let's write a test class that creates a few example employee objects and then uses a stream to process the employees:

```java
import java.util.*;

public class Report {
    List<PaidEmployee> employees = new ArrayList<>();

    void buildEmployeeList() {
        employees.add(new PaidEmployee("Fozzie", 4, 30_000));
        employees.add(new PaidEmployee("Gonzo", 2, 50_000));
        employees.add(new PaidEmployee("Kermit", 1, 60_000));
```

```
    employees.add(new PaidEmployee("Piggy", 3, 80_000));
  }

  public void publishNames() {
    employees.stream().map(e -> e.getName()).forEach(System.out::println);
  }

  public static void main(String args[]) {
    Report r = new Report();
    r.buildEmployeeList();
    r.publishNames();
  }
}
```

The publishNames() method uses map() to take our PaidEmployee object and grab the employee's name. That name (a simple String object) continues on down the stream. With the names available, we could add filters, like our "names with an o" filter from earlier examples, or watch out for duplicate employee records. Any time you need to massage your data, map() is the method to use.

Mapping conversions

In the previous example, we quietly converted our stream from one with PaidEmployee objects to one with String objects. Because both types are reference types, we don't really have to worry about the fact that we have different before and after types. If you need to move from a reference type to a base type—or vice versa—you have to be a little more explicit about the conversion. This is definitely a common task, so Java supplies some handy variations of map() for just this purpose. Let's get a sum of all our employees' annual salaries to know what our wage budget should be:

```
  public void publishBudget() {
    int b = employees.stream().mapToInt(e -> e.getSalary()).sum();
    System.out.println("Annual budget is " + b);
  }
```

Figure 11-2 illustrates the data moving through this budget-calculating stream.

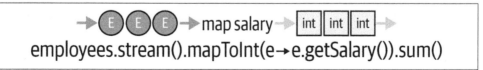

Figure 11-2. Converting between objects and ints in a stream

Similar classes exist for moving to two other base types: mapToDouble() and mapTo Long(). If you already have a stream of numbers and want to move to an object, the base type streams, like IntStream, all include the mapToObj() operation.

Flatmaps

We want to introduce one other type of mapping operation commonly used with streams: the *flatmap*. The flatmap operation takes lumpy inputs and smooths them into a single (you might even say flat!) stream of elements. What do we mean by lumpy input? It's mostly a cute way of saying multidimensional data. Consider the array-of-arrays chessboard we discussed in "Multidimensional Arrays" on page 127. We can play with a similar setup in *jshell* using simple int values. The "board" is an array of rows, where each row is an array of numbers. What happens if we try to start a stream from our two-dimensional array? Let's try it out with a reduced 4 × 4 matrix:

```
jshell> int[][] board = {
   ...>    { 2, 0, 4, 2 },
   ...>    { 0, 3, 0, 1 },
   ...>    { 5, 0, 1, 0 },
   ...>    { 2, 3, 0, 2 } }
board ==> int[4][] { int[4] ... , int[4] { 2, 3, 4, 2 } }

jshell> Arrays.stream(board).forEach(System.out::println)
[I@5a10411
[I@2ef1e4fa
[I@306a30c7
[I@b81eda8
```

Hmm, that appears to be a stream of int[] objects, not individual integers. (Those ugly blobs are Java's default way of printing objects that don't have a pretty toString() method. The format is "object type @ memory address".) What if we try to start a stream from the first row?

```
jshell> Arrays.stream(board[0]).forEach(System.out::println)
2
3
4
2
```

That output looks better—it's a list of our made-up chess piece values, but it's only one row. We could put the stream in the middle of a for loop and process a separate stream for every row, but that seems cumbersome and would make any kind of counting or summing step much more difficult.

For a nice, stream-friendly way to get all of our chess pieces into one stream, we'll use flatMap(), or in our case of going from an object (each row is an array object) to a base type (each chess piece is an int), we'll use flatMapToInt():

```
jshell> Arrays.stream(board).
   ...>    flatMapToInt(r -> Arrays.stream(r)).
   ...>    forEach(System.out::println)
2
3
4
```

```
2
0
0
0
0
0
0
0
0
2
3
4
2
```

Hooray, it worked! We started with a stream of dense objects and broke up those dense objects into a single stream of smaller parts. You can use `flatMap()` and its base-type cousins to toss any tabular, cubic, or generic multidimensional data into a pleasant stream of individual elements.

Let's look at another example that combines several of the stream topics we've covered so far. A common task for system and network administrators is parsing log files. Web servers, for example, log each visitor's Internet Protocol (IP) address and the resource they requested. Here's a small example, with the long lines truncated for readability:

```
54.152.182.118 - - [20/Sep/2020:08:28:46 -0400] "GET / ...
107.150.59.82 - - [20/Sep/2020:09:33:02 -0400] "GET / ...
66.249.65.234 - - [20/Sep/2020:09:33:54 -0400] "GET /robots.txt ...
66.249.65.243 - - [20/Sep/2020:09:33:54 -0400] "GET /robots.txt ...
```

Each line contains lots of information: that IP address, the date and time of the request, what was requested, how it was requested, and (if you peek at the real log file in the *ch11/examples* folder) information about what browser or user agent made the request. Real-world log files can be huge, and admins usually keep them compressed on disk.

Let's use all our stream skills. We'll start with a GZIP file and load its contents with some I/O streams, then break up the uncompressed data into lines. We can use `flatMap()` to turn the functional stream of lines into a stream of space-separated tokens. With our tokens in hand, we can finally get to the information we really want: a count of unique visitor IP addresses:

```java
import java.util.regex.Pattern;
import java.util.stream.Stream;
import java.util.zip.GZIPInputStream;
import java.io.*;

public class UniqueIPs {
  public static void main(String args[]) {
    Pattern separator = Pattern.compile("\\s+");
```

```
    Pattern ipAddress = Pattern.compile("\\d+\\.\\d+\\.\\d+\\.\\d+");
    try {
      // Open the file...
      FileInputStream fis = new FileInputStream("sample-access.log.gz");
      // Then decompress the file with a wrapper...
      GZIPInputStream gis = new GZIPInputStream(fis);
      // Then wrap the decompressed input in a reader
      InputStreamReader ir = new InputStreamReader(gis);
      // Then layer on a buffered reader...
      BufferedReader br = new BufferedReader(ir);

      // That finally gives us our stream!
      // Now let's process that stream to get some interesting information
      long result = br.lines()
          .flatMap(ls -> separator.splitAsStream(ls))
          .filter(word -> ipAddress.matcher(word).matches())
          .distinct()
          .count();
      System.out.println("Found " + result + " unique IPs.");

    } catch (IOException ioe) {
      System.err.println("Oh no! Something went wrong: " + ioe);
    }
  }
}
```

Very nice. Once we have the stream of lines from our decompressed file, we can get our count using the functional approach to processing data with a compact, efficient, and readable list of steps. Again, you do not *have* to use functional streams and lambdas, but more and more programmers are looking into this way of solving problems—even in erstwhile object-oriented languages like Java.

Reducing and Collecting

We've looked at several examples using streams in this chapter. Each example has ended the stream with one of three terminal operations: a forEach() that we typically use to print the elements, a count() to know how many elements there are, or with sum() as a way to add up all of the numerical elements. Counting and summing are examples of *reducing* a stream. You "reduce" all the elements in your stream to a single answer.

Streams in Java have several built-in reducers, as shown in Table 11-1.

Table 11-1. Terminal reduction operations

Operation	Description
count()	Returns the number of elements in the stream
findAny()	Returns an element (if any exist) from the stream
findFirst()	Returns the first element (if it exists) from the stream

Operation	Description
matchAll()	Returns true if all elements of the stream match the given criteria
matchAny()	Returns true if at least one element in the stream matches the given criteria
max()	Using a provided comparator, returns the "largest" element (if any)
min()	Using a provided comparator, returns the "smallest" element (if any)

You might wonder why the sum() operation we've used a few times isn't listed. It is definitely a reducer, but the built-in version is available only on the base-type streams: IntStream, LongStream, and DoubleStream.

Optional values

Before looking deeper at reducers (including how to create a custom reducer), we need to be prepared for a potentially dire outcome: an empty stream.

Any time you filter a stream, it's possible you won't have anything left on the other side of the filter. As a quick example, what if the filter in our names example earlier had been looking for the letter "a" instead of "o"? None of our names contain an "a," so the filter would end up dropping every name from our list. The count() operation can handle that situation fine: it simply returns an answer of zero. But what if we had used min() or findFirst()? Those reducers expect to give you a matching element from your stream. If there are no elements left, what should a reducer return? It might be acceptable in some scenarios to return a null value, but if your stream ends with base-type elements, like int values, you can't use null.

Rather than force you to construct some strange rule or throw an exception, Java streams support the notion of an *optional* answer. These answers are wrapped in a class, appropriately called Optional, from the java.util package. An Optional object has two key methods that we'll work with in this section: isPresent() tells us whether a value exists or not, and get() returns that value. (If you call get() when no value is present, you'll "get" a NoSuchElementException.)

We can test this optional idea by revisiting our name filtering example. Rather than counting the results, though, we'll use findFirst() to return the first matching name. Since there might not be any matches at all, we'll get the result wrapped in an Optional. Feel free to reuse the names collection if it's still in your *jshell*, but here's a quick recap:

```
jshell> List<String> names = new ArrayList<>()
names ==> []

jshell> names.add("Kermit")
jshell> names.add("Fozzie")
jshell> names.add("Gonzo")
jshell> names.add("Piggy")
```

```
jshell> names
names ==> [Kermit, Fozzie, Gonzo, Piggy]
```

Now let's run those names through a filter and look for the first match. We'll try our filter with an "o" (which should have an answer) and then with an "a" (which should not have an answer). Notice how we use the Optional result:

```
jshell> Optional matched = names.stream().
   ...>    filter(n -> n.indexOf("o") > -1).findFirst()
matched ==> Optional[Fozzie]

jshell> System.out.println(matched.isPresent() ?
   ...>    matched.get() : "N/A")
Fozzie

jshell> Optional matched = names.stream().
   ...>    filter(n -> n.indexOf("a") > -1).findFirst()
matched ==> Optional.empty

jshell> System.out.println(matched.isPresent() ?
   ...>    matched.get() : "N/A")
N/A
```

While it makes your code a little more verbose to test if your value isPresent(), Optional provides a clear interface for handling both the good and the "bad" outcomes of your stream processing. And as with so many other classes and methods in this functional arena, you can use the OptionalInt, OptionalLong, and Optional Double classes to catch potentially missing base-type results.

Creating a custom reducer

What if the built-in reducers don't cover your needs? You may not be surprised to learn that you can supply a lambda to create a custom reducer. The Stream class includes a reduce() operation that accepts a lambda with the BinaryOperator shape from the java.util.function package we discussed in "Functional Interfaces" on page 359. BinaryOperator accepts two arguments of the same type and returns a value (also of the same type). Depending on your needs, you can either use reduce() with just the binary operator lambda, or you can use a second form that also takes an initial value of the same type used by the binary operator. Let's try out this second form to create a custom factorial reducer.

Factorials are big numbers—or they can be, anyway. If the term doesn't sound familiar, it's similar to a summing operation, but instead of adding each number in the sequence, you multiply. You typically use the exclamation mark to indicate this operation: 5! (pronounced "five factorial") will multiply 5 and 4 making 20, then 20 × 3 makes 60, then 60 × 2 makes 120, and finally 120 × 1 leaves 120. It may look simple enough, but factorial numbers get very big, very quickly:

```
jshell> 5 * 4 * 3 * 2 * 1
$17 ==> 120

// we already know what 5! is, so reuse that value
jshell> 10 * 9 * 8 * 7 * 6 * 120
$18 ==> 3628800

jshell> 12 * 11 * 3628800
$19 ==> 479001600
```

If you look carefully at the result of 12!, you'll notice it is just under half a billion, so it still fits within the (positive) range of values for the int type. But 13! would be roughly 6.5 billion, so we can't store that answer with ints. We could calculate it with longs, but even that type can't hold anything after 20!. Fortunately, Java is ready with some fun classes from java.math: BigInteger and BigDecimal. These classes can house arbitrarily large values, perfect for removing the limits of base types in our factorial work.

We can use a simple iterator as our source, since multiplication doesn't require a particular order of operations. Our factorial reducer will always produce an answer similar to count() or sum(),[3] so we'll use the second form with a starting value of 1. We can try this out in *jshell*:

```
// First make a quick alias for our "1" value
jshell> one = BigInteger.ONE
one ==> 1

// Test with 12!
jshell> Stream.iterate(one, count -> count.add(one)).
   ...>    limit(12).reduce(one, (a, b) -> a.multiply(b))
$32 ==> 479001600

// It matches. Yay! Can we get 13!?
jshell> Stream.iterate(one, count -> count.add(one)).
   ...>    limit(13).reduce(one, (a, b) -> a.multiply(b))
$33 ==> 6227020800

// Hooray. Big test next, can we get 21!?
jshell> Stream.iterate(one, count -> count.add(one)).
   ...>    limit(21).reduce(one, (a, b) -> a.multiply(b))
$36 ==> 51090942171709440000

// Sure did! Now, just to be silly, try 99!
jshell> Stream.iterate(one, count -> count.add(one)).
   ...>    limit(99).reduce(one, (a, b) -> a.multiply(b))
$37 ==> 9332621544394415268169923885626670049071596826431
```

---

3 A quirk of the factorial process is that 0! is defined as "the number of ways to arrange items in an empty set"—which is exactly one. Even if our stream has no elements, we can still correctly return the starting value.

8162146859296389521759999322991560894146397615651828625369792082722375825118521091686400000000000000000000000

The output of 99! is so large we had to arbitrarily chop it up to make it fit the printed edition of this book.[4] But our custom reducer worked!

You can implement the `BinaryOperator` interface in a class if your reducing logic is too complex for the simple, inline lambda. Then you can supply an instance of that class to `reduce()` instead of the lambdas we used in our examples.

Collectors

The answers that reducers produce are often very useful. How many lines did you process? How many times did you see a particular word? What's the average of some column in tabular data? But what if you want more than a single answer? When filtering, for example, you might want to keep all of the items from the stream that match, rather than counting or summing them.

What if you want a new list of just the names containing the letter "o"? We can use a collector.

The `java.util.stream.Collector` interface allows for some impressive flexibility in how you collect and organize the results of processing your stream. We won't be tackling custom collectors in this book, but happily, the related `Collectors` class includes several common collectors as static methods. For example, we can use one of those static methods to get that list of o-having names we were curious about:

```
jshell> List<String> onames = names.stream().
   ...>    filter(n -> n.indexOf("o") > -1).
   ...>    collect(Collectors.toList())
onames ==> [Fozzie, Gonzo]
```

Excellent. Now `onames` is a regular `List<String>` object that we can use anywhere else we might need it. There are many, many other collecting methods that we encourage you to peek at in the online documentation for `Collectors` (*https://oreil.ly/R3vmF*). The code exercises at the end of this chapter give you the chance to try out another popular collector, `groupingBy()`, but we don't have time to cover all of the other wonderful options available.

---

4 That's 9.3e+155 if scientific notation is easier for you to parse at that size. Popular estimates for the number of atoms in the known universe come in around 10e+82, in case you were wondering just how big 99! really is.

Using Lambdas Directly

We want to highlight one other feature of lambdas in Java: you can use them in your own code. While you will probably start by using lambdas in a few tasks like sorting collections or filtering long streams of data, eventually you may want to write methods that accept a lambda as an argument to be used in the body of that method. Since lambda expressions are just instances of some functional interface, Java makes accepting lambdas fairly straightforward.

Consider a digital sensor: perhaps some gadget attached to a USB port. Many of these sensors are stable and consistent, but they are consistently off by some factor. Maybe a thermometer thinks your home office is always three degrees warmer than it is, or maybe a light sensor underestimates ambient light by 10%. You could write separate adjustment methods that "add 3" to a reading or that "reduce by 10%" every value, but you can also use lambdas to create a generic adjustment method and let the caller supply the adjusting logic.

Let's see how you might write such a method. To make your method accept a lambda, you need to decide what shape it should have. You can always create your own shape, of course, but often you can simply use one of the interfaces from the `java.util.function` package. For our sensor-reading adjustments, we'll use the `DoubleUnaryOperator` shape. (A *unary operator* operates on one value the same way a binary operator works on two.) We'll accept one `double` argument and return an adjusted `double` as the result. We can put our amazingly flexible adjuster in a simple test harness to try out:

```java
import java.util.function.DoubleUnaryOperator;

public class Adjuster {
  public static double adjust(double val,
                              DoubleUnaryOperator adjustment)
  {
    return adjustment.applyAsDouble(val);
  }

  public static void main(String args[]) {
    double sample = 70.2;
    System.out.println("Initial reading: " + sample);
    System.out.print("Adding 3: ");
    System.out.println(adjust(sample, s -> s + 3));
    System.out.print("Reducing by 10%: ");
    System.out.println(adjust(sample, s -> s * 0.9));
  }
}
```

You can see that our `adjust()` method takes two arguments: the value we want to adjust, and the lambda that will do the adjusting. (And yes, you could implement the `DoubleUnaryOperator` in a class and supply an instance of that implementation as an alternative.) When we call `adjust()`, we get to use the same compact syntax that we've seen with other parts of the official JDK. It feels a bit like using forbidden magic, but it is entirely encouraged!

If you compile and run this demo, you should see output similar to this:

```
$ java Adjuster
Initial reading: 70.2
Adding 3: 73.2
Reducing by 10%: 63.18000000000001
```

Exactly what we expected. And we could write other adjustments without having to rewrite our actual `adjust()` method. You probably won't need this type of dynamic logic for every problem you tackle in Java, but it's worth putting this trick into your toolbox so you can pull it out when you do.

Next Steps

As with so many features of Java, we could write an entire book just on lambda expressions or streams. Others have! (*https://oreil.ly/4Eb4c*) We hope this introduction whets your appetite for learning more about FP topics. If you want more interactive practice with these topics, we highly recommend the labs available through O'Reilly's online platform (*https://oreil.ly/gRFDW*). Our own Marc Loy has created two series, one on Java lambdas (*https://oreil.ly/QNmjK*) and another on Java streams (*https://oreil.ly/XquFS*), both with practical examples of the topics we touched on in this chapter. These labs take advantage of O'Reilly's Interactive Learning Environment, where you can edit, compile, and execute Java code right in your browser.

Review Questions

1. Which package contains the majority of functional interfaces introduced in Java 8?

2. Do you need to use any special flags when compiling or running Java applications that use functional features like lambdas?

3. How do you create lambda expressions with multiple statements in the body?

4. Can lambda expressions be void? Can they return values?

5. Can you reuse a stream after you have processed it?

6. How might you take a stream of objects and convert it to a stream of integers?

7. If you have a stream that filters out empty lines from a file, what operation might you use to tell you how many lines had some content?

Code Exercises

1. Our `Adjuster` demonstration allows us to pass any lambda that accepts and returns a `double` value. We aren't restricted to simple changes like adding a fixed amount. Add one more line of output that converts the number from a Fahrenheit reading to Celsius. (As a quick refresher, C = (F – 32) * 5 / 9. Our reading of 70.2 should come out around 21.2.)

2. Using the `PaidEmployee` and `Report` classes from "Mapping object attributes" on page 369, add a simple report similar to `publishBudget()` that displays the average salary of all employees.

Advanced Exercises

1. Let's explore more of the collectors we touched on at the end of the chapter. Add a "role" attribute (of type `String`) to the `PaidEmployee` class. Be sure to update the `buildEmployeeList()` method in the `Report` class to assign roles as well. Feel free to pick whatever roles you like but make sure at least two employees share the same role (for testing purposes).

   Now look at the documentation for the `groupingBy()` collector (*https://oreil.ly/miu1t*). It returns a map of the groups and their members. In our example, the keys of this map will be the roles you created. The associated values will be lists of all the employees who share that role. You can add one more "report" to the `Report` class that creates this map and then prints out the roles and their associated employees.

CHAPTER 12

Desktop Applications

Java leapt to fame and glory on the power of applets—amazing, *interactive* elements on a web page. Sounds mundane these days, but at the time it was nothing short of a marvel. Java also had cross-platform support up its sleeve and could run the same code on Windows, Unix, and macOS systems. The early JDKs had a rudimentary set of graphical components collectively known as the Abstract Window Toolkit (AWT). The "abstract" in AWT comes from the use of common classes (Button, Window, etc.) with native implementations. You write AWT applications with abstract, cross-platform code; your computer runs your application and provides concrete, native components.

Unfortunately, that nifty combination of abstract and native comes with some pretty serious limitations. In the abstract realm, you encounter "lowest common denominator" designs that only give you access to features available on every platform supported by the JDK. In the native implementations, even some features roughly available everywhere were distinctly different when actually rendered on the screen. Many desktop developers working with Java in those early days joked that the "write once, run everywhere" tagline was really "write once, debug everywhere." The Java Swing package set out to ameliorate this woeful state. While Swing didn't solve every problem of cross-platform application delivery, it did make serious desktop application development possible in Java. You can find many quality open source projects and even some commercial applications written in Swing. Indeed, the IDE we detail in Appendix A, IntelliJ IDEA, is a Swing application! It clearly goes toe-to-toe with native IDEs on both performance and usability.[1]

---

[1] If you are curious about this topic and want to see behind the curtains of a commercial, desktop Java application, JetBrains publishes the source code (*https://oreil.ly/YleE5*) for the Community Edition.

If you look at the documentation for the `javax.swing`[2] package, you will see it contains a multitude of classes. You will still need some pieces of the original `java.awt` realm as well. There are entire books on AWT (*Java AWT Reference* (*https://oreil.ly/ppyCu*), Zukowski, O'Reilly) and on Swing (*Java Swing* (*https://oreil.ly/bO7g6*), Loy, et al., O'Reilly), and even on subpackages of the AWT, such as 2D graphics (*Java 2D Graphics* (*https://oreil.ly/o3YxN*), Knudsen, O'Reilly). In this chapter, we'll stick to covering some popular components like buttons and text fields. We'll look at how to lay them out in your application window and how to interact with them. You may be surprised by how sophisticated your application can get with these simple starting topics. If you do more desktop development after reading this book, you may also be surprised by how much more graphical user interface (GUI, or just UI) content is out there for Java. We want to whet your appetite while acknowledging that there are many, *many* more UI discussions we must leave for you to discover later. With that said, let the whirlwind tour commence!

Buttons and Sliders and Text Fields, Oh My!

So where to begin? We have a bit of a "chicken and the egg" problem: we need to discuss the "things" to put on the screen, such as the `JLabel` objects we used in "HelloJava" on page 40. But we also need to discuss what you put those things into. And *where* you put those things also merits discussion, as it's a nontrivial process. We actually seem to have a chicken, egg, and brunch problem. Grab a cup of coffee or a mimosa, and we'll get started. We will cover some popular components (the "things") first, then their containers, and finally the topic of laying out your components in those containers. Once you can put a nice set of widgets on the screen, we'll discuss how to interact with them as well as how to handle user interfaces in a multithreaded world.

Component Hierarchies

As we've discussed in previous chapters, Java classes are designed and extended in a hierarchical fashion. `JComponent` and `JContainer` sit at the top of the Swing class hierarchy, as shown in Figure 12-1. We won't cover these two classes in much detail, but remember their names. You will find several common attributes and methods in these classes as you read the Swing documentation. As you advance in your programming endeavors, you'll likely want to build your own component. `JComponent` is a great starting point. We used `JComponent` when building our graphical `Hello Component` back in Chapter 2.

---

2 The `javax` package prefix was introduced early by Sun to accommodate packages that were distributed with Java but were not "core." The decision was modestly controversial, but `javax` has stuck and has been used with other packages as well.

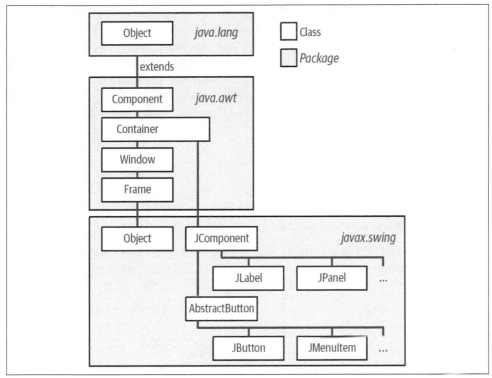

Figure 12-1. Partial (very partial) Swing class hierarchy

We will be covering most of the other classes mentioned in the abridged hierarchy above, but you will definitely want to visit the online documentation (*https://oreil.ly/ H7KhT*) to see the many components we had to leave out.

Model View Controller Architecture

At the base of Swing's notion of "things" is a design pattern known as Model View Controller (MVC). The Swing package authors worked hard to consistently apply this pattern so that when you encounter new components, their behavior and usage should feel familiar. MVC architecture aims to compartmentalize what you see (the view) from the behind-the-scenes state (the model) and from the collection of inter-actions (the controller) that change those parts. This separation of concerns allows you to concentrate on getting each piece right. Network traffic can update the model behind the scenes. The view can be synchronized at regular intervals that feel smooth and responsive to the user. MVC provides a powerful yet manageable framework to use when building any desktop application.

As we look at our small selection of components, we'll highlight the model and the view elements. We'll then go into more detail on the controllers in "Events" on page 413. If you find the notion of programming patterns intriguing, *Design Patterns: Elements of Reusable Object-Oriented Software* (*https://oreil.ly/gt4Pt*) (Addison-Wesley) by Gamma, Helm, Johnson, and Vlissides (the renowned Gang of Four) is the classic work. For more details on the use of the MVC pattern in Swing specifically, see the introductory chapter of *Java Swing* (*https://oreil.ly/ADKQq*), by Loy et al.

Labels and Buttons

The simplest UI component is not surprisingly one of the most popular. Labels are used all over the place to indicate functionality, display status, and draw focus. We used a label for our first graphical application back in Chapter 2. We'll use many more labels as we continue building more interesting programs.

The JLabel component is a versatile tool. Let's look at some examples of how to use JLabel and customize its many attributes. We'll start by revisiting our "Hello, Java" program with a few preparatory tweaks:

```java
import javax.swing.*;
import java.awt.*;

public class Labels {

    public static void main(String[] args) {
        JFrame frame = new JFrame("JLabel Examples");
        frame.setLayout(new FlowLayout());  ❶
        frame.setDefaultCloseOperation(JFrame.EXIT_ON_CLOSE);  ❷
        frame.setSize(300, 150);

        JLabel basic = new JLabel("Default Label");  ❸
        frame.add(basic);
        frame.setVisible(true);
    }
}
```

Briefly, the interesting parts are:

❶ Setting the layout manager for use by the frame.

❷ Setting the action taken when using the operating system's "close" button (in this case, the red dot in the upper-left corner of the window). The action we selected here exits the application.

❸ Creating our simple label and adding it to the frame.

You declare and initialize the label, then add it to the frame. That should be familiar. What is likely new is our use of a FlowLayout instance, which helps us produce the screenshot shown in Figure 12-2.

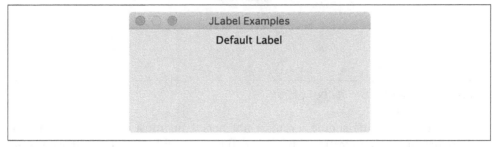

Figure 12-2. A single, simple JLabel

We'll go over layout managers in much more detail in "Containers and Layouts" on page 401, but we need something to get us off the ground that also allows us to add multiple components to a single container. The FlowLayout class fills a container by horizontally centering components at the top, adding from left to right until that "row" runs out of room, then continuing on a new row below. This type of arrangement won't be of much use in larger applications, but it is ideal for getting several things on the screen quickly.

Let's prove that point by adding a few more labels to the frame. Check out the results shown in Figure 12-3:

```
public class Labels {

    public static void main(String[] args) {
        JFrame frame = new JFrame("JLabel Examples");
        frame.setLayout(new FlowLayout());
        frame.setDefaultCloseOperation(JFrame.EXIT_ON_CLOSE);
        frame.setSize(300, 150);

        JLabel basic = new JLabel("Default Label");
        JLabel another = new JLabel("Another Label");
        JLabel simple = new JLabel("A Simple Label");
        JLabel standard = new JLabel("A Standard Label");

        frame.add(basic);
        frame.add(another);
        frame.add(simple);
        frame.add(standard);

        frame.setVisible(true);
    }
}
```

Figure 12-3. Several basic JLabel *objects*

Neat, right? Again, this simple layout is not meant for most types of content you find in production applications, but it's definitely useful as you get started. One more point about layouts that we want to make, as you'll encounter this idea later: FlowLayout also deals with the size of the labels. That can be hard to notice in this example because labels have a transparent background by default. If we import the java.awt.Color class, we can use that class to help make them opaque and give them a specific background color:

```
JLabel basic = new JLabel("Default Label");
basic.setOpaque(true);
basic.setBackground(Color.YELLOW);
JLabel another = new JLabel("Another Label");
another.setOpaque(true);
another.setBackground(Color.GREEN);

frame.add(basic);
frame.add(another);
// other frame setup
```

If we do the same for all of our labels, we can now see their true sizes and the gaps between them in Figure 12-4. But if we can control the background color of labels, what else can we do? Can we change the foreground color? (Yes.) Can we change the font? (Yes.) Can we change the alignment? (Yes.) Can we add icons? (Yes.) Can we create self-aware labels that eventually build Skynet and bring about the end of humanity? (Maybe, but probably not, and certainly not easily. Just as well.) Figure 12-5 shows some of these possible tweaks.

Figure 12-4. Opaque, colored labels

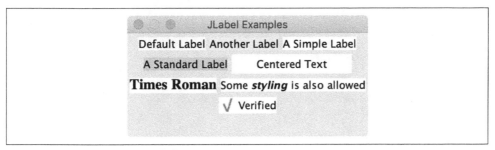

Figure 12-5. More labels with fancier options

And here is the relevant source code that built this added variety:

```
// a white label with a forced size and text centered inside
JLabel centered = new JLabel("Centered Text", JLabel.CENTER);
centered.setPreferredSize(new Dimension(150, 24));
centered.setOpaque(true);
centered.setBackground(Color.WHITE);

// a white label with an alternate, larger font
JLabel times = new JLabel("Times Roman");
times.setOpaque(true);
times.setBackground(Color.WHITE);
times.setFont(new Font("TimesRoman", Font.BOLD, 18));

// a white label using inline HTML for styling
JLabel styled = new JLabel("<html>Some <b><i>styling</i></b>"
    + " is also allowed</html>");
styled.setOpaque(true);
styled.setBackground(Color.WHITE);

// a label with both an icon and text
JLabel icon = new JLabel("Verified",
    new ImageIcon("ch10/examples/check.png"), JLabel.LEFT);
icon.setOpaque(true);
icon.setBackground(Color.WHITE);

// finally, add all our new labels to the frame
```

```
frame.add(centered);
frame.add(times);
frame.add(styled);
frame.add(icon);
```

We used a few other classes to help out, such as java.awt.Font and
javax.swing.ImageIcon. We could review many more options, but we need to look
at some other components. If you want to play around with these labels and try
out more of the options you see in the Java documentation, try importing a helper
we built for *jshell* and playing around.[3] The results of our few lines are shown in
Figure 12-6:

```
$ javac ch12/examples/Widget.java
$ jshell
|  Welcome to JShell -- Version 21-ea
|  For an introduction type: /help intro

jshell> import javax.swing.*
jshell> import java.awt.*
jshell> import ch12.examples.Widget

jshell> Widget w = new Widget()
w ==> ch10.Widget[frame0,0,23,300x150,layout=java.awt.B ... abled=true]

jshell> JLabel label1 = new JLabel("Green")
label1 ==> javax.swing.JLabel[,0,0,0x0,invalid,alignmentX=0. ... ion=CENTER]

jshell> label1.setOpaque(true)
jshell> label1.setBackground(Color.GREEN)

jshell> w.add(label1)
$8 ==> javax.swing.JLabel[,0,0,0x0,...]

jshell> w.add(new JLabel("Quick test"))
$9 ==> javax.swing.JLabel[,0,0,0x0,...]
```

---

3 You'll need to start *jshell* from the top-level directory containing the compiled examples for the book. If you
  are using IntelliJ IDEA, you can start its terminal and switch directories using **cd out/production/Learning
  Java6e**, and then start *jshell*.

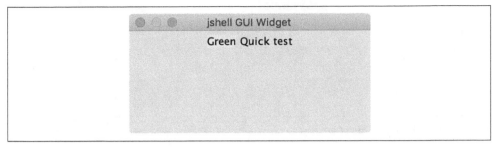

Figure 12-6. Using our `Widget` *class in jshell*

We hope you see how easy it is now to create a label (or other components, such as the buttons that we'll be exploring next) and tweak its parameters interactively. This is a great way to familiarize yourself with the building blocks you have at your disposal for creating Java desktop applications. If you use our `Widget` much, you may find its `reset()` method handy. This method removes all of the current components and refreshes the window so you can start over quickly.

Buttons

The other near-universal component you'll need for graphical applications is the button. The `JButton` class is your go-to button in Swing. (You'll also find other popular button types, such as `JCheckbox` and `JToggleButton`, in the documentation.) Creating a button is very similar to creating a label, as shown in Figure 12-7.

```java
import javax.swing.*;
import java.awt.*;

public class Buttons {
  public static void main(String[] args) {
    JFrame frame = new JFrame("JButton Examples");
    frame.setLayout(new FlowLayout());
    frame.setDefaultCloseOperation(JFrame.EXIT_ON_CLOSE);
    frame.setSize(300, 150);

    JButton basic = new JButton("Try me!");
    frame.add(basic);

    frame.setVisible(true);
  }
}
```

Figure 12-7. A simple `JButton`

You can control the colors, text and image alignment, font, and so on for buttons in much the same way as you do for labels. The difference, of course, is that you can click on a button and react to that click in your program, whereas labels are mostly static displays. Try running this example and clicking on the button. It should change color and feel "pressed," even though it does not perform any other function in our program yet. We want to go through a few more components before tackling that notion of "reacting" to a button click (an "event" in Swing-speak), but you can jump to "Events" on page 413 if you can't wait!

Text Components

It would be impossible to imagine a desktop or web application today without the text input fields. These input elements allow for free-form entry of information and are nearly ubiquitous in online forms. You can grab names, email addresses, phone numbers, and credit card numbers. You can do all that in languages that compose their characters, or others that read from right to left. Swing has three big text components: JTextField, JTextArea, and JTextPane; all extended from a common parent, JTextComponent. JTextField is a classic text field meant for brief, single-word or single-line input. JTextArea allows for much more input spread across multiple lines. JTextPane is a specialized component meant for editing rich text.

Text fields

Let's get an example of text input running in our simple, flowing application. We'll pare things back to two labels and corresponding text fields:

```
import javax.swing.*;
import java.awt.*;

public class TextInputs {
  public static void main(String[] args) {
    JFrame frame = new JFrame("JTextField Examples");
    frame.setLayout(new FlowLayout());
    frame.setDefaultCloseOperation(JFrame.EXIT_ON_CLOSE);
    frame.setSize(400, 200);

    JLabel nameLabel = new JLabel("Name:");
```

```
        JTextField nameField = new JTextField(10);
        JLabel emailLabel = new JLabel("Email:");
        JTextField emailField = new JTextField(24);

        frame.add(nameLabel);
        frame.add(nameField);
        frame.add(emailLabel);
        frame.add(emailField);

        frame.setVisible(true);
    }
}
```

Notice in Figure 12-8 that the size of a text field is dictated by the number of columns we specify in its constructor. That's not the only way to initialize a text field, but it is useful when there are no other layout mechanisms dictating the width of the field. (Here, the FlowLayout failed us a bit—the "Email:" label did not stay on the same line as the email text field. We'll fix that soon as we learn more about layouts.) Go ahead and type something! You can enter and delete text; highlight stuff inside the field with your mouse; and cut, copy, and paste as you'd expect.

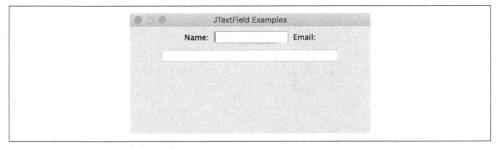

Figure 12-8. Simple labels and JTextFields

If you add a text field to our demo app in *jshell*, as shown in Figure 12-9, you can call its getText() method to see that the content is indeed available to you.

Figure 12-9. Retrieving the contents of a JTextField

```
jshell> w.reset()

jshell> JTextField emailField = new JTextField(15)
emailField ==> javax.swing.JTextField[,0,0,0x0, ... lignment=LEADING]

jshell> w.add(new JLabel("Email:"))
$12 ==> javax.swing.JLabel[,0,0,0x0, ... sition=CENTER]

jshell> w.add(emailField)
$13 ==> javax.swing.JTextField[,0,0,0x0, ... lignment=LEADING]

// Enter an sample address, we typed in "me@some.company"

jshell> emailField.getText()
$14 ==> "me@some.company"
```

Note that the **text** property is read-write. You can call **setText()** on your text field to change its content programmatically. This can be great for setting default values, auto-formatting things like phone numbers, or prefilling a form from information you gather over the network. Try it out in *jshell*.

Text areas

When you need room for more than simple words or even long URL entries, you'll likely turn to **JTextArea** to give the user multiple lines of input space. You can create an empty text area with a constructor similar to **JTextField**. For **JTextArea**, you specify the number of rows in addition to the number of columns. Take a look at the code to add a text area to our text input demo app:

```
JLabel bodyLabel = new JLabel("Body:");
JTextArea bodyArea = new JTextArea(10,30);

frame.add(bodyLabel);
frame.add(bodyArea);
```

The results are shown in Figure 12-10. You can see we have room for multiple lines of text. Go ahead and run this new version and try it yourself. What happens if you type past the end of a line? What happens when you press the Return key? Do you get the behaviors you're familiar with? You still have access to its content just like you do with a text field.

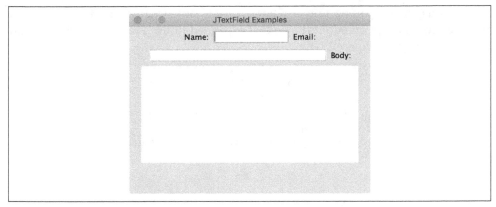

Figure 12-10. Adding a JTextArea

Let's add a text area to our widget in *jshell* so that we can play with its properties:

```
jshell> w.reset()

jshell> w.add(new JLabel("Body:"))
$16 ==> javax.swing.JLabel[,0,0,0x0, ... ition=CENTER]

jshell> JTextArea bodyArea = new JTextArea(5,20)
bodyArea ==> javax.swing.JTextArea[,0,0,0x0, ... word=false,wrap=false]

jshell> w.add(bodyArea)
$18 ==> javax.swing.JTextArea[,0,0,0x0, ... lse,wrap=false]

jshell> bodyArea.getText()
$19 ==> "This is the first line.\nThis should be the second.\nAnd the third..."
```

Great! We can see that the Return key we typed to produce our three lines in Figure 12-11 gets encoded as the \n character in the string we retrieve.

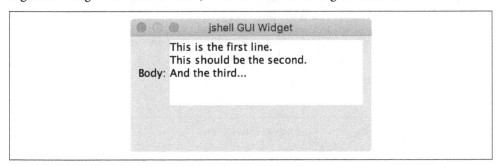

Figure 12-11. Retrieving the contents of a JTextArea

But what happens if you try to type a long, run-on sentence that runs past the end of the line? You may get an odd text area that expanded to the size of your window and beyond, as shown in Figure 12-12.

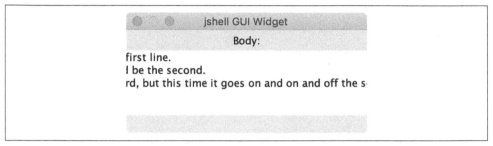

Figure 12-12. An overly long line in a simple JTextArea

We can fix that incorrect sizing behavior by looking at a pair of properties of JTextArea, shown in Table 12-1.

Table 12-1. Wrap properties of JTextArea

Property	Default	Description
lineWrap	false	Whether lines longer than the table should wrap at all
wrapStyleWord	false	If lines do wrap, whether the line breaks should be on word or character boundaries

So let's start fresh and turn on the word wrap. We can use setLineWrap(true) to make sure the text wraps. But that's probably not enough. We'll add a call to setWrapStyleWord(true) to make sure the text area doesn't just break words in the middle. That should look similar to Figure 12-13.

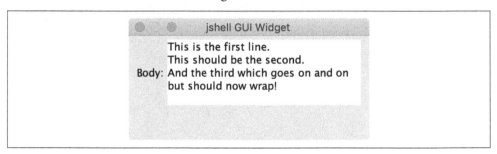

Figure 12-13. A wrapping line in a simple JTextArea

You can try that yourself in *jshell* or in your own app. When you retrieve the text from the bodyArea object, you should *not* see a line break (\n) in line three between the second "on" and the "but."

Text scrolling

What happens if we have too many rows? On its own, JTextArea does that odd "grow until it can't" trick, as shown in Figure 12-14.

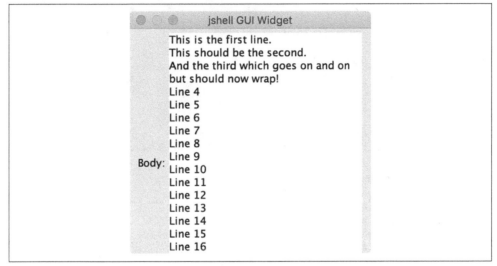

Figure 12-14. Too many lines in a simple JTextArea

To fix this problem, we need to call in some support from a standard Swing helper component: JScrollPane. This is a general-purpose container that makes it easy to present large components in confined spaces. To show you just how easy this is, let's fix our text area:[4]

```
jshell> w.remove(bodyArea); // So we can start with a fresh text area

jshell> bodyArea = new JTextArea(5,20)
bodyArea ==> javax.swing.JTextArea[,0,0,0x0,inval... word=false,wrap=false]

jshell> w.add(new JScrollPane(bodyArea))
$17 ==> javax.swing.JScrollPane[,47,5,244x84, ... ortBorder=]
```

---

4 As we create Swing components for use in these *jshell* examples, we'll be omitting much of the resulting output for the sake of space. *jshell* prints a lot of information about each component, although it also uses ellipses when things get too extreme. Don't be alarmed if you see extra details about an element's attributes while you're experimenting.

You can see in Figure 12-15 that the text area no longer grows beyond the bounds of the frame. You can also see the standard scroll bars along the side and bottom. If you just need simple scrolling, you're done! But like most other components in Swing, JScrollPane has many fine details you can adjust as needed. We won't cover most of those here, but we do want to show you how to tackle a common setup for text areas: line wrapping (breaking on words) with vertical scrolling—meaning no horizontal scrolling.

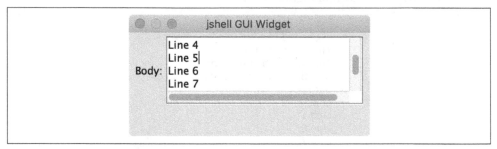

Figure 12-15. Too many lines in a JTextArea embedded in a JScrollPane

```
JLabel bodyLabel = new JLabel("Body:");
JTextArea bodyArea = new JTextArea(10,30);
bodyArea.setLineWrap(true);
bodyArea.setWrapStyleWord(true);
JScrollPane bodyScroller = new JScrollPane(bodyArea);
bodyScroller.setHorizontalScrollBarPolicy(
    JScrollPane.HORIZONTAL_SCROLLBAR_NEVER);
bodyScroller.setVerticalScrollBarPolicy(
    JScrollPane.VERTICAL_SCROLLBAR_ALWAYS);

frame.add(bodyLabel);
// note we don't add bodyArea, it's already in bodyScroller
frame.add(bodyScroller);
```

You should end up with a text area like the one shown in Figure 12-16.

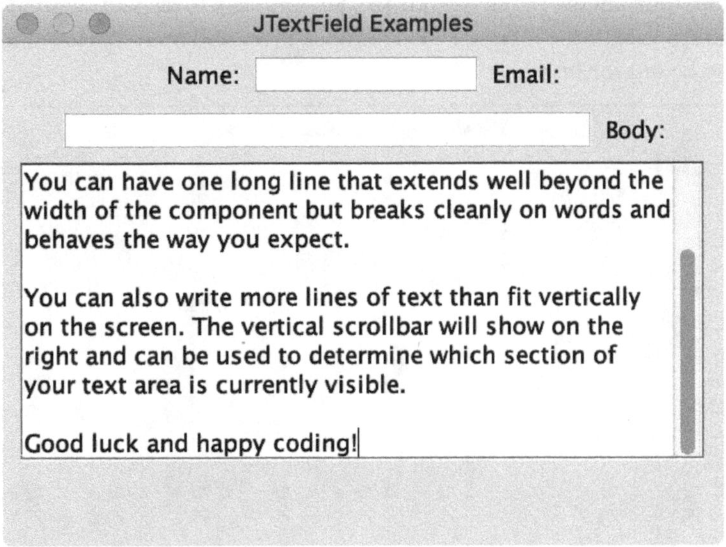

Figure 12-16. A well-formed `JTextArea` *in a* `JScrollPane`

Hooray! You now have a taste of the most common Swing components, including labels, buttons, and text fields. But we really have just scratched the surface of these components. Look over the Java documentation and play around with each of these components in *jshell* or in your own mini applications.

Getting comfortable with UI design takes practice. We encourage you to look up other books and online resources if you will be building desktop applications, but nothing beats time spent at the keyboard.

Other Components

If you've already looked at the documentation on the `javax.swing` package, you know several dozen other components are available. Within that large list, there are a few that we want to highlight.[5]

JSlider

Sliders are a nifty, efficient input component when you want the user to choose from a range of values: for instance, things like font size selectors, color pickers, and zoom selectors. Sliders are perfect for the angle and force values we need in our apple

---

5 We should also note that there are many open source projects with even fancier components for handling things like syntax highlighting in text, various selection helpers, graphs and charts, and composite inputs like date or time pickers.

tossing game. Our angles range from 0 to 180, and our force value ranges from 0 to 20 (an arbitrary maximum). Figure 12-17 shows these sliders in place (ignore how we achieved the layout for now).

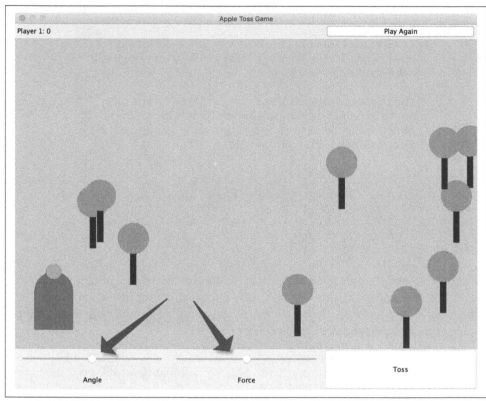

Figure 12-17. Using JSlider in our apple tossing game

To create a new slider, you provide three values: the minimum (0 for our angle slider), the maximum (180), and the initial value (start in the middle for the game at 90). You can add such a slider to our *jshell* playground like this:

```
// reset the widget
jshell> w.reset()

jshell> JSlider slider = new JSlider(0, 180, 90);
slider ==> javax.swing.JSlider[,0,0,0x0, ... ks=false,snapToValue=true]

jshell> w.add(slider)
$20 ==> javax.swing.JSlider[,0,0,0x0, ... alue=true]
```

Scoot the slider around like you see in Figure 12-18, then look at its current value using the `getValue()` method:

```
jshell> slider.getValue()
$21 ==> 112
```

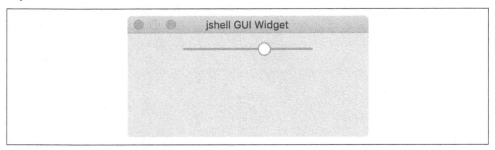

Figure 12-18. A simple `JSlider` in jshell

In "Events" on page 413, we'll see how to receive those values in real time as the user changes them.

The `JSlider` constructors use integers for the minimum and maximum values, and `getValue()` returns an integer. If you need fractional values, that falls to you. The force slider in our game, for example, would benefit from supporting more than 21 discrete levels. We can address that by building the slider with a larger range of integers, then dividing the current value by an appropriate scale factor:

```
jshell> JSlider force = new JSlider(0, 200, 100)
force ==> javax.swing.JSlider[,0,0,0x0, ... ks=false,snapToValue=true]

jshell> w.add(force)
$23 ==> javax.swing.JSlider[,0,0,0x0,invalid ... alue=true]

jshell> force.getValue()
$24 ==> 68

jshell> float myForce = force.getValue() / 10.0f;
myForce ==> 6.8
```

JList

If you have a discrete set of values but those values are not a simple, contiguous range of numbers, the "list" UI element is a great choice. `JList` is the Swing implementation of this input type. You can set it to allow single or multiple selections, and if you dig deeper into Swing's features, you can produce custom views that display the items in your list with extra information or details. (For example, you can make lists of icons, or icons and text, or multiline text, and so on.)

Unlike the other components we've seen so far, `JList` requires a little more information to get started. To make a useful list component, you need to use one of the constructors that takes the data you intend to show. The simplest such constructor accepts an `Object` array. While you can pass an array of objects of any type, the default behavior of `JList` will be to show the output of your objects' `toString()` method in the list. Using an array of `String` objects is very common and produces the expected results. Figure 12-19 shows a simple list of cities.

Figure 12-19. A simple `JList` of four cities in jshell

```
jshell> w.reset()

jshell> String[] cities = new String[] { "Atlanta", "Boston",
   ...>    "Chicago", "Denver" };
cities ==> String[4] { "Atlanta", ..., "Denver" }

jshell> JList cityList = new JList<String>(cities);
cityList ==> javax.swing.JList[,0,0,0x0, ...entation=0]

jshell> w.add(cityList)
$29 ==> javax.swing.JList[,0,0,0x0,invalid ... ation=0]
```

We use the same `<String>` type information with the constructor as we do when creating parameterized collection objects, such as `ArrayList` (see "Type Limitations" on page 217). As Swing was added well before generics, you may encounter examples online or in books that do not add the type information. Omitting it doesn't stop your code from compiling or running, but you will receive the same unchecked warning message at compile time that you saw with the collection classes.

Similar to getting the current value of a slider, you can retrieve the selected item or items in a list at any time using one of four methods:

`getSelectedIndex()`
    For single-select lists, returns an `int`

`getSelectedIndices()`
    For multiselect lists, returns an array of `int`

getSelectedValue()
> For single-select lists, returns an object

getSelectedValues()
> For multiselect lists, returns an array of objects

The main difference is whether the index of the selected item(s) or the actual value(s) is more useful to you. Playing with our city list in *jshell*, we can pull out a selected city like so:

```
jshell> cityList.getSelectedIndex()
$31 ==> 2

jshell> cityList.getSelectedIndices()
$32 ==> int[1] { 2 }

jshell> cityList.getSelectedValue()
$33 ==> "Chicago"

jshell> cities[cityList.getSelectedIndex()]
$34 ==> "Chicago"
```

For large lists, you'll probably want a scroll bar. Swing promotes reusability in its code, so you can use a JScrollPane with JList just like we did for text areas.

Containers and Layouts

That formidable list of components is only a subset of the widgets available. In this section, you'll be laying out the components we've discussed into useful arrangements. Those arrangements happen inside a *container*, which is Java's term for a component that can have (or "contain") other components. Let's start by looking at the most common containers.

Frames and Windows

Every desktop application needs at least one window. This term predates Swing and is used by most graphical interfaces available on the three big operating systems—including Windows (no relation). Swing does provide a low-level JWindow class if you need it, but most likely you will build your application inside a JFrame. Figure 12-20 illustrates the class hierarchy of JFrame. We will stick to its basic features, but as your applications become richer, you may want to create customized windows using elements higher up in the hierarchy.

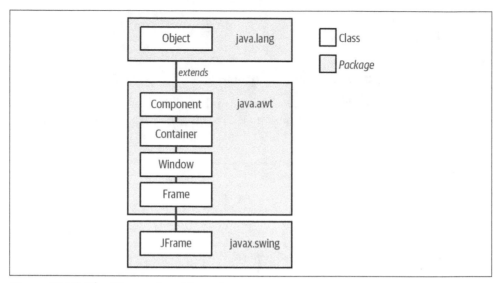

Figure 12-20. The JFrame class hierarchy

Let's revisit the creation of that first graphical application from Chapter 2 and focus a bit more on the JFrame object:

```
import javax.swing.*;

public class HelloJavaAgain {
  public static void main(String[] args) {
    JFrame frame = new JFrame("Hello, Java!");
    frame.setDefaultCloseOperation(JFrame.EXIT_ON_CLOSE);
    frame.setSize(300, 150);

    JLabel label = new JLabel("Hello, Java!", JLabel.CENTER);
    frame.add(label);

    frame.setVisible(true);
  }
}
```

The string we pass to the JFrame constructor becomes the title of the window. We then set a few specific properties on our object. We make sure that when the user closes the window, we quit our program. (That might seem obvious, but complex applications might have multiple windows, such as tool palettes or support for multiple documents. Closing one window in these applications may not mean "quit.")

We then pick a starting size for the window and add our actual label component to the frame (which in turn places the label in its *content pane*, more on that in a minute). Once the component is added, we make the window visible, and the result is Figure 12-21.

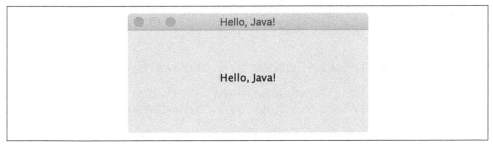

Figure 12-21. A simple JFrame with an added label

This basic process is the foundation of every Swing application. The interesting part of your application comes from what you do with that content pane.

But what *is* that content pane? The frame uses its own set of containers that hold various parts of typical applications. You can set your own content pane to be any object descended from `java.awt.Container`, but we'll be sticking with the default for now.

We are also using a shortcut to add our label. The `JFrame` version of `add()` will delegate to the content pane's `add()`. The following snippet shows how to add the label without the shortcut:

```
JLabel label = new JLabel("Hello, Java!", JLabel.CENTER);
frame.getContentPane().add(label);
```

The `JFrame` class does not have shortcuts for everything, however. Read the documentation and use a shortcut if it exists. If not, don't hesitate to grab a reference via `getContentPane()` and then configure or tweak that container as needed.

JPanel

The default content pane is a `JPanel`, the go-to container in Swing. It is a component just like `JButton` or `JLabel`, so your panels can contain other panels. Such nesting often plays a big role in application layout. For example, you could create a `JPanel` to house the formatting buttons of a text editor in a "toolbar," then add that toolbar to the content pane. This arrangement makes it easy for users to show, hide, or move it around.

`JPanel` lets you add and remove components from the screen. (The methods are inherited from the `Container` class, but we access them through our `JPanel` objects.) You can also `repaint()` a panel if something has changed and you want to update your UI.

We can see the effects of the add() and remove() methods shown in Figure 12-22 using our playground widget in *jshell*:

```
jshell> Widget w = new Widget()
w ==> ch10.Widget[frame0,0,23,300x300, ... kingEnabled=true]

jshell> JLabel emailLabel = new JLabel("Email:")
emailLabel ==> javax.swing.JLabel[,0,0,0x0 ... ition=CENTER]

jshell> JTextField emailField = new JTextField(12)
emailField ==> javax.swing.JTextField[,0,0,0x0, ... LEADING]

jshell> JButton submitButton = new JButton("Submit")
submitButton ==> javax.swing.JButton[,0,0,0x0, ... ble=true]

jshell> w.add(emailLabel);
$8 ==> javax.swing.JLabel[,0,0,0x0, ... ition=CENTER]
// Left screenshot in image above

jshell> w.add(emailField)
$9 ==> javax.swing.JTextField[,0,0,0x0, ... nment=LEADING]

jshell> w.add(submitButton)
$10 ==> javax.swing.JButton[,0,0,0x0, ... pable=true]
// Now we have the middle screenshot

jshell> w.remove(emailLabel)
// And finally the right screenshot
```

Try it yourself! Most applications don't add and remove components willy-nilly. You'll usually build your interface by adding what you need and then leave it alone. You might enable or disable some buttons along the way, but try not to surprise the user with disappearing parts or new elements popping up.

Figure 12-22. Adding and removing components in a JPanel

Layout Managers

Containers like JPanel are responsible for laying out the components you add. Java provides several *layout managers* to help you achieve your desired results.

BorderLayout

You've already seen the FlowLayout in action. You were using another layout manager without really knowing it: the content pane of a JFrame uses BorderLayout by default. Figure 12-23 shows the five areas controlled by BorderLayout, along with their regions. Notice that the NORTH and SOUTH regions are as wide as the application window but only as tall as required to fit the label. Similarly, the EAST and WEST regions fill the vertical gap between the NORTH and SOUTH regions but are only as wide as required, leaving the remaining space to be filled both horizontally and vertically by the CENTER region:

```java
import java.awt.*;
import javax.swing.*;

public class BorderLayoutDemo {
  public static void main(String[] args) {
    JFrame frame = new JFrame("BorderLayout Demo");
    frame.setDefaultCloseOperation(JFrame.EXIT_ON_CLOSE);
    frame.setSize(400, 200);

    JLabel northLabel = new JLabel("Top - North", JLabel.CENTER);
    JLabel southLabel = new JLabel("Bottom - South", JLabel.CENTER);
    JLabel eastLabel = new JLabel("Right - East", JLabel.CENTER);
    JLabel westLabel = new JLabel("Left - West", JLabel.CENTER);
    JLabel centerLabel = new JLabel("Center (everything else)",
        JLabel.CENTER);

    // Color the labels so we can see their boundaries better
    northLabel.setOpaque(true);
    northLabel.setBackground(Color.GREEN);
    southLabel.setOpaque(true);
    southLabel.setBackground(Color.GREEN);
    eastLabel.setOpaque(true);
    eastLabel.setBackground(Color.RED);
    westLabel.setOpaque(true);
    westLabel.setBackground(Color.RED);
    centerLabel.setOpaque(true);
    centerLabel.setBackground(Color.YELLOW);

    frame.add(northLabel, BorderLayout.NORTH);
    frame.add(southLabel, BorderLayout.SOUTH);
    frame.add(eastLabel, BorderLayout.EAST);
    frame.add(westLabel, BorderLayout.WEST);
    frame.add(centerLabel, BorderLayout.CENTER);

    frame.setVisible(true);
  }
}
```

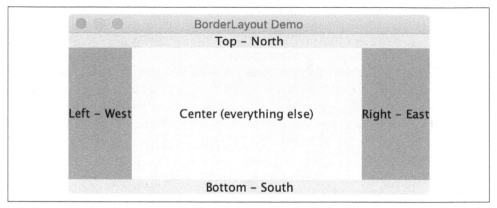

Figure 12-23. The regions available with `BorderLayout`

The `add()` method in this case takes an extra argument and passes it to the layout manager. (Not all managers need this argument, as you saw with `FlowLayout`.)

Figure 12-24 shows an example of nesting `JPanel` objects within an application. We use a text area for a large message in the center and then add some action buttons to a panel along the bottom. Again, without the events we'll cover in the next section, none of these buttons do anything, but we want to show you how to work with multiple containers. And you could continue nesting `JPanel` objects if you wanted.

Sometimes a better top-level layout choice makes your app both more maintainable and more performant:

```
public class NestedPanelDemo {
  public static void main(String[] args) {
    JFrame frame = new JFrame("Nested Panel Demo");
    frame.setDefaultCloseOperation(JFrame.EXIT_ON_CLOSE);
    frame.setSize(400, 200);

    // Create the text area and add it to the center
    JTextArea messageArea = new JTextArea();
    frame.add(messageArea, BorderLayout.CENTER);

    // Create the button container
    JPanel buttonPanel = new JPanel(new FlowLayout());

    // Create the buttons
    JButton sendButton = new JButton("Send");
    JButton saveButton = new JButton("Save");
    JButton resetButton = new JButton("Reset");
    JButton cancelButton = new JButton("Cancel");

    // Add the buttons to their container
    buttonPanel.add(sendButton);
    buttonPanel.add(saveButton);
```

```
        buttonPanel.add(resetButton);
        buttonPanel.add(cancelButton);

        // And finally, add that container to the bottom of the app
        frame.add(buttonPanel, BorderLayout.SOUTH);

        frame.setVisible(true);
    }
}
```

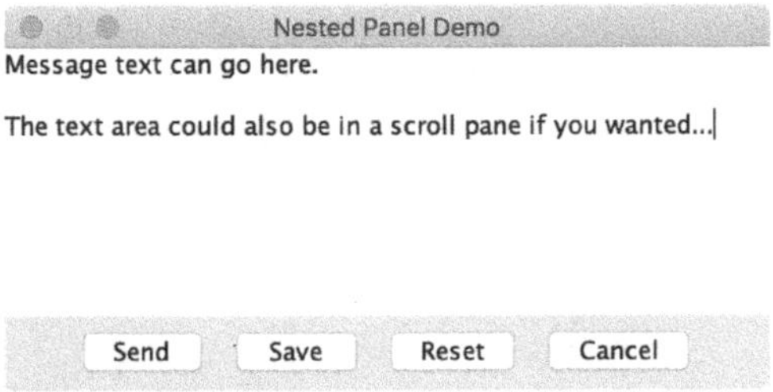

Figure 12-24. A simple nested container example

Two things to note in this example. First, you might see that we did not specify the number of rows or columns when creating our JTextArea object. Unlike FlowLayout, BorderLayout will set the size of its components when possible. For the top and bottom, this means using the component's own height, similar to how FlowLayout works, but then setting the width of the component to fill the frame. The sides use their components' width, but the layout manager sets the height. BorderLayout sets both the width and height of the component in the center.

Second, when we add the messageArea and buttonPanel objects to the frame, we specify the extra "where" argument to the frame's add() method. However, when we are adding the buttons themselves to buttonPanel, we use the simpler version of add() with only the component argument. The container's layout manager dictates which variation of add() we need. So even though the buttonPanel is in the SOUTH region of the frame using BorderLayout, the saveButton and its compatriots are in an enclosing container of their own and don't know or care about what is happening outside that container.

GridLayout

Many times you need (or want) your components or labels to occupy symmetric spaces. Think of the Yes, No, and Cancel buttons along the bottom of a confirmation dialog. (Swing can make those dialogs, too; more on that in "Modals and Pop-Ups" on page 430.) The GridLayout class can help with such even spacing. Let's try using GridLayout for those buttons in our previous example. All we have to do is change one line:

```
// Create the button container. Old version:
// JPanel buttonPanel = new JPanel(new FlowLayout());
JPanel buttonPanel = new JPanel(new GridLayout(1,0));
```

The calls to **add()** remain exactly the same; no separate constraint argument is needed.

As you can see in Figure 12-25, the `GridLayout` buttons are the same size, even though the text of the Cancel button is a bit longer than the others.

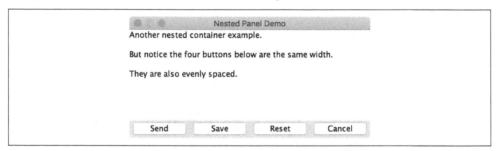

Figure 12-25. Using GridLayout for a row of buttons

In creating the layout manager, we told it we want exactly one row, with no restrictions on how many columns (1, 0). Grids can also be two-dimensional with multiple rows and columns. Figure 12-26 shows the classic phone-keypad layout as an example.

```
public class PhoneGridDemo {
  public static void main(String[] args) {
    JFrame frame = new JFrame("Nested Panel Demo");
    frame.setDefaultCloseOperation(JFrame.EXIT_ON_CLOSE);
    frame.setSize(200, 300);

    // Create the phone pad container
    JPanel phonePad = new JPanel(new GridLayout(4,3));

    // Create and add the 12 buttons, top-left to bottom-right
    phonePad.add(new JButton("1"));
    phonePad.add(new JButton("2"));
    phonePad.add(new JButton("3"));

    phonePad.add(new JButton("4"));
    phonePad.add(new JButton("5"));
    phonePad.add(new JButton("6"));

    phonePad.add(new JButton("7"));
    phonePad.add(new JButton("8"));
    phonePad.add(new JButton("9"));

    phonePad.add(new JButton("*"));
    phonePad.add(new JButton("0"));
```

```
        phonePad.add(new JButton("#"));

        // And finally, add the pad to the center of the app
        frame.add(phonePad, BorderLayout.CENTER);

        frame.setVisible(true);
    }
}
```

Adding the buttons in order from left to right, top to bottom, should result in the app you see in Figure 12-26.

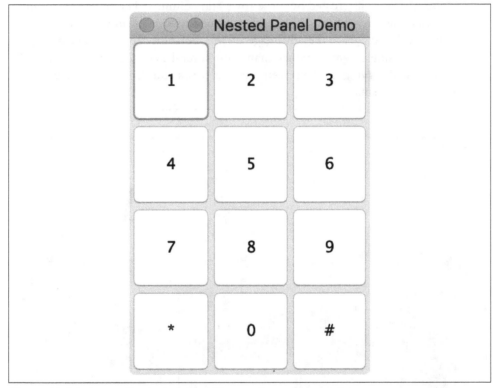

Figure 12-26. A two-dimensional grid layout for a phone pad

Very handy and very easy if you need perfectly symmetric elements. But what if you want a *mostly* symmetric layout? Think of popular web forms with a column of labels on the left and a column of text fields on the right. GridLayout could handle a basic, two-column form like that, but many times your labels are short and simple, while your text fields are wider, giving the user more space to type. How does Java accommodate those layouts?

GridBagLayout

If you need a more interesting layout but don't want to nest lots of panels, consider GridBagLayout. It's more complex to set up, but it allows for intricate layouts that still keep elements aesthetically aligned and sized. Similar to BorderLayout, you add components with an extra argument. The argument for GridBagLayout, however, is a rich GridBagConstraints object rather than a simple String.

The "grid" in GridBagLayout is exactly that, a rectangular container divvied up into various rows and columns. The "bag" part, though, comes from a grab-bag notion of how you use the cells created by those rows and columns. The rows and columns can have their own height or width, and components can occupy any rectangular collection of cells. We can take advantage of this flexibility to build out our game interface with a single JPanel rather than with several nested panes. Figure 12-27 shows one way of carving up the screen into four rows and three columns, and then placing the components.

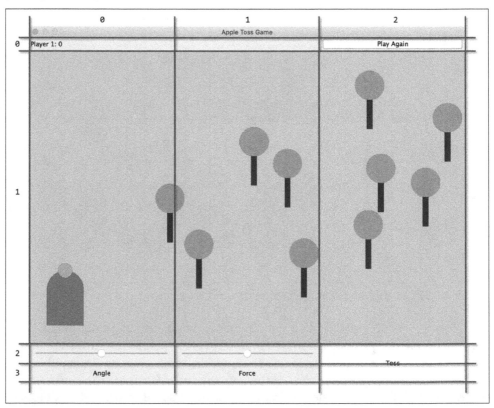

Figure 12-27. An example grid for use with GridBagLayout

You can see the different row heights and column widths. Some components occupy more than one cell. This type of arrangement won't work for every application, but it is powerful and works for many UIs that need more than simple layouts.

To build an application with a `GridBagLayout`, you need to keep a couple of references around as you add components. Let's set up the grid first:

```
public static final int SCORE_HEIGHT = 30;
public static final int CONTROL_WIDTH = 300;
public static final int CONTROL_HEIGHT = 40;
public static final int FIELD_WIDTH = 3 * CONTROL_WIDTH;
public static final int FIELD_HEIGHT = 2 * CONTROL_WIDTH;
public static final float FORCE_SCALE = 0.7f;

GridBagLayout gameLayout = new GridBagLayout();

gameLayout.columnWidths = new int[]
    { CONTROL_WIDTH, CONTROL_WIDTH, CONTROL_WIDTH };
gameLayout.rowHeights = new int[]
    { SCORE_HEIGHT, FIELD_HEIGHT, CONTROL_HEIGHT, CONTROL_HEIGHT };

JPanel gamePane = new JPanel(gameLayout);
```

This step requires a little planning on your part, but it's easy to adjust once you get a few components on the screen. To add those components, you need to create and configure a `GridBagConstraints` object. Fortunately, you can reuse the same object for all of your components—you just need to repeat the configuration portion before adding each element. Here's an example of how you could add the main playing field component:

```
GridBagConstraints gameConstraints = new GridBagConstraints();

gameConstraints.fill = GridBagConstraints.BOTH;
gameConstraints.gridy = 1;
gameConstraints.gridx = 0;
gameConstraints.gridheight = 1;
gameConstraints.gridwidth = 3;

Field field = new Field();
gamePane.add(field, gameConstraints);
```

Notice how we set which cells the field will occupy. We specify the upper-left corner of a rectangle by giving the row (`gridy`) and column (`gridx`). Then we specify how many rows our field will occupy (`gridheight`) and how many columns (`gridwidth`). This is the core of configuring grid bag constraints.

You can also adjust things like how a component will fill the cells it occupies (`fill`) and how much of a margin each component gets. We've settled on simply filling all of the space available in a group of cells ("both" a horizontal fill and a vertical fill), but you can read about more options in the documentation for `GridBagConstraints` (*https://oreil.ly/XwdXt*).

Let's add a scorekeeping label at the top:

```
gameConstraints.fill = GridBagConstraints.BOTH;
gameConstraints.gridy = 0;
gameConstraints.gridx = 0;
gameConstraints.gridheight = 1;
gameConstraints.gridwidth = 1;

JLabel scoreLabel = new JLabel(" Player 1: 0");
gamePane.add(scoreLabel, gameConstraints);
```

For this second component, do you see how similar the setup of the constraints is to how we handled the game field? Any time you see similarities like this, consider pulling those similar steps into a function you can reuse:

```
private GridBagConstraints buildConstraints(int row, int col,
    int rowspan, int colspan)
{
  // Use our global reference to the gameConstraints object
  gameConstraints.fill = GridBagConstraints.BOTH;
  gameConstraints.gridy = row;
  gameConstraints.gridx = col;
  gameConstraints.gridheight = rowspan;
  gameConstraints.gridwidth = colspan;
  return gameConstraints;
}
```

Then you could rewrite the earlier blocks of code for the score label and game field, like this:

```
GridBagConstraints gameConstraints = new GridBagConstraints();

JLabel scoreLabel = new JLabel(" Player 1: 0");
Field field = new Field();
gamePane.add(scoreLabel, buildConstraints(0,0,1,1));
gamePane.add(field, buildConstraints(1,0,1,3));
```

With that function in place, you can quickly add the various other components and labels to complete the game interface. For example, the toss button in the lower-right corner of Figure 12-27 can be set up like this:

```
JLabel tossButton = new JButton("Toss");
gamePane.add(tossButton, buildConstraints(2,2,2,1));
```

Much cleaner! We simply continue creating our components and placing them on the correct row and column, with the appropriate spans. In the end we have a reasonably interesting set of components laid out in a single container.

As with other sections in this chapter, we don't have time to cover every layout manager, or even every feature of the layout managers we do discuss. Be sure to check the Java documentation and try creating a few dummy apps to play with the different layouts. As a starting point, BoxLayout is a nice upgrade to the grid idea, and GroupLayout can produce data-entry forms. For now, though, we're going to move on. Time to get all these components "hooked up" and responding to all the typing and clicking and button pushing—actions that are encoded in Java as events.

Events

As discussed in "Model View Controller Architecture" on page 383, the model and view elements of MVC designs are straightforward. But what about the controller aspect? In Swing (and Java more generally), interaction between users and components is communicated via events. An *event* contains general information, such as when the interaction occurred, as well as information specific to the event type, such as the point on your screen where you clicked your mouse, or which key you typed on your keyboard. A *listener* (or *handler*) picks up the message and can respond in some useful way. Connecting components to listeners is what allows users to control your application.

Mouse Events

The easiest way to get started is just to generate and handle an event. Let's follow in the footsteps of our first, quick applications with a HelloMouse application and focus on handling mouse events. When we click our mouse, we'll use that click event to determine the position of our JLabel. (This will require removing the layout manager, by the way. We want to set the coordinates of our label manually.)

As you look at the source code for this example, pay attention to a few particular items, noted with the numbered callouts:

```
// filename: ch12/examples/HelloMouse.java
package ch10.examples;

import java.awt.*;
import javax.swing.*;
import java.awt.event.MouseEvent;
import java.awt.event.MouseListener;

public class HelloMouse extends JFrame implements MouseListener {❶
    JLabel label;

    public HelloMouse() {
        super("MouseEvent Demo");
        setDefaultCloseOperation(JFrame.EXIT_ON_CLOSE);
        // remove the layout manager
        setLayout(null);
        setSize(300, 100);
```

```
    label = new JLabel("Hello, Mouse!", JLabel.CENTER);
    label.setOpaque(true);
    label.setBackground(Color.YELLOW);
    label.setSize(100,20);
    label.setLocation(100,100);
    add(label);

    getContentPane().addMouseListener(this); ❹
  }

  public void mouseClicked(MouseEvent e) { ❷
    label.setLocation(e.getX(), e.getY());
  }

  public void mousePressed(MouseEvent e) { } ❸
  public void mouseReleased(MouseEvent e) { }
  public void mouseEntered(MouseEvent e) { }
  public void mouseExited(MouseEvent e) { }

  public static void main(String[] args) {
    HelloMouse frame = new HelloMouse();
    frame.setVisible(true);
  }
}
```

❶ As you click, Java picks up low-level events from your hardware (computer, mouse, keyboard) and hands them to an appropriate listener. Listeners are interfaces. You can make special classes just to implement the interface, or you can implement listeners as part of your main application class, like we did here. Where you choose to handle events really depends on what actions you need to take in response to them. You'll see a number of examples of both approaches throughout the rest of this book.

❷ We implemented the MouseListener interface in addition to extending JFrame. We had to provide a body for every method listed in MouseListener, but we do our real work in mouseClicked(). This method takes the coordinates of the click from the event object and uses them to change the position of the label. The MouseEvent class contains a wealth of information about the event: when it occurred, which component it occurred on, which mouse button was involved, the (x,y) coordinate where the event occurred, and so on. Try printing some of that information in some of the unimplemented methods, such as mouseDown().

❸ We added quite a few methods for other types of mouse events that we didn't use. That's common with lower-level events, such as mouse and keyboard events. The listener interfaces are designed to give you a central collecting point for related events. You have to implement every method in the interface, but you can respond to the particular events you care about and leave the other methods empty.

❹ The other critical bit of new code is the call to addMouseListener() for our content pane. The syntax may look a little odd, but it's a standard approach. Using getContentPane() says "this is the component generating events," and using this as the argument says "this is the class receiving (handling) the events." In this example, the events from the frame's content pane will be delivered back to the same class, which is where we put all of the mouse-handling code.

Go ahead and run the application. You'll get a variation on the familiar "Hello, World" graphical application, shown in Figure 12-28. The friendly message should follow your mouse as you click around.

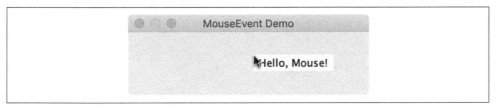

Figure 12-28. Using a MouseEvent to position a label

Mouse adapters

If you want to try the helper-class approach, you could add a separate class to the file and implement MouseListener in that class. If so, you can take advantage of a shortcut Swing provides for many listeners. The MouseAdapter class is a simple implementation of the MouseListener interface, with empty methods written for every event. When you extend this class, you override only the methods you care about. That makes for a clean, concise handler:

```
// filename: ch12/examples/HelloMouseHelper.java
package ch12.examples;

import java.awt.*;
import java.awt.event.MouseEvent;
import java.awt.event.MouseAdapter;
import javax.swing.*;

public class HelloMouseHelper {
  public static void main(String[] args) {
    JFrame frame = new JFrame("MouseEvent Demo");
    frame.setDefaultCloseOperation(JFrame.EXIT_ON_CLOSE);
    frame.setLayout(null);
    frame.setSize(300, 300);

    JLabel label = new JLabel("Hello, Mouse!", JLabel.CENTER);
    label.setOpaque(true);
```

```
        label.setBackground(Color.YELLOW);
        label.setSize(100,20);
        label.setLocation(100,100);
        frame.add(label);

        LabelMover mover = new LabelMover(label);
        frame.getContentPane().addMouseListener(mover);
        frame.setVisible(true);
    }
}

/**
 * Helper class to move a label to the position of a mouse click.
 * Recall from Chapter 5 that secondary classes included in the same
 * public class must not be public themselves. They can be protected,
 * file as private, or package private (with no qualifier).
 */
class LabelMover extends MouseAdapter {
    JLabel labelToMove;

    public LabelMover(JLabel label) {
        labelToMove = label;
    }

    public void mouseClicked(MouseEvent e) {
        labelToMove.setLocation(e.getX(), e.getY());
    }
}
```

Remember that helper classes need to have a reference to every object they touch. We passed our label to the constructor of our adapter. That's a popular way to establish the necessary connections, but you could certainly add the required access later—as long as the handler has a reference to every object it needs before it starts receiving events.

Action Events

While low-level mouse and keyboard events are available on just about every Swing component, they can be a little tedious. Most UI libraries provide higher-level events that are simpler to think about. Swing is no exception. The JButton class, for example, supports an ActionEvent that lets you know the button has been clicked. Most of the time this is exactly what you want. But the mouse events are still available if you need some special behavior, such as reacting to clicks from different mouse buttons or distinguishing between a long and a short press on a touch screen.

A popular way to demonstrate the button click event is to build a simple counter, like the one you see in Figure 12-29. Each time you click the button, the program updates the label. This simple proof of concept shows that you can receive and respond to UI events. Let's see the wiring required for this demo:

```java
package ch12.examples;

import javax.swing.*;
import java.awt.*;
import java.awt.event.ActionEvent;
import java.awt.event.ActionListener;

public class ActionDemo1 extends JFrame implements ActionListener {
  int counterValue = 0;
  JLabel counterLabel;

  public ActionDemo1() {
    super("ActionEvent Counter Demo");
    setDefaultCloseOperation(JFrame.EXIT_ON_CLOSE);
    setLayout(new FlowLayout());
    setSize(300, 180);

    counterLabel = new JLabel("Count: 0", JLabel.CENTER);
    add(counterLabel);

    JButton incrementer = new JButton("Increment");
    incrementer.addActionListener(this);
    add(incrementer);
  }

  public void actionPerformed(ActionEvent e) {
    counterValue++;
    counterLabel.setText("Count: " + counterValue);
  }

  public static void main(String[] args) {
    ActionDemo1 demo = new ActionDemo1();
    demo.setVisible(true);
  }
}
```

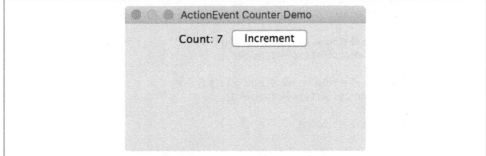

Figure 12-29. Using ActionEvent *to increment a counter*

We update a simple counter variable and display the result inside the actionPer
formed() method, which is where ActionListener objects receive their events. We

used the direct listener implementation approach, but we could just as easily have created a helper class as we did with the LabelMover example in "Mouse Events" on page 413.

Action events are straightforward; they don't have as many details available as mouse events, but they do carry a "command" property. The command in question is just an arbitrary string. It doesn't mean anything to Java, but you can customize this property for your own use. For buttons, Java defaults to using the text of the button's label. The JTextField class also generates an action event if you press the Return key while typing in the text field. In this case, however, the text currently in the field is used for the command. Figure 12-30 shows how to hook up a button and a text field to a label.

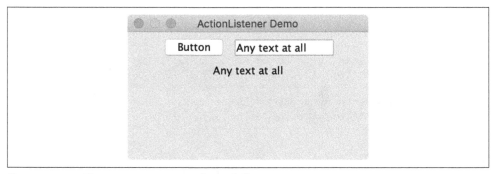

Figure 12-30. Using ActionEvents *from different sources*

```
public class ActionDemo2 {
  public static void main(String[] args) {
    JFrame frame = new JFrame("ActionListener Demo");
    frame.setDefaultCloseOperation(JFrame.EXIT_ON_CLOSE);
    frame.setLayout(new FlowLayout());
    frame.setSize(300, 180);

    JLabel label = new JLabel("Results go here", JLabel.CENTER);
    ActionCommandHelper helper = new ActionCommandHelper(label);

    JButton simpleButton = new JButton("Button");
    simpleButton.addActionListener(helper);

    JTextField simpleField = new JTextField(10);
    simpleField.addActionListener(helper);

    frame.add(simpleButton);
    frame.add(simpleField);
    frame.add(label);

    frame.setVisible(true);
  }
}
```

```
/**
 * Helper class to show the command property of any ActionEvent in a given label.
 */
class ActionCommandHelper implements ActionListener {
  JLabel resultLabel;

  public ActionCommandHelper(JLabel label) {
    resultLabel = label;
  }

  public void actionPerformed(ActionEvent ae) {
    resultLabel.setText(ae.getActionCommand());
  }
}
```

Notice we used one `ActionListener` object to handle the events for *both* the button and the text field. This is a great feature of Swing's listener approach to handling events: any component that generates a given type of event can report to any listener that receives that type. Sometimes your event handlers are unique and you'll build a separate handler for each component. But many applications offer multiple ways to accomplish the same task. You can often handle those different input sources with a single listener. And the less code you have, the less that can go wrong!

Change Events

Another event type that appears in several Swing components is `ChangeEvent`. This is a simple event that lets you know something has, well, changed. The `JSlider` class uses this mechanism to report changes to the position of the slider. The `ChangeEvent` class has a reference to the component that changed (the event's *source*) but no details on what might have changed within that component. It's up to you to go ask the component for those details. That listen-then-query process might seem tedious, but it does allow for efficient notifications that updates are necessary, without creating hundreds of classes with thousands of methods to cover all the event variations that might come up.

We won't reproduce the entire application here, but let's take a look at how the `AppleToss` class uses `ChangeListener` to map the aiming slider to our physicist:

```
// file: ch12/examples/game/AppleToss.java
    gamePane.add(buildAngleControl(), buildConstraints(2, 0, 1, 1));

    // other setup stuff ...

    private JSlider buildAngleControl() {
      // Our aim can range from 0 to 180 degrees
      JSlider slider = new JSlider(0,180);

      // but trigonometric 0 is on the right side, not the left
      slider.setInverted(true);
```

```
    // Any time the slider value changes, update the player
    slider.addChangeListener(new ChangeListener() {
      public void stateChanged(ChangeEvent e) {
        player1.setAimingAngle((float)slider.getValue());
        field.repaint();
      }
    });
    return slider;
}
```

In this snippet, we use a factory pattern to create our slider and return it for use in the add() method of our gamePane container. We create a simple anonymous inner class. Changing our aiming slider has one effect, and there is only one way to aim the apple. Since there is no possibility of class reuse, we chose an anonymous inner class. There is nothing wrong with creating a complete helper class and passing it the player1 and field elements as arguments to a constructor or initialization method, but you will find the approach used above quite often in the wild.

We want to point out one other option for handling simple events like ChangeEvent and ActionEvent. The listeners for these events have a single abstract method. Does that phrase ring a bell? That's how Oracle describes its functional interfaces. So we can use a lambda!

```
    // And now, any time the slider value changes, we should update
    slider.addChangeListener(e -> {
      player1.setAimingAngle((float)slider.getValue());
      field.repaint();
    });
```

Unfortunately, many listeners handle a spectrum of related events. You can't use a lambda with any listener interface that has more than one method. But lambdas work with buttons and menu items, so they can still play a big role in your graphical application if you find them appealing.

Our Widget isn't really good for trying event-related code in *jshell*. While you certainly can write an anonymous inner class or a multiline lambda at a command line, it can be tedious and prone to errors that are not easy to fix from that same command line. It's usually simpler to write small, focused demo apps, like many of the examples in this chapter. While we encourage you to fire up the apple tossing game to play with the slider shown in the code above, you should also try your hand at a few original apps.

Other Events

There are dozens of other events and listeners spread across the java.awt.event and javax.swing.event packages. It's worth peeking at the documentation just to get a sense of the other types of events you might run into. Table 12-2 shows the events and

---

listeners associated with the components we've discussed so far in this chapter, as well as a few that are worth checking out as you work more with Swing.

Table 12-2. Swing and AWT events and associated listeners

S/A	Event class	Listener interface	Generating components
A	ActionEvent	ActionListener	JButton, JMenuItem, JTextField
S	ChangeEvent	ChangeListener	JSlider
A	ItemEvent	ItemListener	JCheckBox, JRadioButton
A	KeyEvent	KeyListener	Descendants of Component
S	ListSelectionEvent	ListSelectionListener	JList
A	MouseEvent	MouseListener	Descendants of Component
A	MouseMotionEvent	MouseMotionListener	Descendants of Component

AWT events (A) from java.awt.event, Swing events (S) from javax.swing.event

If you're unsure what events a particular component supports, check its documentation for methods that look like addXYZListener(). Whatever stands in for XYZ is a clue about where else in the documentation to look. Recall that our slider uses addChangeListener(). So that XYZ is Change in this case. You can infer the event name (ChangeEvent) and the listener interface (ChangeListener) from that clue. Once you have the documentation for the listener, try implementing every method and simply printing which event is reported. You can learn a lot about how the various Swing components react to keyboard and mouse events this way.

Threading Considerations

If you have read any of the JDK documentation on Swing as you've been working through this chapter, you may have come across a warning that Swing components are not thread-safe. As you learned in Chapter 9, Java supports multiple threads of execution to take advantage of modern computer processing power. Multithreaded applications run the risk of allowing two threads to fight over the same resource or update the same variable at the same time but with different values. Not knowing if your data is correct can severely decrease your ability to debug a program or even just trust its output. For Swing components, this warning reminds programmers that their UI elements could be subject to this type of corruption.

To help maintain a consistent UI, Swing encourages you to update your components on the AWT *event dispatch thread*. This is the thread that naturally handles things like button clicks. If you update a component in response to an event (such as our counter button and label in "Action Events" on page 416), you are all set. The idea is that if every other thread in your application sends UI updates to the sole event dispatch thread, no component can be adversely affected by simultaneous, possibly conflicting changes.

A common example of threading in graphical applications is the animated spinner that sits on your screen while you wait for a large file to download. But what if you get impatient? What if it seems like the download has failed but the spinner is still going? If your long-running task is using the event dispatch thread, your user won't be able to click a Cancel button or take any action at all. Long-running tasks should be handled by separate threads that can run in the background, leaving your application responsive and available. But then how do we update the UI when that background thread finishes? Swing has a helper class ready for you.

SwingUtilities and Component Updates

You can use the `SwingUtilities` class from any thread to perform updates to your UI components in a safe, stable manner. There are two static methods you can use to communicate with your UI:

- `invokeAndWait()`
- `invokeLater()`

As their names imply, the first method runs some UI update code and makes the current thread wait for that update to finish before continuing. The second method hands off some UI update code to the event dispatch thread and then immediately resumes executing on the current thread. (The event dispatch thread is sometimes called the *event dispatch queue*. You can append events or updates and the event dispatch thread will get to them in roughly the order they were added, like in a queue.) Which one you use really depends on whether your background thread needs to know the state of the UI before continuing. For example, if you are adding a new button to your interface, you might want to use `invokeAndWait()` so that by the time your background thread continues, it can be sure that future updates will actually have a button to update.

If you aren't as concerned about when something gets updated, but still want it to be handled safely by the dispatch thread, `invokeLater()` is perfect. Think about updating a progress bar as a large file is downloading. Your code might fire off several updates as more and more of the download completes. You don't need to wait for those graphical updates to finish before resuming your download. If a progress update gets delayed or runs very close to a second update, there's no real harm. But you don't want a busy graphical interface to interrupt your download—especially if the server is sensitive to pauses.

We'll see several examples of this type of network/UI interaction in Chapter 13, but let's fake some network traffic and update a small label to show off `SwingUtilities`.

We can set up a Start button that will update a status label with a simple percentage display and kick off a background thread that sleeps for one second, then increments the progress. Each time the thread wakes up, it will update the label using invoke Later() to correctly set the label's text. First, let's set up our demo:

```
package ch12.examples;

public class ProgressDemo {
  public static void main(String[] args) {
    JFrame frame = new JFrame("SwingUtilities 'invoke' Demo");
    frame.setDefaultCloseOperation(JFrame.EXIT_ON_CLOSE);
    frame.setLayout(new FlowLayout());
    frame.setSize(300, 180);

    JLabel label = new JLabel("Download Progress Goes Here!",
        JLabel.CENTER);
    Thread pretender = new Thread(new ProgressPretender(label));

    JButton simpleButton = new JButton("Start");
    simpleButton.addActionListener(e -> {
      simpleButton.setEnabled(false);
      pretender.start();
    });

    JLabel checkLabel = new JLabel("Can you still type?");
    JTextField checkField = new JTextField(10);

    frame.add(label);
    frame.add(simpleButton);
    frame.add(checkLabel);
    frame.add(checkField);
    frame.setVisible(true);
  }
}
```

Most of this should look familiar, but look at how we create our thread. We pass a new ProgressPretender() as the argument to our Thread constructor. We could have broken that call into separate parts, but since we do not refer directly to our ProgressPretender object again, we can stick with this tidier, denser approach. We *do* refer to the thread itself, however, so we make a proper variable for it. We can then start our thread running in the ActionListener for our button. We also disable our Start button at that point. We don't want the user trying to (re)start a thread that is already running!

We added a text field for you to type in. While the progress is being updated, your application should continue responding to user input like typing. Try it! The text field isn't connected to anything, but you should be able to enter and delete text while watching the progress counter slowly climb up, as shown in Figure 12-31.

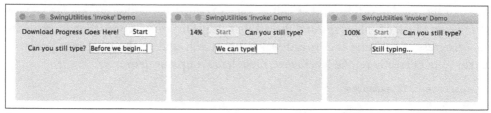

Figure 12-31. Thread-safe updates to a progress label

So how did we update that label without locking up the application? Let's look at the `ProgressPretender` class and inspect the `run()` method:

```
package ch12.examples;

class ProgressPretender implements Runnable {
  JLabel label;
  int progress;

  public ProgressPretender(JLabel label) {
    this.label = label;
    progress = 0;
  }

  public void run() {
    while (progress <= 100) {
      SwingUtilities.invokeLater(
        () -> label.setText(progress + "%");
      );
      try {
        Thread.sleep(1000);
      } catch (InterruptedException ie) {
        System.err.println("Someone interrupted us. Skipping download.");
        break;
      }
      progress++;
    }
  }
}
```

In this class, we store the label passed to our constructor so we know where to display our updated progress. The `run()` method has three basic steps: 1) update the label, 2) sleep for 1,000 milliseconds, and 3) increment our progress.

In step 1, the lambda argument we pass to `invokeLater()` is based on the `Runnable` interface in Chapter 9. We could have used an inner class or an anonymous inner class, but for such a simple task, a lambda is perfect. The lambda body updates the label with our current progress value. The event dispatch thread will execute the lambda. This is the magic that leaves the text field responsive even though our "progress" thread is sleeping most of the time.

Step 2 is standard-issue thread sleeping. The `sleep()` method knows it can be interrupted, so the compiler will make sure you supply a `try/catch` block like we've done above. There are many ways to handle the interruption, but in this case we chose to simply `break` out of the loop.

Finally, we increment our progress counter and start the whole process over. Once we hit 100, the loop ends and our progress label should stop changing. If you wait patiently, you'll see that final value. The app itself should remain active, though. You can still type in the text field. Our download is complete and all is well with the world!

Timers

The Swing library includes a timer that is designed to work in the UI space. The `javax.swing.Timer` class is fairly straightforward. It waits a specified period of time and then fires off an action event (the same type of event as clicking a button). It can fire that action once or repeatedly. You'll find many reasons to use timers with graphical applications. Besides providing an alternative way to drive an animation loop, you might want to automatically cancel some action, like loading a network resource if it is taking too long. Conversely, you might put up a little "please wait" spinner or dialog to let the user know the operation is ongoing. You might want to take down a dialog prompt if the user doesn't respond within a specified time span. Swing's `Timer` can handle all of these scenarios.

Animation with Timer

Let's modify our flying apples from "Revisiting Animation with Threads" on page 281 and try implementing the animation with an instance of `Timer`. The `Timer` class takes care of that detail for us. We can still use our `step()` method in the `Apple` class from our first pass at animation. We just need to alter the start method and keep a suitable variable around for the timer:

```
public static final int STEP = 40;  // frame duration in milliseconds
Timer animationTimer;

// other member declarations ...

void startAnimation() {
  if (animationTimer == null) {
    animationTimer = new Timer(STEP, this);
    animationTimer.setActionCommand("repaint");
    animationTimer.setRepeats(true);
    animationTimer.start();
  } else if (!animationTimer.isRunning()) {
    animationTimer.restart();
  }
}
```

```
    // other methods ...

    public void actionPerformed(ActionEvent event) {
      if (animating && event.getActionCommand().equals("repaint")) {
        System.out.println("Timer stepping " + apples.size() + " apples");
        for (Apple a : apples) {
          a.step();
          detectCollisions(a);
        }
        repaint();
        cullFallenApples();
      }
    }
```

There are two nice things about this approach. It's definitely easier to read because we are not responsible for the pauses between actions. We create the Timer by passing to the constructor the time interval between events and an ActionListener to receive the events—our Field class in this case. We give the timer a simple but unique action command, make it a repeating timer, and start it up!

The other nice thing is specific to Swing and graphical applications: javax.swing.Timer fires its action events *on the event dispatch thread*. You do not need to wrap any of your response in invokeAndWait() or invokeLater(). Just put your timer-based code in the actionPerformed() method of an attached listener and you are good to go!

Because several components generate ActionEvent objects, we did take a little precaution against collisions by setting the actionCommand attribute for our timer. This step is not strictly necessary in our case, but it leaves room for the Field class to handle other events down the road without breaking our animation.

Other Timer uses

Mature, polished applications have a variety of small moments where it helps to have a one-time timer. Our apple game is simple by comparison to most commercial apps or games, but even here we can add a little "realism" with a timer: after tossing an apple, we can pause before allowing the physicist to fire another apple. Maybe the physicist has to bend down and grab another apple from a bucket before aiming or tossing. This kind of delay is another perfect spot for a Timer.

We can add this pause to the bit of code in the Field class where we toss the apple:

```
    public void startTossFromPlayer(Physicist physicist) {
      if (!animating) {
        System.out.println("Starting animation!");
        animating = true;
        startAnimation();
      }
```

```
    if (animating) {
      // Check to make sure we have an apple to toss
      if (physicist.aimingApple != null) {
        Apple apple = physicist.takeApple();
        apple.toss(physicist.aimingAngle, physicist.aimingForce);
        apples.add(apple);
        Timer appleLoader = new Timer(800, physicist);
        appleLoader.setActionCommand("New Apple");
        appleLoader.setRepeats(false);
        appleLoader.start();
      }
    }
  }
```

Notice this time that we set the timer to run only once with the `setRepeats(false)` call. This means that after a little less than a second, a single event will be fired off to our physicist. The `Physicist` class, in turn, needs to add the `implements Action Listener` portion to the class definition and include an appropriate `action Performed()` function, like so:

```
// other imports ...
import java.awt.event.ActionEvent;
import java.awt.event.ActionListener;

public class Physicist implements ActionListener {

  // Current Physicist stuff ...

  // New event handler for getting a new apple
  public void actionPerformed(ActionEvent e) {
    if (e.getActionCommand().equals("New Apple")) {
      getNewApple();
      if (field != null) {
        field.repaint();
      }
    }
  }
}
```

Using `Timer` isn't the only way to accomplish such tasks, but in Swing, the combination of efficient timed events and automatic use of the event dispatch thread make it worth considering. If nothing else, it makes prototyping easy. You can always come back and refactor your application to use custom threading code, if needed.

But Wait, There's More

As we noted at the beginning of the chapter, there are many, many more discussions and topics and explorations available in the world of Java graphical applications. Java has an entire package devoted to storing user preferences (*https://oreil.ly/Vrbfz*), for example. And O'Reilly has an entire book by Jonathan Knudsen devoted to *Java 2D*

Graphics (https://oreil.ly/4xYdN). We'll leave it to you to do that exploring but wanted to go through at least a few key topics worth focusing on first if you have plans for a desktop app.

Menus

While not technically required, most desktop applications have an application-wide menu of common tasks, such as saving changed files or setting preferences. Apps with specific features, like spreadsheets, might have menus for sorting the data in a column or selection. The `JMenu`, `JMenuBar`, and `JMenuItem` classes help you add this functionality to your Swing apps. Menus go inside a menu bar, and menu items go inside menus. Swing has three prebuilt menu item classes: `JMenuItem` for basic menu entries, `JCheckBoxMenuItem` for option items, and `JRadioButtonMenuItem` for grouped menu items like the currently selected font or color theme. The `JMenu` class is itself a valid menu item so you can build nested menus. `JMenuItem` behaves like a button (as do its radio and checkbox compatriots), and you can catch menu events using the same listeners.

Figure 12-32 shows an example of a simple menu bar populated with some menus and items.

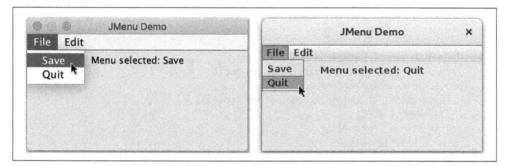

Figure 12-32. JMenu and JMenuItem on macOS and Linux

Here's the source code for this demonstration:

```
package ch12.examples;

import javax.swing.*;
import java.awt.*;
import java.awt.event.ActionEvent;
import java.awt.event.ActionListener;

public class MenuDemo extends JFrame implements ActionListener {
  JLabel resultsLabel;

  public MenuDemo() {
    super("JMenu Demo");
```

```java
        setDefaultCloseOperation(JFrame.EXIT_ON_CLOSE);
        setLayout(new FlowLayout());
        setSize(300, 180);

        resultsLabel = new JLabel("Click a menu item!");
        add(resultsLabel);

        // Now let's create a couple menus and populate them
        JMenu fileMenu = new JMenu("File");
        JMenuItem saveItem = new JMenuItem("Save");
        saveItem.addActionListener(this);
        fileMenu.add(saveItem);
        JMenuItem quitItem = new JMenuItem("Quit");
        quitItem.addActionListener(this);
        fileMenu.add(quitItem);

        JMenu editMenu = new JMenu("Edit");
        JMenuItem cutItem = new JMenuItem("Cut");
        cutItem.addActionListener(this);
        editMenu.add(cutItem);
        JMenuItem copyItem = new JMenuItem("Copy");
        copyItem.addActionListener(this);
        editMenu.add(copyItem);
        JMenuItem pasteItem = new JMenuItem("Paste");
        pasteItem.addActionListener(this);
        editMenu.add(pasteItem);

        // And finally build a JMenuBar for the application
        JMenuBar mainBar = new JMenuBar();
        mainBar.add(fileMenu);
        mainBar.add(editMenu);
        setJMenuBar(mainBar);
    }

    public void actionPerformed(ActionEvent event) {
        resultsLabel.setText("Menu selected: " + event.getActionCommand());
    }

    public static void main(String args[]) {
        MenuDemo demo = new MenuDemo();
        demo.setVisible(true);
    }
}
```

We obviously don't do much with the menu item actions here, but they illustrate how you can start building out the expected parts of a professional application.

Modals and Pop-Ups

Events let the user get your attention, or at least the attention of some method in your application. But what if you need to get the user's attention? A popular UI mechanism for this task is the pop-up window. You'll often hear such a window referred to as a *modal* or *dialog* or even *modal dialog*. The term *dialog* comes from the fact that these pop-ups present some information to the user and expect—or require—a response. Perhaps this quick question and answer process is not as lofty as a Socratic symposium, but still. The *modal* name refers to the fact that some of those dialogs that require a response will actually disable the rest of the application—putting it in a restricted mode—until you provide that response. You may have experienced such a dialog yourself in other desktop applications. If your software requires you to stay up-to-date with the latest release, for example, it might "gray out" the application, indicating you can't use it, and then show you a modal dialog with a button that initiates the update process.

The term *pop-up* is more general. While you can certainly have modal pop-ups, you can also have plain ("modeless") pop-ups that do not block you from using the rest of the application. Think of a search dialog in a word-processing application that you can leave available and just scoot off to the side of your main window.

Swing provides a bare `JDialog` class that you can use to create custom dialog windows. For typical pop-up interactions with your users, including alerts, confirmations, and input dialogs, the `JOptionPane` class has some really handy shortcuts. For simple alerts and error messages, you can use the `showMessageDialog()` call. This type of dialog includes a customizable title, some text, and a button to acknowledge (and dismiss) the pop-up. If you need the user to make a yes-or-no choice, `showCon firmDialog()` is perfect. And if you need short, text-based answers from the user, you'll want to use `showInputDialog()`. Figure 12-33 shows an example of these three dialogs.

Figure 12-33. The main variations of JOptionPane pop-up windows

To create a message dialog, you have to supply four arguments. The first argument refers to the frame or window "owning" the pop-up. `JOptionPane` will attempt to center the dialog over its owner when shown. You can also specify `null` for this argument, which tells `JOptionPane` there is no primary window, so center the pop-up on the user's screen. The second and third arguments are `Strings` for the dialog's message and title, respectively. The final argument indicates the "type" of pop-up, which mostly affects the icon you see. You can specify several types:

- ERROR_MESSAGE, red Stop icon
- INFORMATION_MESSAGE, Duke[6] icon
- WARNING_MESSAGE, yellow triangle icon
- QUESTION_MESSAGE, Duke icon
- PLAIN_MESSAGE, no icon

Head back to your *jshell* and try creating a message pop-up. You can use the handy null option for the owner:

```
jshell> import javax.swing.*

jshell> JOptionPane.showMessageDialog(null, "Hi there", "jshell Alert",
   ...>    JOptionPane.ERROR_MESSAGE)
```

Another common task for pop-ups is verifying the user's intent. Many applications ask if you're sure you want to quit or delete something. JOptionPane has you covered. You can try out this confirmation dialog in *jshell*:

```
jshell> JOptionPane.showConfirmDialog(null, "Are you sure?")
$18 ==> 0
```

The two-argument version of the showConfirmDialog() method produces a pop-up with Yes, No, and Cancel buttons. You can determine which answer the user selected by keeping the return value (an int). We clicked the Yes button, which returns 0, but you don't have to memorize the return values. JOptionPane has constants covering the various responses:

- YES_OPTION
- NO_OPTION
- CANCEL_OPTION
- OK_OPTION
- CLOSED_OPTION

JOptionPane returns the CLOSED_OPTION value if the user closes the dialog using the window controls rather than clicking on any of the available buttons within the dialog. You also have a modicum of control over those buttons. You can use a

---

6 "Duke" is the official Java mascot. You can find out more at the OpenJDK wiki (*https://oreil.ly/jahxA*).

four-argument version that takes a title and a button choice with one of the following values:

- YES_NO_OPTION
- OK_CANCEL_OPTION
- YES_NO_CANCEL_OPTION

In most situations, having both a "No" and a "Cancel" in the same dialog confuses users. We recommend using one of the first two options. (The user can always close the dialog using the standard window controls if they do not want to make a selection.) Let's try creating a Yes/No dialog:

```
jshell> int answer = JOptionPane.showConfirmDialog(null,
   ...>   "Are you sure?", "Confirm", JOptionPane.YES_NO_OPTION)
answer ==> 1

jshell> if (answer == JOptionPane.NO_OPTION)
   ...>   System.out.println("They declined")
They declined
```

Some pop-ups ask for a quick bit of input. You can use the `showInputDialog()` method to ask a question and allow the user to type in an answer. That answer (a `String`) can be stored the same way you keep the confirmation choice. Let's try one more pop-up in *jshell*:

```
jshell> String pin = JOptionPane.showInputDialog(null, "Please enter your PIN:")
pin ==> "1234"
```

Input dialogs are handy for one-off requests, but we don't recommend them if you have a series of questions to ask the user. You should keep modals confined to quick, infrequent tasks. They interrupt the user—by design. Sometimes that interruption is exactly what you need. If you abuse the user's attention, however, you're likely to annoy the user, and they'll learn to simply ignore every pop-up from your application.

The file *ch12/examples/ModalDemo.java* contains a small application that can create a variety of modal dialogs. Feel free to play around with it and try out the different message types or confirmation button options. And don't be afraid of modifying these example applications! Sometimes tweaking a simple app and recompiling is easier than trying to type multiline examples into *jshell*.

User Interface and User Experience

This was a whirlwind tour of some of the more common UI elements for desktop applications, such as JButton, JLabel, and JTextField. We discussed how to arrange those components using layout managers in containers and introduced several other components.

Of course, desktop applications are only part of the story. Chapter 13 covers networking basics, including getting content from the web and simple client/server applications.

Review Questions

1. Which component would you use to display some text to the user?

2. Which component(s) would you use to allow the user to enter text?

3. What event does clicking a button generate?

4. Which listener should you attach to JList if you want to know when the user changes the selected item?

5. What is the default layout manager for JPanel?

6. Which thread is responsible for processing events in Java?

7. What method would you use to update a component like JLabel after a background task completes?

8. What container holds JMenuItem objects?

Code Exercises

1. Create a calculator interface with buttons and a text display. You can use the starter Calculator class in the *ch12/exercises* folder. It extends JFrame and implements the ActionListener interface. The display element should go at the top of the calculator and show right-justified text. The buttons should include the digits 0-9, a decimal point, addition, subtraction, multiplication, division, and an "equals" for showing the results. You can see what it should look like in Figure 12-34.

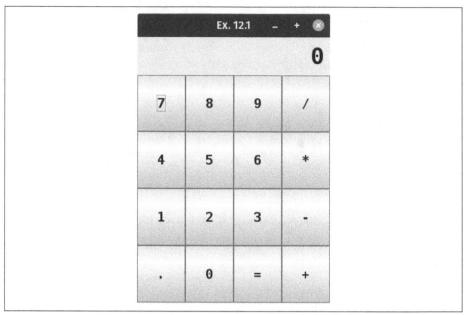

Figure 12-34. An example calculator interface

Don't worry about hooking up the buttons to make the calculator work—yet. We'll tackle that in the advanced exercise.

2. The apple tossing game in the *ch12/exercises/game* folder has sliders and buttons to aim and toss apples. Right now those apples simply fly in an arc and eventually go outside the bounds of our window. Add the necessary code to catch collisions between an apple and an obstacle, like a tree or a hedge. Your solution should remove both the apple and the obstacle and then refresh the screen.

Advanced Exercises

1. Take the visual shell you created for a calculator in the first code exercise and connect the buttons to make it functional. Clicking number buttons should put the corresponding digit in the display. Clicking an operation button (like addition or division) should store the operation to perform and allow the user to enter a second number. Clicking the "=" button should show the results of the operation.

This exercise pulls together several discussions from past chapters. Make incremental changes and don't be afraid to look in "Advanced Exercises" on page 491 for hints on how to proceed.

CHAPTER 13

Network Programming in Java

When you think about the web, you probably think of web-based applications and services. If you are asked to go deeper, you may consider tools such as web browsers and web servers that support those applications and move data around the network. In this chapter, we'll look at how Java interacts with web services. We'll also peek under the hood a bit and discuss some of the lower-level networking classes of the *java.net* package.

Uniform Resource Locators

A *Uniform Resource Locator* (URL) points to an object on the internet. It's a text string that identifies an item, tells you where to find it, and specifies a method for communicating with it or retrieving it from its source. A URL can point to any kind of information source: static data, such as a file on a local filesystem, a web server, or an FTP site. It can point to a more dynamic object, such as an RSS news feed or a record in a database. URLs can also refer to other resources, such as email addresses.

Because there are many different ways to locate an item on the internet, and different mediums and transports require different kinds of information, URLs can have many forms. The most common form has four components as shown in Figure 13-1: a network host or server, the name of the item, its location on that host, and a protocol by which the host should communicate.

Figure 13-1. Common elements of a URL

protocol (also called the "scheme") is an identifier such as http, https, or ftp; *hostname* is usually an internet host and domain name; and the *path* and *resource* components form a unique path that identifies the object on that host.

Variants of this form pack extra information into the URL. For example, you can specify fragment identifiers (those suffixes that start with a "#" character) that reference sections inside documents. Other, more specialized types of URLs exist as well, such as "mailto" URLs for email addresses, or URLs for addressing things like database components. These types of locators may not follow this format precisely, but they generally contain a protocol, host, and path. Some are more properly called *Uniform Resource Identifiers*, or URIs, which can specify more information about the name or the location of a resource. URLs are a subset of URIs.

Because most URLs have the notion of a hierarchy or path, we sometimes speak of a URL that is relative to another URL, called a *base URL*. In that case, we are using the base URL as a starting point and supplying additional information to target an object relative to that URL. For example, the base URL might point to a directory on a web server, and a relative URL might name a particular file in that directory or in a subdirectory.

The URL Class

The Java java.net.URL class represents a URL address and provides a simple API for accessing web resources, such as documents and applications on servers. It can use an extensible set of protocol and content handlers to perform the necessary communication and, in theory, even data conversion. With the URL class, an application can open a connection to a server and retrieve content with just a few lines of code.

An instance of the URL class manages all the component information within a URL string and provides methods for retrieving the object it identifies. We can construct a URL object from a complete string or from component parts:

```
try {
  URL aDoc =
    new URL("http://foo.bar.com/documents/homepage.html");
  URL sameDoc =
    new URL("http","foo.bar.com","/documents/homepage.html");
} catch (MalformedURLException e) {
  // Something wrong with our URL
}
```

These two URL objects point to the same network resource, the *homepage.html* document on the server *foo.bar.com*. We can't know whether the resource actually exists and is available until we try to access it. A new URL object contains only data about the object's location and how to access it. Creating a URL object does not make any network connections.

 Oracle deprecated the URL constructor in Java 20. Deprecation doesn't remove methods or classes, but it does mean you should consider other means of accomplishing your goal. The Javadoc for deprecated items often includes suggested alternatives. In this case, the URI class has better validation code, so Oracle recommends new URI("http://your.url/").toURL() as a replacement.

If you are using Java 20 or later, feel free to update the code examples to use URI if you want to get rid of the compiler's deprecation warnings. As this is a recent deprecation, though, you will still see the URL constructor used widely in online examples.

We can examine the parts of the URL with the getProtocol(), getHost(), and get File() methods. We can also compare it to another URL with the sameFile() method (an unfortunate name for something that may not point to a file), which determines whether two URLs point to the same resource. It's not foolproof, but sameFile() does more than compare the URL strings for equality; it takes into account the possibility that one server may have several names, as well as other factors.

When you create a URL, Java parses the URL's specification to identify the protocol component. It then tries to match what it parses from your URL with a *protocol handler*. A protocol handler is essentially a helper that can speak the given protocol and can retrieve a resource by following the protocol's rules. If the URL's protocol doesn't make sense, or if Java can't find a compatible protocol handler, the URL constructor throws a MalformedURLException.

Java provides URL protocol handlers for http, https (secure HTTP), and ftp, as well as local file URLs and jar URLs that refer to files inside JAR archives. Java also provides the necessary low-level structure for third-party libraries to add support for other types of URLs.

Stream Data

The lowest-level and most general way to get data back from a URL is to ask for an InputStream from the URL by calling openStream(). Getting data as a stream may also be useful if you want to receive continuous updates from a dynamic information source. Unfortunately, you have to parse the contents of this stream yourself. Not all types of URLs support the openStream() method because not all types of URLs refer to concrete data; you'll get an UnknownServiceException if the URL doesn't.

The following code (a simplification of the *ch13/examples/Read.java* file) prints the contents of an HTML file from an imaginary web server:

```java
try {
  URL url = new URL("http://some.server/index.html");

  BufferedReader bin = new BufferedReader(
      new InputStreamReader(url.openStream()));

  String line;
  while ((line = bin.readLine()) != null) {
    System.out.println(line);
  }
  bin.close();
} catch (Exception e) {
  e.printStackTrace();
}
```

In this snippet, we ask for an InputStream from our url with openStream() and wrap it in a BufferedReader to read the lines of text. Because we specify the http protocol in the URL, we enlist the services of an HTTP protocol handler. We haven't talked about content handlers yet. Because we're reading directly from the input stream, we don't need a content handler to transform the content.

Getting the Content as an Object

As we said previously, openStream() is the most general way to access web content, but it leaves the data parsing up to the programmer. The URL class supports a more sophisticated, pluggable, content-handling mechanism, but the Java community never really standardized the actual handlers, so its usefulness is limited.

Many developers are curious about loading objects over the network because they need to load images from URLs. Java provides a few alternative approaches to accomplish this task. The simplest approach is to use the javax.swing.ImageIcon class which has a constructor that accepts a URL:

```
//file: ch13/examples/IconLabel.java
    URL fav = new URL("https://www.oracle.com/.../favicon-192.png");
    ImageIcon image1 = new ImageIcon(fav);
    JLabel iconLabel = new JLabel(image1);
    // iconLabel can be placed in any panel, just as other labels
```

If you need to turn a network stream into some other type of object, you can look into the `getContent()` method of the URL class. You may need to write your own handler, though. For that advanced topic, we recommend *Java Network Programming* (*https://oreil.ly/1GwXT*) by Elliotte Rusty-Harold (O'Reilly).

Managing Connections

Upon calling `openStream()` on a URL, Java consults the protocol handler, and a connection is made to the remote server or location. Connections are represented by a `URLConnection` object, subtypes of which manage different protocol-specific communications and offer additional metadata about the source. The `HttpURLConnection` class, for example, handles basic web requests and also adds some HTTP-specific capabilities, such as interpreting "404 Not Found" messages and other web server errors. We'll talk more about `HttpURLConnection` later in this chapter.

We can get a `URLConnection` from our URL directly with the `openConnection()` method. One of the things we can do with the `URLConnection` is ask for the object's content type before reading data. For example:

```
URLConnection connection = myURL.openConnection();
String mimeType = connection.getContentType();
InputStream in = connection.getInputStream();
```

Despite its name, a `URLConnection` object is initially created in a raw, unconnected state. In this example, the network connection was not actually initiated until we called the `getContentType()` method. The `URLConnection` does not talk to the source until data is requested or its `connect()` method is explicitly invoked. Prior to connection, we can set up network parameters and provide protocol-specific details. For example, we can set timeouts on the initial connection to the server and on read attempts:

```
URLConnection connection = myURL.openConnection();
connection.setConnectTimeout(10000); // milliseconds
connection.setReadTimeout(10000); // milliseconds
InputStream in = connection.getInputStream();
```

As we'll see in "Using the POST Method" on page 441, we can get at the protocol-specific information by casting the `URLConnection` to its specific subtype.

Talking to Web Applications

Web browsers are the universal clients for web applications. They retrieve documents for display and serve as a user interface, primarily through the use of HTML, Java-Script, and linked documents such as images. In this section, we'll write client-side Java code that uses HTTP through the URL class. This combination allows us to work with web applications directly using GET and POST operations to retrieve and send data.

The primary task we discuss here is sending data to the server, specifically HTML form-encoded data. Browsers encode the name/value pairs of HTML form fields in a special format and send them to the server (typically) using one of two methods. The first method, using the HTTP GET command, encodes the user's input into the URL itself and requests the corresponding document. The server recognizes that the first part of the URL refers to a program and invokes it, passing along the information encoded in the other part of the URL as a parameter. The second method uses the HTTP POST command to ask the server to accept the encoded data and pass it to a web application as a stream.

Using the GET Method

You can get going with network resources quite quickly using the GET method of encoding data in a URL. Just create a URL pointing to a server program and use a simple convention to tack on the encoded name/value pairs that make up our data. For example, the following code snippet opens a URL to an old-school CGI program called *login.cgi* on the server *myhost* and passes it two name/value pairs. It then prints whatever text the CGI sends back:

```
URL url = new URL(
  // this string should be URL-encoded
  "http://myhost/cgi-bin/login.cgi?Name=Pat&Password=foobar");

BufferedReader bin = new BufferedReader(
  new InputStreamReader(url.openStream()));

String line;
while ((line = bin.readLine()) != null) {
  System.out.println(line);
}
```

To form the URL with parameters, we start with the base URL of *login.cgi*. We add a question mark (?), which marks the beginning of the parameter data, followed by the first "name=value" pair. We can add as many pairs as we want, separated by ampersand (&) characters. The rest of our code simply opens the stream and reads back the response from the server. Remember that creating a URL doesn't actually open the connection. In this case, the URL connection was made implicitly when we called `openStream()`. Although we are assuming here that our server sends back text, it could send anything, including images, audio, or PDFs.

We have skipped a step here. This example works because our name/value pairs happen to be simple text. If any "nonprintable" or special characters (including ? or &) are in the pairs, they must be encoded first. The `java.net.URLEncoder` class provides a utility for encoding the data. We'll show how to use it in the next example in "Using the POST Method" on page 441.

Although this small example sends a password field, you should never send sensitive data using this simplistic approach. The data in this example is sent in clear text across the network (it is not encrypted). Even using HTTPS (HTTP Secure) won't obscure the URL. And in this case, the password field would appear anywhere the URL is printed as well, including server logs, browser history, and bookmarks.

Using the POST Method

For larger amounts of input data or for sensitive content, you'll likely use the POST option. Here's a small application that acts like an HTML form. It gathers data from two text fields—`name` and `password`—and posts the data to the Postman Echo service[1] URL using the HTTP POST method. This Swing-based client application works just like a web browser and connects with a web application.

Here's the key networking method that performs the request and handles the response:

```
//file: ch13/examples/Post.java

protected void postData() {
    StringBuilder sb = new StringBuilder();
    String pw = new String(passwordField.getPassword());
    try {
        sb.append(URLEncoder.encode("Name", "UTF-8") + "=");
        sb.append(URLEncoder.encode(nameField.getText(), "UTF-8"));
        sb.append("&" + URLEncoder.encode("Password", "UTF-8") + "=");
        sb.append(URLEncoder.encode(pw, "UTF-8"));
    } catch (UnsupportedEncodingException uee) {
        System.out.println(uee);
    }
    String formData = sb.toString();

    try {
        URL url = new URL(postURL);
        HttpURLConnection urlcon =
```

---

1 Postman is a fantastic tool for web developers. You can learn more at the Postman site (*https://oreil.ly/3LKc6*). The testing service they host at postman-echo.com (*https://oreil.ly/hzZpS*) accepts both GET and POST requests, and echoes back the request and any form or URL parameters.

```
          (HttpURLConnection) url.openConnection();
      urlcon.setRequestMethod("POST");
      urlcon.setRequestProperty("Content-type",
          "application/x-www-form-urlencoded");
      urlcon.setDoOutput(true);
      urlcon.setDoInput(true);
      PrintWriter pout = new PrintWriter(new OutputStreamWriter(
          urlcon.getOutputStream(), "8859_1"), true);
      pout.print(formData);
      pout.flush();

      // Did the post succeed?
      if (urlcon.getResponseCode() == HttpURLConnection.HTTP_OK)
        System.out.println("Posted ok!");
      else {
        System.out.println("Bad post...");
        return;
      }

      // Hooray! Go ahead and read the results
      InputStream is = urlcon.getInputStream();
      InputStreamReader isr = new InputStreamReader(is);
      BufferedReader br = new BufferedReader(isr);
      String line;
      while ((line = br.readLine()) != null) {
        System.out.println(line);
      }
      br.close();

    } catch (MalformedURLException e) {
      System.out.println(e);        // bad postURL
    } catch (IOException e2) {
      System.out.println(e2);       // I/O error
    }
  }
}
```

The beginning of the application creates the form using Swing elements, like we did in Chapter 12. All the magic happens in the protected postData() method. First, we create a StringBuilder and load it with name/value pairs, separated by ampersands. (We don't need the initial question mark when we're using the POST method because we're not appending to the URL.) Each pair is first encoded using the static URLEncoder.encode() method. We run the name fields through the encoder as well, even though they contain no special characters in this example. This extra step is a best practice and simply a good habit. The field names may not always be so plain.

Next, we set up the connection to the server. In our previous example, we weren't required to do anything special to send the data because the request was made by the simple act of opening the URL on the server. Here, we have to carry some of the weight of talking to the remote web server. Fortunately, the HttpURLConnection object does most of the work for us; we just have to tell it what type of data we are sending and how we want to send it. We get a URLConnection object via the openConnection() method. We know that we are using the HTTP protocol, so we should be able to cast it to an HttpURLConnection type, which has the support we need. Because HTTP is one of the guaranteed protocols, we can safely make this assumption. (Speaking of safety, we use HTTP here only for demonstration purposes. So much data these days is considered sensitive. Industry guidelines have settled on defaulting to HTTPS; more on that soon in "SSL and Secure Web Communications" on page 444.)

We use setRequestMethod() to tell the connection we want to do a POST operation. We also use setRequestProperty() to set the Content-Type field of our HTTP request to the appropriate type—in this case, the proper media type[2] for encoded form data. (This is necessary to tell the server what kind of data we're sending, "application/x-www-form-urlencoded" in our case.)

For the final configuration step, we use the setDoOutput() and setDoInput() methods to tell the connection that we want to send *and* receive stream data. The URL connection infers from this combination that we are going to do a POST operation and expects a response.

To send data, we get an output stream from the connection with getOutputStream() and create a PrintWriter so that we can easily write our encoded form content. After we post the data, our application calls getResponseCode() to see whether the HTTP response code from the server indicates that the POST was successful. Other response codes (defined as constants in HttpURLConnection) indicate various failures.

Although form-encoded data (as indicated by the media type we specified for the Content-Type field) is common, other types of communications are possible. We could use the input and output streams to exchange arbitrary data types with the server program. The POST operation could send any kind of data; the server application simply has to know how to handle it. One final note: if you are writing an application that needs to decode form data, you can use the java.net.URLDecoder to undo the operation of the URLEncoder. Be sure to specify UTF-8 when calling decode().

The HttpURLConnection

Other information from the request is available from the HttpURLConnection as well. We could use getContentType() and getContentEncoding() to determine the MIME type and encoding of the response. We could also interrogate the HTTP

---

2 You may have heard the phrase "MIME type" before. MIME has its roots in email, and the term "media" is meant to be more generic.

response headers by using `getHeaderField()`. (HTTP response headers are metadata name/value pairs carried with the response.) Convenience methods can fetch integer- and date-formatted header fields, `getHeaderFieldInt()` and `getHeaderFieldDate()`, which return an `int` and a `long` type, respectively. The content length and last modification date are provided through `getContentLength()` and `getLastModified()`.

SSL and Secure Web Communications

Some of the previous examples sent sensitive data to the server. Standard HTTP doesn't provide encryption to hide our data. Fortunately, adding security for `GET` and `POST` operations like this is easy (trivial, in fact, for the client-side developer). Where available, you simply need to use a secure form of the HTTP protocol—HTTPS. Consider the testing URL from the `Post` example:

```
https://postman-echo.com/post
```

HTTPS is a version of the standard HTTP protocol run over Secure Sockets Layer (SSL), which uses public-key encryption techniques to encrypt the browser-to-server communications. Most web browsers and servers currently come with built-in support for HTTPS (or raw SSL sockets). Therefore, if your web server supports HTTPS and has it configured, you can use a browser to send and receive secure data simply by specifying the `https` protocol in your URLs. There is much more to learn about SSL and related aspects of security, such as authenticating to whom you are actually talking, but as far as basic data encryption goes, this is all you have to do. It is not something your code has to deal with directly. Java ships with both SSL and HTTPS support.

Network Programming

The web dominates developer discussions of networking, but there is more out there than just HTML pages! As Java's networking APIs have matured, Java has also become the language of choice for implementing traditional client/server applications and services. In this section, we look at the `java.net` package, which contains the fundamental classes for communications and working with networked resources.

The classes of `java.net` fall into two general categories: the Sockets API, for working with low-level network protocols, and higher-level, web-oriented APIs that work with URLs, as we saw in the previous section. Figure 13-2 shows most of the `java.net` package hierarchy.

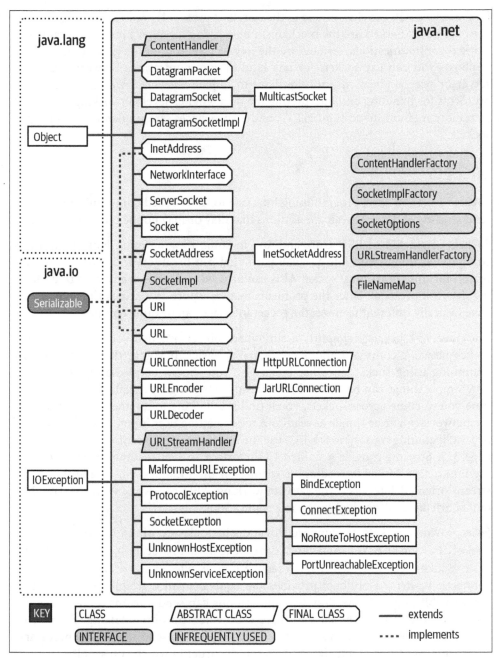

Figure 13-2. Main classes and interfaces of the `java.net` package

Java's Sockets API provides access to the standard protocols used for communications between hosts. *Sockets* are the mechanism underlying all other kinds of portable networked communications. Sockets are the lowest-level tool in the general networking toolbox—you can use sockets for any kind of communications between client and server or peer applications, but you have to implement your own application-level protocols for handling and interpreting the data. Higher-level networking tools, such as remote method invocation, HTTP, and web services, are implemented on top of sockets.

Sockets

Sockets are a low-level programming interface for networked communications. They send streams of data between applications that may or may not be on the same host.

Sockets originated in BSD Unix and are, in some programming languages, messy, complicated things with lots of small parts that can break off and cause havoc. The reason for this is that most socket APIs can be used with almost any kind of underlying network protocol. Since the protocols that transport data across the network can have radically different features, the socket interface can be quite complex.[3]

The `java.net` package supports a simplified, object-oriented socket interface that makes network communications considerably easier. If you've done network programming using sockets in other languages, you should be pleasantly surprised at how simple things can be when objects encapsulate the gory details. If this is the first time you've come across sockets, you'll find that talking to another application over the network can be as simple as reading a file or getting user input. Most forms of I/O in Java, including most network I/O, use the stream classes described in "Streams" on page 313. Streams provide a unified I/O interface so that reading or writing across the internet is similar to reading or writing on the local system. In addition to the stream-oriented interfaces, the Java networking APIs can work with the Java NIO buffer-oriented API for highly scalable applications.

Java provides sockets to support three distinct classes of underlying protocols: `Socket`, `DatagramSocket`, and `MulticastSocket`. In this section, we look at Java's basic `Socket` class, which uses a *connection-oriented* and *reliable* protocol. A connection-oriented protocol provides the equivalent of a telephone conversation. After establishing a connection, two applications can send streams of data back and forth, and the connection stays in place even when no one is talking. Because the protocol is reliable, it also ensures that no data is lost (resending data, as necessary), and that whatever you send always arrives in the order in which you sent it.

---

3 For a detailed discussion of these low-level sockets, see *Unix Network Programming* by W. Richard Stevens et al. (Prentice-Hall).

We'll have to leave the other two classes, which use a *connectionless, unreliable* protocol, for you to explore on your own. (Again, see *Java Network Programming* (*https://
oreil.ly/RzACA*) by Elliotte Rusty-Harold for a detailed discussion.) A connectionless
protocol is like the postal service. Applications can send short messages to each
other, but no end-to-end connection is set up in advance, and no attempt is made
to keep the messages in order. It's not even guaranteed that the messages will arrive
at all. A MulticastSocket is a variation of a DatagramSocket that performs *multicast-
ing*—simultaneously sending data to multiple recipients. Think of the postal service
delivering flyers for the local grocery market to "Resident" addresses throughout a
large neighborhood. Working with multicast sockets is very much like working with
datagram sockets; there are simply more recipients.

In theory, just about any protocol can be used underneath the socket layer. In practice, there's only one important protocol family used on the internet, and only one
protocol family that Java supports: the Internet Protocol (IP). The Socket class speaks
TCP, Transmission Control Protocol, over IP (often lumped together as TCP/IP);
and the connectionless DatagramSocket class speaks *UDP*, User Datagram Protocol,
over IP.

Clients and Servers

When writing network applications, it's common to talk about clients and servers.
The distinction is increasingly vague, but the *client* usually initiates the conversation.
The *server* usually accepts incoming requests. There are many subtleties to these
roles,[4] but for simplicity we'll use this definition.

An important difference between a client and a server is that a client can create
a socket to initiate a conversation with a server application at any time, while a
server must be prepared in advance to listen for incoming conversation requests.
The java.net.Socket class represents one side of an individual socket connection on
both the client and server. In addition, the server uses the java.net.ServerSocket
class to listen for new connections from clients. In most cases, an application acting
as a server creates a ServerSocket object and waits, blocked in a call to its accept()
method, until a request arrives. When a client attempts to connect, the accept()
method creates a new Socket object that the server uses to communicate with the
client. The ServerSocket instance hands over details on the client to the new Socket,
as shown in Figure 13-3.

---

4 A peer-to-peer environment, for example, has machines that simultaneously perform both roles.

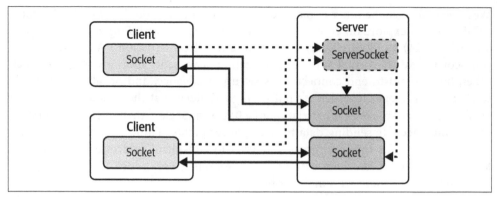

Figure 13-3. Clients and servers using Socket *and* ServerSocket

That socket continues the conversation with the client, allowing the ServerSocket to resume its listening task. In this way, a server can carry on conversations with multiple clients at once. There is still only a single ServerSocket, but the server has multiple Socket objects—one associated with each client.

Clients

At the socket level, a client needs two pieces of information to locate and connect to a server on the internet: a *hostname* (used to find the host computer's network address) and a *port number*. The port number is an identifier that differentiates between multiple network services or connections on the same host.

A server application listens on a prearranged port while waiting for connections. Clients make a request to that prearranged port number. If you think of the host computer as a hotel and the various services available as guests, the ports are like the guests' room numbers. To connect to a service, you must know the hotel name and the right room number.

A client application opens a connection to a server by constructing a Socket that specifies those two bits of information:

```
try {
  Socket sock = new Socket("wupost.wustl.edu", 25);
} catch (UnknownHostException e) {
  System.out.println("Can't find host.");
} catch (IOException e) {
  System.out.println("Error connecting to host.");
}
```

This client-side code fragment attempts to connect a Socket to port 25 (the SMTP mail service) of the host *wupost.wustl.edu*. The client must handle the possibility that the hostname can't be resolved (UnknownHostException) and that the server might

---

not accept a new connection (IOException). Java uses DNS, the standard *Domain Name Service* (DNS), to resolve the hostname to an *IP address* for us.

IP addresses (from the Internet Protocol) are the phone numbers of the internet, and DNS is the global phone book. Every machine connected to the internet has an IP address. If you don't know that address, you look it up with DNS. But if you do know a server's address, the Socket constructor can also accept a string containing a raw IP address:

```
Socket sock = new Socket("22.66.89.167", 25);
```

Regardless of which way you start, after sock connects, you can retrieve input and output streams with the getInputStream() and getOutputStream() methods. The following (rather arbitrary) code sends and receives some data with the streams:

```
try {
    Socket server = new Socket("foo.bar.com", 1234);
    InputStream in = server.getInputStream();
    OutputStream out = server.getOutputStream();

    // write a byte
    out.write(42);

    // write a newline or carriage return delimited string
    PrintWriter pout = new PrintWriter(out, true);
    pout.println("Hello!");

    // read a byte
    byte back = (byte)in.read();

    // read a newline or carriage return delimited string
    BufferedReader bin =
        new BufferedReader(new InputStreamReader(in) );
    String response = bin.readLine();

    server.close();
} catch (IOException e) {
    System.err.println(e);
}
```

In this exchange, the client first creates a Socket for communicating with the server. The Socket constructor specifies the server's hostname (*foo.bar.com*) and a prearranged port number (1234). Once the client connects, it writes a single byte to the server using the OutputStream's write() method. To send a string of text more easily, it then wraps a PrintWriter around the OutputStream. Next, it performs the complementary operations: reading a byte back from the server using InputStream's read() method and then creating a BufferedReader from which to get a full string of text. The client then terminates the connection with the close() method. All these operations have the potential to generate IOExceptions; our snippet handles these checked exceptions by wrapping the entire conversation in a try/catch block.

Servers

On the other side of the conversation, after a connection is established, a server application uses the same kind of Socket object for its communication with a client. However, to accept a connection from a client, it must first create a ServerSocket, bound to the correct port. Let's re-create the previous conversation from the server's point of view:

```java
// Meanwhile, on foo.bar.com...
try {
  ServerSocket listener = new ServerSocket(1234);

  while (!finished) {
    Socket client = listener.accept();  // wait for connection

    InputStream in = client.getInputStream();
    OutputStream out = client.getOutputStream();

    // read a byte
    byte someByte = (byte)in.read();

    // read a newline or carriage-return-delimited string
    BufferedReader bin =
      new BufferedReader(new InputStreamReader(in) );
    String someString = bin.readLine();

    // write a byte
    out.write(43);

    // say goodbye
    PrintWriter pout = new PrintWriter(out, true);
    pout.println("Goodbye!");

    client.close();
  }

  listener.close();
} catch (IOException e) {
  System.err.println(e);
}
```

First, our server creates a ServerSocket attached to port 1234. On most systems, there are rules about which ports an application can use. Port numbers are unsigned, 16-bit integers, which means they can range from 0 to 65,535. Port numbers below 1,024 are usually reserved for system processes and standard, "well-known" services, so we pick a port number outside of this reserved range.[5] We need to create the ServerSocket only once; thereafter, it can accept as many connections as arrive.

Next, we enter a loop, waiting for the accept() method of the ServerSocket to return an active Socket connection from a client. When a connection has been established, we perform the server side of our dialog, then close the connection and return to the top of the loop to wait for another connection. Finally, when the server application wants to stop listening for connections altogether, it calls the close() method of the ServerSocket.

This server is single threaded; it handles one connection at a time, finishing a complete conversation with one client before returning to the top of the loop and calling accept() to listen for another connection. A more realistic server would have a loop that accepts connections concurrently and passes them off to their own threads for processing. Even though we don't plan on creating a MMORPG,[6] we do show how to conduct a conversation using the thread-per-client approach in "A Distributed Game" on page 453. If you want to do a little independent reading, you can also look up the nonblocking, NIO equivalent ServerSocketChannel.

The DateAtHost Client

In the past, many networked computers ran a simple time service that dispensed their clock's local time on a well-known port. The time protocol is a precursor of NTP, the more general Network Time Protocol. We'll stick with the time protocol for its simplicity, but if you do want to synchronize the clocks of networked system, NTP is a better option.[7]

The next example, DateAtHost, includes a subclass of java.util.Date that fetches the time from a remote host instead of initializing itself from the local clock. (See Chapter 8 for a discussion of the Date class, which is still good for some uses but has been largely replaced by its newer, more flexible cousins, LocalDate and LocalTime.)

DateAtHost connects to the time service (port 37) and reads four bytes representing the time on the remote host. These four bytes have a peculiar specification that we decode to get the time. Here's the code:

---

5 For more on well-known services and their standard port numbers, see the official list (*https://oreil.ly/4WCON*) hosted by the Internet Assigned Numbers Authority.

6 Massively Multiplayer Online Role-Playing Game, if, like the authors, you're too old to recognize the acronym. Sigh.

7 Indeed, the publicly available site we use from NIST strongly encourages users to upgrade. See the introductory notes (*https://oreil.ly/hYBSO*) for the NIST Internet Time Servers for more information.

```
//file: ch13.examples.DateAtHost.java
package ch13.examples;

import java.net.Socket;
import java.io.*;

public class DateAtHost extends java.util.Date {
  static int timePort = 37;
  // seconds from start of 20th century to Jan 1, 1970 00:00 GMT
  static final long offset = 2208988800L;

  public DateAtHost(String host) throws IOException {
    this(host, timePort);
  }

  public DateAtHost(String host, int port) throws IOException {
    Socket server = new Socket(host, port);
    DataInputStream din =
      new DataInputStream(server.getInputStream());
    int time = din.readInt();
    server.close();

    setTime((((1L << 32) + time) - offset) * 1000);
  }
}
```

That's all there is to it. It's not very long, even with a few frills. We have supplied two possible constructors for DateAtHost. Normally we'd expect to use the first, which simply takes the name of the remote host as an argument. The second constructor specifies the hostname and the port number of the remote time service. (If the time service were running on a nonstandard port, we would use the second constructor to specify the alternate port number.) This second constructor does the work of making the connection and setting the time. The first constructor simply invokes the second (using the this() construct) with the default port as an argument. Supplying simplified constructors that invoke their siblings with default arguments is a common and useful pattern in Java; that is the main reason we've shown it here.

The second constructor opens a socket to the specified port on the remote host. It creates a DataInputStream to wrap the input stream and then reads a four-byte integer using the readInt() method. It's no coincidence that the bytes are in the right order. Java's DataInputStream and DataOutputStream classes work with the bytes of integer types in *network byte order* (most significant to least significant). The time protocol (and other standard network protocols that deal with binary data) also uses the network byte order, so we don't need to call any conversion routines. Explicit data conversions would probably be necessary if we were using a nonstandard protocol, especially when talking to a non-Java client or server. In that case, we'd have to read byte by byte and do some rearranging to get our four-byte value. After reading the data, we're finished with the socket, so we close it, terminating the connection to the server. Finally, the constructor initializes the rest of the object by calling `Date`'s `setTime()` method with the calculated time value.

The four bytes of the time value are interpreted as an integer representing the number of seconds since the beginning of the 20th century. `DateAtHost` converts this to Java's notion of absolute time—the count of milliseconds since January 1, 1970 (an arbitrary date standardized by C and Unix). The conversion first creates a `long` value, which is the unsigned equivalent of the integer `time`. It subtracts an offset to make the time relative to the epoch (January 1, 1970) rather than the century, and multiplies by 1,000 to convert to milliseconds. The converted time is used to initialize the object.

The `DateAtHost` class can work with a time retrieved from a remote host almost as easily as `Date` is used with the time on the local host. The only additional overhead is dealing with the possible `IOException` that the `DateAtHost` constructor can throw:

```
try {
  Date d = new DateAtHost("time.nist.gov");
  System.out.println("The time over there is: " + d);
}
catch (IOException e) {
  System.err.println("Failed to get the time: " + e);
}
```

This example fetches the time at the host *time.nist.gov* and prints its value.

A Distributed Game

We can use our newfound networking skills to extend our apple tossing game and go two-player. We'll have to keep this foray simple, but you might be surprised by how quickly we can get a proof of concept off the ground. While there are several mechanisms two players could use to get connected for a shared experience, our example uses the basic client/server model we've been discussing in this chapter. One user will start the server, and the second user will be able to contact that server as the client. Once both players are connected, they'll race to see who can clear the trees and hedges the fastest!

Setting up the UI

Let's start by adding a menu to our game. Recall from "Menus" on page 428 that menus live in a menu bar and work with `ActionEvent` objects, much like buttons. We need one option for starting a server and another for joining a game at a server someone has already started. The core code for these menu items is straightforward; we can use another helper method in the `AppleToss` class:

```
private void setupNetworkMenu() {
    JMenu netMenu = new JMenu("Multiplayer");
    multiplayerHelper = new Multiplayer();
```

```
                    JMenuItem startItem = new JMenuItem("Start Server");
                    startItem.addActionListener(
                        e -> multiplayerHelper.startServer());
                    netMenu.add(startItem);

                    JMenuItem joinItem = new JMenuItem("Join Game...");
                    joinItem.addActionListener(e -> {
                      String otherServer = JOptionPane.showInputDialog(
                          AppleToss.this, "Enter server name or address:");
                      multiplayerHelper.joinGame(otherServer);
                    });
                    netMenu.add(joinItem);

                    JMenuItem quitItem = new JMenuItem("Disconnect");
                    quitItem.addActionListener(
                        e -> multiplayerHelper.disconnect());
                    netMenu.add(quitItem);

                // build a JMenuBar for the application
                JMenuBar mainBar = new JMenuBar();
                mainBar.add(netMenu);
                setJMenuBar(mainBar);
              }
```

The use of lambdas for each menu's `ActionListener` should look familiar. We also use the `JOptionPane` discussed in "Modals and Pop-Ups" on page 430 to ask the second player for the name or IP address of the server where the first player is waiting. The networking logic is handled in a separate class.

We'll look at the `Multiplayer` class in more detail in the coming sections, but you can see the methods we'll be implementing. The code for this version of the game (in the *ch13/examples/game* folder) contains the `setupNetworkMenu()` method, but the lambda listeners just pop up an info dialog to indicate which menu item was selected. You get to build the `Multiplayer` class and call the actual multiplayer methods in the exercises at the end of the chapter. But do feel free to check out the completed game—including the networking parts—in the *ch13/solutions/game* folder.

The game server

As we did in "Servers" on page 450, we need to pick a port and set up a socket that is listening for an incoming connection. We'll use port 8677—"TOSS" on a phone number pad. We can create a `Server` inner class in our `Multiplayer` class to drive a thread ready for network communications. The `reader` and `writer` variables will be used to send and receive the actual game data. More on that in "The game protocol" on page 458:

```
class Server implements Runnable {
  ServerSocket listener;
```

```
public void run() {
  Socket socket = null;
  try {
    listener = new ServerSocket(gamePort);
    while (keepListening) {
      socket = listener.accept();  // wait for connection

      InputStream in = socket.getInputStream();
      BufferedReader reader =
          new BufferedReader(new InputStreamReader(in));
      OutputStream out = socket.getOutputStream();
      PrintWriter writer = new PrintWriter(out, true);

      // ... game protocol logic starts here
    }
  } catch (IOException ioe) {
    System.err.println(ioe);
  }
}
}
```

We set up our `ServerSocket` and then wait for a new client inside a loop. While we plan to play only one opponent at a time, this allows us to accept subsequent clients without going through all the network setup again.

To actually start the server listening the first time, we just need a new thread that uses our `Server` class:

```
// from Multiplayer
Server server;

// ...

public void startServer() {
  keepListening = true;
  // ... other game state can go here
  server = new Server();
  serverThread = new Thread(server);
  serverThread.start();
}
```

We keep a reference to the instance of `Server` in our `Multiplayer` class so that we have ready access to shut down the connections if the user selects the "disconnect" option from the menu, like so:

```
// from Multiplayer
  public void disconnect() {
    disconnecting = true;
    keepListening = false;
    // Are we in the middle of a game and regularly checking these flags?
    // If not, just close the server socket to interrupt the blocking
    // accept() method.
```

```
if (server != null && keepPlaying == false) {
  server.stopListening();
}

// ... clean up other game state here
}
```

We mainly use the keepPlaying flag once we're inside our game loop, but it comes in handy above, too. If we have a valid server reference but we're not currently playing a game (keepPlaying is false), we know to shut down the listener socket.

The stopListening() method in the Server inner class is straightforward:

```
public void stopListening() {
  if (listener != null && !listener.isClosed()) {
    try {
      listener.close();
    } catch (IOException ioe) {
      System.err.println("Error disconnecting listener: " +
          ioe.getMessage());
    }
  }
}
```

We do a quick check of our server and try to close listener only if it exists and is still open.

The game client

The setup and teardown of the client side is similar—without the listening Server Socket, of course. We'll mirror the Server inner class with a Client inner class and build a smart run() method to implement our client logic:

```
class Client implements Runnable {
  String gameHost;
  boolean startNewGame;

  public Client(String host) {
    gameHost = host;
    keepPlaying = false;
    startNewGame = false;
  }

  public void run() {
    try (Socket socket = new Socket(gameHost, gamePort)) {

      InputStream in = socket.getInputStream();
      BufferedReader reader =
          new BufferedReader(new InputStreamReader(in) );
      OutputStream out = socket.getOutputStream();
      PrintWriter writer = new PrintWriter(out, true);
```

```
        // ... game protocol logic starts here
      } catch (IOException ioe) {
        System.err.println(ioe);
      }
    }
  }
```

We pass the name of the server to the `Client` constructor and rely on the common `gamePort` variable used by `Server` to set up the socket. We use the "try with resource" technique discussed in "try with Resources" on page 202 to create our socket and make sure it gets cleaned up when we're done. Inside that resource `try` block, we create our `reader` and `writer` instances for the client's half of the conversation, as shown in Figure 13-4.

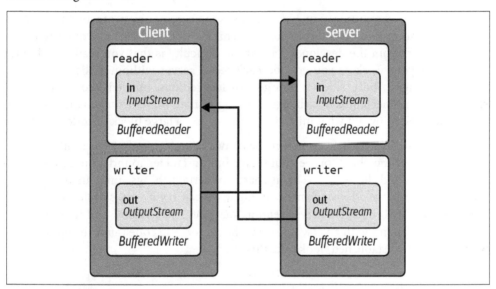

Figure 13-4. Game client and server connections

To get this going, we'll add another helper method to our `Multiplayer` helper class:

```
// from Multiplayer

  public void joinGame(String otherServer) {
    clientThread = new Thread(new Client(otherServer));
    clientThread.start();
  }
```

We don't need a separate `disconnect()` method—we can use the same state variables used by the server. For the client, the `server` reference will be `null`, so we won't attempt to shut down a nonexistent listener.

The game protocol

You likely noticed we left out the bulk of the run() method for both the Server and Client classes. After we build and connect our data streams, the remaining work is all about collaboratively sending and receiving information about the state of our game. This structured communication is the game's *protocol*. Every network service has a protocol. Think of the "P" in HTTP. Even our DateAtHost example uses a (very simple) protocol so that clients and servers know who is expected to talk and who must listen at any given moment. If both sides try to talk at the same time, information will likely be lost. If both sides end up waiting for the other side to say something (for instance, both the server and the client are blocking on a reader.readLine() call), then the connection will appear to hang.

Managing those communication expectations is the core of any protocol, but what to say and how to respond are also important. This portion of a protocol often requires the most effort from the developer. Part of the difficulty is that you really need both sides to test your work as you go. You can't test a server without a client, and vice versa. Building up both sides as you go can feel tedious, but it is worth the extra effort. As with other kinds of debugging, fixing a small incremental change is much simpler than figuring out what might be wrong within a large block of code.

In our game, we'll have the server steer the conversation. This choice is arbitrary—we could have used the client, or we could have built a fancier foundation and allowed both the client and the server to be in charge of certain things simultaneously. With the "server in charge" decision made, though, we can try a very simple first step in our protocol. We'll have the server send a "NEW_GAME" command and then wait for the client to respond with an "OK" answer. The server-side code (after the connection with the client is established) looks like this:

```
// Create a new game with the client
writer.println("NEW_GAME");

// If the client agrees, send over the location of the trees
String response = reader.readLine();
if (response != null && response.equals("OK")) {
  System.out.println("Starting a new game!")
  // ... write game data here
} else {
  System.err.println("Unexpected start response: " + response);
  System.err.println("Skipping game and waiting again.");
  keepPlaying = false;
}
```

If we get the expected "OK" response, we can proceed with setting up a new game and sharing the tree and hedge locations with our opponent—more on that in a minute. (If we don't get an "OK", we show an error and reset to wait for some other attempt.) The corresponding client-side code for this first step flows similarly:

```
// We expect to see the NEW_GAME command first
String response = reader.readLine();

// If we don't see that command, disconnect and return
if (response == null || !response.equals("NEW_GAME")) {
  System.err.println("Unexpected initial command: " + response);
  System.err.println("Disconnecting");
  writer.println("DISCONNECT");
  return;
}
// Yay! We're going to play a game. Send an acknowledgement
writer.println("OK");
```

If you want to try things as they stand, you can start your server from one system and then join that game from a second system. (You can also just launch a second copy of the game from a separate terminal window. In that case, the name of the "other host" would be the networking keyword localhost.) Almost immediately after joining from the second game instance, you should see the "Starting a new game!" confirmation printed in the terminal of the first game. Congratulations! You're on your way to designing a game protocol. Let's keep going.

We need to even the playing field—quite literally. The server will tell its game to build a new field, and then it can ship the coordinates of all the new obstacles to the client. The client, in turn, can accept all the incoming trees and hedges, and place them on a clean field. Once the server has sent all of the trees, it can send a "START" command and play can begin. We'll stick to using strings to communicate our messages. Here's one way we can pass our tree details to the client:

```
gameField.setupNewGame();
for (Tree tree : gameField.trees) {
  writer.println("TREE " + tree.getPositionX() + " " +
      tree.getPositionY());
}
// do the same for hedges or any other shared elements ...

// Attempt to start the game, but make sure the client is ready
writer.println("START");
response = reader.readLine();
keepPlaying = response.equals("OK");
```

On the client side, we can call readLine() in a loop for "TREE" lines until we see the "START" line, like so (with a little error handling thrown in):

```
// And now gather the trees and set up our field
gameField.trees.clear();
response = reader.readLine();
while (response.startsWith("TREE")) {
  String[] parts = response.split(" ");
  int x = Integer.parseInt(parts[1]);
  int y = Integer.parseInt(parts[2]);
  Tree tree = new Tree();
```

```
    tree.setPosition(x, y);
    gameField.trees.add(tree);
    response = reader.readLine();
}
// Do the same for hedges or other shared elements

// After all the obstacle lists have been sent, the server will issue
// a START command. Make sure we get that before playing
if (!response.equals("START")) {
    // Hmm, we should have ended the lists of obstacles with a START,
    // but didn't. Bail out.
    System.err.println("Unexpected start to the game: " + response);
    System.err.println("Disconnecting");
    writer.println("DISCONNECT");
    return;
} else {
    // Yay again! We're starting a game. Acknowledge this command
    writer.println("OK");
    keepPlaying = true;
    gameField.repaint();
}
```

At this point, both games should have the same obstacles, and players can begin clearing them. The server will enter a polling loop and send the current score twice a second. The client will reply with its current score. Note that there are certainly other options for how to share changes in the score. While polling is straightforward, more advanced games, or games that require more immediate feedback regarding remote players, will likely use more direct communication options. For now, we mainly want to concentrate on a good network back-and-forth, so polling keeps our code simpler.

The server should keep sending the current score until the local player has cleared everything or we see a game-ending response from the client. We'll need to parse the client's response to update the other player's score and watch for their request to end the game. We also have to be prepared for the client to simply disconnect. That loop looks something like this:

```
while (keepPlaying) {
    try {
        if (gameField.trees.size() > 0) {
            writer.print("SCORE ");
        } else {
            writer.print("END ");
            keepPlaying = false;
        }
        writer.println(gameField.getScore(1));
        response = reader.readLine();
        if (response == null) {
            keepPlaying = false;
            disconnecting = true;
        } else {
            String parts[] = response.split(" ");
```

```
        switch (parts[0]) {
          case "END":
            keepPlaying = false;
          case "SCORE":
            gameField.setScore(2, parts[1]);
            break;
          case "DISCONNECT":
            disconnecting = true;
            keepPlaying = false;
            break;
          default:
            System.err.println("Warning. Unexpected command: " +
                parts[0] + ". Ignoring.");
        }
      }
      Thread.sleep(500);
    } catch(InterruptedException e) {
      System.err.println("Interrupted while polling. Ignoring.");
    }
  }
```

The client will mirror these actions. Fortunately for the client, it is just reacting to
the commands coming from the server. We don't need a separate polling mechanism
here. We block waiting to read a line, parse it, and then build our response:

```
while (keepPlaying) {
  response = reader.readLine();
  String[] parts = response.split(" ");
  switch (parts[0]) {
    case "END":
      keepPlaying = false;
    case "SCORE":
      gameField.setScore(2, parts[1]);
      break;
    case "DISCONNECT":
      disconnecting = true;
      keepPlaying = false;
      break;
    default:
      System.err.println("Unexpected game command: " +
      response + ". Ignoring.");
  }
  if (disconnecting) {
    // We're disconnecting or they are. Acknowledge and quit.
    writer.println("DISCONNECT");
    return;
  } else {
    // If we're not disconnecting, reply with our current score
    if (gameField.trees.size() > 0) {
      writer.print("SCORE ");
    } else {
      keepPlaying = false;
```

```
      writer.print("END ");
    }
    writer.println(gameField.getScore(1));
  }
}
```

When a player has cleared all of their trees and hedges, they send (or respond with) an "END" command that includes their final score. At that point, we ask if the same two players want to play again. If so, we can continue using the same reader and writer instances for both the server and the client. If not, we'll let the client disconnect and the server will go back to listening for another player to join:

```
// If we're not disconnecting, ask about playing again
if (!disconnecting) {
  String message = gameField.getWinner() +
      " Would you like to ask them to play again?";
  int myPlayAgain = JOptionPane.showConfirmDialog(gameField,
      message, "Play Again?", JOptionPane.YES_NO_OPTION);

  if (myPlayAgain == JOptionPane.YES_OPTION) {
    // If they haven't disconnected, ask to play again
    writer.println("PLAY_AGAIN");
    String playAgain = reader.readLine();
    if (playAgain != null) {
      switch (playAgain) {
        case "YES":
          startNewGame = true;
          break;
        case "DISCONNECT":
          keepPlaying = false;
          startNewGame = false;
          disconnecting = true;
          break;
        default:
          System.err.println("Warning. Unexpected response: "
              + playAgain + ". Not playing again.");
      }
    }
  }
}
```

And one last reciprocal bit of code for the client:

```
if (!disconnecting) {
  // Check to see if they want to play again
  response = reader.readLine();
  if (response != null && response.equals("PLAY_AGAIN")) {
    // Do we want to play again?
    String message = gameField.getWinner() +
        " Would you like to play again?";
    int myPlayAgain = JOptionPane.showConfirmDialog(gameField,
        message, "Play Again?", JOptionPane.YES_NO_OPTION);
```

```
        if (myPlayAgain == JOptionPane.YES_OPTION) {
          writer.println("YES");
          startNewGame = true;
        } else {
          // Not playing again so disconnect.
          disconnecting = true;
          writer.println("DISCONNECT");
        }
      }
    }
```

Table 13-1 summarizes our simple protocol.

Table 13-1. Apple tossing game protocol

Server command	Args (optional)	Client response	Args (optional)
NEW_GAME		OK	
TREE	x y		
START		OK	
SCORE	score	SCORE END DISCONNECT	score score
END	score	SCORE DISCONNECT	score
PLAY_AGAIN		YES DISCONNECT	
DISCONNECT			

Much More to Explore

We could spend much more time on our game. We could expand the protocol to allow multiple opponents. We could change the objective to clear the obstacles and destroy your opponent. We could make the protocol more bidirectional, allowing the client to initiate some of the updates. We could use alternate lower-level protocols supported by Java, such as UDP rather than TCP. Indeed, there are entire books devoted to games, network programming, and programming networked games!

But whew! You made it! Saying we covered a lot of ground is quite an understatement. We hope you have a solid understanding of Java's syntax and core classes. You can use that understanding as you go forward and learn other interesting details and advanced techniques. Pick an area that interests you and go a little deeper. If you're still curious about Java in general, try connecting parts of this book. For example, you could try using regular expressions to parse our apple toss game protocol. Or you could build a more sophisticated protocol altogether and pass small chunks of binary data over the network rather than simple strings. For practice writing more complex programs, you could rewrite some of the inner and anonymous classes in the game to be separate, standalone classes, or even replace them with lambda expressions.

If you want to explore other Java libraries and packages while sticking with some of the examples you have already worked on, you could dig into the Java2D API and make nicer looking apples and trees. You could try out some of the other collection objects, like TreeMap or Deque. You could research the popular JSON format (*https://oreil.ly/oEa0E*) and try rewriting the multiplayer communication code. Using JSON for the protocol will likely give you the opportunity to work with a library as well.

When you're ready to branch out further, you could see how Java works off the desktop by trying some Android development. Or look at large networked environments and the Jakarta Enterprise Edition from the Eclipse Foundation. Maybe big data is on your radar? The Apache Foundation has several projects, such as Hadoop or Spark. Java has its detractors, but it remains a vibrant, vital part of the professional developer world.

Now that we've laid out some avenues for future research, we are ready to wrap up the main part of our book. The Glossary contains a quick reference of many useful terms and topics we've covered. Appendix A has some details on getting the code examples imported into IntelliJ IDEA. Appendix B includes answers to all of the review questions as well as some hints and guidance on the code exercises.

We hope that you've enjoyed this sixth edition of *Learning Java*. This is really the eighth edition of the series that began over two decades ago with *Exploring Java*. It has been a long and amazing trip watching Java develop in that time, and we thank those of you who have come along with us over the years. As always, we welcome your feedback to help us keep making this book better in the future. Ready for another decade of Java? We are!

Review Questions

1. Which networking protocols does the URL class support by default?

2. Can you use Java to download binary data from an online source?

3. What are the high-level steps to send form data to a web server using Java? Which classes are involved?

4. What class do you use to listen for incoming network connections?

5. When creating your own server like you did for the game, are there any rules for picking a port number?

6. Can a server application written in Java support multiple, simultaneous clients?

7. How many simultaneous servers can a given client Socket instance connect to?

Code Exercises

1. Create your own, human-friendly `DateAtHost` client (`FDClient`, Friendly Date Client, in our solutions) and server (`FDServer`). Use the classes and formatters from "Dates and Times" on page 262 to produce a server that sends one line of nicely formatted text containing the current date and time. Your client should read that line after connecting and print it out. (Your client does not need to extend `Instant` or even store the response beyond printing it out.)

2. Our game protocol does not yet include support for the hedge obstacles. (Hedges are still in the game, but they aren't part of the network communications yet.) Review Table 13-1 and add support for a `HEDGE` entry similar to our `TREE` lines. It may be easier to update the client side first, although you will need to update both sides to have the hedges work like the trees for both players.

Advanced Exercises

1. Upgrade your `FDServer` class to handle multiple, simultaneous clients with threads or virtual threads. You can put your client handling code in a lambda, an (anonymous) inner class, or a separate helper class. You should be able to use the same `FDClient` class from the first exercise without recompiling. If you use virtual threads, remember that they may still be a preview feature in your version of Java. Use the appropriate flags when compiling and running. (Our solution for this exercise is in `FDServer2`.)

2. This exercise is more of a nudge to go explore the world of web services now that you have seen some examples of using Java to interact with online APIs. Search online for a service with a free developer account option (signing up may still be necessary), and write a Java client for that service. Many of the services available online require some type of authentication, such as an *API token* or *API key* (usually long strings that work like unique usernames). Sites like random.org (*https://oreil.ly/moEyN*) or openweathermap.org (*https://oreil.ly/8B4rl*) could be fun places to start. (We do provide a completed client, `NetworkInt`, for getting random integers from *random.org* in the solutions. You'll need to provide your own API key in the source for the client to work.)

Code Examples and IntelliJ IDEA

This appendix will help you get up and running with the code examples found throughout the book. Some of the steps here were mentioned in Chapter 2, but we want to go through them a little slower here with specific details on how to use the book examples inside the free Community Edition of IntelliJ IDEA from JetBrains. As noted in "Installing IntelliJ IDEA and Creating a Project" on page 33, you can get IntelliJ from the jetbrains.com (*https://oreil.ly/Lo9Xk*) site. And they have an excellent installation guide (*https://oreil.ly/Fh9fV*) if you need more help setting things up.

Once you have IDEA installed, you'll want to make sure you have a recent version of the JDK selected. (If you still need to install Java itself, "Installing the JDK" on page 28 has details for each of the major platforms.) The File → Project Structure dialog shown in Figure A-1 allows you to select from any JDKs you have installed. For the purposes of this book, you will need at least Java 19. You will also want to set the "Language level" option to the Preview version for your chosen JDK.

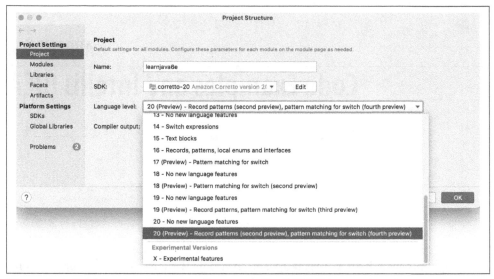

Figure A-1. Enabling Java's preview features in IntelliJ IDEA

In this example, we use Corretto 20 and select the 20 (Preview) language level. If you want more information on enabling Java's preview features in IntelliJ IDEA, check out their preview feature tutorial (*https://oreil.ly/jePVu*) online.

We also want to reiterate that IntelliJ IDEA is not the only Java-friendly integrated development environment out there. It's not even the only free one! Microsoft's VS Code (*https://oreil.ly/pv2JX*) can be quickly configured to support Java. And Eclipse (*https://oreil.ly/zxBL1*), maintained by IBM, remains available. Beginners looking for a tool designed to ease them into both Java programming and the world of Java IDEs can check out BlueJ (*https://oreil.ly/QcZ_I*), created by King's College London.

Grabbing the Main Code Examples

No matter which IDE or editor you use, you'll want to grab the code examples for the book from GitHub. While we often include complete source listings when discussing particular topics, many times we chose to leave out things like import or package statements, or the enclosing class structure for brevity and readability. The downloadable code examples aim to be complete to help reinforce the discussions in the book.

You can visit GitHub in a browser to meander through the individual examples without downloading anything. Just head to the *learnjava6e* repository (*https://git hub.com/l0y/learnjava6e*). (If that link doesn't work, just go to github.com and search for the term "learnjava6e.") It might be worth poking around GitHub generally as it has become the primary watering hole for open source developers and even corporate teams. You can look over the history of a repository as well as report bugs and discuss issues related to the code.

The site's name refers to the *git* tool, a source code control system or source code manager, that developers use to manage revisions among teams for code projects. But recall from Figure 2-14 that you don't have to use *git*. You can just grab the whole batch of examples by downloading the main branch of the project as a ZIP archive (*https://oreil.ly/HoZrA*). Once it's downloaded, just unzip the file into a folder where you can easily find the examples. You should see a folder structure similar to Figure A-2.

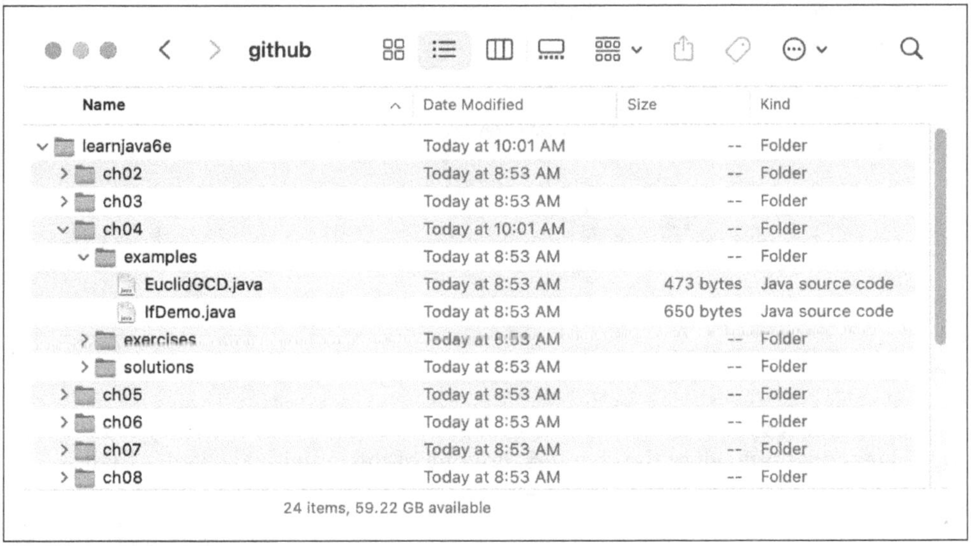

Figure A-2. Folder structure for the code examples

If you're curious about Git but your system does not already have the *git* command available, you can download it from the Git website (*https://oreil.ly/YfF4H*). GitHub has its own site to help you learn about *git* at try.github.io. Once *git* is installed, you can clone the project to a folder on your computer. You can work from that clone or keep it as a clean copy of the code examples. As a small bonus, if we publish any fixes or updates down the road, you can also easily sync your cloned folder.

Importing the Examples

Before we import anything into IntelliJ IDEA, you may want to rename the folder where you downloaded the code examples from GitHub. After cloning or unzipping, you likely have a folder named *learnjava6e-main*. That's a perfectly fine name, but if you want something friendlier (or shorter), go ahead and rename the folder now. We chose to rename the folder *learnjava6e* (without the *-main* suffix).

Start IntelliJ IDEA and select the Open option from the welcome screen shown in Figure A-3. If you have already used IntelliJ IDEA and don't see the welcome screen, you can also select File → Open from the menu bar.

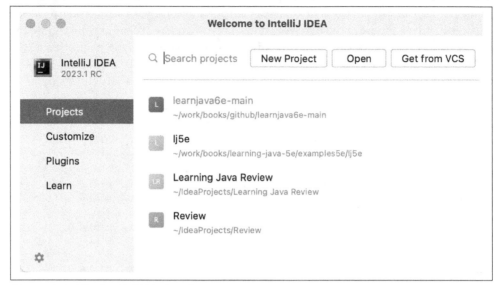

Figure A-3. The IntelliJ IDEA welcome screen

Navigate to your code example folder, as shown in Figure A-4. Be sure you select the top folder containing all of the chapters, not one of the individual chapter folders.

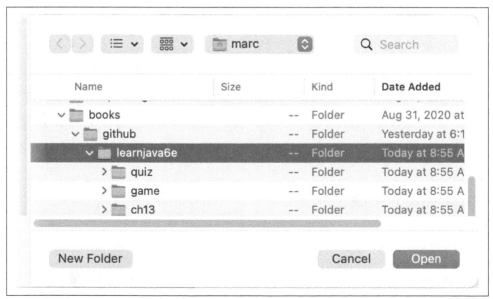

Figure A-4. Importing the code examples folder

After opening the examples folder, you might be asked to "trust" the folder containing the examples. IDEA asks this question to confirm that the potentially executable classes in the folder are safe to run.

You may also need to specify the version of Java you want to use for compiling and running the examples. Using the project hierarchy on the left, open the *ch02/examples* folder and click on the HelloJava class. The source file for our class should appear on the right. If you see a pale yellow banner similar to the one shown in Figure A-5, click on the Setup SDK linked text in the upper-right corner. (*SDK* stands for Software Development Kit, and in our case, it's synonymous with JDK.) Pick the JDK you want to use from the dialog that appears.

Figure A-5. Selecting a JDK

For this example, we chose the long-term support version (21), but you can choose anything version 19 or greater that you may have installed. (You can always change your selection or enable preview features using the File → Project Structure dialog shown in Figure A-1.)

To check that everything is working, right-click on the HelloJava class in the tree on the left and select the Run HelloJava.main() item from the context menu.

Figure A-6. Running an application directly in IDEA

Congratulations! IntelliJ IDEA is set up and ready for you to start exploring the amazing and gratifying world of Java programming.

Exercise Answers

This appendix contains answers (and usually a bit of context) for the review questions at the end of each chapter. The code exercise answers are included with the source download for the example programs, in the *exercises* folder. Appendix A has details on obtaining the source and setting it up inside IntelliJ IDEA.

Chapter 1: A Modern Language

1. Which company currently maintains Java?

   While Java was developed in the 1990s at Sun Microsystems, Oracle purchased Sun (and thus Java) in 2009. Oracle maintains ownership and is an active partner in the development and distribution of its own commercial JDK and the open source OpenJDK.

2. What is the name of the open source development kit for Java?

   The open source version of the JDK is known as the OpenJDK.

3. Name the two main components that play a role in Java's approach to securely running bytecode.

   Java has many features that relate to security, but the main components at play in every Java application are the class loader and the bytecode verifier.

Chapter 2: A First Application

1. What command should you use to compile a Java source file?

   If you are working in a terminal, the *javac* command compiles Java source files. While the details are often hidden when using an IDE like IntelliJ IDEA, the IDE is also using *javac* behind the scenes.

2. How does the JVM know where to start when you run a Java application?

   Any executable Java class must have a main() method defined. The JVM uses this method as the entry point.

3. Can you extend more than one class when creating a new class?

   No. Java does not support direct multiple inheritance from multiple, separate classes.

4. Can you implement more than one interface when creating a new class?

   Yes. Java allows you to implement as many interfaces as needed. Using interfaces provides programmers with most of the useful features of multiple inheritance without many of the pitfalls.

5. Which class represents the window in a graphical application?

   The JFrame class represents the main window used in Java graphical applications, although later chapters will introduce you to some lower-level classes that can also create specialized windows.

Code Exercises

We won't generally list the code solutions in this appendix, but we want to make it easy to check your solution for this first program. The simple text version of "Goodbye, Java!" should look something like this:

```
public class GoodbyeJava {
  public static void main(String[] args) {
    System.out.println("Goodbye, Java!");
  }
}
```

For the graphical version, your code should look similar to this:

```
import javax.swing.*;

public class GoodbyeJava {
  public static void main(String[] args) {
    JFrame frame = new JFrame("Chapter 2 Exercises");
    frame.setSize(300, 150);
    frame.setDefaultCloseOperation(JFrame.EXIT_ON_CLOSE);
    JLabel label = new JLabel("Goodbye, Java!", JLabel.CENTER);
    frame.add(label);
    frame.setVisible(true);
  }
}
```

Note that we added the extra EXIT_ON_CLOSE that we introduced in HelloJava2 so that the app will quit correctly when you close it. If you are using IDEA, you can run either class using the green Play button right inside the IDE. If you are using a terminal, you can change to the directory where *GoodbyeJava.java* is located and type the following commands:

```
% javac GoodbyeJava.java
% java GoodbyeJava
```

Chapter 3: Tools of the Trade

1. What statement gives you access to the Swing components in you application?

   The `import` statement loads information the compiler needs from the specified class or package. For Swing components, you typically import the entire package with `import javax.swing.*;`.

2. What environment variable determines where Java will look for class files when compiling or executing?

   The `CLASSPATH` environment variable holds a list of directories containing the other classes or JAR files available for both compilation and execution. If you are using an IDE, the `CLASSPATH` is still defined, but it is not something you typically edit yourself.

3. What options can you use to look at the contents of a JAR file without unpacking it?

   You can run the following command to show the contents of a JAR file without actually unpacking it into the current directory:

   ```
   % jar tvf MyApp.jar
   ```

   The `tvf` flags represent the table of contents (`t`), verbose (`v`), and file (`f` followed by a filename).

4. What entry is required in the *MANIFEST.MF* file to make a JAR file executable?

   You must include an entry for `Main-Class` that gives the fully qualified name of a class with a valid `main()` method to make a given JAR file executable.

5. What tool allows you to try out Java code interactively?

   You can run *jshell* from a terminal to try simple Java code interactively.

Code Exercises

You will find our solutions to the code exercises in the *ch03/solutions* folder. (Appendix A has details on downloading the examples.) Our solutions are not the only—or even best—way to solve these problems. We try to present clean, maintainable code that follows best practices, but there are always other ways to approach a coding problem. Hopefully you are able to write and run your own answers, but here are a few hints if you are stuck.

To make the executable *hello.jar* file, we'll do all of our work in the *ch03/exercises* folder in a terminal. (You can certainly do this type of work inside IDEA (*https:// oreil.ly/l0akz*) as well.) Go ahead and open a terminal and change into that folder.

Before we create the JAR file itself, we need to edit the *manifest.mf* file. Add the `Main-Class` entry. The final file should look something like this:

```
Manifest-Version: 1.0
Created-By: 11.0.16
Main-Class: ch03.exercises.HelloJar
```

Now you can create and test your JAR file with the following commands:

```
% jar cvmf manifest.mf hello.jar *.class
% java -jar hello.jar
```

Recall that the `m` element in the flags is necessary to include our manifest. It's also worth a reminder that the order of the `m` and `f` flags determines the order of the *manifest.mf* and *hello.jar* command-line arguments that follow. Do you remember how to look at the contents of your newly created JAR to verify the manifest is there?[1]

Chapter 4: The Java Language

1. What text encoding format does JAVA use by default by Java in compiled classes?

   By default, Java uses the 8-bit Unicode Transformation Format (UTF-8) encoding. The 8-bit (or one byte) encoding can accommodate single and multibyte characters.

2. What characters are used to enclose a multiline comment? Can those comments be nested?

   Java borrows from C and C++ for its comment syntax. Single-line comments begin with two slashes (`//`), while multiline comments are enclosed in `/*` and `*/` pairs. The multiline style can also be used to embed small comments in the middle of a line of code.

3. Which looping constructs does Java support?

   Java supports the `for` loop (both traditional C-style, and an enhanced form for iterating over collections), the `while` loop, and the `do/while` loop.

4. In a chain of `if/else if/else` tests, what happens if multiple conditions are true?

---

1 You can look at any JAR or ZIP file with `jar tvf <jarfile>`.

The block associated with the first test that evaluates to true will be executed. After that block completes, control resumes after the entire chain—regardless of how many other tests would have also returned true.

5. If you wanted to store the US stock market's total capitalization (roughly $31 trillion at the close of fiscal year 2022) as whole dollars, what primitive data type could you use?

   You could use the long integer type; it can store numbers up to 9 quintillion (positive or negative). While you could also use the double type, as the numbers get larger, their precision falls off. And since "whole dollars" implies no fractions, an integer type makes more sense.

6. What does the expression 18 - 7 * 2 evaluate to?

   This is an order-of-precedence question to make sure your high school algebra teacher finally gets some credit after all those "but when will I ever use this?" queries. The multiplication of 7 and 2 will occur first, then the subtraction. The final answer is 4. (You might have come up with 22, which results from performing the operations from left to right. If you actually want that result, you could enclose the 18 - 7 portion inside parentheses…just like this aside.)

7. How would you create an array holding the names of the days of the week?

   You can create and initialize an array using curly braces. For the days of the week, we need an array of Strings, like this:

   ```
   String[] dayNames = {
       "Sunday", "Monday", "Tuesday", "Wednesday",
       "Thursday", "Friday", "Saturday"
   };
   ```

   The spacing around the names in the list is optional. You can list everything on one line, list each name on its own line, or some combination as we did here.

Code Exercises

1. There are a number of ways to print the original a and b to the screen along with the calculated greatest common denominator. You could use a print() statement (*not* println()) before you begin calculating, and then use a println() with the answer to finish the output. Or you could store a copy of a and b in a second set of variables before beginning the calculation. After you find the answer, you can print the copied values along with the result.

2. To output the triangular data in a simple row, you can use the same nested loops that you use to fill the triangle:

```
        for (int i; i < triangle.length; i++)
          for (int j; j < triangle[i].length; j++)
            System.out.println(triangle[i][j]);
```

Advanced Exercises

1. To present your output in a visual triangle, use a `print()` statement inside the inner j loop. (Be sure to print a space after each number as well.) After the inner loop finishes, you can use an empty `println()` to terminate the line and be ready for the next row.

Chapter 5: Objects in Java

1. What is the primary organizing unit in Java?

   The main "unit" in Java is a class. Many other structures play important roles, of course, but you can't use any of those other things without at least one class.

2. What operator do you use to create an object (or instance) from a class?

   The `new` operator instantiates an object from a class and calls the appropriate constructor.

3. Java does not support classic multiple inheritance. What mechanisms does Java provide as alternatives?

   Java uses interfaces to accomplish most of the goals of multiple inheritance found in many other object-oriented languages.

4. How can you organize multiple related classes?

   You place related classes in a package. In your filesystem, a package appears as nested folders. In your code, packages use dot-separated names.

5. How do you include classes from other packages for use in your own code?

   You can `import` other individual classes or entire packages for your own use.

6. What do you call a class defined inside the scope of another class? What are some features that make such a class useful in some circumstances?

   A simple class defined within the curly braces of another class (not just in the same file) is called an inner class. Inner classes have access to all the variables and methods of the outer class—including private members. They can be used to help break up your code into manageable and reusable pieces while providing good control over who else can use them.

7. What do you call a method designed to be overridden that has a name, return type, and argument list, but no body?

Methods defined with only their signatures are known as abstract methods. Including an abstract method in a class makes the class abstract as well. The abstract class cannot be instantiated. You must create a subclass and then provide a real body for the abstract method to use it.

8. What is an overloaded method?

Java allows you to use the same method name with different types or numbers of arguments. If two methods share the same name, they are said to be overloaded. Overloading makes it possible to create a batch of methods that do the same logical work on disparate arguments. The classic example of an overloaded method in Java is `System.out.println()` which can take several different types of arguments and convert them all to strings for printing to a terminal.

9. If you want to make sure no other class can use a variable you have defined, what access modifier should you use?

The `private` access modifier for a variable (or a method, or indeed an entire inner class) restricts its use to the class where it is defined.

Code Exercises

1. For the first problem in our `Zoo`, you just need to add a `print()` statement to the empty `speak()` method in the inner `Gibbon` class. Hopefully the `Lion` example is straightforward to follow.

2. Adding another animal should also be straightforward; you can copy the entire `Lion` class. Rename the class and print an appropriate noise in the `speak()` method. You'll also need to replicate a few lines in the `listen()` method so that your animal's sound is added to the output.

3. To refactor the `listen()` method, we noted that the output for each animal is very similar, but the name of the animal obviously changes for each animal. If we move that name into the animals' respective classes, we can create a loop whose body prints out the details (name and noise) for one animal. Then we iterate over our array of animals. If you make another animal, you only have to add an instance of your new inner class to the array.

4. The `AppleToss` class for this exercise is part of the `exercises.ch05` package. (The *game* folder contains the completed game, with all the features we'll be building throughout the book. The classes in that folder are part of the `game` package. You're welcome to compile and run that version, but it has several features we haven't discussed yet.) To compile the game from a terminal, you can either change into the *ch05/exercises* directory and compile the Java classes there, or stay in the top-level folder where you unpacked the source code and give the path when compiling:

```
% javac ch05/exercises/AppleToss.java
```

To run the game, you need to be in that top-level folder. From there, you can run the `exercises.ch05.AppleToss` class with the *java* command.

Advanced Exercises

1. Hopefully, adding a `Hedge` feels straightforward. You can start with a copy of the `Tree` class. Rename the file *Hedge.java*. Edit the class to reflect our new `Hedge` obstacle and update its `paintComponent()` method. Inside the `Field` class, you'll need to add a member variable for the `Hedge`. Create a `setupHedge()` method similar to `setupTree()` and be sure to include your hedge in the `paintCompo nent()` method of `Field`.

   Last, but certainly not least, update the `setupFieldForOnePlayer()` method to call our `setupHedge()` method. Compile and run the game just like you did in the previous exercise. Your new hedge(s) should appear!

Chapter 6: Error Handling

1. What statement do you use to manage potential exceptions in your code?

   You can use a `try`/`catch` block around any statement or group of statements that might generate an exception.

2. Which exceptions does the compiler require you to handle or throw?

   In Java, the term *checked exception* refers to a category of exceptions that the compiler understands and requires the programmer to acknowledge. You can use a `try`/`catch` block within a method where checked exceptions might occur, or you can add the exception to the method's `throws` clause in its signature.

3. Where do you place any "clean-up" code that you always want to run after using some resources in a `try` block?

   The `finally` clause will run at the end of a `try` block regardless of what happens. If there are no problems, the code in the `finally` clause runs. If there is an exception and a `catch` block handles it, `finally` still runs. If an exception occurs that is not handled, the `finally` clause still runs before control is transferred back to the calling method.

4. Do assertions have much of a performance penalty when they are disabled?

   No. This is by design. Assertions are meant to be used more during development or debugging. When you turn them off, they are skipped. Even in a production application, though, you might leave assertions in your code. If a user reports a problem, assertions could be turned on temporarily to allow your user to collect any output and help you find the cause.

Code Exercises

1. To get the *Pause.java* file to compile, you need to add a `try/catch` block around the call to `Thread.sleep()`. For this simple exercise, you only need to encapsulate the `Thread.sleep()` line.

2. The assertions statements we need will have the following form:
   ```
   assert x > 0 : "X is too small";
   assert y > 0 : "Y is too small";
   ```

   The bigger question is: where should we place them? We only need to check the starting position of our message, so we don't want the assertions inside the `paintComponent()` method. A better place would be in the `HelloComponent0()` constructor, perhaps right after we store the supplied `message` argument.

   To test the assertions, you'll need to edit the source file to change the `x` or `y` values and recompile.

Advanced Exercises

1. Your `GCDException` class will probably look something like this:
   ```
   package ch06.exercises;

   public class GCDException extends Exception {
     private int badA;
     private int badB;

     GCDException(int a, int b) {
       super("No common factors for " + a + ", " + b);
       badA = a;
       badB = b;
     }

     public int getA() { return badA; }
     public int getB() { return badB; }
   }
   ```

   You can test the result of your GCD calculation with a simple `if` statement. If the result is 1, you can throw your new `GCDException` with our original `a` and `b` as arguments to its constructor, like this:
   ```
   if (a == 1) {
     throw new GCDException(a1, b1);
   ```

```
    }
    // ...
```

Chapter 7: Collections and Generics

1. If you want to store a contact list with names and phone numbers, which kind of collection would work best?

   A `Map` would do the trick. The keys could be simple strings containing the contact's name, and the values could be a simple (though wrapped) long number. Or you could create a `Person` class and a `PhoneNumber` class, and the map could use your custom classes.

2. What method do you use to get an iterator for the items in a `Set`?

   The imaginatively named `iterator()` method from the `Collection` interface will get your iterator.

3. How can you turn a `List` into an array?

   You can use the `toArray()` method to turn a `List` into either an array of type `Object` or an array of the list's parameterized type.

4. How can you turn an array into a `List`?

   The `Arrays` helper class includes the handy `asList()` method that accepts an array and returns a parameterized list of the same type.

5. What interface should you implement to sort a list using the `Collections.sort()` method?

   While there are many ways to sort collections, a list of `Comparable` objects (meaning objects whose class implements the `Comparable` interface) can use the standard `sort()` method provided by the `Collections` helper class.

Code Exercises

1. As we mentioned in this chapter, you can't directly sort a simple map in the same way you can sort a list or array. Even `Sets` are not typically sortable.[2] You can sort a list, though, so using the `keySet()` method to fill a list should give you what you need:

   ```
   List<Integer> ids = new ArrayList<>(employees.keySet());
   ids.sort();
   for (Integer id : ids) {
   ```

---

2 You could, however, use a `SortedSet` or a `TreeMap`, which both keep their entries sorted. For `TreeMap`, the keys are kept in order.

```
      System.out.println(id + ": " + employees.get(id));
    }
```

2. Hopefully, the expansion to support multiple hedges feels straightforward to you. We mostly just duplicate any code we already have for the trees. And using `Lists` allows us to use the enhanced `for` loop to quickly run through all of our hedges:

```
// File: ch07/exercises/Field.java
  List<Hedge> hedges = new ArrayList<>();
  // ...

  protected void paintComponent(Graphics g) {
    // ...
    for (Hedge h : hedges) {
      h.draw(g);
    }
    // ...
  }
```

Advanced Exercises

1. You can use the `values()` output to create and sort a list similar to the solution for Code Exercise 1. The interesting part of this exercise is implementing the `Comparable` interface with the `Employee` class. (Actually, in the *ch07/solutions* folder, the sortable employee class is `Employee2`. We wanted to leave the original `Employee` class as a valid solution to the first exercise.) Here's an example of doing string comparisons, using the employees' names:

```
public class Employee2 implements Comparable<Employee2> {
  // ...
  public int compareTo(Employee2 other) {
    // Let's be a little fancy and sort on a constructed name
    String myName = last + ", " + first;
    String otherName = other.last + ", " + other.first;
    return myName.compareToIgnoreCase(otherName);
  }
  // ...
}
```

Of course, you could perform other comparisons using the other `Employee` attributes. Try playing around with some other orderings and see if you get the results you expect. And if you want to dig even deeper, take a look at the `java.util.TreeMap` class as a way to store your employees in a sorted manner without needing the list-conversion detour.

Chapter 8: Text and Core Utilities

1. Which class contains the constant π? Do you need to import that class to use π?

The java.lang.Math class contains the constant PI. All of the classes in the java.lang package are imported by default; no explicit import is required to use them.

2. Which package contains newer, better replacements for the original java.util.Date class?

The java.time package contains a wide variety of quality classes for handling dates, times, timestamps (or "instants" consisting of both a date and a time), and time spans or durations.

3. Which class do you use to format a date for user-friendly output?

The DateFormat class in the java.text package has a marvelously flexible (if occasionally opaque) formatting engine for rendering both dates and times.

4. What symbol do you use in a regular expression to help match the words "yes" and "yup"?

You can use the alternation operator, | (vertical pipe), to create an expression such as yes|yup for use as a pattern.

5. How would you convert the string "42" into the integer 42?

The various numeric wrappers all have string conversion methods. For an integer like 42, the Integer.parseInt() method would work. The wrapper classes are all part of the java.lang package.

6. How would you compare two strings to see if they match, ignoring any capitalization, such as "yes" and "YES"?

The String class has two main comparison methods: equals() and equalsIgnoreCase(). The latter would ignore capitalization, as its name suggests.

7. Which operator allows for simple string concatenation?

Java does not generally support operator overloading, but the plus sign (+) performs addition when used with numeric base types, and concatenation when used with String objects. If you use + to "add" a string and a number, the result will be a string. (So 7 + "is lucky" would result in the string "7is lucky." Notice that concatenation does not insert any whitespace. If you are assembling a typical sentence, you must add your own spacing between the parts.)

Code Exercises

There are many ways to accomplish the goals of this exercise. Testing the number of arguments should be straightforward. Then you can use some of the String class features to figure out whether you have the random keyword or a pair of coordinates.

You can split() the coordinates, or craft a regular expression to separate the numeric values. When creating random coordinates, you can use Math.random(), similar to how we positioned the trees for our game in "Math in action" on page 260.

Chapter 9: Threads

1. What is a thread?

   A thread represents a "thread of execution" within a program. Threads have their own state and can run independently from other threads. Typically you use threads to handle long-running tasks that can be put in the background while more important tasks can continue to do their work. Java has both platform threads (tied one-to-one with native threads supplied by the operating system) and virtual threads (pure Java constructs that retain the semantics and benefits of native threads without the operating system overhead).

2. What keyword can you add to a method if you want threads to "take turns" when calling it? (Meaning no two threads should be executing the method at the same time to avoid corrupting shared data.)

   You can use the synchronized modifier on any method that reads or writes shared data. If two threads need to use the same method, the first thread sets a lock that blocks the second thread from calling the method. Once the first thread finishes, the lock is cleared and the second thread can proceed.

3. What flags allow you to compile a Java program that includes preview feature code?

   When compiling a Java class that relies on a preview feature, you must supply the --enable-preview and either the -source or --release flags to *javac*.

4. What flags allow you to run a Java program that includes preview feature code?

   When running a compile class that includes a preview feature, you only need to supply the --enable-preview flag.

5. How many platform threads can one native thread support?

   Just one. Creating a platform thread using the Thread class with a Runnable target or using something like the ExecutorService in the java.util.concurrent package requires the operating system to supply a thread as well.

6. How many virtual threads can one native thread support?

   A single native thread will support many virtual threads. Project Loom set out to separate the threads used in Java programs from the threads managed by the operating system. For certain scenarios, lightweight virtual threads perform much better when Java is responsible for their scheduling. There is no fixed ratio of virtual to native, but the key insight with virtual threads is that the number of virtual threads is not tied to the number of native threads.

7. Is the statement x = x + 1; an atomic action for the int variable x?

No. While it seems like such a small operation, there are several low-level steps involved. Any one of those low-level steps can be interrupted, and the value of x can be adversely affected. You could use an AtomicInteger or wrap the statement in a synchronized block if you need to guarantee a thread-safe increment.

8. What package includes thread-safe versions of popular collection classes like Queue and Map?

The java.util.concurrent package contains several collection classes that Java defines as "concurrent," such as ConcurrentLinkedQueue and ConcurrentHash Map. Concurrency implies a few other behaviors beyond pure thread-safe reads and writes, but thread safety is guaranteed.

Code Exercises

1. You'll do most of your work inside the startClock() method. (You will still have to import anything beyond the AWT and Swing packages that you use, of course.) You can create a separate class, an inner class or an anonymous inner class to handle the clock update loop. Recall that you can request a GUI element refresh by calling its repaint() method. Java supports a few mechanisms for "infinite" loops. You can use something like while (true) { … } or the cleverly named "forever" loop: for (;;) { … }. Don't forget to start your thread once everything is in place!

2. Hopefully, this exercise is fairly simple for you. As a testament to the overall compatibility of virtual threads with the existing codebase in Java, you should have to change only a few lines where the demo apple toss animation starts. In this iteration of the game, all of the setup and kickoff code happens in the Field class. Look for code like new Thread() or new Runnable(). You should be able to reuse the actual animation logic with no alterations.

Chapter 10: File Input and Output

1. How could you check to see if a given file already exists?

There are a number of ways to see if a file exists, but two of the simplest rely on helper methods from either the java.io or java.nio package. An instance of java.io.File can use the exists() method. The static java.nio.file.Files.exists() method can test a Path object to see if a represented file exists.

2. If you have to work with a legacy text file using an old encoding scheme, such as ISO 8859, how might you set up a reader to properly convert that content to UTF-8?

   You can supply an appropriate character set (`java.nio.charset.Charset`) to the constructor of `FileReader` to safely convert the file to Java strings.

3. Which package has the best classes for nonblocking file I/O?

   One of the primary features of the `java.nio` package and its subpackages is support for nonblocking I/O.

4. Which type of input stream might you use to parse a binary file, such as a JPEG-compressed image?

   From `java.io`, you could use the `DataInputStream` class. For NIO, channels and buffers (like `ByteBuffer`) naturally support binary data.

5. What are the three standard text streams built into the `System` class?

   The `System` class gives you access to two output streams, `System.out` and `System.err`, and one input stream, `System.in`. These streams are attached to the OS handles for `stdout`, `stderr`, and `stdin`, respectively.

6. Absolute paths begin at a root (/ or C:\, for example). Where do relative paths begin? More specifically, where are relative paths relative to?

   Relative paths are relative to the "working directory," which is typically where you started the program if you are using the command line to launch your application. In most IDEs, the working directory is something that can be configured.

7. How do you retrieve a NIO channel from an existing `FileInputStream`?

   If you already have an instance of `FileInputStream`, you can use its `getChannel()` method to return a `FileChannel` associated with the input stream.

Code Exercises

1. The first iteration of our `Count` needs only one of the utilities discussed in the chapter. You'll can use the `File` class with the path given as a command-line argument. From there, the `exists()` method will let you know if you can proceed or if you should print a friendly error message, and the `length()` method will give you the file's size, in bytes. (The solution for this example is `Count1.java` in the *ch10/solutions* folder.)

2. For the second iteration that shows the line and word count in the given file, you'll need to read and parse the contents of the file. One of the `Reader` classes would be great, but there are a variety of ways to read text files. However you open the file, you can count each line and then break that line up into words

with something like `String.split()` or a regular expression. (The solution to this exercise is `Count2.java`.)

3. There isn't any new functionality in this third version, but we hope you'll take this chance to try out some of the NIO classes and methods. Take a look at the methods of the `java.nio.file.Files` class. You'll be surprised how much this helper class helps! (The solution to this exercise is `Count3.java`.)

Advanced Exercises

1. For this final upgrade, you get to write to a file or channel. Depending on how you chose to read the contents in version 2 or 3, this may represent a fairly significant addition to our class. You'll need to check to make sure the second argument (if it was given!) is writable. Then use one of the classes that allows appending, such as `RandomAccessFile`, or include the `APPEND` option for a `File Channel`. (The solution to this exercise is `Count4.java`. We used the previous `Count3` with NIO, but you are welcome to start from `Count2` and use the standard I/O classes.)

Chapter 11: Functional Approaches in Java

1. Which package contains the majority of functional interfaces?

   While functional interfaces are scattered throughout the JDK, you will find the bulk of the "official" interfaces defined in the `java.util.function` package. We used qualifying quotes on "official" because any interface with a single abstract method (SAM) can be treated as a functional interface.

2. Do you need to use any special flags when compiling or running Java applications that use functional features like lambdas?

   No. The many FP features currently available in Java are full members of the JDK. There are no preview or feature flags required to compile or execute Java code that uses them.

3. How do you create lambda expressions with multiple statements in the body?

   The body of a lambda expression follows the same rules as the body of something like a `while` loop: single statements do not require enclosing curly braces, but multiple statements do. You can use a curly brace block on the right side of the lambda if you have multiple statements. If your lambda returns a value, you can use the standard `return` statement as well.

4. Can lambda expressions be void? Can they return values?

   Yes on both counts. Lambda expressions run the same gamut of options as methods. You can have lambdas that take no arguments and return no values.

You can have lambdas that consume arguments but produce no results. You can have lambda generators that don't have arguments but do return values. Finally, you can have lambdas that accept one or more arguments and return a value.

5. Can you reuse a stream after you have processed it?

No. Once you start processing a stream, that's it. Attempting to reuse a stream will result in an exception. You can often reuse the original source to create an entirely new but identical stream, if needed.

6. How might you take a stream of objects and convert it to a stream of integers?

You could use one of the mapToInt() variations from the Stream class: map ToInt(), flatMapToInt(), or mapMultiToInt(). The IntStream class, in turn, has a mapToObj() method to convert in the opposite direction.

7. If you have a stream that filters out empty lines from a file, what operation might you use to tell you how many lines had some content?

The easiest way to count the remaining lines would be to use the count() terminal operation. You could also create your own reducer, or use a collector and then query the length of the resulting list.

Code Exercises

1. Hopefully the use of a more interesting formula for our adjustment feels straight-forward. We don't need any alternative syntax or extra methods; we just put the Celsius conversion, C = (F − 32) * 5 / 9, into the body of our lambda, like so:

```
System.out.print("Converting to Celsius: ");
System.out.println(adjust(sample, s -> (s - 32) * 5 / 9));
```

Not very dramatic, but we want to point out that lambdas can open up some really clever possibilities that extend beyond your initial plans.

2. You have a number of choices available to accomplish this averaging task. You could write an averaging reducer. You could collect the salaries into a simpler container and then write your own averaging code. But if you look over the documentation on the different streams, you'll notice that the numeric streams already have the perfect operation: average(). It returns an OptionalDouble object. You'll still need to start the stream and then use something like map ToInt() to get your stream of numeric values.

Advanced Exercises

1. The groupingBy() collector needs a function that extracts a key from each element of the stream and returns a map of the keys paired with a list of all

the elements that have matching keys. For our `PaidEmployee` example, you will probably have something like this:

```
Map<String, List<PaidEmployee>> byRoles =
    employees.stream().collect(
    Collectors.groupingBy(PaidEmployee::getRole));
```

The type of the key in our map must match the type of object we extract in our `groupingBy()` operation. We used a method reference here, but any lambda that returns the role of the employee would also work.

We didn't want to complicate the previous solution, so we made copies of the report and employee classes named `Report2` and `PaidEmployee2`, respectively.

Chapter 12: Desktop Applications

1. Which component would you use to display some text to the user?

   While you could use a variety of text-based components, `JLabel` is the simplest way to show the user some (read-only) textual information.

2. Which component(s) would you use to allow the user to enter text?

   Depending on how much information you expect from the user, you could use either `JTextField` or `JTextArea`. (Other text components exist, but they serve more specialized purposes.)

3. What event does clicking a button generate?

   Clicking a button or any button-like component such as `JMenuItem` generates an `ActionEvent`.

4. Which listener should you attach to `JList` if you want to know when the user changes the selected item?

   You can implement the `ListSelectionListener` from the `javax.swing.event` package to receive list selection (and deselection) events from a `JList` object.

5. What is the default layout manager for `JPanel`?

   By default, `JPanel` uses the `FlowLayout` manager. One notable exception to this default is the content pane of `JFrame`. That pane is a `JPanel`, but the frame automatically changes the pane's manager to `BorderLayout`.

6. Which thread is responsible for processing events in Java?

   The event dispatch thread, sometimes called the event dispatch queue, manages delivery of events and updates to components on screen.

7. What method would you use to update a component like `JLabel` after a background task completes?

You could use `SwingUtilities.invokeAndWait()` if you want to wait for the label to be updated before processing any other events. You could use `Swing Utilities.invokeLater()` if it doesn't matter exactly when the label gets updated.

8. What container holds `JMenuItem` objects?

A `JMenu` object can hold `JMenuItem` objects as well as nested `JMenu` objects. The menus themselves are contained in a `JMenuBar`.

Code Exercises

1. You can tackle the calculator layout one of two ways: you can use nested panels or you can use the `GridBagLayout`. (Our solution in *ch12/solutions/Calculator.java* uses a nested panel for the buttons.) Start simple. Add the text field to the top of the frame. Then add one button to the center. Now decide how you want to handle adding the remaining buttons. If your buttons use the `Calculator` instance (using the keyword `this` we discussed in "Shadowing" on page 146) as their listener, you should see the label of any button you click printed to the terminal.

2. This exercise doesn't require much new graphical code. But you do need to work within the UI event thread to safely alter the obstacles shown on the field. You can start slowly by simply printing a message or using a `JOptionPane` to show an alert any time an apple touches a tree or a hedge. Once you're confident in your distance measuring, review how to remove an object from a list. After removing an obstacle, be sure to repaint the field.

Advanced Exercises

1. The logic for a calculator is relatively straightforward, but it certainly is not trivial. Start by getting the various digit buttons (1, 2, 3, and so on) hooked up to the display. You'll need to append digits to create full numbers. Clicking the 1 button followed by the 2 button should display a 12. When the user clicks on an operation button such as "−", store whatever number is currently displayed as well as the operation to use later. Let the user type in a second number. Clicking the "=" should store this second number and then perform the actual calculation. Put the result in the display and then let the user start over.

There are many (many!) subtleties in a full, professional calculator app. Don't worry if your early attempts impose restrictions like working only with single-digit numbers. The point of this exercise is to practice responding to events. Even just getting a digit to show in the display field after the user clicks a button is worth celebrating!

Chapter 13: Network Programming in Java

1. Which networking protocols does the URL class support by default?

   Java's URL class includes support for the HTTP, HTTPS, and FTP protocols. These three protocols cover a great deal of the resources available online, but you can create your own protocol handler if you deal with systems other than web or file servers.

2. Can you use Java to download binary data from an online source?

   Yes. Byte streams lie at the heart of all network data in Java. You can read the raw bytes, or you can chain some other higher-level stream. For example, InputStreamReader and BufferedReader work great for text. DataInputStream can handle binary data.

3. How do you send form data to a web server using Java? (No need for a fully functional application, we just want you to think about the high-level steps you take and the Java classes involved.)

   You can use the URL class to open a connection to a web server. Before making any requests, you can configure the connection for bidirectional communication. The HTTP POST command allows you to send data to the server in the body of your request.

4. What class do you use to listen for incoming network connections?

   You use the java.net.ServerSocket class to create a network listener.

5. When creating your own server like we did for our game, are there any rules for picking a port number?

   Yes. Port numbers must be between 0 and 65,535 with ports below 1,024 typically reserved for well-known services that often require special permissions to use.

6. Can a server application written in Java support multiple, simultaneous clients?

   Yes. While you can create only one ServerSocket on a given port, you can accept hundreds or even thousands of clients and process their requests in a thread.

7. How many simultaneous servers can a given client Socket instance talk to?

   One. A client socket communicates with one host on one port. A client application may allow multiple, distinct sockets for communicating with multiple servers at the same time, but each socket will still talk to a single server.

Code Exercises

1. Adding a feature to the protocol of our game requires updating both the server and client code. Fortunately we can reuse much of the TREE entry's logic on both

sides. Even more fortunately, all of our network communication code is in the Multiplayer class.

The client and the server are inner classes, creatively named Client and Server, respectively. For the server, add a loop in the run() method to send hedge data right after you have sent the tree data. For the client, add a HEDGE segment to the run() method that accepts the location of the hedge and adds it to the field.

Once the fields are set up for the two players, the in-game portion of the protocol only reports scores and disconnects. We don't have to modify any of this code. Each player will have the same hedge obstacles and the same opportunity to remove them with a tossed apple.

2. A human-readable date/time server should be fairly straightforward, but we want you to practice setting up your own sockets from scratch. You'll need to decide on a port number for the server. 3283 spells "DATE" on a phone keypad if you need a little inspiration. We recommend processing the client request immediately after accepting the connection. (The advanced exercises give you a chance to try the more sophisticated approach of using threads.)

For the client, the only real piece of configurable data is the name of the server. You're free to hardcode "localhost" if you plan to test your solution using two terminal windows on your local machine. Our solution takes an optional command-line argument, defaulting to "localhost" as well if you don't provide an argument.

Advanced Exercises

1. To handle clients using threads, you need to isolate the code responsible for communicating with the client. A helper class (inner, anonymous, or separate are all fine options) or a lambda will work. You still need to let the ServerSocket do its work and accept() a new connection, but you can hand off the accepted Socket object to your helper as soon as you get it.

It'll be hard to really test this class, as you would need many clients all requesting the current date at the same moment. At a minimum, though, your current FDClient class should work with no changes, and you should still receive the correct date.

2. Working with online APIs can be fun, but it also requires paying attention to details. You typically need to answer a few questions as you begin to create your client:

   • What is the base URL for the API?

   • Does the API use standard web form encoding or JSON? If not, is there a library with support for encoding and decoding?

- Are there limits on how many requests you can make or how much data you can download?

- Does the site have good documentation with common examples of sending and retrieving data?

As you practice, you'll develop your own sense of what information you need to start using new APIs. But you do need to practice. After you build your first client, look up another service. Write a client for that API and see if you can already spot common problems, or better, reusable code from your first client.

Glossary

abstract

The `abstract` keyword is used to declare abstract methods and classes. An abstract method has no implementation defined; it is declared with arguments and a return type as usual, but the body enclosed in curly braces is replaced with a semicolon. The implementation of an abstract method is provided by a subclass of the class in which it is defined. If an abstract method appears in a class, the class is also abstract. Attempting to instantiate an abstract class will fail at compile time.

annotations

Metadata added to Java source code using the @ tag syntax. Annotations can be used by the compiler or at runtime to augment classes, provide data or mappings, or flag additional services.

Ant

An older, XML-based build tool for Java applications. Ant builds can compile, package, and deploy Java source code as well as generate documentation and perform other activities through pluggable "targets."

Application Programming Interface (API)

An API consists of the methods and variables programmers use to work with a component or tool in their applications. The Java language APIs consist of the classes and methods of the `java.lang`, `java.util`, `java.io`, `java.text`, and `java.net` packages, and many others.

application

A Java program that runs standalone, as compared with an applet.

Annotation Processing Tool (APT)

A frontend for the Java compiler that processes annotations via a pluggable factory architecture, allowing users to implement custom compile-time annotations.

assertion

A language feature used to test for conditions that should be guaranteed by program logic. If a condition checked by an assertion is found to be *false*, a fatal error is thrown. For added performance, assertions can be disabled when an application is deployed.

atomic

Discrete or transactional in the sense that an operation happens as a unit, in an all-or-nothing fashion. Certain operations in the Java virtual machine (VM) and provided by the Java concurrency API are atomic.

Abstract Window Toolkit (AWT)

Java's original platform-independent windowing, graphics, and UI toolkit.

Boojum

The mystical, spectral, alter ego of a Snark. From the 1876 Lewis Carroll poem "The Hunting of the Snark."

Boolean

A primitive Java data type that contains a `true` or `false` value.

bounds

In Java generics, a limitation on the type of a type parameter. An upper bound specifies that a type must extend (or is assignable to) a specific Java class. A lower bound is used to indicate that a type must be a supertype of (or is assignable from) the specified type.

boxing

Wrapping of primitive types in Java by their object wrapper types. See also *unboxing*.

byte

A primitive Java data type that's an 8-bit two's-complement signed number.

callback

A behavior that is defined by one object and then later invoked by another object when a particular event occurs. The Java event mechanism is a kind of callback.

cast

The changing of the apparent type of a Java object from one type to another, specified type. Java casts are checked both statically by the Java compiler and at runtime.

catch

The Java `catch` statement introduces an exception-handling block of code following a try statement. The `catch` keyword is followed by one or more exception type and argument name pairs in parentheses, and a block of code within curly braces.

certificate

An electronic document using a digital signature to assert the identity of a person, group, or organization. Certificates attest to the identity of a person or group and contain that organization's public key. A certificate is signed by a certificate authority with its digital signature.

certificate authority (CA)

An organization that is entrusted to issue certificates, taking whatever steps are necessary to verify the real-world identity for which it is issuing the certificate.

char

A primitive Java data type; a variable of type char holds a single 16-bit Unicode character.

class

1. The fundamental unit that defines an object in most object-oriented programming languages. A class is an encapsulated collection of variables and methods that may have privileged access to one another. Usually a class can be instantiated to produce an object that's an instance of the class, with its own unique set of data.

2. The `class` keyword is used to declare a class, thereby defining a new object type.

classloader

An instance of the class `java.lang.Class Loader`, which is responsible for loading Java binary classes into the Java VM. Classloaders help partition classes based on their source for both structural and security purposes, and they can also be chained in a parent-child hierarchy.

class method

See *static method*.

classpath

The sequence of path locations specifying directories and archive files containing compiled Java class files and resources, which are searched in order to find components of a Java application.

class variable

See *static variable*.

client

The consumer of a resource or the party that initiates a conversation in the case of a networked client/server application. See also *server*.

Collections API

Classes in the core `java.util` package for working with and sorting structured collections or maps of items. This API includes the `Vector` and `Hashtable` classes as well as newer items such as `List`, `Map`, and `Queue`.

compilation unit

The unit of source code for a Java class. A compilation unit normally contains a single class definition, and in most current development environments is simply a file with a *.java* extension.

compiler

A program that translates source code into executable code.

component architecture

A methodology for building parts of an application. It is a way to build reusable objects that can be easily assembled to form applications.

composition

Combining existing objects to create another, more complex object. When you compose a new object, you create complex behavior by delegating tasks to the internal objects. Composition is different from inheritance, which defines a new object by changing or refining the behavior of an old object. See also *inheritance*.

constructor

A special method that is invoked automatically when a new instance of a class is created. Constructors are used to initialize the variables of the newly created object. The constructor method has the same name as the class and no explicit return value.

content handler

A class that is called to parse a particular type of data and convert it to an appropriate object.

datagram

A packet of data normally sent using a connectionless protocol such as UDP, which provides no guarantees about delivery or error checking and provides no control information.

data hiding

See *encapsulation*.

deep copy

A duplicate of an object along with all of the objects that it references, transitively. A deep copy duplicates the entire "graph" of objects, instead of just duplicating references. See also *shallow copy*.

Document Object Model (DOM)

An in-memory representation of a fully parsed XML document using objects with names like `Element`, `Attribute`, and `Text`. The Java XML DOM API binding is standardized by the World Wide Web Consortium (W3C).

double

A Java primitive data type; a `double` value is a 64-bit (double-precision) floating-point number in IEEE-754 (binary64) binary format.

Document Type Definition (DTD)

A document containing specialized language that expresses constraints on the structure of XML tags and tag attributes. DTDs are used to validate an XML document and can constrain the order and nesting of tags as well as the allowed values of attributes.

Enterprise JavaBeans (EJBs)

A server-side business component architecture named for, but not significantly related to, the JavaBeans component architecture. EJBs represent business services and database components, and provide declarative security and transactions.

encapsulation

The object-oriented programming technique of limiting the exposure of variables and methods to simplify the API of a class or package. Using the private and *protected* keywords, a programmer can limit the exposure of internal ("black box") parts of a class. Encapsulation reduces bugs and promotes reusability and modularity of classes. This technique is also known as *data hiding*.

enum

The Java keyword for declaring an enumerated type. An enum holds a list of constant object identifiers that can be used as a type-safe alternative to numeric constants that serve as identifiers or labels.

enumeration

See *enum*.

erasure

The implementation technique used by Java generics in which generic type information is removed (erased) and distilled to raw Java types at compilation. Erasure provides backward compatibility with nongeneric Java code but introduces some difficulties in the language.

event

1. A user's action, such as a mouse-click or keystroke.

2. The Java object delivered to a registered event listener in response to a user action or other activity in the system.

exception

A signal that some unexpected condition has occurred in the program. In Java, exceptions are objects that are subclasses of Exception or Error (which themselves are subclasses of Throwable). Exceptions in Java are "raised" with the throw keyword and handled with the catch keyword. See also *catch*, *throw*, and *throws*.

exception chaining

The design pattern of catching an exception and throwing a new, higher-level, or more appropriate exception that contains the underlying exception as its *cause*. The "cause" exception can be retrieved if necessary.

extends

A keyword used in a class declaration to specify the superclass of the class being defined. The class being defined has access to all the public and protected variables and methods of the superclass (or, if the class being defined is in the same package, it has access to all nonprivate variables and methods). If a class definition omits the extends clause, its superclass is taken to be java.lang.Object.

final

A keyword modifier that may be applied to classes, methods, and variables. It has a similar, but not identical, meaning in each case. When final is applied to a class, it means that the class may never be subclassed. java.lang.System is an example of a final class. A final method cannot be overridden in a subclass. When final is applied to a variable, the variable is a constant—that is, it can't be modified. (The contents of a mutable object can still be changed; the final variable always points to the same object.)

finalize

A reserved method name. The finalize() method is called by the Java VM when an object is no longer being used (i.e., when there are no further references to it) but before the object's memory is actually reclaimed by the system. Largely disfavored in light of newer approaches, such as the Closeable interface and try-with-resources.

finally

A keyword that introduces the finally block of a try/catch/finally construct.

catch and finally blocks provide exception handling and routine cleanup for code in a try block. The finally block is optional and appears after the try block, and after zero or more catch blocks. The code in a finally block is executed once, regardless of how the code in the try block executes. In normal execution, control reaches the end of the try block and proceeds to the finally block, which generally performs any necessary cleanup.

float

A Java primitive data type; a float value is a 32-bit (single-precision) floating-point number represented in IEEE 754 format.

garbage collection

The process of reclaiming the memory of objects no longer in use. An object is no longer in use when there are no references to it from other objects in the system, and no references in any local variables on any thread's method call stack.

generics

The syntax and implementation of parameterized types in the Java language, added in Java 5.0. Generic types are Java classes that are parameterized by the user on one or more additional Java types to specialize the behavior of the class. Generics are sometimes referred to as *templates* in other languages.

generic class

A class that uses the Java generics syntax and is parameterized by one or more type variables, which represent class types to be substituted by the user of the class. Generic classes are particularly useful for container objects and collections that can be specialized to operate on a specific type of element.

generic method

A method that uses the Java generics syntax and has one or more arguments or return types that refer to type variables representing the actual type of data element the method will use. The Java compiler can often infer the types of the type variables from the usage context of the method.

graphics context

A drawable surface represented by the java.awt.Graphics class. A graphics context contains contextual information about the drawing area and provides methods for performing drawing operations in it.

graphical user interface (GUI)

A traditional, visual user interface consisting of a window containing graphical items such as buttons, text fields, pull-down menus, dialog boxes, and other standard interface components.

hashcode

A random-looking identifying number, based on the data content of an object, used as a kind of signature for the object. A hashcode is used to store an object in a hash table (or hash map). See also *hash table*.

hash table

An object that is like a dictionary or an associative array. A hash table stores and retrieves elements using key values called hashcodes. See also *hashcode*.

hostname

The human-readable name given to an individual computer attached to the internet.

Hypertext Transfer Protocol (HTTP)

The protocol used by web browsers or other clients to talk to web servers. The simplest form of the protocol uses the commands GET to request a file and POST to send data.

Integrated Development Environment (IDE)

A GUI tool such as IntelliJ IDEA or Eclipse that provides source editing, compiling, running, debugging, and deployment functionality for developing Java applications.

implements

A keyword used in class declarations to indicate that the class implements the named interface or interfaces. The `imple ments` clause is optional in class declarations; if it appears, it must follow the `extends` clause (if any). If an `implements` clause appears in the declaration of a non-`abstract` class, every method from each specified interface must be implemented by the class or by one of its superclasses.

import

The `import` statement makes Java classes available to the current class under an abbreviated name, or disambiguates classes imported in bulk by other `import` statements. (Java classes are always available by their fully qualified name, assuming the appropriate class file can be found relative to the `CLASSPATH` environment variable and that the class file is readable. `import` doesn't make the class available; it just saves typing and makes your code more legible.) Any number of `import` statements may appear in a Java program. They must appear, however, after the optional `package` statement at the top of the file, and before the first class or interface definition in the file.

inheritance

An important feature of object-oriented programming that involves defining a new object by changing or refining the behavior of an existing object. Through inheritance, an object implicitly contains all of the non-`private` variables and methods of its superclass. Java supports single inheritance of classes and multiple inheritance of interfaces.

inner class

A class definition that is nested within another class or a method. An inner class functions within the lexical scope of another class.

instance

An occurrence of something, usually an object. When a class is instantiated to produce an object, we say the object is an *instance* of the class.

instance method

A non-`static` method of a class. Such a method is passed an implicit `this` reference to the object that invoked it. See also *static, static method*.

instanceof

A Java operator that returns `true` if the object on its left side is an instance of the class (or implements the interface) specified on its right side. `instanceof` returns `false` if the object isn't an instance of the specified class or doesn't implement the specified interface. It also returns `false` if the specified object is `null`.

instance variable

A non-`static` variable of a class. Each instance of a class has an independent copy of all of the instance variables of the class. See also *class variable, static*.

int

A primitive Java data type that's a 32-bit two's-complement signed number.

interface

1. A keyword used to declare an interface.

2. A collection of abstract methods that collectively define a type in the Java language. Classes implementing the methods may declare that they implement the interface type, and instances of them may be treated as that type.

internationalization

The process of making an application accessible to people who speak a variety of languages. Sometimes abbreviated I18N.

interpreter

The module that decodes and executes Java bytecode. Most Java bytecode is not, strictly speaking, interpreted any longer, but is compiled to native code dynamically by the Java VM.

introspection

The process by which a JavaBean provides additional information about itself, supplementing information learned by reflection.

ISO 8859-1

An 8-bit character encoding standardized by the ISO. This encoding is also known as Latin-1 and contains characters from the Latin alphabet suitable for English and most languages of western Europe.

JavaBeans

A component architecture for Java. It is a way to build interoperable Java objects that can be manipulated easily in a visual application builder environment.

Java beans

Java classes that are built following the JavaBeans design patterns and conventions.

JavaScript

A language developed early in the history of the web by Netscape for creating dynamic web pages. From a programmer's point of view, it's unrelated to Java, although some of its syntax is similar.

Java API for XML Binding (JAXB)

A Java API that allows for generation of Java classes from XML DTD or Schema descriptions and the generation of XML from Java classes.

Java API for XML Parsers (JAXP)

The Java API that allows for pluggable implementations of XML and XSL engines. This API provides an implementation-neutral way to construct parsers and transforms.

JAX-RPC

The Java API for XML Remote Procedure Calls, used by web services.

Java Database Connectivity (JDBC)

The standard Java API for talking to an SQL (Structured Query Language) database.

JDOM

A native Java XML DOM created by Jason Hunter and Brett McLaughlin. JDOM is easier to use than the standard DOM API for Java. It uses the Java Collections API and standard Java conventions. Available at the JDOM Project site (*http://www.jdom.org*).

Java Web Services Developer Pack (JDSDP)

A bundle of standard extension APIs packaged as a group with an installer from Sun. The JWSDP includes JAXB, JAX-RPC, and other XML and web services-related packages.

lambda (or lambda expression)

A compact way to put the entire definition of a small, anonymous function right where you are using it in the code.

Latin-1

A nickname for ISO 8859-1.

layout manager

An object that controls the arrangement of components within the display area of a Swing or AWT container.

lightweight component

A pure Java GUI component that has no native peer in the AWT.

local variable

A variable that is declared inside a method. A local variable can be seen only by code within that method.

Logging API

The Java API for structured logging and reporting of messages from within application components. The Logging API supports logging levels indicating the importance of messages, as well as filtering and output capabilities.

long

A primitive Java data type that's a 64-bit two's-complement signed number.

message digest

A cryptographically computed number based on the content of a message, used to determine whether the message's contents have been changed in any way. A change to a message's contents will change its message digest. When implemented properly, it is almost impossible to create two similar messages with the same digest.

method

The object-oriented programming term for a function or procedure.

method overloading

Provides definitions of more than one method with the same name but with different argument lists. When an overloaded method is called, the compiler determines which one is intended by examining the supplied argument types.

method overriding

Defines a method that matches the name and argument types of a method defined in a superclass. When an overridden method is invoked, the interpreter uses *dynamic method lookup* to determine which method definition is applicable to the current object. Beginning in Java 5.0, overridden methods can have different return types, with restrictions.

MIME (or MIME type)

A media type classification system often associated with email attachments or web page content.

Model-View-Controller (MVC) framework

A UI design that originated in Smalltalk. In MVC, the data for a display item is called the *model*. A *view* displays a particular representation of the model, and a *controller* provides user interaction with both. Java incorporates many MVC concepts.

modifier

A keyword placed before a class, variable, or method that alters the item's accessibility, behavior, or semantics. See also *abstract, final, native method, private, protected, public, static, synchronized.*

NaN (not-a-number)

This is a special value of the double and float data types that represents an undefined result of a mathematical operation, such as zero divided by zero.

native method

A method that is implemented in a native language on a host platform, rather than being implemented in Java. Native methods provide access to such resources as the network, the windowing system, and the host filesystem.

new

A unary operator that creates a new object or array (or raises an OutOfMemoryExcep tion if there is not enough memory available).

NIO

The Java "new" I/O package. A core package introduced in Java 1.4 to support asynchronous, interruptible, and scalable I/O operations. The NIO API supports nonthreadbound "select" style I/O handling.

null

null is a special value that indicates that a reference-type variable doesn't refer to any object instance. Static and instance variables of classes default to the value null if not otherwise assigned.

object

1. The fundamental structural unit of an object-oriented programming language, encapsulating a set of data and behavior that operates on that data.

2. An instance of a class, having the structure of the class but its own copy of data elements. See also *instance.*

package

The package statement specifies the Java package for a Java class. Java code that is part of a particular package has access to all classes (public and non-public) in the package, and all non-private methods and fields in all those classes. When Java code is part of a named package, the compiled class file must be placed at the appropriate position in the CLASS PATH directory hierarchy before it can be accessed by the Java interpreter or other utilities. If the *package* statement is omitted from a file, the code in that file is part of an unnamed default package. This is convenient for small test programs run from the command line, or during development because it means that the code can be interpreted from the current directory.

parameterized type

A class, using Java generics syntax, that is dependent on one or more types to be specified by the user. The user-supplied parameter types fill in type values in the class and adapt it for use with the specified types.

polymorphism

One of the fundamental principles of an object-oriented language. Polymorphism states that a type that extends another type is a "kind of" the parent type and can be used interchangeably with the original type by augmenting or refining its capabilities.

Preferences API

The Java API for storing small amounts of information on a per-user or system-wide basis across executions of the Java VM. The Preferences API is analogous to a small database or the Windows registry.

primitive type

One of the Java data types: boolean, char, byte, short, int, long, float, and double. Primitive types are manipulated, assigned, and passed to methods "by

value" (i.e., the actual bytes of the data are copied). See also *reference type*.

printf

A style of text formatting originating in the C language, relying on an embedded identifier syntax and variable-length argument lists to supply parameters.

private

The private keyword is a visibility modifier that can be applied to method and field variables of classes. A private method or field is not visible outside its class definition and cannot be accessed by subclasses.

protected

A keyword that is a visibility modifier; it can be applied to method and field variables of classes. A protected field is visible only within its class, within subclasses, and within the package of which its class is a part. Note that subclasses in different packages can access only protected fields within themselves or within other objects that are subclasses; they cannot access protected fields within instances of the superclass.

protocol handler

A URL component that implements the network connection required to access a resource for a type of URL scheme (such as HTTP or FTP). A Java protocol handler consists of two classes: a StreamHandler and a URLConnection.

public

A keyword that is a visibility modifier; it can be applied to classes and interfaces and to the method and field variables of classes and interfaces. A public class or interface is visible everywhere. A non-public class or interface is visible only within its package. A public method or variable is visible everywhere its class is visible. When none of the private, protected, or public modifiers are specified, a field is visible only within the package of which its class is a part.

public-key cryptography

A cryptographic system that requires public and private keys. The private key can decrypt messages encrypted with the corresponding public key, and vice versa. The public key can be made available to the public without compromising security, and used to verify that messages sent by the holder of the private key must be genuine.

queue

A list-like data structure normally used in a first-in, first-out fashion to buffer work items.

raw type

In Java generics, the plain Java type of a class without any generic type parameter information. This is the true type of all Java classes after they are compiled. See also *erasure*.

reference type

Any object or array. Reference types are manipulated, assigned, and passed to methods "by reference." In other words, the underlying value is not copied; only a reference to it is. See also *primitive type*.

reflection

The ability of a programming language to interact with structures of the language itself at runtime. Reflection in Java allows a Java program to examine class files at runtime to find out about their methods and variables, and to invoke methods or modify variables dynamically.

regular expression

A compact yet powerful syntax for describing a pattern in text. Regular expressions can be used to recognize and parse most kinds of textual constructs, allowing for wide variation in their form.

Regular Expression API

The core `java.util.regex` package for using regular expressions. The regex package can be used to search and replace text based on sophisticated patterns.

Schema

XML Schemas are a replacement for DTDs. Introduced by the W3C, XML Schema is an XML-based language for expressing constraints on the structure of XML tags and tag attributes, as well as the structure and type of the data content. Other types of XML Schema languages have different syntaxes.

Software Development Kit (SDK)

A package of software distributed by Oracle for Java developers. It includes the Java interpreter, Java classes, and Java development tools: compiler, debugger, disassembler, applet viewer, stub file generator, and documentation generator. Also called the JDK.

SecurityManager

The Java class that defines the methods the system calls to check whether a certain operation is permitted in the current environment.

serialize

To serialize means to put in order or make sequential. Serialized methods are methods that have been synchronized with respect to threads so that only one may be executing at a given time.

server

The party that provides a resource or accepts a request for a conversation in the case of a networked client/server application. See also *client*.

servlet

A Java application component that implements the `javax.servlet.Servlet` API, allowing it to run inside a servlet container or web server. Servlets are widely used in web applications to process user data and generate HTML or other forms of output.

servlet context

In the Servlet API, this is the web application environment of a servlet that provides server and application resources.

The base URL path of the web application is also often referred to as the servlet context.

shadow

To declare a variable with the same name as a variable defined in a superclass. We say the variable "shadows" the superclass's variable. Use the super keyword to refer to the shadowed variable or refer to it by casting the object to the type of the superclass.

shallow copy

A copy of an object that duplicates only values contained in the object itself. References to other objects are repeated as references and are not duplicated themselves. See also *deep copy*.

short

A primitive Java data type that's a 16-bit two's-complement signed number.

signature

1. Referring to a digital signature. A combination of a message's message digest, encrypted with the signer's private key, and the signer's certificate, attesting to the signer's identity. Someone receiving a signed message can get the signer's public key from the certificate, decrypt the encrypted message digest, and compare that result with the message digest computed from the signed message. If the two message digests agree, the recipient knows that the message has not been modified and that the signer is who they claim to be.

2. Referring to a Java method. The method name and argument types and possibly return type, collectively uniquely identifying the method in some context.

signed applet

An applet packaged in a JAR file signed with a digital signature, allowing for authentication of its origin and validation of the integrity of its contents.

signed class

A Java class (or Java archive) that has a signature attached. The signature allows the recipient to verify the class's origin and that it is unmodified. The recipient can therefore grant the class greater runtime privileges.

sockets

A networking API originating in BSD Unix. A pair of sockets provide the endpoints for communication between two parties on the network. A server socket listens for connections from clients and creates individual server-side sockets for each conversation.

spinner

A GUI component that displays a value and a pair of small up and down buttons that increment or decrement the value. The Swing JSpinner can work with number ranges and dates as well as arbitrary enumerations.

static

A keyword that is a modifier applied to method and variable declarations within a class. A static variable is also known as a class variable as opposed to non-static instance variables. While each instance of a class has a full set of its own instance variables, there is only one copy of each *static* class variable, regardless of the number of instances of the class (perhaps zero) that are created. static variables may be accessed by class name or through an instance. Non-static variables can be accessed only through an instance.

static import

A statement, similar to the class and package import, that imports the names of static methods and variables of a class into a class scope. The static import is a convenience that provides the effect of global methods and constants.

static method

A method declared *static*. Methods of this type are not passed implicit this references, and may refer only to class variables and invoke other class methods of the current class. A class method may be invoked through the class name, rather than through an instance of the class.

static variable

A variable declared *static*. Variables of this type are associated with the class, rather than with a particular instance of the class. There is only one copy of a static variable, regardless of the number of instances of the class that are created.

stream

A flow of data, or a channel of communication. All fundamental I/O in Java is based on streams. The NIO package uses channels, which are packet oriented. Also a framework for functional programming introduced in Java 8.

string

A sequence of character data and the Java class used to represent this kind of character data. The String class includes many methods for operating on string objects.

subclass

A class that extends another. The subclass inherits the public and protected methods and variables of its superclass. See also *extends*.

super

A keyword used by a class to refer to variables and methods of its parent class. The special reference super is used in the same way as the special reference this is used to qualify references to the current object context.

superclass

A parent class, extended by some other class. The superclass's public and protected methods and variables are available to the subclass. See also *extends*.

synchronized

A keyword used in two related ways in Java: as a modifier and as a statement. First, it is a modifier applied to class or instance methods. It indicates that the method modifies the internal state of the class or the internal state of an instance of the class in a way that is not thread-safe. Before running a synchronized class method, Java obtains a lock on the class to ensure that no other threads can modify the class concurrently. Before running a synchronized instance method, Java obtains a lock on the instance that invoked the method, ensuring that no other threads can modify the object at the same time. Synchronization also ensures that changes to a value are propagated between threads and are eventually visible throughout all your processor cores.

Java also supports a synchronized statement that serves to specify a "critical section" of code. The synchronized keyword is followed by an expression in parentheses and a statement or block of statements. The expression must evaluate to an object or array. Java obtains a lock on the specified object or array before executing the statements.

TCP (Transmission Control Protocol)

A connection-oriented, reliable protocol. One of the protocols on which the internet is based.

this

Within an instance method or constructor of a class, this refers to "this object"—the instance currently being operated on. It is useful to refer to an instance variable of the class that has been shadowed by a local variable or method argument. It is also useful to pass the current object as an argument to static methods or methods of other classes. There is one additional use of this: when it appears as the first statement in a constructor method, it refers to one of the other constructors of the class.

thread

An independent stream of execution within a program. Because Java is a multithreaded programming language, more than one thread may be running within the Java interpreter at a time. Threads in Java are represented and controlled through the `Thread` object.

thread pool

A group of "recyclable" threads used to service work requests. A thread is allocated to handle one item and then returned to the pool.

throw

The `throw` statement signals that an exceptional condition has occurred by throwing a specified `Throwable` (exception) object. This statement stops program execution and passes it to the nearest containing `catch` statement that can handle the specified exception object.

throws

The `throws` keyword is used in a method declaration to list the exceptions the method can throw. Any exceptions a method can raise that are not subclasses of `Error` or `RuntimeException` must either be caught within the method or declared in the method's `throws` clause.

try

The `try` keyword indicates a guarded block of code to which subsequent `catch` and `finally` clauses apply. The `try` statement itself performs no special action. See also *catch* and *finally* for more information on the `try`/`catch`/`finally` construct.

try-with-resources

A `try` block that also opens resources implementing the `Closeable` interface for automatic cleanup.

type instantiation

In Java generics, the point at which a generic type is applied by supplying actual or wildcard types as its type parameters. A generic type is instantiated by the user of the type, effectively creating a new type in the Java language specialized for the parameter types.

type invocation

See *type instantiation*. The term *type invocation* is sometimes used by analogy with the syntax of method invocation.

User Datagram Protocol (UDP)

A connectionless, unreliable protocol. UDP describes a network data connection based on datagrams with little packet control.

unboxing

Unwrapping a primitive value that is held in its object wrapper type and retrieving the value as a primitive.

Unicode

A universal standard for text character encoding, accommodating the written forms of almost all languages. Unicode is standardized by the Unicode Consortium. Java uses Unicode for its `char` and `String` types.

UTF-8 (UCS transformation format 8-bit form)

An encoding for Unicode characters (and more generally, UCS characters) commonly used for transmission and storage. It is a multibyte format in which different characters require different numbers of bytes to be represented.

variable-length argument list

A method in Java may indicate that it can accept any number of a specified type of argument after its initial fixed list of arguments. The arguments are handled by packaging them as an array.

varargs

See *variable length argument list*.

vector

A dynamic array of elements.

verifier

A kind of theorem prover that steps through the Java bytecode before it is run and makes sure that it is well behaved and does not violate the Java security model. The bytecode verifier is the first line of defense in Java's security model.

Web Applications Resources file (WAR file)

A JAR file with additional structure to hold classes and resources for web applications. A WAR file includes a *WEB-INF* directory for classes, libraries, and the *web.xml* deployment file.

web application

An application that runs on a web server or application server, normally using a web browser as a client.

web service

An application-level service that runs on a server and is accessed in a standard way using XML for data marshalling and HTTP as its network transport.

wildcard type

In Java generics, a "*" syntax used in lieu of an actual parameter type for type instantiation to indicate that the generic type represents a set or supertype of many concrete type instantiations.

XInclude

An XML standard and Java API for inclusion of XML documents.

Extensible Markup Language (XML)

A universal markup language for text and data, using nested *tags* to add structure and meta-information to the content.

XPath

An XML standard and Java API for matching elements and attributes in XML using a hierarchical, regex-like expression language.

Extensible Stylesheet Language/XSL Transformations (XSL/XSLT)

An XML-based language for describing styling and transformation of XML documents. Styling involves simple addition of markup, usually for presentation. XSLT allows complete restructuring of documents, in addition to styling.

Index

Symbols

$ (dollar sign), position marker, 249
% (percent) operator, 115
&& logical AND in regular expression, 249
* (asterisk)
    any number of character iterations, 250
    wildcard type, 70, 162, 508
+ (plus) operator, 102, 115, 238, 240, 250
-> (arrow operator)
    lambda expressions, 356
    switch expressions, 108
. (dot) (see dot (.) notation/operator)
.* (dot star) notation, 51
/** (doc comments), 89
// or /* (comment syntax), 88
<> (angle brackets), type parameter, 221
<String> object, 221, 400
= (assignment operator), 116
== (equals operator), 240
> (comparison operator), 109
>>, right-arithmetic-shift operator, 115
>>>, operand as unsigned number, 115
? (question mark), zero or one iteration, 250
?d (Unix lines flag), 252
?i (case-insensitive flag), 251
?m (multiline flag), 252
?s (dot all flag), 252
@ (tags or annotations), 90-91, 495
[] (index operator), 121, 248
\ (backslash), preceding escape sequences, 246, 323
\b or \B (word boundary position marker), 249
\d or \D (digit or nondigit character), 248
\s or \S (whitespace or nonwhitespace character), 248
\s or \s* (single or multiple whitespace), 245
\w or \W (word or nonword) character, 248
^ (carat)
    inverting character class, 249
    position marker, 249
{x,} (range), at least x or more iterations, 251
{} (curly braces), code blocks, 103
| (vertical bar)
    alternation, 251
    or syntax, 194
' ' (single quotes), enclosing character literals, 98
" " (double quotes), enclosing string literals, 238

A

abs() method, Math, 259
absolute file path, 325
abstract, 508
abstract classes, 172-180
    anonymous inner classes, 177, 179-180
    inner classes, 177-178
    and interfaces, 12, 174-177
    streams, 313, 314
abstract keyword, 495
abstract methods, 172-174, 315, 360, 420
abstract modifier, 172, 175
Abstract Window Toolkit (AWT), 381, 495
accept() method, ServerSocket, 447, 451
access modifiers, 16, 141, 164
accessor methods, 181, 298
action events, 416-419

ActionEvent class, 58
ActionEvent interface, 416-419, 426
ActionListener interface, 360, 417-419, 423, 426
actionPerformed() method, ActionListener,
  360, 417, 426
ad hoc polymorphism, 154
adapter classes, 59
adaptive compilation, 7
add() method
  BorderLayout, 406
  Collection, 213
  JFrame, 403
  JPanel, 403
  List, 214, 218
  Queue, 215
addAll() method, Collection, 213
addMouseListener() method, 415
addMouseMotionListener() method, 57
ahead-of-time (AOT) compilation, 7
algorithm, assembling, 118
allocate() method, Buffer, 343
alternation (|), regular expressions, 251
Amazon Corretto, installing, 28-33
angle brackets (<>), type parameter, 221
animation, 142, 281-283, 425-427
Animator class, 276-278
Annotation Processing Tool (APT), 495
annotations, 91, 495
anonymous inner classes, 177, 179-180
Ant build tool, 495
AOT (ahead-of-time) compilation, 7
applets, 2
Application Programming Interface (API), 495
  (see also specific APIs by name)
applications, 27-62, 495
  (see also desktop applications; web services)
  collections, 233-235
  HelloJava, 40-53
  HelloJava2, 53-62
  Java tools and environment for, 27-40
  running, 35-39, 67-68
apply() method, IntFunction, 360
APT (Annotation Processing Tool), 495
arbitrary-precision math, 261
argument list, 145, 507
arguments
  and events, 58
  in lambda expressions, 356
  method, 55, 100, 145, 151-152

and parameters, 56
passing, 46
running applications, 67-68
taking label as an argument, 112
ArithmeticException, 257, 259
Array class, 121
arraycopy() method, 125
ArrayList, 218, 221, 226-228
arrays, 15, 101, 120-130
  anonymous, 126
  versus buffers, 339
  and collections, 211, 229, 230
  creation and initialization, 122-124
  multidimensional, 127-129, 371
  types, 121
Arrays class (utility), 126
Arrays helper class, 231
ASCII character encoding, 86
asList() method, 231
assert keyword, 205
AssertionError type, 190, 205
assertions, 204-207, 495
assignment (=) operator, 116
associative array (see Map interface)
asterisk (*)
  any number of character iterations, 250
  wildcard type, 70, 508
asynchronous channels, 337, 339
AsynchronousFileChannel, 339
atomic convenience classes, 307
atomic operations, 298, 306, 495
AtomicBoolean class, 307
attributes
  chaining of, 119
  getting information on file, 322
  in JAR manifests, 81
  mapping object, 369
autoboxing, 153, 222
AutoCloseable interface, 203
available() method, InputStream, 329
availableCharsets() method, 344
AWT (Abstract Window Toolkit), 381, 495

B
background threads, 195, 274, 281, 285, 422
backgrounds, GUI, 386-388
backslash (\), preceding escape sequences, 246, 323
base classes, 14

E

F

just-in-time (JIT) compilation, 6
JVM (Java Virtual Machine), 5-8, 66, 298, 302
JWindow class, 401

K

key-value pairs, Map, 217, 232
KeyEvent class, 58
keySet() method, Map, 216, 232
Knudsen, Jonathan, 427

L

labels, GUI, 134, 384-389
lambda expressions (lambdas), 354-363, 501
    in event code, 420
    expression bodies, 358
    functional interfaces, 359
    and inner classes, 177, 358
    method references, 361
    passing arguments, 356
    returning values, 359
    sorting a list with, 362
    and streams, 363-377
    using directly in code, 378-379
last in, first out (LIFO), queues, 214
last() set call, 213
lastIndexOf() method, String, 242
lastModified() method, File, 325
late binding languages, 13
Latin-1, 501
layout managers, 404-413, 501
length() method
    File object, 325, 329
    String class, 117, 238
length, array, 120
LIFO (last in, first out), queues, 214
lightweight component, 501
limit() method
    ByteBuffer, 340
    java.util.stream, 367
    Stream, 365
line comments, 88
LinkedList class, 294
Linux, 29-29, 323
Lisp, 11, 353
List interface, 214
    erasure, 224-225
    and generics, 220-221, 227-229
list() method, File, 326
listener interface, event handling, 58, 413-421

listFiles() method, File, 326
ListIt class, 329
listRoots() method, File, 324
lists, GUI component, 399-401
literal strings, 241
little-endian and big-endian approaches to byte
    order, 320, 342
loadFile() method, 196
local dates and times, 263-264
local variables, 55, 96, 145, 146, 149-150, 501
LocalDate class, 263, 269
LocalDateTime class, 263
localization, path, 323-325
LocalTime class, 263, 269
Lock class, 305
lock() method, FileChannel, 347
locking files, NIO package, 338
locking threads, 292, 302
LockSupport class, 305
log() method, Math, 259
Logging API, 501
Long class, 244
long primitive type, 502
long value, integer literals, 96
longValue() method, Number, 152
lookingAt() method, Matcher, 255

M

macOS, 30-31, 69, 323
main() method, 40, 43-44, 67
make utility, 12
MalformedURLException, 189, 437
Manifest class, 82
manifest, JAR file, 81-82
Map interface, 215-216, 222, 305
map() method, Stream, 368, 370
mapped files, NIO package, 338
MappedByteBuffer class, 338
mapping streams, 368-373
Matcher class, regular expressions, 255
matches() method, Pattern, 253, 255
Math class, 147, 258-261
math utilities, 257-262
Maven: The Definitive Guide (Van Zyl), 166
max() method, Math, 259
memory allocation and deallocation, 155
memory-mapped files, NIO package, 338
menus, GUI, 428
message digest, 502

O

Object class, 134
Object set() method, List, 214
ObjectInputStream class, 313
ObjectOutputStream class, 313
objects, 133-184, 502
    (see also reference types)
    classes (see classes)
    constructors, 55-58, 118, 155-158, 497
    creating, 118, 155-158
    destroying, 158-160
    methods (see methods)
    and packages, 160-166
    as strings, 239
octal numbers, 96
of() method, dates and times, 263
offer() method, Queue, 215
OffsetDateTime class, 265
ofPattern() method, dates and times, 266
OOP (object-oriented programming), 354
open() method, FileChannel, 345
openConnection() method
    try/catch, 195
    URLConnection, 442
openStream() method, 438
operations, stream, 363
operators, list of Java, 114
or syntax (|), 194
Oracle Corporation, 4
OutputStream class, 313
OutputStreamWriter class, 313, 317, 330
overloading constructors, 157-158
overloading methods, 154-155, 171, 259, 502
overloading strings or numbers, 102
overriding methods, 48, 53, 155, 171-172, 502

P

package statement, 160, 503
packages, 16
    and class files, 12, 50-52, 134, 160
    compiling with, 166
    custom, 163-164
    importing, 162
    modifiers in, 164
    naming, 50, 67
    and objects, 160-166
    organizing objects in, 180
paintComponent() method, 52
panels, GUI, 403

parallel programming, 16, 273, 307
parameterized types, 101, 214, 217, 227-229, 503
    (see also generics)
parent class, 99
parse() method, dates and times, 263, 266
ParseException, 199
parsing
    dates and times, 266-268
    primitive numbers, 243
passing arguments, 151-152, 356
path
    absolute, 325
    classpath, 69-71, 496
    relative, 325
    URL, 436
Path interface, 332
path localization, 323-325
pathnames, separator variable for, 323
patterns in regular expressions, 246, 250, 252-255
peek() method, Queue, 215
percent (%) operator, 115
performance
    and immutability of Strings, 237
    exceptions, 204
    lambdas, 355
    NIO package, 338
    threads, 302-305
Pipe.SinkChannel, 338
Pipe.SourceChannel, 338
PipedInputStream class, 314
PipedOutputStream class, 314
PipedReader class, 314
PipedWriter class, 314
plus (+) operator, 102, 115, 238, 240, 250
plus() method, dates and times, 264
poll() method, Queue, 215
polymorphism, 48, 154, 171, 217, 503
pop-up windows, GUI, 430-432
port number, 448, 449
position markers, regular expressions, 249
position() method, ByteBuffer, 340
POST method, HTML environment, 441-443
postconditions, method, 207
postData() method, 442
Postman Echo service, 441
pow() method, Math, 259
preconditions, method, 207

signed applet, 505
signed class, 505
simplicity principle of Java, 11
single abstract method (SAM), 360
single inheritance, 167
single quotes (' '), enclosing character literals,
    98
size() method, FileChannel, 347
sleep() method, Thread, 278, 279
sliders, GUI component, 397-399, 419
Smalltalk, 11, 13
Socket class, 446, 448-450
Socket object, 203
SocketChannel, 338
sockets, 446-462, 505
    clients and servers, 447-451
    DateAtHost client, 451-453
    distributed game setup, 453-462
Software Development Kit (SDK), 504
sort() method, Collections, 232, 362
SortedMap class, 216
SortedSet class, 213, 214
-source flag, 288
spinner, 505
split() method, String, 256
sqrt() method, Math, 259
SSL (Secure Sockets Layer), 444
SSLException, 194
stack traces, 189, 195
StackTraceElement objects, 196
start() method
    Animator, 278
    Matcher, 256
    Thread, 276
startsWith() method, String, 241
startVirtualThread() method, 356
statements
    break/continue, 111-113
    do/while loops, 108-109
    for loops, 109-111
    if/else conditionals, 104-105
    switch statements, 105-108
    unreachable, 113
static (class) methods, 142, 147-149, 505
static (class) variables, 142, 144, 298, 506
static imports, 505
static keyword, 142, 505
static members of classes, 142-144
static versus dynamic languages, 12, 93

stop() method, Thread, 278
stream() method, Collection, 363
Stream.of() method, 363
streams (java.io), 313-331, 506
    (see also java.util.stream package)
    character, 317-318
    data streams, 319
    File class, 322-327
    file streams, 328-330
    PrintWriter and PrintStream, 321
    RandomAccessFile, 330
    stream wrappers, 318-322
strictfp keyword, 95
String arrays, 121, 256
String class, 237-245, 506
    (see also regular expressions)
    and CharBuffer, 342
    comparing strings, 240-241
    constructing strings, 238-239
    for error messages, 198
    and file constructing, 323
    instance variables, 54
    method summary, 242
    objects and primitive types as strings, 239
    and overloading methods, 154
    parsing primitive number types, 243
    searching strings for substrings, 241
    splitting strings, 256
    tokenizing text, 244
    Unicode support, 86
StringBuilder, 442
strings
    reading and writing with java.io, 317-318
    splitting in regular expressions, 256
    text (see text)
    type system, 101
Stroustrup, Bjarne, 17
structured concurrency, 307
StructuredTaskScope class, 308
subclasses, 99, 506
    and abstract method, 173
    in class hierarchy, 48-50
    and inheritance, 167-172
    overriding methods, 171-172
subMap() method, 216
subSet() method, 213
substrings, 117, 241
subtype polymorphism, 99, 171
Sun Microsystems, 2

super reference, 157, 170, 506
superclass, 157, 167, 171-172, 506
Supplier interface, 365
suspend() method, Thread, 278
Swing API, 302
    (see also desktop applications)
    IntelliJ IDEA, 33-35, 467-471
    and thread death hangups, 285
SwingUtilities class, 422-425
switch expressions, 107
switch statements, 105-108
synchronization, threads, 16, 274, 290-298, 305
synchronized keyword, 292-293, 506
System class, 315
system properties, JVM, 68
System.err variable, 315
System.in variable, 315, 317
System.out variable, 315
systemDefault() method, dates and times, 265

T

tailMap() method, 216
tailSet() method, 213
TCP/IP (Transmission Control Protocol/Internet Protocol), 447, 506
templates, 217
terminal operations, 367
text areas, 392-395
text blocks, Strings, 238
text encoding, 86-88
text fields, GUI, 390-392, 418
text processing, 237-272
    components, 390-397
    dates and times, 262-270
    math utilities, 257-262
    regular expressions, 245-257
    scrolling, 395-397
    String class, 237-245
    tokenizing text, 244
this constructor, 506
this reference, 57, 146, 151, 358
this() method, 157, 506
Thread class, 275-278
thread pools, 303, 507
threads, 16, 273-309, 506
    animation with, 281-283
    and asynchronous I/O, 337
    background, 195, 274, 281, 285, 422
    concurrency utilities, 305-308

and desktop applications, 421-427
    lambdas with, 355-359
    locking, 292, 302
    methods to control, 278-280
    multithreading, 298, 421
    performance, 302-305
    scheduling and priority, 298-302
    synchronization of, 274, 290-298, 302, 305
    termination of, 284-285
    thread state, 299
    time-slicing, 300-301
    virtual, 285-290, 297, 299, 304
throw statement, 197, 507
throw/catch, exceptions, 189
Throwable class, 190, 196, 200
throwaway arrays, 126
throwing exceptions, 204
throws keyword, 197, 507
time zones, 265
time-slicing, threads, 290, 300-301
Timer class, javax.swing, 425-427
timers, threading considerations, 425-427
timestamps, 270
tokenizing text, 244
toString() method, 240
toURL() method, 327
Transmission Control Protocol/Internet Protocol (TCP/IP), 447, 506
truncate() method, FileChannel, 347
try creep, 200-201
try keyword, 507
try with resources, 202-204, 317, 507
try/catch blocks, 191-195, 197, 200-204
type instantiation, 507
type parameters, 219
    (see also parameterized types)
type parameters, generics, 219
type state, 19
type system, 93-102
    character literals, 98
    collections, 213-215
    floating-point literals, 98
    floating-point precision, 95
    generics in, 219-223
    inferring types, 100
    integer literals, 96-98
    limitations on types in collections, 217-219
    Math class, 147, 258-261
    method binding, 13

parameterized types, 101, 214, 217, 227-229, 503
primitive types (see primitive data types)
raw types, 225-226, 504
reference type (see reference (class) types)
safety of, 12-14, 229
strings, 101
variable declaration and initialization, 95

U

UDP (User Datagram Protocol), 447, 507
UI (user interface), 433
(see also desktop applications; web services)
unary operator, 378
unboxing, 507
unchecked and checked exceptions, 196
unchecked warning, 226
Unicode, 86, 237, 507
Uniform Resource Identifiers (URIs), 436
Uniform Resource Locators (URLs), 333, 435-437
Unix lines flag (?d), 252
Unix, CLASSPATH on, 69
UnknownServiceException, 438
unreachable statements, 113, 159
upper bound of type, 226
URIs (Uniform Resource Identifiers), 436
URL class, 436-439
    getting content as object, 438
    managing connections, 439
    stream data, 438
URLConnection object, 439
URLDecoder class, 443
URLEncoder class, 441
URLProducer class, 295
URLs (uniform resource locators), 333, 435-437
User Datagram Protocol (UDP), 447, 507
user interface (UI), 433
(see also desktop applications; web services)
UTF-16, 87
UTF-32, 87
UTF-8, 87, 507

V

valueOf() method, String, 239
values() method, Map, 216, 232
Van Zyl, Jason, 166
variable-length argument list, 507
variables

accessing, 116
and class types, 45
and constants, 91-93
declaring, 95, 135
final variables in lambdas, 358
float, 142
initializing, 95, 149-150
instance, 146, 298, 500
local, 145, 146, 149-150, 501
separators for pathnames, 323
shadowing, 146, 169-170
static, 142, 144, 298, 506
Vector class, 211
vectors, 507
verifiers, 18-19, 507
vertical bar (|)
    alternation, 251
    or syntax, 194
virtual threads, 285-290, 297, 299, 304
VirtualDemo class, 287
visibility modifiers, 141, 156, 164, 175, 502
void add() method, List, 214
void return type, 144

W

wait() method, 108, 278, 279
Watchable interface, 333
web application, 508
Web Applications Resources file (WAR file), 508
web services, 435-444
    GET method, 440
    HttpURLConnection, 443
    POST method, 441-443
    SSL and secure web communications, 444
    URLs, 435-437
whitespace or nonwhitespace character (\s or \S), 248
whitespace, single or multiple (\s or \s*), 245
wildcard (*) type, 70, 162, 508
wildcard instantiations, 228, 233
Windows, 32-33, 70, 323
withZoneSameInstant() method, dates and times, 265
word boundary position marker (\b or \B), 249
word or nonword (\w or \W) character, 248
wrap properties, JTextArea, 394
wrap() method, Buffer, 343
wrappers

for primitive types, 152-153
for streams, 318-322
write once, run away, regular expressions, 246
write() method
buffering, 321
FileOutputStream, 330
try/catch, 195
Writer class, 313, 317
writeUTF() method, DataOutputStream, 320

X

x-y (range notation), regular expressions, 249
XInclude, 508

-Xlint:preview, 288
-Xlint:unchecked, 226
XML (Extensible Markup Language), 508
XPath, 508
XSL/XSLT (Extensible Stylesheet Language/XSLTransformations), 508

Z

ZIP file compression, 79
ZipException, 194
ZonedDateTime class, 265, 267
ZoneID class, 265

About the Authors

Marc Loy caught the Java bug after seeing a beta copy of the HotJava browser showing a sorting algorithm animation back in 1994. He developed and delivered Java training classes at Sun Microsystems back in the day and has continued training a (much) wider audience ever since. He now spends his days consulting and writing on technical and media topics. He has also caught the maker bug and is exploring the fast-growing world of embedded electronics and wearables.

Patrick Niemeyer became involved with Oak (Java's predecessor) while working at Southwestern Bell Technology Resources. He is the CTO of Ikayzo, Inc., and an independent consultant, and author. Pat is the creator of BeanShell, a popular Java scripting language. He has served as a member of several JCP expert groups that guided features of the Java language and is a contributor to many open source projects. Most recently, Pat has been developing analytics software for the financial industry as well as advanced mobile applications. He currently lives in St. Louis with his family and various creatures.

Dan Leuck is the CEO of Ikayzo, Inc., a Tokyo- and Honolulu-based interactive design and software development firm with customers that include Sony, Oracle, Nomura, PIMCO, and the federal government. He previously served as senior vice president of research and development for Tokyo-based ValueCommerce, Asia's largest online marketing company; global head of development for London-based LastMinute.com, Europe's largest B2C website; and president of the US division of DML. Dan has extensive experience managing teams of 150-plus developers in 5 countries. He has served on numerous advisory boards and panels for companies such as Macromedia and Sun Microsystems. Dan is active in the Java community, is a contributor to BeanShell and the project lead for SDL, and sits on numerous Java Community Process expert groups.

Colophon

The animals on the cover of *Learning Java*, Sixth Edition, are a Bengal tiger and her cubs. The Bengal is a subspecies of tiger (*Panthera tigris tigris*) found in Southern Asia. It has been hunted practically to extinction and now lives mostly in natural preserves and national parks, where it is strictly protected. It's estimated that there are fewer than 3,500 Bengal tigers left in the wild.

The Bengal tiger is reddish orange with narrow black, gray, or brown stripes, generally in a vertical direction. Males can grow to 9 feet long and weigh as much as 500 pounds; they are the largest existing members of the cat family. Preferred habitats include dense thickets, long grass, or tamarisk shrubs along river banks. Maximum longevity can be 26 years but is usually only about 15 years in the wild.

Tigers most commonly conceive after the monsoon rains; the majority of cubs are born between February and May after a gestation of three and a half months. Females bear one litter every two to three years. Cubs weigh under three pounds at birth and are striped. Litters usually consist of one to four cubs, but it's unusual for more than two or three to survive. Cubs are weaned at four to six months but depend on their mother for food and protection for another two years. Female tigers are mature at three to four years, males at four to five years.

Bengals are an endangered species threatened by poaching, habitat loss, and habitat fragmentation. Many of the animals on O'Reilly covers are endangered; all of them are important to the world.

The color illustration is by Karen Montgomery, based on a black and white engraving from a loose plate, source unknown. The cover fonts are Gilroy Semibold and Guardian Sans. The text font is Adobe Minion Pro; the heading font is Adobe Myriad Condensed; and the code font is Dalton Maag's Ubuntu Mono.

Printed in the USA
CPSIA information can be obtained
at www.ICGtesting.com
JSHW052332010923
47738JS00007B/10